MEDICAL NEGLIGENCE

Cavendish
Publishing
Limited

MEDICAL NEGLIGENCE

Malcolm Khan, LLB (Hons) DUNELM,
Barrister at Law
Principal Lecturer in Law
University of Northumbria at Newcastle

Michelle Robson, LLB, Solicitor,
Senior Lecturer in Law
University of Northumbria at Newcastle

Cavendish
Publishing
Limited

First published in Great Britain 1997 by Cavendish Publishing Limited, The Glass House, Wharton Street, London WC1X 9PX
Telephone: 0171-278 8000   Facsimile: 0171-278 8080

Khan, Malcolm
Medical Negligence – (Medico-Legal Series)
I Title II Robson, Michelle III Series
344.106332

ISBN 1 85941 022 7

Printed and bound in Great Britain by
Biddles Ltd, Guildford and King's Lynn

PREFACE

Why? We have asked ourselves this question on many occasions as yet another weekend was spent correcting the ninety-third draft. Yet even as our caffeine levels reached dangerous proportions and our friends questioned our sanity we lost none of our original enthusiasm for this project.

Our aim in writing this book is to provide practitioners and students with the beginnings of their tools of the trade, the trade in question being the practice of medical negligence litigation. Why another book when there is already a plethora of work on medical negligence litigation? It is true that the vast majority of these publications are excellent, but we felt (rightly or wrongly) that there was a space for a book that was neither wholly substantive nor procedural but a marriage of the two, a book where practitioners would find advice on the merits of their client's case and guidance on how to progress it; a student would find a clear, comprehensible account of the subject. Additionally, we wanted to encourage argument, to stimulate new ideas about to how to beat the problems of causation and *Bolam*. By providing all the materials in one place, we hope that even the most jaded practitioners will take the time to remind themselves why they chose to practice in this area of the law with all its fascinations and frustrations, and encourage the new medical lawyers of the future.

Once we had decided on the aim we then asked ourselves what should be the format and our inspiration came from two sources – *The White Book* and Dicey and Morris's *Conflict of Laws*. By setting out the basic principles as a series of rules followed by explanatory notes and references, we hope to cater for most tastes. Anyone who simply wants to check a principle or a reference can just read the relevant paragraph, whereas the lawyer who wants to know, for example, how to try and circumvent the *Bolam* rule can spend more time in reading the commentary.

Readers will note that there is a great deal of cross referencing. We hope that this does not detract from the reading or become too irritating. Unfortunately many of the authorities spring up in more than one chapter and as yet we have not thought of another way to combat this problem.

We have tried to keep our own opinions about the defects in the law and what it should be to a minimum. In addition, although we have attempted to provide advice on tactics and arguments on how to meet particular situations, the aim of this book is to state what the law is, not what we think it should be. To this end we hope we have been successful.

Although the book concentrates on civil negligence, we thought it appropriate to include two other major subjects, medical confidentiality and consent. Consent to medical treatment is never far from the news and, although not as commonplace as the negligence action, the claim for trespass is equally important. A claim for breach of confidence may still be thought of as unusual, but in these days of AIDS and sexual and physical violence health carers need reassurance about their legal position and, conversely, the patient may need advice about breach of confidence.

As a final note, we refer throughout the book to people like 'health carers', 'doctors', 'defendants'. All the principles discussed (unless indicated otherwise) refer to all participants involved in the health care of the individual.

The law is as stated at 1 October 1996. As always, we expect to be corrected, and we apologise in advance for any errors that may be lurking in the following pages.

Malcolm Khan
Michelle Robson

ACKNOWLEDGMENTS

The authors gratefully acknowledge the permission which has been given by the following bodies/persons for reproduction of their material:

Action for Victims of Medical Accidents

Butterworths (County Court Rules 1981 as taken from County Court Practice 1996)

Crown copyright material is reproduced with the permission of the Controller of Her Majesty's Stationary Office

General Medical Council

Law Society (Protocol for obtaining Hospital Medical Records: Appendix H)

Loomba & Burke, Solicitors, Newcastle upon Tyne

Lord Chancellor's Department

Sweet & Maxwell (Rules of the Supreme Court 1965 and notes thereto taken from the Supreme Court Practice 1997)

Voluntary Euthanasia Society

* * * * *

And now to thank certain individuals without whom this book would never have made it to print and who helped keep the authors sane. In the former category come Diane Lightburn and Linda Gallant; in both categories fall Michael Stockdale and Andrea O'Cain.

Malcolm Khan extends his heartfelt thanks to all administrative staff within the School of Law who, at varying times, helped with his typing and put up with his tantrums. This book is dedicated to his deceased parents.

Michelle Robson wishes to personally thank Margaret and Derek Robson and Jacqueline Robson for their unfailing interest and support, and a special thanks must go to Tim Clarke for his endless patience and encouragement and to whom she dedicates this book.

ABBREVIATIONS

ABI	Association of British Insurers
AHA	Area Health Authority
AVMA	Action for Victims of Medical Accidents
BMA	British Medical Association
CHC	Community Health Council
CRU	Compensation Recovery Unit
DSS	Department of Social Security
DVLC	Driver and Vehicle Licensing Centre
FHSA	Family Health Services Authority
GMC	General Medical Council
GP	General Practitioner
HA	Health Authority
LREC	Local Research Ethics Committee
NHS	National Health Service

CONTENTS

TABLE OF CASES

TABLE OF STATUTES

TABLE OF STATUTORY INSTRUMENTS

STOP PRESS

Solicitors should also note the following recent developments.

Procedure/Statutes

Practice Direction No 49 Medical Negligence (see Law Gazette 6 November 1996)

From 1 November 1996, Master Foster has been assigned to hear all interlocutory applications in medical/clinical negligence actions. The practice direction lists a series of points designed to produce more effective case management in keeping with the Woolf reforms.

Damages Act 1996

In force from 24 September 1996. The Act permits the Lord Chancellor to set rates of return to be expected from investment monies. This would be achieved by consulting with the Government Actuary and Treasury. However, for the present, it seems that the rate will still be determined by judges, see, for example, *Page v Sheerness* Chapter 7, Damages, p 207.

Consent

Re T (a minor) (1996) The Times, 27 October

A parent refused to give consent to her child undergoing a liver transplant as she did not wish the child to suffer the pain and distress of invasive surgery. The Court of Appeal held that the 'mother and this child are one' and the court had to consider whether it was in the child's best interests for his mother to be forced to agree to the surgery and consequently be committed to caring for him long term. It held that the interests of the child would be best served by leaving his treatment in the hands of his parents.

Comment. The full implications of this decision have yet to be determined. However, we are of the opinion that this decision is fundamentally flawed. The 'best interests' test should be solely applied to the patient, the views of the parents being persuasive only. The future care of the patient should be determined by what is best for him; here, the evidence indicated that the operation had a good chance of success and the long term prospects were good. Whilst we profoundly sympathise with the parents' wishes, the welfare of the child should not depend on his mother: they should not be 'treated as one'.

Negligence

Damages

Frost and Others v Chief Constable of South Yorkshire Police and others (1996) The Times, 5 November

The plaintiffs were five policemen who were on duty at Hillsborough football ground in 1989 when several people were killed and injured as the result of crushing caused by the police decision to open an outer gate to the ground whilst failing to close the access to spectator pens from which there was no exit. The plaintiffs alleged that they had suffered post-traumatic stress disorder as a result of the horrifying events they had witnessed. The Court of Appeal held that a duty of care existed between the plaintiffs and the defendant and consequently the defendant was liable for any psychiatric injury caused to an employee as a result of fear for himself or through witnessing what had happened to his colleagues.

Comment. The court was at pains to stress that no special rule was being formulated for plaintiffs who happened to be police officers. Essentially any rescuer may recover against the tortfeasor for injury sustained during a rescue. In this particular case, the police officers could also establish that their employer was in breach of its duty of care and therefore could bring a claim for injuries caused during the course of their employment. Only where the plaintiff is a mere bystander must he then seek to establish a degree of love and affection towards the primary victim and come within the aftermath principle as enunciated by *McLoughlin, Alcock* and the like. This may seem particularly harsh for those relatives of victims who were denied compensation in *Alcock*.

McFarlane v Tayside Health Board (1996) The Times, 11 November

In this Scottish case, the pursuers had sued the defenders for the upkeep of their child who was born after the first pursuer had undergone a vasectomy at the defenders' hospital. There had been an administrative error in the subsequent tests of the first pursuer's sperm following the vasectomy; consequently he had been wrongly advised that he no longer needed to take any contraceptive precautions. Lord Gill, in dismissing the pursuers claim for damages, held that:

(i) the conception of the child was not an injury to the wife, and although pregnancy and labour were painful they were natural processes resulting in a happy outcome; and

(ii) the joy of the child's existence completely outweighed the costs of rearing the child.

Comment. This case is of interest in two respects. First, it is in direct contrast to the English case of *Walkin v South Manchester Health Authority* [1996] considered at Chapter 4, Limitation, p 90, which held that wrongful conception could be viewed as an injury as the woman had to endure the pain and inconvenience associated with the pregnancy. Second, the decision not to award damages is in direct contrast to that of *Allen v Bloomsbury Health Authority* [1993] Chapter 7, Damages, p 214, where the plaintiffs were allowed to recover the costs of the upkeep of a healthy child. This case was considered by Lord Gill in *McFarlane* but he held that it would be distasteful for the court to have to assess the value of a child's life as that this may mean the court concluding that the value of a child's life was less than the cost of rearing him. Moreover, he considered that damages of this type were greater in the English cases if the parents were more affluent. In Lord Gill's opinion, more affluent parents should derive greater satisfaction from the fact that they could offer greater opportunities to their child. We would hope these arguments remain confined to the Scottish courts. Clearly, the woman should be compensated for the pain associated with an unwanted pregnancy; it may be a natural occurrence but it has been brought about by the negligence of the defendant. Further, we do not see any reason why damages cannot be assessed; the plaintiffs simply want compensation for the extra mouth to feed. True the child may now be very much wanted but at the time of the negligence the child was very much unwanted and the plaintiffs should not be penalised for putting their wishes to one side and caring for this unplanned addition to the family.

CHAPTER 1

MEDICAL CONFIDENTIALITY

RULE 1(A)

Health care personnel owe both a legal and an ethical duty of confidentiality. In practical terms this means that a doctor must not disclose (except in defined circumstances) information regarding his patient to a third party, whether that third party be a relative or a stranger.

Commentary

This rule is frequently expressed as if it were a self-sustaining proposition. In fact, while there is no doubting the ethical origins of the rule, its legal origin is somewhat difficult to state with any degree of certainty.

Ethically the duty exists because such declarations as the Hippocratic Oath, the Declaration of Geneva and GMC and BMA guidelines say so. For example, in the GMC's booklet on Good Medical Practice, para 16 says:

> Patients have a right to expect that you will not pass on any personal information which you learn in the course of your professional duties, unless they agree. If in exceptional circumstances you feel you should pass on information without a patient's consent, or against a patient's wishes, you should read our booklet 'Confidentiality' and be prepared to justify your decision.

The justification for this information being kept confidential is that it enhances the doctor–patient relationship. Without the rule, it is said, the patient might not entrust full, potentially intimate, details to the doctor with the result that the treatment given might not be appropriate. It is to be stressed that the rule is not dependent on any conscious wish of the patient for confidentiality; it arises from the existence of the relationship. Thus, while a patient may fervently hope that a discussion with the doctor about an embarrassing problem will go no further and may indeed ask the doctor that it should be kept confidential, in less embarrassing situations the doctor's obligation to respect the confidence will still exist even though the patient may not consciously look for confidentiality.

This ethical rule applies to all branches of health carers, eg nurses, physiotherapists, etc. If a disclosure is made in unauthorised circumstances, then disciplinary action may follow if a complaint is lodged. The 'punishment' will very much depend on the code of the particular branch of the profession involved. Thus, if a GP were carelessly to divulge confidential information, a complaint to the Family Health Services Authority or the Community Health Council or (in an extreme case) the GMC would be in order. In the latter case, although no appeal exists against its findings, an ordinary civil action could still be pursued (see below at Rule 1(B)). Again, if the disclosure occurred against the background of hospital treatment, then the hospital complaints procedure could be invoked. While it is more than likely that the patient's first thoughts will turn to the profession's complaints machinery, legal redress will be available for those situations where the patient may be dissatisfied with the internal handling of his complaint, or where the disclosure has resulted in serious consequences for the patient and there is such a legal requirement to respect the confidence of the patient.

What is the legal basis for the rule? It cannot be the ethical codes (see above) as these all lack legal status. Given that there is as yet no statutory provision against unauthorised disclosure, is it contractual, tortious, equitable, fiduciary or *sui generis*? What remedy is available to the disgruntled patient?

As regards a private patient the answer is clear: a claim lies in contract because there is a contractual relationship between the patient and the hospital and/or the health staff, and that contract will either contain an express term of confidentiality or the courts will 'read in' an implied term to that effect in appropriate circumstances.

But what of the NHS patient, who has no contract with the hospital or its staff? As there is no specific tort of breach of confidence, could the legal underpinning of the rule lie in the tort of negligence, so that non-disclosure might be seen as part of the doctor's overall duty of care to the patient? Probably not, since negligence implies a certain degree of inadvertence whereas in the case of an unauthorised disclosure the actions of the person disclosing are invariably deliberate. To this extent, the New Zealand case of *Furniss v Fitchett* [1958] NZLR 396 may now be regarded as founded on an unsound legal premise. In that case the unauthorised disclosure was followed by a successful negligence claim using the argument that it was reasonably foreseeable that the disclosure would cause physical harm to the patient. Furthermore, if negligence were to be considered the correct form of action then it would follow that the *Bolam* rule would be applicable (see Chapter 5, Standard of Care, p 121), and that in turn would mean that a GP would not be liable for any unauthorised disclosure provided that a responsible body of medical opinion would have made the disclosure in similar circumstances.

Could medical confidentiality be regarded as an independent duty (ie not as part of the doctor's overall duty of care)? It is an interesting thought and one which, if true, could have a profound effect on the general legal liability of the medical profession. It would then be possible to argue that, instead of one indivisible duty owed to the patient with one standard of care (the *Bolam* standard), in reality, there were separate duties owed, not all of which need necessarily attract the *Bolam* standard (see, for example, the Australian case of *Rogers v Whittaker* [1993] 4 Med LR 79). But to do so would mean ignoring the House of Lords approach in *Sidaway v Board of Governors of the Bethlem Royal Hospital and the Maudsley Hospital* [1985] AC 871; where it was said that the doctor's duty to his patient was legally indivisible.

Is there a 'tort' of breach of confidence which, if committed, could give rise to such remedies as an injunction or damages? According to some of the standard works on tort the answer is yes. Seemingly, there are three questions which have to be answered:

(1) Was the relevant information of a confidential nature?

(2) Was it entrusted in such circumstances that the other person knew that it was not to be disclosed without prior permission, ie was there a special relationship between the giver and receiver of the information?

(3) Was it in the public interest that the information should not be divulged?

If the answer to all three questions is yes, then a claim can be brought in equity. This conclusion is supported by various statements made by Scott J in *W v Egdell* [1989] 1 All ER 1089, (at p 1101):

> Counsel for W relies on two sources for the obligation of confidence or of non-disclosure on which W's action against Dr Egdell is based. One source is implied contract, the other is equity. The two sources will in most cases cover the same ground. It is convenient for me first to ask myself what duty of confidence a court of equity ought to regard as imposed on Dr Egdell by the circumstances in which he obtained information from and about W and prepared his report.

Again, he said (at p 1105):

> In my judgment ... the circumstances of this case did not impose on Dr Egdell an obligation of conscience, an equitable obligation to refrain from disclosing his report ...

It is submitted that the whole tenor of Scott J's judgment in the *Egdell* case is to suggest that the legal basis for non-disclosure is in equity and not tort, with the principal remedy being one of injunction, but that damages may be awarded in appropriate circumstances. The success of the claim will rest not so much on the nature of any specific agreement between the parties but on the plaintiff establishing that the information was imparted in confidence and that the receiver should not, in the circumstances, have taken advantage of it. That the law should still be in this unsatisfactory state is surprising given that in 1981 the Law Commission actually recommended the abolition of the present law on breach of confidence and replacing it with a statutory tort. An action in the courts would then lie where the information involved was:

(1) secret, ie not in the public domain;

(2) something other than personal knowledge, skill or experience acquired in the course of work; and

(3) such that, on the balance of public interests, ought to be protected from disclosure.

REFERENCES

English case law

(1) Bolam v Friern Hospital Management Committee [1957] 1 WLR 582; [1957] 2 All ER 118

See Chapter 5, Standard of Care, p 121.

(2) Sidaway v Board of Governors of the Bethlem Royal Hospital and the Maudsley Hospital [1985] AC 871; [1985] 1 All ER 643

See Chapter 3, Duty, p 63.

(3) W v Egdell [1989] 1 All ER 1089 affirmed at [1990] 1 All ER 835

See Rule 1(D)(v), at p 23.

See also *AG v Guardian Newspapers (No 2) [1988] 3 All ER 545*

On the question of whether the plaintiff need show detriment, Lord Keith commented that the erosion of privacy was a sufficient reason for the court to act as it is in the public interest.

Note: There is as yet to right to privacy.

Foreign case law

AUSTRALIA

Rogers v Whittaker [1993] 4 Med LR 79; [1992] 3 Med LR 331; (1992) 109 ALR 625

See Chapter 3, Duty, at pp 64, 67.

NEW ZEALAND

Furniss v Fitchett [1958] NZLR 396

The defendant doctor wrote a letter stating that in his opinion the plaintiff was exhibiting signs of paranoia and should be examined by a psychiatrist. The defendant passed this letter to the plaintiff's husband (both the plaintiff and her husband were patients of the defendant), who then used this letter in separation proceedings. The plaintiff sued the defendant for breach of confidence.

Held: the defendant ought to have reasonably foreseen that the letter might come to his patient's knowledge and that if it did it might injure her health. He did not have to foresee the precise way in which it came to the plaintiff's attention. The defendant was therefore in breach of his duty of care to the plaintiff, and she recovered damages for her physical injuries.

UNITED STATES

Morris v Consolidation Coal Co (1994) 446 SE (2d) 648

The Supreme Court of Appeal of West Virginia considered the relationship between a treating physician and his patient and recognised it as being of a fiduciary nature. It was further held that a third party who induces the physician to breach the confidence of his patient may be liable to that patient. Such a claim will exist when the third party is aware of the physician–patient relationship and the information is wrongfully disclosed.

Statutes / statutory instruments

(1) LAW COMMISSION REPORT NO 110 BREACH OF CONFIDENCE (CMND 838, 1981)

(2) EUROPEAN CONVENTION ON HUMAN RIGHTS, ARTICLE 10

Freedom of expression but disclosure of information should not occur where the information was given in confidence.

RULE 1(B)

If the plaintiff's legal claim for an unauthorised disclosure is successful then the court is entitled to grant an injunction and/or award damages.

Commentary

Injunction

Under s 37 Supreme Court Act 1981, an injunction can be granted in all cases where it appears to the court to be just and convenient to do so. (See also s 38 County Courts Act 1984 which gives a similar jurisdiction to the county court.) Breach of the injunction is punishable as contempt of court.

The courts will only act at the instance of the party to whom the duty of confidence is owed. In the case of an injunction, it matters not whether the parties' relationship is in contract or in tort (ie whether the plaintiff is a private patient or a NHS patient); what is required is that the person who possesses the confidential information must be under an obligation to maintain that confidence.

The injunction will be an interlocutory, prohibitory injunction. It may be qualified, eg to prevent the defendant disclosing information to the press but to permit disclosure to the appropriate authorities who should receive the information in the public interest (see Rule 1D(v)). It may be refused altogether where the court considers damages to be an adequate remedy, whether or not the plaintiff has applied for damages in his statement of claim (see s 50 Supreme Court Act 1981).

The precise circumstances in which an injunction may be granted are as follows:

(1) where there is serious harm which is likely to continue; or

(2) where the harm is irreparable or cannot be quantified in financial terms; or

(3) where the defendant does not have the means to pay damages.

Additionally, before granting an injunction the court will require an undertaking from the plaintiff to compensate the defendant for any harm caused by the injunction at a later date. This requirement will not apply, however, where the order is in the nature of a final order which, it is suggested, the majority of claims for breach of confidence will be.

If it is intended to proceed to trial the principles laid down in the case of *American Cyanamid v Ethicon* [1975] AC 396 will need to be followed (see RSC Ord 29, r 1). This means the plaintiff will have to show the following:

(1) He has a good arguable claim to the right he seeks to protect, ie it is not frivolous or vexatious.

(2) There is a serious action to be tried. (This means the court will be looking to see if the plaintiff has a good arguable case, not that he will necessarily win.)

(3) If the plaintiff satisfies (1) and (2), then whether or not the court chooses to exercise its discretion depends on the balance of convenience. The court will consider (i) are damages an adequate remedy and/or is the defendant able to pay them; (ii) whether the damages are an appropriate remedy (see below at p 6); and (iii) whether more harm will be done by granting or refusing an injunction.

If all things are equal, the court will favour maintaining the *status quo*. It will take into account social and economic factors and the relative strength of the respective parties' cases. If it is not self-evident that the injunction should be granted on the criteria stated above then it can be influenced by the fact that one of the parties has a stronger case.

The most obvious reason for applying for an injunction is to prevent a breach of confidence taking place. But will this ever happen? How will the plaintiff know that the defendant is about to breach confidence? There may be some warning but if not then the action will always be for a past breach. Where the confidence has already been breached then the person to whom the confidence is owed may still be entitled to an injunction, eg to prevent the defendant from continuing to disclose the information or disclosing further information. However, it will perhaps be thought that damages, in these circumstances, are a more appropriate remedy. Interestingly, in the notes to RSC Ord 29, *The White Book* (29/1/3) points out that, in assessing the balance of convenience test, damages may not be an appropriate remedy if the damage is:

(a) irreparable; or

(b) outside the scope of pecuniary compensation; or

(c) too difficult to assess.

It seems apparent that for the majority of claims for breach of confidence, the damage done will be irreparable.

Alternatively, if the intention is not to proceed to trial then invariably the plaintiff will want the matter decided once and for all. *The White Book*, at 29/1/2, provides that where neither side is interested in monetary compensation and the decision on the application will be the equivalent of a final judgment, then the court should assess the relative strength of each side's case before deciding whether the injunction should be granted, see *Cambridge Nutrition Ltd v BBC* [1990] 3 All ER 523. Admittedly, this principle is more often to be found where the case concerns a public broadcast (see *Cambridge*) or article but it is suggested that the same could equally apply in a breach of confidence case where the plaintiff is not looking for financial compensation.

We would argue, however, that although technically the courts may consider the principles stated in *Cambridge*, in a breach of confidence claim the court should favour the plaintiff every time and grant an interlocutory injunction. As for the defendants, they will have ample time to justify their actions at the trial or at a later interlocutory hearing by showing that their conduct comes within one of the GMC exclusion criteria (see further, at p 14 *et seq*).

Damages

Damages are appropriate to compensate for a past breach of confidence where there is no likelihood of the breach recurring and where the court deems an injunction to be inappropriate. The award of damages may be made up of any of the following:

(1) mental distress, injury to feelings or annoyance resulting from the breach;

(2) loss of society;

(3) loss of employment;

(4) any adverse effect on promotion prospects.

It is at this point that a distinction begins to emerge depending on the legal relationship of the parties, ie whether the patient is being treated privately or under the NHS. In a contractual claim, the courts have held that damages will not be awarded in contract for mental distress or injury to feelings (see *W v Egdell* [1990] 1 All ER 835) unless the contract itself was a contract to provide peace of mind or freedom from distress (see *Jarvis v Swan Tours* [1973] 1 QB 233). As regards the other heads of damages, they could be substantial and, under general contract principles, will lie for all those losses which flow naturally from the breach, eg if it is revealed that the plaintiff is HIV positive his business may suffer and his insurance may be affected, etc.

There is some confusion over what damages are available in a non-contractual relationship, eg where a NHS patient is involved. Certainly, the English courts have recognised that damages may be an appropriate remedy, as illustrated in the case of *X v Y* [1988] 2 All ER 648. Furthermore, the defendant in a breach of confidence claim will need to account for a loss of profits. However, the courts are also able to award damages not based on any loss of profit (see *Seager v Copydex* [1967] 2 All ER 415); these should be assessed on the basis of reasonable compensation for the use of the confidential information. In reality, however, a plaintiff's claim for breach of confidence by a doctor is unlikely to be concerned primarily with loss of profit.

An equity-based claim should not be affected by the ruling in *W v Egdell* [1990] 1 All ER 835 which ruled out damages for mental distress in a contractual claim, although there are comments in this case which seem to imply that the position would be the same in equity. Moreover, there is no tort remedy in damages for mental distress falling short of a recognised psychiatric illness, see *McLoughlin v O'Brian* [1983] AC 410; *Alcock v Chief Constable of South Yorkshire* [1992] 1 AC 310 and Chapter 7, Damages, at p 215 *et seq*.

Apart from damages for mental distress, what other compensation will the plaintiff receive? As the claim is in equity (as opposed to contract or tort) the position appears to be that he will not recover financial losses flowing from the breach. However, it does seem inequitable that a private patient, suing in contract, could recover such a loss whereas a NHS patient could not. To be 'equitable', the plaintiff should be able to recover for all foreseeable loss as a result of the breach of confidence whether the claim is in contract, tort or equity.

REFERENCES

English case law

(1) American Cyanamid v Ethicon [1975] AC 396; [1975] 1 All ER 504

See above, at p 5.

(2) Cambridge Nutrition Ltd v BBC [1990] 3 All ER 523

The plaintiff brought an action against the BBC for an injunction to prevent the BBC broadcasting a programme about the 'Cambridge diet'.

Held: the subject of the program was in the public interest and the action failed. It was also held that the *American Cyanamid* principle was not of universal application and in this instance Kerr LJ said (at p 536):

... I do not think that it makes any difference whether this case is decided in accordance with the *Cyanamid* test or not. On either basis the answer is the same.

Gibson LJ said the case came within the category stated in *American Cyanamid*, namely (at p 543):

... many other special factors to be taken into consideration in the particular circumstances of individual cases.

In this case because the loss was said to be uncompensatable and the action would not proceed to trial the court was not bound by the *American Cyanamid* principle.

(3) W v Egdell [1990] 1 All ER 835

See Rule 1(D)(v), at p 23 *et seq*.

(4) Jarvis v Swan Tours [1973] 1 QB 233

Here, for breach of a holiday contract costing £63.45, the court awarded £125 damages. As Stephenson LJ said (at pp 240–41):

> I argue that ... there may be contracts in which the parties contemplate inconvenience or breach which may be described as mental frustration, annoyance, disappointment and as Mr Thompson accedes that this is such a contract, the damages for breach of it should take wider inconvenience or discomfort into account.

(5) X v Y [1988] 2 All ER 648

See Rule 1(D)(v), at p 23 *et seq.*

(6) Seager v Copydex [1967] 2 All ER 415

The plaintiff had told the defendants about a new type of carpet grip; the defendants then developed the idea which had been given to them in confidence. The plaintiff was awarded damages for their having used the idea without paying for it.

(7) McLoughlin v O'Brian [1983] AC 410; [1982] 2 All ER 298

See Chapter 7, Damages, at p 215 *et seq.*

(8) Alcock and others v Chief Constable of South Yorkshire [1992] 1 AC 310; [1991] 4 All ER 907

See Chapter 7, Damages, at p 215.

Statutes / statutory instruments

(1) RSC ORD 29

(2) LAW COMMISSION REPORT NO 110 'BREACH OF CONFIDENCE, CMND 838, 1981

This recommended that damages for mental distress caused by breach of confidence should be available. However, to date this recommendation has not been acted upon.

(3) MEDICAL (PROFESSIONAL PERFORMANCE) ACT 1995

Discussed below.

Professional / ethical guidelines

- If legal redress is not to be sought, a complaint may be lodged with the GMC accusing the doctor of 'serious professional misconduct'.

    The GMC's Good Medical Practice lists the type of conduct which is capable of being labelled 'an abuse of the doctor's professional opinion' (serious professional misconduct). A breach of medical confidentiality falls within this definition (see para 17 of the GMC's Good Medical Practice). It is abundantly clear that the outcome of such disciplinary procedure will have considerable evidential value in any subsequent civil proceedings and, even though there is no right of appeal against the GMC's findings (judicial review may be available), the unsuccessful patient may still pursue a civil claim for breach of confidence. However, although the courts can depart from the GMC's decision, in practice this is unlikely to happen (see *W v Egdell* [1990] 1 All ER 835 and *X v Y* [1988] 2 All ER 648 discussed at Rule 1D(v), at p 23 *et seq*).

    Faced with the criticism that the phrase 'serious professional misconduct' was being given too narrow a meaning, eg it was alleged to be more focused on the sexual behaviour of the medical profession than its professional performance, the GMC published in May 1992, a consultative paper, 'Proposals for New Performance Procedures'. Out of that paper came the Medical (Professional Performance) Act 1995, which widens the GMC's jurisdiction. Now, in addition to 'serious professional misconduct', the GMC can take jurisdiction where the doctor's performance is 'seriously deficient'. Although this phrase has deliberately not been defined, it is doubtful, given the tenor of the debates in Parliament, whether 'seriously deficient' is intended to cover such matters such as the breaking of a medical confidence. See also, the National Health Service (Service Committees) and Tribunal Regulations 1992 SI 1992/664. These regulations deal with complaints to the FHSA. The complaint must relate to a breach by the GP of his terms of service as laid down in the National Health Service (General Medical Services) Regulations 1992 SI 1992/635 Schedule 2.

Practice points

- Injunction – The application should be made by motion to the Chancery Division or *ex parte* on affidavit. If the application is made *ex parte*, it must be made promptly and there must be strong grounds to justify its being made *ex parte* (see *The White Book* 29/1/8). Clearly, the application will be made *ex parte* to preserve the element of surprise or where speed is essential. An application can only be made *ex parte* if:

  (1) giving notice to the opponent would cause injustice to the applicant because either the situation is urgent or it is imperative to preserve the element of surprise; and

  (2) the risk of damage to the opponent is compensatable by damages or is less than the potential risk to the applicant if the order is not granted.

- All the facts must be laid before the court and nothing suppressed (see *R v Kensington Income Tax Commissioners* [1917] 1 KB 486). The applicant has a duty to make any material disclosure, and there are severe penalties should he fail to comply with this obligation.

- The writ with the affidavit should be delivered to the court office the day preceding the application, although in practice as the application will be made *ex parte* the documents should be taken to the court as soon as practicable. Note that any application should explain why the opponent was not given notice.

  If the writ has not been issued the solicitor must undertake to issue the writ 'forthwith' or 'as soon as practicable'.

- An undertaking as to damages ought to be given on every interlocutory injunction though not where the order is in the nature of a final order (see *Fenner v Wilson* [1978] 2 Ch 656, and above, at p 5).

- The injunction must be served personally indorsed with a penal notice (see *The White Book* 45/7/6; County Court Form N77 and RSC Ord 45, r 7; CCR Ord 29, r 1).

- In law, it seems that the doctor's duty of confidence does not survive a patient's death (like an action for defamation) unlike the ethical obligation imposed by the GMC. Para 13 of 'Confidentiality' (part of the 'Duties of a doctor' series of publications) states:

  > You still have an obligation to keep information confidential after a patient dies. The extent to which confidential information may be disclosed after a patient's death will depend on the circumstances. These include the nature of the information, whether that information is already public knowledge, and how long it is since the patient died. ...

  Query – will a defence try and drag out the case as long as possible until the patient has died, and therefore escape legal, if not professional, liability?

- In *X v France European Court Of Human Rights* (1992) *The Times*, 20 April (see (PMILL) Vol 8 No 9 1992, at p 71), it was held that the excessive length of proceedings brought to obtain compensation before the French administrative authorities and the Paris administrative court violated an AIDS sufferers' rights under Article 6 para 1 of the European Convention on Human Rights. The applicant had developed full AIDS and the court held that, because of his reduced life expectancy, exceptional diligence was called for in this instance.

In this case, it was the administrative court that was penalised; however, we can see no reason why this principle should not be applied to an unscrupulous defence lawyer. Perhaps this area of the law will be amended to come into line with negligence, ie the Law Reform (Miscellaneous Provisions) Act 1934: after all, it is usually the family who will suffer after the plaintiff's death.

- While it may be possible to prove the doctor has made an error in breaching the patient's confidence, one should always stress to the patient that the damage has been done and an action which may drag the whole matter up again, perhaps even bring it to the attention of the media, should not be undertaken lightly.

- Note that the plaintiff may have a claim in defamation in addition to a breach of confidence claim. However, a claim in defamation is likely to be a rare occurrence for a number of reasons. First, legal aid is not available for an action for defamation, an obvious deterrent to many would-be litigants. Second, with the exception of those actions that are actionable *per se* in England, the law of slander requires that the plaintiff should be able to prove special damage, ie pecuniary losses. This latter point will effectively rule out those cases which are simply a claim for mental distress and anguish.

Finally, if the defendant has acted responsibly he is likely to have a defence. If what he stated is true then he will have a complete defence, and even if it is found that part of the statement is not true, provided he had reasonable grounds for holding that belief and he communicated the information to the proper authorities he will not be found liable. For example, in a suspected child abuse case, informing the police or the social services would be protected by the defence of qualified privilege. However, the defendant who informs an employer that his employee is HIV positive treads an unstable path. The courts will again look at whether the disclosure was justified along the same principles as those used for a breach of confidence claim, see disclosure in the public interest at Rule 1(D)(v), at p 23 *et seq*. We believe that it will only be the reckless defendant or the defendant motivated by malice who will find himself liable.

- See the end of this chapter for checklist, draft pleadings and order regarding breach of confidence.

RULE 1(C)

If a doctor decides not to disclose information he will not be liable to a third party who is subsequently harmed by the patient.

Commentary

In deciding whether or not to disclose information a doctor will undoubtedly consider the risk posed by the patient, weigh the duty to the patient against the harm that could be done to society (and that includes the third party), and consider whether disclosure is necessary. If this approach is adopted, then the doctor should not be held culpable by the courts. In English law, it is still the position that one person will not usually be held liable for harm done by another person (see *Smith v Littlewoods Organisation Ltd* [1987] 1 All ER 710 and

Hill v Chief Constable of West Yorkshire [1988] 2 All ER 238). Only where the doctor exercises control over the patient will a duty be imposed (see *Holgate v Lancashire Board* [1937] 4 All ER 19 and *Home Office v Dorset Yacht Co Ltd* [1970] AC 1004). If the doctor acts in the public interest, then that will excuse a breach of confidence, but the public interest does not impose a new duty on the doctor. Hence, while the doctor can foresee a risk to a third party, eg the spouse of an AIDS patient, that does not place him under a duty to disclose to the third party. If such a duty were imposed on a doctor then it could place him in the difficult position of being forced to juggle his respective obligations. It is suggested that this should never occur because the duty of confidence is paramount and can only be breached where it is in the public interest to do so: disclosure is the exception not the rule.

In certain states of the United States, a different approach is evident. In *Tarasoff v Regents of the University of California* (1976) 551 P(2d) 334, a medical centre was found liable to a third party in negligence for failing to disclose information to the third party. In this case, the Supreme Court of California held a psychiatrist liable for the actions of his student patient who murdered his girlfriend in a case of unrequited love. The girl was identifiable and identified and it was clear that the relationship between the psychiatrist and the patient was one in which the patient was under the control of the health professional. More recently, in *Bradshaw v Daniel* (1994) *Med L Rev* 237, the Supreme Court of Tennessee, following *Tarasoff*, imposed a similar duty on a physician where, although there was an identifiable plaintiff, there was no control. In this case, a woman died from a non-contagious disease, Rocky Mountain Spotted Fever. The defendant physician had been treating the woman's husband for the same disease from which he had died shortly before the wife began to show symptoms of the disease. The court held that the physician–patient relationship was sufficient to impose upon the physician a positive duty to warn identifiable third parties in the patient's immediate family against foreseeable risks resulting from the patient's illness; here, although it was not a contagious disease, members of the family were in danger of contracting the disease.

On the other hand, in *Webb v Jarvis* (1991) 575 NE (2d) 992, the plaintiff had been shot by a patient who was being treated by the defendant physician. He brought an action in negligence against the defendant arguing that:

(1) the physician had a duty to administer medical treatment to a patient in such a way as to take into account possible harm to unidentifiable third persons;

(2) the defendant had breached this duty by prescribing anabolic steroids which had made the patient violent; and

(3) the defendant had a duty to warn others of the patient's propensity for violence.

The Supreme Court of Indiana dismissed the plaintiff's claim. In deciding whether the defendant owed a duty it took into account three factors:

(1) The relationship between the parties. The court ruled that a professional person had no duty to a third party unless the former had actual knowledge that the latter was relying on him to render professional services. Here there was no evidence that the plaintiff was in fact relying on the defendant in this

way. This is somewhat different from the *Tarasoff* case where the defendant must have been aware that the third party was relying on his treatment of the patient. Does this therefore mean that a spouse who wishes to claim against her husband's doctor for failing to warn her that her spouse was infected with HIV would have to show not only that the doctor knew of her existence but also that she was relying on the doctor who was treating her husband? How would she demonstrate such reliance?

(2) The duty of care was only owed to a foreseeable victim and the particular harm must have been foreseeable. Whether or not the third party was a foreseeable victim was a matter for the jury. In *Webb*, it was held it was not reasonably foreseeable that prescribing steroids would make the patient dangerous, as a matter of law. But is this not a question for the medical experts to answer?

(3) Public policy dictated that the physician should not be liable. It would, it was said, impose too onerous a burden on the physician to predict a patient's reaction to medication and to identify possible plaintiffs who might be at risk.

One has to ask whether that would always be the case? If the doctor knew that, by prescribing a certain treatment to his patient, there was a high degree of risk that the patient would harm a third party, should he not be under a moral/legal duty to warn that third party?

What clearly emerges from these cases is that some American courts see no objection in principle in imposing what may be called a third party positive duty on a doctor. What is less clear are the circumstances which must prevail for such a duty to exist. In our view the cases suggest that:

(1) A reasonably foreseeable identifiable individual must be at risk. In *Tarasoff*, there was such an individual while in Bradshaw the members of the family (a distinct and identifiable group) were the people at risk. If the patient in *Tarasoff* had uttered threats of a general nature, eg to society as a whole, then we would have expected a different decision because it would not have been possible to isolate any specific identifiable third party at risk. While not a perfect analogy, it could be said that one of the reasons why Mrs Hill failed in her claim against the police in *Hill v Chief Constable of West Yorkshire* [1988] 2 All ER 238 was that she was 'at no special or distinctive risk', ie she was not sufficiently identifiable.

(2) Some control is exercisable over the patient, and exercised by the defendant doctor. It is our contention that the nature of this control needs to be of the type which existed in *Tarasoff*, bearing in mind the nature of the patient's illness rather than the 'normal control' which exists between any doctor and his patient. To this extent the nature of the illness will play a significant part in determining whether the duty does exist.

Demonstrating that the duty exists in some American states is one thing; arguing from that premise that English law is wrong in denying the existence of such a duty is a more difficult proposition. While it is correct to say that at present the American approach is unlikely to be followed in the United Kingdom, we would argue that where a defendant exercising control over an individual can reasonably foresee that the individual's actions will harm identifiable third parties, then a duty should be imposed on the defendant to warn that third party. We would extend this principle to the situation where a defendant, by his own actions over an individual, creates the risk that an identifiable third party may be harmed. When this approach is applied to doctors we do not give much credence to the argument that the doctor would be placed under too onerous a duty to predict a patient's reaction to medication: surely this is the doctor's job? We would further extend the duty to all identifiable third parties whether or not they are immediate members of the family, because any attempt to limit the duty to family members would, in our opinion, be unfairly restrictive and vague (eg who are members of the family – only those living in the same household?). The doctor could comply with his obligations by informing the third party or the appropriate authorities, see Rule 1(F), at p 29.

This is how we believe the law should develop. The bottom line still appears to be that the doctor must act in what he perceives to be the public interest, even if this does not accord with the majority's view of how he should have acted. If the doctor does so and harm befalls a third party, it seems that at present the doctor will not be held liable.

See also Chapter 3, Duty, at p 71 *et seq*.

REFERENCES

English case law

(1) Smith v Littlewoods Organisation Ltd [1987] 1 All ER 710

The defendants purchased a cinema intending to demolish it and build a supermarket. The property, however, remained empty for over a month, during which time vandals entered the property and attempted to start fires. Neither the defendants nor the police were informed of this. Eventually the vandals were successful in starting a fire, and as a result the plaintiff's adjoining property was damaged. The plaintiff brought an action against the defendants in negligence.

Held: there was no general duty of care to prevent third parties from causing damage. The foreseeability of the damage is not in itself sufficient to create a positive duty on the defendant to act.

(2) Hill v Chief Constable of West Yorkshire [1988] 2 All ER 238

The plaintiff was the mother of the Yorkshire Ripper's thirteenth victim and alleged that the West Yorkshire police force had breached their duty of care to her daughter by failing to apprehend the Ripper earlier. The court dismissed the action partly on the ground that the victim 'was one of a vast number of the female general public who might be at risk from his activities but was at no special distinctive risk ... ' (*per* Lord Keith, at p 243).

(3) Holgate v Lancashire Mental Hospitals Board [1937] 4 All ER 19

The defendant was held liable for negligently releasing a dangerous patient who had been compulsorily detained following convictions for violent offences. The patient subsequently assaulted the plaintiff.

(4) Home Office v Dorset Yacht Co Ltd [1970] AC 1004; [1970] 2 All ER 294

Borstal trainees escaped due to the negligence of Borstal officers. The trainees caused damage to the plaintiff's yacht.

Held: the Borstal authorities were responsible for the damage caused by the trainees. Note that there was a high degree of control being exercised by the officers over the trainees.

Foreign case law

UNITED STATES

(1) Tarasoff v Regents of the University of California (1976) 551 P (2d) 334

In *Tarasoff*, it was held that a psychiatrist had a duty to inform a third party of the threats made against her by his patient. The patient had repeatedly told his psychiatrist that he intended to kill his former girlfriend. He in fact did carry out his threat and the woman's family brought a successful negligence claim against the medical centre.

(2) Bradshaw v Daniel [1994] Med L Rev 237

See Commentary above, at p 11.

(3) Webb v Jarvis (1991) 575 NE (2d) 992

See Commentary above, at p 11. See also *Saur v Probes (1991) 476 NW (2d) 196*

The plaintiff's wife had petitioned the court to have the plaintiff involuntarily hospitalised for psychiatric treatment. The plaintiff's psychiatrist disclosed communications which had been made to him several months earlier. On appeal, the plaintiff succeeded in an action for negligence against his psychiatrist.

Held: the duty of confidentiality may be breached in the following instances:

(1) voluntary waiver by the patient;

(2) waiver by operation of law;

(3) disclosure which is justified in the supervening interests of society, of a third party, or of the patient. This was a matter for the jury, and it had not been established in this instance.

In commenting on the duty of the doctor to act in such instances, the court stated that the 'overriding public or private interests to which we refer merely excuse the psychiatrists breach of duty to maintain confidentiality, and do not impose a new duty on the psychiatrist or affect any pre-existing duties'. This is in line with the English position, ie a doctor has discretion to breach his duty of confidentiality; he is never under a duty to do so.

RULE 1(D)

The rule against disclosure is not an absolute rule. There are exceptions to it.

Commentary

The rules about to be discussed are based upon the GMC and the BMA ethical guidelines. Although the point that we are about to make is, strictly speaking, a practice point it seems appropriate to make it here. In all cases, the GMC advise that, should the doctor decide to disclose confidential information, he must be prepared to explain and justify his decision. We suggest that any doctor should discuss his intended disclosure of information with a colleague or seek advice from, eg the Medical Defence Union. Moreover, any defence practitioner should advise his client to do just that, if the breach has not yet taken place. If it has, then his first question to the defendant should be: did he consult the aforesaid persons or bodies? While these guidelines are not legally binding, the courts have tended, as in most cases involving medical matters, to follow the lead given by the medical profession.

Rule 1(D)(i)

A doctor is legally and ethically justified in disclosing confidential information about his patients, should that patient willingly consent to the disclosure.

Commentary

Both the legal rules and the ethical guidelines state that, in well-defined circumstances, a disclosure can be made by either the doctor or someone in receipt of confidential information from the doctor. One such situation is where the patient willingly consents. Since the confidence is that of the patient, the doctor should be seen as the temporary custodian of that confidence: as such, the patient is free to do whatever he (the patient) wishes with the information. Consequently, any adult patient ie one who is 16 years of age or over, can give oral or written, express or implied, consent for disclosure and the doctor will be bound to acquiesce to those wishes. No court, it is submitted, will uphold the argument that in the doctor's view the disclosure would not have been in the patient's best interests; that would be taking paternalism too far. Having said that, it is clear that the consenting patient must fully understand both the nature and the consequences of the disclosure, eg what is to be revealed and who is the intended recipient, etc; also the consent has to be freely and willingly given. Finally, there is no reason why the consent may not be conveyed to the doctor by a third party, eg a relative or a legal adviser, on behalf of the patient. In such circumstances, however, the doctor would be well advised to ascertain the relationship between the patient and the third party and to note this information on the patient's records.

Where a patient is in the vulnerable position of lying in a hospital bed, he may not know whether the person having a conversation with him and trying to elicit his consent is his consultant, or a fellow doctor, or a social worker. Clearly, patients have no problem with their consultants sharing information with fellow health carers. But will patients feel equally content if they learn that the person with whom the information is being shared is a medical student or a social worker? Probably not, which is why it is important for the doctor or consultant not to assume that consent exists or will be given if sought; it is safer and ethically correct to seek the patient's consent. Again, where a doctor asks whether medical students can watch the procedure being undertaken, the patient is unlikely to refuse, but one must query whether the consent is truly voluntary. The doctor may genuinely feel that the patient has consented to student observation when in fact that is not the case. See further Rule 1(D)(ii), at p 16.

Can a patient under the age of 16 consent to disclosure? It is arguable that, since the *Gillick* case permits the mature under-16 to consent in law to medical treatment without parental permission, then such a person should be able to consent to any confidential information being disclosed or not as the case may be. Were this not so the situation would be reached where a doctor could rely on the patient for consent to treat but would have to turn to the parents for permission to disclose information about the said treatment. In fact, this could very well be the present state of the law since in *Re W (a minor) (medical treatment)* [1992] 4 All ER 627, the courts said that, although a mature under-16 can consent to treatment he has no right to refuse to be treated. This would suggest that such patients have limited rights. Maybe they do. But a denial of the right to refuse to be treated does not necessarily mean that, when properly treated, confidentiality can be ignored simply because you are under 16 years of age. Fortunately, new guidelines issued by the BMA, the Royal College of General Practitioners, the Family Planning Association and the Brooke Advisory Centres (and supported by the government funded Health Education Authority) now advise that the under-16s' confidentiality should be respected and that parents should only be informed in 'exceptional circumstances'. Although these guidelines relate specifically to young girls seeking contraceptive advice, it is submitted that capacity to consent to medical treatment will carry with it confidentiality.

REFERENCES

English case law

(1) Gillick v West Norfolk and Wisbech Area Health Authority [1986] AC 112; [1985] 3 All ER 402

See Chapter 2, Consent, at p 50.

(2) Re W (a minor) (medical treatment) [1992] 4 All ER 627

The Court of Appeal held that, although a competent minor can give consent to medical treatment, he does not have an absolute right to refuse treatment where his parent/guardian has consented to the treatment, see further, at p 46. This decision seems to take paternalism to even greater heights!

See also the cases discussed in Chapter 2, Consent, at p 48.

Professional / ethical guidelines

GMC's 'Confidentiality' booklet para 2

The GMC recognise that information may be disclosed 'in strict accordance with the patient's consent, or the consent of a person properly authorised to act on the patient's behalf'.

Rule 1(D)(ii)

The doctor may disclose confidential information to other persons responsible for the clinical treatment of the patient; ideally the patient should give his consent.

Commentary

Here the points made in Rule 1(D)(i) in relation to whether or not the patient is competent to give consent to disclosure to third parties apply, ie the consent could be express or implied, oral or written. Disclosure is permitted to third parties whether they are just involved in an isolated act of treatment or responsible for the continuing care of the patient. If the patient had to be consulted every time the doctor liaised with a fellow professional the doctor's job, if not impossible, would be difficult; therefore, it is taken that disclosure can be made to, eg nurses, radiologists, physiotherapists, etc, whenever the best interests of either the patient or the fellow health carers (see below, at p 18 *et seq*) so demand.

The doctor's duty is to ensure that the third party appreciates that the information is being imparted in strict confidence, although it seems unlikely that any claim will succeed against the doctor should the third party decide not to maintain the confidence. Perhaps the only grounds on which a claim could succeed are that:

(1) the doctor failed to state that the information was of a confidential nature (unlikely, given the nature of the information being disclosed; and a health care professional in any event would, it is suggested, be bound to assume that the information is confidential); or

(2) where the third party is outside the permitted group to which the doctor can disclose.

As regards the latter it is not certain to what extent people outside the medical profession can receive such information. For example, can social workers be told the specific details of a patient's illness? We suggest that in cases involving terminal illnesses they should be told, in the absence of which they may not be able to participate in providing the palliative care the patient requires. The decision, however, will be the doctor's and, providing he has acted in accordance with good clinical management, it is unlikely that he will be held to account for the misdemeanours of his fellow professionals.

The GMC issued guidelines in October 1995 for doctors treating HIV patients. On the subject of disclosing information to fellow health carers the relevant guidelines say significantly that, in all cases, the doctor must first try and persuade the patient that disclosure is necessary; the extent of that persuasion is unknown, but we suggest that the doctor will have to try and persuade on more than one occasion and explain fully the difficulties in treating the patient should he refuse to consent to such disclosure.

If the patient should steadfastly refuse to give consent then the doctor can disclose the confidential information when he believes the health of any of his fellow professionals is at risk. Note that the disclosure must only take place in exceptional circumstances. In effect, this is little more than a restatement of the public interest defence, (see further Rule 1(D)(lv), at p 23); the doctor again must balance the risk to the individual as against the public interest in maintaining the confidence of his patient. What if the doctor acts too late? Will his fellow colleague, affected by this inactivity, have any recourse against his silent colleague? We would say not, in line with the position of third parties who allege that the doctor owes them a duty of care to breach the patient's confidence (see Rule 1(C), at p 10). However, the court may feel inclined to treat the patient slightly differently given the identity of the third party, ie if the third party is a GP then in most cases there is a much higher degree of intimate contact (eg blood) than there would be between someone diagnosed as HIV positive and his work colleagues.

With regard to infected health care workers, the Department of Health Guidance AIDS–HIV Infected Health Care Workers (December 1991), in its amended statement of June 1993 and, more recently, in the booklet 'HIV and

AIDS: the ethical considerations' states that health carers have the same rights to confidentiality as a patient. However, the clear difference is that these persons could put patients at risk and this is recognised by the GMC who stress the need for a health carer to seek counselling and to inform the appropriate authority should he suspect a colleague is no longer fit. If a health carer fails to do this then he will be clearly in breach of his ethical obligations.

REFERENCES

Professional / ethical guidelines

GMC's 'Confidentiality' booklet paras 3–8

This deals with disclosure to other members of the health team. In particular, it notes that the doctor must explain to the patient why such disclosure is necessary; that in limited circumstances, eg an emergency, the patient's consent to disclosure need not be obtained; that if the patient refuses permission his decision will be respected, and that all members of the team have a duty to ensure their colleagues understand the obligation of confidentiality. For the position of the health carer and his rights to confidentiality, see above, at p 17.

Rule 1(D)(iii)

When a doctor considers it undesirable for medical reasons to seek the patient's consent or where the patient refuses consent to the disclosure of information, then, if the doctor considers it in the patient's best interests, he may disclose that information to a third party or a relative.

Commentary

What circumstances fall within this rule? The GMC say that it is where it is in the patient's best interests and it then goes on to list the following examples:

(1) in cases of neglect, physical or sexual abuse to the patient;

(2) where the patient is immature;

(3) where the nature of the patient's illness, including mental illness, precludes their giving consent.

We suggest that these exceptions will cover the majority of situations a doctor is likely to face, but before considering each in detail there are three general points that should be borne in mind:

(1) a properly considered clinical decision, in accordance with this guideline, cannot be unethical and therefore would not give rise to a claim;

(2) as regards consent to treatment, relatives have no special status, although it is more likely than not that the disclosure will be made to a relative;

(3) if the patient were to place a total ban on communication that would have to be respected in line with patient autonomy; however, in exceptional cases, disclosure may be made even if it is contrary to the patient's wishes.

Many of the situations about to be discussed could be said to come within the public interest defence (see Rule 1(D)(v), at p 23). However, it is possible to differentiate between the two categories of exceptions: the doctor can rely on the public interest defence where a third party is at risk; disclosure under the present rule is where it is supposedly in the patient's best interests.

Sexual/ physical abuse

The doctor's situation may differ with the identity of the patient; in the case of an adult woman usually she has the ability to sort out her own situation by either informing the police or seeking the protection of the law (see Domestic Violence and Matrimonial Proceedings Act 1976). It is suggested that all a doctor can do here is advise and help the patient; disclosure will only be justified if the doctor is of the opinion that the woman's life is at risk.

In the case of child abuse, the situation is different because the patient invariably cannot give consent; therefore the doctor will have to act on the basis of the best interests of the child and inform the proper authorities. Obviously, a case misdiagnosed could lead to an action for defamation but it is likely that the doctor would also have a defence under the public interest exception providing that he discloses the information to the proper authorities. Given that some authorities may undertake not to disclose the name of the informant, this is something which may encourage the doctor to act. The GMC's 'Confidentiality' booklet reiterates that disclosure should only be made, without the patient's consent, if the patient is unable to give consent and such disclosure is in the patient's best interests.

Immaturity

Generally, the duty owed to a person under the age of 16 is the same as that owed to any other patient. Relying on the GMC guidelines and the BMA advice published in consultation with, among others, the Health Education Authority (see Rule 1(D)(iii) above, at p 18) disclosure without consent would only be justified where the patient does not have sufficient understanding to appreciate what the advice or the treatment sought may involve and cannot be persuaded to involve another person in the consultation, and it would, in the doctor's opinion, be in the best interests of the child. The GMC stress that any disclosure must be based on an assessment of the patient's ability to understand the treatment and not solely their age.

One would have thought that where the patient is competent to consent to treatment then he will be entitled to have his confidence maintained, and that if he is not competent then that will entitle the doctor to breach the confidence. Not so; even where the patient is too immature to consent to treatment, confidentiality should still be maintained unless there are convincing arguments to the contrary.

This throws up an intriguing proposition. The BMA guidance is in particular targeted at under-age sexual relations. As such, we suggest that the main areas where doctors are likely to come into conflict with their young patients is in relation to sexual relations, contraception and abortion. Let us therefore take an example. A girl whom the doctor does not consider competent and therefore unable to consent to treatment would still be entitled to have her confidence maintained. But suppose she refuses to have her parents involved. She leaves the surgery and the doctor fears that she will have unprotected sexual intercourse. The consultation, according to the BMA, must remain confidential. Would the doctor be justified in breaching the confidence? Perhaps yes – if he believes that she is being sexually abused or exploited. But is a 14 year old who is in a steady relationship with another 14 year old being sexually abused or exploited? Is the risk of pregnancy sufficient for the doctor to be able to justify breaching her confidence? What if the 14 year old is well aware that a pregnancy may result but does not perceive this as a problem, as all her sisters had children when they were very young? Should the doctor take it upon himself to be that girl's moral guardian and breach her confidence, because although she does not see pregnancy as something that should be avoided, the doctor does? Perhaps the doctor would be justified in breaching the confidence because of the serious risk of a sexually transmitted disease, although if the patient has only one sexual partner this may again be unjustifiable.

However, the above situation may never arise, because one of the factors that a doctor must take into account is whether the patient is likely to continue having sexual intercourse without contraception should he refuse to prescribe it. We therefore suggest, in line with the government's wish to reduce teenage pregnancies, that the doctor will generally prescribe contraceptives, despite the fact that the teenager may not be *Gillick* competent.

Take another example: a 15 year old girl who wants an abortion. Abortion differs in one major respect from prescribing the pill in that it is an invasive procedure. The girl in question views the fact that she is pregnant as merely a way of life: her sisters have had abortions. The girl always forgets to take the pill, is simply having a good time and wants the abortion over with so she can get on with her life. She does not appear to understand the nature and risks associated with the abortion procedure. If the doctor does not help her she will go to a back street abortionist. In this situation, the doctor would probably agree to the abortion even though she is not *Gillick* competent. If he did breach her confidence, on what basis would that breach be justified? Clearly, if there was a risk to her health posed by the back street abortionist then the disclosure would be justified, not only under this heading but also in the public interest. But could he disclose on the grounds of the possibility of a future pregnancy if the girl did not perceive it as a risk? For that matter, if the parents did not see it as a problem, to whom would he disclose the information?

As regards boys and their sexual relationships, clearly since the boy can go into a supermarket and buy condoms it is unlikely he will ever need to go to a doctor for the prescription of contraceptives. But what would happen if he were to reveal that he is in a homosexual relationship? Could the doctor breach his confidence? It is likely, given that the age of consent for gay sex is 18, that if the doctor chose to breach the confidence he would be justified under this particular exception. But if the boys were both 15 and mature and in a steady relationship, it is suggested that the doctor could not justify the disclosure on grounds of exploitation, and any disclosure would have to be justified under the public interest argument. In our opinion, although the courts would probably sanction such a disclosure, ethically the doctor should maintain the confidence of his patient.

Having outlined some of the potential problems the doctor may face, it has to be said that it will be unusual for a minor to bring a claim, because in both the High Court and the county court he must sue by his next friend (see RSC Ord 80; CCR Ord 10). A next friend is an officer of the court appointed to take all steps for the benefit of the person he represents; thus, he has conduct of the litigation on the minor's behalf. In the case of a guardian *ad litem* (someone who is acting for the minor who is being sued) the court would prefer him to be a 'substantial person', namely a relative or a person connected with the family, rather than a mere volunteer. It is submitted that this will apply equally to the choice of next friend. In most cases, the next friend will be a parent or guardian, but in a breach of confidence case it is suggested that the parents will never agree to bring an action on behalf of their child because they are the very people who would have wanted the doctor to breach the confidence. Consequently, the minor will have to ask someone else to act on his behalf. It is suggested that this will never occur; in any event will the minor realise that he has a claim for breach of confidence? Probably not.

Illness

The GMC indicate that disclosure may be permitted where, because of illness, the patient lacks the capacity to consent. If that were the case, it is submitted that, as the patient would no longer be able to consent to treatment, the doctor would be forced to consult either a relative or a third party in the patient's best interests. Disclosure may also take place where the doctor judges that it would be damaging to the patient to seek consent to such disclosure.

REFERENCES

English case law

Gillick v West Norfolk and Wisbech Area Health Authority [1986] AC 112; [1985] 3 All ER 402

See Chapter 2, Consent, at p 50.

Statutes / statutory instruments

(1) DOMESTIC VIOLENCE AND MATRIMONIAL PROCEEDINGS ACT 1976

Section 1 grants the ability to apply for an injunction to restrain the other party to the marriage from molesting the applicant or a child or to exclude him or her from the matrimonial home. Section 2 extends this provision to a man and wife living together as though they were parties to the marriage.

(2) RULES OF THE SUPREME COURT

RSC Ord 80 (litigants under a disability) see Appendix D, at p 372.

Professional / ethical guidelines

GMC's 'Confidentiality' booklet paras 10–12

This deals with disclosure without the patient's consent. Generally, it echoes the exceptions as discussed in the preceding paragraphs. *Note* also that at para 9 it deals with disclosure to employers and insurance companies; it reminds doctors in these circumstances that they should only carry out an assessment of the patient's condition for these bodies with the patient's written consent.

Rule 1(D)(iv)

Information may be disclosed for the purposes of teaching and medical research, providing that that research is approved by a local clinical research ethical committee.

Commentary

This exception recognises that there is a public interest in properly conducted medical research. The research must be sanctioned by an approved ethical committee or, in the case of the National Cancer Registry, by the Chairman of the BMA's Central Ethical Committee or his nominee.

Paragraph 15 in the GMC's 'Confidentiality' booklet discusses confidentiality and research. Where consent cannot be obtained, it will be the research ethics committee which will decide whether the research comes within the public interest exception.

The GMC consider that where the information is used in a form that does not enable persons to be identified then technically there is no breach of confidence, eg where a doctor writes an article about a patient's condition without identifying the specific individual. But where the information would reveal the identity of one or more individuals, the researcher must obtain the patients' consent. We suggest that the consent sought should be an express written consent given at that time the research is to be conducted.

There is, however, one aspect of the GMC's statement with which we disagree. Whether or not the patient's identity is revealed is immaterial – there has still been a breach of confidence. Should, however, the patient's consent be sought prior to the breach; and furthermore is there any damage caused by the breach?

As this type of research often occurs sometime after the relevant entry in the patient's records has been made, any prior consent from the patient would be meaningless. As for any damage caused to the patient then this must be minimal: the patient is only known by the researcher for a short period, it is likely his name will be one of many and, providing the researcher undertakes not to make an unauthorised disclosure and does use the information for the public benefit, then we would support such research. We do not see that there is any advantage to be gained from seeking the patient's consent for the reasons outlined above.

The government has provided additional guidance in the document Local Research Ethics Committee HSG 91(5). Among its recommendations are the following:

(1) no individual should be recognisable from the research without their explicit consent and the information should be destroyed when it is no longer needed;

(2) where a situation arises where it would be impracticable to seek a patient's consent the LREC must be satisfied that the research is in the public interest, albeit that if the patient has indicated that he does not want his records released this should be respected;

(3) information should not be obtained without the consent being obtained from the health care professional and no approach should be made to the patient without the consent of the health care professional responsible for his care.

We endorse this approach and cannot see the law penalising any breach of confidence where the identity of an individual is not revealed. Obviously, if an individual is named our answer would be the opposite.

One point which is perhaps worthy of note relates to the number of medical students who, as part of their studies, carry out active research in hospitals. There are no guidelines governing the use of this information. We can only speculate whether the patient has given his consent freely to the general publication of such information.

REFERENCES

Professional / ethical guidelines

GMC's 'Confidentiality' booklet paras 15–17

Patients must be informed of their rights to withhold consent to disclosure. Where consent cannot be obtained then the research ethics committee must decide whether the public interest in the research outweighs the public interest in the preservation of the patient's confidence. The patient's consent must be obtained for use of confidential information in teaching unless such information is anonymous.

Rule 1(D)(v)

A doctor will have a defence to an action for breach of confidence if it can be shown that the disclosure of information was in the public interest. In determining whether or not the disclosure was in the public interest, the court will balance the harm that would have resulted had the doctor not disclosed the information against the public interest in maintaining the doctor–patient confidence.

Commentary

In establishing the parameters of this exception, the courts have over the years relied heavily on the guidance within the GMC's 'Blue Book' Professional Conduct: Fitness to Practice and the BMA's Handbook of Medical Ethics (see now the GMC's 'Confidentiality' booklet, paras 18–19). In balancing the various public interests, the courts have demonstrated certain definite approaches. They will have regard to the following.

Public interest

Disclosure of the information must be in the public interest; it is not sufficient that the information is interesting to the public. In *X v Y* [1988] 2 All ER 648, a health authority successfully obtained an injunction prohibiting a tabloid newspaper from publishing the names of two doctors who were being treated for AIDS. While the information would have been of interest to the public, public interest maintained that their identities should not be revealed, as this could have potentially discouraged fellow AIDS sufferers from seeking treatment.

The doctor should also be able to rely on this public interest defence where the duty of confidence is breached to protect an individual from harm; there is a public interest in protecting the safety of an individual. Hence, the HIV patient who refuses to inform his sexual partner is unlikely to succeed in an action against his doctor if that doctor breaches his duty of confidence and informs the partner. But for this defence to be available there must be a specific individual at risk. If the HIV patient is sexually promiscuous or is unattached, so that there is no identifiable third party at risk, then the doctor could only encourage the patient to seek help.

Risk

How great must the risk to the public be for the doctor to rely on this defence? In *W v Egdell* [1990] 1 All ER 835, a psychiatrist was found not liable for breach of confidence. The court endorsed his actions in sending a report he had prepared on W, a prisoner in a secure hospital, to the director of the hospital, who then passed it to the Home Secretary. Dr Egdell had been asked by W's legal advisers to prepare a report in support of W's application for a transfer to a regional secure unit. His report was unfavourable to W and, as a result, W abandoned his application for a transfer. Dr Egdell, however, was concerned that W might make a further application for a transfer at a later date, and that his report would not be included in the patient's notes. He considered that W would be a danger to the public if he was ever released, hence he breached his duty of confidence. The Court of Appeal, relying on the GMC guidelines, held that the doctor was justified in disclosing the information.

This case was followed in *R v Crozier* [1991] Crim LR 138 where a psychiatrist acting for the accused handed his report to the prosecutor for the Crown. The Court of Appeal held that there was a stronger interest in the public knowing that the appellant was a danger to the public than in the confidence being maintained.

What these cases reveal is that there must be a risk of harm to the public and that it must be necessary for the information to be disclosed. Even if the exact degree of risk to the public or the individual is uncertain, that is irrelevant; all that matters is that there should be some definite risk of danger to the public.

Practical application of the above

Below we consider certain common situations where the doctor will be faced with these two competing public interests.

Crime

The GMC say a breach of confidence is justified if there is a risk of harm to a third party or if there is a risk of a serious crime being committed (see Appendix F, at p 389). Note the use of the word 'serious'; a doctor is unlikely to be able to rely on the public interest defence if the crime which has been committed or is threatened is of a trivial nature. The fact that the patient has committed a crime, or is about to commit a crime, does not change the nature of the doctor–patient relationship. However, in cases such as rape or child abuse, a doctor would be justified in disclosing such information because of the serious risk to the public and/or a specific individual. Child abuse is particularly difficult because often not only the child but also the rest of the family are patients of the doctor. The paramount duty of the doctor is to secure the safety of the child, so he must admit the child to hospital and consult with a paediatrician. Given these circumstances, if the doctor should choose not to disclose the information it is submitted that the law will be powerless against his inactivity, except as prescribed by statute; however, he may be censored for professional misconduct.

AIDS

Although in law AIDS has to be treated in the same way as any other contagious disease, because it is incurable and can be transmitted via venereal or blood contact it raises special dilemmas. Simply being tested for AIDS can lead to an assumption that the person must be in a high risk category, and consequently is leading a dubious lifestyle. This may have repercussions in relation to such matters as employment, life insurance and mortgages.

The GMC has published a separate booklet on the treatment of AIDS and HIV and the ethical ramifications these illnesses pose for the doctor (see 'HIV & AIDS: the ethical considerations').

The doctor may disclose information:

(1) to a GP and/or other health care professionals responsible for the care of the HIV patient; or

(2) to the patient's sexual partner/spouse, ie a specific identifiable individual.

In both instances, the disclosure can only be made after the patient has received counselling from the doctor in charge of his case and has refused to give his consent to the disclosure. In line with the defence of disclosure in the public interest, there must be a serious risk of injury involved and it must be an urgent situation; hence a doctor will only be a permitted to inform a specific individual or individuals, eg if several members of the health care team are at risk. With regard to disclosure by the doctor to the patient's sexual partner, where the patient is not in a permanent relationship and it is not clear whether or not the risk may materialise, then there is not the same degree of urgency about the situation. In addition, it is in the public interest that, as far as possible, the confidences of such patients should be maintained, or else patients may feel disinclined to seek treatment. In both the above examples, the advice from the GMC is intended to be binding; in all cases the doctors must make their own judgment. However, it is submitted that should a doctor follow such advice then he will not be subject to the wrath of the courts or the profession.

Finally, we consider the situation where it could be said that certain individuals consent to run the risk of contracting diseases and infections, etc namely sportspersons. The two infections that they are most at risk of are HIV and HBV (Hepatitis B Virus); HBV can be cured, to date HIV cannot. Should the sports doctor disclose the fact that one member of the team has the HBV/HIV virus to his other team mates? Is this situation any different because each player implicitly consents to run the risks associated with the sport? Could it be argued that the sportsperson affected has not given true consent because he does not know of the risk?

Unlike other health care professionals the sports doctor is not subject to the the National Health Service Trust (Venereal Diseases) Regulations 1991 SI 1991/29. It therefore seems apparent that the sports doctor will not be placed under any more of an onerous obligation than his NHS counterpart. As a matter of routine, sportsmen/women should be vaccinated against HBV, although there is little that can be done to prevent the spread of HIV except screening, which has obvious drawbacks.

As a final point perhaps the obligation for sportsperson's safety lies solely with the employer – they are the ones who make the profits, so perhaps they should bear the risk. See further A A McConnell and M G Mackay in *Medicine, Science and the Law* (1995) Vol 35, No 1, at p 45.

REFERENCES

English case law

(1) X v Y [1988] 2 All ER 648

This case is also referred to at Rule 1(B). A tabloid newspaper had acquired information identifying two GPs as HIV positive. The newspaper argued that the public had a right to know the names of the said individuals because they were continuing to practice and were therefore a risk to the public. The court rejected this argument in favour of the Health Authority, who argued that where a doctor had received proper counselling the risk to the public was negligible. Furthermore, great emphasis was placed upon maintaining the confidence of AIDS sufferers, otherwise there was a substantial risk they would not seek treatment.

(2) W v Egdell [1990] 1 All ER 835

For the facts of this case, see Commentary above. W brought an action in contract and equity alleging breach of confidence. The court relied on the advice of the GMC in particular paras (b) and (g) of r 81 of the Blue Book, and found that the public interest in disclosure outweighed W's private interest. Dr Egdell was correct in disclosing his report on W to the appropriate authorities, as W posed a danger to the public should he ever be released.

(3) R v Crozier [1991] Crim LR 138

For the facts of this case, see p 24.

Held: the psychiatrist had acted reasonably and in the public interest.

Foreign case law

UNITED STATES

(1) *Saur v Probes (1991) 476 NW (2d) 196*

This case is considered, at p 14.

Statutes / statutory instruments

NATIONAL HEALTH SERVICE TRUST (VENEREAL DISEASES) REGULATIONS 1991 SI 1991/29

Professional / ethical guidelines

GMC's 'Confidentiality' booklet paras 18–19; and 'HIV and AIDS: The Ethical Considerations' paras 15–19

In the former publication, three situations are highlighted which may justify disclosure in the interests of others:

(1) disclosure to the DVLC where the patient continues to drive contrary to medical advice;

(2) where a medical colleague is ill and is placing patients at risk; and

(3) where disclosure is necessary to prevent crime.

With regard to AIDS, the advice is that disclosure should only be made to the patient's sexual partner where the patient has refused to consent to such disclosure and there is a serious and identifiable risk to a specific individual. Disclosure is also permitted to members of the health care team if the doctor judges their health is at risk.

RULE 1(E)

A doctor will have to breach the confidentiality of a patient if he is ordered to do so by the courts or if legislation (primary or delegated) so requires.

Commentary

Two separate sets of circumstances are envisaged here.

Court orders

A court, in the course of legal proceedings, may order a doctor who is either a witness or a defendant to disclose information about his patient. In doing so, the court will have to strike a balance between the need for all relevant information to be disclosed, thereby ensuring justice is done, against the need to keep the patient's confidence secret. The decision to order disclosure will not be taken lightly, but if the court so orders then, subject to the rules of legal professional privilege, the doctor has no choice: he must answer or be in contempt of court.

Further, the rules of court provide for the pre-trial disclosure of such things as expert medical reports on which one or other party is seeking to rely. If this is so then again the doctor has no choice: his report will be made public. As Sir John Donaldson said in *Naylor v Preston Area Health Authority* [1987] 1 WLR 958 (at p 967):

> ... the general rule is that, whilst a party is entitled to privacy in seeking out the 'cards' for his hand, once he has put his hand together, the litigation is to be conducted with all the cards face up on the table. Furthermore, most of the cards have to be put down well before the hearing.

Furthermore, the courts held in *Hay v University of Alberta Hospital* [1991] 2 Med LR 204 that where the nature of the plaintiff's action is against either his doctor or the health authority for damages then the plaintiff implicitly consents to the defence having access to his medical records and discussing the case with the physicians who treated him.

Legislation

There are Acts of Parliament and delegated legislation which require disclosure to be made. Among the more familiar are the Public Health (Infectious Diseases) Regulations 1988 (SI 1988/1546) and the Abortion Regulations 1991 (SI 1991/499). Among the less familiar of these are s 18 Prevention of Terrorism (Temporary Provisions) Act 1989 and s 8 Police and Criminal Evidence Act

1984. It would be futile to look for a common thread running through these various measures; suffice to say that Parliament usually regards such disclosures as being necessary in the interests of society as a whole.

REFERENCES

English case law

Naylor v Preston Area Health Authority [1987] 1 WLR 958

See above, at p 27.

Foreign case law

AUSTRALIA

Australian Red Cross Society v BC [1992] 3 Med LR 273

Court ruled that the identity of a blood donor should be revealed to the plaintiff in the interests of justice. This outweighed the public interest in maintaining the confidentiality of blood donors.

CANADA

Hay v University of Alberta Hospital [1991] 2 Med LR 204

See above, at p 27.

Statutes / statutory instruments

(1) PREVENTION OF TERRORISM (TEMPORARY) PROVISIONS ACT 1989

18(1) A person is guilty of an offence if he has information which he knows or believes might be of material assistance:

  (a) in preventing the commission by any other person of an act of terrorism connected with the affairs of Northern Ireland; or

  (b) in securing the apprehension, prosecution or conviction of any other person for an offence involving the commission, preparation or instigation of such an act,

and fails without reasonable excuse to disclose the information as soon as reasonably practicable ...'

(2) POLICE AND CRIMINAL EVIDENCE ACT 1984

See in particular ss 8, 9, 11 and 12.

Section 8 allows a justice of the peace to issue a search warrant where he is satisfied that a serious arrestable offence has been committed and that there is material on the premises which is likely to be of substantial value in the investigations and which is not subject to legal privilege. See further ss 9 and 11 for what material may be seized. Note that an application may be made to seize 'excluded material' such as personal records, human tissue, etc. The government's objective in these sections is to protect the relationship of the person so affected with the community. According to s 12, 'personal records' means documentary and other records concerning an individual (whether living or dead) and includes those records relating to his physical or mental health. The provisions may apply to medical records and human tissue fluid taken for the purpose of diagnostic or medical treatment.

(3) PUBLIC HEALTH (CONTROL OF DISEASE) ACT 1984 supplemented by PUBLIC HEALTH (INFECTIOUS DISEASES) REGULATIONS 1988 (SI 1988/1546)

(4) ABORTION REGULATIONS 1991 (SI 1991/499)

(5) NATIONAL HEALTH SERVICE (NOTIFICATION OF BIRTHS AND DEATHS) REGULATIONS 1982 (SI 1982/286)

(6) MISUSE OF DRUGS (NOTIFICATION OF, AND SUPPLY TO ADDICTS) REGULATIONS 1973 (SI 1973/799)

(7) NATIONAL HEALTH SERVICE TRUST (VENEREAL DISEASES) REGULATIONS 1974 (SI 1974/29)

Note that these regulations are said to apply to a sexually transmitted disease; would this apply to someone who is infected with HIV following a blood transfusion?

Practice points

In any legal proceedings medical evidence will remain privileged unless that privileged is waived, usually because the party wishes to adduce the evidence at trial and therefore must disclose it to the other side in accordance with RSC Ord 38, rr 36–44; CCR Ord 20, rr 20, 28. In fact, the disclosure of medical evidence will be one of the directions sought in the summons for directions in the High Court (RSC Ord 25) and is included in the automatic directions in the county court (CCR Ord 17, r 11).

Professional / ethical guidelines

GMC's 'Confidentiality' booklet paras 20–22

Note that disclosure should be confined to information which is necessary and should not be given in the absence of a court order.

RULE 1(F)

Even if the circumstances permit disclosure, a doctor must ensure that the information is disclosed only to the appropriate person or authority.

Commentary

If the doctor chooses to broadcast the confidential information to all and sundry then his actions will be reprimanded by both the courts and his profession. Consequently, in the case of an epileptic driver, disclosure should be made to the DVLC as the appropriate body and, in cases of child abuse, the appropriate social services body or the NSPCC should be informed. As such, the doctor not only has the difficult decision of whether or not to disclose, he must be certain that he is revealing the information in the correct format and to the correct person(s); he must tread carefully at all times. Again, if he is preparing a report on a patient for the patient's employer or insurance company, he owes a legal and ethical duty to the recipients of the report and should, in such circumstances, only examine the patient on the clear understanding that the patient is aware of the report, with its confidential information, will be forwarded to the employer, etc.

REFERENCES

English case law

(1) W v Egdell [1990] 1 All ER 835

Dr Egdell was not in breach of his duty of confidence because he had disclosed the information to the 'proper authorities' (see the judgment of Bingham LJ, at p 853).

(2) X v Y [1988] 2 All ER 648

Disclosure could not be authorised to a tabloid newspaper; it was a matter for the health authority who were responsible for GPs and their patients.

Foreign case law

NEW ZEALAND

Duncan v Medical Practitioners' Disciplinary Committee [1986] 1 NZLR 513

A GP was found 'guilty of professional misconduct in that he breached professional confidence in informing lay people of his patient's personal medical history'.

The patient, a bus driver, had undergone a triple coronary bypass operation and was certified fit to drive by his surgeon. However, his GP asked that the patient's driving licence be withdrawn and, in addition, warned the patient's passengers of the potential danger. The decision of the Disciplinary Committee was the subject of judicial review and the court duly commented:

> I think a doctor who has decided to communicate should discriminate and ensure the recipient is a responsible authority.

Professional / ethical guidelines

GMC's 'Confidentiality' booklet para 18

This notes that disclosure in the interests of others should be made to the appropriate person or authority.

CHECKLIST FOR PATIENT / PLAINTIFF'S SOLICITOR

(1) Is the plaintiff:
    (a) a patient?
    (b) a third party injured by the defendant following a refusal to breach the confidence (claim unlikely to succeed see Rule 1(C), at p 10)?
    (c) a minor (who is acting by his or her next friend)?
    (d) a person under a disability (see (c) above)?
    (e) dying (is there a need for urgency)?
    (f) dead, ie is the claim being brought by dependants (note that only the ethical obligation survives death)?
    (g) a patient being treated privately (claim will be brought in contract) or under the NHS (claim in equity)?

(2) Is the proposed defendant:
    (a) a GP?
    (b) a consultant?
    (c) other health care professional?
    (d) a third party, ie was the information disclosed to a third party who then breached the confidence?
    (e) a health authority?

(3) What does the client want:
- (a) an apology/explanation?
- (b) disciplinary action against the defendant?
- (c) financial compensation?
- (d) an injunction to either:
    - (i) prevent the breach occurring; or
    - (ii) prevent further breaches?
- (e) an action for defamation?

(4) Has the breach already taken place?

If yes:
- (a) when did it occur?
- (b) what was the nature of the breach?
- (c) to whom was the disclosure made?
- (d) did the defendant attempt to persuade the patient to consent to the disclosure earlier?
- (e) did the plaintiff know the defendant was going to breach his confidence?

If not:
- (a) how does the plaintiff know the defendant is about to breach his confidence?
- (b) has the defendant tried to persuade the plaintiff to give his consent to the disclosure?
- (c) to whom will the disclosure be made?
- (d) is the plaintiff still under the care of the defendant?

(5) What happened/will happen as a result of the breach? Did the plaintiff:
- (a) write a letter of complaint to the defendant?
- (b) use the internal complaints machinery?
- (c) lose his job?
- (d) suffer distress, inconvenience, illness?
- (e) sustain damage to his business, eg loss of profit?

Furthermore:
- (f) was the information disclosed accurate? Was it defamatory?

(6) Does the defendant have any defence?
- (a) did the plaintiff consent to the disclosure?
- (b) is the information confidential?
- (c) was the information imparted in the context of a doctor–patient relationship?
- (d) did the defendant have just cause for disclosing the information
    - (i) in the patient's best interests?
    - (ii) in the public interest?
    - (iii) to another health carer?
    - (iv) for research purposes?
- (e) was the information disclosed not by the defendant but by a third party?

(7) Do immediate steps need to be taken, eg an *ex parte* injunction?

CHECKLIST FOR DEFENDANT'S SOLICITOR

Refer to the plaintiff's checklist, with the following amendments.

(1) Points 1 and 2 will be reversed, ie the client is the defendant and will want to know who is the alleged plaintiff.

(2) At point 3 the question will be what is the alleged claim?

(3) Refer to points 4, 5 and 6 but in addition:

   (a) Did the defendant consult with any bodies/organisations before the disclosure, eg Medical Defence Union, BMA, etc? If yes, what was the nature of their advice?

   (b) How often did he try (if he did) to persuade the patient to allow him to disclose the information?

   (c) On what basis will he try and justify the disclosure?

(4) What emergency steps (if any) are required?

SUGGESTED PRECEDENTS TO BE USED IN A BREACH OF CONFIDENCE CLAIM

DOCUMENT 1

IN THE HIGH COURT OF JUSTICE   1996–S–No 1234
CHANCERY DIVISION
NEWTOWN DISTRICT REGISTRY
(Writ issued the 13th day of May 1996)
BETWEEN

STANLEY SMITH	PLAINTIFF
and	
(1) DR FRANCIS FINLAY	
(2) DR MARY FERGUSON	
(3) DR HANNAH HYDE	
(4) DR JAMES BELLAMY	DEFENDANTS

STATEMENT OF CLAIM

1 At all material times the First Defendant was a medical general practitioner practising at Willow Surgery, Grey Street, Newtown, Blankshire in partnership with the Second to Fourth Defendants.[1]

2 At all material times the Plaintiff was a patient under the care of the First Defendant and as such a doctor–patient relationship existed between the Plaintiff and First Defendant ('the relationship').

3 It was an implied term of the relationship that all and any information imparted by the Plaintiff to the First Defendant was of a private and personal nature ('the information') which would be treated by the First Defendant as confidential and would not be communicated in any form to any other party.

4   In breach of the obligation pleaded at para 3 the First Defendant has communicated certain of the information to other parties without the consent of the Plaintiff or other good cause.

PARTICULARS

(i) On or about 4th March 1996 the First defendant divulged in writing information concerning the Plaintiff's medical condition and treatment to the Plaintiff's then employer.

(ii) On or about the 5th May 1996 the First Defendant divulged in writing the same information to the Plaintiff's wife.

5   By reason of the aforesaid breaches the Plaintiff has suffered loss and damage.

PARTICULARS

(i) On 7th May 1996 the Plaintiff's then employer dismissed the Plaintiff from employment justifying such dismissal on grounds based on information from the First Defendant.

(ii) On or about 6th May 1996 the Plaintiff's wife left the matrimonial home and has since that date refused to cohabit with the Plaintiff justifying such action on grounds based on the information from the First Defendant.

(iii) The Plaintiff has suffered mental distress and anguish.

6   Further, by reason of the First Defendant's breach the Plaintiff believes that unless restrained by injunction the First Defendant will commit further breaches of the implied term.

AND the Plaintiff claims:

(1) An injunction to restrain the First Defendant whether by himself or by his servants or agents or otherwise from communicating or disclosing in any form whatsoever to any party or parties whomsoever the information.

(2) Against all Defendants damages and interest thereon pursuant to section 35A of the Supreme Court Act 1981 for such a period and at such a rate as the court consider just.

(3) Further, or other relief.[2]

Robson and Khan ....(signed)

Served the 13th day of June 1996 by Robson & Khan of 301 Sutherland House, Newtown, Blankshire, Solicitors for the Plaintiff.

Notes

1   The action is being brought against all of the partners in the practice, enabling the plaintiff to enforce any award of damages against any or all of the partners.

2   It is usual to include this all embracing claim in the writ and statement of claim. It is possible that the court will order an enquiry as to what damages the plaintiff has sustained by reason of the defendants' breach.

DOCUMENT 2

THE WRIT

1   Set out brief facts and your relief.

2   For the appropriate headings see the Statement of Claim in document 1.

Below is an example of a suggested indorsement:

The Plaintiff's claim is for an injunction and damages due to the First Defendant's breach of the implied duty of confidentiality arising in the course of the relationship between the parties of the Plaintiff as patient and the First Defendant as doctor and the Second to Fourth Defendants as partners to the First Defendant.

DOCUMENT 3

IN THE HIGH COURT OF JUSTICE   1996–S–No 1234

CHANCERY DIVISION

NEWTOWN DISTRICT REGISTRY

Before Mr Justice Henry

This 3rd day of August 1996

BETWEEN

STANLEY SMITH	PLAINTIFF
and	
(1) DR FRANCIS FINLAY	
(2) DR MARY FERGUSON	
(3) DR HANNAH HYDE	
(4) DR JAMES BELLAMY	DEFENDANTS

ORDER[1]

UPON THE TRIAL OF THIS ACTION

AND UPON READING the documents in the Court File recorded as having been read.

AND UPON HEARING Counsel for the Plaintiff

IT IS ORDERED that:-

1   The First Defendant be restrained whether by himself or by his servants or agents or otherwise howsoever from communicating or disclosing in any form whatsoever to any party or parties whomsoever the information imparted by the Plaintiff to the First Defendant of a private or personal nature as described in the Statement of Claim dated 13th June 1996.[2]

2   An inquiry be taken and made as to what damages the Plaintiff has sustained by reason of the acts the repetition of which is restrained by this Order.

     AND in taking such inquiry[3] the Defendants are to be charged with interest at the rate of 8% per annum on all items of such damages from the date when the same were respectively sustained by the Plaintiff.

3   The Defendants do jointly and severally pay such damages to the Plaintiff as he may be found to have sustained under para 2 of this Order.

4   The Defendants do pay to the Plaintiff the costs of this action down to the date of the Order to be taxed.

Notes

1   This Order is equally applicable to an interlocutory matter and should be amended as appropriate.

2   Delete 'The statement of claim' and substitute 'in the affidavit of Stanley Smith' as the case may be. Also delete the reference as to trial.

3   See Document 1 note 2 (above).

DOCUMENT 4

IN THE HIGH COURT OF JUSTICE   1996–S–No 1234
CHANCERY DIVISION
NEWTOWN DISTRICT REGISTRY
BETWEEN

          STANLEY SMITH   PLAINTIFF
          and
          (1) DR FRANCIS FINLAY
          (2) DR MARY FERGUSON
          (3) DR HANNAH HYDE
          (4) DR JAMES BELLAMY   DEFENDANTS

NOTICE OF MOTION

TAKE NOTICE that this Court will be moved on Monday the 20th day of June 1996 at 2 o'clock at the sitting of the Court or so soon thereafter as Counsel can be heard, by Counsel for the above-named Plaintiff for an Order that the First Defendant whether by himself his servants or agents or otherwise be restrained by injunction until judgment in this action or further Order from communicating to any party whomsoever the information imparted by the Plaintiff to the First Defendant of a private or personal nature.

AND that the costs of and incidental to this application may be paid by the Defendants.

AND FURTHER take notice that the grounds of this application are as set out in the affidavit of the Plaintiff sworn on 10th June 1996 a copy of which is served herewith.

DATED the 13th day of June 1996

Robson & Khan of Sutherland House, Newtown, Blankshire

Solicitors for the Plaintiff Stanley Smith whose address is 34 Northside, Newtown, Blankshire.

To the Defendants and to Shady and Co, of Nixon Building, Newtown, Blankshire, their Solicitors.

DOCUMENT 5

Plaintiff: Stanley Smith: 1st
Sworn:
Exhibits SS 1 & 2
1996–S–No 1234

IN THE HIGH COURT OF JUSTICE
CHANCERY DIVISION
NEWTOWN DISTRICT REGISTRY
BETWEEN

STANLEY SMITH		PLAINTIFF
and		
(1) DR FRANCIS FINLAY		
(2) DR MARY FERGUSON		
(3) DR HANNAH HYDE		
(4) DR JAMES BELLAMY		DEFENDANTS

AFFIDAVIT OF STANLEY SMITH

I, Stanley Smith, of 34 Northside, Newtown, Blankshire, Head Chef, MAKE OATH and say as follows:–

1   I am the Plaintiff in this action.

2   I first met the First Defendant about 10 years ago and since then I have been a patient under the care of the First Defendant.

3   During the years I was under the care of the First Defendant I disclosed to the First Defendant information of a private and personal nature ('the information') on the implicit understanding that the information would be treated by the First Defendant as confidential and would not be communicated in any form to any other party.

INSERT HERE THE EXACT NATURE OF THE BREACH, eg WHAT INFORMATION WAS DISCLOSED, EXHIBIT LETTERS, etc.

4   I have been informed by a Mr James Brown, a friend of the First Defendant[1] and verily believe that the First Defendant intends to disclose the information to other parties without my consent or otherwise good cause and I respectfully ask this court that an injunction be granted in the terms specified in the notice of motion herein pending trial or further Order.

SWORN by the above named defendant

at

in the .... of

this ...... day of .... 199_

Before me   Solicitor/Commissioner for Oaths.

Notes

1   It may be that the Plaintiff has been informed by the Defendant that he intends to disclose the information, or he may have been informed by a Third Party.

Whatever the source of his belief, we think it unlikely that the Plaintiff will be granted an injunction unless he can produce substantial evidence that the Defendant is intending to breach his confidence, ie the Plaintiff will not be granted an injunction if he is merely apprehensive that the Defendant will breach his confidence because the information is highly confidential.

DOCUMENT 6

THE DEFENCE

We have not thought it necessary to include a defence or an affidavit in reply to the Plaintiff's affidavit opposing an application for an interlocutory injunction restraining breach of confidence. However, any defence/affidavit would, it is suggested, be along the following lines:

1   That the defendant did not/does not owe the Plaintiff a duty of confidence (unlikely to figure much in a doctor–patient action)

2   That the breach never took place, ie that the breach occurred without the fault of the Defendant. This could be a possible defence where the information was imparted to a Third Party in confidence, who subsequently disclosed the information. However, it is possible the doctor could still be liable for the Third Party's breach.

3   That the information was not confidential – ie was public property. The Defendant here may rely on the public interest defence at Rule 1(D)(v), at p 23.

4   The Plaintiff consented to the disclosure.

5   That the Defendant had just cause to disclose the information. In this instance, the Defendant will attempt to rely on one of the defences to a breach of confidence claim (see Rules 1(D)(i) to (v), at p 14 *et seq*).

CHAPTER 2

CONSENT

RULE 2(A)

Since most forms of medical treatment will involve some touching of the patient, then any touching without the express or implied consent of the patient will be actionable as trespass to the person. There is no need for the plaintiff to show hostile intent on the part of the health carer.

Commentary

In England an adult patient is invariably said to have complete autonomy over his body to the extent that he can consent to any form of medical treatment and no one can veto that consent. (In reality, patients have never had complete autonomy, eg they cannot consent to treatment which would constitute a criminal act.) What the rule means is that a patient can choose whether to have the treatment on offer or not, even if, without that treatment, his condition may worsen to the point where he may die. Consequently, before treating a patient, the health carer must ensure that he has the patient's express or implied consent. This can be given verbally, in writing, or a combination of the two.

In the Canadian case of *Malette v Shulman* [1991] 2 Med LR 162, the plaintiff, who was seriously injured in a road accident, was taken to a hospital where she was treated by the defendant. As her condition worsened and she lapsed into unconsciousness, the need to treat her as an emergency arose; in particular, it became necessary to give her a blood transfusion. A Jehovah's Witness card was found among her belongings which, when translated, read as follows:

NO BLOOD TRANSFUSION

As one of the Jehovah's Witnesses with firm religious convictions, I request that no blood products be administered to me under any circumstances. I fully realise the implications of this position but I have absolutely decided to obey the Bible command ...

The defendant was made aware of both the card and its contents but, as the patient's condition deteriorated, he decided to administer blood. The patient's daughter, on arrival at the hospital, confirmed her mother's wish not to be given a blood transfusion and actually signed a 'consent to treatment and a release of liability form'. Despite this the defendant continued to administer the blood. The Ontario Court of Appeal held that the defendant was liable in trespass. As Robins JA said (at p 166): 'the instructions imposed a valid restriction on the emergency treatment that could be provided ... and precluded blood transfusions.'

In our view, this case accurately represents the position in English law: any unauthorised touching is technically a battery and a civil claim can be maintained even if there is no evidence of damage to the plaintiff. It may seem harsh to conclude that a defendant is legally liable in damages when the only thing that he is 'guilty' of is trying to help another human being. But a person's choice, however misguided, must be respected if autonomy is to have any meaning. Although English law has not been entirely consistent in its approach when autonomy is taken to its logical conclusion, eg in the area of euthanasia, it is clear that an adult, conscious patient can choose his treatment. This explains why the court in *Re C* [1994] All ER 819 decided that a paranoid schizophrenic who chose not to have his leg amputated when gangrene was diagnosed, should be left alone and not treated. It also explains why patients who, for religious reasons or otherwise, choose not to undergo a particular form of treatment, must have their wishes respected.

Patients may give consent thereby negativing any trespass. They frequently do so impliedly, eg when their GP asks to examine their throat; certainly they do so expressly when, in a hospital and prior to undergoing surgery, they sign a consent form (see Appendix H, p 415). At this point, hospitals may both be surprised and disturbed to learn that a signed consent form is not conclusive that there has been no trespass; it is, however, very strong evidence that consent has been given for the invasive treatment. Therefore, where a patient consents to treatment A and, during that treatment, B is also effected, *prima facie,* a trespass claim could be maintained in respect of B, unless the defendant could show that the additional treatment was immediately vital. For example, a hysterectomy performed while a woman is in the operating theatre having a foetus removed following a miscarriage is actionable if the woman has not consented to the hysterectomy and it could not be shown that that treatment was immediately necessary.

Consent obtained by fraud or misrepresentation should be treated as no consent and therefore a trespass claim should be possible. But, as the next rule will show, health carers can obtain true consent without revealing all known risks to the patient and in the full knowledge that they are not disclosing everything to the patient. They may later justify their actions either by arguing that it was not therapeutically beneficial to the patient to know everything or that, as accepted medical practice, the particular risk or type of risk would not have been revealed. Furthermore, according to the decision in *Blyth v Bloomsbury Health Authority* [1993] 4 Med LR 151; if it was also accepted practice not to answer the patient's questions fully and/or truthfully, medical practitioners may again obtain true consent to treat based on a patient having less than full knowledge. Is this fraud? Is this misrepresentation? Legally it is not; the practitioner is only complying with the law. But it would be fraudulent and misrepresenting the situation to tell a patient that procedure A was going to be carried out in the full knowledge that it was not and that it was procedure B that was going to be effected; a rare situation indeed.

REFERENCES

English case law

(1) Re C [1994] 1 All ER 819

C, a 68 year old patient suffering from paranoid schizophrenia, developed gangrene in his foot; the diagnosis was that he was likely to die immediately if the leg was not amputated below the knee. C refused the amputation.

Held:: C was capable of making the decision whether to receive treatment or not; having decided that he did not want to be treated, that decision had to be respected.

(2) Blyth v Bloomsbury Health Authority [1993] 4 Med LR 151

See p 43 for the facts of this case.

Per Neill LJ (at p 160):

> ... I do not understand that in the decision of the House of Lords in *Sidaway* ... either Lord Diplock or Lord Bridge were laying down any rule of law to the effect that where questions are asked by a patient, or doubts are expressed, a doctor is under any obligation to put the patient in possession of all the information on the subject which may be available in the files of the consultant ... The amount of information to be given must depend upon the circumstances, and as a general proposition it is governed by what is called the *Bolam* test.

(3) Devi v West Midlands Area Health Authority (1981) Kemp and Kemp Vol 2 F5–018 and F5–017

The plaintiff, aged 29, had four children and hoped for more. Her religious beliefs precluded sterilisation and contraception. She was admitted to hospital for a minor operation on her womb. In the course of the operation her womb was found to be ruptured. Without her consent or knowledge the surgeons decided to sterilise here because they feared that if she became pregnant again her womb could rupture. Although acting in the patient's best interests there was no immediate urgency to perform the operation without permission. The defendants admitted liability and damages of £4,000 were awarded.

Foreign case law

CANADA

(1) Malette v Shulman [1991] 2 Med LR 162

See above, at p 39 for facts.

> The principles of self-determination and individual autonomy compel the conclusion that the patient may reject blood transfusions even if harmful consequences may result and even if the decision is generally regarded as foolhardy.

(2) Murray v McMurchy [1949] 2 DLR 442

During a caesarean operation a doctor tied the patient's fallopian tubes as he was concerned about the consequences of a second pregnancy. No consent had been given. As there was no evidence of immediate danger, liability existed.

(3) Marshall v Curry [1933] 3 DLR 260

In the course of a hernia operation, the patient's diseased testicle was removed.

> *Held::* there was no liability because this was an emergency.

(4) Allen v Mount Sinai Hospital [1980] 109 DLR (3d) 634

Battery was committed when a patient expressly instructed a doctor not to give her an anaesthetic in her left arm and he subsequently did.

RULE 2(B)

The consent required to defend a trespass claim is true consent.

Commentary

Commentators have not always been consistent in deciding whether the consent the patient has to give is to be termed 'informed consent', 'valid consent', 'true consent', 'real consent' or, simply, 'consent'. In our view, the only meaningful distinction that can and should be made is the one between 'informed consent' and 'true consent'. 'Informed consent' is an American concept (see *Reibl v Hughes* (1980) 114 DLR (3d) 1 for the Canadian version and *Rizzo v Schiller* [1995] 6 *Med L Rev* 209 for the Virginia Supreme Court's view of 'informed consent') which requires all material risks to be disclosed to a patient; furthermore, a risk is to be treated as material 'when a reasonable person, in what the physician knows or should know to be the patient's position, would be likely to attach significance to the risk ... in deciding whether or not to forgo the proposed therapy': see *Canterbury v Spence* (1972) 464 F (2d) 772 and the judgment of Lord Scarman in *Sidaway* where he said ([1985] 1 AC 871, at p 889):

> To the extent that I have indicated I think that English law must recognise a duty of the doctor to warn his patient of risk inherent in the treatment which he is proposing: and especially so, if the treatment be surgery. The critical limitation is that the duty is confined to material risk. The test of materiality is whether in the circumstances of the particular case the court is satisfied that a reasonable person in the patient's position would be likely to attach significance to the risk.

In effect, this means that the patient in the United States, before consenting, will be in receipt of the information which the health carer thinks he, as a patient, would want to have. Because as a rule American health carers are ever conscious of the financial consequences of getting it wrong, they are more likely to err on the side of caution and to give more information (a good illustration of a defensive medicine attitude). In England, on the other hand, 'informed consent' was categorically ruled out by the majority of the House of Lords in *Sidaway* where only Lord Scarman was prepared to adopt the transatlantic doctrine. The English approach is best evidenced by the judgment of Bristow J in *Chatterton v Gerson* [1981] QB 432, later approved by the House of Lords in *Sidaway*, and it is this: the patient need only be informed in broad terms as to the nature of the proposed treatment; in turn, that will be determined by what other responsible practitioners, in similar circumstances, would have done. If the patient has been so informed and thereafter gives his consent he cannot subsequently sue in trespass, although if the procedure is not properly carried out, he will be able to sue in negligence. In short, the patient in England is not as well informed as his American counterpart and the decision as to what he is to be told is definitely that of the health carer. For these reasons we argue for an acceptance of a distinction between 'true consent' and 'informed consent' and the adoption of the term 'true consent' in so far as UK law is concerned.

What has so far been discussed relates to the types of information which must be voluntarily disclosed, ie without any questions being asked by the patient. But what about the 'concerned' patient who, before signing the consent form, asks specific questions relating to his treatment which demand information that would not otherwise voluntarily be disclosed? What is the health carer to do? According to Lord Bridge in *Sidaway*:'... when questioned specifically by a patient of apparently sound mind about risks involved in a particular treatment proposed, the doctor's duty must ... be to answer both truthfully and as fully as the questioner requires' [1985] 1 AC 871, at p 898. But in *Blyth v Bloomsbury Health Authority* [1993] 4 Med L Rev 151; the Appeal Court seemingly took a different view. There the patient, a nurse, was admitted to hospital for antenatal care. It was diagnosed that she had no or insufficient immunity to rubella, but because of the late stage of her pregnancy, a rubella vaccination could not be administered; also the vaccine, if given, could adversely affect a foetus if she became pregnant again within three months. However, as it was essential that she be provided with contraceptive protection, the decision was made to use a progesterone-only contraceptive, Depo-Provera. Unlike many patients she had specifically and repeatedly questioned the doctor beforehand as to the risks associated with the drug. In his summary of the facts Kerr LJ (at p 154) noted that the particulars of negligence included the following allegation:

> (iv) failing to answer the plaintiff's enquiries concerning Depo-Provera accurately and of failing to obtain answers to her questions before attempting to give her the said assurances about the said drug.

In giving judgment for the defendants this point was answered by Kerr LJ this way (at p 157):

> As regards the judge's repeated reference to the need to give a full picture in answer to a specific enquiry, it must borne in mind ... that no specific enquiry was found to have been made ... Secondly, I think the judge's conclusions equally cannot properly be based on the remarks of Lord Diplock and Lord Bridge in *Sidaway*. The question of what a plaintiff should be told in answer to a general enquiry cannot be divorced from the *Bolam* test, any more that when no such enquiry is made. In both cases, the answer must depend upon the circumstances, the nature of the enquiry, the nature of the information which is available, its reliability, relevance, the condition of the patient and so forth.

The distinction being drawn by both Lord Bridge and Kerr LJ is the difference between a general enquiry ('Will I get better?' 'Are there likely to be any complications?') and a specific enquiry ('Will my spinal cord be damaged?'). In the former, the *Bolam* rule will apply and the defendant need only respond in the way a responsible group of his peers would reply; thus, if they would not have answered truthfully and/or fully, the defendant likewise does not. But in the situation of the specific enquiry it seems that the question must be answered truthfully, etc. But is this not subject to the further proposition that, if the truth is not therapeutically beneficial to the patient, specific questions need not be answered truthfully? Either way the patient is completely in the hands of the health carer. Is this true consent? Doubtful, in our view.

REFERENCES

English case law

(1) *Sidaway v Board of Governors of the Bethlem Royal Hospital and the Maudsley Hospital [1985] AC 871; [1985] 1 All ER 643*

See p 65 for facts of this case.

(2) Chatterton v Gerson [1981] 1 All ER 257

The plaintiff sued in trespass and negligence. She alleged that she had not been warned of the side effects of the treatment, namely, loss of muscle power. In finding for the defendant, Bristow J said (at p 265):

> In my judgment, once the plaintiff is informed in broad terms of the nature of the procedure which is intended, and gives her consent, that consent is real, and the cause of action ... is negligence, not trespass ...

> ... even taking the plaintiff's evidence at its face value, she was under no illusion as to the general nature of what an intrathecal injection of phenol solution nerve block would be, and in the case of each injection her consent was not unreal.

(3) Blyth v Bloomsbury Health Authority [1993] 4 Med LR 151

See above, at p 43.

(4) Bolam v Friern Hospital Management Committee [1957] 1 WLR 582; [1957] 2 All ER 118

See Rule 5(A), at p 121.

Foreign case law

CANADA

Reibl v Hughes (1980) 114 DLR (3d) 1

See p 147 for facts of this case.

Per Laskin CJC:

> In saying that the test is based on the decision that a reasonable person in the patient's position would have made, I should make it clear that the patient's particular concerns must also be reasonably based; otherwise there would be more subjectivity than would be warranted under an objective test ... In short, although account must be taken of a patient's particular position, a position which will vary with the patient, it must be objectively assessed in terms of reasonableness.

UNITED STATES

(1) Rizzo v Schiller [1995] 6 Med L Rev 209; Supreme Court of Virginia (1994) 445 S E (2d) 153

Informed consent by the law of Virginia.

(2) Canterbury v Spence (1972) 464 F (2d) 772

Per Robinson J (at p 787):

> [A] risk is ... material when a reasonable person in what the physician knows or should know to be the patient's position, would be likely to attach significance to the risk or cluster of risks in determining whether or not to forego the proposed therapy.

(3) Arato v Avedon (1994) 6 Med L Rev 230

The Supreme Court of California held that informed consent required the disclosure of all material information the patient needed to make an informed decision, but it did not require any particular species of information to be disclosed. This was because material information in any given context was to be assessed by the clinical setting, informational needs and the degree of the patient's dependency. The court also made it clear that the informed consent doctrine did not apply to the disclosure of non-medical interests, eg business and/or investment interests.

RULE 2(C)

A patient who has given true consent to medical treatment cannot have that consent vetoed by another person. This rule applies with equal force whether the patient is a mature adult or a 16 year old.

Commentary

Those who are related to patients, whether by blood or marriage, may view this rule with some disquiet and surprise. Probably the most vivid illustration of the legal thinking behind it involves the case of a woman seeking a legal abortion. Here the courts have held that neither the woman's spouse nor her partner can legally object to the abortion on the ground that their rights are being ignored, see *Paton v British Pregnancy Advisory Service* [1978] 2 All ER 987. What the court is upholding is the right of a woman to determine for herself what should or should not be done to her body. Ethically, partners or spouses should be involved in the discussions preparatory to procedures such as abortions, sterilisations and vasectomies; but that is, in our submission, the limit of their involvement. Sir George Baker, in *Paton*, said (at p 990):

> No court would ever grant an injunction to stop sterilisation or vasectomy. Personal family relationships in marriage cannot be enforced by the order of the court.

In *Gillick v West Norfolk and Wisbech Area Health Authority* [1986] AC 112, the House of Lords held that a mature girl under the age of 16 could seek contraceptive advice and treatment from a health carer without her parents' knowledge and involvement, although every effort should be made by the health carer to encourage the girl to involve them. Ultimately, however, the decision is that of the patient, and no one else.

REFERENCES

English case law

(1) Paton v British Pregnancy Advisory Service [1978] 2 All ER 987

Mr Paton's wife, having discovered she was pregnant, obtained a certificate to a legal abortion. Mr Paton, the plaintiff, sought an injunction to restrain his wife and the defendants from proceeding with the abortion. The court refused to grant the injunction.

See also *Arndt v Smith* [1996] 7 Med LR 35, where Hutchinson J (at p 40) quoted the following statement from the Canadian Supreme Court's decision in *Tremblay v Daigle* (1989) 62 DLR (4th) 634 (at p 665):

> No court in Quebec or elsewhere has ever accepted the argument that a father's interest in a foetus which he helped create could support a right to veto a woman's decision in respect of the foetus she is carrying.

The court went on to hold that, while a doctor has a duty to warn obstetric patients, ie the mother, of the material risks faced by the unborn foetus, no such duty was owed to the prospective father.

(2) Gillick v West Norfolk and Wisbech Area Health Authority [1986] AC 112; [1985] 3 All ER 402

See below, at p 50.

RULE 2(D)

A patient does not have an unfettered right to refuse treatment. In appropriate circumstances a refusal to be treated may be ignored.

Commentary

It might seem self-evident that any legal system which supports the contention that 'every adult has the right and capacity to decide whether or not he will accept medical treatment' (*per* Lord Donaldson MR in *Re T* [1992] 3 Med LR 306, at p 313) must then equally uphold the rule that a person has a right to refuse treatment, whether that decision is founded on a rational or an irrational reason. In the case of *Re C* [1994] 1 WLR 290, that is exactly what the court did. There a 68 year old schizophrenic patient with a gangrenous leg refused to give permission ever to amputate his leg; the prognosis was – and this was never doubted – that, without the operation, he would die (he did later agree to some treatment which meant that the immediate threat to his life had receded). Thorpe J held that the mere fact that the patient was a schizophrenic did not necessarily mean he lacked the capacity to consent and, as there was insufficient evidence to show that he did lack capacity, the patient had a right to refuse treatment.

But in three recent cases *Re T* [1992] 3 Med LR 306, *Re W (a minor) (medical treatment)* [1992] 4 All ER 627 and *Re S* [1992] 4 All ER 671, the patients' wishes not to be treated were not obeyed. In *Re T*, a pregnant woman's decision not to have a blood transfusion on religious grounds, while given careful consideration by the court, was ultimately ignored on the ground that she lacked the capacity to make the particular decision. While the judge at first instance based his decision on the fact that the treatment was in the patient's best interests, the Appeal Court adopted a slightly different stance. They queried whether the refusal was meant to apply in the circumstances which subsequently arose; in other words, a refusal given at a certain point in time when a particular set of circumstances were in existence might not be intended to apply when later the patient's condition worsened. (There was also some evidence to suggest that the woman's will was overborne by that of her mother, to the extent that it was seriously doubted whether it was her decision.)

In *Re W*, a 16 year old girl suffering from anorexia nervosa refused to undergo a particular form of treatment. Again, a strong Appeal Court held that she should be treated since, by the time the case came before the court, her condition had deteriorated to the point where there was a real fear that her future capacity to bear children would be seriously in jeopardy and ultimately non-treatment would threaten her life. The decision has also been explained on the ground of the patient's lack of capacity, namely that she was not old enough to refuse treatment. The implication of the case is that, while a person may be mature enough at the age of 16 to consent to treatment without parental involvement (see the *Gillick* case below), at that same age a person is not sufficiently mature to decide to refuse to be treated.

In *Re S*, a declaration was granted allowing a hospital to perform a non-consensual caesarean operation on a pregnant woman. This was done in the interests of both the woman and her unborn baby since, according to the evidence, without the operation both would have died. While the court in this case was seemingly 'prepared' to accede to the mother's choice were she the only person involved, they were certainly not prepared to do so given that her decision impacted on the life of a third party, ie the foetus. This particular decision is unfortunate for two reasons. First, it elevates the rights of the foetus to a superior status over the mother's rights: a doubtful proposition. Secondly, the reliance on the American case of *Re AC* (1990) 573 A (2d) 1235 was regrettable because that case ultimately rejected the notion of compulsory treatment, except in extreme circumstances.

Whatever the merits (or lack of merits) of the above cases it seems clear that English courts are not prepared to accept complete patient autonomy in the case of a refusal to be treated. At present, lack of capacity would seem to be the main reason why compulsory treatment will be ordered but, additionally, if the refusal would adversely affect a third party, whether that person is an unborn foetus or a living person, then the refusal will be ignored.

REFERENCES

English case law

(1) Re T [1992] 3 Med LR 306; [1992] 4 All ER 649

T, an adult who was 34 weeks pregnant, was injured in a road traffic accident. The case report indicates that she was not a Jehovah's Witness, although she was brought up by her mother who was a fervent member of that faith. T indicated that she did not want a blood transfusion; shortly before so deciding she had been alone with her mother. A decision was taken to deliver the baby by caesarean section. A refusal to consent to a blood transfusion form was signed by T, although it was never explained to her that it might be necessary to give her a transfusion to prevent injury to her health or even to preserve her life. The caesarean section was performed but the baby was stillborn. As T's condition deteriorated a declaration was made by Ward J that it would not be unlawful to administer blood in the circumstances as that would be in her best interests. Two days later he ruled as follows:

(a) although T was under the influence of her mother, she did reach the decision of no treatment on her own;

(b) T was misinformed as to the availability and effectiveness of alternative procedures;

(c) T's refusal of a blood transfusion did not extend to the question of whether she should have a transfusion in the extreme situation which subsequently arose;

(d) since T was no longer able to express any view the doctors could lawfully treat her in her best interests.

With this, the Appeal Court agreed. On the issue of patient autonomy versus society's interests in keeping the patient alive, Lord Donaldson MR said (at p 312):

The patient's interest consists of his right to self-determination, his right to live his own life how he wishes ... society's interest is in upholding the concept that all human life is sacred and that it should be preserved if at all possible. It is well established that in the ultimate the right of the individual is paramount. But this merely shifts the problem where the conflict occurs and calls for a very careful examination of whether, and if so the way in which, the individual is exercising that right. *In case of doubt, that doubt falls to be resolved in favour of the preservation of life* ...

(2) Re C [1994] 1 WLR 290

See p 46.

(3) Re J [1992] 3 Med LR 317

J, aged 16, was suffering from anorexia nervosa. Cazalet J granted the local authority leave under s 100(3) Children Act 1989 to apply for the exercise of the inherent jurisdiction of the High Court. The local authority duly applied for leave to give the minor medical treatment without her consent.

Held:: leave would be given. Lord Donaldson MR said (at p 325):

No minor of whatever age has power by refusing consent to treatment, to override a consent to treatment by someone who has parental responsibility for the minor ...

See also *Re S (A Minor) (Consent to Medical Treatment)* [1994] 2 FLR 1065.

(4) Re R [1992] 3 Med LR 342

R, a girl aged 15 years and 10 months, was in voluntary care. As doubts crept in about her mental state she was compulsorily admitted to a hospital under the Mental Health Act 1983. The unit there wanted to use medication to control her, but she refused. Wardship proceedings ensued and the local authority applied to the courts for leave to be given to the unit to administer medication, including anti-psychotic drugs, without R's consent.

Held:: The court had the power to consent to the making of the necessary order and it would do so, in these circumstances. On the issue of autonomy of someone who is '*Gillick* competent', Lord Donaldson MR said (at p 347):

... in *Re E* [unreported, 21 September 1990], the judges treated *Gillick* as deciding that a '*Gillick* competent' child has a right to refuse treatment. In this I consider that they were in error. Such a child can consent, but if he or she declines to do so or refuses, consent can be given by someone else who has parental rights or responsibilities. The failure or refusal of the '*Gillick* competent' child is a very important factor in the doctor's decision whether or not to treat, but does not prevent the necessary consent being obtained from another competent source.

(5) Re S [1992] 4 All ER 671; [1993] 4 Med LR 28

S and her husband were 'born-again Christians' and as such were opposed to anything other than natural childbirth. Thus, S refused to consent to an emergency caesarean section when her baby was overdue and in danger of being born dead. In her doctor's opinion, the section was necessary both in the mother's and the unborn baby's interests.

Held:: following the American decision of *Re AC* (1990) 573 A (2d) 1235, a declaration would be granted for an emergency caesarean operation.

Foreign case law

UNITED STATES

Re AC (1990) 573 A (2d) 1235

In an unusual set of circumstances involving (*inter alia*) the patient being resuscitated and indicating that she did not wish to undergo a caesarian section, the court nevertheless ruled that a pregnant woman suffering from cancer should undergo a caesarian operation. All the available evidence at the time indicated that she would probably not withstand the operation. As it turned out, both the baby and the mother died shortly after surgery.

Associate Judge Nebeker:

> The fundamental right to bodily integrity encompasses an adult's right to refuse medical treatment, even if the refusal will result in death ... The state's interest in protecting third parties from an adult's decision to refuse medical treatment ... may override the interest in bodily integrity.

RULE 2(E)

True consent can be given by a conscious, competent, adult patient voluntarily. Such a person must also be in possession of a certain amount of information relating to his treatment and it must be established that the patient has understood the information given.

Commentary

For true consent to exist six conditions have to be met. The person giving the consent must:

(1) be an adult, ie aged 16 or over as laid down in s 8 Family Law Reform Act 1969.

(2) be competent, ie not subject to any disability which would make suspect his decision on his treatment;

(3) be conscious;

(4) be in possession of a certain amount of information on which to base his decision (see previous rule);

(5) have understood the information provided;

(6) have given the consent voluntarily.

RULE 2(F)

True consent can be given by a patient of adult years ie someone aged 16 or over. But a mature person under the age of 16 may consent to treatment without involving their parents or guardians.

Commentary

According to s 8 Family Law Reform Act 1969, a patient aged 16 or over is competent to consent to surgical, medical or dental treatment which, 'in the absence of consent, would constitute a trespass ... and the consent given is effective as it would be if he were of full age'.

Taken at face value s 8 would seem to be suggest that anyone aged 16 or over can consent to any form of medical treatment. That would be misleading since it is generally accepted that an adult cannot consent to treatment which would otherwise be a criminal act; that much is clear. What is less clear is whether all non-criminal treatment can be agreed to by an adult as defined above; eg could a 16 year old consent to organ donation or cosmetic surgery?

We would argue that such a question should be answered no for one good reason. Section 8 refers to consenting to 'treatment'; is organ donation or cosmetic surgery 'treatment'? It may be therapeutically beneficial for a person to donate a kidney to his brother or sister or it may make a person feel better to have his nose straightened, but it is our contention that 'treatment' should be taken to mean a procedure which necessarily makes someone physically or mentally better; procedures such as cosmetic surgery are generally undertaken by choice. Consequently, our suggestion is that, legally and ethically, even a mature 16 year old should be refused cosmetic surgery and denied the ability to donate an organ. Although there is no 'magic' in attaining the age of 18, it is submitted that should represent the minimum age for non-necessary medical treatment.

Additionally, patients under the age of 16 can consent to treatment without their parents' involvement provided they are 'Gillick mature'. This was the decision of the House of Lords in Gillick v West Norfolk and Wisbech Area Health Authority [1986] AC 112 where Lord Fraser laid down the following guidelines for determining and assessing maturity in the context of contraceptive counselling and advice. He said (at p 174) that the doctor had to be:

(1) satisfied that the patient understood his advice;

(2) prepared to try and persuade her to tell her parents or let him do so; only if she refused would he then be entitled to proceed with the treatment;

(3) of the opinion that she was very likely to have sexual intercourse with or without the contraceptive advice or treatment;

(4) of the opinion that, unless she had the advice, etc her physical or mental health or both would suffer;

(5) sure that the girl's best interests required the advice, etc.

The ratio of Gillick should not be construed as being restricted to contraceptive counselling and advice; at no stage did the Law Lords try to so limit it. As Lord Scarman said (at pp 188–89):

> ... I would hold that as matter of law the parental right to determine whether or not [a] minor child below the age of 16 will have medical treatment terminates if and when the child achieves a sufficient understanding and intelligence to enable him or her to understand fully what is proposed.

Consequently, mature under 16s can consent to medical treatment to the same extent as someone aged 16 or over subject to what was said earlier about the limitations on the latter group.

It follows that the consent for treatment, in respect of non-mature under 16s, rests with parents or guardians. But again it must be stressed that this should not be seen as an absolute rule. The courts should not allow parents to have such a complete domination over the health of their children; treatment should be in the child's best interests and probably sanctioned by the courts. This certainly is the position where parents, for religious or other reasons, refuse blood transfusions for their children; the child will be made a ward of court and, in his best interests, the blood transfusion will be administered. We see no difference in approach between that situation and the one where a parent consents to a son donating a kidney to his brother or sister; in both, it should be in the best interests of the donor child.

REFERENCES

English case law

Gillick v West Norfolk and Wisbech Area Health Authority [1986] AC 112; [1985] 3 All ER 402

A circular was issued by the DHSS to area health authorities advising them that, if a girl under 16 consulted a doctor at a family planning clinic seeking contraceptive counselling and advice, in exceptional cases the treatment could be provided without consulting the parents or obtaining their consent. The plaintiff, a mother of five daughters, sought a declaration that the circular was *ultra vires* and unlawful.

The House of Lords held that it was lawful.

Statutes / statutory instruments

(1) FAMILY LAW REFORM ACT 1969

8(1) The consent of a minor who has attained the age of 16 years to any surgical, medical or dental treatment which, in the absence of consent, would constitute a trespass to his person, shall be as effective as it would be if he were of full age; and where a minor has by virtue of this section given an effective consent to any treatment it shall not be necessary to obtain any consent for it from his parent or guardian.

(2) In this section, 'surgical, medical or dental treatment' includes any procedure undertaken for the purposes of diagnosis, and this section applies to any procedure (including, in particular, the administration of an anaesthetic) which is ancillary to any treatment as it applies to that treatment.

(3) Nothing in this section shall be construed as making ineffective any consent which would have been effective if this section had not been enacted.

RULE 2(G)

The patient must be conscious to be able to consent. If the patient is unconscious, treatment can only be administered if it is in his best interests.

Commentary

A conscious patient can make a rational or irrational decision regarding his treatment. But the unconscious patient lacks this luxury; he cannot articulate his wishes (however, see below, at p 52 *et seq*) and yet he may require treatment. It would be most unwise for the health carer to work on the premise that, if he were to treat the patient, when the patient recovers consciousness and learns that he has been treated, he will be eternally grateful to the medical profession. The health carer might just find that the patient did not want the particular treatment in question and would have said so had he been conscious (see *Malette v Shulman* [1991] 2 Med LR 162).

As such, the rule to which the health carer must normally adhere is, 'act in the best interests of the patient'. This means that the unconscious patient can be treated (he can even have invasive treatment) provided the treatment is necessary to save his life 'or to ensure improvement or prevent deterioration in [his] physical or mental health' (*per* Lord Brandon in *Re F* (Mental Patient Sterilisation) [1989] 2 WLR 1025, at p 1067) and is in the best interests of the patient. Or, as Lord Goff put it, at pp 1086–87):

> Where, for example, a surgeon performs an operation without his consent on a patient temporarily rendered unconscious in an accident, he should do no more than is reasonably required in the best interests of the patient, before he recovers consciousness ... but where the state of affairs is permanent or semi-permanent, as may be so in the case of a mentally disordered person, there is no point in waiting to obtain the patient's consent. The need to care for him is obvious; and the doctor must then act in the best interests of his patient just as if he had received the patient's consent so to do.

If these criteria exist then the consent or wishes of the relatives, although respected, will not amount to a pre-requisite to treatment. The treatment provided will depend on the injuries sustained and the length of time the patient is like to remain in an unconscious condition, but clearly the courts will draw a distinction between what is necessary pending the patient recovering consciousness and a non-temporary state of unconsciousness where more permanent treatment may legally be administered in the patient's interests.

The real difficulty for all concerned is to decide how the patient's best interests are to be determined and who is to make the judgment. In some cases the health carers themselves will make the decision and decide on the appropriate treatment using their professional expertise and acting in the patient's best interests. In any subsequent litigation they will have to justify their actions accordingly. But with certain forms of treatment the decision has often (not always) been correctly left to the courts which, if the circumstances are right, will grant declarations permitting treatment in the patient's best interests. In doing so the courts will invariably be guided by experts within the medical profession; these experts should be other than and additional to the patient's health carers. What the courts will be looking for is evidence of the following:

(1) the inability of the patient to make the decision for himself;

(2) whether the patient had earlier expressed any choice as to his proposed treatment;

(3) the need for that particular treatment to alleviate the particular condition;

(4) the consequences should the treatment not be administered; and

(5) the wishes of those closest to him, eg a spouse or relative.

Consequently, in cases where the compulsory sterilisation of mentally handicapped females is deemed to be in their best interests, prior permission from the courts is rightly sought (see *Re F* [1989] 2 WLR 1025 and Practice Note (Minors and Mental Health Patients: Sterilisation) [1993] 3 All ER 222).

An approach similar to the one described in *Re F* has been adopted in the treatment of patients described as being in a persistent vegetative state (PVS). This somewhat indelicate term describes patients who are not clinically dead but have 'lost the function of the cognitive part of the brain' (BMA Consultation Paper on Treatment of Patients in Persistent Vegetative State, September 1992). Put another way, they are patients who are unable to do anything for themselves, are almost totally dependant on various life support machines and the prognosis is that they will be in that condition for the foreseeable future. As the patient is unable to give his consent to anything, common law jurisdictions have resorted to the rule of allowing the health carers to do what is in the patient's best interests. To date this has resulted, via applications to the court, in hydration and nutrition being lawfully withdrawn (see *Airedale NHS Trust v Bland* [1993] 2 WLR 316 and *Re G* [1995] Med L Rev 80), gastrostomy tubes not being replaced when they have become dislodged (see *Frenchay Healthcare NHS Trust v S* [1994] 2 All ER 403, and artificial ventilatory support being withdrawn (*Auckland Area Health Board v AG* [1993] NZLR 235).

On occasions, given the right circumstances, eg the need to move quickly, health carers may treat without obtaining the court's prior approval; here, if the health carer can subsequently justify his actions on the ground not only that it was in the patient's best interests but also that it accorded with accepted medical practice, then it is doubtful if any court will hold the health carer liable in civil law. This is even when it is hydration, etc that is to be withdrawn from PVS patients with its inevitable consequences. As Sir Thomas Bingham MR (*obiter*) said in *Frenchay Healthcare NHS Trust v S* [1994] 2 All ER 403 (at p 409):

> I have in mind the acute emergency when a decision has to be taken within minutes or at most hours as to whether treatment should be given or not, whether one form of treatment should be given or another, or as to whether treatment should be withheld.

Given the serious consequences of this type of 'treatment', it is fervently to be hoped that the *Frenchay* case will not be followed in future for two reasons. The first is that it is questionable whether PVS cases should be treated as emergencies; after all, the circumstance in which the patient now finds himself is one which was known for some time, so why the rush? Secondly, in an emergency the Official Solicitor – the one person who is likely to argue against the proposed action – will be denied that very opportunity. Should not the PVS patient have his day in court, figuratively speaking? Is that not in his best interests?

What the PVS cases demonstrate is that, in respect of such patients:

(1) The courts will closely scrutinise the medical profession's prognosis and diagnosis that the patient is in a PVS state. To this end the BMA have suggested that:

   (a) every effort should be made to rehabilitate the patient for at least six months from the date of the injury;

   (b) a PVS diagnosis should not be confirmed until at least one year has elapsed from the date of the injury; and

   (c) a PVS diagnosis should be confirmed by two other independent doctors.

   Despite this, both the courts and the BMA have recently become alarmed at the news that two PVS patients have started to communicate with their families and health carers after periods of seven and two years respectively.

(2) The views of the relatives are important and indeed it is good medical practice to discover those views, but ultimately it is the health carer's duty to decide what is in the patient's best interests (subject to (4) below). So far in almost all cases the relatives and the doctors have been in complete agreement, but in *Re G* [1995] Med L Rev 10, the patient's wife agreed with the doctors while the mother disagreed.

(3) With PVS patients the courts have decided that what they have to determine is whether the continuation of medical treatment is in the patients best interests, ie is it medically pointless to continue the treatment? It is interesting to speculate what the actions of health carers should be once a diagnosis of PVS is made and upheld by the courts: must the treatment be discontinued immediately or can it legally be continued? In the light of the English decisions we would suggest that health carers should discontinue the treatment even if such action were to be taken in the face of opposition from the relatives. This is because the court's decision, made in the patient's interests, must be obeyed; it could hardly be said to be in his interests to continue a treatment which both the medical and legal professions have decreed is futile.

(4) An application must be made to the High Court for a declaration to discontinue the treatment (see above). Each case will be treated on its own merits.

One thing which would certainly assist the courts in determining the patient's best interests is the discovery of whether the patient had ever voiced his views on what treatment should or should not be administered to him at some time in the future and, more significantly, whether treatment should ever continue or be discontinued in a given situation. But, accepting that the patient is incapable of articulating his views, where is this knowledge to come from? It could come from having communicated his views to friends or relatives; it would be much better if the patient had taken the trouble to put his views in written form. The issue then is the legal effect which should be accorded to such written views.

In some American States, advance directives on future medical treatment (or 'living wills') are legally acceptable (see the Patient Self-Determination Act 1991). In Denmark, they have been accorded limited recognition. In England, some degree of legal recognition has already been accorded to advance directives. In *Bland [1993] 2 WLR 316*, two of the Law Lords (*obiter*) approved the use of living wills as a way of informing the medical profession about future treatments. Lord Keith said (at pp 360–61):

> The first point to make is that it is unlawful ... to administer medical treatment to an adult, who is conscious and of sound mind, without his consent ... This extends to the situation where the person, in anticipation of his ... entering into a condition such as PVS, gives clear instructions that in such event he is not to be given medical care, including artificial feeding, designed to keep him alive.

In similar vein, Lord Goff said (at p 367):

> On this basis, it has been held that a patient of sound mind may, if properly informed, require that life support and should be discontinued. ... Moreover, the same principle applies where the patient's refusal has been expressed at an earlier date, before he became unconscious or otherwise incapable of communicating it ...

In our view, a strong argument already exists for their legal acceptance in English law; can it be seriously questioned that there is any meaningful difference between the direction issued by the plaintiff in *Malette v Shulman* (see above) and the directions found in 'living wills'? (see the efforts of the Voluntary Euthanasia Society in this field and Appendix H for a sample advance directive.) Their 'introduction' should be by way of legislation, if only because there will need to be clear, unambiguous safeguards, eg minimum age, provided to counter potential abuse. As such, we would contend that the legislation should lay down a standard form of words to be used (for example, 'I do not want any life sustaining treatment to be administered to me if any disease or illness or cardiac arrest or accident or other similar conditions result in such a severe state of disability that I will thereafter be permanently, physically and mentally, unable to look after myself.') Further, the legislation should demand that the patient makes a clear statement that the nature and effect of making a living will has been explained to him; that there should be two independent witnesses (not members of his family – the word family would need to be defined) to the patient's signature (who sign themselves). Finally, there should be a standard form of words which would have to be used and signed by two medical practitioners that the medical conditions set out in the living will have been reached. When the above factors exist, the legislation should then decree that the patient is not to be given any life extending treatment nor should he be given anything, eg lethal injection, which would hasten his death. Instead, he is to be left for nature to take its course. (See the Law Commission's 1995 Report on Mental Incapacity along with the draft bill. Under those proposals, patients would have had a statutory right to make advance directives. To the consternation of many interest groups, the Lord Chancellor announced in January 1996 that the Government was not intending to introduce legislation to implement the proposals in their present form. This is an unfortunate state of affairs because it means that in future every time an advance directive is to be acted upon or is acted upon the English courts will have to pronounce on its validity.)

REFERENCES

English case law

(1) Re F [1989] 2 WLR 1025

A 36 year old mentally handicapped woman, who was a voluntary in-patient in a mental hospital, formed a sexual relationship with a male partner. It was the professional opinion of the hospital staff that she would be unable to cope with the effects of pregnancy and childbirth; since all other forms of contraception were unsuitable, sterilisation should be resorted to. The House of Lords agreed with the hospital. As Lord Bridge said (at p 1063):

> ... I agree ... that the court has jurisdiction to declare the lawfulness of such an operation proposed to be performed on the ground that it is ... in the best interests of the woman.

(2) Airedale NHS Trust v Bland [1993] 2 WLR 316

A patient, aged 17, was seriously injured in the Hillsborough football disaster of 1989. As a result he was left in a PVS condition. The prognosis was that there was no hope of any improvement in his condition. declarations were sought that the hospital could lawfully discontinue all life sustaining treatment.

Held:: the declarations would be granted. Lord Goff said (at p 371):

... the question is not whether it is in the best interests of the patient that he should die. The question is whether it is in the best interests of the patient that his life should be prolonged by the continuance of this form of medical treatment or care. The correct formulation of the question is of particular importance in a case such as the present, where the patient is totally unconscious or where there is no hope whatsoever of any amelioration of his condition. In circumstances such as these, it may be difficult to say that it is in his best interests that the treatment should be ended. But if the question is asked ... whether it is in his best interests that treatment which has the effect of artificially prolonging his life should be continued, that question can sensibly be answered to the effect that his best interests no longer require that it should be.

(3) Frenchay Healthcare NHS Trust v S [1994] 2 All ER 403

The Appeal Court upheld a declaration that it would be lawful not to reconnect a feeding tube, which had become dislodged, to a PVS patient.

(4) Re G [1995] Med L Rev 80

The Hospital Trust sought a declaration that it would be lawful to withdraw artificial hydration and nutrition from a PVS patient. The matter was discussed with the patient's wife and she agreed that it would not be in her husband's best interests to continue the artificial feeding, etc but the patient's mother disagreed.

Held:: the declaration would be granted. The doctors had to act in the patient's best interests, although the views of relatives would not be ignored.

(5) Swindon and Marlborough NHS Trust v S [1995] Med L Rev 84

The principles applicable to PVS patients apply whether they are being treated in a hospital or at home. In either case it was to do what was in the patient's best interests. Ward J held that, in treating such a patient, if a doctor were to follow the practice of the Medical Ethics Committee of the BMA, he would be acting in accordance with a responsible and competent body of relevant professional opinion.

(6) Re C (1995) Guardian, 18 November

A High Court judge, Johnson J, sanctioned the withdrawal of artificial feeding from a patient who was diagnosed as PVS. He said he was sure that C's interests required the withdrawal.

(7) Lybert v Warrington Health Authority [1996] 7 Med LR 71

Negligence was upheld where the evidence pointed to the fact that no reasonable steps had been taken by the defendants to ensure that the plaintiff understood a warning was being issued. See further, at p 142.

See also Morland J in *Smith v Tunbridge Wells Health Authority* [1994] 5 Med LR 332 (at p 339):

When recommending a particular type of surgery or treatment, the doctor, when warning of the risks, must take reasonable care to ensure that his explanation of the risks is intelligible to his particular patient. The doctor should use language, simple but not misleading, which the doctor perceives from what knowledge and acquaintanceship that he may have of the patient (which may be slight), will be understood by the patient so that the patient can make an informed decision ...'

Foreign case law

CANADA

(1) *Malette v Shulman [1991] 2 Med LR 162*

See p 39.

NEW ZEALAND

Auckland Area Health Board v AG [1993] 1 NZLR 235

A declaration was granted by the New Zealand High Court permitting the withdrawal of artificial ventilation from an incompetent adult patient, even though it was inevitable that such action would lead to his death. The court stressed that sanctity of life was not an absolute; fundamental values of human dignity and personal privacy also had to be obeyed.

SOUTH AFRICA

Clarke v Hurst [1994] 5 Med LR 177

The court held that a patient who had made a 'living will' could have artificial feeding discontinued.

Practice Directions / Notes

Practice Note (Minors and Mental Health Patients) [1993] 3 All ER 222

Statutes / Statutory Instruments

Foreign Statutes

PATIENTS SELF-DETERMINATION ACT 1991 (USA)

Practice points

See Appendix H for sample advance directive, at p 413.

RULE 2(H)

The patient must be in possession of a certain amount of information prior to giving true consent.

Commentary

See Rules 2(A) and (B).

RULE 2(J)

The patient must have understood the information provided.

Commentary

In the multicultural society in which we live, it would be most surprising if all patients had the same level of capacity for reading, writing or understanding the English language. So, what does true consent mean for the patient from Vietnam or Bangladesh who cannot speak or write English? What should the health carer do to satisfy himself that the patient has reasonably understood what is being said to him? Furthermore, what if the information is imparted in complex technical jargon so that even an English-speaking person would not understand what was been said?

In our view, the information should be given in non-technical English language accompanied, if necessary, by diagrams or charts. The health carer needs only to be reasonably (not absolutely) assured that the patient has understood; this may be achieved by simply asking if he has any questions or if he has understood everything. However, to comply with this standard more needs to be done if, because of the patient's ethnic origins, the health carer is of the opinion that the information has not been understood. In most situations where this is likely to occur relatives may be resorted to as interpreters; in extreme circumstances, professional interpreters may be used. Certainly, some of the more commonplace information which has to be imparted to patients, eg their rights of complaint, could and should be in a number of languages.

It is our contention that, if the above minimum criteria have not been observed, then there will be a strong argument for saying that true consent has not been obtained.

RULE 2(K)

The patient must give his consent voluntarily.

Commentary

As a general rule a patient's ability to consent voluntarily to treatment is not determinable by his status at the particular time. Consequently, a detained prisoner of sound mind has the same right to consent or refuse consent to treatment as a 'free' person and that right has to be respected by all (see *Home Secretary v Robb* [1995] 1 All ER 677).

The position is less straightforward when dealing with patients subject to detention under the Mental Health Act 1983. The basic rule is that treatments, other than those covered by ss 57 and 58, do not require the patient's consent. Section 57, which involves such treatments as psychosurgery and hormone implants to reduce the male sex drive, does require the patient to give his consent to the Regional Medical Officer who will subsequently inform the Mental Health Act Commission. Section 58 stipulates that treatments such as ECT (electro convulsive therapy) and drug treatment after three months or more have elapsed since drugs were first given during the detention period, also require the patient's consent. A consent can extend over more than one of these treatments and it can be limited to a specified period, but it can also be withdrawn at any time; in such circumstances the treatment will have to stop at once unless to do so would cause serious suffering to the patient. Overreaching both ss 57 and 58 is s 63 which defines the circumstances when these treatments can be given without the patient's consent, eg where it is 'immediately necessary to save the patient's life' (see *B v Croydon Health Authority* [1995] 2 WLR 294).

REFERENCES

English case law

(1) Home Secretary v Robb [1995] 1 All ER 677

A prisoner of sound mind had a right to refuse nutrition.

(2) B v Croydon Health Authority [1995] 2 WLR 294

B, who suffered from a psychopathic disorder, was compulsorily detained under the Mental Health Act 1983. One of her symptoms was a compulsion to hurt herself; as such she had stopped eating to a point where her weight fell to a dangerous level. The hospital decided to feed her by nasogastric tube without her consent.

Held:: tube feeding was medical treatment for the purposes of s 63 and could therefore lawfully be carried out without B's consent.

(3) SW Hertfordshire Health Authority v Brady [1994] Med L Rev 208

As regards a patient who was anorexia nervosa, feeding by nasogastric tube was treatment under s 63 of the Mental Health Act 1983 and consequently did not require the patient's consent. (See also *Re VS (Adult: Mental Disorder)* [1995] Med LR 292.)

Foreign case law

UNITED STATES

Thor v Supreme Court [1994] Med L Rev 220

The Supreme Court of California held that a prisoner, who was a quadriplegic but mentally competent, could decide for himself whether life-sustaining medical treatment should be given or withheld. His right did not depend on the nature of the treatment.

Statutes / statutory instruments

(1) MENTAL HEALTH ACT 1983

Treatment requiring consent and a second opinion

57 (1) This section applies to the following forms of medical treatment for mental disorder:

 (a) any surgical operation for destroying brain tissue or for destroying the functioning of brain tissue; and

 (b) such other forms of treatment as may be specified for the purposes of this section by regulations made by the Secretary of State.

(2) Subject to s 62 below, a patient shall not be given any form of treatment to which this section applies unless he has consented to it and:

 (a) a registered medical practitioner appointed for the purposes of this part of this Act by the Secretary of State (not being the responsible medical officer) and two other persons appointed for the purposes of this paragraph by the Secretary of State (not being registered medical practitioners) have certified in writing that the patient is capable of understanding the nature, purpose and likely effects of the treatment in question and has consented to it; and

 (b) the registered medical practitioner referred to in paragraph (a) above has certified in writing that, having regard to the likelihood of the treatment alleviating or preventing a deterioration of the patient's condition, the treatment should be given.

(3) Before giving a certificate under subsection 2(b) above the registered medical practitioner concerned shall consult two other persons who have been professionally concerned with the patient's medical treatment, and of those persons one shall be a nurse and the other shall be neither a nurse nor a registered medical practitioner.

(4) Before making any regulations for the purpose of this section the Secretary of State shall consult such bodies as appear to him to be concerned.

Treatment requiring consent or a second opinion

58(1) This section applies to the following forms of medical treatment for mental disorder:

    (a) such forms of treatment as may be specified for the purposes of this section by regulations made by the Secretary of State;

    (b) the administration of medicine to a patient by any means (not being a form of treatment specified under paragraph (a) above or s 57 above) at any time during a period for which he is liable to be detained as a patient to whom this part of this Act applies if three months or more have elapsed since the first occasion in that period when medicine was administered to him by any means for his mental disorder.

(2) The Secretary of State may by order vary the length of the period mentioned in subsection (1)(b) above.

(3) Subject to s 62 below, a patient shall not be given any form of treatment to which this section applies unless:

    (a) he has consented to that treatment and either the responsible medical officer or a registered medical practitioner appointed for the purposes of this part of this Act by the Secretary of State has certified in writing that the patient is capable of understanding its nature, purpose and likely effects and has consented to it; or

    (b) a registered medical practitioner appointed as aforesaid (not being the responsible medical officer) has certified in writing that the patient is not capable of understanding the nature, purpose and likely effects of that treatment or has not consented to it but that, having regard to the likelihood of its alleviating or preventing a deterioration of his condition, the treatment should be given.

(4) Before giving a certificate under subsection (3)(b) above the registered medical practitioner concerned shall consult two other persons who have been professionally concerned with the patient's medical treatment, and of those persons one shall be a nurse and the other shall be neither a nurse nor a registered medical practitioner.

(5) Before making any regulations for the purposes of this section the Secretary of State shall consult such bodies as appear to him to be concerned.

Urgent treatment

62(1) Sections 57 and 58 above shall not apply to any treatment:

    (a) which is immediately necessary to save the patient's life; or

    (b) which (not being irreversible) is immediately necessary to prevent a serious deterioration of his condition; or

    (c) which (not being irreversible or hazardous) is immediately necessary to alleviate serious suffering by the patient; or

    (d) which (not being irreversible or hazardous) is immediately necessary and represents the minimum interference necessary to prevent the patient from behaving violently or being a danger to himself or to others.

(2) Sections 60 and 61(3) above shall not preclude the continuation of any treatment or of treatment under any plan pending compliance with s 57 or 58 above if the responsible medical officer considers that the discontinuance of the treatment or of treatment under the plan would cause serious suffering to the patient.

(3) For the purposes of this section treatment is irreversible if it has unfavourable irreversible physical or psychological consequences and hazardous if it entails significant physical hazard.

Treatment not requiring consent

63 The consent of a patient shall not be required for any medical treatment given to him for the mental disorder from which he is suffering, not being treatment falling within s 57 or 58 above, if the treatment is given by or under the direction of the responsible medical officer.

Practice points

- On occasions, the courts have expressed a preference for claims to be brought in negligence as opposed to trespass where the argument is that the defendant has failed to carry out his duty to inform in order to obtain the patient's consent; in our view, the choice is straightforward: either there is consent or there is no consent.
- If true consent is given, the claim should be in negligence.
- If true consent is not given, the claim should be in trespass.
- Note the advantages of trespass over negligence. In trespass:
  (1) mere touching, without damage, is actionable;
  (2) fault does not need to be established;
  (3) the *Bolam* rule is of no importance (see further, at p 121);
  (4) there is no need for the plaintiff to argue that consent would have been denied if sought;
  (5) the defendant is liable for all direct damage, not just damage which is reasonably foreseeable.
- If there is no true consent, then the health carer should 'back off' or risk being sued, unless the patient is unconscious or it is an emergency in which event the health carer can carry out such procedures as are in the patient's best interests. By all means, listen to the wishes of the relatives, etc but, at the end of the day, the health carer must comply with this principle and should be prepared to support his actions at a later date in a court of law. Doing what other health carers would have done in the circumstances is not a defence to a trespass claim.
- True consent is obtained when the patient agrees to treatment after information, relating to his procedure, has been communicated to him in broad terms. Not every risk has to be notified voluntarily; this may be because it is not in the patient's interests to tell him or because it is not something which the profession would do in the circumstances. In short, this is a clear case where the health carer is deemed to know best.
- True consent from a patient carries with it confidentiality. Consequently, if a 15 year old girl is considered to be '*Gillick* mature' and is subsequently treated without her parents' consent or knowledge, then she is further entitled to the confidentiality of the health carer, ie the latter should not inform the parents about the treatment.
- True consent to be treated cannot be vetoed, but a refusal to be treated can be vetoed in certain circumstances. These latter circumstances, although clearly defined by case law, are not exhaustive. It is therefore possible for a practitioner to argue other occasions where the consent not to be treated can be ignored, eg where the refusal is likely to cause harm to a third party. Conversely, it is still

open to argue that, if true consent is given, a refusal to be treated should be respected.

- In PVS cases, recent incidents should have alerted all concerned to the fact that the present legal and ethical rules are not satisfactory; the 12 month 'wait' rule, as suggested by the BMA, is clearly not enough.

- Practitioners and health carers should not be afraid to use advance directives. If properly drawn up, it is our contention that the courts will give them legal validity. To wait for legislation is to fail in your ethical duty to the patient concerned.

CHAPTER 3

DUTY

RULE 3(A)

A patient is owed a legal duty of care by a health carer. This duty is a single, indivisible duty.

Commentary

Whether or not a duty of care is owed in any given situation will be determined as an issue of law by the English courts. As patients using National Health Service or Trust facilities have no contract with the NHS or the Trust (see *Pfizer Corpn v Ministry of Health* [1965] AC 512) they can only look to the law of tort (in particular the tort of negligence) for redress. For the private patient, ie the person who is being treated privately, the law of contract exists as an additional alternative to this tort liability. If the claim is brought in contract, then cases such as *Thake v Maurice* [1986] QB 644; *Scuriaga v Powell* [1979] 123 SJ 406 and *Eyre v Measday* [1986] 1 All ER 488 will be most instructive to the plaintiff's lawyers. What these cases demonstrate is that, in the absence of contrary evidence, the contract will be interpreted as one to treat the patient with reasonable skill and care, not as one guaranteeing a successful outcome. However, should a health carer, orally or in writing, go further and guarantee an outcome, eg permanent sterility and should that outcome fail to materialise, then the defendant will be liable in contract. As Kerr LJ said in *Thake* (at p 678):

> ... it seems to me that the plaintiffs could not reasonably have concluded anything other than that his agreement to perform the operation meant that ... he had undertaken to render Mr Thake permanently sterile.

The legal duty of care in the tort of negligence is regarded by the English courts as a single duty, broken down for convenience into individual duties such as a duty to diagnose, a duty to treat, etc. The consequence of this is that there will, again according to the courts, be only one standard of care. But what if that standard should prove to be unsatisfactory or, at the very least, questionable in its application? Should the standard be redefined? Or might it be argued that, in law, the duty owed is not the single indivisible duty which, admittedly, the House of Lords did confirm in *Sidaway v Board of Governors of the Bethlem Royal Hospital and the Maudsley Hospital* [1985] AC 871? In that case, Lord Diplock unhesitatingly said (at p 895):

> In English jurisprudence, the doctor's relationship with his patient which gives rise to the normal duty of care to exercise his skill and judgment to improve the patient's health ... has hitherto been treated as a single comprehensive duty ... This general duty is not subject to dissection into a number of component parts to which different criteria ... apply ...

The difficulty with this approach lies, to a large extent, with the standard applied to this single duty: the *Bolam* standard (see Chapter 5, at p 121). It has been argued, successfully in the Australian courts, that the *Bolam* standard places too much control into the hands of the medical profession and results in the English courts declining to impose an objective standard which could and would lead to the conclusion that standard medical practice is negligent. The reluctance of English courts to adopt this objective approach could be the result of not wishing to impose their judgment in matters of life and death (see, however, the judgment of Roch LJ in the recent case of *Joyce v Merton, Sutton and Wandsworth Health Authority* [1996] 7 Med LR 1. But even accepting the merits of that particular argument it is, however, questionable whether the same reasoning could be applied where the negligence results from the doctor's failure to warn the patient about the risks of, eg invasive surgery. Certainly, the Australian courts in *Rogers v Whittaker* [1993] 4 Med LR 79; [1992] 3 Med LR 331; (1992) 109 ALR 625 took the view that, as part of the medical treatment, disclosing risks associated with the procedure could and should be treated differently from diagnosis and treatment and, while they were prepared to apply the *Bolam* rule to the latter two areas, they were not prepared to apply the same rule exclusively in the area of risks.

It is not too late for the English courts to follow the approach in *Rogers v Whittaker* and hold that a health carer's duty is not single and indivisible, but it is extremely unlikely that they will because, apart from the 'neatness' of the English rule, it is evident that a legal objective standard will only serve to increase the number of instances where a health carer might be held negligent and this, in turn, could result in defensive medicine – something which is generally regarded as unwelcome in England. But as cases such as *Rogers v Whittaker* and *Hucks v Cole* (1968) reported at [1993] 4 Med LR 393 gain a wider audience it is possible that more and more plaintiffs' lawyers will argue that a distinction can and should be drawn between diagnosis, treatment, etc and the risks and that, for the latter, an objective standard should be adopted (see the judgments of Morland J in *Smith v Tunbridge Wells Health Authority* [1994] 5 Med LR 334 and Rougier J in *McAllister v Lewisham and North Southwark Health Authority* [1994] 5 Med LR 343).

REFERENCES

English case law

(1) Pfizer Corporation v Ministry of Health [1965] AC 512; [1965] 2 WLR 387

Lord Pearce (at p 548):

> There is no consensual bargain between the patient and the Minister or his agent. The Minister is by statute bound to provide the drug and the patient is entitled to receive it.

Lord Upjohn (at p 552):

> When the National Health Service Act 1952, authorised the Minister to make 'a charge' it seems to me that the basic nature of the transaction was not ... turned from a statutory relationship into a contractual relationship of bargain and sale.

(2) Thake v Maurice [1986] QB 644; [1986] 2 WLR 337; [1986] 1 All ER 479

The plaintiff had four children and a fifth was on the way. It was agreed that the surgeon, M, would perform a vasectomy on the husband. The husband had been told that the operation was irreversible but he was not warned that there was a small chance that the vasectomy would not sterilise him. When late recanalisation occurred and the wife found herself pregnant, the plaintiffs sued for breach of contract and negligence.

Held:: there was no breach of contract but there was negligence. Nourse LJ said ([1986] QB 644, at p 688):

> In my view, a doctor cannot be objectively regarded as guaranteeing the success of any operation or treatment unless he says as much in clear and unequivocal terms.

(3) Scuriaga v Powell [1979] 123 SJ 406

The defendant doctor agreed to terminate a pregnancy by a legal abortion. He performed the operation but it failed to terminate the pregnancy. The plaintiff then gave birth to a healthy child by caesarean section. Subsequently, she claimed damages for breach of contract arguing that the doctor had negligently performed the operation and had failed to carry out the necessary further investigations, procedures and treatment.

Held:: the plaintiff succeeded. Watkins J considered that the sole and effective cause of the continuation of the pregnancy was the breach of contract.

(4) Eyre v Measday [1986] 1 All ER 488

The defendant gynaecologist agreed to perform a sterilisation operation on the plaintiff. The nature of the operation was explained including the fact that it was irreversible but he did not tell the plaintiff that there was a small risk of pregnancy occurring after the operation. The plaintiff subsequently became pregnant and an action was brought for damages for *(inter alia)* breach of contract.

Held:: judgment for the defendant. The contract was to carry out a particular type of operation and not to render the plaintiff absolutely sterile.

(5) Sidaway v Board of Governors of the Bethlem Royal Hospital and the Maudsley Hospital [1985] AC 871; [1985] 2 WLR 840; [1985] 1 All ER 643

During an operation to relieve the plaintiff of persistent pain in her back and shoulder, her spinal cord was damaged. Her claim in damages was based not on the operation being performed negligently, but rather on the failure by the surgeon to warn her of the risk of damage to the spinal cord, which, at the trial, was agreed to be less that 1%. Her claim was dismissed; the court ruled that, since there was a responsible body of medical opinion who would have warned the plaintiff in substantially similar terms to those used by the defendant, the latter was not negligent. Lord Diplock said (at [1985] 1 AC 871 at p 895):

> To decide what risks the existence of which a patient should be voluntarily warned and the terms in which such warning, if any, should be given ... is as much an exercise of professional skill and judgment as any other part of the doctor's comprehensive duty of care ... The *Bolam* test should be applied.

(6) Bolam v Friern Hospital Management Committee [1957] 1 WLR 582; [1957] 2 All ER 118

The plaintiff was treated for depression by ECT (electro convulsive therapy). No relaxant drugs were administered nor was any form of manual restraint used; this was in line with the hospital's practice. During the treatment the patient suffered severe injuries. In directing the jury, McNair J (at p 587) uttered the oft-quoted words, 'A doctor is not guilty of negligence if he has acted in accordance with a practice accepted as proper by a responsible body of medical men skilled in that particular art ...'. See further Chapter 5, Standard of Care, at p 121.

(7) Hucks v Cole (1968) reported at [1993] 4 Med LR 393

During and after her confinement the plaintiff was under the control and care of the defendant, a GP. When her finger became swollen the doctor reassured her that there was nothing to worry about. After the hospital had diagnosed her to be suffering from fulminating septicaemia and prescribed an antibiotic, the GP failed to start her on a course of penicillin treatment. Ultimately the plaintiff's voice was permanently damaged.

Holding the doctor negligent, Sachs LJ said (at p 397):

> When the evidence shows that a lacuna exists by which risks of great danger are knowingly taken, then, however small the risks, the courts must anxiously examine that lacuna – particularly, if the risks can be easily and inexpensively avoided.
>
> If the court finds, on an analysis of the reasons given for not taking precautions that, in the light of current professional knowledge, there is no proper basis for the lacuna, and that it is definitely not reasonable that those risks should be taken, its function is to state that fact and where necessary to state that it constitutes negligence. In such a case the practice will no doubt there after be altered to the benefit of patients.
>
> On such occasions the fact that other practitioners would have done the same thing as the defendant practitioner is a very weighty matter to be put in the scales on his behalf; but it is not ... conclusive.

See further Chapter 5, at p 140.

(8) Joyce v Merton and Sutton and Wandsworth Health Authority [1996] 7 Med LR 1; [1995] 6 Med LR 60

Per Roch LJ (at pp 13–14):

> The second misdirection of which complaint is made, is ...:
>
>> In the field of diagnosis and treatment, a defendant is not guilty of negligence if his acts or omissions were in accordance with accepted clinical practice.
>
> Had that been the totality of the judge's direction to himself on the law I would have agreed that it amounted to a misdirection. However, the judge added these words:
>
>> Provided that clinical practice stood up to analysis and was not unreasonable in the light of the state of the medical knowledge at the time.
>
> *The addition is very important because without it, it leaves the decision of negligence or no negligence in the hands of the doctors, whereas that question must at the end of the day be one for the courts. In my view, the judge's direction would have been better phrased if, instead of the words:*
>
>> ... if his acts or omissions
>
> he had used the words:
>
>> ... if his acts or decision not to act
>
> because it is to be hoped that an omission would never be part of accepted clinical practice. In the present case, the question was not whether Dr Stewart had omitted to re-explore the artery but whether his decision was not to re-explore because there was a palpable pulse, albeit of small volume, was in accordance with accepted clinical practice and whether that clinical practice stood up to analysis.

See further Chapter 5, at p 142.

(9) Smith v Tunbridge Wells Health Authority [1994] 5 Med LR 334

In this case, Morland J held a consultant negligent for not giving a patient a warning of a particular risk even though it was agreed and accepted that, in failing to do so, the defendant was doing what other experienced, competent surgeons would have done. *Per* Lord Morland (at p 388):

I accept the defendant's submission that Mr Cook's [the consultant] personal view as to his duty is not definitive evidence that in law he owed that duty. In my judgment, it is, however, cogent evidence that general surgeons in 1988 ... would have regarded it as the proper and accepted practice to warn such a patient of the risk of impotence.

Why was *Bolam* not regarded as conclusive? Was it because this case had to do with risks? See further Chapter 5, at p 141.

(10) McAllister v Lewisham & North Southwark Health Authority [1994] 5 Med LR 343

Here, Rougier J held a senior consultant neurosurgeon liable in negligence for failing to disclose adequate information regarding the risks associated with a particular operation. *Per* Rougier J (at p 352):

I have come to the conclusion that those who say that the warnings given ... were inadequate were right ... It is in this sphere that I am compelled to hold that Mr Strong [consultant neurosurgeon] fell below the standard which could have been expected from him.

Is it a coincidence that like the *Smith* case (*supra*), disclosure of risks was involved here?

Foreign case law

AUSTRALIA

(1) Rogers v Whittaker [1993] 4 Med LR 79; [1992] 3 Med LR 331; (1992) 109 ALR 625

The plaintiff, who was almost blind in one eye, consulted the defendant, an ophthalmic surgeon, about an operation and the possible risks associated with such an operation. However, she omitted to ask specifically whether sympathetic ophthalmia (damage to the good eye) would result. The Australian High Court held that the surgeon was under a duty to inform the patient of the slight risk to the good eye.

Per Mason CJ (at p 82):

In Australia, it has been accepted that the standard of care to be observed by a person with some special skill or competence is that of the ordinary skilled person exercising and professing to have that special skill. But, that standard is not determined solely or even primarily by reference to the practice followed or supported by a responsible body of opinion in the relevant profession or trade. Even in the sphere of diagnosis and treatment ... the *Bolam* principle has not always been applied. Further, and more importantly, particularly in the field of non-disclosure of risk and the provision of advice and information, the *Bolam* principle has been discarded and, instead, the courts have adopted the principle that, while evidence of acceptable medical practice is a useful guide for the courts, it is for the courts to adjudicate on what is the appropriate standard of care ...

See further Chapter 5, at p 143.

(2) F v R (1983) 33 SASR 189

After an unsuccessful tubal ligation, a woman became pregnant. She brought a negligence action alleging a failure by the medical practitioner to warn her of the procedure's failure rate. In refusing to apply the *Bolam* rule, King CJ said (at p 194):

the ultimate question, however, is not whether the defendant's conduct accords with the practices of his profession or some part of it, but whether it conforms to the standard of reasonable care demanded by the law. That is a question for the court and the duty of deciding it cannot be delegated to any profession or group in the community.

CANADA

Brushett v Cowan [1991] 2 Med LR 271

Per Marshall JA (at p 275):

Whether a particular relationship gives rise to a duty of care owed by one to another is a question of law. That question was not in issue since the existence of legal obligations of a surgeon towards his or her patient in relation to post operative care is not really subject to dispute.

RULE 3(B)

The legal duty of care arises as soon as medical treatment is undertaken by the health carer.

Commentary

This means that patients who register with doctors, patients seen by doctors but not registered with them, eg where medical care is administered at the roadside consequent on a motorway pile up, patients who enter the Accident and Emergency ward of a hospital, are all owed the duty of care, because they either have a legal right to be treated or have actually been treated; in other words, their treatment has been undertaken. BMA Guidelines (Medical Ethics: Its Practice and Philosophy [1993], at p 180) indicate that the doctor has an *ethical* duty not to drive past, eg the injured victims of a motorway crash ('In an emergency all doctors would be expected to offer assistance, but the extent of care provided will depend on the nature of the emergency ...') but, in truth, there is no *legal* duty to stop and treat such victims. One exception to this rule relates to GPs. According to Schedule 1, para 4(1)(h) of the terms of their contract with the FHSA, if an emergency were to occur in his practice area, then a GP has no choice but to render emergency assistance if requested; if the emergency were to occur outside his practice area then there must be prior agreement to provide emergency cover before the legal obligation will arise.

The word 'treatment' includes diagnosis and suggested courses of action to follow, whether the patient is seen or not seen by the doctor; eg the doctor in the casualty department of a busy hospital who instructs a nurse via the telephone of the treatment which the patient is to undergo (see *Morrison v Forsyth* [1995] 6 Med LR 6). But the legal duty will not arise where the person has been examined by a health carer for some purpose other than to receive medical advice and treatment, eg someone who is being examined for drunkenness at a police station or who is being assessed for the purposes of insurance cover. Having said that, there is a fine line between the doctor–patient duty and the general duty of care owed by one person to another which the health carer would still clearly owe to the person being examined or assessed; consequently tort liability will exist in the non-doctor–patient relationship if, in taking a sample of blood, a broken needle was carelessly left in the person's arm by the health carer. The difference relates to the standard of care required in the two sets of circumstances; with the doctor–patient relationship the doctor owes the *Bolam* standard of care, ie to act as a responsible group of health carers, similarly qualified, would have acted, whereas in the non-doctor–patient relationship the duty is to act as a reasonable person would act in the circumstances.

For the sake of completeness it should be emphasised that the duty of care is owed by all categories of health carers, eg doctors, nurses, physiotherapists, irrespective of their experience. Thus the junior doctor owes the same duty of care to the patient as his more experienced senior colleague; this must be right since the patient expects a certain standard of care when he puts himself in the hands of the hospital authority or health carer. From a practical standpoint this means that the hospital or health authority should never place the health carer in a position where, unassisted, he will have to do things which are beyond his abilities. Furthermore, the employer of such health carers, ie the health authority, owes a direct, as opposed to a vicarious, duty of care to the patient. In *Wilsher v Essex Area Health Authority* [1986] 3 All ER 801, two of the Appeal Court judges positively asserted that such a duty did exist. The Vice Chancellor's approach was that '... a health authority which so conducts its hospital that it fails to provide doctors of sufficient skill and experience to give the treatment offered ... may be directly liable in negligence to the patient ... I can see no reason why, in principle, the health authority should not be so liable if its *organisation* is at fault' (at p 833). Glidewell LJ expressed it this way (at p 831): '... there seems to be no reason in principle why, in a suitable case ... a hospital management committee should not be held directly liable ... for failing to provide sufficient qualified and competent staff.'

In fairness, this direct duty is not a recent creation of the courts. In *Cassidy v Ministry of Health* [1951] 2 KB 343, Denning LJ had already signalled that such a duty existed. To paraphrase what he said (at p 365), when a patient puts himself in the hands of a hospital he expects there to be sufficiently qualified people and adequate facilities to look after him properly and hopefully make him better; if that fails to materialise then it is fitting that the health authority should be made liable. In many ways, the word 'organisation' used by the Vice Chancellor in *Wilsher* is the most significant; if the hospital 'set up' is inadequate so that, eg the patient on the ward becomes vulnerable to attacks by other patients or members of the public then the duty is owed and broken. It was because of the breakdown in its organisational set-up that the health authority in *Bull and another v Devon Area Health Authority* [1993] 4 Med LR 117 was held liable to the patient; their system of cover in the field of obstetrics had produced a real risk of danger to their patients.

The legal duty continues as long as the patient is being treated; it ends when the treatment is completed or the patient or the doctor dies. But it can also come to an end when, having been referred by a GP to a hospital or a consultant, the GP then writes and informs the hospital or the consultant that the patient does not need to be seen any longer; or, having been told to return for further treatment the patient fails to reattend. In the latter case, most health carers should try to find out, either by contacting the GP or writing direct to the patient, why the patient was unable to attend. However, it is not being suggested that an infinite number of reappointments should be made; there will come a point in time, dictated by hospital practice and common sense, when the patient's non-attendance will release the health carer and the hospital from their legal duty of care.

REFERENCES

English case law

(1) Bolam v Friern Hospital Management Committee [1957] 1 WLR 582; [1957] 2 All ER 118

See above.

(2) Morrison v Forsyth [1995] 6 Med LR 6

The defendant was covering for the plaintiff's GP. In response to the plaintiff's account of his symptoms, he telephoned the local pharmacy to make a prescription available. The plaintiff's symptoms worsened and he eventually died. The plaintiff's widow and children brought an action contending:

(1) that a reasonably competent GP would not have relied upon taking a history and issuing a prescription over the telephone; and

(2) that the GP was negligent in not asking further questions, particularly as the patient was reduced to communicating via an intermediary.

The action failed as the plaintiff failed to show that on the facts given it was negligent to have given medical advice and further that a doctor exercising reasonable care would have questioned the plaintiff further.

(3) Wilsher v Essex Area Health Authority [1986] 3 All ER 801

The plaintiff was born three months prematurely with breathing problems, as a result of which he needed extra oxygen. To monitor the partial pressure of oxygen in the arterial blood of a baby, the standard practice is to pass a catheter through the umbilical artery into the aorta. Regrettably, a house officer in the special care baby unit inserted the catheter into a vein; the outcome was that false readings of the level of oxygen were shown. The plaintiff contracted retrolental fibroplasia and was nearly blind. In a negligence claim, the Appeal Court held that inexperience (on the part of the house officer) was no defence. In a dissenting judgment, the Vice Chancellor considered that it was more appropriate to sue the health authority directly as opposed to vicariously, on the ground that it had run the hospital in such a way that it had failed to provide doctors of sufficient skill and experience to give the necessary treatment.

See further Chapter 5, at p 124.

(4) Cassidy v Ministry of Health [1951] 2 KB 343; [1951] 1 All ER 574

The plaintiff was diagnosed as suffering from Dupuytren's Contracture (forward curvature of one or more fingers). After the operation his hand and arm were bandaged by a nurse. Following complaints that he was suffering excruciating pain it was found, on removal of the splint, that he had lost the use of four of his fingers. The Appeal Court held that there was a *prima facie* case of negligence.

Denning LJ (at p 365–66):

> If the plaintiff had to prove that some particular doctor or nurse was negligent, he would not be able to do it. But he was not put to that impossible task: he says, 'I went into the hospital to be cured of two stiff fingers. I have come out with four stiff fingers, and my hand is useless. That should not have happened if due care had been used ...' I am quite clearly of opinion that that raises a *prima facie* case against the health authorities.

(5) Bull and another v Devon Area Health Authority [1993] 4 Med LR 117

Where it took 68 minutes between the spontaneous delivery of one twin and the surgical delivery of the other resulting in serious damage to the latter, the Appeal Court held that the liability on the Area Health Authority was direct for failing to have a registrar in attendance at a critical period in the second delivery.

Statutes / statutory instruments

Terms of service for doctors in general practice (issued pursuant to the NATIONAL HEALTH SERVICE (GENERAL MEDICAL PHARMACEUTICAL SERVICES) REGULATIONS 1974 (as amended) (SI 1974/160). Schedule 1, para 4(1) says that a doctor's patients include:

(h) persons to whom he may be requested to give treatment which is immediately required owing to an accident or other emergency at any place in his practice area if:

(i) he is not a doctor to whom paragraph 5 applied, and

(ii) he is not, at the time of the request, relieved under paragraph 16(2) of his obligation to give treatment personally, and

(iii) he is available to provide such treatment,

or any persons to whom he may be requested, and he agrees, to give treatment which is immediately required owing to an accident or other emergency at any place in the locality of any Committee on whose medical list he is included, provided, in either case, that there is no doctor who, at the time of the request, is under an obligation otherwise than under this subparagraph to give treatment to that person, or there is such a doctor but, after being requested to attend, he is unable to attend and give treatment immediately required.

Professional / ethical guidelines

BMA Guidelines/Medical Ethics: Its Practice and Philosophy [1993].

See p 68 above.

RULE 3(C)

In appropriate circumstances the legal duty of care may be owed by the health carer to a third party affected by the patient's acts or omissions.

Commentary

This rule is stated with a certain degree of caution since the significant medical authorities to support it are almost exclusively foreign. To illustrate the problem, consider the following two scenarios.

Scenario 1

A is B's patient. In the course of his treatment for depression A tells B that he is very much in love with C but that C sees him only as a friend not a lover. He further reveals to B that if he cannot be with C as a lover then she (C) would be 'better off dead'. Although alarmed, B decides that the confidentiality of his patient is paramount and therefore he does not inform C or her parents or the authorities of A's threat. A subsequently kills C. Could C's relatives pursue a civil claim against B arguing that C was owed a duty of care by B?

Scenario 2

X is Y's patient. Tests reveal that X is HIV positive. Y knows that X has a regular partner, that the union has produced two children and that the parties have a healthy sex life. Y counsels X as regards his future life style, including advice as to what and how to tell his partner of his illness. X agrees to think about it. Some months later Y discovers that X has not told his partner of his illness. X, however, is adamant that he, not Y, will tell the partner. If X still does not inform his partner and she subsequently tests positive for HIV, could she bring a claim in negligence against Y alleging that he owed her a duty of care?

In two cases in the American courts it has been held that a positive legal duty can be owed by the doctor to the third party; in both cases the harm that was sustained by the third party was said to outweigh the confidentiality owed to the patient. In *Tarasoff v Regents of the University of California* (1976) 551 P(2d) 334, the facts of which are similar to those in Scenario 1, the Supreme Court of California held that the defendant health carer could not escape liability by simply arguing that the third party was not his patient; there was a positive obligation to use reasonable care to protect the undefended victim from the source of the danger. In *Bradshaw v Daniel* [1994] Med L Rev 237, the facts of which are reminiscent to those in Scenario 2 except that the case involved Rocky Mountain Spotted Fever, the Supreme Court of Tennessee held that a physician did owe a duty to a non-patient third party in respect of injuries caused by the physician's negligence, in circumstances where that injury could have been reasonably foreseen. Writing in the *Medical Law Review* (1994, at p 239), Ian Kennedy noted that 'English law has yet to decide whether to recognise such a duty of affirmative action', but ventured to suggest:

> [it] may well be, however, that the availability of limits, established by cases such as *Gamill* and reflected in the instant case, would persuade an English court to recognise the duty and hence impose liability for its breach if damage occurred.

In general, the English courts have been reluctant to impose a duty in respect of third parties who have suffered harm as a result of the actions of someone who is being 'looked after' by the defendant. This could be explained on the basis either that the reasonable foresight test for a duty situation has not been satisfied or that it was not fair, just or equitable to impose a duty in the particular circumstance. In non-medical cases, a duty to a third party has been upheld, eg in *Home Office v Dorset Yacht Co Ltd* [1970] AC 1004 where liability was imposed for the negligent supervision of borstal trainees by Home Office employees. There, it could be argued that there was an element of control exercised by the defendants over the perpetrators. (The same could also be said of *Tarasoff* given the nature of the student's illness.) If the 'modern' test for establishing a duty is said to be proximity/reasonable foresight/just and equitable, then we are suggesting that a duty should be owed where harm to *identifiable* and *identified* third parties is foreseen. Will the English courts lay down such a general principle? At present they give no indication that they will and we can only conclude that, as a matter of policy, they are unwilling to impose additional duties on a profession which, in their view, already carries a heavy responsibility in respect of matters of life and death.

To revert briefly to the subject of HIV/AIDS, it is to be noted that the new GMC's guidelines (HIV and AIDS; the Ethical Considerations, para 19) permit disclosure of clinical details to a patient's spouse or other sexual partner in the following circumstances:

> Questions of conflicting obligations also arise when a doctor is faced with the decision whether the fact that a patient is HIV positive or suffering from AIDS

should be disclosed to a third party, other than another health care professional, without the consent of the patient. The GMC has reached the view that there are grounds for such a disclosure only where there is a serious and identifiable risk to a specific individual who, if not so informed, would be exposed to infection. Therefore, when a person is found to be infected in this way, the doctor must discuss with the patient the question of informing a spouse or other sexual partner. The GMC believes that most such patients will agree to disclosure in these circumstances, but where such consent is withheld the doctor may consider it a duty to seek to ensure that any sexual partner is informed, in order to safeguard such persons from infection.

See also Rule 1 (D)(v), at p 23.

REFERENCES

English case law

(1) Home Office v Dorset Yacht Co Ltd [1970] AC 1004; [1970] 2 WLR 1140; [1970] 2 All ER 294

The allegation here was that, while officers in charge of some borstal trainees were asleep, the trainees escaped and caused damage to property. The House of Lords held that a duty of care was owed by the appellants (employers of the officers) to the persons whose property was damaged.

Per Lord Reid (at p 1026):

> The case for the Home Office is that under no circumstances can Borstal Officers owe any duty to any member of the public to take care to prevent trainees under their control or supervision from injuring him or his property.

and he continued (at p 1032):

> It is argued that it would be contrary to public policy to hold the Home Office or its officers liable ... The basic question is who should bear the loss caused by that carelessness – the innocent respondents or the Home Office, who are vicariously liable for the conduct of their careless officers?

(2) Goodwill v British Pregnancy Advisory Service [1996] 7 Med LR 129

The Court of Appeal held that a woman, who became pregnant by a man who had had a vasectomy some years before he started a relationship with her, could not sue the defendants who had performed the vasectomy and had assured him it had been successful. One reason was that no duty was owed to her by the defendants. As Thorpe LJ said (at p 133):

> In my judgment on the plaintiff's pleading the defendants were not in a sufficient or any special relationship with the plaintiff such as gives rise to a duty of care. I cannot see that it can properly be said of the defendants that they voluntarily assumed responsibility to the plaintiff when giving advice to Mr MacKinlay. At that time, they had no knowledge of her, she was not an existing sexual partner of Mr MacKinlay but was merely, like any other woman in the world, a potential future sexual partner of his, that is to say a member of an indeterminably large class ... I find it impossible to believe that the policy of the law is or should be to treat so tenuous a relationship ... as giving rise to a duty of care ...

Foreign case law

UNITED STATES

(1) Tarasoff v Regents of the University of California (1976) 551 P (2d) 334

A student psychiatric patient was receiving therapy at the University's hospital. He informed his therapist (an employee of the University) that he was going to kill an unnamed but readily identifiable young lady. At no time was the young lady or her parents informed of the threat. The threat was carried out and the plaintiffs (the parents) sued the therapist and the University in negligence. It was held by the Supreme Court of California that a duty was owed to the young lady; in the circumstances the confidentiality due to the patient was outweighed by the duty to the third party.

Per Justice Tobriner:

> ... When the avoidance of foreseeable harm requires a defendant to control the conduct of another person, or to warn of such conduct, the common law has traditionally imposed liability only if the defendant bears some special relationship to the dangerous person or the potential victim. Since the relationship between a therapist and his patient satisfies this requirement, we need not here decide whether foreseeability alone is sufficient to create a duty to exercise reasonable care to protect a potential victim of another's conduct.

> Although the California decisions that recognise this duty have involved cases in which the defendant stood in a special relationship ... we do not think that the duty should logically be constricted to such situations. Decisions of other jurisdictions hold that the single relationship of a doctor to his patient is sufficient to support the duty to exercise reasonable care to protect others against dangers emanating from the patient's illness.

(2) Bradshaw v Daniel [1994] Med L Rev 237

A woman died from a non-contagious disease, Rocky Mountain Spotted Fever. It transpired that the defendant physician had been treating the woman's husband for the same disease from which he had died shortly before the wife started to show symptoms of the disease. The plaintiff (the son) argued that the defendant had been negligent in failing to warn the mother of the risks of exposure to the disease. The Supreme Court of Tennessee agreed. It reasoned that the physician-patient relationship was sufficient to impose on the physician a positive duty to warn identifiable third parties in the patient's immediate family against foreseeable risks resulting from the patient's illness.

Professional / ethical guidelines

GMC Guidelines.

(HIV and AIDS: the ethical considerations.)

Para 19 – see above.

RULE 3(D)

Employers of health carers will be held vicariously liable for negligence committed by the health carer in the course of the latter's employment.

Commentary

It is a well established rule of common law that a Health Authority, a Trust, a GP or a medical practice can and will be held legally responsible for the negligence of the health carers it employs, be they medical (including consultants, nursing, paramedical staff), or support staff (receptionists, secretaries) provided the wrong was done in the course of the employee's duties (*Cassidy v Ministry of Health* [1951] 2 KB 343; *Roe v Minister of Health* [1954] 2 QB 66). We do not intend to go into the details of what constitutes an employee or what is meant by the phase 'in the course of employment'; other, fuller works, such as *Street on Torts*, should be consulted. What does need emphasising is that consultants are regarded as employees even though the idea of any form of control being exercised over them by the hospital authorities is illusory. As Denning LJ said in *Cassidy* (at p 362):

> ... I can see no possible reason why they [hospital authorities] should not also be responsible for the house surgeons and resident medical officers on their permanent staff ... where the doctor or surgeon, be he a consultant or not, is employed and paid not by the patient but by the hospital authorities.

Although this rule is well tested and uncontroversial, some relationships in the field of medical negligence do require special attention.

Locums

From time to time a GP or a medical practice may have to use the services of a qualified doctor to act as a temporary replacement for the GP or one of the doctors in the practice. The responsibility of the GP or the practice is to ensure that a suitably qualified person is appointed to deputise; failure to do so will result in direct liability (not vicarious). If the locum is negligent when treating a patient, there will be no vicarious liability on the GP or the practice since the relationship between the parties is not one of employer/employee; instead, the locum is in the position of an independent contractor and therefore any action should be brought against the locum in his personal capacity. The conclusion is the same where the GP arranges with a deputising service for cover and the service allocates a doctor as and when the need arises.

Agency nursing staff

Hospitals and medical practices frequently use the services of nursing staff supplied by an agency. In the event of negligence by such staff it is submitted that whether direct or vicarious liability exists and, if so, against whom it exists, may well depend on the cause of the negligence, the terms of the contract between the agency and the nurse and the relationship between the agency and the hospital. For example, if the agency chosen is not a reputable/reliable one or if the hospital fails to instruct the nurse adequately in her duties, then we submit that a direct action will lie against the health authority. But if the agency is reputable and the nurse has been properly instructed but is nonetheless negligent we contend that since the agency nurse has become, albeit temporarily, an integral part of the hospital set-up and is acting under the control of and in the interests of the health authority at the point of the delivery of the treatment, then the health authority, not the agency, should be held vicariously liable.

NHS staff treating private patients

It is not unknown for some beds on a ward in a NHS hospital or even a whole ward to be reserved for private patients under an agreement between the health authority and the private provider. In these circumstances, that agreement will be the determining factor as to who will be ultimately responsible for the negligence of the doctors, etc treating the private patients.

Honorary medical personnel

In *Ellis v Wallsend District Hospital* [1990] 2 Med LR 103, the surgeon involved was described as an honorary medical officer in that, although he had his own specialist medical practice, he had an agreement with the hospital to use their facilities to carry out surgery. The agreement stipulated that the surgeon undertook to treat, free of charge, patients who applied directly to the hospital for relief; in return the surgeon received operating privileges, nursing care and accommodation for his own patients. Assuming negligence by the surgeon towards one of his 'own' patients while the patient was in the hospital, was the hospital vicariously liable? The New South Wales Appeal Court held that since at the moment of treatment the surgeon was engaged in his own business as opposed to that of the hospital, there was no vicarious liability.

REFERENCES

English case law

(1) Cassidy v Ministry of Health [1951] 2 KB 343; [1951] 1 All ER 574

See above.

(2) Roe v Minister of Health [1954] 2 QB 66; [1954] 2 WLR 915; [1954] 2 All ER 131

The plaintiff was given an injection of Nupercaine at the hospital. The Nupercaine was stored in glass ampoules which were, prior to use, immersed in a phenol solution. Unfortunately, some phenol had leaked into the syringe and this resulted in the patient's paralysis. At that time it was not known that phenol could leak into syringes through invisible cracks. The Appeal Court held that there was no negligence; the defendant's conduct had to be judged by the standard of a reasonable person with the knowledge available at the time.

See also Chapter 5, Standard of Care, at pp 133, 135.

Foreign case law

AUSTRALIA

Ellis v Wallsend District Hospital [1990] 2 Med LR 103

Per Samuels JA (at p 126):

> ... I would reduce my question to more fustian terms by asking whether: in treating the appellant was Dr Chambers engaged in his own business or the hospital's ...

And (at p 127):

> Considering the totality of the relationship ... I conclude that it points convincingly to the conclusion that in treating the appellant Dr Chambers was engaged in his own business and not the hospital's. He was conducting his independent practice as a neurosurgeon and his relationship was not one of employer and employee.

RULE (3)(E)

A legal duty of care is owed to an embryo.

Commentary

What any health carer will want to know here is whether he can be sued by a child born with disabilities resulting from the negligence of the health carer towards the mother. It should be clear from the earlier discussion that a duty is owed to the pregnant mother: she is being treated. But can it be said that a duty is also owed to the embryo/foetus while it is in the mother's womb?

According to the Appeal Court decisions in *Burton v Islington Health Authority; De Martell v Merton and Sutton Health Authority* [1993] 4 Med LR 8; a claim can be brought in respect of the child's injuries but only after the child has been born. In *Burton's* case, the negligence was said to have occurred during a dilation and curettage operation; in *De Martell* the child was born with brain damage following a failed forceps delivery and a subsequent delivery by a caesarean section. The courts in effect said two things. First, a duty is owed to an embryo but it is a contingent one which will only be fulfilled when the child is born alive; secondly, again because of the contingent nature of the duty, the mother is unable to bring a claim for and on behalf of her unborn baby. As Potts J said in the *Burton* case [1991] 2 Med LR 133 (at p 136):

> In my view, the actual damage suffered by the plaintiff, that is being born suffering from physical abnormalities, was 'potential damage which was foreseeable' and was the result of the breach of a 'possible duty'. The fact that the plaintiff was undefined in law and without status ... is neither here nor there.

And later:

> However, what had been a 'potential' or 'contingent' duty vested on the birth of the live plaintiff ... (at p 136)

But what if the scenario is taken one stage further back; is there a common law duty to avoid pre-conception negligence? In the Australian case of *X and Y v Pal and others* [1992] 3 Med LR 195, X became pregnant in January 1973. Unknown to her she was at that time suffering from syphilis. In March 1973, she consulted P, an obstetrician and gynaecologist, who submitted her to a number of tests but none for syphilis. In October 1973, she gave birth to a child which subsequently died from gross hydrocephaly and other physical deformities. Reassured in mid-1974 that there was no reason why she could not have a child, she became pregnant in September 1974. The child, Y, was born in March 1995, dysmorphic and mentally retarded. Shortly after the birth it was discovered that both X and Y were suffering from syphilis. Y's action against P and the other doctors was that her abnormalities stemmed from the failure of all the doctors to submit her mother, X, for syphilis testing. One of the issues which the New South Wales court had to determine was whether a duty was owed to a person conceived *subsequent* to the act/omission alleged to be the breach. At first instance, Sully J held that a duty was not owed; this was reversed on appeal. Clarke JA voiced the Appeal Court's approach thus (at p 205):

> In principle ... it should be accepted that a person may be subjected to a duty of care to a child who was neither born nor conceived at the time of his careless act

or omissions such that he may be found liable in damages to that child. Whether or not that duty will arise depends upon whether there is a relevant relationship between the careless person and the class of person to whom the child is one.

Does such a duty in principle exist in English law? In *Reay v BNF plc; Hope v BNF plc* [1994] 5 Med LR 1, the plaintiffs brought their actions against the defendants under the Fatal Accidents Act 1976 and the Law Reform (Miscellaneous Provisions Act) 1934 alleging paternal preconception irradiation (PPI) which, they said, caused mutation in their fathers' sperm which in turn caused a predisposition to leukaemia and/or non-Hodgkin's lymphoma in the next generation. Judgment was given for the defendants principally on the ground that the plaintiffs had failed, on the balance of probabilities, to show causation. Although French J did not specifically consider the duty issue, *obiter* he did say that, if PPI had been found to cause or materially contribute to the resultant illnesses, he would have found for one of the plaintiffs (the other plaintiff would still have lost but not because a duty was not owed).

This suggests that the court did not have a problem with imposing a duty in law on the defendant. But it does not necessarily follow that a similar duty would or should be imposed on the medical profession. English courts are not renowned for extending the liability of the medical profession; public policy has played a conspicuous part in circumscribing that profession's duties. A closer look at the judgment of Clarke JA in *Pal* reveals that what he did say was that there was no reason *in principle* why a duty could not be owed; but that is some way from saying that a duty will be owed in any given situation. In English law, proximity is only one factor in determining duty situations; reasonable foresight and public policy are other very important issues and it is submitted that public policy will prevent a duty being owed by the medical profession in these circumstances.

Under the Congenital Disabilities (Civil Liability) Act 1976 a statutory duty of care is owed to an embryo. This Act applies to births occurring after the passage of the Act, ie 22 July 1976; for births before that date the common law rules apply (above). According to the Act, the child has a claim if he was born disabled as a result of an occurrence before his birth and someone (other than the mother) was answerable to the child for that occurrence; in such circumstances the child's disabilities are to be regarded as stemming from the wrongful act of that person (s 1(1)). An occurrence is defined as one which:

(a) affected either parent of the child in his or her ability to have a normal, healthy child' (this would cover pre-conception negligence, but causation would still be an important issue); or

(b) affected the mother during her pregnancy, or affected her or the child in the course of its birth, so that the child was born with disabilities which would not otherwise have been present (s 1(2)).

Linking these provisions with the requirements that the defendant must be liable or would be liable in tort to the parent (if sued in time) (s 1(3)) and that the child must have been alive (s 4(2)(a)), the following emerge as the conditions for a claim under the 1976 Act:

(1) The doctor must have owed a duty to the parents which is subsequently broken and would have therefore given rise to liability;

(2) As a result of that breach, a child is born disabled;

(3) The child is born alive (ie no claim can be brought while the child is in the mother's womb even if damage to the embryo is ascertainable).

The disability envisaged by the Act is prescribed by s 4(1) and it is 'any deformity, disease or abnormality, including predisposition ... to physical or mental defect in the future'. From this it would appear that the resultant injury must be quantifiable in monetary terms, thus ruling out, after 22 July 1976, a claim by a child for 'wrongful life', ie that life with all its disabilities is or would be so awful that it would be better off dead, since such claims are considered to be impossible to quantify in money terms.

As regards 'wrongful life' claims before 22 July 1976, the case of *McKay v Essex Area Health Authority* [1982] QB 1166 decided that such claims were not possible in English law. In addition to the reason that such claims were impossible to quantify, the court used the floodgates argument, ie that to allow this type of the claim would simply open the way to many other claims, but also the public policy argument, ie that to allow the claim would send out the wrong signal – that English courts preferred no life to a wretched life. None of these arguments is totally convincing. The courts could have drawn a distinction between some existence and a very poor existence; why did it have to be a contrast between a poor existence and no existence at all? Furthermore, how many more cases could be envisaged if the claim in *McKay* was upheld? Ten? Twenty? Whatever the figure it seems scandalous that a meritorious argument should fail simply because there exist other meritorious claims. Finally, can it really be said that English law is consistent in preferring some life to no life? What about cases where lifesaving machines are turned off or nutrition withheld because the patient's quality of life is said to be very poor?

REFERENCES

English case law

(1) Burton v Islington Health Authority [1993] 4 Med LR 8

This was an appeal against a decision to strike out the plaintiff's statement of claim as disclosing no cause of action. The appeal was dismissed. *Per* Dillon LJ (at p 11):

> ... I think it would be open to the English courts to apply the civil law maxim directly to the situations we have in these two appeals, and treat the two plaintiffs as lives in being at the times of the events which injured them as they were later born alive, but it is not necessary to do so directly in view of the effect which the *Montreal Tramways* case has already had on the development of the common law in this field in other common law jurisdictions.

(2) De Martell v Merton and Sutton Health Authority [1993] 4 Med LR 8

Here the defendants were appealing against a finding on a preliminary issue. The issue was whether, assuming the allegations set out in the statement of claim, the defendants were liable in tort to the plaintiff for acts and omissions committed before the plaintiff's birth. The appeal was dismissed.

(3) Reay v BNF plc; Hope v BNF plc [1994] 5 Med LR 1

Per French J (at p 53):

> As to Vivien, she was brought up until the age of six in Drigg, a village rather over two miles to the south of Seascale. When she was six years old her family

moved to and remained in Seascale and Vivien's NHL (non-Hodgkins Lymphoma) was diagnosed when she was living there.

Thus, she did not satisfy the Gardner study criterion of being born as well as diagnosed in Seascale. Nonetheless, had I been satisfied that NHL was properly to be considered as a form of leukaemia and had I been satisfied that PPI did cause or contribute to the Seascale excess including NHL, I would have found that Vivien Hope was part of the excess and her claim ... would have succeeded ...

(4) McKay v Essex Area Health Authority [1982] QB 1166; [1982] 2 WLR 890; [1982] 2 All ER 771

The plaintiff's claim in negligence was that while in her mother's womb she was infected with rubella (German measles) as a result of negligence by an employee of the health authority. Specifically the claim was that the doctor, who had taken blood samples and sent them for laboratory analysis, had not informed the mother that she and the unborn baby were infected. Consequently, the plaintiff was born with severe disabilities. Part of the claim was 'for entry into a life in which her injuries are highly debilitating ...' (ie 'wrongful life').

Held:: to uphold such a claim would be contrary to public policy. Further, such a claim would be incapable of quantification of damages as it involved comparing existence with non-existence. Ackner LJ said (at p 1188):

I cannot accept that the common law duty of care to a person can involve, without specific legislation to achieve this end, the legal obligation to that person, whether or not *in utero*, to terminate his existence. Such a proposition runs wholly contrary to the concept of sanctity of human life.

Per Stephenson LJ at (p 1180):

But, because a doctor can lawfully by statute do to a fetus what he cannot lawfully do to a person who has been born, it does not follow that he is under a legal obligation to a foetus to do it and terminate its life, or that the fetus has a legal right to die.

Foreign Law Case

AUSTRALIA

(1) X and Y v Pal and others [1992] 3 Med LR 195

The New South Wales Court of Appeal held that a gynaecologist and an obstetrician owed a duty of care to an unborn child or a child not conceived at the time of the negligence.

Per Clarke JA (at p 203):

I would express the position in these terms – A may be liable in damages to B notwithstanding that B had not been conceived at the time A acted carelessly if the following conditions be satisfied:

(a) In all the circumstances A owed a duty to take care to a particular class of persons;

(b) A breached that duty;

(c) B was subsequently born suffering from damage which was causally related to those acts/omissions of A which constituted the breach of duty to the particular class of persons; and

(d) B was a member of the relevant class of persons.

(2) Lynch v Lynch and Government Insurance Office of NSW [1992] 3 Med LR 62

A pregnant woman was held to owe a duty of care to her unborn child.

Per Grove J (at p 66):

> ... I would hold that an injury to an infant suffered during the stages of the journey through life between conception and parturition is not an injury to a person devoid of personality ... Nicole's personality was identifiable and recognisable ... Second, it does not seem to me to be contrary to any principle that in the class of unborn persons to whom a duty to take reasonable care is undoubtedly owed ... there should be included those children who will be born out of the tortfeasor's own body.

CANADA

Montreal Tramways v Leveille [1933] 4 DLR 337

The majority of the Canadian Supreme Court held that when a child, not actually born at the time of an accident, was subsequently born alive and viable, it was clothed with all the rights of action it would have had if actually in existence at the date of the accident to the mother.

GENERAL PRACTICE POINTS – RULES 3(A)–3(E)

Costs

Medical negligence claims can be both costly and lengthy. Plaintiffs should therefore try to discover from their solicitors, at the first interview, the probable cost to them of going to court and the length of time it may take for their claim to be heard and determined. Any plaintiff who is not going to be in receipt of legal aid has the choice of either funding the claim privately (in some cases, if they belong to a professional body such as a trade union, funding may be provided for them) or accepting the path of non-litigation. In the latter case, this could mean a complaint to the FHSA, the GMC, the Health Ombudsman or, in appropriate cases, making use of the Hospital Complaints Procedure Act 1985. These non-litigious approaches are invariably quicker and less formal but they will not provide the plaintiff with financial compensation; what they may offer is an explanation of why things went wrong and, in some circumstances, this explanation may shed light on the negligence issue, eg the hospital report may indicate that a nurse had queried the doctor's recommended treatment. Many plaintiffs may have sought the aforementioned explanations before consulting their solicitors; therefore, as a solicitor, one of your first tasks at the initial interview is to ascertain whether, following a complaint, the plaintiff has or is aware of a report of the investigation.

For those claims which are going to be funded privately, the client should expect to spend at least between £1,000 and £2,000 before discovering whether he has a viable medical negligence claim. Some of that money will be spent on the initial letter(s) which have to be written to obtain voluntary pre-trial disclosure of the medical records and the medical reports. How should the client thereafter decide whether to continue with his action? If, in his solicitors's opinion, there is more than a 50% chance of success. Furthermore, a private client should bear in mind that, even if he is successful, he may not recover all the costs of the action from the losing side: The recent advent of conditional fee arrangements, introduced by s 58 Courts and Legal Services Act 1990 (see also Conditional Fee Agreements Order 1995 (SI 1674) and Conditional Fee Agreements Regulations 1995 (SI 1675)) will be of the utmost significance to private clients and their solicitors in the future as they plan their strategy. A conditional fee arrangement (to be distinguished from a contingency fee arrangement under which the solicitor receives, as his fee, a proportion of the successful plaintiff's damages) is a method by which, in the event of a claim succeeding, the successful client's solicitor, by prior agreement with the client, is rewarded by an enhanced fee based on a percentage of the costs to which he would otherwise be entitled. Currently fees may be increased by a maximum of 100%. Conversely, if the claim is lost then, under the agreement, the solicitor will not recover any costs; however, the client will still be responsible for the disbursements and his opponent's costs and disbursements. Clients may take out insurance to meet this latter eventuality in a claim for personal injuries; however, currently this sort of insurance is not available for medical negligence and pharmaceutical, drug or tobacco-related actions. The Law Society has published a model agreement for personal injury cases (*Law Society Gazette*: 28 June 1995). It is more than likely that private clients will see this type of agreement as the ideal way to fund their action.

If the client is eligible for Legal Aid then any initial discussion will centre on the Green Form Scheme and then the Legal Aid Scheme itself. The former will enable the client to receive up to two hours' help and advice during which the solicitor will obtain a proof of evidence and submit the client's application for legal aid. Assuming the client comes within the current financial limits and the claim looks as if it is worth pursuing, then an application for legal aid should be made as soon as possible after the initial interview. *Note*, that the solicitor should not delay in issuing proceedings until legal aid is obtained if the limitation period is about to expire or has expired. In any event, the solicitor should try to obtain emergency legal aid, see further Chapter 4, Limitation, at p 89. It is more than likely, however, that the Legal Aid Board will, in the first instance, issue a limited certificate; only when a favourable opinion from counsel on liability is obtained will a 'full' certificate be granted.

How long will the case take?

With a contentious claim a plaintiff could expect to be involved in litigation for 3–4 years. That it should take so long is due to a variety of factors, eg good medical experts are invariably busy people who may take up to three months to prepare a medical report; conferences with counsel and experts could take up to four months; in some cases, the true extent of the injuries will be unknown for some considerable period. Changes to the procedural rules in the last four years have made little real impact on the sort of aforementioned issues. But it must be conceded that some of the new rules have improved the situation concentrating as they do on a 'cards on the table' approach as opposed to 'ambush' tactics. Furthermore, Lord Taylor's *Practice Direction (Civil Litigation: Case Management)* [1995] 1 WLR 262 – see Appendix C, at p 347) now ensures that lawyers know exactly what must be done in managing a case and what are the consequences if it is not properly managed, eg not to conduct a case economically could be visited by appropriate orders for costs, including wasted costs orders. Again, if Lord Woolf's proposals in his final report should be implemented (see Appendix H, at p 408) then parties may eagerly look forward to the day of the speedy, economical and fair civil hearing. For example, Lord Woolf wants the courts not only to determine the procedure suitable for each case but also to set timetables for the conduct of the case. Whether these reforms will actually speed up the procedure for medical negligence cases remains be seen.

Access to medical records

A patient has no common law right of access to his medical records; any access exists by way of voluntary disclosure or statutory provisions. This is because the patient does not own his medical records; hospital records are the property of the Health Authority or Trust, while a GP's records are owned by the FHSA. Moreover, the courts have held that a refusal of access to one's records is not a denial of respect for a person's private life or a breach of Article 8 of the European Convention on Human Rights, see *R v Mid-Glamorgan FHSA and another ex parte Martin* [1994] 5 Med LR 383. Solicitors should also realise that the Patient's Charter is of limited help. Although it says that a patient has a right to see his medical records, not all records can or will be seen.

So how does the solicitor obtain the medical records? First, he should make sure he has written permission from the patient to write to the appropriate record holders (who may or may not turn out to be the defendants) requesting that the records be released to him (the solicitor). Then he should write to the relevant defendant(s) asking for voluntary disclosure of the medical records. While the style and contents of such a letter will vary from one legal practice to another, there are certain things which should never be left out of this early communication (see Appendix H, at p 410):

(1) The names of the health carers, dates of treatment and the patient's hospital number (if known);

(2) Enough factual information to convince the defendant(s) that a negligence claim is viable;

(3) A statement that the information should be disclosed to you, the practitioner, and not to a nominated medical adviser; this is because it is the job of the solicitor to ascertain from the records whether there is a possible claim in negligence and to prepare the appropriate memorandum for the medical expert. Also, there seems little point in announcing to the defendants in advance who your medical expert will be.

(4) A statement that if voluntary disclosure is not forthcoming within a reasonable period of time (six weeks is usually considered appropriate) then compulsory disclosure will be sought under ss 33(2) and 34(2) Supreme Court Act 1981 and RSC Ord 24, r 7A, applicable in the county court by virtue of s 76 CCA 1984. These provisions are available against a person likely to be a party to the proceedings (not necessarily a defendant) and someone who is not going to be involved in the ensuing litigation but has relevant documents in his possession.

(5) A statement to the effect that, if compulsory disclosure has to be invoked, costs will sought. In *Hall v Wandsworth Health Authority* (1985) 129 SJ 188, the

plaintiff's solicitors gave the defendant health authority six weeks to comply with voluntary disclosure. When that failed and the Supreme Court Act had to be resorted to, the court upheld a claim for costs against the defendants. It ruled that, while the defendant would normally have his costs paid for by the plaintiff in this type of application: 'in a small number of cases, the conduct of the defendant will justify the court in ordering him to pay his own costs. Mrs Hall's case was [the] worse example of dilatory conduct by the defendants.'

(6) List clearly and fully, preferably in the form of a schedule to your letter, the documents you are requesting. There is enough concrete evidence to suggest that you will only get from the defendant health authority what you ask for; if, through inexperience or carelessness, you have to write more than one pre-writ letter then you are wasting your client's time and you may fall foul of the limitation period. In August 1995, the Civil Litigation Committee of the Law Society produced a protocol for obtaining hospital medical records (see Appendix H, at p 404). This is an extremely useful alternative to your own pre-writ letter, but there is no obligation on you, as a solicitor, to use it.

The main statutory provision which allows the patient access to his own medical records is the Access to Health Records Act 1990. Before that there was the Data Protection Act 1984 which, while allowing a patient access to his computerised medical records, ensured there was no general right to see all the records, eg access could be refused if it was considered that the information would cause serious harm to the physical or mental health of the person requesting access. Then came the Access to Personal Files Act 1987 and the Access to Medical Reports Act 1988 which, combined, allowed the patient sight of his medical records in certain well defined circumstances, eg if the report had been prepared for insurance or employment purposes.

The more far-reaching statute is the Access to Health Records Act 1990 which came into force on 1 November 1991. In many respects this Act is most beneficial to the patient since it applies to non-computerised health records made by or on behalf of a fairly comprehensive list of health professionals, ranging from doctors through to speech therapists. But in other aspects the Act follows the pattern of the earlier Data Protection Act 1984 in that there are circumstances where access can and will be refused, eg where there is a genuine risk to the physical or mental health of either the applicant or an identifiable third party. Furthermore, there is no statutory right to see anything which was written prior to 1 November 1991, unless it explains something written after that date. Since most medical information in this day and age is likely to be computerised, patients (and solicitors) may do well to focus on the 1984 Act. In the event of an unfavourable reply to a subject access request, redress is possible through the courts or by way of a complaint to the Data Protection Registrar. The significance of these Acts it that they provide an exceptionally useful alternative to the solicitor's pre-writ letter for obtaining the medical records.

Privilege

The defendant in a medical negligence action may claim privilege in respect of some or all of the documents sought. According to RSC Ord 24, r 7A(6), he may refuse to hand over documents on the ground that they are privileged communications, ie that the documents represent communication(s) between the defendants (as clients) and their legal representatives. In *Waugh v British Railways Board* [1980] AC 521, the House of Lords in a non-medical case ruled that where the prepared document had two objectives (to communicate with solicitors and to improve matters internally) then the document's main purpose had to be the communication to the solicitor for the privilege to exist. If the main purpose was not that but rather to improve matters within the organisation in question, as in *Lask v Gloucester Health Authority* (1985) *The Times*, 13 December, the privilege will not attach; furthermore, the court showed in that case that it was prepared to go behind the veil of privilege to examine the true purpose of the communications. Consequently, patients could feel quietly confident about the way in which the law on privilege was being interpreted. But in *Lee v SW Thames Regional Health Authority* [1985] 1 WLR 845, the Appeal Court handed down a ruling which, in some respects, gave the initiative back to the defendants. There a plaintiff, who was badly burnt, was taken to a hospital run by Health Authority A. On the same day he was transferred to the burns unit of a hospital run by Health Authority B. After he developed respiratory problems, he was put on a respirator and sent back to the first hospital in an ambulance whose service was in the control of Health Authority C. Three days later he was found to have been severely brain damaged, very likely through a lack of oxygen when he was in the ambulance. The claim was brought against Health Authority C, but pre-action discovery was sought from all three Health Authorities. It soon became evident that one vital piece of evidence was a memorandum which had been prepared by the ambulance crew at the request of Health Authority B in the event of litigation against them; Health Authority C (the defendants) claimed privilege for the memorandum. In effect, what Health Authority C was claiming was the privilege of Health Authority B, since at no time was it ever suggested that the memorandum in question was prepared for impending litigation against Health Authority C. The Court of Appeal held that privilege did exist. It ruled that the action against Health Authority C arose out of the same set of circumstances which made Health Authority B a likely defendant; it went on to argue that, to say evidence was privileged if the action was against Health Authority B but not if the action was against Health Authority C, would be to defeat the whole purpose of privileged communications. For the plaintiff this was a harsh decision; the real evidence as to what may have caused the brain damage was not available and so the decision about whether to bring an action had to depend on less weighty evidence.

Public interest immunity

Plaintiffs may also find themselves confronting the public interest immunity argument which says that documents, if revealed, may prove either embarrassing for the defendants or damaging to the public interest. The Department of Health unsuccessfully raised this defence in *Re HIV Haemophiliac Litigation* (1990) 140 NLJ 1349 (see also Chapter 5, at p 136). There the plaintiffs, who had been infected with the AIDS virus as a result of being treated with contaminated blood from the United States, sought disclosure of various documents relating to the policy of self-sufficiency in blood products. But they were met with the public interest defence: that to reveal the information would hinder the proper functioning of the National Blood Transfusion Service and the need for effective, candid advice and discussion between ministers and their advisers. The Court of Appeal disagreed and ordered disclosure, arguing that the public interest in having a full, fair trial overrode the Department's claim for secrecy.

Who to sue?

Practitioners for plaintiffs should always consider suing an employing health authority in tort either on the ground of vicarious liability or on the ground that the authority breached its direct duty to provide reasonable care for the patient. In such circumstances, it is inadvisable to sue the individual health carer additionally if only because any award of damages may go unsatisfied: one could go further and advise that the health carer's name should not even be added as a second defendant. But in the situation where there is no employing health authority, then the action must be against the GP or locum personally.

Form of action

Whenever the opportunity presents itself lawyers for private patients should consider using contract rather than tort as the form of action. Although the limitation period will be the same, namely three years if the claim is for a breach of contract resulting in personal injuries, yet if the claim is for damages for loss of earnings following a failed sterilisation then it may be possible to argue that the limitation period should be six years. However, this has now been put in doubt following the decision in *Walkin v South Manchester Health Authority* [1996] 7 Med LR 211, see Chapter 4, Limitation, at p 90). Also in a contractual claim the terms of the agreement dominate and the problems associated with the *Bolam* rule will be largely ignored.

REFERENCES

English case law

(1) *R v Mid-Glamorgan FHSA and another ex parte Martin* [1995] 1 WLR 110; [1994] 5 Med LR 383

The respondents held the medical records of the appellant which included reports on his psychiatric behaviour. Numerous requests had been made by the appellant to see his records but, for a variety of reasons, they were not released. The appellant then sought judicial review of the respondent's decisions but both Popplewell J and the Appeal Court held that:

(a) he had no common law right to see his records; and

(b) there had been no breach of Article 8 of the European Convention for the Protection of Human Rights and Fundamental Freedoms. (Article 8 says, 'Everyone has the right to respect for his private and family life, his home and his correspondence.')

(2) *Hall v Wandsworth Health Authority* (1985) 129 SJ 188

Where the plaintiff started proceedings for the production of documents in a personal injury case, costs could be awarded against the defendant where the defendant had, without excuse, delayed the production of the documents.

(3) Waugh v British Railways Board [1979] 3 WLR 150; [1980] AC 521

Following an accident which resulted in the death of the plaintiff's husband, the Board conducted an internal enquiry and produced a report. The report was headed, 'Further information of the Board's solicitors'. However, the affidavit produced by the Board showed that the report had two objectives: to establish the cause of the accident (and consequently take the necessary safety measures to avoid future accidents) and to enable the solicitors to advise in the likelihood of litigation. The House of Lords held that a document would only be privileged if the purpose of its preparation was that it would be submitted to the legal advisor for advice. Since on the evidence that was not the purpose of this report, the claim for privilege failed.

(4) Lask v Gloucester Health Authority (1985) The Times, 13 December

The Appeal Court held that where NHS circulars require health authorities to prepare confidential accident reports, both for the use of solicitors in the event of litigation and to prevent a repetition of the accidents, those reports would not attract legal professional privilege.

(5) Lee v SW Thames Regional Health Authority [1985] 2 All ER 385

Per Lord Donaldson MR (at p 389):

> ... we consider that the appeal has to be decided by reference to principle rather than authority. The principle is that a defendant or potential defendant shall be free to seek evidence without being obliged to disclose the result of his researches to his opponent. Hillingdon can certainly waive its rights and, were it to do so, the memorandum would clearly be disclosable by SW Thames. However, it has not done so. Furthermore, it would, we think, be impossible to seek in this case to impose a term that disclosure should take place after all proceedings against Hillingdon are terminated or abandoned. If Hillingdon is to be sued as well as SW Thames, the actions must be tried together. SW Thames and their employees have no rights as witnesses, but we can see no way of protecting the rights of Hillingdon as potential defendants if disclosure is ordered against SW Thames.

(6) Re HIV Haemophiliac Litigation (1990) 140 NLJ 1349

The Appeal Court held that even if the National Health Service Act 1977 did not confer a right to claim damages, a private individual could, on the same facts, sue in negligence.

(7) Walkin v South Manchester HA [1996] 7 Med LR 211

See Chapter 4, at p 90.

(8) Bolam v Friern Hospital Management Committee [1957] 1 WLR 582; [1957] 2 All ER 118

See Chapter 5, at p 121.

Foreign case law

AUSTRALIA

(1) Breen v Williams [1995] 6 Med LR 385

The New South Wales Appeal Court held that a patient had no (common law) right to inspect or obtain access to her medical files; nor did she have any proprietary rights over the contents of her file. Further, the court refused to imply a term into the contract to the effect that she had such a right.

Statutes / statutory instruments

(1) SECTION 58 COURTS AND LEGAL SERVICES ACT 1990

See Appendix A, at p 301.

(2) CONDITIONAL FEES AGREEMENTS ORDER 1995 (SI 1674)

See Appendix B, at p 339.

(3) CONDITIONAL FEE AGREEMENTS REGULATIONS 1995 (SI 1675)

See Appendix B, at p 340.

(4) SECTIONS 33(2) AND 34(2) SUPREME COURT ACT 1981

See Appendix A, at p 279.

(5) SECTION 76 COUNTY COURTS ACT 1984

See above, at p 83.

(6) RSC ORD 24, R 7A

See Appendix D, at p 358.

(7) ACCESS TO HEALTH RECORDS ACT 1990

See Appendix A, at p 294.

(8) DATA PROTECTION ACT 1984

See Appendix A, at p 287.

(9) ACCESS TO PERSONAL FILES ACT 1987

(10) ACCESS TO MEDICAL REPORTS ACT 1988

See Appendix A, at p 290.

Practice Directions / Notes

Practice Direction (Civil Litigation: Case Management) [1995] 1 WLR 262; [1995] 1 All ER 385

See Appendix C, at p 347.

CHAPTER 4

LIMITATION

RULE 4(A)

A medical negligence claim must be commenced within three years of:

(1) the date on which the cause of action accrued; or

(2) if later, the date of knowledge of the existence of the cause of action.

Commentary

Since a medical negligence claim is a claim normally involving personal injuries or death, it falls within ss 11–14 Limitation Act 1980. The court has a discretion to extend this three year period by virtue of s 33 of the Act (this is considered at Rule 4(B)). Section 11 covers personal injury actions, while s 12 deals with fatal accidents (see Rule 4(B), at p 104 *et seq* for commentary on this section.) Only by issuing proceedings will time cease to run; therefore, the issue of proceedings and not the service must be within the limitation period, although the proceedings must be served within four months of issue (see RSC Ord 6, r 8; CCR Ord 7, r 20(1)).

The three year period applies to personal injury actions resulting from negligence, nuisance, breach of contract (eg private patients) or breach of the duty of care, but not to those injuries resulting from a deliberate assault. In *Stubbings v Webb* [1993] AC 498, the plaintiff sued in respect of psychiatric harm which she had suffered as a result of sexual and physical abuse during childhood. The court held that the three year period did not apply because she had been injured deliberately; her case should have been pleaded as a battery and consequently she had six years to commence the action (see further s 2 of the Act). This case may have considerable implications for a claim brought against a doctor for battery. If he proceeds to carry out treatment without the consent of the patient, conceivably he comes within the ambit of the decision in *Stubbings*; after all, his conduct can be said to be intentional. Hence, our advice is that when the solicitor is faced with a potential claim where the allegation is that the patient did not consent to the procedure, the claim should be framed as a claim in trespass and not in negligence. This approach would also extend to those situations where the patient has consented to the treatment but, for some reason, the doctor goes beyond the ambit of the consent, eg removing an ovary when he suspects cancer rather than simply performing a diagnostic operation. In this example, the doctor's defence may be that it was implied in the patient's consent that he would remove the ovary if he thought it necessary. The patient may counter this by saying that the information about the possibility of removal of her ovaries was not disclosed to her, in which case a claim could be brought in negligence, the doctor having breached his standard of care in relation to disclosure of information. However, a claim may also be brought in trespass because the patient did not consent to the procedure. Solicitors should always take the trespass option where there is a choice, not only to take advantage of the decision in *Stubbings*, but also to avoid the often insurmountable problems posed by the *Bolam* and causation rules.

Personal injuries are defined by s 38(1) as being 'any disease and any impairment of a person's physical or mental condition'. It had been thought that where the claim was limited to financial losses the three year period would not apply; however, this may not now be the case if a recent authority is followed. In *Walkin v S Manchester Health Authority* [1996] 7 Med LR 211, the negligence claim was for a failed sterilisation and was limited to financial losses consequent on the treatment; no compensation was sought for pain, suffering or inconvenience. The court held that this was a claim for personal injuries and was therefore statute barred. Potter J argued that, unlike a failed vasectomy, a failed sterilisation involves the mother suffering an unwanted birth and that brought it within the ambit of s 11; Mrs Walkin had simply abandoned her claim for personal injuries following the birth but was still claiming a loss consequent on that injury. It may seem strange to view pregnancy as an injury. Not all of the judges in the subsequent Court of Appeal hearing took the view that it was; Auld LJ held that the distinction made by Potter J between a vasectomy and a sterilisation was artificial – in each case the personal injury was the unwanted pregnancy. Roch LJ had, he confessed, great difficulty in appreciating a normal conception and pregnancy as a disease or impairment when the only reasons for the pregnancy being unwanted were purely financial ones. All their lordships agreed, however, that because the pregnancy was unwanted the woman had been injured. This must be right and it is perhaps worth noting that as every pregnancy carries recognised risks, then where the woman suffers an unwanted pregnancy, clearly she has been injured. In any event, it is true to say that whilst the plaintiff may not have specifically claimed damages for personal injuries, the damages she was claiming were as a consequence of the injury. The Appeal Court therefore held that the cause of action arose on the unwanted conception though time would not begin to run until the woman had knowledge of the pregnancy. (See also *Howe v David Brown Tractors (Retail) Ltd (Rustons Engineering Co Ltd; third party)* [1991] 4 All ER 30.) These decisions appear to conflict with the case of *Pattison v Hobbs* (1985) *The Times*, 11 November, see p 98.

On the other hand, where a plaintiff had been wrongly informed that he had inoperable cancer and as a result had closed down his engineering business, sold his house and gone abroad, it was said the claim was for financial and consequential losses, not personal injuries (see *Whiteford v Hunter* [1950] WN 553).

Accrual of the cause of action

Normally in a medical negligence claim this will be fairly uncontroversial: it will arise when the damage occurs; but the damage must not fall within the *de minimis* rule, ie trivial damage will be ignored. However, in some cases the damage might occur some time after the breach, eg in relation to industrial deafness. In such a case providing the breach is a continuing one, the court will generally find that a new cause of action accrues each time the damage reoccurs as a result of a wrongful act. In any event, in most claims this point is irrelevant as time will inevitably begin when the plaintiff has knowledge.

Date of knowledge

Under s 11(4) time begins to run from the date of knowledge as defined by s 14(1) and (3). Essentially, the plaintiff is deemed to have knowledge when he has knowledge of the following facts (s 14(1)):

(a) that the injury in question was significant; and

(b) that the injury was attributable in whole or in part to the act or omission which is alleged to constitute negligence, nuisance or breach of duty; and

(c) the identity of the defendant; and

(d) if it is alleged that the act or omission was that of a person other than the defendant, the identity of that person and the additional facts supporting the bringing of an action against the defendant; and

knowledge that any acts or omissions did or did not, as a matter of law, involve negligence, nuisance or breach of duty is irrelevant.

By virtue of s 14(3), knowledge includes constructive knowledge. This means that the plaintiff is deemed to have knowledge from the facts which he might reasonably be expected to acquire:

(a) from facts observable or ascertainable by him; or

(b) from facts ascertainable by him with the help of medical or other appropriate expert advice which it is reasonable for him to seek;

but a person shall not be fixed under this subsection with knowledge of a fact ascertainable only with the help of expert advice so long as he has taken all reasonable steps to obtain (and, where appropriate, to act on) that advice.

The significance of the injury (s 14(1)(a), (2))

The injury will be thought of as significant if the particular plaintiff would have thought it so serious as to justify instituting proceedings for damages against a defendant who did not dispute liability and was able to satisfy a judgment. Whether or not the plaintiff had other personal reasons for not commencing proceedings is irrelevant (although the court may invoke s 33: see Rule 4(B), at p 104). The court is only concerned with whether 'the particular plaintiff', not some hypothetical plaintiff, thought it reasonable to sue. In *Stephen v Riverside Health Authority* [1990] 1 Med LR 261, the plaintiff did not sue in respect of her erythema and anxiety. She began the proceedings only when she knew that the overdose of radiation she had been subjected to could cause cancer. The court held that this was reasonable.

As most injuries will be deemed to be significant in monetary terms, the plaintiff should begin the proceedings as soon as he suspects the injury. Even if a more serious injury should develop later, time begins to run from the date of the lesser injury. Similarly, if the plaintiff knows there is a risk of deterioration, a claim should be brought in respect of that risk even though it may not yet have materialised. In the case of injuries caused by the side effects of drugs, time will not start to run until the plaintiff knows that the side effects are dangerous and not just an accepted consequence of using the drug (see *Nash v Eli Lilly* [1992] 3 Med LR 353). In *Dobbie v Medway HA* [1994] 5 Med LR 160 (discussed in detail at p 93), the court reiterated that 'significance' referred to the *quantum* of the claim and not the plaintiff's belief as to its cause. The Master of the Rolls said (at p 165):

> Time does not run against a plaintiff, even if he is aware of the injury, if he would have reasonably have considered it insufficiently serious to justify proceedings against an acquiescent and credit-worthy defendant if (in other words) he would reasonably have accepted it as a fact of life or not worth bothering about. It is otherwise if the injury is reasonably to be considered as sufficiently serious within the statutory definition: time then runs (subject to the requirement of attributability) even if the plaintiff believes the injury normal or properly caused.

That the injury was caused by the defendant's act or omission (s 14(1)(b), (3))

There are two points to consider here:

(1) Does the plaintiff have the degree of knowledge to satisfy s 14 (1)(b) (*actual knowledge*)?

(2) Failing that, will the court deem that the plaintiff had the requisite constructive knowledge as required by s 14(3) (*constructive knowledge*)?

Actual knowledge

(i) The first point which should be emphasised is, as a matter of law, knowledge that the acts or omissions did or did not constitute negligence, nuisance or breach of duty is irrelevant, as stated in s 14 of the Act. The plaintiff must merely have knowledge that the defendant's acts might have caused his injuries. Furthermore, according to *Nash v Eli Lilly* [1992] 3 Med LR 353, the court said that knowledge meant more than just 'some vague and generalised conduct', eg knowing that something had gone wrong as a result of an operation at a hospital would not amount to knowledge under s 14(1). Rather, knowledge referred to some specific factor as Purchas LJ put it (at p 368):

> What is required is knowledge of the essence of the act or omission to which the injury is attributable.

On the other hand, it does not mean that the plaintiff is required to have knowledge of every specific act or omission contained within the statement of claim. In *Nash*, a case which concerned claims against the manufacturers of the drug Opren, the crucial acts/omissions were:

(1) providing for the use of patients a drug which was unsafe in that it was capable of causing persistent photosensitivity in those patients; and/or

(2) failing to discover that that was the case so as to properly protect those patients (see Hidden J at [1991] 2 Med LR 183).

The appeal court held that (1) and (2) above were all that the plaintiff was required to know. She was not required to know, eg that the marketing of an unsafe drug was due to a lack of care in testing or in informing the medical profession about it. *Nash* was applied in the important case of *Broadley v Guy Clapham & Co* [1993] 4 Med LR 328. In *Broadley*, the plaintiff underwent an operation in 1980 to remove a foreign body from her knee. For seven months after the operation she could only walk with the aid of two sticks, as she was suffering from foot drop. The plaintiff's claim was against her solicitor for failing to issue a writ within the limitation period (see further, at p 99). The court held that s 14(1) required it to look at the way the plaintiff put her case and whether she had broad knowledge of the facts on which the complaint was based. As such the plaintiff must have realised something was wrong by virtue of the fact that she realised she could not walk unaided seven months after the operation. A reasonable person in her position should have sought further legal and medical advice, and that would bring her within the ambit of constructive knowledge under s 14(3). The plaintiff, however, did not have sufficient knowledge to fall within s 14(1). The court, applying *Nash*, stating that she would have had to have *'knowledge of the essence of the act or omission to which the injury is attributable'* ([1993] 4 Med LR 328, at p 334 and see *Nash*, at p 368). This, of course, begs the question; what is meant by the 'essence of the act'? In this case, the court held that the essence of the plaintiff's complaint was that her nerve was damaged during the course of her operation.

In *Dobbie v Medway Health Authority* [1994] 5 Med LR 160, the plaintiff claimed damages for an operation negligently performed in 1973. The plaintiff underwent a lumpectomy, however, the surgeon went on to remove her whole breast, a procedure to which she had not consented. The growth was later discovered to be benign and the plaintiff was told by the surgeon and a nurse that she was fortunate that the growth had not proved to be malignant. She went on to suffer considerable psychiatric stress in reaction to the unnecessary removal of her breast. She did not, however, progress her claim until 1988 when she heard of a similar case where a woman successfully sued. The court ruled, however, that the claim was statute barred. At [1994] 5 Med LR 160, at p 166 *per* Beldam LJ:

> The personal injury on which the plaintiff seeks to found her claim is the removal of her breast and the psychological and physical harm which followed. She knew of this injury within hours, days or months of the operation and she at all times considered it to be significant. She knew from the beginning that this personal injury was capable of being attributed to, or more bluntly, was the clear and direct result of an act or omission of the health authority. *What she did not appreciate until later was that the health authority's act or omission was (arguably) negligent or blameworthy. But her want of that knowledge did not stop time beginning to run.*

But, more recently, *Dobbie* was considered in the Lloyds underwriters case of *Hallam-Eames and Others v Merrett* [1996] 7 Med LR 122. The Court of Appeal said that *Dobbie* had been misinterpreted. At p 125, Hoffmann LJ said the plaintiff must,

> have known the facts which can fairly be described as constituting the negligence of which he complains. It may be that knowledge of such facts will also serve to bring home to him the fact that the defendant has been negligent or at fault. But that is not in itself a reason for saying that he need not have known them.

In *Hallam-Eames*, the court was at pains to point out that it was not enough for Mrs Dobbie to know that her breast had been removed; rather that it was a healthy breast that had been removed. At [1995] 7 Med LR 122, at p 125, Hoffmann LJ said:

> If all that was necessary was that a plaintiff should have known that the damage was attributable to an act or omission of the defendant, the statute would have said so. Instead, it speaks of the damage being attributable to 'the act or omission

which is alleged to constitute negligence.' In other words, the act or omission of which the plaintiff must have knowledge must be that which is casually relevant for the purposes of an allegation of negligence.

And at p 126, Hoffmann LJ, continuing in his review of *Broadley* and *Dobbie*, said:

> If one asks what is the principle of common sense on which one would identify Mrs Dobbie's complaint as the removal of a healthy breast rather than simply the removal of a breast, it is that the additional fact is necessary to make the act something of which she would *prima facie* seem entitled to complain.

Similarly, Mrs Broadley's complaint was that the surgeon had caused damage to her foot when he was supposed to be treating her knee. It is these additional facts - namely the removal of a healthy breast in *Dobbie* and the damage to a knee instead of a foot which gave the plaintiff knowledge.

This view appears to be the current position – see *Smith v West Lancashire Health Authority* [1995] PIQR 514 where the court held that merely because the plaintiff has knowledge that an operation was not performed or that treatment has failed, does not necessarily imply that he has knowledge that an operation should have been performed or that the treatment given was negligent.

(ii) Also, the knowledge required will depend on the plaintiff's state of mind, his ability to understand the information and the strength of his belief. To quote from Purchas LJ, again in the *Nash* case (at p 365):

> Whether or not a state of mind for this purpose is properly to be treated by the court as knowledge seems to us to depend, in the first place, upon the nature of the information the plaintiff received, the extent to which he pays attention to the information as affecting him, and his capacity to understand it ... The court must assess the intelligence of the plaintiff; consider and assess his assertions as to how he regarded such information as he had; and determine whether he had knowledge of the facts by reason of his understanding of the information.

The court then went on to state that in some cases the plaintiff would not acquire knowledge until he had received expert advice:

> If it appears that a claimant, while believing that his injury is attributable to the act or omission of the defendant, realises that his belief requires expert confirmation before he acquires such a degree of certainty of belief as amounts to knowledge, then he will not have knowledge until that confirmation is obtained (*per* Purchas LJ, at p 366).

See further on this point *Khan v Ainslie* [1993] 4 Med LR 319, *Baig v City and Hackney Health Authority* [1994] 5 Med LR 221 and *Forbes v Wandsworth Health Authority* [1996] 7 Med LR 175.

The latter case is of particular importance. The writ was issued 10 years after the allegedly negligent treatment. The complaint was that had the defendant operated sooner, the plaintiff's leg need not have been amputated. At first instance, it was held that the plaintiff had neither actual nor constructive knowledge until he received an expert report. The Court of Appeal agreed that the plaintiff did not have actual knowledge until he received the expert report but held that he had constructive knowledge. This is discussed below, at p 95 and see further, at p 101. The case makes some useful points for the plaintiff so far as actual knowledge is concerned. Discussing knowledge of an omission, Stuart-Smith LJ said that the plaintiff could not know there has been an omission until he was aware that there had been 'a lost opportunity to prevent the injury which he later suffered.' Stuart-Smith went on to say (at p 185):

> The fact that in such cases it may be necessary for the plaintiff also to know of the negligence before he can identify the omission alleged to have been negligent is nothing to the point.

As far as actual knowledge is concerned, this approach is in line with the decisions in *Hallam-Eames v Merrett* [1996] 7 Med LR 122 and *Smith v Lancashire Health Authority* [1995] PIQR 514 and is in conflict with the *Dobbie* decision. In the latter, the Court of Appeal held that Gatehouse J had erred at first instance in holding that Mrs Dobbie had to know that her breast had been 'unnecessarily removed'; for the purpose of actual knowledge that was irrelevant.

(iii) Finally, in *Nash,* it was decided that if the plaintiff had taken legal advice and instituted proceedings he will be deemed to have knowledge. This seems fairly logical, although it is to be hoped that time will not start to run from the moment the patient asks for legal assistance because clearly at that stage he may have no idea that he has a viable claim (contrary to the decisions in *Stephen v Riverside Health Authority* [1990] 1 Med LR 261 and *Davis v Ministry of Defence* (1985) *The Times,* 7 August, see p 101).

The Court of Appeal in *Nash* also doubted the proposition put forward in *Davis v Ministry of Defence* (1985) *The Times,* 7 August, that the plaintiff lost the knowledge he had previously acquired if he subsequently received expert advice which contradicted his belief that he may have had a claim. That proposition had been endorsed in the case of *Bentley v Bristol and Western Health Authority* [1991] 2 Med LR 359, where Hirst J said that broad knowledge that the injury was caused by the operation was not enough; time did not start to run until the plaintiff became aware of the act or omission which could have caused the negligence. Usually such information would only be acquired when the plaintiff had consulted an expert, and the views of such an expert would often determine whether the plaintiff had knowledge.

Constructive knowledge

If the plaintiff does not have actual knowledge then the court will consider whether he has constructive knowledge. In *Broadley,* the plaintiff was held to have such knowledge because she could have ascertained with the aid of medical advice that an injury had been caused to her nerve. In considering this particular question, *Nash v Eli Lilly* [1992] 3 Med LR emphasised that the character and intelligence of the plaintiff had to be taken into the equation. At p 368, Purchas LJ, in discussing constructive knowledge, said:

> The standard of reasonableness in connection with the observations and/or the effort to ascertain are therefore finally objective but must be qualified to take into consideration the position, and circumstances and character of the plaintiff.

This proposition is now in doubt following the decision in *Forbes v Wandsworth Health Authority* [1996] 7 Med LR 175, see p 101 for the facts. By the time the case had come to trial the plaintiff had died. The Court of Appeal, considering the test for constructive knowledge, held that the test should be solely objective and the characteristics of the particular plaintiff were irrelevant. By a majority of 2–1, the plaintiff was held to have had constructive knowledge. Stuart-Smith LJ gave the example of a man who, following an operation on his leg which he expected to be successful, discovers that he now has only one leg instead of two. After the initial shock the patient then has a choice, either (1) to simply accept it as a cruel blow and not to make any inquiry or, (2) to decide that something is not right and to investigate further. In Stuart-Smith LJ's view, this choice would be made about 12–18 months after the injury. At p 185 he said:

> ...where, as here, the plaintiff expected or at least hoped that the operation would be successful and it manifestly was not, with the result that he sustained a major injury, *a reasonable man* of moderate intelligence, such as the deceased, if he thought about the matter, would say that the lack of success was 'either just one of those things a risk of the operation or something may have gone wrong and there may have been want of care; I do not know which, but if I am ever to make a claim I must find out'.

Roch LJ dissented from this view and held that if such a test applied then many patients would feel compelled to seek a second opinion following an unsuccessful operation. At p 192, he said:

> In my view, it would be unfortunate if the question asked in s 14(3)(b) were to be resolved by imputing to a would-be plaintiff an unconscious decision to do nothing and then requiring him to stand by that 'decision'. Such an approach would encourage those undergoing medical treatment, which did not achieve the desired result, to go automatically to another specialist for an opinion whether the treatment given could have been more effective.

There certainly seems something to be said for Roch LJ's argument. As we have seen in *Dobbie*, many patients do not even recognise that they have been injured rather than treated, let alone make a decision that their predicament is simply a cruel twist of fate as opposed to their carer's negligence. Additionally, to place a time limit on this decision and to ignore the characteristics of the particular plaintiff appears to be totally unrealistic. In the same way as everyone reacts differently to the death of a loved one and copes with grief, patients will come to terms with their unforeseen injury in an entirely individual way. We would also suggest that here the nature of the injury must be considered. Mrs Dobbie was completely traumatised after the masectomy, even if she had been aware that she had been injured rather than treated, would she have been rational enough to choose within the 18 months? Perhaps there should be a separate rule for the 'Dobbie-like' cases and those cases where the complaint is caused by the side-effect of surgery rather than a definite injury, or would this be too complex?

Finally, what if the plaintiff does seek medical advice? Can he always rely on it or must he seek further advice in given circumstances? In *Smith v West Lancashire Health Authority* [1995] PIQR 514, the court held that as the plaintiff had been reassured by his GP that his treatment was appropriate for his condition then he was not caught by s 14(3) which states that a plaintiff will be deemed to have constructive knowledge if he failed to seek medical advice. This must be right otherwise it would seem that the plaintiff can never rely on the reassurances of the medical profession and that he must obtain several opinions before he can be satisfied that he has taken all steps in accordance with s 14(3). However, in *Gregory v Ferro (GB) Ltd* [1995] 6 Med LR 321, the plaintiff relied on assurances from her GP that the pain in her leg was caused by her recurrent arthritis. The Court of Appeal held that she had constructive knowledge and they took into account that the plaintiff was 'an intelligent woman' who doubted whether the continuing pain was solely attributable to her arthritis. In both these cases the plaintiff relied on the reassurances of their GP. Could the defendant argue that in all cases the plaintiff should obtain the advice of a specialist to totally fulfil the requirements of s 14(3)?

Is the position any different where the plaintiff seeks legal advice? As a general principle, the plaintiff will be fixed with the knowledge ascertained by his solicitor. What, however, if the solicitor fails to find out the facts of the case; will the plaintiff still have constructive knowledge? This is different from the point discussed above, ie that the plaintiff receives negative advice. The answer is far from certain but, in line with s 14(3), we would argue that the plaintiffs' knowledge includes only that which 'he might reasonably be expected to acquire' and that he shall not be fixed with knowledge only ascertainable with expert help 'if he has taken all reasonable steps to obtain ... that advice.' Clearly, by taking legal advice, the plaintiff will have taken all reasonable steps and cannot be found wanting for his solicitor's inactivity.

From the above, the following principles emerge:

(1) If the patient knows that he has been injured by an operation/treatment which is unexpected and knows in general terms how the injury occurred, then the limitation period may begin to run or at the very least the patient will be under an obligation to make further enquiries.

(2) A patient should always seek further advice if he has any reason to suspect that he has suffered an injury which would not normally have occurred. If the plaintiff, in the court's opinion, has failed to act reasonably in an attempt to obtain information the court may fix him with constructive knowledge (s 14(3)). From *Forbes*, it now appears that where the plaintiff undergoes a medical procedure, which does not achieve its desired result, that may be sufficient to put him on enquiry.

(3) If the patient fails to obtain further advice then whether or not the patient is deemed to have knowledge will be determined by reference to s 14(1)(b).

The identity of the defendant (s 14(1)(c))

In a medical negligence case this should not pose too many problems given that the health authority will be vicariously liable for its nursing and medical staff. In the case of a private patient, the individual surgeon or physician may be sued in addition to the hospital or clinic. The only potential difficulty with identifying the defendant is where a claim is one for product liability. For example, more than one company may produce the drugs which caused the injury and it may be difficult to ascertain exactly who is responsible for its manufacture. If a claim is brought under the Consumer Protection Act 1987 (see Rule 4(C), at p 112) the defendant could be:

(1) the producer of the product; or

(2) anyone who holds himself out as a producer; or

(3) an importer; or

(4) a supplier.

The plaintiff may bring a claim against any of the above; if the claim is brought against the supplier, then it is highly likely he will seek an indemnity from the importer and so on.

Summary

To date this is an unclear area of law, and it would be premature to try and state with absolute certainty how the court would view each individual case. Therefore, the reader should consider the cases listed below and at Rule 4(B), in conjunction with the principles that have emerged from the decisions in *Nash*, *Broadley*, *Dobbie* and the like. It seems clear, however, that the trend of judgments is against the plaintiff, which is patently demonstrated by the cases discussed below, and see in particular *Dobbie v Medway Health Authority* [1994] 5 Med LR 160, and *Forbes v Wandsworth Health Authority* [1996] 7 Med LR 175.

REFERENCES

English case law

(1) Stubbings v Webb [1993] AC 498

See p 89.

(2) Bolam v Friern Hospital Management Committee [1957] 1 WLR 582; [1957] 2 All ER 118

See Chapter 5, Standard of Care, at p 121.

(3) Walkin v S Manchester Health Authority [1996] 7 Med LR 211

Here there was a failed sterilisation. The plaintiff's claim was for the upkeep of her child.

Held:: damages for loss of earnings fell within the meaning of s 11(1) of the Act and the limitation period ran from the moment of conception.

(4) Howe v David Brown Tractors (Retail) Ltd (Rustons Engineering Co Ltd; third party) [1991] 4 All ER 30

The plaintiff was injured by some defective agricultural machinery. He claimed damages for negligence as part of a partnership.

Held:: a claim for financial loss resulting from physical injuries is a claim for damages in respect of personal injuries. The plaintiff could not circumvent the three year rule by seeking damages only for his loss of earnings.

(5) Pattison v Hobbs (1985) The Times, 11 November

A claim arising out of a failed vasectomy was not a personal injury claim.

(6) Whiteford v Hunter [1950] WN 553; 94 SJ 758

See p 90.

(7) Stephen v Riverside Health Authority [1990] 1 Med LR 261

The plaintiff underwent a mammography in which the radiographer took 10 films instead of the usual four or six. She was told that there was a danger from the effects of radiation. She began proceedings nearly 11 years later in respect of her increased risk of developing cancer.

Held:: although she had a suspicion or belief that she did have cancer, contrary to what the experts had told her this did not amount to knowledge and therefore her claim was not statute barred.

(8) Nash v Eli Lilly [1992] 3 Med LR 353

The plaintiffs claimed that as a result of being prescribed the drug Opren they had suffered side effects. The drug had been prescribed to relieve arthritic pain and was withdrawn in August 1982 amid intense publicity. The side effects included skin sensitivity to sunlight and in some cases any sort of bright light, acute red rashes, injury to eyes, abnormal hair growth and liver and kidney failure.

See also *Hepworth v Kerr* [1995] 6 Med LR 135: the limitation issue here was tried as a preliminary issue. The plaintiff alleged that his paraplegia was caused by the negligence of the defendant anaesthetist in 1979. In the operation notes a diagnosis was made that there may have been an anterior spinal artery thrombosis (the hospital rejected this claim). Soon after this operation the plaintiff was examined by Dr Cook, a neurologist who formed the opinion that the plaintiff's condition was not the result of the operation. The plaintiff subsequently showed this report to a solicitor in 1980 who said that there was nothing more to be done.

In 1987, the plaintiff changed his GP and saw solicitors who obtained his medical records. They commissioned a new medical report which attributed the plaintiff's injuries to the operation. The plaintiff's action was commenced within three years of this date.

The defence argued that the plaintiff's claim was statute barred, because the solicitor in 1979 should have requested the hospital notes and realised that Dr Cook was the wrong expert. Consequently, the plaintiff had the requisite knowledge at that time. The court dismissed this argument holding that Dr Cook was not simply acting as an expert, he was acting as a clinician attempting to identify the cause of the plaintiff's condition. Furthermore, it was unreasonable to require the plaintiff or his solicitor to question whether Dr Cook had obtained the notes. Accordingly, the plaintiff would not be fixed with knowledge pursuant to s 14(3) of the Act which he might reasonably be expected to acquire with the help of his solicitor because it was not the sort of knowledge that would have reasonably been ascertained with the help of a solicitor.

(9) Dobbie v Medway Health Authority [1994] 4 All ER 450; [1994] 5 Med LR 160

See above, at p 93 and at Rule 4(B), at p 105.

(10) Broadley v Guy Clapham & Co [1993] 4 Med LR 328

The plaintiff underwent an operation on her knee in 1980 and afterwards suffered from foot drop. In June 1983, the plaintiff saw a solicitor who consulted an expert who told the plaintiff that the operation might have been performed negligently (no report was obtained). The plaintiff consulted new solicitors in August 1990 who began proceedings.

Held:: time started to run immediately after the operation (the plaintiff must have known that something was wrong when she was compelled to walk with sticks for seven months). Therefore, the claim was statute barred.

(11) Hallam-Eames v Merrett [1996] 7 Med LR 122

At first instance, the claims against the underwriters were held to be statute barred. However, in the Court of Appeal, it was held that *Dobbie* had been misinterpreted at first instance, for time to start running, the plaintiff must realise not only that something had gone wrong but also that the defendant's act or omission had caused that wrong. See p 93.

(12) Smith v West Lancashire Health Authority [1995] PIQR 514

In 1981, the plaintiff attended an accident and emergency department complaining of an injury to his right hand. The plaintiff was X-rayed and reviewed over the next few weeks but no change was made in his treatment until eight weeks after the injury when he was advised that the treatment had not worked and he required an urgent operation. The plaintiff continued to see his GP after the operation but was never told that the operation should have been performed shortly after the injury and not some eight weeks later. As a result of the failure to operate promptly, the plaintiff sustained pain and degenerative changes.

Held: that the plaintiff had been reassured by his GP that he had been given the appropriate treatment, therefore, he would not be deemed to have constructive knowledge.

(13) Khan v Ainslie [1993] 4 Med LR 319

The plaintiff had been suffering from acute angle glaucoma which the defendant optician had been treating by the administration of mydriatic fluid. For some time the plaintiff had believed that it was negligent to administer the fluid notwithstanding expert evidence to the contrary. His real complaint, however, was only revealed when he received a further expert report which indicated that the defendant had failed to recognise the glaucoma and should have referred the plaintiff to hospital immediately. The plaintiff was held to have acquired knowledge on receipt of the later report.

(14) Baig v City and Hackney Health Authority [1994] 5 Med LR 221

The plaintiff had suffered from chronic partial deafness. In 1973, an ear nose and throat surgeon performed a stapedectomy on the plaintiff's ear. The plaintiff alleged that within a matter of weeks all his hearing had been lost. He returned to Pakistan in 1976 and did not return to the United Kingdom until 1984. In 1985, he wrote to the defendant alleging negligence. In 1986, he consulted solicitors but it was not until 1989 that he received an optimistic report confirming that the operation was the cause of his handicap. The writ was issued in 1991.

Limitation was tried as a preliminary issue. The court first considered whether the plaintiff had knowledge sufficient to satisfy s 14(1). Rougier J held that knowledge equated with a 'sufficiently firm conviction' and that conviction must be right in accordance with specialist opinion. In any event, the plaintiff must know in general terms what it was that the defendant had done or failed to do which had caused the damage. The court held that the plaintiff's position was analogous to *Broadley v Guy Clapham & Co* [1993] 4 Med LR 328 and consequently the plaintiff did not have knowledge pursuant to s 14(1). However, the plaintiff was held to have constructive knowledge pursuant to s 14(3). The plaintiff was an educated man capable of reading his own case notes; thus, when an operation which he had been assured was virtually certain of success was a disaster this should have put him on enquiry. Shortly after the operation he should have sought professional help but he did nothing until 1985.

In refusing to exercise its discretion under s 33, the court gave the following reasons:

(a) There was considerable and inordinate delay;

(b) The defendant was responsible for six months' delay in providing the medical records but that appears to have been a genuine mistake;

(c) One of the plaintiff's arguments was that the defendant had failed to warn him of the dangers of the operation. The evidence depended on personal recollection and as such the defendant would be unduly prejudiced given the length of time that had elapsed, much more so than the plaintiff for whom this was a 'one-off' event.

(d) The defendant's insurance arrangements had changed. (See *Antcliffe v Gloucester Health Authority* [1992] 1 WLR 1044.)

(e) There was considerable delay in issuing the writ when the plaintiff did find out the position.

(f) The plaintiff's chances of success were doubtful, he had one favourable report as opposed to three unfavourable reports.

See further Rule 4(B), at p 106.

(15) Forbes v Wandsworth Health Authority [1996] 7 Med LR 175

The plaintiff had a history of circulatory problems and underwent a bypass operation in October 1982. This was unsuccessful and so another operation was carried out the next day. The plaintiff was informed that his leg would have to be amputated to prevent gangrene.

In 1991, the plaintiff consulted his solicitor to obtain financial advice. His medical notes and an expert report was obtained and a writ issued the following year.

The Court of Appeal held that the plaintiff had constructive knowledge in 1982 and declined to exercise it's discretion under s 33. For further commentary, see p 110.

(16)Davis v Ministry of Defence (1985) The Times, 7 August

The plaintiff firmly believed that his dermatitis was the result of his employment, but he accepted medical and legal advice that it was not. He subsequently experienced another far more severe attack and received further expert advice which confirmed his original belief that the dermatitis was caused by his work conditions.

Held:: he did not acquire knowledge within the meaning of s 14(1)(b) until he received this second expert advice.

(17) Bentley v Bristol and Western Health Authority [1991] 2 Med LR 359

The plaintiff had received negative medical and legal advice.

Held:: it was only when she received a positive report that she acquired knowledge.

(18) Gregory v Ferro (GB) Ltd [1995] 6 Med LR 321

See above, at p 96.

See also *Burton v Islington Health Authority; De Martell v Merton and Sutton Health Authority [1993] 4 Med LR 8; [1995] 6 Med LR 234*

The plaintiff's mother became pregnant in 1966 as a result of a secret liaison with her uncle. Due to the alleged negligence of the defendant in the plaintiff's delivery he was born with athetoid cerebral palsy. The plaintiff was 18 years of age on 5 February 1985 but the writ was not issued until 15 November 1988. The defendant contended that the plaintiff must have known that something must have happened at his birth at an earlier age when he realised his disability. The plaintiff contended that he did not learn the truth until 1987 when he requested a medical report before undertaking a pioneering trip to Hungary for further treatment. The court accepted this argument. The plaintiff had adduced evidence that his birth was never discussed in the household because of the secret surrounding his conception. It was only when he had the chance of further treatment that he felt bound to investigate the circumstances of his birth.

In this case, if it was necessary, the court would have applied s 33. The court did not feel that the defendants would have been unduly prejudiced as they had confessed they had no recollection of the plaintiff's birth; therefore, any further delay was irrelevant.

See also *Driscoll-Varley v Parkside Health Authority* [1991] 2 Med LR 346 where the court accepted that the plaintiff did not seek further advice as to the merit of her treatment because she was terrified of having her leg amputated and wished to retain her present surgeon. She had absolute faith and trust in him and therefore did not question his acts.

Query – Could this not be applied to the vast majority of patients, ie they hold the belief that their doctor can do no wrong? Or will it only apply to the less intelligent patient?

Statutes / statutory instruments

CONSUMER PROTECTION ACT 1987

For persons who may be liable, see s 2 of the Act and Rule 4(C), at p 112.

RULE 4(B)

The three year rule for commencing a medical negligence / personal injury claim will not apply in the following instances:

(1) **In the case of person under a disability time will not start to run until the plaintiff dies or ceases to be under the disability, whichever occurs first (s 28(1), (6)).**

(2) **Where an action is brought under the Fatal Accidents Act 1976 or the Law Reform (Miscellaneous Provisions) Act 1934 time will start to run from the date of the deceased's death, or the date of the dependants' or personal representatives' knowledge, whichever is the later (ss 11(5), 12).**

(3) **By virtue of s 33, the court may disapply the limitation period if it is equitable to do so.**

(4) **Where the defendant has deliberately concealed any fact from the plaintiff which would have notified him that he has a right of action time does not start to run until the plaintiff discovers or could, with reasonable diligence, have discovered the nature of the concealment (s 32(1)).**

Commentary

Plaintiffs under a disability

A person is under a disability if he is an infant (ie under the age of 18, see s 1(1) Family Law Reform Act 1969) or is of unsound mind (ie someone who, under the Mental Health Act 1983, is incapable of managing or administering his property affairs – s 1(2)). As stated above, time will not start to run until the plaintiff ceases to be under the disability or dies; thus, a child can commence an action any time before he attains the age of 21 (ie 18 plus three years limitation period); while a person who comes within s 1(2) Mental Health Act 1983 can bring an action within three years of becoming sane. Although the plaintiff may be suffering from a mental illness, he may still be capable of managing his own affairs and, if this is indeed the case, s 28 will not apply and he will be subject to the usual three year rule. If the person will never recover from his mental disability the limitation period may never run. It is interesting to note that in *Headford v Bristol and District Health Authority* [1995] 6 Med LR 1, the court held that it did not matter how long those caring for a plaintiff under a disability took to issue proceedings. In that case, the delay was 28 years but it might well have been 40, 50 or greater (see p 108 for the facts of this case). This will undoubtedly place the defendant under an awesome burden; imagine how difficult it will be to locate medical records and witnesses from several decades previously.

A plaintiff may still commence an action while under a disability (see RSC Ord 80; Appendix D, at p 372). If the action itself caused the mental disability time will not run providing the disability was immediate. However, where the disability occurs after the cause of action accrued time will still run, although in such a case it is highly probable that the court will exercise the s 33 discretion.

An interesting point in this area was raised by the case of *Colegrove v Smyth* [1994] 5 Med LR 111. The plaintiff, born in 1959, claimed for negligent delay in the diagnosis of a congenital displacement of the hip. She alleged that the defendant should have diagnosed the condition when she was 12 months of age instead of at three years of age; consequently, the plaintiff had suffered ever since from a debilitating condition. The plaintiff succeeded on the limitation issue, since the court held that she was under the impression that she had simply been born with a disability until, applying for a job in 1984, an examining doctor suggested to her that that might not be have been the case. In fact, even this was said not to have given the plaintiff knowledge until she had the condition confirmed by an expert report. What is significant is the treatment by the court of the knowledge the plaintiff acquired while she was a minor. The plaintiff admitted that, at the age of eight, a doctor had basically said the very same thing which was said to her in 1984, and furthermore that she understood what he was saying. However, the court held that this neither constituted knowledge nor put the plaintiff under an obligation to enquire further when she came of age. The court ruled that the doctor's statement merely indicated that there had been a delay in diagnosis and nothing further. This is contrary to the decision in *Nash* which states that knowledge once acquired cannot be lost. As a matter of policy, however, it appears that the court will not attribute knowledge to a child which is recalled on the age of majority. In any event, it appears that the court in *Colegrove* would have resorted to their s 33 discretion, if necessary.

How does this decision fit with the decision in *Gillick v West Norfolk and Wisbech Area Health Authority* [1986] AC 112? *Gillick* is widely thought of as being the seminal case in the area of children consenting to medical treatment. Is it the case that a child, although *Gillick* competent, will never be regarded as having acquired knowledge for the purposes of the Limitation Act 1980? In *Colegrove*, it appears that the child may have been '*Gillick* competent'; however, that in itself did not put her under any obligation to make further enquiries when something went wrong. It is a curious situation but we suggest that both legally and ethically it must be correct; we would never advocate that merely because a child can take an active part in deciding the nature of his treatment that he should be placed under an obligation to make further enquiries when something goes wrong.

Fatal Accidents, etc

For limitation purposes, these claims are dealt with under ss 11, 12 and 13 of the Limitation Act 1980. Claims brought on behalf of the estate under the Law Reform (Miscellaneous Provisions) Act 1934 are governed by s 11(5) and those claims brought on behalf of the dependants under the 1976 Act fall under s 12. Effectively both ss 11 and 12 state that the three year limitation period begins at the date of death or, if later, the date of knowledge of either the dependants or personal representatives depending on which Act the claim is being made under. If there is more than one dependant and each has a different date of knowledge, then different limitation periods apply (s 13(1)), whereas if the personal representatives have different dates of knowledge then time runs from the earliest date (s 11(7)). If the claim is not brought within this period then it is *prima facie* statute barred, although the court may invoke s 33. If the three year period had expired before the deceased's death, any action brought by the personal representatives/dependants will be statute barred. No account is taken of the possibility that the deceased could have invoked s 33. However, the court may, of its own accord, invoke s 33 in favour of the deceased's dependants or personal representatives.

The s 33 discretion

By virtue of s 33 the court may allow an action to continue notwithstanding that it is outside the limitation period, if it would be equitable to do so having regard to the prejudice caused to both the plaintiff and the defendant if the action were not allowed to proceed. The question is not whether the claim itself is equitable, but whether it would be equitable to allow it to proceed (see *Ward v Foss and Heathcote* (1993) *The Times*, 29 November). Section 33(3) (set out in full at Appendix A, at p 275) states that, in deciding whether or not to exercise its discretion, the court must consider a number of factors including the length and the reasons for the plaintiff's delay, the effect the delay has had on the evidence, the defendant's conduct (eg did he respond to any requests the plaintiff made for information?), whether or not the plaintiff was suffering from any disability after the cause of action accrued, and, once the plaintiff realised that he had a claim, the speed of his actions and in particular the steps he took to obtain advice. The court will not consider any of these points in isolation; it will have regard to the circumstances of the claim as a whole and may take into account any factors not specifically listed at s 33(3).

The length of delay (s 33(3)(a))

This refers to the time that elapses between the expiry of the limitation period and the issue of a writ. However, in *Donovan v Gwentoys Ltd* [1990] 1 All ER 1018, the court said the whole period, ie the delay from the commencement of the limitation period must be taken into account in assessing prejudice to the defendant, see further, at p 109. A short delay will not usually prejudice the claim, as illustrated in *Hartley v Birmingham District Council* [1992] 2 All ER 213 (where the writ was issued only one day late), and *Hendy v Milton Keynes Health Authority* [1992] 3 Med LR 114 (a delay of nine days). What is more important are the reasons for the delay and in assessing these the court will look at why the plaintiff acted as he did.

The plaintiff's reasons for the delay (s 33(3)(a))

In *Dale v British Coal Corporation* (1992) *The Times*, 2 July, the plaintiff was advised by Arthur Scargill in 1975 that he had a good case but he did not act on that advice, and did not see a solicitor until 1987. The court ruled in favour of the defendant, holding that the claim was now so stale it would be unfairly prejudicial for the defendant to defend it, given that 15 years had elapsed and the plaintiff had known he had a cause of action since 1975.

In *Dobbie v Medway Health Authority* [1994] 5 Med LR 160, the court held that Mrs Dobbie knew she had a cause of action in 1973 and it refused to exercise its discretion under s 33; after all, the plaintiff knew that her breast had been wrongly removed in 1973 and consequently a delay of 16 years was inexcusable. Perhaps the court should have taken into account the fact that the plaintiff was under great emotional strain immediately after the lumpectomy and had been told in effect that she should not complain – after all, she might be minus a breast but at least she did not have cancer! In fact, the evidence indicates that she repeatedly overdosed and was admitted to psychiatric hospitals after the loss of her breast. In our opinion, this case is harsh in the extreme.

We contend that Mrs Dobbie did not appreciate that something had gone wrong and was therefore unaware that she had suffered an injury as opposed to having been treated. In 1973, it would have been unheard of to question the actions of the medical profession. Unfortunately, the Court of Appeal in *Dobbie* did not share this view. (See also *Baig v City and Hackney Health Authority* [1994] 5 Med LR 221, at p 100.) Generally, where the delay is the result of a discouraging expert opinion or incompetent legal advice, the court will favour the plaintiff though a delay because of fear of what the legal action will cost is unlikely to find favour. However, the court must be satisfied the plaintiff took steps to obtain expert advice or, if he did not, that he had a cogent reason for not doing so.

The evidence (s 33(3)(b))

In *Hartley v Birmingham City District Council* [1992] 2 All ER 213, the court held that problems associated with the evidence were the most significant issues for consideration in the exercise of its discretion. (See also *Dale v British Coal Corporation* (1992) *The Times*, 2 July.) Further, in *Forbes v Wandsworth Health Authority* [1996] 7 Med LR 175, the court noted that the factual evidence of the case was highly questionable and this together with the fact that the plaintiff was legally aided placed a heavy burden on the defendant which ultimately persuaded the court not to exercise it's discretion. In *Dobbie*, the fact that the documentary evidence was still available, was not enough to persuade the court to exercise its discretion. Furthermore, in *Whitfield v N Durham Health Authority* [1995] 6 Med LR 32, the court still felt that there would be difficulties in reconstructing the events despite the fact that the relevant documents and the original slide on which the diagnosis was made were still available. Generally, where there has been a long delay, the courts will favour the defendant with one notable exception; in the case of minors, where there has already been a considerable delay before beginning proceedings (see p 102 *et seq*), the courts sensibly have decided that any extra delay which was avoidable is unlikely to have any effect on the cogency of the defendant's evidence (see *Doughty v North*

Staffordshire Health Authority [1992] 3 Med LR 81 and *Colegrove v Smyth* [1994] 5 Med LR 111).

Another factor the solicitor must bear in mind is the nature of the claim being pursued. Where, for example, the claim is for a failure to treat, the action is more likely to be allowed to proceed since the evidence is usually contained in available medical notes, etc. However, where the claim is based on a failure to disclose a risk then the evidence is often based on the recollections of witnesses and the court will take into account the number of patients who will inevitably have passed through the doctor's door since the relevant incident, plus the fact that most people are normally forgetful.

How did the defendant respond? (s 33(3)(c)

The defendant can expect to be penalised where the delay is of his own making. Instances where this may occur are failing to supply the plaintiff with his medical records promptly or failing in any way to respond to reasonable requests from the plaintiff. In *Atkinson v Oxfordshire Health Authority* [1993] 4 Med LR 18, the court held that it would have exercised its discretion because a large part of the delay had been caused by the defendant's failure to inform the plaintiff's mother what had happened during a second operation. The defendant cannot lie to the plaintiff, but at the same time does not have to volunteer information, as aptly illustrated by *Dobbie* above, at p 105.

Was the plaintiff under a disability? (s 33(3)(d))

This is considered at p 102 above. *Note* that the court is only concerned with a disability that arises after the date of the accrual of the cause of action.

What steps did the plaintiff take to investigate the claim? (s 33(3)(e),(f))

In particular, what steps did he take to obtain legal/medical advice, and if he did take such steps, what was the nature of the advice? This section should be read in conjunction with the section on constructive knowledge, at p 95. The court will consider how quickly the plaintiff progressed his case once he was aware he had a cause of action. In particular, the court will be interested to see whether the plaintiff obtained medical and/or legal advice and whether that advice was negative. In *Nash*, Purchas LJ had indicated that the plaintiff may not acquire knowledge until he received a positive expert report (see p 94 and *Baig v City and Hackney Health Authority* [1994] 5 Med LR 221, *Bentley v Bristol and Western Health Authority* [1991] 2 Med LR 359 and *Khan v Ainslie* [1993] 4 Med LR 319, at p 94.) Generally, if the plaintiff can show that he was attempting to progress the case the court will rule in his favour.

Other matters the court may consider are set out below.

The alternative remedy

Can the plaintiff substitute his solicitor as the defendant for failing to bring proceedings within the limitation period? This alternative remedy is something which the courts will consider. The two factors which are significant in deciding whether the plaintiff should pursue this alternative remedy are:

(1) would the plaintiff suffer any unfair prejudice in suing his solicitors as opposed to the defendant?

(2) whether the defendant, if deprived of the limitation defence, was nonetheless insured and hence would be able to claim on his insurance.

Two cases on this point have favoured the plaintiffs continuing their action against the defendants notwithstanding that there was a viable claim against the plaintiff's solicitors. In *Ramsden v Lee* [1992] 2 All ER 204, the accident occurred in September 1985 and the writ was issued in April 1989, but the defendants had been notified of the plaintiff's claim within two months of the accident and had themselves done a substantial amount of work investigating the accident and had, additionally, made a voluntary interim payment. In refuting recourse to the alternative remedy the court held that to find for the defendant would be to provide them with 'an undeserved windfall'. The court also took into account the fact that the plaintiff's solicitors might have known of some weaknesses in the plaintiff's case and, as such, could exploit these facts in defending any action that might be brought against them.

In *Hartley v Birmingham District Council* [1992] 2 All ER 213, the court noted that the defendants were insured and hence the plaintiff was allowed to proceed with the claim notwithstanding that he had a good claim against his solicitors. The courts obviously felt that there was no good reason why the burden should be shifted to the solicitor's insurers instead of being met by the defendant's insurers.

The 'sword of damocles'

Effectively what this means is that the courts will at some stage rule that the defendant has been threatened with the issue of proceedings for too long and that threat must be removed (see *Biss v Lambeth Health Authority* [1978] 1 WLR 382, at p 111). In *Dobbie*, the court said that the defendant could not use this argument when the doctor had absolutely no idea that there was any threat of litigation hanging over him. Surely this argument must hold good for the majority of cases, the exception being when the defendant is fearful that there may have been negligence, but does not reveal this to the plaintiff in the hope that it will remain undiscovered. Perhaps this is another reason for placing defendants under a duty to disclose their mistakes!

The 'Crown indemnity prejudice'

Increasingly, the court will take into account 'crown indemnity prejudice'. This is where the defendant argues that its resources are in effect prejudiced by the operation of the Crown indemnity rule in that any judgment which it is ordered to meet must now come out of its budget whereas, had the plaintiff prosecuted his claim earlier, any damages award would have been met by the Medical Defence Union. See on this point *Antcliffe v Gloucester Health Authority* [1993] 4 Med LR 14 and *Whitfield v North Durham Health Authority* [1994] 6 Med LR 32 and, more recently, *Forbes v Wandsworth Health Authority* [1996] 7 Med LR 175.

Beginning and discontinuing

Finally under this section, for the sake of completeness, we consider the effect of beginning an action, discontinuing it and then issuing for a second time, where those second proceedings are outside the limitation period. This is what happened in *Walkley v Precision Forgings Limited* [1979] 1 WLR 606 where the court refused to exercise its discretion under s 2D Limitation Act 1939 (the forerunner of the 1980 Act). Therefore, if the solicitor fails to start an action and the limitation period expires the court retains a discretion to invoke s 33. If, however, the writ was issued but not served or, if the writ was served only for the action to be discontinued or struck out at a later date, the court has no discretion to reinstate the action. In *Walkley*, the court indicated that even in the last mentioned scenario it can exercise its discretion if there are exceptional circumstances, such as where the plaintiff has been encouraged to discontinue the action because of the misrepresentations of the defendant. But beware the moral of this tale – the plaintiff does not get two bites at the cherry!

Concealment

There are two points to make under this heading:

(1) Concealment does not necessarily mean fraud. It could simply be an assurance from the defendant 'not to concern yourself' when the plaintiff asks if something has gone wrong.

(2) In personal injury claims, the plaintiff will not normally have to invoke s 32 because he will be deemed not have acquired the knowledge as required by s 14. Nonetheless, s 32 may be relevant for non-personal injury claims since in those cases time will start to run from the date on which the action accrued. In the case of *Sheldon and others v RHM Outhwaite (Underwriting Agencies) Ltd and others* [1995] 2 WLR 570, the court held that the deliberate concealment of a cause of action which occurred after the accrual of the cause of action postponed the running of the limitation period.

REFERENCES

English case law

(1) Headford v Bristol and District Health Authority [1995] 6 Med LR 1

The plaintiff underwent an operation in 1964 as a baby during which he suffered a cardiac arrest and brain damage. Proceedings were not issued until 1992, the plaintiff relying on s 28 of the Act. The defendant succeeded before the deputy judge in their claim to strike out the action as an abuse of process. The judge held that the defendant was prejudiced because of the 28 year delay because several witnesses had died, medical records had been lost, medical practice had changed since the incident as had the defendant's insurance arrangements. The plaintiff appealed to the Court of Appeal.

Commenting on the application of s 28, the court made the following points:

(a) Section 28 of the Act was not to be compared to s 33. The court was not interested in the degree of prejudice that would be suffered by either party should the action be allowed to proceed, or struck out.

(b) As Parliament had already legislated to allow an action to proceed within six years of the disability, ie 28 years after the incident, then there was no objection to a delay of 28 years or longer.

(c) Section 28(1) contained no long stop provision as per s 28(4).

(d) Generally, s 28 was permissive; however, it conferred a right in general to bring proceedings during the period of continuing disability.

(e) Any prejudice arising to the defendant from a change in their insurance arrangements (ie the introduction of Crown indemnity) was immaterial.

(f) The case was distinguishable from *Hogg v Hamilton & Northumberland HA* [1993] 4 Med LR 370. The plaintiff had suffered brain damage in 1976, a writ was issued in 1978. In January 1982, the claim was struck out for want of prosecution. The plaintiff later instructed a second firm of solicitors who, whilst investigating the alleged negligence of the plaintiff s former solicitors, asked the health authority responsible for the plaintiff's treatment for disclosure of the plaintiff's medical records. The plaintiffs solicitors gave an assurance that he would not sue the health authority in return for disclosure of the said records. The action was struck out as an abuse of process. Merely issuing fresh proceedings itself within a current limitation period would not necessarily amount to an abuse but it could do depending on the circumstances of the case and where the previous action had been struck out for want of prosecution.

(2) Colegrove v Smyth [1994] 5 Med LR 111

See above, at p 103.

(3) Nash v Eli Lilly [1992] 3 Med LR 353

See above, at p 103.

(4) Gillick v West Norfolk and Wisbech Area Health Authority [1986] AC 112; [1985] 3 All ER 402

See p 50 for the facts of this case.

(5) Ward v Foss and Heathcote (1993) The Times, 29 November

See above, at p 104. After the death of their parents in 1982, actions were commenced on behalf of the dependent children seven years later under the Law Reform (Miscellaneous Provisions) Act 1934 for the benefit of the estate and under the Fatal Accidents Act 1976 for the benefit of the children. The claim under the Fatal Accidents Act was within time; however, the estates claim was statute barred and therefore an application was made under s 33.

Section 4(2) Administration of Justice Act 1982, which applies to all actions after 1 January 1983, prevents an award of damages for loss of income in respect of any period after the death of the injured person. The court had to decide whether the injustice caused by this provision should dictate whether or not it was 'equitable' pursuant to s 33 to disapply the limitation period. The court ruled that the question was not whether the claim was equitable or not but whether it was equitable to allow the claim to proceed. Here it held there was little prejudice to the defendant despite the delay and, further, that the claims had been promptly notified in 1982; consequently, the claim was allowed to proceed.

(6) Donovan v Gwentoys Ltd [1990] 1 All ER 1018

See above, at p 104. The plaintiff, then aged 16, suffered an accident in 1979. The limitation period therefore began in 1981 and in 1984 a writ was issued, five months after the limitation period had expired. Due to the various ineptitudes of the plaintiff's solicitors the defendant only learned of the nature and date of the accident in June 1987. Therefore, the defendants were faced with a claim which was now eight years old. The court held that it would be unfairly prejudicial for the defendants to have to defend the claim.

Note that the plaintiff's solicitors were criticised in this case for not obtaining emergency legal aid and issuing a protective writ. Waiting for legal aid should not prevent issuing within the limitation period.

(7) Hartley v Birmingham District Council [1992] 2 All ER 213

See above, at p 104. The writ was issued one day late. This insignificant delay did not really have any prejudicial affect on the defendant.

(8) Hendy v Milton Keynes Health Authority [1992] 3 Med LR 114

See above, at p 104.

(9) Dale v British Coal Corporation (1992) The Times, 2 July

See above, at p 105. The court held that the test as to whether the plaintiff had acted reasonably was an objective one.

(10) Dobbie v Medway Health Authority [1994] 4 All ER 450; [1994] 5 Med LR 160

See above, at p 105.

See also *Whitfield v North Durham Health Authority* [1995] 6 Med LR 32 below and at p 111.

(11) Baig v City and Hackney Health Authority [1994] 5 Med LR 221

See Rule 4(A), at p 100 and above, at p 106.

(12) Forbes v Wandsworth Health Authority [1996] 7 Med LR 175

See p 14. In considering whether to exercise it's discretion under s 33, the court took into account the fact that the plaintiff had now died. It also took into account the prejudice caused to the defendant by changed insurance arrangements, missing medical records and changing medical standards.

(13) Whitfield v North Durham Health Authority [1995] 6 Med LR 32

The plaintiff's solicitors had negligently omitted to issue proceedings against one of the defendants, the cytologist. As to the courts discretion under s 33 the following points were made:

(a) The court held that it would be inequitable to allow the plaintiff to gain an advantage from the negligence of his solicitors. Although this was not conclusive, the court had to take this into account in assessing whether to exercise its discretion.

(b) As to Crown indemnity prejudice, the trial judge had erred in assuming altruism on the part of patients whose expectations of prompt medical treatment would be lessened because of the use of part of the health authority resources to pay damages to the plaintiff.

(c) The plaintiff's conduct could not be considered in isolation. The court had to look at her conduct in conjunction with the conduct of her legal advisers.

(d) The paramount question was whether it would be equitable to allow the action to proceed having regard to all the circumstances together with the plaintiff's and her advisers' conduct.

(e) The medical evidence on which the defendant relied was still available but the court should take into account the fact that the delay must have had some prejudicial effect.

The court considered the prejudice to both parties, and refused to exercise its discretion.

Note that the court is not concerned with any hardship caused to either party but with what is fair in the circumstances. Therefore, the plaintiff cannot rely on the default of his solicitors, notwithstanding that there is still prejudice to the defendant.

Note that this case also is relevant in considering the application of s 14, the court ruling that it is sufficient for the plaintiff to have 'a generalised sense of grievance'.

(14) Doughty v North Staffordshire Health Authority [1992] 3 Med LR 81

The court was faced with a 28 year old claim brought on behalf of a minor which could have been commenced 17 years earlier. The court held that where minors were involved there would always be considerable delay, any extra delay will be largely insignificant. The court refused to penalise the plaintiff's mother for not progressing the case as quickly as she could since much of her time was taken up with looking after her child.

(15) Atkinson v Oxfordshire Health Authority [1993] 4 Med LR 18

See p 106.

(16) Bentley v Bristol and Western Health Authority [1991] 2 Med LR 359

See Rule 4(A), at 95.

(17) Khan v Ainslie [1993] 4 Med LR 319

See Rule 4(A), at p 100.

(18) Ramsden v Lee [1992] 2 All ER 204

See above, at p 107.

(19) Biss v Lambeth, Southwark and Lewisham Health Authority [1978] 1 WLR 382

In considering an application to strike out for want of prosecution, the court said that there would be prejudice to the defendants where they lived in fear of an action hanging over them.

(20) Antcliffe v Gloucester Health Authority [1992] 4 Med LR 14

Scott LJ held that if, as a consequence of the delay in bringing proceedings, the defendant suffered prejudice because of his business or insurance arrangements, the court should consider that prejudice.

(21) Walkley v Precision Forgings Limited [1979] 1 WLR 606

See above, at p 107. The plaintiff issued and served a writ in 1971 and later discontinued that action. He sought to commence proceedings again in 1977. The court refused to exercise its discretion. The result is that if proceedings are issued and not served or the action is discontinued then any future action outside the limitation period will not be allowed.

See also *Whitfield v North Durham Health Authority* [1995] 6 Med LR 32, at p 110. The plaintiff underwent surgery to remove what was thought to be a malignant lump from her neck. During the operation, damage was caused to the plaintiff's nerve causing neurological damage. It later transpired that the lump was benign. The plaintiff had taken medical and legal advice early on and knew that the original diagnosis was wrong but proceedings were not instituted until six years and nine months after the operation. During these six years, the plaintiff had consulted a first set of solicitors who had issued a writ for personal injuries but had failed to issue it as counsel had advised the plaintiff did not have a claim. The plaintiff subsequently instructed a second set of solicitors. By this time the writ had expired. The plaintiff argued that the principle in *Walkley* was not applicable, however, the court decided differently – although the proceedings had not been discontinued but remained alive (the court could still renew the writ) the *Walkley* principle was relevant. Furthermore, the court held that where an action against a second defendant in respect of the same cause of action was not begun at the time of the first action because of the default of the plaintiff's first solicitors, the plaintiff should not be entitled to take advantage of s 33 to exclude the limitation period as against that second defendant.

(22) *Sheldon and others v RHM Outhwaite (Underwriting Agencies) Ltd and others [1995] 2 WLR 570*

The plaintiffs issued proceedings against the defendant in April 1992 for breaches of contract and duty by the defendants in or before 1982. The defendants asserted that the claim was statute barred. The plaintiffs contended that pursuant to s 32(1)(b) of the Act the limitation period had been postponed because the defendants had deliberately concealed facts relevant to their cause of action, and consequently time did not start to run until such concealment was discovered which occurred less than six years before the issue of the writ.

At first instance, the plaintiffs were successful. However, the Court of Appeal allowed the defendants' appeal holding that s 32(1)(b) could not be relied upon when the limitation period had already begun to run. The House of Lords overturned the Court of Appeal decision by a majority of 3–2.

Section 32(1)(b) of the Act provides that time shall not run when, 'any fact relevant to the plaintiff's right of action has been deliberately concealed from him by the defendant'. The House of Lords ruled that this provision covered both where the concealment was contemporaneous with the accrual of the cause of action and where the concealment occurred some time later. The court relied on s 1(2) of the Act, namely that if the case fell within the ambit of s 32, then the ordinary time limits would be excluded until the discovery or imputed discovery of the facts by the plaintiffs. Browne-Wilkinson LJ's opinion was that it would be absurd that a plaintiff, who had been prevented by the dishonourable conduct of the defendant from learning the facts, should not be entitled to the full six year period from the date of the discovery of such concealment. However, it would be equally absurd if the plaintiff's right of action became time barred before he became aware of the full facts of the case because of the deliberate concealment of the defendant, an argument endorsed by the Court of Appeal.

RULE 4(C)

A claim brought under the Consumer Protection Act 1987 for personal injuries must be brought within three years of the date when the damage occurred or the date of knowledge of the claim, whichever is the later, subject to a maximum time limit of 10 years.

Commentary

For the purposes of the 1987 Act, the date of knowledge is interpreted in much the same way as under the 1980 Act: see s 14(1)(A). However, the main difference is with regard to personal injury claims, which must be brought within 10 years of the product being put into circulation. The court has no discretion to overrule this time limit irrespective of the substance of the mitigating factors (s 33(1A)), or if the plaintiff is under a disability (s 28(7)) or has been the victim of fraud or concealment (s 32(4A)). Therefore, to rely on the courts' s 33 discretion, many plaintiffs will be forced to sue in negligence or to ensure that the application under s 33 is made before the limitation period expires.

REFERENCES

Statutes / statutory instruments

(1) LIMITATION ACT 1980

See Appendix A, at p 267.

(2) CONSUMER PROTECTION ACT 1987

Persons who may be liable under the Consumer Protection Act 1987

(2)

(a) the producer of the product;

(b) any person who, by putting his name on the product or using a trade mark or other distinguishing mark in relation to the product, has held himself out to be the producer of the product;

(c) any person who has imported the product into a member State from a place outside the member States in order, in the course of any business of his, to supply it to another.

(3) ... any person who supplied the product (whether to the person who suffered the damage, to the producer of any product in which the product in which the product in question is comprised or to any other person) shall be liable for the damage if ...

Note that this section then continues to state that a supplier shall be held liable if he fails, within a reasonable time of a request by the person who suffered the damage to identify the person to whom subsection (2) applies, ie the producer of the product.

RULE 4(D)

A claim for latent damage must be brought within six years from the date when the cause of action accrued or three years from the date on which the plaintiff discovered or ought to have discovered the damage, subject to an absolute time limit of 15 years from the date of the defendant's negligence (s 1 Latent Damage Act 1986; ss 14A, 14B Limitation Act 1980).

Commentary

Rules 4(A)–(C) have essentially dealt with the limitation periods applicable to claims for personal injuries which will make up the vast majority of all medical negligence claims. As we have seen, at p 89, where a claim is for pure financial loss only then a six year limitation period will apply whether the claim is in contract or in tort (s 2).

The six year period runs from the date on which the damage occurs or in the case of a number of negligent acts, the last instance on which damage occurs or three years from the starting date (see s 14A (3),(4) below), whichever expires later. The 'starting date' is defined in s 14A(5), (6) and (8) as the time the plaintiff must have had knowledge of the material facts about the damage and that it was caused by the defendant's negligence. The degree of knowledge is defined at s 14A(7), but is similar to that specified in s 14(2).

The 15 year time bar on latent damage claims is laid down in s 14B and is an absolute bar, notwithstanding that the cause of action or the damage may not have occurred yet or the damage is still latent. The two exceptions to this rule are where the action has been concealed or the plaintiff is under a disability (see Rule 4(B), at p 102 et *seq* and ss 28A, 32(5) of the Act).

We have not dealt with latent damage in great detail as this rule will only be applicable in limited circumstances, eg where the plaintiff, relying on the negligent diagnosis of a doctor, gave up work, and subsequently suffered loss of earnings for more than six years only then to find out that the diagnosis was negligent.

REFERENCES

Statutes / statutory instruments

(1) Section 14A LIMITATION ACT 1980

See Appendix A, at p 270.

GENERAL PRACTICE POINTS – RULES 4(A)–4(D)

We strongly advise any solicitor to bear in mind the following points in relation to limitation:

(1) Ascertain from the facts when the cause of action accrued and when the plaintiff had knowledge. When these dates have been decided diarise the earlier of the two as the date from which the limitation period will run, and consequently when the limitation period will expire or has expired. *Note* that this date may have to be revised on receipt of further evidence, eg medical records. The plaintiff's medical records will often confirm whether or not the plaintiff had knowledge, eg did the plaintiff make any complaint after the procedure or visit his GP on several occasions.

(2) Late instructions from the client can cause obvious problems. The solicitor should adopt the following measures:

(a) Obtain emergency legal aid (if appropriate).

(b) Obtain medical records and contact a medical expert.

(c) Inform the intended defendant immediately of the claim. If there is any doubt as to the contractual relationship between the managers or owners of the hospital and their staff, then seek clarification from the managers.

(d) Issue the writ/summons within limitation period if at all possible. Time will stop running on issue of the proceedings. Even if a medical report confirming the merit of the plaintiff's claim is not yet available, always issue (even though the client may have to fund this particular step himself). If the writ has been issued without a medical report, in actions in the High Court the court will grant an extension of time for service of the writ (ie beyond the usual four months) provided evidence is adduced to show that all steps have been taken to progress the matter: in the county court an explanatory letter should be put before the court explaining why the medical report is not yet available. As an alternative, when serving the writ/summons attach a report from the patient's GP – so long as he is not the defendant!

If acting for the defendant, remember that in the case of third party proceedings time will stop on issue of the third party notice.

(3) If the limitation period has expired, notify the intended defendant of the claim and issue proceedings. *Note* that the court will not refuse to issue a writ/summons which is to be served out of time. If the defendant fails to raise the limitation point the court will not raise it of its own motion.

A limitation point must be specifically pleaded, see RSC Ord 18, r 8(1). Thus, in an action for personal injuries or under the Fatal Accidents Act 1976, the plaintiff who alleges that he was entitled to commence the action within three years from the date of knowledge which is later than the date when the cause of action accrued, he must in his statement/particulars of claim plead the facts which support his contention. He should not wait for the defendant to plead the defence of limitation and then reply alleging the grounds on which he is entitled to bring his action out of time. The plaintiff should plead in the statement of claim, as precisely as he can, the date when he first knew of the facts and matters as specified in s 14 and the facts which led to such knowledge.

The defendant should plead positively, ie the date on which the defendant alleges that the plaintiff had knowledge should be specified in particular; if the defendant intends to assert that the plaintiff had constructive knowledge pursuant to s 14(3) he must plead those facts.

Finally, if the plaintiff intends to resort to s 33, all facts on which he intends to rely in asserting that ss 11 and 12 of the Act do not apply must be pleaded and, conversely, the defendant should plead all facts in support of the argument that the court should not exercise its discretion.

Not only will the action continue until limitation is pleaded in the defence but, additionally, the plaintiff may make an application for pre-action disclosure despite the fact the action appears statute barred (see *Harris v Newcastle Area Health Authority* [1989] 1 WLR 96).

(4) Before serving the proceedings the plaintiff's solicitors must consider the likelihood of the s 33 application succeeding (see p 104 *et seq*) and the costs implications should the plaintiff fail. The solicitor should explain this to the client in writing. However, while the solicitor must consider the merits of a s 33 application he must endeavour to serve the proceedings as soon as possible after they are issued. Once proceedings have been issued the court will not invoke its s 33 discretion in any subsequent proceedings. In any event, proceedings must be served within the four month time limit as prescribed by the rules (see RSC Ord 6, r 8, Appendix D, at p 351 and CCR Ord 7, r 20(1)) and the court will only extend this period if the plaintiff's solicitors can establish a good reason for non-service (see *Harris v Lopen Group Ltd* [1993] PIQR PI and RSC Ord 6, r 8). Obviously, if the limitation is about to expire do not serve the writ/summons by post but use personal service.

The court may have reference to the criteria for extending the limitation period as laid down under s 33, RSC Ord 32, r 9A, Appendix D, at p 364; CCR Ord 15, r 1 (see p 104 *et seq*). More generally, the court will examine the potential hardship to the parties (eg where the plaintiff is legally aided the court will have regard to the fact that the defendant is unlikely to recover his costs (see *Lye v Marks and Spencers plc* (1988) *The Times*, 15 February)) and, where the limitation period has now expired, the reason why the plaintiff's solicitors failed to apply for an extension of the time for service of the writ within the time as prescribed by the rules, eg where the parties have agreed to defer service of the writ, or the defendant has assured the plaintiff that the writ need not be served and the plaintiff has relied on this to his detriment, that may suffice. However, the fact that the plaintiff delayed serving until legal aid was obtained, or that the non-service was accidental is unlikely to convince the court to renew the writ. The moral is: serve as soon as possible!

The s 33 procedure

See generally on this area Butterworths, *Personal Injury Litigation Service* Vol 1 VI [1011–1506] and Butterworths, *Personal Injury Encyclopaedia*, Vol IV [1022–1071].

The application

The application is dealt with under RSC Ord 32, r 9A; CCR Ord 13, r 1. The defendant must plead limitation in the defence to rely on it and consequently in reply the plaintiff will apply on summons (or notice of application in the county court) for the limitation period to be disapplied. Following the recent Court of Appeal decision, *Hughes v Jones* (1996) *The Times*, 18 July, it now seems that the application is within the jurisdiction of a district judge in the county court only if the claim is worth less than £5,000, or the parties agree that the district judge should determine the limitation issue. The reason behind this decision is that an application to disapply the limitation period is not an interlocutory application as defined by RSC Ord 59, r 1A, but a final application. Although the Supreme Court Rules grant Queen's Bench Masters the right to hear such applications there is no equivalent provision in the County Court. In any event, the application was often made direct to a High Court judge in chambers because in the event of an appeal (which is very common considering the entire action rests on the matter), the issue will be brought before him and thus the parties may agree to him dealing with the question from the outset.

In some cases, the limitation issue will not be dealt with until trial and will be taken as a preliminary issue. This may seem rather late in the day but it is often not until discovery and other interlocutory procedures are completed that the degree of prejudice to both parties becomes apparent; in particular, the exchange of witness statements often clarifies any remaining ambiguities. A case on this point is *Fletcher v Sheffield Health Authority* [1994] 5 Med LR 156, at p 118. The procedure for split trials and dealing with preliminary issues is detailed at RSC Ord 33, r 3; CCR Ord 13, r 2(2)(c).

The affidavit

(a) The affidavit should cover the material as required by s 33 (see p 104 and RSC Ord 32, at p 364; CCR Ord 15, r 1).

(b) If the limitation period has been missed due to the error of the solicitors, the affidavit should specify these facts (after the solicitors have agreed the matter with the other partners and insurers).

(c) Always check that the affidavit explains why the action was not brought within the limitation period; if it was the fault of the solicitors they should appear suitably apologetic. Whatever the facts, a full chronology should be set out detailing the plaintiff's character, in particular, his ability to understand legal or medical advice and the reason for any delays. The affidavit should also cover events prior to the expiry of the limitation period.

The plaintiff should also detail the defendant's conduct, eg was there prompt disclosure of medical records, replies to letters, etc. The defendant often argues that because of the delay there are problems in collecting the evidence. The plaintiff can, however, counter that as soon as the defendant was notified of the claim the latter should have been on notice to begin this procedure.

Once the plaintiff has acquired knowledge the affidavit should detail all the steps he took regarding medical and legal advice, etc. If the plaintiff is under a disability (and that began after the limitation period started to run) then the next friend should show that they acted with diligence and sought to prosecute the case.

The order

The order is a final order, consequently, any party can appeal without leave (see RSC Ord 59, r 1A(3) and the notes in *The White Book* at 59/1A/19). Only where a county court judge is acting in an appellate capacity ruling on a decision from the district judge will leave be required before an appeal to the Court of Appeal (see County Court Appeals Order 1991, reg 2(1)(b)).

(5) When acting as the defendant's solicitor, always consider an application to strike out (see RSC Ord 18, r 19; CCR Ord 13, r 50, although it is unclear as to whether this is really appropriate. Remember that the burden of proof is on the plaintiff to show that he did not have knowledge until a time which decrees that the commencement of proceedings was within the limitation period. *Note*, however, that if an application is made to strike out for want of prosecution and it is made before the expiry of the three year period the plaintiff will simply bring fresh proceedings unless there are exceptional circumstances, eg that the plaintiff has indicated that he is abandoning the action. Where the limitation period has expired, the crucial question to be answered is whether the delay has caused any extra prejudice to the defendant. In the county court, pursuant to the automatic directions, the action will be struck out if the plaintiff does not apply for a hearing date within 15 months of the close of pleadings (see CCR Ord 17, r 11). If the case has been struck out under this provision and the limitation period has expired, the court is unlikely to allow an application to restore. However, if the limitation period has not expired then the plaintiff may commence a second action and this will not generally be regarded as an abuse of process (see *Gardner v Southwark London Borough Council No 2* [1996] 1 WLR 575). If the plaintiff has been successful in his application under s 33, then if he fails to comply with all time limits subsequently, the defendant may strike out for want of prosecution (see *Biss v Lambeth HA* [1978] 2 All ER 125).

(6) Ensure that the action is commenced in the right court pursuant to the High Court and County Court Jurisdiction Order 1991 SI 1991/724 (ie any personal injury action of value less than £50,000 should be begun in the county court, see Article 5 and RSC Ord 6, r 2(f)), although should the solicitor issue in the wrong court, the court would probably exercise its discretion to transfer the action despite the fact that it may be outside the

limitation period at the date of transfer, see *Restick v Crickmore* [1994] 2 All ER 12.

(7) The plaintiff must prove that all relevant parties are joined in the action (see *Welsh Development Agency v Redpath Dorman Long Ltd* (1994) *The Times*, 4 April). The court will not add another party to the action after the limitation period has expired unless the case falls within one of the exceptions in s 35(3). The court may allow an amendment introducing a new cause of action after the limitation period has expired 'if the new cause of action arises out of the same facts or substantially the same facts as a cause of action' (see RSC Ord 20, r 5(5) and *Sion v Hampstead Health Authority* [1994] 5 Med LR 170).

REFERENCES

English case law

(1) Harris v Newcastle Area Health Authority [1989] 1 WLR 96

See above, at p 115.

(2) Harris v Lopen Group Ltd [1993] PIQR PI

The writ was posted by first class mail on 3 May but delivered on 8 May, one day out of time for service – the court extended the time for service.

(3) Lye v Marks and Spencers plc (1988) The Times, 15 February

See above, at p 115.

(4) Hughes v Jones, The Times, 18 July 1996

Where the application was currently in process, the Court of Appeal issued the following guidelines. Where the application has already been heard by the district judge and the time for appealing has expired, then the court will infer the parties agreement to him acting in a final capacity. If an appeal is still outstanding to a circuit judge, then the application should be treated *de novo* unless he is satisfied that the district judge had jurisdiction.

(5) Fletcher v Sheffield Health Authority [1994] 5 Med LR 156

The plaintiff was born jaundiced with rhesus incompatibility. She alleged negligence by the defendant at her birth and also during a series of leg operations carried out when she was aged 16–17 (in 1975). The question the court had to resolve was whether the plaintiff should have knowledge of the alleged negligence during 1975 and whether that should have led her to discover the alleged negligence at birth and therefore whether she had constructive knowledge.

The court was asked to determine whether the limitation issue should be tried as a preliminary issue or whether it was so closely bound up with the evidence that it should be dealt with at the trial.

Held:: the limitation issue and the substantive issues overlapped: the same experts would be required to cover both the alleged negligence at birth and in 1975/76, and therefore all matters should be dealt with at the trial.

This will usually be the case where causation is at issue.

(6) Gardner v Southwark London Borough Council No 2 [1996] 1 WLR 575

See above, at p 117.

(7) Restick v Crickmore [1994] 2 All ER 12

The Court of Appeal considered whether a personal injury action which had been commenced in the wrong court should be struck out or merely transferred. The court said that the usual sanction would be in costs. Only where the action had been begun in the High Court in an attempt to harass the defendant or where the solicitors had previously been warned about the correct venue but persistently commenced cases in the wrong court would the drastic sanction of striking out be invoked.

(8) Welsh Development Agency v Redpath Dorman Long Ltd (1994) The Times, 4 April

The plaintiff's claim was for breach of contract and negligence, and in July 1992 sought leave to add claims of negligent misstatement. The judge at first instance ruled that the claim was statute barred from September 1992. The plaintiff's appeal was dismissed.

Held:: a new claim under s 35(3) Limitation Act 1980 could not be 'made' by amendment until the pleading was actually amended, therefore, unless the claim fell within s 35(5) or RSC Ord 20, r 5(5), leave could not be given, even if at the date of the application for leave to amend the limitation period had not expired. This case overrules *Kennet v Brown* [1988] 1 WLR 582.

(9) Sion v Hampstead Health Authority [1994] 5 Med LR 170

The plaintiff's original action was under the Fatal Accidents Act 1976 and Law Reform Miscellaneous Provisions Act 1934. The plaintiff amended his statement of claim to include a claim for psychiatric illness. The defendant argued that the amendment should be allowed as it introduced a new cause of action after the expiration of the limitation period. The plaintiff relied on RSC Ord 20, r 5(5) which reads:

> An amendment may be allowed under paragraph (2) notwithstanding that it is alleged that the effect of the amendment will be to add or substitute a new cause of action if the new cause of action arises out of the same facts or substantially the same facts as a cause of action in respect of which relief has already been claimed in the action by the party applying for leave to make the amendment.

The defendant argued that RSC Ord 20, r 5(5) could only be invoked if the original claim disclosed no cause of action.

The Court of Appeal dismissed this argument. It held that if the statement of claim fails to disclose a cause of action but by some amendment can be made to do so on substantially the same facts then notwithstanding the limitation period has expired the amendment should be allowed.

See further Chapter 7, Damages, at pp 217, 223.

CHAPTER 5

STANDARD OF CARE

RULE 5(A)

To establish negligence the plaintiff must show that the defendant's acts fell below the required standard of care. The standard of care applicable to the medical profession is that stated by McNair J in *Bolam v Friern Hospital Management Committee* [1957] 1 WLR 582, at pp 587–88, now commonly known as the *Bolam* test:

> A doctor is not guilty of negligence if he has acted in accordance with a practice accepted as proper by a responsible body of medical men skilled in that particular art.

Commentary

To establish negligence on the part of the defendant the plaintiff must show:

(1) what is the standard of care; and

(2) on the facts of the case, that the defendant's conduct fell below this standard.

In the field of medical negligence the *Bolam* test is now recognised as almost determinative of liability; moreover it has been held that the *Bolam* test is not restricted to doctors but is of general application to any branch of the medical profession (see *Gold v Haringey Health Authority* [1987] 2 All ER 888).

In *Bolam* the plaintiff was given electro convulsive therapy and as a result of this treatment sustained fractures. He argued that the doctor was negligent first in not giving him relaxant drugs (which admittedly would have excluded the risk of fracture); secondly, if drugs were not used, in failing to restrain him manually; finally, in not warning him of the risks involved in the treatment. There were different opinions in the medical field as to whether the plaintiff should have been given relaxant drugs and whether he should have been so warned. The defendant doctor was found not negligent because he had acted in accordance with the accepted practice of his peers.

The defendant doctor will be tested against the standard of the doctor in his particular field of medicine, eg the GP must meet the standard of the reasonably competent GP, likewise, the consultant must meet the standard of his reasonably competent fellow consultant. A patient suffering from a rare skin disorder cannot expect his GP to be an expert dermatologist unless the GP held himself out as having that degree of skill. This principle is nothing new – in all professional negligence cases like is compared with like.

The defendant is not to be judged by the standards of the most experienced, or or most skillful, nor by the standards of the least qualified and experienced. In accordance with *Bolam*, the standard is that of the ordinary competent practitioner in the defendant's field of medicine; 'the norm'. The standard of care is to be judged by reference to the status of the defendant, and not his personality. No allowance is made for the personal idiosyncrasies or, for that matter, the physical or mental illness of the defendant (see *Nickolls v Ministry of*

Health (1955) *The Times*, 4 February and *Barnett v Chelsea and Kensington Hospital Management Committee* [1969] 1 QB 428).

Moreover, the standard of care does not differ because of the unique circumstances the defendant is placed in, eg an emergency situation. The standard is that dictated by *Bolam*. Sensibly, the court will not expect a doctor working in extreme conditions to achieve the same results as his colleague operating within the confines of a hospital and will not judge the defendant's conduct too harshly simply because, with hindsight, a different course would have been adopted had the situation not been an emergency. However, the defendant may be held negligent if, knowing that an emergency situation might develop, he did not cater for that emergency (see *Bull and another v Devon Area Health Authority* [1993] 4 Med LR 117 and Chapter 3, Duty, at p 69).

Nor does the standard change depending on the nature of the medical treatment. It is still *Bolam* irrespective of whether the defendant is dealing with a diagnosis or a disclosure of information or post operative care. Attempts have been made to introduce a different standard of care in the realms of disclosure of information and giving advice, and in some jurisdictions they have been successful, see *Rogers v Whittaker* [1993] 4 Med LR 79 and the doctrine of informed consent (see Chapter 2, at p 42); however, to date the English judiciary have only sparingly deviated from the *Bolam* standard (see, for example, *Hucks v Cole* (1968) reported at [1993] 4 Med LR 393, *Clarke v Adams* (1950) 94 SJ 599, *DeFreitas v O'Brien and Connolly* [1995] 6 Med LR 108 (discussed at p 132) and r 5(D)).

Do the personal idiosyncrasies of the plaintiff have any bearing on the standard of care? In English law the answer given is that it does not. In *Blyth v Bloomsbury Area Health Authority* [1993] 4 Med LR 151, Mrs Blyth alleged that her doctor was negligent in not informing her of the potential side effects of the contraceptive drug Depo-Provera. Unlike many patients she had specifically and repeatedly questioned the doctor beforehand as to the risks associated with Depo-Provera. The court ruled that the defendant had complied with accepted practice, there was no obligation to pass on to the patient all the information available to the hospital. Kerr LJ held (at p 157):

> The question of what a plaintiff should be told in answer to a general enquiry cannot be divorced from the Bolam test, any more than when no such enquiry is made.

In the same case, Balcombe LJ said (at p 160) that there was no rule of law that if the patient asks questions or had doubts a doctor must disclose all the information he possesses on the subject to the patient:

> Furthermore, I do not understand that the decision of the House of Lords in *Sidaway v Governors of Bethlem Royal Hospital* [1985] AC 871 ... either Lord Diplock or Lord Bridge were laying down any rule of law to the effect that where questions are asked of a patient, or doubts are expressed, a doctor is under an obligation to put the patient in possession of all the information on the subject ... The amount of information to be given must depend on the circumstances, and as a general proposition it is governed by what is called the *Bolam* test.

Readers will note that by relying exclusively on accepted medical practice the courts in medical negligence are doing little more than playing lip service to the usual approach in negligence, gauging whether or not the defendant fell below the required standard of care. Normally the court will consider the following:

(1) The magnitude of the risk (see, for example, *Paris v Stepney Borough Council* [1951] AC 367). The more serious the damage to be prevented, the greater the precautions that must be taken. When determining this equation the court must also consider the likelihood of the damage occurring and the foreseeability of that risk. *Vernon v Bloomsbury Health Authority* [1995] 6 Med LR 297 is an interesting and pertinent example of the courts applying the risk/benefit analysis. In this case, the court found the defendant not negligent notwithstanding that the administration of the drug in question was in excess of the manufacturer's guidelines. The court applied a risk/benefit approach – the plaintiff was suffering from a serious illness, and medical experts confirmed that higher dosages of the drug than recommended by the manufacturer had been prescribed on other occasions. The lesson being, therefore, that it is dangerous to solely rely on guidelines and the like – whether the defendant is in breach will be a question of fact.

(2) The availability and practicability of the precautions which can be taken in order to prevent the potential damage occurring (see, for example, *Latimer v AEC Ltd* [1953] AC 643 where the only precaution which was available to the employer was to close down his factory, which the court held was not commercially viable).

(3) Usual and accepted practice. This will usually be considered after (1) and (2) above. However, following accepted practice will not always exculpate the defendant. The court will consider whether it is reasonable practice or whether it is *Wednesbury* unreasonable (see *Associated Provincial Picture Houses v Wednesbury Corporation* [1948] 1 KB 223). *Note*, however, the application of this test to medical negligence cases has recently been doubted in *Joyce v Wandsworth Health Authority* [1996] 7 Med LR 1. Unfortunately in a medical negligence case somewhere along the line (1) and (2) tend to become blurred and consequently the courts usually consider not the degree of risk, or the precautions that should have been followed, but simply whether the defendant acted in accordance with accepted practice in the particular circumstances. The courts shy away from their self-appointed role of assessors and instead simply ask the defendant's peers if this particular defendant acted in accordance with accepted practice. In a medical negligence case the courts argue that they are advised by medical experts on the degree of risk and the measures which could have been taken to avoid the damage. This in itself may not be too damaging a consequence except that in matters of medical judgment the judiciary place too much emphasis on who is giving the opinion rather than considering whether the opinion is a reasonable one. Although the courts have substituted their opinion for the views of experts in non-medical fields, they show unparalleled reluctance to use the same initiative in the world of the medical expert. For those instances where the court has departed from the medical experts view, see p 139 *et seq* and in particular *Hucks v Cole* (1968) reported at [1993] 4 Med LR 393.

Finally, an error of judgment does not of itself amount to negligence; it may be indicative of such, but the *Bolam* test should be applied. In *Whitehouse v Jordan*

[1981] 1 WLR 246, Lord Denning argued in the Court of Appeal that an error of clinical judgment by a medical practitioner did not amount to negligence. He indicated that the law allowed for errors of judgment which did not of themselves amount to negligence. The House of Lords rejected Lord Denning's interpretation and stated that some errors of judgment may be negligent and some may not. Whether or not a defendant committed an error of judgment may be indicative of negligence, but the proper test to be applied was the *Bolam* test.

Below we consider the standard of care expected of health carers with different levels of experience.

Specialists

A specialist must exercise the standard of care of a reasonably competent specialist in his field. If a GP embarked on a specialist task he would be judged by the standards of that speciality. To date the courts have shied away from demanding a higher standard of care from a specialist (ie higher than the standard of a reasonably competent specialist): see *Ashcroft v Mersey Regional Health Authority* [1983] 2 All ER 245. We submit that in certain circumstances the defendant's specialism should warrant a higher degree of care because the plaintiff expects more of the defendant due to his apparent expertise. However, there is a potential problem with imposing this higher standard of care and it revolves around the distinction between the private patient and the NHS patient. Clearly, any contractual term could be implied (subject to the reasonableness requirement) into a contract, consequently, it could be argued that a higher degree of care could be demanded from the private specialist than his NHS counterpart, thus placing the private patient in a better position. For this reason the courts are unlikely to change the current standards.

The novice

With regard to the junior doctor inexperience is no defence. The defendant must meet the standard of care expected of his rank/status. This is nothing new in the law of tort (see *Nettleship v Weston* [1971] 2 QB 691 where the same standard of care was expected of a learner driver as of an experienced driver).

The leading authority on this point in the medical context is *Wilsher v Essex Area Health Authority* [1986] 3 All ER 801. Martin Wilsher was born prematurely suffering from various illnesses including oxygen deficiency. He was placed in a special care baby unit at the hospital. While he was in the unit a catheter was twice inserted into a vein rather than an artery and on both occasions he was given excess oxygen. The doctors administering the oxygen were a junior and an inexperienced doctor respectively. The position of the catheter was not in itself negligent as it was a mistake a reasonably competent doctor could make. The catheter could be checked by means of an X-ray, which was in fact done in this case; however, the senior registrar failed to spot the mistake. The baby was subsequently found to be suffering from retrolental fibroplasia, which causes blindness.

In the Court of Appeal, it was argued that the standard of care expected of the junior doctor was not the same as that of his experienced counterpart. It was said that a junior doctor had to learn on the job, otherwise it would be impossible for medicine to develop and function; it was therefore unavoidable that mistakes would be made. Sir Nicholas Browne-Wilkinson VC agreed with this argument (stating at p 833):

> ... a doctor ... should only be held liable for acts and omissions which a careful doctor with his qualifications and experience would not have done or omitted.

But the majority of the Court of Appeal dismissed this argument. Glidewell LJ applied the *Bolam* test commenting (at p 831) that if there was not a uniform standard of care then:

> ... inexperience would frequently be urged as a defence to an action for professional negligence.

The solicitor should bear in mind that:

(1) The judgment of Glidewell LJ sums up the current legal position. What is reasonable conduct on behalf of the defendant will not change with the post he held nor with his level of inexperience. It may be that the hospital was at fault in placing the junior doctor in such a situation (see Chapter 3, Duty, at p 69 for direct liability on health authorities); however, the wrong inflicted on the junior doctor should not be remedied at the expense of the patient.

(2) Once a doctor performs a task, the patient can assume he has the competence to perform the task with care and skill. If the doctor either unwittingly or knowingly attempts a task beyond his experience then that will constitute a breach of the standard of care. (Refer to Chapter 3, Duty, at p 69.)

(3) The junior doctor will not be liable if he seeks the advice of a senior/more experienced colleague (as was the case in *Wilsher*). The liability will then fall upon the shoulders of the more experienced doctor for lack of supervision. A common illustration of inexperience is that often the doctor does not realise that the task at hand is beyond his capabilities and therefore does not seek help. In the Canadian case of *Fraser v Vancouver General Hospital* (1951) 3 WWR 337, the court held that an intern had to exercise the 'ordinary skill of a junior doctor' and must have an appreciation of his own limitations. Quite what this means is uncertain: it is all very well saying that a doctor must have appreciated his own capabilities but in most situations the junior doctor is already acting under the firm belief that this is in fact what he is already doing.

(4) The more experienced doctor could be held liable for failing to reasonably supervise the junior doctor, or the hospital could be made directly liable for placing the junior doctor in a position with which he was not qualified to cope (see *Bull and another v Devon Area Health Authority* [1993] 4 Med LR 117, at p 69). We urge that the latter of these options be resorted to: we have no qualms about placing the health authorities under this onerous obligation, it may even make them consider the working environment of junior doctors more closely. However, we are wary of increasing the demands on their colleagues, as it seems to us that the only way in which they could escape liability would be to place their inexperienced staff under constant supervision: not only would this increase the pressure on the supervisors but also it might make the inexperienced staff insecure.

(5) What about the converse situation where the doctor again either knowingly or unwittingly holds himself out as being more experienced than he actually is? The position seems clear – once the doctor has held himself out as possessing that degree of skill and knowledge, has accepted the responsibility and undertaken the treatment, he must reach that standard (see *R v Bateman* (1925) LJKB 791).

What if the patient accepts the treatment knowing that the doctor does not have that skill? Will this prevent the patient from bringing an action in negligence against the doctor should something go wrong? It is suggested that the particular factual situation will be all important. If it is an emergency situation then the patient may have had no alternative. However, if the patient has a range of available options then could it be said he must have consented to run the risk, ie *volenti non fit injuria*? Perhaps the situation can be likened to where a person accepts a lift from a drunken driver (see *Owens v Brimmell* [1977] 1 QB 859). However, we suggest that the two situations cannot be held to be truly analogous: the patient does not really have a choice; he requires treatment and he does not really have knowledge of what the doctor can and cannot do; the passenger clearly has a choice and a great deal more knowledge about his situation. We therefore contend that *volenti* is inappropriate, although contributory negligence may be considered.

Recently, the courts have again looked at the question of inexperience in relation to the standard of care to be expected. In *Bouchta v Swindon HA* [1996] 7 Med LR 62, the junior operating surgeon was under the supervision of a more senior surgeon. The court held that at a certain time during the operation, despite the supervision of the senior surgeon, the junior surgeon failed to exercise reasonable care. In *Wilsher*, it was accepted that had the junior doctor sought supervision then he might have escaped liability. The junior surgeon was under constant supervision in *Bouchta* but despite this he was still liable. In *Wilsher*, the court went on to say that the senior doctor could be held liable for failing to supervise adequately – this point was either not discussed in *Bouchta* or the court was satisfied with the level of supervision that took place; indeed, the report states that the senior surgeon 'supervised as far as he could'. The court went on to say that had the senior doctor carried out the operation it would have been difficult to reach the same conclusion – why? If the more senior surgeon had acted as his junior counterpart why would the decision have been any different? (See also *Djemal v Bexley Health Authority* [1995] 6 Med LR 269.)

The medical student

To our knowledge there is no case law concerning the medical student; but it is our contention that *Wilsher* should apply and that the student's inexperience should not be a defence. Furthermore, there is the guidance given by the DHSS to health authorities in September 1971 (DS 256/71). Essentially this states that the consultant in charge has overall supervisory responsibility, that a student should not initiate treatment for the patient on his own diagnosis but should have that diagnosis confirmed by a registered medical practitioner, that he is not to be regarded as a locum and that he should not prescribe or request X-rays.

The nurse

Finally, what about the legal position of the nurse? She should show the standard expected of a reasonably competent nurse. If she finds herself in a difficult position should always seek the advice of her superiors; this could be a line manager or a doctor depending on the nature of the difficulty. The nurse should act on the doctor's instructions but should not follow those instructions if they are clearly erroneous or criminal. The nurse is responsible not only for her own actions but also for those of her team.

REFERENCES

English case law

(1) Bolam v Friern Hospital Management Committee [1957] 1 WLR 582; [1957] 2 All ER 118

See Commentary above, at p 121.

(2) Gold v Haringey Health Authority [1987] 2 All ER 888

There is no difference in the standard of care between advice given in a therapeutic context and advice given in a contraceptive context. The judge at first instance in this case preferred one body of medical opinion to the other. The Court of Appeal dismissed this approach and held that the test to be applied was *Bolam*. For further details see Chapters 2, Consent and 5, Standard of Care.

(3) Nickolls v Ministry of Health (1955) The Times, 4 February

The surgeon was suffering from cancer, and operated on the plaintiff. The court held that he was in a fit condition to operate and consequently was not negligent.

(4) Barnett v Chelsea and Kensington Hospital Management Committee [1969] 1 QB 420

A casualty officer who was unwell refused to see three nightwatchmen in casualty.

Held:: he was negligent in telling them to go home and contact their own doctors.

Note the case eventually failed on causation as the court found that even if the men had been treated they would have still died from arsenic poisoning.

(5) Bull and another v Devon Area Health Authority [1993] 4 Med LR 117

Refer to Chapter 3, Duty, at p 69 and this chapter, at p 162 – failure of hospital administration/organisation.

(6) Hucks v Cole [1993] 4 Med LR 393; (1968) 112 SJ 483

For a detailed commentary, see p 140.

(7) Clarke v Adams (1950) 94 SJ 599

See p 145.

(8) DeFreitas v O'Brien and Connolly [1995] 6 Med LR 108

See r 5(B), at p 132.

(9) Blyth v Bloomsbury Area Health Authority [1993] 4 Med LR 151; (1989) 5 PN 169

See Chapter 2, Consent, at p 43.

(10) Paris v Stepney Borough Council [1951] AC 367

The plaintiff was already blind in one eye when a scrap of metal fell into his good eye during the course of his employment. His employer had not provided him with safety goggles, although that was in accordance with accepted practice.

Held:: the defendant employer was negligent in failing to provide goggles: he owed a duty of care to each individual employee. Consequently the employer must take account of the degree of risk posed to each employee, ie the employer must take greater care over the precautions for a partially sighted man.

(11) Latimer v AEC Ltd [1953] AC 643

A factory floor became very slippery after a heavy rainfall which resulted in water mixing with oil. Despite the fact that the defendant had covered the floor with sawdust the plaintiff slipped. It was argued that the factory should have been closed down. However, the court held that this was not commercially practicable.

(12) Associated Provincial Picture Houses v Wednesbury Corporation [1948] 1 KB 223

See above at p 123.

(13) Joyce v Merton, Sutton and Wandsworth Health Authority [1996] 7 Med LR 1; [1995] 6 Med LR 60

See r 5(D) and p 142.

(14) Vernon v Bloomsbury Health Authority [1995] 6 Med LR 297

See above, at p 123.

(15) Whitehouse v Jordan [1981] 1 WLR 246; [1981] 1 All ER 267

See above, at p 124.

(16) Ashcroft v Mersey Regional Health Authority [1983] 2 All ER 245

Per Kilner-Brown J (at p 247):

The more skilled a person is, the more care that is expected of him.

The plaintiff's case failed in this instance because expert evidence was divided, namely there was a body which stated that the damage could occur without negligence and a body which stated that the injury occurred because of the fault of the defendant. The plaintiff had sustained severe damage to his ear, despite the fact it was a relatively simple operation. However, Kilner-Brown J indicated, as stated above, that the court would expect a high degree of care from someone professing to be a specialist.

(17) Nettleship v Weston [1971] 2 QB 691

Held:: a learner driver must meet the standard of care of a qualified driver even vis-à-vis his instructor. The Court of Appeal was heavily influenced by the presence of compulsory insurance.

Note that the High Court of Australia has refused to follow this decision (see *Cook v Cook* (1986) 68 ALR 353) holding that it was 'contrary to what is common sense'.

See also *Philips v William Whiteley Ltd* [1938] 1 All ER 566 where the court held that a jeweller piercing ears is not bound to take the same precautions as a surgeon but must meet such standards as may reasonably be expected of a jeweller. In this day of AIDS and other highly infectious diseases we submit that the standard of a jeweller would be rather high.

(18) Wilsher v Essex Area Health Authority [1988] 2 WLR 557; [1988] 1 All ER 871; [1986] 3 All ER 801

See above, at p 124.

See also on this point the following five cases:

Burgess v Newcastle Health Authority [1992] 3 Med LR 224

Whether the doctor is sufficiently competent and experienced to carry out an operation unsupervised is a matter of fact and degree on the evidence.

Jones v Manchester Corporation [1952] 2 All ER 125

A doctor was found negligent, and it was held that inexperience is no defence. The hospital board was also found negligent for not supervising the defendant.

Payne v St Helier Group Hospital Management Committee (1952) The Times, 12 November

A casualty officer was held to be negligent for failing to detain a patient for examination by a doctor of consultant rank.

Sa'ad v Robinson [1989] 1 Med LR 41

In the case of a junior doctor, a failure to summon a senior colleague might constitute negligence even though the problem was not unusual or did not appear complicated or a senior colleague might not have been able to do anything in the circumstances. (See further, at p 151.)

Scott v Bloomsbury Health Authority [1989] 1 Med LR 214

Failure to summon a senior colleague might not constitute negligence, it will depend on all the circumstances of the case.

(19) Bouchta v Swindon Health Authority [1996] 7 Med LR 62

The plaintiff sustained damage to her ureter. The court held that as damage to a ureter was a well known risk of hysterectomies, the degree of care must reflect that risk. See above and Chapter 6, Causation, at p 189.

(20) Djemal v Bexley Health Authority [1995] 6 Med LR 269

The defendant contended that the standard of care and skill to be applied was that of a reasonably competent senior officer of about 4 months experience on the job. The court, applying *Wilsher*, said that the test was that of a reasonably competent houseman acting as a casualty officer without any reference to the length of experience.

(21) R v Bateman (1925) LJKB 791

See above, at p 126.

Foreign case law

Readers will note that other jurisdictions do not adhere as stringently to the *Bolam* test as their English counterparts (see p 143).

AUSTRALIA

Rogers v Whittaker [1993] 4 Med LR 79; [1992] 3 Med LR 331; (1992) 109 ALR 625 discussed in Chapters 2, Consent, at p 64 and 5, Standard of Care, at p 143.

CANADA

(1) Crits v Sylvester (1956) 1 DLR (2d) 502

Held:: an anaesthetist handling dangerous substances which he knew to be highly inflammable was subject to a proportionately higher degree of care and consequently he was bound to take special precautions to prevent injury. It was stated (at p 508):

> Every medical practitioner ... is bound to exercise that degree of care and skill which could reasonably be expected of a normal, prudent practitioner of the same experience and standing, and if he holds himself out as a specialist, a

higher degree of skill is required of him than of one who does not profess to be so qualified by special training and ability.

(2) Fraser v Vancouver General Hospital (1951) 3 WWR 337; affirmed [1952] 3 DLR 785

A patient was admitted to casualty after being involved in a road accident. He was examined by junior doctors, X-rays were taken and examined, and the plaintiff was then sent home. The patient subsequently died.

Held:: the junior doctors were negligent in attempting to read the X-rays themselves and failing to consult a specialist. The negligence was failing to ask the advice of the radiologist and relying on their own knowledge.

Statutes / statutory instruments

(1) UNFAIR CONTRACT TERMS ACT 1977

Section 2(1) governs excluding liability for death or personal injuries. A private patient has a contractual relationship with his doctor and as such is technically free to negotiate the terms, but this is subject to the Unfair Contract Terms Act 1977 which states that a doctor will not be able to exclude any liability for his negligence which results in death or personal injuries. In reality the court will imply a term into the contract that the doctor must reach the same standard of care as his NHS contemporary.

(2) EMERGENCY TREATMENT AND GPS

Note that although it is stated that there is no legal duty on a GP to be a good Samaritan, the GP must give treatment to anyone in an emergency in his practice area (National Health Service (General Medical Pharmaceutical Services) Regulations 1974, SI 1974/160, Sched 1, para 4(h)), providing the doctor is available and the patient's own doctor is not available to give immediate treatment. See also the National Health Service (General Medical Services) Regulations 1992 paras 40–41 which state that the doctor is 'requested to give treatment which is immediately required owing to an accident or other emergency at any place in his practice area'.

(3) MEDICAL (PROFESSIONAL PERFORMANCE) ACT 1995

This Act came into force on 1 May 1995 and amends the Medical Act 1983. Section 1 of the Act gives the GMC power to act where the doctor's conduct is found to be 'seriously deficient' in performance of his professional duties. To date, the guidelines for what will constitute a seriously deficient performance are yet to be finalised but it appears that it will not cover individual mistakes nor conduct matters. When the guidelines are drafted, it may be that they will have some bearing on medical negligence claims as there will be clear guidelines for all specialties and grades, though the assessment of whether someone has been negligent as opposed to seriously deficient may differ. See also Chapter 1, Confidentiality, at p 8.

Professional/ethical guidelines

The GMC has recently published a series of pamphlets under the general title 'Duties of a Doctor'. One of the booklets is entitled 'Good Medical Practice' and deals which what it suggests to be a good standard of practice and care. In particular, the booklet categorises what it deems to be good clinical care, which includes an adequate assessment of the patient's condition, providing or arranging necessary investigations or referring the patient to another practitioner. Further, it states that practitioners must appreciate their own limitations and be willing to consult others. The booklet stresses the need to keep accurate records and, interestingly, to consider the appropriate use of resources.

Practice points

- The effect of the Patient's Charter (HMSO 1991) on the patient's right to sue in negligence is unknown. We suggest that at present breach of the charter will only add evidential weight to the plaintiff's allegations. As yet there is no organisational body behind the charter to enforce the standards it contains, therefore the benefit to the plaintiff is minimal. In a similar vein we suggest that the solicitor may make use of the GMC guidance on Good Practice as detailed above.

- Know your specialisms. If you are claiming against a specialist then it is vitally important to use an expert in the specialist's field. (See Appendix H, at p 403.)

- Although the degree of the defendant's experience and rank is relevant when evaluating whether the defendant has been negligent, ie specialists will be compared with specialists, etc, in practice it does not matter whether the breach of duty was that of the novice or the specialist; the standard of care will be determined by the *Bolam* test.

RULE 5(B)

Accepted practice means practice accepted as proper by the defendant's peers. If the defendant has complied with this practice then that is strong evidence that he is not negligent, if he does not then it is likely he will be negligent.

Commentary

In ascertaining whether or not the defendant has met the appropriate standard of care the court is governed by the *Bolam* test. This test demands that the defendant acts in accordance with accepted practice, which means the practice followed by a responsible body of medical opinion. It does not matter that there is a body of medical opinion which takes the contrary view or that there is more than one accepted practice. The rationale for the *Bolam* rule is that the courts are not the appropriate forum for the medical profession to squabble over what is the 'right practice'. Perhaps the judiciary were of the same opinion when they decided that they were not competent to rule on what is the best practice in medical law. This is evident from cases such as *Sidaway v Board of Governors of the Bethlem Royal Hospital and the Maudsley Hospital* [1985] AC 871, where Lord Scarman stated (at p 881):

> In short, the law imposes the duty of care but the standard is a matter for medical judgment.

Although this statement has been endorsed by many cases, eg *Maynard v West Midlands Regional Health Authority* [1984] 1 WLR 634, many commentators have said that the decision in *Bolitho v City and Hackney Health Authority* [1993] 4 Med LR 381, together with some recent decisions, have made serious inroads into this principle. (This is discussed in detail in Chapter 6, Causation, at p 196.)

Most recently, in *Djemal v Bexley Health Authority* [1995] 6 Med LR 269 (also discussed at p 129), the judge rejected the evidence of both defence experts who were of the opinion that the defendant had acted in accordance with the *Bolam* test and preferred the evidence of the plaintiff. The judgment, however, fails to reveal any facts which may enlighten the reader as to why the court took this step. Clearly, this approach is in contrast with *Maynard*.

Perhaps the most interesting word on this matter belongs to the case of *DeFreitas v O'Brien and Connolly* [1995] 6 Med LR 108. The Court of Appeal held that a small number of medical practitioners could constitute a 'responsible body of medical opinion against which the practices of a doctor could be measured'. The plaintiff sought to argue that although a small number of surgeons could be considered responsible, nevertheless they had to be a substantial body. In support of this contention the plaintiff relied on the judgment of Hirst J in *Hills v Potter* [1984] 1 WLR 641 (at p 653):

> I do not accept that ... by adopting the *Bolam* principle, the court in effect abdicates its power of decision to the doctors. In every case the court must be satisfied that the standard contended for on their behalf accords with that upheld by a substantial body of medical opinion, and that this body of medical opinion is both respectable and responsible, and experienced in this particular field of medicine.

This approach was also applied in the Irish case of *Dunne v National Maternity Hospital and Jackson* [1989] IRLM 735 where Findlay CJ said (at p 746):

> General and approved practice need not be universal but must be approved of and adhered to by a substantial number of reputable practitioners holding the relevant specialist or general qualifications.

The court in *DeFreitas* rejected this approach, ruling that 'substantial' did not simply refer to numbers. The issue could not be determined by counting heads – it was a question of fact. However, we submit that numbers must play a part in determining whether or not the practice is accepted and responsible. Referring to the *dicta* of Hirst J in *Hills v Potter* [1984] 1 WLR 641, we find it difficult not to construe the word 'substantial' as meaning 'of a great number'. Just how many this number is, however, is irrelevant to the argument. However, we submit that the greater the number the higher the degree of respectability it is likely to attract. In the light of *DeFreitas* conceivably there is now a situation where a 'body' of two medical practitioners could outweigh the views of a group of 50. This cannot be what McNair J intended in *Bolam*. In determining whether or not a practice is responsible, the first thing the court should do is to see who has adopted the practice and count heads. It follows that the greater the number adopting a practice the more likely it is that the practice is both accepted and responsible. What is not being advocated is that the matter can be determined *solely* by counting heads: before anything else the court should examine the risk in relation to the precautions adopted, if any. *DeFreitas* sets a worrying precedent in that perhaps now a small fringe group practising experimental techniques can legitimately constitute a responsible body despite being contrary to the norm. This interpretation of the *DeFreitas* case may seem radical but there is no reason to draw any other conclusion; certainly case law to date does not persuade us to change our view. As always, however, we urge solicitors to prove us wrong!

Complying with accepted practice is strong evidence that the defendant is not negligent, but it is not conclusive, otherwise adopting a practice and calling it 'accepted' would exculpate the defendant every time. However, in all but a few cases accepted practice will get the seal of approval from the courts. As has been mentioned before, courts in other jurisdictions have not accepted this approach without reservation, and in some cases have actually held it not to be appropriate to the case in question (see p 143 *et seq*). The concept of accepted practice is nothing new in the law of tort, what is different in this field of the law is the reluctance of the court to challenge the 'accepted practice'.

The accepted practice must be the current practice. This requires the health carer to keep up to date with new developments in his field of medicine (see *Hepworth v Kerr* [1995] 6 Med LR 139, at p 139). The medical practitioner cannot stick steadfastly to the principles learnt in his training, he must endeavour to keep up with new developments. But this does not mean he must read everything published within a few weeks of its publication; all he is required to do is to act responsibly and reasonably. Like any other practice, medical practice will be judged by the standard of care prevailing at the time of the incident, not at the time of the trial. In *Roe v Minister of Health* [1954] 2 QB 66, anaesthetic was kept in glass ampoules stored in disinfectant; the disinfectant seeped through cracks into the anaesthetic. This was impossible to detect at the time, and so the defendant was found not negligent. (See also *Re HIV Haemophiliac Litigation* (1990) 140 NLJ 1349 and *ter Neuzen v Korn* (1993) 103 DLR (4th) 473.) This principle has found its way into the Consumer Protection Act 1987. This Act is important in the medical field as it covers pharmaceutical products, in particular contraceptive drugs, appliances and possibly even blood. While purporting to be a strict liability Act, under s 4(1)(e) a producer can escape liability if it can be shown that the state of scientific knowledge was not such that the defendant could have been expected to have knowledge of the defect (the development risks defence). Thus, a defendant can escape liability if, for example, it can be shown that the defect constituting a breach in 1993 was not generally known until 1995. This seems to go against the very spirit of the Act and perhaps will not prevent a 'thalidomide' tragedy occurring again. The Consumer Protection Act is soon to be reviewed, and it is to be hoped that English law falls in line with European law. France, Belgium, Greece and Luxembourg are among the Member States which do not permit the development risks defence, whereas Germany will not permit it in respect of death or personal injury from pharmaceuticals. As the law now stands, it would be right to conclude that Britain is little more than a testing ground for new drugs.

The problem for any solicitor who alleges that the defendant has been negligent in failing to adopt a new practice is to determine when the defendant should have adopted the new practice, ie how long does a health carer have before he is found negligent in not adopting a new technique? Each case will have to be judged on its own facts but we submit that the court will look at:

(1) how widespread the knowledge is;

(2) the length of time it has been available;

(3) if the new practice is a precaution, the expense of adopting that precaution, the practicality of doing so and the benefit to the patient.

However, at the end of the day, the *Bolam* test will be applied. Consequently, there could be the bizarre situation when a health carer is clearly following an old practice, but because he can find others who are equally behind the times, in accordance with the *Bolam* rule he will not be negligent. Can this be logical? Is this what *Bolam* intended? It may be that the court will, in these circumstances, intervene and hold that the practice is now not reasonable for a responsible body of medical opinion to hold and cannot therefore be accepted practice. If so, it will be one of those rare instances like *Hucks v Cole* (1968) reported at [1993] 4 Med LR 393 where the court has chosen to intervene. Dillon LJ said in *Bolitho v City and Hackney Health Authority* [1993] 4 Med LR 381 (at p 392) (commenting on the judgment of Sachs LJ in *Hucks*):

> In my judgment, the court could only adopt the approach of Sachs LJ and reject medical opinion on the ground that the reasons of one group of doctors do not really stand up to analysis, if the court, fully conscious of its own lack of medical knowledge and clinical experience, was none the less clearly satisfied that the views of that group of doctors were *Wednesbury* unreasonable, ie views such as no reasonable body of doctors could have held ...

This could happen only where the old practice is blatantly dangerous; where the practice is old and has merely been superseded by some new approach, the court should regard this as a situation where there are two accepted practices and it not for the court to intervene. This bodes well for the slow reading doctor!

Finally, whose practice is being referred to when the phrase 'accepted practice' is being used? Is it an English practice only, or can the practices in other jurisdictions be looked at? In the Canadian case of *ter Neuzen v Korn* (1993) 103 DLR (4th) 473 (see p 137), the court said that although Canadian doctors were not expected to be aware of the practices of their Australian counterparts, they should be aware of the American guidelines. However, it is submitted that to be judged negligent in not following an accepted practice, the court must have regard to an English accepted practice; otherwise we could be faced with a situation where, for example, an English doctor could be held negligent for failing to operate because it was an accepted practice in, say, the United States. Conversely, could a doctor 'save himself' by saying, for example, that his practice was an accepted practice in another country? Would it matter which country had adopted his practice? If we accept that a doctor will not be held negligent for not following a foreign accepted practice then surely he should not be permitted to rely on a foreign medical practice as a last ditch attempt to escape liability.

REFERENCES

English case law

(1) Bolam v Friern Hospital Management Committee [1957] 1 WLR 582; [1957] 2 All ER 118

See p 121.

(2) Sidaway v Board of Governors of the Bethlem Royal Hospital and the Maudsley Hospital [1985] AC 871; [1985] 1 All ER 643

See p 154.

(3) Maynard v West Midlands Regional Health Authority [1984] 1 WLR 634; [1985] 1 All ER 635

The plaintiff was provisionally diagnosed as having TB, although this was far from certain – she could have been suffering from Hodgkins disease. It was agreed that further tests should be carried out and in the course of a biopsy the recurrent larungeal nerve was damaged and the patient rendered hoarse. The plaintiff based her case on the grounds that the diagnosis was so obvious that the operation should never have been performed.

The case eventually went to the House of Lords. There was two schools of thought, one of which supported the plaintiff, the other the defendant. Lord Scarman said (at [1984] 1 WLR 634, at p 639):

a judge's 'preference' for one body of distinguished professional opinion to another also professionally distinguished is not sufficient to establish negligence in a practitioner whose actions have received the seal of approval of those whose opinions, truthfully expressed, honestly held, were not preferred ... For in the realms of diagnosis and treatment negligence is not established by preferring one respectable body of professional opinion to another. Failing to exercise the ordinary skill of a doctor (in the appropriate speciality, if he be a specialist) is necessary.

Consequently, as the defendant's conduct was approved by a body of medical opinion then the plaintiff's action ultimately failed.

(4) Bolitho v City and Hackney Health Authority [1993] 4 Med LR 381

This case is dealt with in detail in Chapter 6, Causation, at p 196.

See also *Joyce v Wandsworth Health Authority* [1996] 7 Med LR 1; [1995] 6 Med LR 60, a case which applied *Bolitho*. The court applied the *dicta* of Farquharson LJ in *Bolitho*, at p 386 where he said when the court was faced with a breach of duty which consisted of an omission, the court had to decide 'what course of events would have followed had the duty been discharged'.

(5) Djemal v Bexley Health Authority [1995] 6 Med LR 269

See above, at p 129.

(6) DeFreitas v O'Brien and Connolly [1995] 6 Med LR 108

The plaintiff had suffered from intense back pain since 1981. She had exploratory surgery which later became infected. Her condition deteriorated and eventually she was discharged from hospital suffering from chronic arachnoiditis.

She alleged that her exploratory operation should not have been carried out because there was insufficient clinical or radiological evidence to warrant such an operation.

Held::

- The *Bolam* test did not impose any burden of proof upon the defendant to show that the diagnosis/treatment would be acceptable to a responsible body of medical opinion. The burden of proof was on the plaintiff.
- That the body of spinal surgeons did not have to be substantial. It was sufficient that the court was satisfied that it was a responsible body.

(7) Hills v Potter [1984] 1 WLR 641; [1983] 3 All ER 716

See p 154.

(8) Hepworth v Kerr [1995] 6 Med LR 139

See p 139.

(9) Roe v Minister of Health [1954] 2 QB 66; [1954] 2 All ER 131

The events giving rise to the action occurred in 1947. The plaintiff had a spinal anaesthetic administered to him in preparation for a minor operation. The anaesthetic was contained in a glass ampoule which had been stored in a solution of phenol. Some of the phenol had penetrated the ampoule which contaminated the anaesthetic. As a result the plaintiff was paralysed from the waist down. The ampoule had been inspected prior to the operation. However, the possibility of invisible cracks was not yet known.

Held:: the defendant was not negligent as the risk of invisible cracks was not apparent to the profession until 1951. Current practice is not retrospective. The standard of care is to be judged at the date of the incident not the date of the trial. See the following cases.

Crawford v Charing Cross Hospital (1953) *The Times,* 8 December concerning the liability of an anaesthetist. He failed to read an article in *The Lancet* which had been published 6 months earlier concerning the best position of the arm when using a drip. The Court of Appeal found him not negligent. Failure to read one article in the current medical press was not negligent neither was the failure to implement it immediately.

Whiteford v Hunter [1950] WN 553; 94 SJ 758 concerning a mistaken diagnosis of cancer. If the defendant had the instrument commonly used in the United States and had been aware of the American way of diagnosing such a condition the mistake would not have been made. However, both the instrument and method were rarely used in England and the defendant was held not negligent. This illustrates that doctors are not negligent if they fail to keep up to date with foreign practices.

Gold v Haringey Health Authority [1987] 2 All ER 888 concerning the appropriate standard regarding disclosure of information – to be judged by 1979 standards not the standards applicable at the time of the trial.

(10) Re HIV Haemophiliac Litigation (1990) 140 NLJ 1349

Plaintiffs sued the government in negligence and for breach of statutory duty under the National Health Service Act 1977 for infecting them with the HIV virus (which leads to AIDS) after receiving Factor 8 (the clotting agent) which had been imported from the United States. The case eventually settled, hence it was still remains uncertain whether the government were negligent in failing to implement screening processes for blood in the early 1980s.

Foreign case law

AUSTRALIA

(1) Dwan v Farquhar [1988] Qd R 234

An article published in March 1983 about the risk of contacting AIDS from blood transfusions. The patient contracted AIDS from a blood transfusion performed in May 1983. The defendant was held not to be negligent.

(2) H v Royal Alexandra Hospital for Children [1990] 1 Med LR 297

An infant haemophiliac was infected with the HIV virus from blood products during Factor 8 replacement therapy.

Held:: the plaintiff was owed a duty of care by the treating hospital, the manufacturer and the distributor of the product. However, the evidence did not establish that in March 1982 when the incident took place that the defendant had been negligent in excluding certain groups (notably homosexuals) from the blood donor pool. It was not until June 1983 that the Australian Red Cross Society had recommended that, as an interim measure, blood or blood components should not be collected from certain groups of people until tests for AIDS became available.

The court also held that even where the risk of transmitting AIDS through blood products was known it was not practicable to recall the products.

(3) E v Australian Red Cross Society [1991] 2 Med LR 303

The applicant E received a transfusion of frozen human plasma which was HIV infected. E commenced proceedings against three respondents, the Australian Red Cross Society, the New South Wales Division of the Society and, the Central Sydney Service which was created by statute in 1986 to take over responsibilities for the liabilities of hospitals. The appellant alleged that the Society had been negligent in the collection and distribution of blood.

Note that the court did not apply the *Bolam* rule but instead applied the test as enunciated in *F v R* (1983) 33 SASR 189, at p 194:

> The ultimate question, however, is not whether the defendant's conduct accords with the practices of his profession or some part of it, but whether it conforms to the standard of reasonable care demanded by the law. That is a question for the court and the duty of deciding it cannot be delegated to any profession or group in the community.

The court, ruling on the decision to introduce surrogate testing earlier, held that a 5% reduction in the blood supply (which would have occurred had the testing been implemented) would endanger life and therefore was not practicable.

Note that the American practice was to the contrary. However, the court ruled that this in itself was not decisive.

CANADA

ter Neuzen v Korn (1993) 103 DLR (4th) 473

Plaintiff contracted HIV from an artificial insemination procedure carried out in 1985. The risk of transmission of HIV by this procedure was known in Australia since late 1984, but this information did not filter through to British Columbia until mid 1985. At first instance, the defendant was found liable in negligence. On appeal the court said the test should be whether the defendant had conducted himself as a reasonable doctor would have done in similar circumstances and as such the jury had to look at the prevailing standards of practice at that time.

Held:: the practice of the Canadian practitioners had acted in accordance with accepted practice at that time, therefore the only question was whether the doctor had failed to protect his patients against sexually transmitted diseases, if he failed to do so then he would be negligent even if he did not foresee the risk of HIV.

Note that the court said that although it was not expected that Canadian doctors should be aware of the practices of their Australian counterparts, they should be aware of any published guidelines in the United States.

IRELAND

(1) Dunne v National Maternity Hospital and Jackson [1989] IRLM 735

See above, at p 132.

(2) Best v Wellcome Foundation [1993] IR 421; [1994] 5 Med LR 81

See Chapter 6, Causation, at p 178.

Note that in determining the appropriate standard of care the court held that simply complying with the requirements imposed by health authorities would not necessarily amount to a sufficient degree of care. This would be the minimum requirements only.

Statutes / statutory instruments

(1) CONSUMER PROTECTION ACT 1987

The state of the art defence

4(1) ...

    (e) that the state of scientific and technical knowledge at the relevant time was not such that a producer of products of the same description as the product in question might be expected to have discovered the defect if it had existed in his products while they were under his control.

(2) MEDICINES (LABELLING) AMENDMENT REGULATIONS 1992 (SI 1992/3273) and MEDICINES (LEAFLETS) AMENDMENT REGULATIONS 1992 (SI 1992/3274)

From 1 January 1994, drug manufacturers must with any new product supply an information leaflet. All existing drugs will have to comply with this when the product license is renewed, such renewal takes place on a five year interval.

Professional / ethical guidelines

Solicitors should refer to the pamphlet 'Good Medical Practice' published by the GMC. With regard to keeping up to date the GMC stress the need for practitioners to participate in educational activities, to work with colleagues and take part in regular audits and to keep up to date with any laws affecting their practice.

Practice points

In any case where the allegation is that the defendant has failed to keep up-to-date with current practice, it is vitally important to obtain the latest medical publications, eg *The Lancet*, government guidelines, etc and to ascertain how long these publications have been in circulation. The recent case of *Hepworth v Kerr* [1995] 6 Med LR 139 is, we think, worth reading. *Note* also, in accordance with *Vernon v Bloomsbury HA* [1995] 6 Med LR 297, complying with guidelines may not necessarily be determinative of liability.

RULE 5(C)

A health carer may be held liable in negligence when he departs from accepted practice. This will be determined as a question of fact.

Commentary

Departing from approved practice is in itself not negligent. As the reader will have observed, if the defendant conforms with accepted practice legally he may well have the 'seal of approval' and escape liability. If he departs from the approved practice, providing he can justify his actions he will not be negligent, but if he cannot justify his departure from the accepted practice the plaintiff should have little difficulty in establishing negligence. The negligent performance of an approved practice will also constitute a departure. Generally, the more severe the resulting damage, the more difficult it will be for the defendant to justify his actions. The rationale behind the principle is that the medical profession should not be discouraged from trying new innovative techniques and that the development of medical science should be encouraged.

However, neither should patients be subjected to reckless experimentation.

The latter point has recently been explored in the case of *Hepworth v Kerr* [1995] 6 Med LR 139 where an anaesthetist was found negligent for reducing a patient's blood pressure to a level lower than the accepted norm. The fact that the defendant argued he had performed the technique on 1,500 patients was not enough to show that he had proper scientific validation of his technique, which begs the question what will be and when will a technique be deemed accepted practice (see further, at p 133). In *Hepworth,* the court, did give some guidance: the defendant had failed to follow up any of his previous 1,500 patients; there was no expert support or endorsement of the defendant's work; it was not known how many of the defendant's previous 1,500 patients had the characteristics of the plaintiff; the defendant had no safety margin for error; and there should have been a proper validation of the technique.

REFERENCES

English case law

(1) Hepworth v Kerr [1995] 6 Med LR 139

See also *Clark v McLennan [1983] 1 All ER 416.*

The plaintiff suffered from stress incontinence after the birth of her first child. The defendant operated one month and 11 days after the birth to repair the weakness in her bladder and muscles. The operation and a subsequent operation were unsuccessful. Accepted practice was that the operation should not be performed until at least three months after the birth.

Held:: where the defendant has failed to take a precaution and the very damage occurs which the precaution was designed to prevent then the burden of proof is on the defendant to show he is not in breach of duty and did not cause the damage. Pain J said (at p 425):

> ... in a situation in which a general duty of care arises and there is a failure to take a precaution, and that very damage occurs against which the precaution is designed to be a protection, then the burden lies on the defendant to show that he was not in breach of duty as well as to show that the damage did not result from his breach of duty.

Note that this decision has been severely criticised, most notably in *Wilsher v Essex Area Health Authority* [1986] 3 All ER 801. Mustill LJ (at pp 814–15) denied that in such a situation the burden of proof was reversed.

In *Robinson v Post Office* [1974] 2 All ER 737; [1974] 1 WLR 1176, a doctor waited only a minute instead of the usual half hour before administering a tetanus injection after the usual test. Doctor found negligent in not conforming with accepted practice. (The case failed on causation, see p 178.)

RULE 5(D)

If the accepted practice itself is negligent then the courts will intervene and condemn that practice.

Commentary

An accepted practice must meet certain basic criteria. There are a number of cases, albeit outside the area of medical law, where the courts have readily intervened and held a practice to be negligent (see *Re Herald of Free Enterprise* (1987) *The Independent*, 18 December and *Edward Wong Finance Co Ltd v Johnson, Stokes and Master* [1984] AC 296). In the area of medical law, however, the cases are few and far between, but there are the decisions in *Clarke v Adams* (1950) 94 SJ 599 and *Anderson v Chasney* (1949) 4 DLR 71. As these cases predate *Bolam*, they should be viewed with some caution, although McNair J in *Bolam* did state that the *Bolam* principle was nothing new and was simply restating the law as of old. The case which is now the standard bearer for those in the anti *Bolam* camp is the 1968 case of *Hucks v Cole* reported at [1993] 4 Med LR 393. There a GP was found negligent for failing to treat Mrs Hucks with penicillin and, as a result, septicaemia developed. Mrs Hucks had recently given birth and developed puerperal fever, a condition which had been extremely common before the Second World War but was very rare in the 1960s. The defendant said he acted in accordance with the reasonable practice of other doctors with obstetric experience. It was said that this was no defence; the doctor should have taken the requisite steps when he could see that the absence of treatment posed a serious risk to the woman's health. Sachs LJ said (at p 397):

> When the evidence shows that a lacuna in professional practice exists by which risks of grave danger are knowingly taken, then, however small the risks, the courts must anxiously examine that lacuna – particularly if the risks can be easily and inexpensively avoided. If the court finds on analysis of the reasons given for not taking those precautions that, in the light of current professional knowledge, there is no proper basis for the lacuna, and that it is definitely not reasonable that those risks should have been taken, its function is to state that it constitutes negligence. In such a case the practice will no doubt thereafter be altered to the benefit of the patients.

In *Hucks v Cole*, the correct approach was adopted by the court; it focused on the magnitude of the risk involved and the ease of avoiding it. The pathologist's report had signalled that a form of septicaemia infection was present while the expert evidence was that it should have been treated. Dr Cole had received the test results indicating the infection but had done nothing. The court considered the likelihood of death resulting and the extent of the foreseeability of the risk; although the possibility of fulminating septicaemia was extremely rare, where the infection occurred in a maternity ward the consensus of the experts was that it should be treated. Also, the court considered the practicality of the precautions: penicillin was readily available and posed no danger to the patient's health. Bearing all this in mind the court decided that the precautions should have been taken; as they were not, Dr Cole was held to be negligent. It is worthwhile noting that at no time in their judgment did the court refer to the *Bolam* principle.

Hucks v Cole was cited in *Bolitho v City and Hackney Health Authority* [1993] 4 Med LR 381. This case is noteworthy for its application – wrongly, in our view – of the *Bolam* principle in the area of causation. But when referring to the judgment of Sachs LJ in *Hucks v Cole*, Dillon LJ said (at p 392) that the court could only reject medical opinion if, conscious of its own lack of knowledge and clinical experience, it was satisfied that 'the reasons of one group of doctors do not really stand up to analysis' and that the views of that group of doctors were *Wednesbury* unreasonable. On the one hand, this phrase adds nothing new to the debate – the courts have often intervened and rejected an accepted practice which no reasonable person would have followed. Taking into account Dillon LJ's statement that the court had to be cautious in view of their lack of clinical knowledge (a somewhat ambiguous phrase since the courts have no knowledge of plumbing or architecture but will readily rule their practices as unacceptable), we could assume that nothing has changed and that the courts will only depart from a medical opinion in the most exceptional cases. On the other hand, Dillon LJ could be suggesting that the courts should examine the expert evidence in relation to the facts and then reject it if they deem it unsatisfactory. If so, the courts are effectively substituting their own judgment for that of the medical profession and, according to cases such as *Maynard v West Midlands Regional Health Authority* [1984] 1 WLR 634, that is not allowed. In that case Lord Scarman said (at p 639):

> a judge's preference for one body of distinguished professional opinion to another also professionally distinguished is not sufficient to establish negligence in a practitioner whose actions have received the seal of approval of those whose opinions, truthfully expressed, honestly held, were not preferred.

In the *Bolitho* case, Farquharson LJ said that it was not enough for the defendant to call a number of experts to say that they would have acted in accordance with clinical practice; it is for the judge to consider the evidence and decide whether the patient was unnecessarily put at risk. To do this, Farquharson LJ would have had to look at the facts. However, he held that he was not required to do this in *Bolitho* because the trial judge had found that the defendant's expert evidence did constitute a reasonable body of medical opinion. Had the court investigated whether the practice put the plaintiff at risk it would have meant that the court was substituting its judgment for the medical opinion, and as a matter of law they should not do so. Why, if the medical opinion is thought of as wrong, can the judge not intervene? Naturally, any intervention should be made cautiously.

There have been some recent decisions by the lower ranks of the judiciary which may give hope to the luckless plaintiff's solicitor. In *Smith v Tunbridge Wells Health Authority* [1994] 5 Med LR 334, the court readily found the defendant negligent for failing to disclose a risk despite the fact that the defendant had acted in accordance with accepted practice. Morland J seemingly applied *dicta* from *Sidaway* and concluded that the plaintiff required the information to make an informed decision. It also seemed that, despite the fact the defendant had acted in accordance with accepted practice in not disclosing the risk, the judge could find no plausible reason for the risk not being disclosed; in other words, the defendant's conduct failed the risk/benefit analysis. He said (at p 339):

> In my judgment, by 1988, although some surgeons may still not have been warning patients similar in situation to the plaintiff of the risk of impotence, that omission was not reasonable nor responsible.

The implications of this decision are slowly being worked out but there appears to be no reason why it should be confined within any definite parameters, in other words, it should apply to any area of medical negligence. This is discussed further, at p 155. The following cases indicate that the tide could be beginning to turn. In *Gascoigne v Ian Sheridan & Co and Latham* [1994] 5 Med LR 437, Mitchell J held that a group of doctors giving similar evidence did not necessarily constitute an alternative school of thought of medical opinion, ie the fact that there are two schools of thought does not necessarily preclude any agreement being reached. In *Joyce v Merton and Sutton and Wandsworth Health Authority* [1995] 6 Med LR 60, Overend J, at first instance, pointed out that the medical practice must stand up to analysis in the light of knowledge at the time. He said (at p 64):

> ... in the field of diagnosis and treatment, a defendant is not guilty of negligence if his acts or omissions were in accordance with accepted clinical practice, provided that clinical practice stood up to analysis and was not unreasonable in the light of the state of medical knowledge at the time.

In reaching his conclusion, the judge referred to what he called the 'gloss on *Bolam*' and in particular, the cases of *Hucks*, *Bolitho* and *Maynard*. In his view, there was no inconsistency between *Maynard* and *Hucks* because:

> ... It is not enough for a defendant to call a number of doctors to say that what he had done or not done was in accord with accepted clinical practice. It is necessary for the judge to consider the evidence and decide whether that clinical practice puts the patient unnecessarily at risk. (At p 64.)

The Court of Appeal upheld in part the first instance decision. Commenting on the treatment of the evidence at first instance, Hobhouse LJ made some interesting observations (at p 17):

> ... the judge has fallen into error ... He has based his findings, not upon evidence regarding what actually occurred on the occasions in question but rather, upon criteria of subsequent reputation and how the witness impressed him at trial over seven years later. The scope for error in adopting this approach is particularly obvious where the person concerned was at the time in training and relatively inexperienced.

This statement has got to be good news for the plaintiff – evidence of accepted practice is useful but it cannot take precedence over the evidence of witnesses of what they actually did at the time nor contemporaneous documentary evidence.

There has also been some attempt to put a gloss on *Bolam* in the failed vasectomy/sterilisation cases. In *Newell & Newell v Goldenberg* [1995] 6 Med LR 371, the defendant attempted to rely on the *Bolam* test, in that a warning of the risk of the vasectomy failing was usual practice in 1985. He accepted, however, that normally he would have given a warning by sending the patient an information leaflet and it was simply an oversight that he did not do so on this occasion. Mantell J at [1995] 6 Med LR 371 said (at p 374):

> The *Bolam* principle provides a defence for those who lag behind the times. It cannot serve those who know better.

Finally, in *Lybert v Warrington Health Authority* [1996] 7 Med LR 71, the judge held that the warning given by the defendant was inadequate. The plaintiff had already been on a waiting list for a sterilisation operation but became pregnant with her third child. For each pregnancy she had to have a caesarian section – hence, she was anxious to avoid further pregnancies. She requested a hysterectomy after her third child but was told that this was not possible but that she could be sterilised. At no time previously had this possibility been discussed with her or her husband. There then was some dispute as to what warning, if any, was given to the plaintiff after the operation though the defendant maintained that he did warn her of the risk of conception and indeed, there was an entry in the notes to this effect. Despite this, the court found that the defendant was in breach, the warning should have been given orally and in writing, and should have been given before the plaintiff was admitted or before she agreed to the sterilisation or before she was discharged. The court, therefore, chose to apply a judicial standard as to what should have been done and not simply rely on the evidence.

With regard to the latter two cases, it may be that they signify the beginnings of a different rule for at least elective surgical procedures. In *Newell*, the court differentiated between an elective surgical procedure and one which is necessary in the interests of the patient. Where the procedure is an elective one, it may be that a warning must be given notwithstanding *Bolam*.

Perhaps the English judiciary are beginning to realise that there is life beyond *Bolam*; or are they perhaps at last taking notice of the inroads made into the *Bolam* principle by the Australian courts? In the case of *Rogers v Whittaker* [1993] 4 Med LR 79, the plaintiff, who was nearly blind in her right eye, developed an extremely rare condition in her left eye. After a routine checkup she was referred to the defendant for possible surgery. He advised that she should have surgery on the right eye to remove scar tissue which would improve its appearance and restore significant sight to the eye as well as hopefully prevent the onset of glaucoma. The plaintiff agreed to an operation on this eye. She did not ask whether the operation could cause damage to her 'good' eye. However, the evidence at the trial showed that she had questioned the defendant repeatedly as to any possible complications and was very concerned that her good eye could be injured. In fact, an entry had been made in the hospital notes indicating that the plaintiff was concerned that her 'good eye' would be operated on by mistake. Following the operation the plaintiff developed an inflammation in her treated eye which caused a condition, sympathetic ophthalmia, in her left (good) eye which resulted in almost a total loss of sight in this eye, consequently rendering her nearly blind. There was a one in 14,000 chance of this sympathetic ophthalmia developing, but this was not mentioned by the defendant. Had the defendant disclosed the risk, the plaintiff contended she would not have undergone the operation. She claimed the defendant had been negligent for failing to disclose the risk. The High Court of Australia ruled in her favour. It rejected the *Bolam* test and instead applied the test already entrenched in a number of Australian cases and endorsed the dissenting judgment of Lord Scarman in *Sidaway* (see p 42). Mason CJ, commenting on the standard of care said (at p 83):

> ... that standard is not determined solely or even primarily by reference to the practice followed or supported by a responsible body of opinion in the relevant profession or sphere ... Further ... in the field of non-disclosure of risk and the provision of advice and information, the *Bolam* principle has been discarded and instead, the courts have adopted the principle that, while evidence of acceptable medical practice is a useful guide for the courts, it is for the courts to adjudicate

on what is the appropriate standard of care after giving weight to 'the paramount consideration that a person is entitled to make his own decisions about his life'.

The Australian court consequently held that they would adjudicate on the appropriate standard of care and that evidence of accepted practice was a useful, but not conclusive, guide. In determining whether the defendant was in breach the factors it would consider would vary depending on whether it was a case concerning diagnosis, treatment, or the provision of information and advice. It refused to go the way of fully informed consent, as their American counterparts have done, but Mason CJ had this to say (at p 83) (see p 42):

> The law should recognise that a doctor has a duty to warn a patient of a material risk inherent in the proposed treatment; a risk is material if, in the circumstances of the particular case, a reasonable person in the patient's position, if warned of the risk, would be likely to attach significance to it or if the medical practitioner is or should reasonably be aware that a particular patient, if warned of the risk, would be likely to attach significance to it.

This is somewhat different to the English standard, for example, *Whitehouse v Jordan* [1981] 1 WLR 246 and *Sidaway v Board of Governors of the Bethlem Royal Hospital and the Maudsley Hospital* [1985] AC 871 which state that the *Bolam* test is appropriate to all stages of medical treatment, although we now suggest with the caveat that things might have changed since the decision in *Smith v Tunbridge Wells Health Authority* [1994] 5 Med LR 334, above.

Until the English courts unequivocally throw off their reserve, as the Australian courts have done, the concept of accepted practice lives on. It has to be said that the Australian judiciary have for some time used *Bolam* more as an evidential tool rather than a binding rule of law. Some might say that it is totally unrealistic to expect that a patient like Mrs Whittaker should be warned of such a remote risk, yet she had on several occasions expressed how important the risk was to her.

At present, the solicitor is stuck with *Bolam*, although there is nothing to be lost from trying to circumvent the *Bolam* rule in the hope that a member of the English judiciary will be tempted to follow their Australian colleagues. To do so, the plaintiff's solicitor can only rely on pre-*Bolam* case law, the minority of cases that have not followed *Bolam*, and foreign case law. However, on an optimistic note, we would encourage the solicitor to try this tack; not all members of the judiciary are blinded by *Bolam* and some might throw caution to the wind. It is up to solicitors to seek these rare individuals out and put the *Bolam* rule on its rightful footing.

REFERENCES

English case law

(1) Re Herald of Free Enterprise (1987) The Independent, 18 December

This case was appeal following the ferry disaster at Zeebrugge. Although the court agreed that it was common practice that masters did not check the bow doors to confirm that they were closed, there had been a failure to adopt the necessary precautions which were required for the safety of the ship.

(2) Edward Wong Finance Co Ltd v Johnson, Stokes and Master [1984] AC 296

Conveyancing practice in Hong Kong was held negligent despite the fact it was followed by other solicitors.

(3) Clarke v Adams (1950) 94 SJ 597

A physiotherapist was found negligent despite the fact that he had acted in accordance with the practice approved by the Chartered Society of Physiotherapists. The plaintiff was being treated for a fibrotic condition of the heel and was advised to indicate if he felt anything other than a comfortable warmth – the plaintiff suffered severe injury.

(4) Bolam v Friern Hospital Management Committee [1957] 1 WLR 582; [1957] 2 All ER 118

See p 121.

(5) Hucks v Cole [1993] 4 Med LR 393

See above, at p 140.

(6) Bolitho v City and Hackney Health Authority [1993] 4 Med LR 381

See p 196.

(7) Maynard v West Midlands Regional Health Authority [1984] 1 WLR 634; [1985] 1 All ER 635

See p 134.

(8) Smith v Tunbridge Wells Health Authority [1994] 5 Med LR 334

See p 155.

(9) Sidaway v Board of Governors of the Bethlem Royal Hospital and the Maudsley Hospital [1985] AC 871; [1985] 1 All ER 643

In a case about disclosure of information, Lord Bridge stated that the courts might depart from the standards set by the profession, where (at p 663):

> ... disclosure of a risk was so obviously necessary to an informed choice on the part of the patient that no reasonably prudent medical man would fail to make it.

Lord Templeman stated that it is (at p 665):

> ... for the courts to decide, after hearing the doctor's explanation, whether the doctor has in fact been guilty of a breach of duty with regard to information.

(10) Gascoigne v Ian Sheridan & Co (a firm) and Latham [1994] 5 Med LR 437

See above, at p 142.

(11) Joyce v Merton and Sutton and Wandsworth Health Authority [1996] 7 Med LR 1; [1995] 6 Med LR 60

See above, at p 142.

(12) Newell and Newell v Goldenberg [1995] 6 Med LR 371

See above, at p 142.

(13) Lybert v Warrington Health Authority [1996] 7 Med LR 71

See above, at p 142.

(14) Whitehouse v Jordan [1981] 1 WLR 246; [1981] 1 All ER 267

See p 124.

Foreign case law

AUSTRALIA

(1) Rogers v Whittaker [1993] 4 Med LR 79; [1992] 3 Med LR 331; (1992) 109 ALR 625

See p 143.

(2) Ellis v Wallsend District Hospital [1990] 2 Med LR 103; (1989) 70 NSW LR 553

The plaintiff had a background of intractable and severe neck pain, she was dependent on drugs and had overdosed. All other treatment had failed. She was advised to have a five nerve separation microsurgery. The evidence was that the operation carried a remote risk of paralysis but a more substantial risk that it would fail to cure the pain. The plaintiff contended that had she known of the risk then she would not have undergone the operation. Although the case failed on causation the court made some interesting comments re disclosure of risk. The judge at first instance, relying on Lord Scarman's dissent in *Sidaway v Board of Governors of the Bethlem Royal Hospital and the Maudsley Hospital* [1985] AC 871 and the judgment of King CJ in *F v R* (1983) 33 SASR 189, at p 192–94 held that the doctor was in breach of duty in failing to warn of the risk of paralysis and of failure to obtain relief from pain. This decision was not challenged on appeal.

As a result the defendant was found to be in breach of his duty to warn of the risks involved in the operation, despite medical evidence to the contrary in support of non-disclosure.

(3) F v R (1983) 33 SASR 189

The case concerned a failed tubal ligation. The plaintiff's husband had queried whether he should have a vasectomy instead. The plaintiff alleged that the defendant had been negligent for failing to warn of a less than 1% failure rate.

No alternatives were discussed with the patient as the operation was carried out at the same time as a caesarian section. Although the defendant was found not negligent the court had the following comments on the standard of care:

King CJ:

The ultimate question, however, is not whether the defendant's conduct accords with the practice of his profession or some part of it, but whether it conforms to the standard of reasonable care demanded by law. That is a question for the court and the duty of deciding it cannot be delegated to any profession or group in the community.

Per Bollen J:

... nothing in *Bolam* ... which justifies any suggestion that evidence of the practice obtaining in the medical profession is automatically decisive of any issue in an action ... for damages in negligence.

This case on first reading seems to make great inroads into the *Bolam* principle. However, it was uncertain as to the scope of the judgment, namely was it confined to the disclosure of information which was the issue here. See *Sidaway v Board of Governors of the Bethlem Royal Hospital and the Maudsley Hospital* [1985] AC 871 which also comments on the standard of care required for disclosure of information.

CANADA

(1) Anderson v Chasney (1949) 4 DLR 71

A surgeon was found negligent after leaving a sponge in the base of a child's nostrils following a tonsillectomy. His defence was that it was not his practice nor the hospitals practice to use sponges with ties on nor to keep a count of the number of sponges used.

Held:: complying with general practice does not constitute a complete defence. The court reasoned that if common/accepted practice was always a defence then a group of operators by adopting an accepted practice could avoid liability even if that practice was clearly negligent.

Note that this case pre-dates *Bolam.*

(2) Reibl v Hughes (1980)114 DLR (3d) 1

The defendant did not disclose the risk of a stroke resulting from surgery. The risk was rare and might not have affected the plaintiff's decision but for the fact that he was nearing retirement and would have been eligible for a full pension. The risk of the stroke was therefore very significant to him as he could not risk the loss of his pension, and consequently the court ruled that it should have been disclosed if a reasonable patient in the position of the plaintiff would not have undergone the operation.

This case is most known for its application of the doctrine of informed consent. With regard to disclosure of information this case emphasised that current medical practice is persuasive but not conclusive of the matter. If the court feels that practice is lacking in some respect then it may intervene.

See also Chapter 2, Consent, at p 44.

(3) Meyer Estates v Rogers [1991] 2 Med LR 370; [1991] 78 DLR (4th) 307; (1991) 6 CCLT (2d) 114

The Canadian Association of Radiologists specifically warned that a particular risk should not be disclosed for fear the patient would not consent (risk of death from the injection of a contrast dye, Hypaceque). The court rejected the defence of therapeutic privilege.

Held:: doctors had a duty of disclosure, the risk was material risk in accordance with *Reibl v Hughes.* (The risk was between 1 in 40,000 and 1 in 100,000.) The recommendation of the Canadian Association of Radiologists is in direct contravention to the standard required by *Reibl v Hughes.*

Practice points

See Commentary above for suggestions as to possible ways to circumvent the *Bolam* rule.

STANDARD OF CARE IN PARTICULAR INSTANCES

As discussed in the preceding paragraphs the same standard of care is applicable no matter what the stage, nature or context of medical treatment, namely the *Bolam* standard. However, for ease of reference the cases below are split into the following categories; diagnosis, treatment, disclosure of information, and prescriptions.

RULE 5(E)

A health carer may be held liable for a faulty diagnosis, etc.

Commentary

First a health carer may fail to consider the patient's medical history. A doctor is under an obligation to give the history his full consideration for obvious reasons, eg the patient may be allergic to a particular drug, be suffering from a pre-existing illness or may have had treatment for the condition previously. In any event common sense says that it is inherently dangerous to attempt to make a diagnosis without first considering the patient's medical records, and then asking him relevant questions (see *Cassidy v Ministry of Health* [1951] 2 KB 343). The doctor must listen to the patient's account of the illness, while being careful not to attach too much significance to the patient's self-diagnosis, eg the patient who says he has pains in his chest and that it is probably due to indigestion. The doctor must examine the patient and come to his own diagnosis.

An error in diagnosis will not necessarily amount to negligence (see *Whitehouse v Jordan* [1981] 1 WLR 246). The court will take into consideration the nature of the symptoms present (if any), the difficulty in making the diagnosis (see *Hulse v Wilson* (1953) 2 BMJ 890), what further tests may be appropriate and the actual steps required to make an accurate diagnosis, eg the use of diagnostic aids (see *Whiteford v Hunter* [1950] WN 553). A common area for mistaken diagnosis is in the area of fractures (see *Fraser v Vancouver General Hospital* (1951) 3 WWR 337 and *Hotson v East Berkshire* [1987] AC 750). It could be said that in all cases where there is a suspected fracture the defendant should avail himself of X-rays, bearing in mind such a precaution is readily available. In *Hucks v Cole* [1993] 4 Med LR 393, Sachs LJ said (at p 140) that where the precaution was readily available and relatively inexpensive then it would seem sensible that the defendant doctor should avail himself of it.

Another area which causes problems is the diagnosis of cancer. Breast cancer has been subject to a great deal of publicity and yet cases still arise of missed diagnosis (see *Judge v Huntingdon Health Authority* [1995] 6 Med LR 223). The problem here is that, notwithstanding the cancer, the breast itself often contains lumps and therefore an accurate diagnosis can often be difficult without an operation which the patient and the doctor may be loathe to undertake. In *Judge,* an experienced surgeon was convinced of the innocence of the lump even after the second referral. Delay in diagnosis of cancer often leads to another problem, namely how to estimate the damage to the patient's chance of survival, which is considered at p 182 *et seq.* Lack of physical signs of injury or illness is not of itself determinative of liability (see *Bova v Spring* [1994] 5 Med LR 120); what is important is the whole picture as presented by the facts.

Apart from the medical factors the court will have regard to the practicality and the expense of the precautions (see *Latimer v AEC Ltd* [1953] AC 643 and the discussion on p 123). However, the solicitor must always remember that the test is what a reasonable doctor would have done by reference to the *Bolam* test, ignoring the fact that the precaution may seem sensible to him and was readily available.

In some cases, the allegation of negligence is not that the diagnosis was incorrect but that the plaintiff's condition appeared so serious that the defendant should have referred the plaintiff to a specialist or, at the very least, carried out further tests (see *Dale v Munthali* (1976) 78 DLR (3d) 588, *Gordon v Wilson* [1992] 3 Med LR 401 and National Health Service (General Medical and Pharmaceutical Services) Regulations (SI 1974/160) (as amended)). The doctor is advised that where he suspects that the condition is more serious he must carry out further tests even though there is a viewpoint which suggests that the doctor could be sued for over testing. We suggest that such cases would be few and far between and that, in view of the consequences if the doctor failed to test, he should always err on the side of caution.

In determining whether the doctor has failed to reach the requisite standard of care, health carers would do well to bear in mind that diagnosis is an on going factor. A doctor who refuses to budge from his initial assessment of the plaintiff's condition, notwithstanding the patient's apparent deterioration, is at risk of being negligent (see *Stacey v Chiddy* [1993] 4 Med LR 345). At all stages, the treating doctor should be alert to the patient's response to the treatment prescribed and whether he has the expertise to continue to treat the patient, ie should the patient be referred to a specialist. In *Judge v Huntingdon HA* [1995] 6 Med LR 223, the court found the specialist at fault for failing to arrange with the plaintiff to see her again, taking into consideration that the plaintiff was adamant that the lump in her breast was painful and the letter of referral from her GP. GPs, however, usually see their patients over a long period of time; they should therefore continually be monitoring the patient's condition (see *Langley v Campbell* (1975) *The Times*, 6 November). Although the patient may have difficulty in establishing negligence after one visit to his GP, the greater the number of visits and the longer the time before the correct diagnosis is made, the more likely a negligence claim becomes. The moral for the defendant is: if the patient's symptoms persist, think twice. At the very least the health carer should make an accurate note of why he did not refer a patient to a specialist.

Having made the diagnosis that the patient has to be, eg referred to hospital, what if the hospital then fails to give the patient an appointment? Although the GP who made the referral would not be responsible for the hospital's failure, he would be liable for failing to make the hospital aware that the patient's condition was serious or had become so while waiting for the appointment (see *Coles v Reading and District Hospital Management Committee* (1963) 107 SJ 115).

Refer to Chapter 3, Duty, at p 69.

Finally, another area which has attracted media headlines is the number of incidences where patients have caught infections while in hospital, notably from blood transfusions (see *Re HIV Haemophiliac Litigation* (1990) 140 NLJ 1349 and *H v Royal Alexandra Hospital for Children* [1990] 1 Med LR 297). Whether the defendant is negligent will often turn on what he could have reasonably been expected to do at the time of the alleged incident, for example, in *ter Neuzen v Korn* (1993) 103 DLR (4th) 473, the question was whether the defendant should have known in 1985 that there was a risk of HIV infection from artificial insemination. For full details see p 133.

REFERENCES

English case law

(1) Cassidy v Ministry of Health [1951] 2 KB 343; [1951] 1 All ER 574

Hospital staff failed to listen to plaintiff's complaints of excessive pain, see further, at p 69.

See also *Payne v St Helier Group Hospital Management Committee* (1952) *The Times*, 12 November, where the plaintiff was admitted to casualty after being kicked by a horse. He was sent home and subsequently died. The casualty officer was found negligent in failing to examine the plaintiff.

See also *Barnett v Chelsea and Kensington Hospital Management Committee* [1969] 1 QB 420; [1968] 2 WLR 427 on the obligation of casualty officers.

(2) Whitehouse v Jordan [1981] 1 WLR 246; [1981] 1 All ER 267

Child suffered brain damage at birth as a result of the obstetrician's negligence in his use of forceps. In the Court of Appeal, Lord Denning expressed the opinion that a mere error of judgment did not amount to negligence. The House of Lords forcibly stated that whether or not the practitioner was negligent depended on if he had exercised reasonable care. It was held that he had, because the error was one that could have been made by any of his contemporaries.

(3) Hulse v Wilson (1953) 2 BMJ 890

Held: that it was not unreasonable on the part of the defendant not to diagnose cancer of the penis because it was so unusual in a man of the plaintiff's age.

See also *Thornton v Nicol* [1992] 3 Med LR 41 where the doctor diagnosed conjunctivitis but failed to diagnose meningitis. He failed to refer the patient (a baby) to hospital. Meningitis was diagnosed by a subsequent doctor; however, earlier diagnosis would have avoided the worst consequences. The earlier doctor was found not negligent – the patient did not appear so ill that the doctor should have immediately referred him to hospital.

(4) Whiteford v Hunter [1950] WN 553; 94 SJ 758

Availability of diagnostic aids, see p 136 and *Robinson v Post Office* [1974] 1 WLR 1176; [1974] 2 All ER 737.

(5) Hotson v East Berkshire Health Authority [1987] AC 750; [1987] 2 All ER 909

A young boy fell from a tree and hurt his leg. His Accident and Emergency Department failed to X-ray him and he was sent home. After several days he went back and a fracture of the femur was diagnosed. The plaintiff succeeded in showing that the failure to X-ray him on his first visit was negligent. The case later failed on causation (see p 182 *et seq*).

See also *Wood v Thurston* (1951) *The Times*, 5 May where the patient entered hospital in an intoxicated condition. He was allowed to go home and died the next day. It was revealed that he had several injuries. The defendant argued that the deceased's intoxicated condition had dulled his sensitivity to pain. The defendant was held liable for not examining the deceased thoroughly notwithstanding that he might have been misled by the deceased's intoxicated condition.

(6) Hucks v Cole [1993] 4 Med LR 393

See p 140.

(7) Judge v Huntingdon Health Authority [1995] 6 Med LR 223

See Chapter 6, Causation, at p 186.

(8) Bova v Spring [1994] 5 Med LR 120

The plaintiff had been moving concrete and had developed pains in his chest. A week later his GP was called. The plaintiff complained of diarrhoea, breathlessness and of feeling shivery, and also of increased pain on movement. The GP diagnosed a muscular strain and attributed the other symptoms to a virus infection. He did not arrange a further appointment. The plaintiff collapsed and died two days later. The cause of death was suppurative lobar pneumonia.

The defendant GP was accused of negligence in that he did not arrange a follow-up appointment. Expert evidence indicated that had the plaintiff been examined the following day his condition would have indicated that urgent treatment was required.

Held:: the defendant had been negligent in failing to arrange a follow-up appointment.

See also *Sutton v Population Services Family Planning Programme Ltd* (1981) *The Times*, 7 November which involved a failure to follow up a diagnosis of cancer. For a detailed commentary, see Chapter 6, Causation, at p 186.

Other cases involving the diagnosis of cancer include: *Phillips v Grampian Hospital Board* [1991] 3 Med LR 16; *Gascoine v Ian Sheridan & Co and Latham* [1994] 5 Med LR 437; *Judge v Huntingdon Health Authority* [1995] 6 Med LR 223 and *Stacey v Chiddy* [1993] 4 Med LR 216.

In *Sa'ad v Robinson* [1989] 1 Med LR 41, a GP was held negligent for failing to refer to hospital a child who had sucked hot tea from a teapot. The GP had merely prescribed some medication to soothe the child. The child's mother telephoned the surgery some hours later and reiterated her child's symptoms. The duty doctor instructed that the child should be propped up with pillows, but he did not visit the child. Eventually the duty doctor was called to the house and the child was admitted to hospital onto the paediatric ward and later referred to casualty where she had an anoxic fit and suffered irreversible brain damage.

The court ruled that the GP was negligent in failing to realise that in sucking tea from a hot spout the child might have inhaled steam which could reach her throat directly without burning her mouth. The duty doctor was also found negligent in failing to visit the child immediately and for not admitting the child to casualty, or emphasising the seriousness of her condition.

(9) Latimer v AEC Ltd [1953] AC 643

See r 5(A), at p 123.

(10) Bolam v Friern Hospital Management Committee [1957] 1 WLR 582

See r 5(A), at p 121.

(11) Gordon v Wilson [1992] 3 Med LR 401

The plaintiff had visited her GP on several occasions complaining of deafness and difficulties with balance, and that her vision was impaired, and she found eating and drinking difficult. She was eventually referred to a specialist who removed a benign melanoma from her brain. She sued the GP alleging that her symptoms were such that she should have been referred at an earlier stage. The court accepted that her combination of symptoms should have prompted her GP to refer her to a specialist at an early stage.

See also *Chin Keow v Government of Malaysia* [1967] 1 WLR 813 (failure to inquire into family history–inquiry would have revealed that the plaintiff was allergic to penicillin – patient died from an allergic reaction to the drug); *Gardiner v Mountford* [1989] 1 Med LR 205 (doctor failed to listen to the patient's suggestion that she could be pregnant).

(12) Langley v Campbell (1975) The The Times, 6 November

This case concerned a failure to diagnose malaria. The GP diagnosed the patient as having influenza.

Held:: although the GP did not routinely come across malaria, the fact that the plaintiff's symptoms persisted and that the plaintiff had recently returned from Uganda, coupled with the fact that his family had told the GP that the plaintiff had suffered from malaria previously and had himself suggested blood tests, should have alerted the GP that he might be dealing with a tropical disease.

See also *Meyer v Gordon* (1981) 17 CCLT 1 (failure to consider the patient's previous obstetric history which would have revealed that the patient's previous labour was rapid).

(13) Coles v Reading and District Hospital Management Committee (1963) 107 SJ 115

The deceased suffered a finger injury and went to the local cottage hospital for treatment. He was advised to go to the main hospital for a tetanus injection but failed to do and instead visited his GP. His GP failed to inquire what treatment the patient had undergone at a cottage hospital. The patient died of toxaemia, neither the treating hospital nor the GP gave the patient a tetanus injection. The cottage hospital was found negligent in failing to communicate the plaintiff's symptoms, and the GP for not inquiring what treatment the plaintiff had received and for not contacting the cottage hospital.

(14) Re HIV Haemophiliac Litigation (1990) 140 NLJ 1349

See p 136.

Foreign case law

AUSTRALIA

(1) Stacey v Chiddy [1993] 4 Med LR 216, affirmed [1993] 4 Med LR 345

The plaintiff visited her GP after finding two lumps in her breast. The GP arranged a mammogram and an ultra sound scan which gave normal results, but did not confirm that the lumps were cystic. The plaintiff reattended her GP on several occasions. However, he failed to re-examine her breasts for lumps and relied on the inconclusive ultrasound scan. Eventually the plaintiff was referred to a specialist where it was established that the cancer had spread to her spine. In the New South Wales Supreme Court the GP was held negligent for placing too much reliance on inconclusive results and for failing to re-examine the plaintiff. The court held that although the defendant had not acted irresponsibly with his advice he should have taken into consideration the magnitude of the risk to which the appellant was exposed if the diagnosis was incorrect. The action failed on causation.

(2) Giurelli v Girgus (1980) 24 SASR 261

A doctor failed to listen to the patient complaints about persistent pain, claiming that the patient was difficult.

(3) H v Royal Alexandra Hospital for Children [1990] 1 Med LR 29

See p 136.

CANADA

(1) Dale v Munthali (1976) 78 DLR (3d) 588

The plaintiff complained of aching all over and later developed diarrhoea and began vomiting. He also had difficulty in hearing. The plaintiff was diagnosed as suffering from influenza. The plaintiff's condition deteriorated over the next two days and he was admitted to hospital where meningitis was diagnosed. The plaintiff later died.

Held:: the defendant GP was not negligent for failing to diagnose meningitis, but the plaintiff's symptoms were so severe that he should have carried out further tests.

(2) Layden v Cope (1984) 28 CCLT 140

The plaintiff had a history of gout. He complained of a sore foot and the GP diagnosed gout. The plaintiff's condition deteriorated but the doctor continued the treatment for gout. He was eventually diagnosed as having blood poisoning which resulted in his leg being amputated below the knee.

Held:: the defendant was negligent in failing to revise his initial diagnosis in the light of the plaintiff's deterioration.

(3) ter Neuzen v Korn (1993) 103 DLR (4th) 473

See p 137.

Statutes / statutory instruments

NATIONAL HEALTH SERVICE (GENERAL MEDICAL AND PHARMACEUTICAL SERVICES) REGULATIONS (SI 1974/160) (as amended) and NATIONAL HEALTH SERVICE (SCOTLAND) (GENERAL MEDICAL AND PHARMACEUTICAL SERVICES) REGULATIONS (SI 1974/506)

These regulations apply to NHS patients and provide for GPs terms of service to include a condition that they must give to their patients 'all necessary and appropriate personal medical services of the type usually provided by general medical practitioners including arranging for the referral of patients as necessary to any other services provided under the Health Services Acts.

RULE 5(F)

A health carer may be held liable for failing to disclose to the patient the risks associated with the treatment.

Commentary

All medical treatment will involve some side effects and/or risks, ranging from the trivial to the not so trivial. Consequently in treating a patient two things need to be borne in mind:

(1) what are chances of the side effects/risks occurring and are they reasonably foreseeable; and

(2) what are the consequences of those side effects?

Those issues will have a direct bearing on the nature of information to be imparted to the patient prior to the treatment being undertaken. At the same time, this information itself could depend on such things as the treatment involved and the characteristics of the particular plaintiff (see *Blyth v Bloomsbury Health Authority* [1993] 4 Med LR 151 and *Chatterton v Gerson* [1981] QB 432). The general rule is that disclosure of risks is governed by the *Bolam* rule, *viz* the health carer need only disclose what would have been disclosed by similarly qualified people in similar circumstances. Attempts to introduce the American concept of informed consent (see further, at p 42) have so far met with little success except in the judgment of Lord Scarman in the *Sidaway* case (see p 42).

Where the plaintiff claims that he was not given sufficient information about the procedure then, technically, he may be able to claim in either battery or negligence. In *Hills v Potter* [1984] 1 WLR 641, the court held that where there was a lack of information as to the nature of the procedure the claim should be brought in battery, but where the claim was based on the failure of the doctor to disclose the risks inherent in the procedure the claim should be brought in negligence. While this distinction appears to be clear and firmly entrenched (see, for example, *Sidaway*), it is not without its problems. For example, it has been said that some inherent risks are so significant that they go to the very nature of the procedure. Our advice to the doctor is that where the risk is common, even if it is trivial, then it should be disclosed. However, where it is not certain how serious the risk could be the issue is more problematical. One approach would be to instruct the patient to return if certain symptoms appear; in that case if the patient fails to return he could be regarded as contributorily negligent (see further, at p 200).

If the consent is induced by fraud or misrepresentation it will be invalid. However, for a claim in negligence, it does not really matter why the risks have not been disclosed; what matters is that they have not been disclosed and that, if they had been, the patient would not have consented to the procedure. This latter point is crucial; many claims fail because the plaintiff is unable to show that, even if disclosure had taken place, he would not have consented to the procedure (see *Goorkani v Tayside Health Board* [1991] 3 Med LR 33, and p 176). Where the doctor lies to the patient in response to a question he may be able to escape liability if he can rely on the defence of therapeutic privilege or show that other doctors would have done the same.

The leading authority on disclosure of information is *Sidaway v Board of Governors of Bethlem Royal Hospital and the Maudsley Hospital* [1985] AC 871. The plaintiff underwent an operation on her spine to relieve pressure on one of the nerve roots. Unfortunately, during the operation her spinal cord was damaged leaving her disabled. The neurosurgeon had told her about the risk of damage to the nerve root (a risk of about 2%) but had not told her about damage to the spinal cord (a risk of 1%). There was no evidence that the operation had been carried out negligently. The plaintiff, however, argued that the defendant had been negligent in not telling her of the risk of damage to the spinal cord. The claim failed. The court said that it was a matter for the doctor's clinical judgment which risks should be disclosed to enable the patient to make a rational decision. This case demonstrates how much English courts favour the medical profession as the body to determine the level of information to be disclosed as opposed to the 'what would the patient need to know' approach canvassed in *Rogers v Whittaker* [1993] 4 Med LR 79.

Real innovations with regard to the standard of disclosure have been in other jurisdictions. In *Rogers v Whittaker* [1993] 4 Med LR 79, the court held that the *Bolam* test was inappropriate to cases concerning disclosure of information. What was important was whether the risk was material and, if the answer to that question was yes, then that risk should be disclosed. A risk was material if a person in the position of the plaintiff, when warned, would deem it significant or if the medical practitioner would know that if the plaintiff was warned of this particular risk he would attach significance to it. With such an approach the court is not really applying the doctrine of informed consent; it is simply saying that the risk of sympathetic ophthalmia was a risk that the plaintiff should have been informed about in order to make a reasoned decision about the procedure. The fact that the plaintiff had repeatedly questioned the defendant regarding the procedure and whether there was any incidental risk to her good left eye was significant. In making this decision the court departed from the previously established view that asking questions made no difference in determining the standard of care. See, for example, *Blyth v Bloomsbury Health Authority* [1993] 4 Med LR 151 where Kerr LJ said (at p 157):

> The question of what a plaintiff should be told in answer to a general enquiry cannot be divorced from the *Bolam* test, any more than when no such enquiry is made ... Indeed, I am not convinced that the *Bolam* test is irrelevant even in relation to what answers are properly to be given to specific enquiries ...

The court in *Rogers* rightly held that the question was not whether the defendant's conduct was in accordance with accepted practice, but whether the defendant had met the standard of care required by law which was a question to be determined by the court; see, however, the recent cases discussed at r 5D which perhaps indicate that finally the English courts are moving towards this approach. It then went on to distinguish between cases concerning diagnosis and treatment and the present one. In the former, the professional standards of the time would have a large part to play in determining whether the defendant was in breach; however, in cases concerning the apparent failure to disclose information, they were not really about what was accepted practice except for those instances where therapeutic privilege were involved. What was important was whether the defendant communicated the relevant information to enable the plaintiff to make an informed decision. In *Rogers*, the plaintiff expressed concern about the possible danger to her one good eye and therefore that risk was material; however, there was a body of medical opinion which held that the defendant should only have revealed information about damage to the plaintiff's good eye if the latter had specifically asked about damage to her good eye. This was held to be untenable as this would in effect require the plaintiff to have specific knowledge of medical matters (see *Hollis v Dow Corning Corpn* (1993) 103 DLR 520, at p 339).

One decision from which the solicitor for the plaintiff may take heart is *Smith v Tunbridge Wells Health Authority* [1994] 5 Med LR 334. Morland J said (at p 339):

> When recommending a particular type of surgery or treatment, the doctor, when warning of the risks, must take reasonable care to ensure that his explanation of the risks is intelligible to this particular patient. The doctor should use language, simple but not misleading, which the doctor perceives from what knowledge and acquaintanceship that he may have of the patient (which may be slight), will be understood by the patient so that the patient can make an informed decision as to whether or not to consent to the recommended surgery or treatment.

This is an interesting comment. The judge is stressing that the doctor's duty is not simply to provide adequate information but also that the information must be intelligible; and whether it will be intelligible will be determined by the characteristics of the particular patient. At present the doctor, in his opinion, must reasonably believe that the information is understood by the patient.

In addition to warning about risks before treatment, the doctor also has a duty to inform the patient if something goes wrong. It would seem to be the rule that whether or not the doctor decides to tell the patient what has been done to him will still be a matter of clinical discretion and as such determined by the *Bolam* test. However, given the current trend that a patient does have a right to know and the general importance attached to patients' rights as evidenced by the Patients' Charter, it would seem likely that a court would hold that a doctor who failed to disclose a medical error had not met the required standard of care. In some instances, the health carer may be able to rely on the defence of therapeutic privilege; however, although this concept has been widely accepted by American courts, it has been soundly rejected by other jurisdictions, notably Canada, where it was held that it could not be used as an excuse for non-disclosure (see *Meyer Estate v Rogers* [1991] 78 DLR (4th) 307). An important point to bear in mind is that many medical negligence cases will fail on the issue of causation; therefore if the damage has already occurred then the plaintiff's ignorance through non-disclosure will be immaterial. In Canada, the test is that of materiality (see *Reibl v Hughes* (1980) 114 DLR (3d) 1), namely that if an error would be material to a patient, then disclosure must be made.

One notable decision on non-disclosure of an error is the Canadian case of *Stamos v Davies* (1985) 21 DLR 4th 507. In that case, the plaintiff was to have a biopsy of the lung. Unfortunately in error, the biopsy tissue that was obtained was not of the lung but of the spleen which resulted in the spleen being removed. The plaintiff was not informed of the mistake and the court found that the physician had breached his duty to disclose. However, the plaintiff's case failed because he was unable to show a causal connection between the loss of the spleen and the fact that the physician did not tell him that his spleen had been injured. In *Kueper v McMullin* (1986) 37 CCLT 318, a dentist performing a root canal left a piece of the drill bit in the plaintiff's mouth. Although aware of the error he left the bit in place and simply filled the tooth. Eventually X-rays taken by another dentist revealed the drill bit. The court was faced with the issue as to whether the dentist should have disclosed the error. The question they asked was: what would a reasonable patient choose to do, knowing that the drill bit was there and that there was only a minimal risk if it was left alone. The court held that the reasonable patient would have left it there; consequently, the defendant was not liable for non-disclosure.

The plaintiff may take a risk or follow a certain type of lifestyle that he would not otherwise have done had the risk been disclosed. In *Gregory v Pembrokeshire Health Authority* [1989] 1 Med LR 81, the patient was never informed that an amniocentesis test had failed to elicit a result. After giving birth to a Down's Syndrome child, she alleged that, if she had been informed, then she would have undergone a second test, and if that proved positive, had an abortion. The case failed because on the evidence it appeared that she would not have had a second test so late on in the pregnancy in accordance with the doctor's advice.

Whether or not a person would have asked the health carers to do something different or refused further treatment or asked for further tests should be regarded as immaterial in determining whether a medical error ought to have been disclosed. By his inadvertence the health carer has created the dilemma/risk/injury; therefore he should be accountable for his actions. Is this too harsh an approach? Not if there is no other way of ensuring unrestricted flow of information is maintained. In the United States, this principle has been adopted in some cases where the court's reasoning is that the health care provider, rather than 'the individual consumer who is entirely without fault,' should legally bear the consequences. In our opinion, if disclosure is not made, it should be assumed that the health care professional will assume responsibility for anything that does go wrong.

A health carer has a duty to liaise with other health professionals; indeed it is one of the exceptions to the strict confidentiality rule (see p 16). The most obvious case of communication is between the hospital and the GP who has referred the patient to the hospital's outpatient department. The duty demands that the referral letter should be sufficiently detailed for the specialist to be fully familiar with the facts. Initially, the GP may choose to telephone the hospital but this should be followed up by a letter. If the letter is found to be inadequate the question becomes one of whether the hospital's treatment would have been different if the correct information had been communicated.

The patient who has attended a hospital will be given a letter indicating the treatment received which he is then required to take to his GP or another hospital if he is to receive further treatment. What if he does not do this? If the treatment is not yet complete, it should be stressed to him that he must seek further treatment; if there is a danger that he may suffer further injury after discharge, a method by which the patient can contact the treating doctor should be put in place. Is it enough to tell the patient in very strong terms in an attempt to transfer the onus to the patient? What if the patient lives on his own? Is there an obligation to check up on the patient? What if the patient cannot contact the relevant health carer and, in his ignorance, decides not to pursue his enquiry? The extent of this obligation is still, in our opinion, to be clarified. In *Coles v Reading and District Hospital Management Committee* (1963) 107 SJ 115, the patient was not given any document to place before either another hospital or his GP; neither did the GP make any enquiry as to what treatment he had received at the hospital. As a result, the plaintiff was not given a tetanus injection and subsequently died. Both the hospital and the GP were found liable for lack of communication.

If it is alleged that the doctor failed to discharge his responsibility with regard to a follow-up the plaintiff will have to establish that a further appointment would have made a difference. Causation is considered in greater detail in Chapter 6, but for the present it is sufficient to say that the plaintiff will have to show that:

(1) if there had been a follow-up the treatment he received would have been different; and

(2) if he had been contacted for a follow-up his prognosis would have been significantly more optimistic.

Within the hospital itself there must be an adequate system of communication between the various professional groups; likewise there must be a good system of communication between the GP and his employees. There has been an obvious welcome trend to place more emphasis on the role of the nurse/employee; they are not blindly to follow orders but should question matters where they fear for the patient's safety. One area where a GP has to be extremely careful is in the writing of his prescriptions. In *Prendergast v Sam and Dee Ltd* [1989] 1 Med LR 36, a GP was found liable in part when a pharmacist misread his prescription with fatal results for the patient.

The doctor has a duty to give appropriate instructions to his patient. In some cases, this may simply amount to a warning that should symptoms persist he should return to the surgery or instructions as to the dosage and frequency of the medication. Whatever the instructions the doctor must reasonably be convinced that the patient understands these instructions.

REFERENCES

English case law

(1) Blyth v Bloomsbury Health Authority (1987) reported at [1993] 4 Med LR 151; (1989) 5 PN 169

See p 43.

(2) Chatterton v Gerson [1981] QB 432; [1981] 1 All ER 257

The plaintiff was suffering from severe pain. She was injected once near the spinal cord to destroy nerve fibres, but the pain returned. She consented to a further injection which resulted in numbness to her leg. The defendant had indicated that the procedure might involve temporary numbness and the court held that it was sufficient 'that a patient need only be informed in broad terms of the nature of the procedure'.

(3) Bolam v Friern Hospital Management Committee [1957] 1 WLR 582; [1957] 2 All ER 118

See r 5(A), at p 121.

(4) Sidaway v Board of Governors of the Bethlem Royal Hospital and the Maudsley Hospital [1985] AC 871; [1985] 1 All ER 643

See above, at p 154.

See also *McAllister v Lewisham and North Southwark Health Authority* [1994] 5 Med LR 343 which involved a plaintiff suffering from a serious neurological condition. The defendant advised an operation which carried a 20% chance that the condition of her leg would deteriorate, but failed to inform her that the risk also applied to her arm. The said risk materialised.

Held:: although the decision to operate was not negligent, applying *Sidaway*, the defendant was in breach for failing to disclose adequate information.

(5) Hills v Potter [1984] 1 WLR 641; [1983] 3 All ER 716

The plaintiff was left paralysed after an operation on her neck. This was an inherent risk which the defendant had not disclosed, however, he was deemed to have acted in accordance with the *Bolam* standard.

(6) Goorkani v Tayside Health Board [1991] 3 Med LR 33

The patient was diagnosed as suffering from Behcet disease. By 1981, he had lost the sight in one eye. After other treatment failing he was eventually given Chlorambucil which was successful in the treatment of the eye but had the side effect of rendering the patient infertile.

The defendant was found negligent after failing to warn of the risks of infertility which was a known side effect from the long term use of the drug Chlorambucil. The court ruled that the defendant had failed to exercise what skill he had with reasonable care and diligence. Interestingly, the court held that it was not concerned with what was accepted practice.

The case later failed on causation because the pursuer had not proved that had the discussion taken place the outcome would be any different (see generally Chapter 6, Causation, at p 176 *et seq*).

(7) Smith v Tunbridge Wells Health Authority [1994] 5 Med LR 334

See above, at p 155.

(8) Gregory v Pembrokeshire Health Authority [1989] 1 Med LR 81

See above, at p 156.

(9) Coles v Reading and District Hospital Management Committee (1963) 107 SJ 115

See p 157.

(10) Prendergast v Sam and Dee Ltd [1989] 1 Med LR 36

The plaintiff was prescribed amoxil tablets for asthma. The pharmacist misinterpreted the prescription and prescribed daonil. The plaintiff suffered brain damage.

Held::

- the GP was negligent for failing to write clearly;
- the pharmacist was negligent for blindly following the prescription (he prescribed 21 tablets of 250 mg strength instead of the usual 100 tablets of five mg strength).

Foreign case law

AUSTRALIA

Rogers v Whittaker [1993] 4 Med LR 79; [1992] 3 Med LR 331; (1992) 109 ALR 625

See p 154.

CANADA

(1) Hollis v Dow Corning Corporation (1993) 103 DLR (4th) 520

The plaintiff had implants manufactured by the defendant company inserted surgically into her breasts. The implants later ruptured. The plaintiff sued the surgeon for failing to warn her of the risk of rupture.

Held:: as the risk of rupture was well known at the time of the plaintiff's surgery, albeit the risk was comparatively rare, the doctor had a duty to disclose. The company too had a duty to disclose the risks of rupture which were well known to it and could not rely on the medical profession to disclose the risks for them. Consequently, both the doctor and manufacturing company were liable.

(2) Meyer Estates v Rogers [1991] 78 DLR (4th) 307; [1991] 2 Med LR 370

The plaintiff was suffering from an urinary tract problem and consented to an operation, an IVP (intravenous pyelogram) which was a diagnostic procedure. During the course of the operation a dye, hypaque, was administered to the patient which caused an allergic reaction resulting in death. (The case ultimately failed on causation.)

The Canadian Association of Radiologists divided procedures into high and low risk. For a high risk procedure a full informed consent was required, for a low risk procedure such as IVP the association felt that the risks associated with fully informing the patient outweighed the risk of not informing the patient.

Held:: this position contravened the standard as required by *Reibl v Hughes* (1980) 114 DLR (3d) 1 which held that for a patient's consent to be informed all material risks should be disclosed and hence the risk of death was a material risk.

The court went on to reject the defence of therapeutic privilege quoting the judgment of Lord Scarman in *Sidaway* holding that the defence only relates to psychological harm to the patient.

(3) Reibl v Hughes (1980) 114 DLR (3d) 1

See pp 156, 177.

(4) Stamos v Davies (1985) 21 DLR (4th) 507

See above, at p 156.

(5) Kueper v McMullin (1986) 37 CCLT 318

See above, at p 156.

Professional / ethical guidelines

The GMC publication 'Good Medical Practice' (paras 34–36) gives advice for referring patients between GPs and specialists. Generally, the GP has an obligation to give the specialist all relevant information about the patient's history and current condition; the specialist in turn has a duty to provide the GP with details of the care he provided. Normally, the specialist should not accept the patient without a referral from the GP. However, if he does, then he should inform the patient's GP before embarking on treatment unless the patient requests him not to or the patient has no GP. In such cases the specialist will be responsible for the patient's aftercare.

These guidelines are persuasive only; as yet they have no legal status.

RULE 5(G)

The health carer may be held liable for errors in treatment, etc.

Commentary

An error in treatment, eg prescribing the wrong drug is not of itself negligence (see *Whitehouse v Jordan* [1981] 1 WLR 246). Again, it is not necessarily negligent to depart from accepted treatment; the defendant may have had very good reasons for not following what is commonly regarded as the norm (see r 5(C), at p 138).

Many medical people, and different branches of the profession may be involved in the treatment. All the NHS patient has to show is that someone involved in his treatment did something wrong; the hospital will then be vicariously liable. However, where the patient is being treated privately it will be important to ascertain what went wrong and exactly who was at fault it could be the surgeon or it could be a lack of facilities of the private hospital, etc. If a member of the treatment team is at fault he cannot hide behind his superior's instructions; if in doubt the instructions should be queried (see *Collins v Hertfordshire County Council* [1947] 1 KB 598 and see r 5(A) and the discussion of the relationship between junior doctors and their more senior colleagues, at p 124).

A number of cases have arisen where the claim is that during the course of the treatment something was left in the patient, eg a needle or swabs. Generally, if the defendant did not avail himself of the usual precautions that could be taken such as using swabs with tapes, holding a count, and checking the patient before closing, it is likely the court will find him negligent. The two most well known swab cases are *Anderson v Chasney* (1949) 4 DLR 71 and *Mahon v Osborne* [1939] 2 KB 14. In *Anderson*, a child died after a sponge was left in the base of his nostrils following an operation on his tonsils. The defendant was found negligent for failing to adopt the simple precaution of attaching tapes to the sponge. (*Note* this was in spite of the fact that the defendant had followed the hospital's accepted practice.) However, in *Mahon*, the surgeon was found not negligent for leaving a swab inside a patient. The judge directed the jury that they should consider that this had been an emergency operation and that the surgeon had been anxious to conclude the operation. However, it is suggested that this case would be unlikely to be followed now.

REFERENCES

English case law

(1) Whitehouse v Jordan [1981] 1 WLR 246; [1981] 1 All ER 267

See r 5(A) and p 150.

(2) Bolam v Friern Hospital Management Committee [1957] 1 WLR 582; [1957] 2 All ER 118

See r 5(A), at p 121.

(3) Collins v Hertfordshire County Council [1947] 1 KB 598

Junior medical officer misheard an instruction to supply procaine as cocaine. The pharmacist at the hospital did not question the unusual dosage and the surgeon did not check.

Held:: the surgeon, medical officer and hospital were all liable.

(4) Mahon v Osborne [1939] 2 KB 14

See above and p 189.

Foreign case law

CANADA

Anderson v Chasney [1949] 4 DLR 71

See p 146.

RULE 5(H)

A health carer may be liable for faulty prescribing.

Commentary

Here a defendant could be negligent in a number of ways:

(1) failing to appreciate the possible side effects of the prescribed drug;

(2) prescribing the wrong drug or giving the wrong dosage;

(3) writing a prescription illegibly.

The defendant can escape liability if he has acted in accordance with the *Bolam* test. In prescribing drugs a doctor has a duty to pay heed to any instructions given by the manufacturer. The manufacturer will not normally be liable if the drugs have a written warning: that will discharge his liability.

There have been a number of recent cases where the plaintiff has alleged that they 'woke up' in the middle of an operation primarily due to failure of the anaesthetist to administer the correct dosage of anaesthetic (see *Ludlow v Swindon Health Authority* [1989] 1 Med LR 104 and *Taylor v Worcester and District Health Authority* [1991] 2 Med LR 215). If the evidence shows there was consciousness at the relevant time, then the issue again turns on the *Bolam* rule.

REFERENCES

English case law

(1) Ludlow v Swindon Health Authority [1989] 1 Med LR 104

See Chapter 6, Causation, at p 189.

(2) Taylor v Worcester and District Health Authority [1991] 2 Med LR 215

The plaintiff alleged that she was awake during a caesarian operation and she experienced intense pain and terror. The action failed because the court could not find that the anaesthetic technique did not depart from accepted practice. Even if it had been proved that the plaintiff had been awake during the operation the defendant would not have been negligent.

(3) Bolam v Friern Hospital Management Committee [1957] 1 WLR 582; [1957] 2 All ER 118

See r 5(A), at p 121.

RULE 5(I)

The defendant health authority may be directly liable to the patient on the ground that it failed to provide reasonable care and treatment.

Commentary

The final area to be considered is where the negligence claim is targeted at the organisation and/or administration of the hospital. Such claims are canvassed as direct liability claims against the hospital, as opposed to vicarious liability. In practice, it does not matter whether the hospital is vicariously or directly liable, the damages will be the same in both cases. The main hurdle in bringing a direct liability claim is that it often brings into focus the level of resources both personal and physical and in these matters the court is exceedingly reluctant to intervene, seeing them as administrative matters. In *Wilsher*, the court suggested that where a hospital failed to provide doctors with sufficient skill and care, the hospital may be directly liable to the patient. This statement was taken one step further in the case of *Bull and another v Devon Area Health Authority* [1993] 4 Med LR 117 where the health authority was held liable for not having an adequate system to cater for an obstetric emergency. Devon Health Authority had argued that their levels of staffing were no different to any other hospital in the vicinity; the court was unimpressed with this argument, although it did acknowledge that these matters may raise important issues of social policy which the court might have to address. In fact, the courts have had to question social policy in two recent cases, the first involving hole in the heart babies and delays in their treatment and the second concerning the question of an expensive treatment for leukaemia for a child, and in both the plaintiffs lost. These social policy cases can be distinguished from *Bull*, in that in those cases the negligence is in failing to provide the service, whereas in *Bull* it was failing to carry out an already existing service properly. Only in the latter cases are the courts tempted to intervene. See further Chapter 3, Duty, at p 69.

REFERENCES

English case law

(1) Wilsher v Essex Area Health Authority [1988] 1 All ER 871; [1988] 2 WLR 557; [1986] 3 All ER 801

See p 124.

(2) Bull and another v Devon Area Health Authority [1993] 4 Med LR 117

See Chapter 3, Duty, at p 69. During the delivery of twins, it was alleged that there was a delay and inadequate supervision. On appeal, the Court of Appeal held that the health authority were in breach of duty to the plaintiff. Such breach of duty had to be decided according to the standards prevailing in 1970. The health authority had failed to discharge the evidential burden of justifying why the registrar or consultant did not attend. *Note*, however, that the trial judge had erred in holding that it was incumbent on the defendant to ensure that assistance was readily available.

(3) R v Secretary of State for Social Services ex parte Hincks (1979) 123 SJ 436

(4) R v Central Birmingham Health Authority ex parte Walker (1987) 3 BMLR 32; The Times, 26 November 1987

In both these cases, the parents of the children concerned failed in their applications for judicial review. The parents contended that the hospitals concerned should provide the necessary facilities to enable heart surgery to be carried out on their respective children. The court held that it would not intervene in questions of the allocation of resources.

(5) R v Cambridge Health Authority ex parte B (a Minor) [1995] 6 Med LR 250

B, a child aged 10½ was originally suffering from non-Hodgkins lymphoma with common acute lymphoblastic leukemia in 1990. At first, the treatment seemed successful but in 1993 she developed myeloid leukemia. She underwent chemotherapy, total body irradiation and a bone marrow transplant and the disease went into remission, but she suffered a further relapse in January 1995. She was given six to eight weeks to live, no further treatment was deemed appropriate by the doctors who were treating her. B's father, however, found two medical experts who were prepared to treat B, the treatment costing £75,000. B's health authority refused to fund the further treatment. The chances of the treatment being successful was estimated at 10–20% for the chemotherapy and then if a successful remission was achieved, 10–20% chance of a successful bone marrow transplant.

The Court of Appeal held that it was not for it to decide how the defendant's health authority limited budget should be allocated. The court found that the defendant's health authority had acted reasonably, taking into consideration the chances of the proposed treatment being successful, and the suffering it would cause to B.

GENERAL PRACTICE POINTS – RULES 5(A)–(I)

It is assumed at this stage that the solicitor will have identified the parties likely to be at fault, obtained the medical records, etc and is therefore ready to choose his medical expert to evaluate whether or not the defendant fell below the required standard of care.

Choosing your expert

The right expert can make or break your case.

DO NOT USE ANYONE:

- who is involved in the case;
- who works at the same defendant hospital/health authority/Trust;
- who works in the same area;
- simply because you have used him before (attitudes change);
- who is already treating the client – they may have an unduly optimistic opinion of how the treatment is progressing, and could be unduly critical of the patient, thus ruining the doctor–patient relationship.

USE:

The right expert and an independent expert.

SELECT FROM:

- your own list of experts (choose people who are known to have advised plaintiffs properly);
- an expert who has successfully appeared against you;
- an expert you know (because you are qualified to judge);
- AVMA (ACTION FOR VICTIMS OF MEDICAL ACCIDENTS). This is an organisation set up to help victims of medical accidents. They have an extensive pool of experts on their files. Members have access to these files and AVMA will be pleased to assist with selecting the appropriate expert;
- APIL (The Association of Personal Injury Lawyers) now has a database of medical experts. *Note* that these experts may or may not be appropriate to deal with medical negligence cases;
- The Law Society Helpline/Law Society's Directory of Expert Witnesses. The new directory has been published in November 1996 and costs £60.00. In addition to the Directory, the Law Society Helpline will make a search of its database and send out details the same day. There is a charge for this service which is reduced if the solicitor has a copy of the Directory;
- professional journals, ie *The Lancet*, *BMJ*, etc;
- experts you have seen in other case reports which have dealt with the same issues that are facing you now;
- UK Register of Expert Witnesses (see *Law Society Gazette*, the *Solicitors Journal*).

The letter of instruction to the expert

What follows below incorporates the recent advice for doctors and lawyers involved in the preparation of medico–legal reports and is contained in a publication by the Law Society titled, 'Code Of Practice For Medico–Legal Reports In Personal Injury Cases'. This publication is supplemental to the publication 'Medical Evidence: Guidance For Doctors and Lawyers' produced jointly by the BMA and the Law Society. It is strongly recommended that all solicitors familiarise themselves with both publications.

Before instructing your expert it is vital to consider what type of expert you require:

- What medical expert(s) are you concerned with?
- Do you require more than one expert?
- Are separate reports needed on causation and prognosis?
- Did the plaintiff undergo any supervening treatment or suffer a later illness which could have affected the plaintiff's present condition?

Instruct an expert conversant with the plaintiff's treatment.

Check that the expert will accept the case either by telephoning him or, preferably, by a short letter of inquiry. The purpose of such a letter is to deal with the following matters:

- Ascertaining whether the expert will accept this type of case.
- Obtaining the expert's full CV or appropriate evidence of the expert's qualifications. Once received these should be checked against the appropriate entries in the Medical Directory.

  When these details are received consider:

  - what is the degree of experience of the expert, is he still practising, if he is not, only instruct an expert who retired recently as he will still be up-to-date with common practices;
  - if instructing more than one expert, whether they are from different generations and whether they will work well together;
  - whether the expert is up-to-date in the relevant field;
  - try and match experts with the intended defendant.

- Determining his likely fee. Medical experts can be expensive and reports prepared for a medical negligence case are likely to be even more expensive. Ask the expert to give an estimate of his likely fee and his hourly rate. Tell the expert whether the client is paying privately or is legally aided and, consequently, what is limit on the legal aid certificate.

- Obtaining a time estimate: While medical experts will take their time you do not want to be waiting indefinitely. Tell the expert when the limitation period expires and the date when you want the report.

- Determining how long it will be before he can see the client.

- Informing the expert of the nature of the problem, and the parties involved, ie which hospital, etc. It may be that he feels he cannot act against the potential defendant.

- Ascertaining whether the expert has any special requirements regarding instructions.

Once a favourable response has been received to the letter of inquiry, think about drafting the letter of instruction, which should contain the following matters.

- The name, address, date of birth and telephone number of the client.
- What are the issues/facts? Outline the allegations of negligence, eg disclosure of information, inexperience, etc and a brief description of how it is alleged that the injury was caused and what the injury is.
- Reiterate the test for negligence, ie *Bolam*. (Stress to the expert that the defendant will not be negligent if he can show that an accepted body of medical opinion would have acted as the defendant did. Although the expert is probably familiar with *Bolam*, remind him of it.)
- Liability/causation. Ask the expert whether it is clear from the evidence that the alleged negligence caused the damage or whether it is impossible to establish liability.
- Condition/prognosis. Ask the expert to estimate what the client's chances are for a complete recovery, or whether his disability will be permanent. This is obviously required to establish the quantum of damages.
- Whether there are any factors peculiar to the client's case which the expert is required to deal with such as medical history, contributory negligence, and any allegations or reports the defendant has made.
- Progress of the litigation (this should be read in conjunction with the comments on limitation).
- Whether an examination is required and if so what issues are to be addressed.

In addition, any of the issues that were not mentioned in the initial enquiry to the expert should be included. With regard to the medical records, although it is possible to simply provide the expert with an authority to obtain the records, in our opinion, the better option is for the solicitor to provide the records with the letter of instruction. This is because:

- it allows the solicitor to read the records before the expert;
- the solicitor can take a copy of the records, so he is able to identify easily any problem the expert has with the records; and
- the solicitor is able to sort the records before they are sent to the expert.

What should be sent to the expert accompanying the letter of instruction? A file should be sent containing, in paginated and chronological order, the documents listed below.

- Hospital records, eg X-rays and medical notes, nursing kardex, any specialist results of histology, myelograms, blood analyses, etc. Check with your expert that copies will suffice. A copy of the notes should be sent to the expert annotated with the plaintiff's comments and any admissions or comments made by the defendant.
- Case notes and GP's records, eg record cards, correspondence, reports.

- Proof of evidence by the plaintiff and any other relative, if appropriate, plus any recent photographs or videos taken of the client's injuries which may indicate to the expert whether or not the surgery has healed as it should.

- A copy of any current pleadings.

- Any previous expert reports and statements. Tell the expert whether or not they have been disclosed.

- The client's authority to obtain the medical records (if appropriate).

- Experts should be well aware of the format of the report but it may be prudent for the solicitor to send a copy of the recommended format in the Code of Practice for Medico-Legal Reports.

What can the solicitor expect of the expert?

The Code of Practice for Medico–Legal Reports sets out at part 4 the obligations of the medical expert on receipt of his instructions from the solicitor. Briefly, he should expect that:

- the instructions are promptly acknowledged;

- an estimate is given as to costs involved and the time needed to prepare a report;

- an indication will be given if further investigations, eg X-rays are likely to be required;

- the client be seen in sufficient time to allow the report to be prepared;

- the report will be sent to the solicitor within 4 weeks of the date of the examination together with the medical records if these have been provided by the solicitor.

It may be that if the chosen expert fails to comply with these minimum requirements the solicitor will think twice before instructing that particular expert again.

The expert's report

For guidance on the format and general principles concerning expert evidence, see *National Justice Compania Naveria SA v Prudential Assurance Co Ltd (The Ikarian Reefer)* [1993] 2 Lloyd's Rep 68 (a commercial case which is said to be of general application) and the Appendix in the Code of Practice for Medico–Legal Reports in Personal Injury Cases. We have included a brief paragraph as to the format of the report itself so a practitioner can see at glance whether all is right with his expert's report. As a precursor the report should be printed on A4, double spaced, and numbered and should be clear and comprehensible.

A INTRODUCTION

This should contain the personal details of the expert and of the patient. It should also state the date of the accident, when the patient was examined and if any other persons were present.

B PAST MEDICAL HISTORY

This should give a chronological account of the present complaint and a history of the accident and all relevant events subsequent thereto.

C THE EXAMINATION

An account should be given of what examination took place and the particular condition being treated.

D OPINION AND PROGNOSIS

This will form the main body of the report. Obviously, the first question it should address is, is there a claim to answer, or is it impossible to give a firm opinion at this stage. Hence the report should deal with the current position and the expert's prognosis, if possible giving a % chance for further complications. Finally, the report should cover the overall effect of the injury on the patient's life, eg what is his life expectancy, what are his employment prospects, does he have any special needs, etc.

E CONCLUSION

If the report is dealing with liability then somewhere it should state (if appropriate) that 'the doctor(s) have fallen below the standard of care to be expected from a reasonably competent doctor in this field in the following respects ...'

Once the report is received

Once the solicitor has obtained the report he will be expected to take the following steps.

- Read it carefully with the assistance of a medical dictionary, eg *Pears' Medical Encyclopaedia*.

- Check whether the report has dealt with all the issues raised in the letter of instruction; if not be prepared to send a follow-up letter to the expert.

- Ascertain whether any part of the report requires clarification, eg if the claim is for a delay in diagnosis how much earlier would the diagnosis have had to be made to avoid the injury?

- Does the report indicate that the alleged negligence has merely exacerbated a pre-existing condition? Is the client's present condition solely attributable to the alleged negligence, or would his condition have deteriorated in any event? It is important to be aware of the difficulties of establishing causation at an early stage and to be alive to the fact that it could ultimately reduce the level of damages.

- Ask yourself if you need another report. Does the present report throw up issues that would be best dealt with by an expert in a different field of medicine? Do you need a psychiatrist's report, eg has the client suffered from depression since the incident? If yes, then the psychiatrist will require access to all records that you have sent to your first expert. Ensure that if you are acting for a private client he agrees to this further expenditure. If the client is legally aided then you will need the authority of the Legal Aid Board. If this is the case describe the report as a 'supplementary report' rather than a second report. The Legal Aid Board may be more receptive to your application.

- Do you need a second opinion because you are not happy with the report for some reason, eg is it entirely objective? Obviously, if there is anything in the report that you cannot understand then go back to the expert, but if you conclude that you need a second opinion then apply the same criteria to the second expert. If you are acting for a private client then obtain his authority for this extra expenditure. If the client is legally aided, you will have to seek the authority of the Legal Aid Board, if you are refused then you will have to advise the client that he will have to pay for a second report privately (or possibly consider a conditional fee arrangement) and arrange for his certificate to be discharged.

- If the expert has indicated that the evidence is incomplete, eg further proofs of evidence are required, there are missing medical records, etc or for that matter, a different expert is required, ensure that all of these matters are attended to before the conference with counsel.

All of these matters should be attended to before the conference with counsel.

Finally, make one last check that there is nothing in the report which would lower your client's level of damages; if there is, go back to the expert for further comment.

If appropriate, send a copy to your client for his comments. You should advise the expert that the report will be shown to the client and therefore the report should not contain anything which the expert would feel uneasy about the client seeing.

The next step is to arrange a conference with counsel. By this time it should be clear to you whether the client has a good case; you may therefore consider that there is little point in going to counsel if the report is unfavourable. However, it is advantageous to have a conference at this stage with counsel, the expert and the client even if the report is unfavourable for the following reasons:

- It provides a chance to clear up any ambiguities within the report.

- It allows counsel the chance of taking the client through his version of events while at the same time inviting comment from the expert. Counsel will be able from this to estimate how the client and the expert perform as witnesses, and this may ultimately affect what advice he gives, ie if the client is a poor witness, counsel may advise settlement at an early stage.

- A conference at an early stage provides an opportunity for the 'team' to meet; it gives you an opportunity to iron out any problems with your 'team' and the client can see that his case is being well-run.

Selecting counsel

Many of the criteria used for selecting an expert apply equally to your choice of counsel. Unfortunately, we do not as yet have a scheme in place similar to the Law Society's specialist medical negligence panel, although all firms who are franchised and are members of the Personal Injury Panel will have a list of approved counsel. However, as a brief guide, the solicitor should consider the points listed below.

- Choose from your own list, counsel who specialise in this field. Be wary of relying on the advice of counsel's clerks, especially if you know nothing about the particular barrister. If relying on the advice of counsel's clerks, it is worthwhile asking questions like how many medical negligence cases that particular counsel has dealt with and what proportion of them were settled or went to trial.
- Consult Lawyers Directories, etc.
- Consult law reports, journals for the names of counsel. You should be looking for a recent case similar to the one you are dealing with.
- AVMA; APIL; Law Society Helpline (see p 164).
- Consult other solicitors who may be more experienced than you in the field of medical negligence.

The conference

Preparation

To a large extent many of the problems that will arise, eg the expert being suddenly called away, are unavoidable. However, to try and minimise these problems the conference should be timetabled well in advance at the most convenient venue for all the parties, eg if the client is severely disabled it may be difficult for him to travel very far. In selecting the venue the paramount concerns are time and costs. With regard to time this is to a large extent dictated by train/air times; as to costs, bear in mind that the Legal Aid Board are questioning more and more the level of costs incurred, eg would it have been cheaper to travel by train rather than to drive? As a final thought think about using video facilities.

What to tell counsel

How much information do you include in your instructions? The most important item is a chronology of events, especially when several matters occurred close together. By doing this the solicitor ensures that counsel has a clear picture of the events. The instructions should basically reiterate the history and identify the issues. Obviously, every solicitor has his own way of identifying these issues but as a minimum the instructions should state:

- what documents are enclosed;
- the facts of the case;
- how far the litigation has progressed;
- if the client is legally aided, what limitations there are;
- what counsel is being instructed to do and if there is any urgency;
- what documents are enclosed.

With regard to the last point, ensure that the following are included:

(1) all proofs of evidence from the client and witnesses;

(2) all medical reports, together with copies of any supplemental documentation referred to in the report, eg medical texts;

(3) all correspondence between the parties if relevant;

(4) a brief schedule on the estimated damages claim;

(5) a copy of the legal aid certificate plus any amendments to see if relevant.

Make sure that the records used by the solicitor, expert, and counsel are identical, sorted and paginated. Finally, it must be clear what counsel is being asked to do; it is to see if there is a claim to answer.

The conference meeting

It is not our intention to discuss in detail what should be the main priorities of the conference as we are sure that all solicitors have their own way of conducting a conference. However, by way of a brief reminder we will make the following point: before the conference all papers should be read in advance, along with the relevant medical texts and, if appropriate, think about drafting the allegations of negligence.

If the client is in attendance, the solicitor's first priority will be to explain how the conference will proceed and to put the client at ease. It is important that the client feels involved at an early stage; at all times the solicitor should remind himself that the client has already been let down by one group of professionals and may find it difficult to place his trust in another. The client should be encouraged to correct what he perceives to be mistakes and to ask questions. It may be that he feels rather intimidated by the other professionals present so again be alert to this and work to put the client at ease.

During the conference the solicitor should ensure that a contemporaneous note is taken from which future action will be decided and the issues of negligence will be formulated. It is a good idea to have the latter in mind during the progress of the discussion. After the conference it is important that the solicitor's note is circulated to all those who were present to avoid any misunderstanding and to facilitate further discussion.

After the expert advice has been dealt with there must be a discussion on how the case should progress, eg is further advice necessary, does the solicitor need to go back to the Legal Aid Board and have the limitation on the certificate removed, etc.

CHAPTER 6

CAUSATION

RULE 6(A)

The plaintiff must prove, on a balance of probabilities, that the defendant's breach caused the damage. The plaintiff will succeed if he can show that:

(1) the damage would not have occurred but for the defendant's negligence; or

(2) the defendant's negligence materially contributed to or materially increased the risk of injury; or

(3) if the claim is for negligent non-disclosure, had he been adequately informed he would not have accepted the treatment.

Commentary

This is the third step in a negligence claim and perhaps the most problematic of all. Once the plaintiff has overcome the difficulties posed by *Bolam* (see Chapter 5, Standard of Care, at p 121 *et seq*) then he must face the hurdle of causation. The plaintiff must show that the damage he suffered was caused by the defendant's negligence. It is not for the defendant to prove that his negligence did not cause the damage (although in some instances a case could be made out for asserting that that should be the rule, see pp 196–98).

The problem with a medical negligence claim is that there are often several possible factors involved and/or the actual cause of the damage may be unknown. For example, the plaintiff may have been suffering from an ongoing disease; however, he must still show that the medical negligence caused the damage complained of. In some cases where the medical evidence is conflicting the court will probably find that the plaintiff has failed to prove that the defendant's breach was responsible for the ensuing damage (see the whooping cough litigation, and the case of *Loveday v Renton* [1990] 1 Med LR 117).

Below we examine the various ways in which the plaintiff can establish causation.

The 'but for' test

The plaintiff is here saying that 'but for' the defendant's negligence, he would not be in the predicament he is in now in which case it is for him to show that the damage which occurred would not have occurred 'but for' that negligence. The defendant's conduct need not be the sole cause of the damage, there may be other factors which also contributed to the damage (see (2) below). However, the existence of those contributory factors will more often than not make it impossible for the plaintiff to overcome the evidential burden posed by this test. One such example is *Barnett v Chelsea and Kensington Hospital Management Committee* [1969] 1 QB 428 where the plaintiff attended the casualty department of his local hospital complaining of vomiting. The casualty officer failed to examine him, and the nurse in attendance sent him home with the instruction to see his own doctor. Shortly afterwards the plaintiff died of arsenic poisoning. There was no dispute that the casualty officer was negligent in failing to see and examine the patient; however, his lack of care did not cause the plaintiff's death because the arsenic poisoning was too far advanced for any treatment to have prevented his death (see also *Robinson v Post Office* [1974] 1 WLR 1176, at p 178).

The material contribution – materially increasing the risk test

The 'but for' test will only work in a minority of cases. Where there are two or more contributing factors, only one of which is the defendant's negligence, it is enough for the plaintiff to establish that the negligent act materially contributed to the damage. This test was first canvassed in *Bonnington Castings Ltd v Wardlaw* [1956] AC 613. In that case, the plaintiff contracted pneumoconiosis from inhaling silica dust at his workplace. The dust he inhaled came from two sources: the first as a result of the production process for which the defendant could not be held responsible, the second as a result of the defendant's breach of statutory duty in failing to have adequate extraction fans. Medical evidence indicated that both sources contributed to the plaintiff's disease even though the greater amount of dust came from the innocent source. The court held that the plaintiff need only prove on a balance of probabilities that the defendant's negligence materially contributed to the damage to recover the whole of his loss. In this instance the court were prepared to draw an inference that the defendant's breach had materially contributed to the damage even though in reality it was impossible to say. (See, however, *Bolitho v City and Hackney Health Authority* [1993] 4 Med LR 381, at p 196 where the court shied away from developing this approach.)

The question which follows from this test is: just what is a material contribution? In *Bonnington*, Lord Reid indicated that it was anything that did not come within the *de minimis* rule. Exactly what this means in terms of percentages is somewhat uncertain. It may seem somewhat harsh that a defendant who was only 10% liable could be held responsible for all the ensuing damage; however, if the defendant creates the risk it seems unjust that he should escape liability merely because there happens to be another concurrent cause (see further, at p 176).

Bonnington was applied in the other influential case in this area, *McGhee v National Coal Board* [1973] 1 WLR 1. Here the pursuer alleged that as a result of the defender's failure to provide washing facilities he had contracted dermatitis. The defender admitted negligence; however, the evidence was inconclusive as to whether the pursuer would still have contracted the disease. This case differed from *Bonnington* in that it was not being argued that the defender's breach materially contributed to the damage since no one could say that had washing facilities been available the end result would have been different; all that was certain was that there was an increased risk of contracting dermatitis although the exact percentage of increase was unknown. The House of Lords said that this did not matter; a failure to take steps to reduce the risk was the same as a material contribution to the injury. Lord Reid said (at p 5):

> From a broad and practical viewpoint I can see no substantial difference between saying that what the defender did materially increased the risk of injury to the

pursuer and saying that what the defender did made a material contribution to the injury.

We submit that this reasoning does not hold up. Materially increasing the risk is distinguishable from materially contributing to the damage. A risk may or may not materialise in damage; merely to increase the likelihood that something might happen is very different from positively contributing to the actual damage. The defender in *McGhee* merely increased the chance of the plaintiff's contracting dermatitis.

McGhee is also renowned for this policy statement of Lord Wilberforce who said (at p 6):

> And if one asks which of the parties, the workman or the employers, should suffer from this inherent evidential difficulty, the answer as a matter of policy or justice should be that it is the creator of the risk who, *ex hypothesi*, must be taken to have foreseen the possibility of damage, who should bear its consequences.

This statement would seem to indicate the burden of proof is reversed, ie the plaintiff need only show that the defendant's breach had increased the risk; that done, it was for the defendant to rebut the inference. This approach was not new; in *McWilliams v Sir William Arrol & Co Ltd* [1962] 1 WLR 295, a case concerning an employer's breach of duty, Lord Hodson said that the onus was on the defendant to show the plaintiff would not have used the safety equipment had it been available. Again, in *Clark v McLennan* [1983] 1 All ER 416 (a case concerning breach of duty), Pain J said (at p 427):

> It seems that it follows from *McGhee* that where there is a situation in which a general duty of care arises and there is a failure to take a particular precaution, and that very damage occurs against which the precaution is designed to be a protection, then the burden lies on the defendant to show that he was not in breach of duty as well as to show that the damage did not result from his reach of duty.

This approach was severely criticised in *Wilsher v Essex Area Health Authority* [1988] 2 WLR 557. (For the facts of this case see p 124.) The House of Lords firmly quashed any belief that the burden of proof can be reversed at all times. They ruled it remains with the plaintiff, who must establish that the defendant's breach was at least a contributory cause of the harm. Lord Bridge expressed the following sentiments (at p 569):

> ... *McGhee v National Coal Board* [1973] 1 WLR 1 laid down no new principle of law whatever. On the contrary, it affirmed the principle that the onus of proving causation lies on the pursuer or plaintiff. Adopting a robust and pragmatic approach to the undisputed primary facts of the case, the majority concluded that it was the legitimate inference of fact that the defenders' negligence had materially contributed to the pursuer's injury.

McGhee is therefore still good law, subject to the cautionary note in *Wilsher*.

Wilsher also demonstrated the difference between consecutive and discrete contributory factors. In distinguishing *Wilsher* from *McGhee*, the court ruled that where the plaintiff's injury could have resulted from a number of causes, that did not give rise to a presumption that the injury was caused by the defendant's breach of duty. As Browne-Wilkinson V-C had said in the Court of Appeal ([1986] 3 All ER 801, at p 835):

... A failure to take preventive measures against one out of five possible causes is no evidence as to which of those five caused the injury.

In *Wilsher*, there was a 20% chance that the defendant's breach had caused the damage; the court interpreted this to mean that what the defendant had done was to add to the factors which could have caused the damage. To succeed, the plaintiff would have to establish that the defendant's breach did cause or materially contribute to the damage; here the defendant had not increased an existing risk but had simply created a further risk. It was a pity that the words of Wilberforce LJ in *McGhee* were not adopted and that the creator of the risk was not held to account for his actions.

How then does *Wilsher* compare with *McGhee*? In *McGhee*, the defendant increased an already existing risk: in *Wilsher* he increased the number of risks. In *McGhee*, the exposure to the risk was consecutive: in *Wilsher*, there were five possible discrete causes of the retrolental fibroplasia. *McGhee* succeeded: *Wilsher* failed. Why? On a question of semantics only? For some reason the Court of Appeal wanted to distinguish between the enhancement of an existing risk and merely adding to other risks. In both *McGhee* and *Wilsher* the defendant had increased the risk, whether by increasing the likelihood of an existing risk occurring or by adding to a list of possible factors which might have caused the damage; whatever the interpretation both increased the risk to the plaintiff. In neither case could the plaintiff show that the defendant's breach materially caused the damage, but in *McGhee* the court was prepared to infer that it did. Is this because they were only faced with two factors as opposed to five in *Wilsher*? Why should it make any difference how many factors there are as long as it can be said that the particular breach by the defendant does not fall within the *de minimis* rule?

In reality, in neither case could it be said that the defendant's breach materially contributed to the damage, yet it is apparent that both materially increased the risk. Consequently, it is illogical and plainly wrong that the courts were prepared to adopt a robust approach in *McGhee* but not in *Wilsher*. Our advice to the plaintiff's solicitor is never be caught out by *Wilsher* – always assert that the defendant's breach materially increased the risk and therefore materially contributed to the damage, thus adopting a robust and pragmatic approach so much favoured by the courts.

Other jurisdictions adopt a much more innovative approach to the issue of causation. In *Snell v Farrell* (1990) 72 DLR (4th) 289, the Supreme Court of Canada ruled that causation need not be determined with scientific precision; it was not essential that the plaintiff's case should be supported by a firm expert opinion.

Causation and non-disclosure

This section should be read in conjunction with Chapters 2 (Consent) and 5 (Standard of Care), at p 42 *et seq* and at p 153 *et seq*. Readers will already have noted that in Chapter 4, at p 89, we advised the solicitor that, wherever possible to frame a claim for non-disclosure of risks as a trespass claim rather than as a negligence claim, in order to avoid the problems of causation. Where the claim is brought in negligence, once the plaintiff has overcome the *Bolam* test, he must then prove that if he had been warned about the inherent risk in the procedure he would not have accepted the treatment. In the majority of cases the plaintiff's claim will fail at this juncture because the court will hold that, on balance the plaintiff would still have undergone the operation. In the English courts a subjective test is applied: would *this plaintiff* have accepted this treatment?

Although at first glance this test would seem unduly favourable to the plaintiff, case law demonstrates that the courts apply the test stringently (see *Chatterton v Gerson* [1981] QB 432; [1981] 1 All ER 257, *Hills v Potter* [1984] 1 WLR 641 and *Smith v Barking, Havering and Brentwood Health Authority* [1994] 5 Med LR 285). In *Chatterton v Gerson* [1981] QB 432 (an action brought in battery), the defendant had explained to the plaintiff that the treatment would involve some numbness and possibly a temporary loss of muscle power to her leg. However, the plaintiff suffered total numbness in her leg which affected her mobility. She argued that she had not given her consent to the operation because the doctor had not informed her of the inherent risks associated with the procedure. The court ruled that since the plaintiff had been informed in broad terms of the nature of the procedure her consent was real, and any claim should have been brought in negligence. The court remained unconvinced that the plaintiff would not have proceeded with the procedure had she received more information about it.

However, there have been some successes. In *Thake v Maurice* [1986] QB 644, the plaintiff did succeed, although the case can perhaps be distinguished on the grounds that here the claim was not that the male plaintiff would not have had a vasectomy had he been informed of a risk of reversal, but that if his wife had been given this advice, she would have realised that she had subsequently fallen pregnant earlier than she did, and consequently she could have sought an abortion.

In other jurisdictions, notably Canada, an objective test is applied, see, for example, *Reibl v Hughes* (1980) 114 DLR (3d) 1, where the court asked whether a reasonable person in the plaintiff's situation, knowing of the risks, would have declined the treatment. In *Reibl's* case, the plaintiff succeeded largely because of the high risk of a stroke resulting (10%) and the fact that the plaintiff was only about a year-and-a-half away from being eligible for a full pension, consequently this information was very important to him. However, in most cases where an objective test is applied, causation becomes even more burdensome to the plaintiff, and tends to obscure what the real issue is, namely: what would the plaintiff have done had he possessed all the relevant information?

Although there is a difference between the subjective and objective tests, in practical terms whether one or the other is applied will make little difference – the plaintiff must still convince the court that he would not have had the treatment had the risks been disclosed. The court will therefore look at the plaintiff's evidence and weigh up its credibility by reference to the reasonable man and by looking at the risks attached to the particular procedure. Indeed, if cases such as *Smith v Barking, Havering and Brentwood Health Authority* [1994] 5 Med LR 285 are to be followed, it would seem that in reality the English courts are applying an objective test and will be persuaded to adopt a subjective approach only on very rare occasions, see the cases immediately below. Accordingly, the court will assess whether or not the plaintiff's decision was reasonable by reference to what the reasonable man would have done. In practice, this is no different from cases such as *McWilliams v Sir William Arrol & Co Ltd* [1962] 1 WLR 295, although there the burden was on the defendant to show that the plaintiff would not have used the safety equipment, whereas in an action for non-disclosure the burden falls squarely on the plaintiff to show that he would not have consented to the treatment. In practice, many cases will fail because the court will rule that the risk is so small it would not have affected the plaintiff's decision (see *Chatterton v Gerson* [1981] QB 432, *Meyer Estates v Rogers* [1991] 78 DLR (4th) 307 and *Ciarlariello v Schacter* [1991] 2 Med LR 391).

On the issue of burden of proof and non-disclosure, perhaps the better recommendation is that at the very least the burden should be equally shared. Thus the defendant should have to produce substantial evidence to indicate that the plaintiff would still have undergone the treatment by reference to the plaintiff's previous decisions regarding treatment (if any) or the plaintiff's character or, perhaps, the decisions of others in a similar position to the plaintiff. At the same time, the plaintiff would have to adduce evidence in support of his decision to refuse medical treatment, referring to his past decisions, etc.

REFERENCES

English case law

(1) Bolam v Friern Hospital Management Committee [1957] 1 WLR 582; [1957] 2 All ER 118

See Chapter 5, Standard of Care, at p 121.

(2) Loveday v Renton [1990] 1 Med LR 117

The plaintiff failed to establish that pertussis (the whooping cough vaccine) caused meningitis.

For a more optimistic decision from the plaintiff's viewpoint, see *Best v Wellcome Foundation Ltd* [1993] IR 421; [1994] 5 Med LR 81.

Note that the court at no time referred to the decision in *Loveday*. In finding the defendant negligent, the court held that it was not their role to resolve scientific disputes, rather it was to apply common sense and logic.

(3) Barnett v Chelsea and Kensington Hospital Management Committee [1969] 1 QB 428; [1968] 1 All ER 1068

See above, at p 173 and Chapter 5, Standard of Care, at p 127.

(4) Robinson v Post Office [1974] 1 WLR 1176; [1974] 2 All ER 737

While at work, the plaintiff slipped from an oily ladder injuring his shin. He was given an anti tetanus injection by his GP. In giving the injection the GP did not administer a test dose nor did he wait the customary half hour to see whether the plaintiff had any adverse reaction.

Held: he had been negligent for failing to adhere to accepted practice; however, the case failed on causation. The plaintiff's reaction was so severe that it would not have shown itself in the half hour.

(5) Bonnington Castings Ltd v Wardlaw [1956] AC 613; [1956] 1 All ER 615

See above, at p 174.

(6) Bolitho v City and Hackney Health Authority [1993] 4 Med LR 381

See Chapter 5, Standard of Care, at pp 140, 141 and below, at p 196 *et seq.*

(7) McGhee v National Coal Board [1973] 1 WLR 1; [1972] 3 All ER 1008

See above, at p 174 *et seq.*

(8) McWilliams v Sir William Arrol & Co Ltd [1962] 1 WLR 295; [1962] 1 All ER 623

The plaintiff sued his employer in negligence and for breach of statutory duty for failing to provide safety helmets. It was accepted that if the safety helmet had been worn the plaintiff would not have sustained his head injuries he did. However, the case failed on causation because the defendant successfully proved that, even if helmets had been provided, the plaintiff would not have worn one.

(9) Clark v McLennan [1983] 1 All ER 416

After giving birth, the plaintiff was found to be suffering from stress incontinence. The defendant performed an anterior colporrhapy four weeks after the birth. This operation and further operations were unsuccessful and the plaintiff's incontinence became permanent. It was accepted practice that the plaintiff should not have been operated on until three months after the birth. The plaintiff succeeded on causation. *Note*, however, that the defendant was able to prove that even with the operation at the correct time, there was a 33% chance that the plaintiff's incontinence would still have persisted. Accordingly, the court reduced the damages by one-third. See further Chapter 7, Damages, at p 213.

(10) Wilsher v Essex Area Health Authority [1988] 2 WLR 557; [1988] 1 All ER 871; [1986] 3 All ER 801

See Chapter 5, Standard of Care, at p 124 and above, at p 175 *et seq.*

(11) Chatterton v Gerson [1981] QB 432; [1981] 1 All ER 257

See p 42. Bristow J was not satisfied that the defendant was in breach of duty for failing to inform the plaintiff, but even so, as he explained (at [1981] QB 432, p 445):

> ... the plaintiff had not proved that, even if she had been further informed, she would have chosen not to have the operation. The whole picture is on the evidence of a lady desperate for pain relief.

(12) Hills v Potter [1984] 1 WLR 641; [1983] 3 All ER 716

See Chapter 5, Standard of Care, at p 154. The plaintiff underwent an operation to cure a neck deformity, she was rendered paralysed. The defendant had told the plaintiff there was a small risk of her dying and a risk of paralysis which might be temporary or transient.

Held: the defendant had acted in accordance with accepted practice and, furthermore, the plaintiff had failed to show that if the risks had been disclosed she would not have consented to the operation.

(13) Smith v Barking Havering and Brentwood Health Authority [1994] 5 Med LR 285

The plaintiff had undergone an operation as a child to drain a cyst on her spinal cord. At the age of 18, she began to experience problems again and she was advised to have a further operation in the hope of alleviating her condition, without which she would have been in a wheelchair within three months and a tetraplegic within six months. It was accepted there was a 50% chance that the second operation could immediately worsen the condition; this in fact happened and the plaintiff was rendered a tetraplegic immediately. It was admitted that the defendant was negligent in failing adequately to disclose to the plaintiff the risks involved in the procedure. However, the plaintiff's case failed on causation.

The court applied a subjective test and held that the plaintiff would have consented to the operation because if nothing was done she faced disability within three months anyway. She would have trusted the defendant as representing the only chance she had to postpone her inevitable disability.

Note that Hutchinson J urged caution in considering the plaintiff's evidence in 'a wholly artificial situation' ie in the witness box. The court should consider the evidence objectively, asking what would a reasonable plaintiff had done. Only if there were other unique factors such as religious beliefs or other social considerations and these assertions were stated immediately following the operation, should the court be persuaded by such evidence.

(14) Thake v Maurice [1986] QB 644; [1986] 1 All ER 479

The plaintiff underwent a vasectomy operation. The operation failed and the plaintiff's wife gave birth to a fifth child. The plaintiff sued the defendant in contract and negligence for failing to warn him of the possibility that the vasectomy might not render him irreversibly sterile. The claim in contract failed, the court ruling that a reasonable man would not have understood the defendant as giving an absolute guarantee that the operation would be successful. The claim in negligence succeeded, the court ruled the defendant had fallen below the standard of care and had the plaintiff appreciated that the operation was not foolproof, then Mrs Thake would have suspected she was pregnant at an earlier stage and consequently sought an abortion.

See also *Goorkani v Tayside Health Board* [1991] 3 Med LR 33 in Chapter 5, Standard of Care, at p 158.

Foreign case law

AUSTRALIA

Ellis v Wallsend District Hospital [1990] 2 Med LR 103; (1989) 70 NSW LR 553

For the facts of this case see Chapter 5, Standard of Care, at p 146. On appeal the court held that the judge at first instance was correct in applying a subjective rather than an objective test to the question whether the plaintiff would have undergone the operation had she been fully informed of the risk of paralysis and the failure to relieve pain. However, at first instance, the judge had held that the plaintiff had failed to establish a causal link between the negligence and the damage. This was reversed on appeal. The court held that, although there was no rule of law which said the judge was bound to accept the plaintiff's evidence because it was not challenged on cross-examination, since the plaintiff's evidence was not 'inherently incredible' or 'inherently improbable' the judge could not dismiss the evidence without an explanation and hence the decision at first instance would be reversed.

CANADA

(1) Snell v Farrell (1990) 72 DLR (4th) 289

The respondent had problems with her right eye and was advised to have surgery to remove a cataract. The appellant explained the operation and the risks involved. The plaintiff lost the sight in the eye following the operation. The trial judge found that the defendant had acted negligently in continuing the operation after noticing a haemorrhage in the plaintiff's eye. The medical evidence was that the operation was a possible but not definite cause of the loss of sight. The trial judge held that the burden had shifted to the defendant to disprove causation, that this burden had not been discharged, and therefore the defendant was liable. The defendant's appeal to the New Brunswick Court of Appeal was dismissed, as was a further appeal to the Supreme Court.

Held: the burden throughout was on the plaintiff to show that the defendant's negligence had caused her loss, but the evidence adduced by the plaintiff was sufficient to support an inference of causation based on common sense despite the absence of positive medical opinion. It was stated (at p 300):

> Causation need not be determined by scientific precision. It is as stated by Lord Salmon in *Alphacell Ltd v Woodward* [1972] 2 All ER 475, at p 490 'essentially a practical question of fact which can best be answered by ordinary common sense rather than abstract metaphysical theory' ... the allocation of the burden of proof is not immutable. Both the burden and standard of proof are flexible concepts.

And (at p 301):

> The legal or ultimate burden remains with the plaintiff but, in the absence of evidence to the contrary adduced by the defendant, an inference of causation may be drawn, although positive or scientific evidence of causation has not been ... This is, I believe, what Lord Bridge had in mind in *Wilsher* when he referred to a 'robust and pragmatic approach to the facts'.

(2) Patterson v Dutton (1991) 79 DLR (4th) 705

During an operation a congenital displacement of the plaintiff's spine was aggravated and she suffered immediate paralysis. The plaintiff alleged that the defendant had been negligent in failing to make a prompt diagnosis of the spinal displacement and the court found the surgeon had been negligent in the plaintiff's post operative care. However, medical evidence was divided as to whether the plaintiff's paralysis could have been avoided. The court adopted a 'robust and pragmatic' approach, applying *Snell* (see above) stating (at p 717):

> Here, we know what caused the paralysis – it was the compression of the spinal cord. What we do not know with certainty was whether the breach of duty, ie the failure of timely diagnosis made even partial recovery impossible ... What we do not know with certainty is whether if there had been no breach of duty she would have had some recovery.

It was impossible to determine exactly how much traction should have been applied to the plaintiff to prevent the paralysis and consequently it would be unfair to require the plaintiff to prove something which scientifically is incapable of proof. As it was very difficult to determine what would have happened had the correct treatment been given, much more so than determining the effect of something which ought not to have been done, the court was prepared to draw an inference and find for the plaintiff.

Query – is this a loss of chance case? See Rule 6(B), below.

(3) Reibl v Hughes (1980) 114 DLR (3d) 1

See Chapter 5, Standard of Care, at p 147 for the facts of this case.

(4) Ciarlariello v Schacter [1991] 2 Med LR 391; [1994] 5 Med LR 213

It was held that the risk of a reaction to angiography was less than risk of death caused by subarachnoid haemorrhage, consequently, the plaintiff would still have consented to treatment even if the risk had been disclosed.

(5) Meyer Estates v Rogers [1991] 2 Med LR 370

See Chapter 5, Standard of Care, at p 147. The risk of reaction from an intravenous pyelogram was one in 2,000 and the risk of death between one in 40,000 and one in 1,100,000.

Practice points

The plaintiff's solicitor should point out to any prospective plaintiff, the problems associated with a claim for non-disclosure. If the claim proceeds, the solicitor should ensure the plaintiff has a plausible argument as to why he would not have accepted the treatment. If the plaintiff's decision is contrary to the view taken by the reasonable man, the evidence will have to be extremely cogent to convince a sceptical judiciary.

RULE 6(B)

Where the nature of the plaintiff's claim is that the defendant's breach deprived him of the opportunity of making a full recovery from his original illness or injury, the plaintiff must establish on a balance of probabilities that, but for the defendant's negligence, his chances of making a full recovery exceeded 50%.

Commentary

These 'loss of chance' cases are perhaps most closely associated with the area of diagnosis, with the plaintiff alleging that, had the diagnosis been made earlier, then the condition would have been treated in time and he might have made a complete recovery. For example, a man visits his GP's surgery on several occasions complaining of severe headaches; the GP negligently fails to examine him or to ask him whether he has any other symptoms or to refer him to a specialist; he attributes the cause of the headaches to stress. Eventually the patient collapses and a brain tumour is diagnosed. The tumour is now so far advanced that the patient's condition is terminal. The GP is not negligent for failing to make the diagnosis, but he is in breach for failing to revise his initial diagnosis. The question is what difference would an earlier diagnosis have made? Would it have given the patient a chance of a full recovery and, if so, how great a chance?

The leading case in this area is *Hotson v East Berkshire Health Authority* [1987] AC 750. After sustaining a fall the plaintiff was taken to hospital where he was examined and sent home without being X-rayed. Five days later he went back to the hospital complaining of persistent pain; he was again X-rayed and a fracture of the neck of the femur was now diagnosed. Although treatment was undertaken the plaintiff later developed avascular necrosis, a medical condition causing deformity of the hip joint and permanent disability. The defendant admitted negligence; however, the question to be resolved was, what was the plaintiff's loss? Since expert evidence established that even with treatment there was a 75% chance of avascular necrosis developing, the plaintiff's argument was that the defendant's negligence had deprived him of a 25% chance of a cure. Consequently, the trial judge and the Court of Appeal worked on the principle that the plaintiff was entitled to 25% of the damages in proportion to the 25% chance of the recovery he had lost.

The House of Lords reversed this decision, holding that the proportionate approach was incorrect; the plaintiff should recover all or nothing. What the plaintiff had to establish, on the proper application of *Bonnington*, was that the delay in treating him had at least materially contributed to the damage, in this instance, it had been established there was a 75% chance the plaintiff would have contracted avascular necrosis in any event. The plaintiff had to establish at least a 51/49 likelihood that had the defendant not been negligent he would have made a full recovery. Once it had been established that the avascular necrosis was the result of the defendant's negligence, then the court could go on to assess damages.

The following points emerge from this decision:

(1) The House of Lords refused to answer the question whether a claim formulated as a loss of chance claim was recognised by the law of tort. However, *Hotson* has been regarded as tolling the death knell in tort for loss of chance cases (this is endorsed by other jurisdictions: see *Lawson v Lafferiere* (1991) 78 DLR (4th) 609. In fact, although the court said that it would not rule that the plaintiff could never bring such a claim and succeed (at p 786 Lord Mackay said, *'I consider that it would be unwise in the present case to lay down as a rule that a plaintiff could never succeed by proving loss of a chance in a medical negligence case'*) the likelihood of success seems increasingly remote.

(2) The plaintiff's claim was whether through the defendant's negligence he had lost the chance of a recovery. Once this was established the court should have gone on to see whether the defendant's negligence caused the damage. The House of Lords approached the problem on the basis that either the plaintiff's original injury (the fall) or the misdiagnosis caused the injury. Having effectively found that, on a balance of probabilities, it was the fall that caused the injury, it then became immaterial to consider how negligent the defendant had been: the plaintiff had to fail unless he could establish that without the negligence he would have had a 51% chance of making a full recovery. However, in the majority of cases the plaintiff will never be able to prove this because the defendant's negligence will usually be such that it is impossible to say whether the plaintiff would have made a full recovery. What seems certain is that a claim for less than a 50% chance is doomed to failure. Can this be right? – see our recommendations, at practice points, at p 199.

(3) Perhaps the plaintiff in this case would have succeeded had he relied on *McGhee* and argued that the defendant's conduct had materially increased the risk. On the facts of *Hotson*, it is possible to argue that the defendant's negligence increased the risk from 75%–100%, but it is impossible to say that the defendant's negligence materially contributed to the damage. However, in *McGhee*, it could not be said that the provision of washing facilities would have made any difference. So why the different outcomes? Is it because in *McGhee* the degree of risk was unknown, whereas in *Hotson* the percentages were clearly known? Why does this make any difference? Although we have stated that 'loss of chance' claims in medical negligence form the basis of a separate rule in the causation section, we suggest that the claim should not be formulated as a loss of chance claim, but rather along the lines of *McGhee*.

It is worth noting that the courts have not always rejected the loss of chance approach; however, the majority of claims have been brought in contract (see *Chaplin v Hicks* [1911] 2 KB 786). This point was expressly recognised in the Court of Appeal in *Hotson* [1987] AC 750. Dillon LJ said (at p 764):

> ... what is the damage the plaintiff has suffered? Is it the onset of the avascular necrosis or is it the loss of chance of avoiding that condition? In my judgment, it is the latter.

> I see no reason why the loss of chance which is capable of being valued should not be capable of being damage in a tort case just as much as in a contract case such as *Chaplin v Hicks* [1911] 2 KB 786. If that is right, there is no difficulty over causation. Causation – that the damage was caused by the wrongful act of the defendant – has to be proved on the balance of probabilities, but by that standard of proof it was amply proved in the present case that the choice which the plaintiff on the judge's findings had had was lost by the admitted negligence of the doctor.

It is also relevant to note that in solicitors' negligence cases the plaintiff in effect is bringing a loss of chance claim, eg where a solicitor has been negligent in failing to issue proceedings within the limitation period, the plaintiff's claim is for the loss of opportunity in bringing a claim for which he can only estimate the chance of success; he is not required to prove that he would have won his case (see *Kitchen v Royal Air Force Association* [1958] 1 WLR 563). Can an analogy be drawn between the solicitor–client and doctor–patient relationships? If it can, then the plaintiff in *Hotson* should have succeeded. In the House of Lords in *Hotson* [1987] 3 WLR 232, Lord Bridge referred to both *Chaplin* and *Kitchen*, but was of the opinion that any analogy with *Hotson* was only 'superficially attractive' and that there were 'formidable difficulties' in accepting an analogy between these cases and *Hotson*. Why the Court of Appeal could draw the analogy but the House of Lords could not is difficult to see.

We must also ask why, ultimately, the House of Lords rejected the approach of apportioning damages. In the Court of Appeal, the Master of the Rolls indicated that the plaintiff had lost the benefit of timely treatment and that it would be unjust to deprive the plaintiff of a claim simply because the chance of the treatment being successful was less than 50%. Equally, a plaintiff should not succeed on 100% liability where the chances of success or cure only marginally exceeded 50%. It was indicated in *Hotson* that the proportionality approach posed too many problems in assessing damages. This argument is untenable. In *Bagley v North Herts Health Authority* (1986) 136 NLJ 1014, the court reduced the plaintiff's damages by 5% to reflect the medical evidence which indicated that she would still have had a stillbirth had the defendant provided adequate treatment; in *Clark v McLennan* [1983] 1 All ER 416, the plaintiff's damages were reduced by 33%. Ackner LJ in *Hotson* [1987] 3 WLR 232, at p 248) was of the opinion that *Bagley* had been wrongly decided, holding that causation had been fully established by the plaintiff and therefore there should be no discount. These cases, however, appear not to have been categorised as loss of chance cases and, consequently, the courts did not feel that they were playing a game of chance – yet another reason for suggesting that the solicitor should think twice before labelling a claim as the loss of chance.

The loss of chance approach has also fallen on stony ground in other jurisdictions. In *Lawson v Lafferiere* (1991) 78 DLR (4th) 609 (the facts of which are set out below), the court rejected it, especially since the damage had already occurred, ie the plaintiff had died. The plaintiff, however, was allowed to recover for the psychological damage she had suffered and the better quality of life she would have enjoyed (lost years) if the defendant had not been negligent. This claim for lost years was also successful in the English case of *Sutton v Population Services Family Planning Programme Ltd* (1981) *The Times*, 7 November (see p 186).

Finally, it seems somewhat unjust that a patient who has a good chance of recovery, say as great as 49%, and is deprived of this chance by the defendant's negligence will not be able to recover any compensation because it is not possible to say with certainty that the negligence caused the damage. In our view, that negligence did cause the damage and therefore there should be liability. Also, if death is the natural result of the negligence, then any lay person would say that the defendant has caused the death of the patient. Recently the court has again looked at loss of chance in non-medical cases. See *Allied Maples Group Ltd v Simmons & Simmons* [1995] 1 WLR 1602, *Stovold v Barlows* (1995) NPC 154 and *First Interstate Bank of California v Cohen Arnold & Co* (1995) *The Times*, 11 December. In the latter case, the Court of Appeal asserted that a loss of chance claim was recognisable in tort. The chance lost had to be 'real or substantial' and in this particular case was valued at 66%. The chance lost, however, does not necessarily have to be 50% or greater. This argument was put forward in *Allied Maples* and failed. However, the situation remains unresolved as to whether a loss of chance claim is sustainable in medical negligence. Hopefully the court will soon see the injustice of this situation and the loss of chance claim will become more than virtual reality.

REFERENCES

English case law

(1) Hotson v East Berkshire Health Authority [1987] AC 750; [1987] 3 WLR 232

See above, at p 182 *et seq.*

(2) Bonnington Castings Ltd v Wardlaw [1956] AC 613; [1956] 1 All ER 615

See above, at p 174.

(3) McGhee v National Coal Board [1973] 1 WLR 1; [1972] 3 All ER 1008

See above, at p 174 *et seq.*

(4) Chaplin v Hicks [1911] 2 KB 786

The plaintiff entered into a contract with the defendant as a result of which she might have won a prize. The defendant subsequently broke the contract and the plaintiff sought damages for the loss of a chance of winning the prize. The court assessed her chances of winning and then assessed her damages to reflect the lost chance. It was stated (at p 797):

> The contract gave the plaintiff a right of considerable value, one for which many people would give money; therefore to hold that the plaintiff was entitled to no damages for being deprived of such a right because the final result depended on a contingency or chance would have been a misdirection.

(5) Kitchen v Royal Air Force Association [1958] 1 WLR 563

A claim succeeded against a firm of solicitors for the loss of a chance of bringing litigation.

See also *Kenyon v Bell* (1953) SC 125 where the plaintiff sustained an eye injury because of the defendant's negligence. However, the defendant established that even without the negligence there was a more than 50% chance that the plaintiff would have lost her sight. The court held it was an all or nothing approach and consequently found for the defendant.

(6) Bagley v North Herts Health Authority (1986) 136 NLJ 1014

See above, at p 184. The plaintiff successfully sued the defendant for failure to carry out blood tests during her pregnancy when they knew the plaintiff had a blood disorder. Liability was admitted by the hospital for failing to carry out the tests and to perform a caesarian section. If the hospital had not been negligent the plaintiff would have had a 95% chance of a successful pregnancy. The plaintiff's award of damages was made up of the following:

(a) the loss of satisfaction in bringing her pregnancy to a successful conclusion;

(b) compensation for the loss of bringing up an ordinary healthy child (the plaintiff had decided not to attempt a further pregnancy);

(c) physical illness and suffering caused by the loss of the child (relying on *Kralj v McGrath and St Theresa's Hospital* [1986] 1 All ER 54. See Chapter 7, at p 243).

(7) Clark v McLennan [1983] 1 All ER 416

See above, at p 184 and Chapter 5, Standard of Care, at p 139.

(8) Sutton v Population Services Family Planning Programme Ltd (1981) The Times, 7 November

The plaintiff was suffering from cancer. Due to the negligence of a nurse, the cancer was detected too late. However, as the cancer was highly malignant, an earlier diagnosis would not have prevented it but only meant that the onset of the cancer would have been delayed for four years. Additionally, the plaintiff's menopause was brought forward. The plaintiff was compensated for the loss of the four years during which she could have led a normal life. See further Chapter 7, Damages, at p 213.

See also *Judge v Huntingdon Health Authority* [1995] 6 Med LR 223 where the plaintiff attended her GP's surgery with a lump in her left breast. Her GP referred her to a surgeon who examined her and indicated that he found no discrete lump. The plaintiff attended her GP's surgery again some months later, complaining that a lump in her breast was painful. She was again referred to a surgeon who this time removed grade two cancer lump which also had a lymphatic permeation. She later underwent a mastectomy and extensive treatment and her life expectancy was substantially reduced. On causation the court held there was an 80% chance of a cure had the cancer been diagnosed on first referral.

Note that there was a conflict of lay evidence and medical evidence as to whether there was a lump present at the first examination by the surgeon and whether the lymph nodes were present at that time. The court did not take into account the possibility of the cancer recurring and affecting the plaintiff' s life in assessing damages.

See also *Phillips v Grampian Hospital Board* [1991] 3 Med LR 16; *Gascoine v Ian Sheridan & Co and Latham* [1994] 5 Med LR 437.

(9) Allied Maples Group Ltd v Simmons and Simmons [1995] 1 WLR 1602

The plaintiff (a retailing company) alleged that the defendant solicitors had deprived it of the chance that a third party would have given the plaintiff an indemnity for assets the plaintiff had purchased from the third party. Commenting on a loss of chance claim, the Court of Appeal held that the plaintiff must prove that he had lost a real or substantial chance as opposed to a speculative one. Should the plaintiff fulfil this requirement then the court will assess the value of that chance as part of the assessment of *quantum*.

(10) Stovold v Barlows [1995] NPC 154; (1995) The Times, 30 October

The plaintiff claimed the defendant's negligence resulted in the sale of his house falling through. The court found that there was a 50% chance of the sale going through but for the negligence of the defendant. The Court of Appeal therefore awarded the plaintiff damages assessed at 50% of the loss.

(11) First Interstate Bank of California v Cohen Arnold & Co (1995) The Times, 11 December

The plaintiff bank lent money to the defendant accountant's client. As a large proportion of the loan remained outstanding, the plaintiff enquired of the defendant what it's client net worth amounted to. The defendant misrepresented it's client's net worth and as a result the plaintiff, relying on this representation, did not begin marketing the property on which the loan was secured until September. The plaintiff obtained a price of £1.4 million for the property and contended that had it not relied on the defendant's representation that it would have called in the loan in June and sold the property for £3 million. The Court of Appeal held that this was a loss of a 'real or substantial' chance which the law would recognise.

Foreign case law

AUSTRALIA

See *Stacey v Chiddy* [1993] 4 Med LR 345 in Chapter 5, Standard of Care, at p 152.

Note that on appeal the court refused to consider a claim for loss of chance (the doctor had failed to diagnose a malignant tumour) as it had not been explored at trial. As the plaintiff was found to be suffering from an aggressive tumour it was doubtful whether an earlier diagnosis would have made much difference anyway.

CANADA

(1) Lawson v Lafferiere (1991) 78 DLR (4th) 609, also noted at [1994] 5 Med LR 185

The defendant failed to inform the plaintiff of a biopsy result which confirmed the plaintiff had cancer. The plaintiff did not learn of the result until four years later, by which time the cancer had spread throughout her body. She died three years later.

In the Quebec Court of Appeal she was compensated for loss of a chance, but the defendant successfully appealed to the Supreme Court of Canada. The majority of that court held the loss of chance claim should not be introduced into Quebec law, at least where the damage in question had already occurred.

Note that the plaintiff was awarded compensation for the psychological damage that she suffered as a result of the defendant's failure to her inform her of the result. She was also awarded damages for the better quality of life she would have enjoyed had the defendant not been negligent.

In discussing the 'loss of chance' claim, the court held in this instance the damage had already occurred and therefore the court was simply concerned as to whether or not the defendant's negligence had affected the plaintiff's condition and thus the question was one of probability and not loss of chance. In doing so, the court was not persuaded simply by statistical evidence; it would have found for the plaintiff even if the statistical evidence was poor.

See also *Snell v Farrell* (1990) 72 DLR (4th) 289 and *Patterson v Dutton* (1991) 79 DLR (4th) 705, at pp 180, 181.

UNITED STATES

Herskovits v Group Health Cooperative of Puget Sound (1993) 664 P (2d) 474

The plaintiff (the widow of the deceased) brought a claim alleging the defendant had been negligent in failing to diagnose her husband's cancer at an earlier stage. It was accepted that had the cancer been diagnosed at an earlier stage then Mr Herskovits' chances for survival would have been 39%, but the delay reduced his chances to 25%. The plaintiff recovered damages only for her husband's early death, eg loss of earnings, etc. Dole J said (at p 477):

> To decide otherwise would be a blanket release from liability for doctors and hospitals any time there was less than a 50% chance of survival, regardless of how flagrant the negligence.

RULE 6(C)

Where the plaintiff cannot explain how the accident occurred he may rely on the principle of *res ipsa loquitur*. The defendant must then rebut the inference of negligence.

Commentary

In all tort cases the burden of proof is on the plaintiff who must show, on a balance of probabilities, that the defendant's negligence caused the damage. As has already been seen, this may be supremely difficult; the patient might be unconscious at the time of the alleged negligence and therefore oblivious as to what actually happened and who gave the treatment, or the procedure being complained of might have been routine, as a result of which there may be very little in the way of written evidence as to how it was carried out. In such circumstances the plaintiff may rely on the evidential principle of *res ipsa loquitur*. It should be noted that the principle does not shift the burden of proof, it merely raises the inference of negligence which the defendant must rebut (see *Ng Chun Pui v Lee Chuen Tat* [1988] RTR 298). Although reliance on the principle will in effect give the plaintiff a more than equal chance of succeeding the burden still remains with him to establish that the defendant was negligent.

In order to rely on *res ipsa* the plaintiff must essentially prove two things:

(1) that the defendant had control of the situation; and

(2) that the damage would normally not have occurred in the ordinary course of events.

The most apt illustration of the principle at work is the case of *Cassidy v Ministry of Health* [1951] 2 KB 343. The plaintiff was suffering from Dupuytren's contracture and two of his fingers were operated on. After the operation he found that four of his fingers were stiff. In the Court of Appeal, Denning LJ held that *res ipsa* was appropriate because the result of the operation was highly indicative of negligence; the defendant was in control of the situation as it was responsible in law for all of the people involved in the procedure.

In *Mahon v Osborne* [1939] 2 KB 14, where a swab was left inside the patient's body, Scott LJ (in a strong dissenting judgment) said that it was wrong to apply the doctrine as a matter of course; the plaintiff had to prove that the accident was caused by the defendant's want of care. This statement should be borne in mind by a solicitor seeking to rely on *res ipsa*. If the operation is not routine but has associated risks, it may be difficult for the reasonable person to draw the necessary inference. Similarly, the principle should not be used as a stop gap in lieu of a closer investigation of the evidence. In practice, where an object is found in the plaintiff's body which clearly should not be there, it is most unlikely that any defendant is going to spend a vast amount of time and money in defending a negligence claim.

In *Delaney v Southmead Health Authority* [1995] 6 Med LR 355, the court held that *res ipsa loquitur* would rarely be of assistance after all the evidence had been adduced. Furthermore, the defendant could rebut the inference by either giving a reasonable explanation (the usual 'defence' to *res ipsa*), or by showing that he had exercised reasonable care (which is what happened in this case). As regards the second limb of the test, all the defendant did in this case (which satisfied the court) was to demonstrate that it had followed accepted practice despite the fact that this did not accord with the scientific evidence. This is in line with the decision of *Ng v Lee* (see above); the defendant merely has to show that it has taken care, ie provided an explanation, not that it has taken all reasonable care. See also the recent case of *Bouchta v Swindon Health Authority* [1996] 7 Med LR 62 which, like *Delaney*, again demonstrates the reluctance of the court to apply *res ipsa* to medical negligence actions. Commenting on the *res ipsa*, Judge Sumner said (at p 65):

I am reluctant to apply such a test to issues of medical judgment unless I am compelled to do so.

The courts will only entertain *res ipsa* in the most clear cut cases. In *Ludlow v Swindon Health Authority* [1989] 1 Med LR 104, the plaintiff alleged that the defendant had failed to administer halothane during a caesarian operation. Although she was able to describe the symptoms of a caesarian operation and she had experienced the pain, because she had been under the influence of drugs the court doubted the reliability of her version of events. Had the plaintiff been able to establish conclusively that she had been conscious and had suffered pain the court held, *obiter*, that *res ipsa* would have applied.

Once *res ipsa* has been held to apply, the defendant must seek to rebut the inference by offering a reasonable explanation. In *Saunders v Leeds Western Health Authority* (1984) 129 SJ 225, a child suffered cardiac arrest during an operation. The defendant sought to explain it by suggesting that the child's heart had suddenly stopped. This was rejected as implausible by the court.

If the defendant succeeds in rebutting the inference of negligence (see *Roe v Ministry of Health* [1954] 2 QB 66 and *Brazier v Minister of Defence* [1965] 1 Lloyd's Rep 26), the plaintiff must then, as for a 'normal' negligence case, prove that the defendant acted without reasonable care. It is submitted that it will be very difficult for him to do this since, if he had evidence of the defendant's want of care, it is unlikely that he would have relied on *res ipsa* in the first instance.

REFERENCES

English case law

(1) Ng Chun Pui v Lee Chuen Tat [1988] RTR 298; (1988) 132 SJ 1244

The first defendant was driving a coach owned by the second defendant when it crossed the central reservation, colliding with a public bus. The action was brought by the personal representatives of passengers who were killed or injured for damages for negligence. At first instance, judgment was given for the plaintiffs. The plaintiffs had relied on *res ipsa* and the judge had held that the burden of disproving negligence was on the defendants who had failed to discharge it. The Court of Appeal reversed the decision, holding that the defendant had exercised reasonable care in the circumstances. The Judicial Committee upheld this decision. Commenting on *res ipsa*, Lord Griffiths held that the burden of proving negligence rested throughout on the plaintiff. If the defendant adduced evidence, this had to be evaluated to see if it was still reasonable to draw the inference of negligence from the mere fact of the accident.

(2) Cassidy v Ministry of Health [1951] 2 KB 343; [1951] 1 All ER 574

Commenting on the plaintiff's claim Lord Denning said (at p 365):

> I went into hospital to be cured of 'two stiff fingers'; I have come out with 'four stiff fingers'. That should not have happened if due care had been used. Explain it, if you can.

(3) Mahon v Osborne [1939] 2 KB 14

See above, at p 189 and Chapter 5, Standard of Care, at p 161.

> *Note* that there was a strong dissenting judgment of Goddard LJ who thought that *res ipsa* might apply.

(4) Delaney v Southmead Health Authority [1995] 6 Med LR 355

The plaintiff underwent a cholocystectomy under general anaesthetic which was in itself successful, however, it was later discovered that the plaintiff had sustained a lesion of the brachial plexus. The plaintiff contended that as she had suffered a fracture of her clavicle in 1975 which had been plated resulting in substantial callous formation and reduction of the thoracic outlet; that the defendant should have refrained from using her left arm or hand for the administration of the general anaesthetic. As an alternative, the plaintiff argued that her left arm had been hyper abducted resulting in excessive strain and stretch on the nerve. The plaintiff argued that once it was accepted that an injury to the brachial plexus had occurred during the operation and there was no narrowing of the thoracic outlet then the principle of *res ipsa loquitur* was appropriate. The Court of Appeal doubted whether *res ipsa* was appropriate to a medical negligence case (see above, at p 189) and also the recent case of *Hay v Grampian Health Board* [1995] 6 Med LR 128. Here, a voluntary patient who was known to be at a high risk of suicide hung herself resulting in irreversible brain damage. At the time of the incident, the patient was left unattended, the two ward nurses were occupied with other patients. An action for damages was brought and the plaintiff established liability but it was held that the doctrine of *res ipsa loquitur* was inappropriate. Here, the facts were known, the patient had been left unsupervised which had resulted in her attempted suicide.

(5) Bouchta v Swindon Health Authority [1996] 7 Med LR 62

See Chapter 5, Standard of Care, at p 129. The plaintiff suffered damage to her ureter during a routine hysterectomy. Negligence was established though the doctrine of *res ipsa* was held inappropriate.

(6) Ludlow v Swindon Health Authority [1989] 1 Med LR 104

See Chapter 5, Standard of Care, at p 162.

See also *Taylor v Worcester and District Health Authority* [1991] 2 Med LR 215, Chapter 5, Standard of Care, at p 162.

(7) Saunders v Leeds Western Health Authority (1985) 129 SJ 225

See above, at p 189.

(8) Roe v Minister of Health [1954] 2 QB 66; [1954] 2 All ER 131

See Chapter 5, Standard of Care, at p 135.

(9) Brazier v Ministry of Defence [1965] 1 Lloyds Rep 26

The plaintiff was injected with penicillin. During the injection the needle broke off and lodged in his right buttock. He suffered severe pain and was compelled to give up work. He sued the Ministry of Defence, relying on *res ipsa*. The defendant, however, successfully rebutted the inference by showing that the accident was the result of a latent defect in the needle.

(10) Glass v Cambridge HA [1995] 6 Med LR 91

The plaintiff suffered a cardiac arrest whilst under a general anaesthetic resulting in severe brain damage. *Res ipsa* was held to apply. The defendant's explanation that a gas embolism had occurred when hydrogen peroxide was used to clean the patient's wound was rejected as the medical evidence did not support this explanation. If the defendant had proffered a reasonable explanation the inference of negligence would have been rebutted.

Practice points

It is not necessary to plead *res ipsa* – see the notes to RSC Ord 18, r 8 at *The White Book* 18/8/16.

RULE 6(D)

The defendant will only be held to have caused that damage which was reasonably foreseeable. The defendant, however, must take his victim as he finds him.

Commentary

As with other areas of tort the defendant will not be held responsible for all ensuing damage which befalls the plaintiff but only for that which is reasonably foreseeable as per *The Wagon Mound* [1961] AC 388. Furthermore, neither the extent of the damage nor the manner of its occurrence need be foreseen (see *Hughes v Lord Advocate* [1963] AC 837 and *Crossley v Rawlinson* [1982] 1 WLR 369). However, the foreseeable damage must be of the same kind as that which occurred.

The defendant must take his victim as he finds him. This is endorsed by the operation of the 'eggshell skull' rule, the two most important cases in this area being *Bourhill v Young* [1943] AC 92 and *Smith v Leech Brain & Co Ltd* [1962] 2 QB 405. In the latter, an employee who was burnt on the lip by a piece of molten metal contracted cancer as a result of the burn which led eventually to his death. The court held that 'the amount of damage which he suffers as a result of that burn, depends upon the characteristics and constitution of the victim' (at p 415). What is important is that some damage was foreseeable as a result of the defendant's negligence; provided that requirement is satisfied, the defendant is responsible for all the ensuing damage.

How this test fits in with the remoteness test based on foreseeability is speculative to say the least; however, it is apparent that the courts have held that the principle remains unaffected by *The Wagon Mound* decision. In *Page v Smith* [1995] 2 WLR 644, the plaintiff was involved in a road traffic accident with the defendant. Before the accident the plaintiff had been suffering from ME (chronic fatigue syndrome or post viral fatigue syndrome), which he claimed had become chronic and permanent as a result of the sudden shock caused by the accident. The Court of Appeal held that the plaintiff's psychiatric illness, which had not resulted from physical injury but from the nervous shock he sustained, was not reasonably foreseeable and the plaintiff could therefore only recover damages for the harm he suffered if the incident giving rise to the claim would have caused a person of ordinary fortitude to be similarly affected. However, in the House of Lords, the plaintiff was ultimately successful on a 3–2 majority. The two dissenting Lords applied an objective test and held that a reasonable person in the position of the defendant would not have foreseen that such an accident might inflict on a person of normal susceptibility such mental trauma and nervous shock as to result in illness. The majority, however, took the view that any driver should be able to foresee that driving carelessly might cause physical or psychiatric injury or both, and accordingly restored the award of damages.

The full implications of this decision have yet to be determined; however, it would seem that the court quashed any idea that the eggshell skull rule might not apply where the damage is psychiatric in nature. With this we agree. It is possible that the defendant could not have reasonably foreseen that the plaintiff was suffering from ME; however, we imagine that the defendant in *Smith v Leech Brain & Co Ltd* [1962] 2 QB 405 did not for one moment foresee that the plaintiff could contract cancer as a result of a minor burn. In our opinion, the two scenarios are indistinguishable, and there is no justification for applying different rules dependent on whether the damage is physical or psychiatric. It is to be hoped that the majority view of the House of Lords in *Page v Smith* continues to prevail.

See also nervous shock, at p 215.

REFERENCES

English case law

(1) *Overseas Tankship (UK) v Morts Dock & Engineering Co (The Wagon Mound)* [1961] AC 388; [1961] 1 All ER 404; [1961] 2 WLR 126

OT Ltd were demise charterers of *The Wagon Mound* which was moored at the C Oil Co's wharf to take on fuel oil. OT's employees negligently spilt oil onto the water and this spread to MD's wharf where another ship was moored undergoing repair. MD's manager asked C Oil Co whether he should stop the repairs and their answer, together with his own opinion, led him to order that the repairs should continue, taking extensive precautions. However, two days later the oil caught fire causing extensive damage to MD's wharf.

Held:

(a) it was unforeseeable that the fuel oil spread on the water would catch fire; and

(b) the damage which was caused to MD's wharf was foreseeable.

On appeal the Privy Council found for the defendant. The applicable test was the foresight of the reasonable man. It was also said that the damage that occurs must be of the same kind as that which was foreseeable.

(2) Hughes v Lord Advocate [1963] AC 837

A manhole was left open, covered only by a canvas shelter and surrounded by warning paraffin lamps. It was left unattended in the evening. The plaintiff, a child of eight, took one of the lamps and entered the shelter. He fell into the manhole causing an explosion and sustained severe burns.

It was held that it was unforeseeable that the lamp would explode but it was foreseeable that by leaving the shelter unattended someone might take a lamp and enter. So although the exact sequence of events was unforeseeable, the resulting damage clearly was and thus the defendant was liable.

(3) Crossley v Rawlinson [1982] 1 WLR 369

The plaintiff fell when running to put out a fire caused by the defendant's negligence. The court ruled that for the plaintiff to recover it had to be foreseeable that his injuries were caused by falling, it was not enough that it was foreseeable that he might be injured.

(4) Bourhill v Young [1943] AC 92

The plaintiff, a pregnant fishwife, was standing about 45 ft from a motorcycle accident. She heard a noise although she did not see the accident and suffered a fright which resulted in severe nervous shock. She gave birth to a stillborn child.

Held: the driver of the motorcycle owed no duty to her as she was not within an area of potential danger resulting from the negligence.

(5) Smith v Leech Brain & Co Ltd [1962] 2 QB 405

See above, at p 192.

(6) Page v Smith [1995] 2 WLR 644; [1995] 2 All ER 736

Note that the majority judgment distinguished between primary and secondary victims, an example of the latter being the spectators in *Alcock v Chief Constable of South Yorkshire* [1992] 1 AC 310, whereas someone directly involved in the accident would be regarded as a primary victim. Where the plaintiff is a secondary victim and is bringing a claim for nervous shock, the damage must be foreseeable – something which does not arise in the case of the primary victim. The court affirmed the decision in *Brice v Brown* [1984] 1 All ER 997 where a mother and daughter were involved in a car accident. The mother was awarded damages for her own shock and also the shock she suffered as a result of being aware of her daughter's predicament. As a result of *Page* the mother can be seen as both the primary and secondary victim.

RULE 6(E)

The plaintiff's claim will fail on causation if:

(1) there was a break in the chain of causation; or

(2) the defendant's breach of duty amounts to an omission and the plaintiff cannot show that the defendant's actions were contrary to accepted medical practice.

Commentary

The break in the chain

This is where an act by a third party supersedes the original negligent act of the defendant. The court must decide whether the original act of the defendant was responsible for the damage or if the intervening act constitutes a *novus actus interveniens*, ie the second act caused the damage. The second act could be an intervening act by a third party or an intervening act by the plaintiff himself.

By a third party

A good illustration of this principle is the case of *Prendergast v Sam and Dee* [1989] 1 Med LR 36. There a GP's writing was so bad that a prescription was misread by a pharmacist with the result that the patient suffered brain damage. The doctor alleged that the pharmacist's failure to query his illegible handwriting constituted a break in the chain of causation. This argument failed because the court ruled that it was foreseeable that the pharmacist would prescribe the wrong drug because of the GP's illegible handwriting.

The damage must in some way be caused by the initial negligence. So where a GP failed to diagnose appendicitis but the plaintiff's resulting damage was caused by the negligence of the operating surgeon, the GP could not be said to have caused that damage (see *Yepremian v Scarborough General Hospital* (1980) 110 DLR (3d) 513). This is different from the situation where a doctor negligently fails to diagnose a fracture and then the plaintiff is negligently treated by a second doctor for that fracture. In that situation, as in *Prendergast*, it is clearly foreseeable that the second doctor will rely on the negligent diagnosis of the first doctor.

Where the plaintiff's original injuries are exacerbated by negligent medical treatment, is the chain of causation broken? In *Hogan v Bentinck West Hartley Collieries Ltd* [1949]1 All ER 588, the court ruled that the chain would only be broken where the treatment was unreasonable or lacking in care. Just what will constitute an unreasonable intervention is not defined but we submit that it must mean any treatment contrary to accepted practice.

An interesting point is whether the same principles apply where the supervening act constitutes an omission. Generally, no liability attaches where the negligence constitutes an omission unless the doctor has a duty to treat. Usually the defendant can only rely on the omission where it is totally independent of the original act. It seems apparent, however, that any failure by the doctor to treat should be seen as a failure to minimise the damage rather than a failure to act, and that both the original tortfeasor and the negligent health carer should be held responsible. This results from the application of the 'but for' test, ie but for the original negligence the plaintiff would not have been placed in this predicament, but the health carer by his omission has exacerbated the damage and consequently must be held to account for his lack of action.

By the plaintiff

In some cases the defendant will try to argue that the plaintiff's conduct amounts to a *novus actus*. For example, the plaintiff may refuse to follow the prescribed treatment or fail to return to his GP when the very symptoms he has been told to watch out for reappear. Whether such conduct amounts to a *novus actus* must depend to a large extent on whether the patient's conduct is regarded as reasonable. In *Emeh v Kensington and Chelsea Area Health Authority* [1985] QB 1012, a woman sued in respect of the birth of her severely handicapped child following a negligently performed sterilisation operation. She had discovered that she was pregnant at about 20 weeks but decided not to undergo an abortion; this, the defendant argued, amounted to a *novus actus*. At first instance, this argument was accepted by the court but was rightly rejected on appeal. Slade LJ stated that the defendant had by his own negligence caused the plaintiff to be 'faced with the very dilemma she had sought to avoid by having herself sterilised' (at p 1053). The court doubted that such a decision could amount to a *novus actus* 'save in the most exceptional circumstances'. Quite what these exceptional circumstances are is unknown but we submit that a woman's decision not to have an abortion should never amount to a *novus actus*; there should never be a duty on a woman to abort.

An area which may cause problems is where the patient refuses treatment on religious grounds. In the criminal case of *R v Blaue* [1975] 1 WLR 1411, it was held that refusal to undergo a blood transfusion did not constitute a *novus actus*. This decision was clearly made on policy grounds, but it can be said to illustrate that the court will be reluctant to regard a decision based on religious grounds as unreasonable.

It is worth noting that the plaintiff need only take reasonable steps to mitigate his damage, consequently, it should never be unreasonable to make a decision according to one's religion. Also in cases of medical negligence (excepting in emergency situations) it is more than likely that the defendant will have discussed the variety of treatments available with, for example, a Jehovah's Witness patient and therefore should be able to foresee how the patient would react in any given situation. In this regard, it could not be said to be a totally independent act and consequently a *novus actus*.

We think it unlikely that the defendant will be able to rely on the principle of *novus actus*, because the court will be reluctant to hold that either the plaintiff or, for that matter, a third party should be penalised for not taking some step to minimise the damage caused by the defendant. At best the defendant should concentrate on those cases where a blatant lack of care by the plaintiff or a third party has resulted in damage which could have been avoided; as a defendant he should be relying on the principle of contributory negligence (see p 200).

The Bolitho defence

What could be termed the *Bolitho* exception is something new in medical negligence and whether it will become entrenched in English law remains to be seen. It stems from the decision in *Bolitho v City and Hackney Health Authority* [1993] 4 Med LR 381 where the plaintiff (a minor) was admitted to hospital with breathing difficulties. The paediatric registrar failed to attend the child after being summoned by the sister and it was admitted that this was negligent. However, the court could not say that that negligence caused the plaintiff's injuries because it was not apparent what the registrar would have done had she responded. The plaintiff's solicitors contended that had she attended she would have intubated the patient which would have prevented the ensuing injury; the defendant argued that she would not have intubated. Both arguments were endorsed by experts. The court held that where the breach of duty consisted of an omission, it had to be decided what course of events would have followed had the duty been discharged. To do so the court was bound to rely on the evidence of experts. As there was a conflict of medical opinion on the appropriate treatment then, since the plaintiff could not prove that failure to intubate was contrary to medical practice (ie the *Bolam* test), the claim failed. This means that the probability game canvassed in cases such as *Bonnington* and *McGhee* was now redundant; where there are two possible alternatives as to what could have happened, the defendant must now simply show that:

(1) he has acted in accordance with one of them; and

(2) he has acted in accordance with medical practice.

The *Bolam* test is now universally applicable to the standard of care and causation stages!

What does this mean for the medical negligence solicitor? Apparently all the defendant's solicitors must now do, where there is a dispute over causation, is to put forward a scenario that is endorsed by a body of medical opinion (see *DeFreitas v O'Brien and Connolly* [1995] 6 Med LR 108 – two or three can constitute a responsible body of medical opinion – see p 132). The facts of the case will now seemingly count for nothing.

The only thread of hope that remains for the plaintiff's solicitor is to try and persuade the court that the dissenting judgment of Simon Brown LJ in *Bolitho* should be applied in the case in hand. He chose to adopt the robust and pragmatic approach of *McGhee* and said that it was a matter of common sense to infer that a reasonable doctor would have intubated had he attended. It is possible that he reached this decision out of sympathy, but it can be justified using the risk versus precautions approach:

(1) The sister caring for the plaintiff would not have summoned assistance unless treatment was required; from the evidence she was of the opinion that there was something wrong and was sufficiently worried to order a nurse to stay with the plaintiff.

(2) It was an accepted fact that intubation would have benefited the plaintiff. Furthermore, intubating would have resulted in less risk to the plaintiff than not intubating.

(3) The plaintiff had a known history of respiratory problems. One month previously he had undergone a serious operation and had recently recovered from an attack of the croup.

(4) The plaintiff had been admitted to hospital after collapsing and making wheezing sounds. His medical notes indicated reduced air supply.

If point (2) is acceptable, is it wrong to infer the very thing which would have most benefited the plaintiff? As Simon Brown LJ pointed out, this approach had been taken in other cases. Unfortunately, even if this approach had been generally adopted in *Bolitho*, the majority decision would still have been that the defendant had discharged his burden by demonstrating that failure to intubate was in accordance with accepted practice.

Bolitho has recently been approved in the case of *Joyce v Merton, Sutton and Wandsworth Health Authority* [1996] 7 Med LR 1 (see Standard of Care, at p 142). There, the plaintiff established negligence but failed on causation because even if the occlusion had been discovered earlier, a surgeon would not have operated in time to remove the blockage and, furthermore, it would not have been negligent not to have done so. The fact the court found that the defendant would not have operated is a simple application of the 'but for' test but the court then went on to approve *Bolitho*. Hobhouse LJ said (at p 20):

> Thus, a plaintiff can discharge the burden of proof on causation by satisfying the court either that the relevant person would in fact have taken the requisite action (although she would not have been at fault if she had not) or that the proper discharge of the relevant person's duty towards the plaintiff required that she take that action ... Properly viewed, therefore, this rule is favourable to the plaintiff because it gives him two routes by which he may prove his case – either proof that the exercise of proper care would have necessitated the relevant result, or proof that if proper care had been exercised, it would in fact have led to the relevant result.

Later in his judgment, he continued and said:

> In assessing what the exercise of proper care necessitates, no different test is to be applied to that to be applied in any case where professional negligence is alleged, essentially the so called *Bolam* test. This is because it is the same question as is involved in the initial allegation of fault; the causation question merely extends the ambit of fault. The plaintiff's case is still based upon saying what the exercise of proper care required and saying that if proper care had been exercised in all respects and had continued to be exercised, the plaintiff would not have suffered the injury. Nor do any different principles of burden of proof apply; the plaintiff has the same general burden but can rely on evidential inferences to discharge that burden. In my judgment, it does not assist to introduce concepts from administrative law such as the *Wednesbury* test ...

Hobhouse LJ is actually saying that the '*Bolitho* rule' is favourable to the plaintiff because he now has two alternatives to prove his case. Favourable? Surely not. It is difficult, in the authors view, to see what advantage the plaintiff gains by the introduction of the '*Bolitho* rule'. The plaintiff has always had the opportunity to demonstrate that but for the defendant's omission he would not have suffered injury because the defendant would have taken action. That is nothing new, so the first alternative is merely restating the law as we know it to be. But the second? The plaintiff is being asked to prove not one but two negligent acts: (1) the original breach of duty (in this case the fact that the plaintiff was not given adequate post-operative care and was discharged) and (2) that had the original breach of duty not taken place that it was negligent not to intervene. A double edged sword? Hobhouse LJ says the causation question 'merely extends the ambit of the allegation of fault.' Surely, however, the 'fault' has already been established – in *Bolitho*, it was the non-attendance, in *Joyce* it was the discharge of the plaintiff without adequate care. Once this fault had been established to then go on and say that the plaintiff must now further establish a second fault, namely that the defendant would have fallen below the *Bolam* standard had he not acted, if given the chance, seems to us to be particularly absurd. Whatever happened to the rules about balance of probabilities and inferring what would have happened, (see r 6(A)) with ideally conferring most benefit on the plaintiff? Clearly, in *Bolitho,* on the evidence (see above, at p 196), it was open to the court to infer that the plaintiff would have been intubated, in *Joyce,* the evidence pointed the other way. Whatever the outcome, the court must not fight shy of it's role as speculators where there is more than one possible version of what would have happened, always of course with reference to the evidence. But to state that, where there is more than one version of what could have happened, the plaintiff will have to establish that the defendant's chosen option is wrong in accordance with *Bolam*, in addition to establishing the defendant's original breach of duty is not only unfair but wrong. *Bolam* has already been elevated to a position that overstates its importance; we cannot let it encroach into another link in the medical negligence chain. Once and for all, the courts must recognise that *Bolam* and causation do not mix.

REFERENCES

English case law

(1) Prendergast v Sam and Dee [1989] 1 Med LR 36

See above, at p 194.

(2) Hogan v Bentinck West Hartley Collieries Ltd [1949] 1 All ER 588

Held: an operation that had been unreasonably recommended by a doctor broke the chain of causation. If the treatment had been properly carried out, however, the original tortfeasor would still have been liable for any damage that resulted from the treatment.

(3) Emeh v Kensington and Chelsea and Westminster Area Health Authority [1985] QB 1012; [1984] 3 All ER 844

See above, at p 195.

(4) R v Blaue [1975] 1 WLR 1411

The plaintiff was stabbed by the defendant. She refused to undergo a blood transfusion because she was a Jehovah's Witness, and this resulted in her death.

Held: this did not break the chain of causation. The stab wound caused her death and the defendant could not contend that the plaintiff's religious beliefs were unreasonable.

(5) Bolitho v City and Hackney Health Authority [1993] 4 Med LR 381

See above, at p 196 *et seq* and Chapter 5, Standard of Care, at p 140 *et seq*.

(6) Bolam v Friern Hospital Management Committee [1957] 1 WLR 582; [1957] 2 All ER 118

See above and r 5(A), at p 121.

(7) Bonnington Castings Ltd v Wardlaw [1956] AC 613; [1956] 1 All ER 615

See p 174.

(8) McGhee v National Coal Board [1973] 1 WLR 1; [1972] 3 All ER 1008

See p 174.

(9) DeFreitas v O'Brien and Connolly [1995] 6 Med LR 108

See Chapter 5, Standard of Care, at p 132 for a more detailed analysis of the case. Briefly, the plaintiff's claim was that a group of 11 spinal surgeons could not constitute a group for the purposes of the *Bolam* rule; the group had to be substantial as in the *dicta* of Hirst J in *Hills v Potter* [1984] 1 WLR 641. This argument was rejected by the court, which held that whether or not the group was responsible could not be determined by 'counting heads'.

(10) Joyce v Merton, Sutton and Wandsworth Health Authority [1996] 7 Med LR 1; [1995] 2 Med LR 60.

See above, at p 197 and Chapter 5, Standard of Care, at p 142.

Foreign case law

AUSTRALIA

(1) Rogers v Whittaker [1993] 4 Med LR 79; [1992] 3 Med LR 331; (1992) 109 ALR 625

See pp 63, 67.

CANADA

(1) Yepremian v Scarborough General Hospital (1980) 110 DLR (3d) 513

The first doctor (G) was negligent in his treatment of the plaintiff's diabetes. The plaintiff subsequently suffered a cardiac arrest as a result of the negligence of a second doctor (R) after the diabetes had been diagnosed. Consequently, G was not responsible for R's negligence; however, the court indicated that had the cardiac arrest been the result of untreated diabetes then G would have been held liable notwithstanding R's subsequent negligence.

Practice points

The only recommendation we can make to help the hapless plaintiff's solicitor avoid the operation of the *Bolitho* exception is to use existing case law and try and argue material contribution. In reality, a defendant in breach by non-attendance has materially contributed to the damage in exactly the same way as the employer who failed to provide an extractor fan did in *Bonnington*. To quote Lord Simon in *McGhee* ([1973] 1 WLR 1, at p 8) 'a failure to take steps which would bring about a material reduction of the risk involves ... a substantial contribution to the injury'. However, this approach may only work when there is a choice of two alternatives. What about the situation as demonstrated by *Wilsher*? What if the defendant could have chosen any one of, say, five options had he attended? Argue that the defendant's actions materially increased the risk of damage occurring (which the court have held is the same as a material contribution – see p 174, *et seq*). Anything that does not fall within the *de minimis* rule is a material contribution. If the defendant then raises the argument of accepted practice, ie even if he had attended he would have done nothing and that his action (or lack of) is endorsed by a responsible group of medical opinion, the plaintiff's solicitor, in reply, should argue the risk versus precautions theory. The greater the likely risk if the defendant fails to act and the simpler the precautions available to avoid the ensuing damage, the stronger the argument that the court should be able to infer that the defendant would have chosen the option which would have prevented the resulting damage. This approach is not foolproof, but at the moment this is the only viable option we can see.

RULE 6(F)

If the plaintiff's injuries were caused partly by his own fault and partly by the fault of the defendant, the plaintiff's damages may be reduced by such an amount as the court thinks just to reflect the plaintiff's responsibility for the damage.

Commentary

Although contributory negligence may have a only a limited part to play in a medical negligence claim, it should still be borne in mind by any solicitor, especially when it is clear that the plaintiff himself is not totally blameless.

The Law Reform (Contributory Negligence) Act 1945 defines fault as: 'negligence, breach of statutory duty or other act or omission which gives rise to a liability in tort.' After some debate it now appears that the Act also applies in cases of trespass to the person (see *Murphy v Culhane* [1977] QB 94 and *Barnes v Nayer* (1986) *The Times*, 19 December) and in contractual claims where, although the defendant's liability is in contract, the same liability would have arisen in tort independently of any contractual liability. In medical negligence, this means that the Act will apply equally to claims arising out of negligent treatment under the NHS and in private treatment. This accords with the court's intention that private patients should be not be given preferential treatment.

When the defence is raised in a medical negligence claim, the defendant will have to establish that the plaintiff's conduct contributed to the damage (see *Jones v Livox Quarries Ltd* [1952] QB 608) and that he has failed to take reasonable care for his own safety. The plaintiff need not owe any duty to the defendant. The standard of care expected of the plaintiff is measured objectively and is the same as for negligence itself, although there is of course some discretion in relation to children and those plaintiffs under a disability.

If a solicitor wishes to rely on this defence, then he should look to the Canadian courts for guidance on how the principle may be applied. In *Crossman v Stewart* (1977) 82 DLR (3d) 677, a patient was rendered almost blind from chloroquine retinopathy, the drug having been prescribed for a skin disorder. However, the plaintiff's damages were reduced by two-thirds because she had obtained some of her supplies of the drug from an unknown source and failed to obtain prescription renewals or to consult her treating physician.

Whether the defence would be appropriate in, for example, a situation where the plaintiff fails to return to his GP's surgery for follow-up visits is debatable, and we think it could only be invoked where the plaintiff has been specifically and repeatedly warned to return if certain symptoms persist and these symptoms are of a serious nature. Other than that, it would be unwise to place too much emphasis on this defence, primarily because the court will always view the doctor's duty to his patient as paramount and will be reluctant to hold the patient culpable because of his lack of knowledge and lack of control over any given situation. Also, any defendant who pleads contributory negligence may find that the burden of proof is back on him. For example, if the defendant alleges that the plaintiff failed to read the prescription properly or return to the surgery if his condition deteriorated, the court may question what advice the defendant gave to the patient regarding the medication condition and whether this advice was adequate.

As to how damages are apportioned if this defence is successfully pleaded see Chapter 7, Damages, at p 203.

REFERENCES

English case law

(1) Murphy v Culhane [1977] QB 94

The plaintiff (widow of the deceased) brought an action against the defendant. The deceased was killed during an assault by the defendant. The defence argued that the assault occurred during and as part of a criminal affray begun by the plaintiff.

Held: the defendant could rely on the defence of *volenti non fit injuria* and that even if the plaintiff had been entitled to damages they would have been reduced in consequence of his own fault pursuant to the Law Reform (Contributory Negligence) Act 1945.

(2) Barnes v Nayer (1986) The Times, 19 December

See above, at p 200.

(3) Jones v Livox Quarries Ltd [1952] QB 608

The plaintiff was riding on the towbar of a 'traxcavator' vehicle when the driver of another vehicle drove into the back of him.

Held: the plaintiff had exposed himself not only to the risk of being thrown off but also to the risk of being run into from behind.

Foreign case law

CANADA

(1) Crossman v Stewart (1977) 82 DLR (3d) 677

See above, at p 200.

(2) Fredette v Wiebe (1986) 29 DLR (4th) 534

The plaintiff underwent an abortion. She was advised by her GP to return two weeks after the operation to check that the procedure had been successful, and the GP was supposed to check the laboratory report relating to the tissue removed at the operation. The plaintiff did not return and the GP failed to check the report. In fact, the plaintiff was still pregnant.

Held: the plaintiff was contributorily negligent in failing to return to her GP.

Note that this case is similar to *Emeh v Kensington and Chelsea and Westminster Area Health Authority* [1985] QB 1012; [1984] 3 All ER 844 where the court held that the plaintiff was not liable for failing to mitigate her damage by not having an abortion on discovering that she was still pregnant. The court ruled that it is one thing to seek an abortion in the early stages of pregnancy but the plaintiff might feel quite different as the pregnancy advanced.

Practice points

- Contributory negligence must be specifically pleaded by the defendant, see RSC Ord 18, r 12; *The White Book* 18/8/5, 18/12/5. If it is not pleaded, it is not open to the court to find the plaintiff has been contributory negligent.
- For other practice points, see Chapter 5, Standard of Care, at p 164 *et seq*. Readers will note on reading this section that many of the points about commissioning an expert report, etc apply equally at this stage of the proceedings.

CHAPTER 7

DAMAGES

RULE 7(A)

Once the plaintiff has established that the defendant's lack of care caused his injuries he is entitled to be compensated for all of his losses which are attributable to those injuries. In a case for personal injuries, damages are divided into two categories: special damages and general damages. The plaintiff may also be awarded interest on these damages.

Commentary

The basic principle in awarding compensation is to put the plaintiff in the position he would have been had the tort not occurred. Obviously, although the purpose is to compensate the plaintiff for his injuries, in reality no amount of money can compensate for the pain and suffering sustained. But once liability is established or admitted, the principle *restitutio in integrum* applies and the court must award damages – there is no discretion.

There are various categories of damages and these are discussed under separate headings below with the last three being distinct claims in their own right, ie the loss of a chance claim (see *Hotson v East Berkshire Health Authority* [1987] AC 750 in Chapter 6, Causation, at p 182 *et seq*); the claim for wrongful life/birth (refer to Chapter 3, Duty, at p 79) and the claim for nervous shock.

Pain and suffering

Damages for pain and suffering will form part of the general damages award. Damages are assessed at the date of the trial and not the date of injury (see *Jobling v Associated Dairies Ltd* [1982] AC 794). Generally, the court will not draw a distinction between damages awarded for pain and suffering and damages for loss of amenity – they tend to be awarded as a global sum. It is unlikely that any injury will not result in some degree of pain and suffering; therefore as a rule the courts do not recognise the injury itself as a separate head of damage, except where it is specific, eg loss of an arm or leg where there are recommended awards for such injuries. Solicitors will be familiar with texts such as *Kemp and Kemp, Current Law, Halsbury's Monthly Review* and the Judicial Studies Board Guidelines for the Assessment of Damages which detail the awards.

Pain is suffered as a consequence of the injury; that suffering includes anxiety, embarrassment, etc caused by the injury, and the court will also take into account any shock suffered by the plaintiff. The award will be tailored to meet the characteristics of the particular plaintiff; consequently, if a plaintiff suffers no pain or is incapable of experiencing pain (eg someone who is unconscious or paralysed) there will be no award. As with most claims the plaintiff must present evidence that he suffered pain; in *Hicks and others v Chief Constable of the South Yorkshire Police* [1992] 2 All ER 65, the personal representatives of relatives who were crushed to death at the Hillsborough Stadium claimed damages under the Law Reform (Miscellaneous Provisions)

Act 1934 for the pain and suffering alleged to have been sustained immediately prior to their relatives' death. That claim was rejected by the House of Lords who ruled that prior to the deaths the victims suffered fear which in their view was a normal human reaction and as such damages could not be awarded. This decision was clearly a matter of policy since the court was concerned that if they had taken the opposite stance this would in effect have meant that the people who had escaped the Hillsborough disaster would have had a claim for the distress they had suffered, which was an earlier view expressed by the Court of Appeal. It seems rather harsh that a plaintiff can suffer appalling treatment but, because of his extraordinary fortitude, not suffer any shock or psychiatric illness and is therefore not compensated. Generally, only where the plaintiff suffers from a recognisable psychiatric illness as a result of his injuries will the court award compensation (see the commentary on nervous shock claims below, at p 215). However, the plaintiff may be able to recover in a situation where mental distress and grief caused by the death of someone close to him prevents a normal recovery (see *Rourke v Barton* (1982) *The Times*, 23 June).

Other factors which the courts will consider are the degree of pain already suffered and the plaintiff's future prospects. As regards the latter obviously the plaintiff's age and life expectancy are determinative but, additionally, the court will consider the way in which the plaintiff reacted to his predicament.

Medical negligence cases where damages seem to be awarded purely for pain and suffering include:

(1) where a plaintiff was awake during an operation due to the negligence of the anaesthetist, eg conscious during a caesarean section;

(2) where a plaintiff has suffered an appalling time during the delivery of her child. See *Kralj v McGrath and St Theresa's Hospital* [1986] 1 All ER 54; *Ackers v Wigan Health Authority* [1991] 2 Med LR 232; *Phelan v East Cumbria Health Authority* [1991] 2 Med LR 295 and *Cooper v Nottingham Health Authority* (1989) *The Times*, 17 March; or

(3) where a child suffers injuries in the womb and is born disabled as a result he has a claim for pain and suffering in respect of those injuries under the Congenital Disabilities (Civil Liability) Act 1976. This rule is also now enshrined in the common law. See *Burton v Islington Health Authority* and *De Martell v Merton and Sutton Health Authority* [1993] 4 Med LR 8.

Loss of amenity

Damages under this head will compensate the plaintiff for his loss of enjoyment as a result of the accident ie when can he no longer do the things he was accustomed to doing. Damage within this category will include loss of any of the five senses, loss of sex drive, damage to the plaintiff's marriage prospects, loss of enjoyment of hobbies, employment and, indeed, loss of any facet of life. The court may also make an award for loss of congenial appointment when a plaintiff can no longer carry out work which he particularly enjoyed, or for loss of leisure time caused by having to work longer. The court will take into account how long the plaintiff will be deprived of these amenities; if it is for the rest of his life the amount of damages will be awarded in proportion to the plaintiff's age and life expectancy. However, age is not necessarily the determinative factor

– loss of amenity in an elderly patient can have drastic effects and give rise to high awards of damages.

The plaintiff need not be aware of the loss of amenity; what matters is that the amenity is lost, eg someone who is rendered permanently unconscious is still entitled to an award under this head. See *Wise v Kaye* [1962] 1 QB 368 where the plaintiff remained unconscious from the moment of the accident, was deprived of all the attributes of life and was awarded of £15,000. In *H West & Son Ltd v Shepherd* [1964] AC 174, the plaintiff sustained severe head injuries, cerebral atrophy and paralysis of all four limbs. There was no chance that her condition would improve; her life expectancy was reduced to five years. She was unable to speak although the evidence indicated that she might appreciate her condition. The House of Lords upheld an award of £17,500 for loss of amenity.

Whether damages should be awarded in such situations is debatable. Clearly, such a plaintiff is in reality in no different a position than a dead plaintiff. It seems illogical that a plaintiff who feels nothing should be awarded the same as a plaintiff who will have to suffer the loss for the remainder of his life. The Law Commission, however, recommended no change, although the Pearson Commission thought otherwise. Furthermore, in *Lim Poh Choo v Camden and Islington Area Health Authority* [1980] AC 174, the House of Lords refused to endorse any change, ruling that it was a matter for the legislature although they did reduce the award. We do not recommend that the award for the plaintiff who is permanently unconscious should be reduced; rather, we advocate that the award to a conscious plaintiff should be increased to take into account the length of his deprivation.

Finally, pursuant to s 1(1)(b) Administration of Justice Act 1982, for all actions arising after 1 January 1983 the court will make an award to a plaintiff whose expectation of life has been reduced because of his injuries. Before 1983 this was a separate award; now the courts simply take this factor into account in awarding general damages. Any claim for loss of expectation of life will inevitably be coupled with a claim for bereavement which will now be brought under the Fatal Accidents Act 1976.

Loss of future earnings

This head is an exception to the general rule that pecuniary losses fall into the special damages category. The reason is that it is often impossible to say what the plaintiff's future loss would have been but for his injuries. For example, it may be unclear how long he will require medical attention or when or if he will ever return to work. Furthermore, if he does return to work it is most unlikely that his wage will remain constant. In general, the court will apply the same rules for the assessment of past and future loss of earnings, although obviously there is more guess work involved in the latter. The court's main problem is how to take into account the receipt of a lump sum in advance of future losses. The policy operated by the court is that each future payment will be subject to a reduction or a discount to reflect the fact that the plaintiff is actually receiving his compensation before the loss or expense has occurred.

As personal injury solicitors will be aware, future loss of earnings and expenses are assessed at the date of trial by reference to a multiplicand and a multiplier. The multiplicand will be the plaintiff's net annual loss which in practice will already have been calculated in determining the special damages schedule (see p 211). The courts will then apply a multiplier – the figure is an arbitrary one calculated as from the date of trial. The multiplier will be arrived at by reference to the Pearson Commission data, possibly government actuary tables (which are now specifically admissible, see p 225) and previously decided cases. The multiplier is supposed to cover the period from the date of trial up to the time when the loss of earning or expenditure would cease. What is certain is that the court will not fix the multiplier as the number of years from the trial until retirement or death as that would result in over compensation. The general principle is that the interest and capital should be exhausted at the same time as the plaintiff's need is extinguished. Additionally, the court will have to assess what is the real return after tax, national insurance and inflation, and on investment of the money. In looking at the plaintiff's life expectancy, account will be taken of the general vicissitudes of life, and the fact that the lump sum can immediately be invested. In estimating the real return of money a discount rate of 4.5%, has been adopted (see, for example, *Cookson v Knowles* [1979] AC 566). In other words, according to the Pearson Commission data, the court will assume that the plaintiff who receives compensation will subsequently invest it and receive a rate of return of 4.5% per annum after tax and inflation are taken into account.

The above mechanisms have come in for criticism in two reports from the Law Commission, 'Structured Settlements and Interim and Provisional Damages' (No 224) and 'Personal Injury Compensation: How Much is Enough?' (No 225). The second paper concluded that the existing levels of compensation are often insufficient to meet the continuing needs of the victim as time passes. In paper No 224 at para 6.1, the Law Commission recommended that the 'actuarial tables published by the Government Actuary's Department (known as the Ogden tables) should be admissible in any proceedings for damages for personal injury ...' Unfortunately the use of such tables has been discouraged, partly because of the cost involved and partly because the evidence is compiled by insurers, who have an interest in such evidence. In reality, the present approach often will lead to under compensation and therefore anything which will result in greater accuracy in awards must be seen as beneficial.

The Ogden tables are based on English Life Tables which contain information on contingencies other than mortality, eg illness, employment and a list of justifiable deductions in respect of those contingencies. This would seem infinitely preferable to the present position where the court will only take into account mortality and apply a discount for a lump sum and, as a rule of thumb, a deduction of 10% will be made for those other contingencies. At present, a rather bleak view is taken of the plaintiff's future prospects, ie his earnings are not expected to increase drastically, it is not expected that he will live to a great age. If, however, the plaintiff lives longer than expected his compensation will be exhausted before the scheduled time.

The courts have already started to have regard to the Ogden tables, see the first instance decision in *Page v Sheerness Metal plc* [1996] PIQR 261 (but see below and p 219) and now pursuant to s 10 Civil Evidence Act 1995 (see further p 225), the Ogden tables are admissible as of right in civil proceedings.

The Law Commission has also been critical of the rule which says that the plaintiff will receive a 4.5% real return on money. Clearly, the real return on money will depend on how the plaintiff chooses to invest his money. The Law Commission Report No 225 analysed what some plaintiffs did with their money. The most common method of saving was to use a building society account followed by a bank account. Advice was most commonly sought from a bank or building society, though there was still a high percentage of respondents who received no advice. For example, of those who were awarded over £100,000, 16% took no investment advice. In their summary of recommendations, the Law Commission in Report No 224 para 6.2 recommended that legislation should be implemented requiring the court to consider the net return on an index-linked government security ('gilts' – these are published in the *Financial Times*) subject to evidence demonstrating that a different rate is more appropriate in any given case. However, the Court of Appeal has now stated that gilts are inappropriate, in deciding the level of damages the court would assume that the plaintiff acted as a prudent investor, eg invested his money on the stock market, see *Wells v Wells*; *Thomas v Brighton Health Authority*; *Page v Sheerness Steel Co plc* (1996) *The Times*, 23 October. The conventional guidelines were still applicable and the court would continue to adopt a discount rate of 4.5%. We await further developments when these cases reach the House of Lords.

Finally, note that the plaintiff will also be able to recover damages for either the loss of a pension or any reduction in his pension (see further *Auty v National Coal Board* [1985] 1 WLR 784).

Damages for handicap in the labour market – the Smith v Manchester award

Damages under this head are often referred to as damages for loss of a person's earning capacity. A true award under this head is made to a plaintiff who is able to return to his employment but his injuries mean that he is more likely to lose his job in the event of redundancies and/or he is plainly at a disadvantage in the labour market, eg predisposition to similar injury or has been unemployed through his disabilities since the injury (see *Smith v Manchester Corporation* [1974] 17 KIR 1; *Moeliker v A Reyrolle Co Ltd* [1976] ICR 253; *Foster v Tyne & Wear County Council* [1986] 1 All ER 567).

The lost years

These damages are incapable of any precise calculation and form part of the general damages award. The claim is made by a living plaintiff for the 'lost years' ie the period by which his life has been shortened because of his injuries and during which he would have received remuneration. In *Pickett v British Rail Engineering Ltd* [1980] AC 136, the court allowed such a claim overruling previous decisions to the contrary. Damages will be dependent on the plaintiff's date of birth and his expectation of life at the date of trial.

The claim is not restricted to lost earnings, although that is the basis of the usual claim. No deduction is to be made in respect of expenditure that the plaintiff would have incurred on behalf of his dependants during the lost years, but a deduction will be made to reflect the actual living expenses of the plaintiff (see *Harris v Empress Motors Ltd* [1984] 1 WLR 212). It is important to note that the courts are concerned to ensure that the only sums to be deducted are those that were necessary to maintain the plaintiff in the standard of life to which he was accustomed and, furthermore, any joint expenditure between the plaintiff and others should only be deducted to the extent of the plaintiff's share. It therefore follows that a much larger deduction may be made in respect of a single person, and that in the majority of cases where children are involved there will be no deduction.

Loss of a pension will fall under this head of damages in most cases, except where the plaintiff has reached pensionable age; in that case, his past losses will come under the sphere of special damages, while his future loss will form part of his general damages. The court must consider what the plaintiff's pension would have been had he not been injured. Generally, quotations are sought from life insurance companies to calculate this loss, and a comparison is made between the pension the plaintiff could have expected had he not been injured with the pension he can now expect. Recently, the court has again looked at damages under this head. In *Phipps v Brooks Dry Cleaning Services, The Times*, 16 July 1996, the plaintiff's life expectancy had been curtailed as a result of coming into contact with asbestos dust during his employment with the defendant. The court applied the judgment of *Harris v Empress Motors* [1984] which concerned the assessment of damages under the Law Reform (Miscellaneous Provisions) Act 1934. In this case, O'Connor J, discussing what amounted to living expenses, said:

> ... in relation to a man's net earnings that any proportion thereof that he saves or spends exclusively for the maintenance or benefit of others does not form part of his living expenses. Any proportion that he spends exclusively on himself does. In cases where there is a proportion of the earnings expended on what may conveniently be called shared living expenses, a *pro rata* part of that proportion should be allocated for deduction.

The Court of Appeal held that the rationale expressed in *Harris* also applied where the plaintiff was still living. Hence, a living plaintiff who lives with one dependant, eg his wife, will not only have his multiplicand reduced by one-third to reflect his share of the household expenses, but also by half of one-third to represent his share of the joint expenditure: the total deduction being approximately half. This is in contrast to the position of a wife claiming under the Fatal Accidents Act 1976 (see p 244 *et seq*) where her dependency would normally be two-thirds of his net annual earnings.

Past and future expenses

The rule for calculating pecuniary loss is as stated in *McGregor on Damages* (15th edition, para 1450):

> The plaintiff will recover, subject to the rules on remoteness and mitigation, full compensation for the pecuniary loss he has suffered.

In assessing these losses it must be noted that there is no difference between past and future losses; the damages are dealt with under the same categories and the same deductions and/or contingencies are taken into account. The main item under this head will be medical expenses, both past and future. Future medical expenses and any other future expenses will be assessed as part of the plaintiff's general damages; those which have already been incurred will form part of the special damages.

The most important aspect of future expense is how long should the expense last and what discount is appropriate. As for loss of earnings, the expenses will be assessed using the multiplicand/multiplier approach. Generally, a greater multiplier will be applied here than for loss of earnings since it is assumed that most expenses will be permanent future expenses, except where the plaintiff's expectation of life is short, in which case his loss of earnings will be greater.

One of the matters which falls to be determined in estimating the plaintiff's future medical expenses and loss of earnings is his life expectancy. This is often difficult to determine and it will be the area which will cause most disagreement between the respective parties. For example, in the case of a plaintiff who has suicidal tendencies, the defendant may argue that the plaintiff's life expectancy is limited; the plaintiff's argument, however, would be that with round the clock nursing the risk could be minimised.

Below some of the more usual expenses are discussed in greater detail.

Accommodation

One of the major expenses the plaintiff may incur is buying new accommodation or adapting his present accommodation. At present, society encourages the care of the disabled at home wherever possible, but the problem the court faces in assessing damages under this head is how to provide for the plaintiff's reasonable needs without providing a windfall to his estate. This problem was considered in *Roberts v Johnstone* [1988] 3 WLR 1247 where the extra cost of special accommodation was converted into an annual loss, the general multiplier being used to arrive at the sum awarded, and the plaintiff was allowed to recover the cost of moving and any new furniture. The dominant principle in *Roberts* was to avoid over compensation and to ensure that any award was exhausted at the death of the plaintiff. It could be argued that housing costs are special damages in that they are pre-trial costs, thereby removing their speculative nature. The court should also recognise that often a house which has been adapted to cater for the plaintiff's disabilities may be worth less when sold because of those alterations. Thus, not only will the plaintiff fail to recoup his expenditure but he will also lose the opportunity to invest a proportion of the award because it is tied up in the house. Perhaps the time has come for the courts to reassess the principles by which they make these awards.

Where the plaintiff intends to purchase new accommodation, the court must take into consideration the cost of the property as against the benefit of having a new asset. In *Roberts v Johnstone* [1988] 3 WLR 1247, the court ruled that the purchase of residential property should be regarded as the equivalent of buying an investment secured against the risk of inflation. Damages were assessed by taking 2% of the cost of the property and multiplying it by the multiplier. However, this approach may not always be appropriate because the value of property has fallen considerably since 1989 when the case was decided.

Nursing care

Where the plaintiff is being cared for in a private institution, damages awarded under this category must be set off against any domestic savings. However, where the plaintiff is being cared for at home, the cost may be recovered notwithstanding that it would be cheaper if he was in an institution. This is also the case where the help is provided gratuitously, eg by a family or friend (see *Donnelly v Joyce* [1974] QB 454 and *Housecroft v Burnett* [1986] 1 All ER 332). In the former case, the plaintiff's mother gave up work to nurse him and the court ruled that the plaintiff was entitled to recover damages in respect of the reasonable cost of the special attention required. The one exception to this rule is where the services are provided by the tortfeasor, see *Hunt v Severs* [1994] 2 All ER 385 in which the court ruled that any damages paid to the plaintiff under this head were paid under the assumption that the plaintiff would hold them in trust for his carer. It follows that the bizarre situation could be reached where the defendant could be required to pay the plaintiff damages under this head only for the plaintiff to repay him at some future date. This decision has serious implications for victims of road traffic accidents where the driver and the injured passenger are often related, but it has limited application in medical negligence claims where the tortfeasor is usually the NHS, a Trust, etc. However, conceivably there could be a situation where a GP is sued by a relative and the GP goes on to provide care for his relative. In such a situation the solicitor should advise that the care be provided by a relative other than the defendant or, alternatively, that the services be provided pursuant to a contract between the defendant and the victim, as it appears that this would remain unaffected by the decision in *Hunt*.

The carer may recover for any loss of earnings suffered as a result of caring for the plaintiff; however, he will not be able to recover for both loss of earnings and the cost of caring for the plaintiff, because this would amount to double recovery. One exception to this rule is where:

(1) the value of the carer's loss of earnings is more than the cost of care (providing that the carer's decision in giving up his job was reasonable in all the circumstances); and

(2) only the carer can provide that care, eg a father looking after his children after the death of their mother (see *Mehmet v Perry* [1977] 2 All ER 529).

The other main award under this head is in respect of any special facilities the plaintiff has required in respect of the alterations to existing accommodation, eg a lift.

Medical expenses

These are recoverable provided they are reasonable and were incurred as a result of the injuries. They can take any form, eg treatment, medicine, appliances, etc. Often in a medical negligence claim as a result of the defendant's negligence the plaintiff will require further surgery, eg a repeat abortion or sterilisation. The plaintiff will be awarded the cost of the extra surgery (see *Emeh v Kensington and Chelsea and Westminster Area Health Authority* [1985] QB 1012; [1984] 3 All ER 844) where the plaintiff was awarded the cost of a second sterilisation operation. If the plaintiff requires further medical treatment then, pursuant to s 2(4) Law Reform (Personal Injuries) Act 1948, he may claim the cost of private medical treatment notwithstanding that the same treatment is available on the NHS. The court, however, will take into account that if the plaintiff has spent time in a NHS hospital or its equivalent then he must give credit for the savings in his living expenses (see s 5 Administration of Justice Act 1982 and p 224).

Other expenses

There are many other pecuniary items which the solicitor should consider; they are not dealt with here but readers are advised to consult *Kemp and Kemp*, Vol 1, Chapter 5, and in particular paras 5–011–5–0112. By way of quick reference, damages may be awarded for any of the following items:

- Clothes.
- Costs of extra home help.
- Costs of special equipment.
- Postal charges.
- Telephone charges.
- Costs of alterations to car or a new car or car hire.
- Any other pecuniary losses, eg the value of free accommodation, any concessionary fares, a trip abroad, the loss of a job, etc.
- Court of Protection fees where the plaintiff becomes unable to look after his own affairs; the cost here is dependent on the estate to be administered, *Roberts v Johnstone* [1988] 3 WLR 1247 (also applicable where the plaintiff is a minor).
- The extra costs of running a household.
- The cost of buying a second home as a consequence of the breakdown of a marriage. This may occur where, as a result of his injuries, the plaintiff undergoes a complete personality change and the spouse has to move out of the marital home. Although in *Jones v Jones* [1984] 3 WLR 862 the court awarded damages to the plaintiff's spouse for this very loss, that decision was rejected in *Pritchard v Parrot* (1985) *The Times*, 27 September where the court held that the loss was too remote. For any solicitor looking to prove such a claim it is important that the loss is capable of proof.

Loss of earnings (past)

See Practice Direction (Damages: Personal Injuries) [1984] 1 WLR 1127. In calculating lost earnings they will be net of tax and national insurance contributions and the plaintiff's contributions to a compulsory pension scheme, with any loss of pension rights calculated separately. For the position as regards social security benefits, see p 227 *et seq*. The plaintiff's loss is calculated tax year by tax year. In addition, the plaintiff must give credit for any sums that he would have incurred in earning the income, eg travelling expenses (see *Lim Poh Choo v Camden and Islington Area Health Authority* [1980] AC 174).

Normally, special damages are agreed and there is little dispute about what the plaintiff would have earned until trial. The plaintiff should be asked to estimate his loss of earnings over the period and then the employer should be asked to do the same. If there is a difficulty in calculating the amount the plaintiff would have earned as overtime, a comparison can usually be made with a fellow employee. In comparing the plaintiff's loss of earnings with a fellow employee, it is important that the figures are gross not net because special factors, eg individual tax circumstances distorting the true picture. Other considerations the court will take into account in assessing both actual and future loss of earnings are whether the plaintiff's earnings would have been less as a result of factors other than his injuries, whether he receives any commission, whether it was likely that the plaintiff would have been promoted, etc.

Solicitors should study the contract of employment; it may be that the plaintiff was entitled to be paid while he was off work, but this is often subject to a clause in the contract of employment that the plaintiff will seek to recover these sums (see further, at p 228).

As regards statutory sick pay the employee will be entitled to this payment for the first 28 weeks of absence in any three years. At the end of this period he is no longer eligible to statutory sick pay and so will have to claim DSS benefits (see p 228). Until April 1994, any statutory sick pay paid by the employer was refunded by the state and in these cases the employer must repay to the Compensation Recovery Unit all payments made to the client, (see further, at p 228).

In the case of a self-employed plaintiff the services of an accountant will be required and the court will effectively be required to evaluate the loss of a chance of those earning.

Interest

Pursuant to s 35A Supreme Court Act 1981 and s 69 County Courts Act 1984, if the award is £200 or greater then the plaintiff is entitled to interest on the damages awarded from the date of issue until trial, unless the court in its discretion decides there are reasons not to make such an award. The guidelines for the award of interest are found in cases such as *Wright v British Railways Board* [1983] 2 AC 773 and *Pickett v British Rail Engineering Ltd* [1980] AC 136. In essence, the rules are as follows:

(1) on damages for pain and suffering and loss of amenity, interest is awarded at 2%;

(2) for future pecuniary loss inclusive of possible future handicap on the labour market there is no award; and

(3) for special damages interest is awarded at half the court's special account rates applicable during the period. This rate was reduced to 8% on 1 February 1993. The relevant rates since 1965 are set out in *The White Book* at note 12, RSC Ord 6, r 2. (Solicitors should also refer to Rodney Nelson-Jones annual ready reckoner tables in the *Law Society Gazette* (latest edition 25 September 1996). Since June 1987, interest has been paid daily on 1/365

basis, even in a leap year. In *Roberts v Johnstone* [1988] 3 WLR 1247, the court held that damages awarded for unpaid past care and attendance should be treated as special damages for this purpose and that interest should be awarded accordingly. The dates on which interest begins to run will differ depending on the category of damages. For general damages, interest runs from the date of service of the proceedings; for special damages it runs from the date of the accident.

Loss of chance

This claim is dealt with in detail in Chapter 6, Causation, at p 182, *et seq*. It has to be said that it remains uncertain whether damages for loss of chance can ever be awarded in a medical negligence case, even though they have been awarded in contract cases. To have any chance of success the plaintiff must be able to prove that, but for the defendant's negligence, he would have had at least a 51% chance of making a full recovery (see *Hotson v East Berkshire Health Authority* [1987] AC 750). *Hotson* did not rule out the possibility of a loss of chance case, but neither did it endorse it. It also appears that the proportionality approach used by the courts in cases such as *Bagley v North Herts Health Authority* (1986) 136 NLJ 1014 and *Clark v McLennan* [1983] 1 All ER 416 will not, in the light of *Hotson*, find any favour with the courts. The courts in those cases assessed damages on a percentage basis to reflect the chance the plaintiff had lost because of the defendant's negligence. Where the claim is that, had it not been for the defendant's negligence, the plaintiff would have enjoyed a better quality of life for a longer period the courts are prepared to compensate the plaintiff for this loss (see *Sutton v Population Services Family Planning Programme Ltd* (1981) *The Times*, 7 November).

There are more recent cases in which the courts have considered the loss of chance claim in a non-medical context. In *Allied Maples Group v Simmons and Simmons* [1995] 1 WLR 262, the court held that if the plaintiff could establish that he had lost a real or substantial chance then the court must evaluate that chance in the assessment of damages, In *Stovold v Barlows* (1995) *The Times*, 30 October, the defendant's alleged negligence caused the sale of the plaintiff's house to fall through; the Court of Appeal held that had the defendant not been negligent, there was a 50% chance that the sale would have occurred and therefore the plaintiff was entitled to half the award. See further Chapter 6, Causation.

Until this matter is once and for all resolved, the solicitor should think twice before labelling a claim as loss of chance claim and would be better advised to bring the claim within the ambit of *McGhee v National Coal Board* [1973] 1 WLR 1.

Wrongful life/birth

Before an examination is made of the damages that are awarded under this head, it is necessary first to distinguish between a wrongful life claim and a claim for wrongful birth. The former action is disallowed by the courts since the plaintiff (the handicapped child) is in effect saying that I was better off dead than being born the way I am – because of your negligence I was not aborted. This was the nature of the claim in *McKay v Essex Area Health Authority* [1982] QB 1166 where tests on a pregnant woman failed to disclose rubella resulting in the child being born disabled. The court held that a doctor did not have a duty of care to the child to advise the mother to have an abortion. However, the claim should have been framed differently, namely that the mother was deprived of the loss of an opportunity to have an abortion which is implicitly recognised by the Abortion Act 1967. The court refused to award damages on the following policy grounds:

(1) it would have meant assessing the life of a handicapped child as less worthy than that of a normal child;

(2) the child might have sued the mother for failing to abort;

(3) it was impossible to assess damages as it would mean comparing non-existence with existence.

The Congenital Disabilities (Civil Liability) Act 1976 is said to replace any law in force before 1976; consequently it is thought that it prevents any common law action. In McKay, the court said that a wrongful life claim could not be brought under the Act, but it is unclear whether that also includes those claims under s 1A. This section, introduced by s 44 Human Fertilisation and Embryology Act 1992, extends the provisions of the Act to children born disabled as a result of negligent fertility treatment, eg placing a damaged embryo in the womb.

With a wrongful birth claim, the allegation is that a sterilisation operation, vasectomy or abortion was negligently performed and consequently the plaintiff became pregnant. Initially, there was some reservation about awarding damages for the birth of a healthy child but this has now been resolved by *Allen v Bloomsbury Health Authority* [1993] 1 All ER 651 – such damages can be awarded on the grounds listed below:

(1) Pain and suffering associated with the continuance of the pregnancy and birth (although the benefit of not having to undergo an abortion should be offset against this award).

(2) Damages for the cost of bringing the child up to adulthood according to their station in life. Damages under this head include the cost of private education if appropriate and damages may be awarded for additional anxiety and distress at having to bring up a handicapped child.

The plaintiff may also be able to recover for the cost of a second abortion/sterilisation.

If the mother has to give up work she will be able to recover for her loss of earnings or the cost of maintaining the child but not for both, as this would amount to double recovery (see *Fish v Wilcox* [1994] 5 Med LR 230).

The Australian courts have also looked recently at the recoverability of damages following the birth of a healthy but unwanted child in *CES v Superclinics (Australia) Pty Ltd* [1996] Med L Rev. By a majority of 2–1, the court held that awarding damages under this head was not contrary to public policy though the quantification would depend on the facts of the case. Kirby P said that the court was not required by social policy to view the birth of a healthy child as a blessing. Further, in addition to awarding damages for any financial losses sustained by the parents, the court said that damages should be recoverable for the distress and burden of raising the child without any off-set for the joy and blessing of bringing up the child. This is somewhat different to the position in English law where such benefits are off-set except perhaps where the child is disabled and hence causes fresh anxieties for the parents. The argument that such an award might cause the child to feel unwanted was rejected, the court reasoning that many children were unplanned and if damages were not awarded then it may cause more family difficulties. Meagher JA, in his dissent, said that the sanctity of human life rendered any such award 'improper to the point of obscenity'. Priestley JA said that, whilst he agreed with Kirby J, the damages should not be assessed on the grounds that the plaintiff had failed to mitigate her loss, she had chosen to keep the child. Damages could be awarded, however, for any anguish and distress caused by giving the child up for adoption. It is unlikely that the English courts would follow such an abhorrent approach; they have already rejected the argument that a plaintiff may be under an obligation to terminate the unwanted pregnancy (see *Emeh*, at p 195) and presumably this reasoning would be given equally short shrift.

Nervous shock

Because of the imprecise nature of the damages awarded and the abundance of case law in this area we think it appropriate to look at damages for nervous shock separately.

The first point to note is that there must be some recognisable psychiatric illness; damages will not be awarded for emotional distress or grief unless this leads to a recognisable psychiatric illness. In *Hicks v Chief Constable of South Yorkshire* [1992] 2 All ER 65 (see p 203), the victims of the Hillsborough disaster were trapped for several hours before dying from asphyxia. It was held that they had suffered from grief and distress and as such this was not recoverable (see also *Reilly & Reilly v Merseyside Regional Health Authority* [1995] 6 Med LR 246). However, it has to be said that in cases where the victim suffers some other injury the court will take into account any mental distress in assessing general damages for pain and suffering. For example, in *Kralj v McGrath and St Theresa's Hospital* [1986] 1 All ER 54 (see r 7(D), at pp 242, 243), the court ruled that if the plaintiff's injuries were exacerbated because of the grief she was suffering at that time the court could take that into account. The court ruled that aggravated damages were inappropriate and instead increased the award for pain and suffering. A case which seems to go further is *Salih v Enfield Health Authority* [1991] 2 Med LR 235 where, as a result of a negligent diagnosis, the plaintiff gave birth to a child suffering from congenital rubella syndrome. She was awarded £5,000 for pain and suffering, although it is to be noted that there was no evidence of any psychological effects or physical defects as a result of the injury. Finally, in *Grieve v Salford Health Authority* [1991] 2 Med LR 295, the plaintiff, who it was admitted had a vulnerable personality, was awarded £12,500 general damages. This award was for having to undergo a caesarean section after an aborted attempt at forceps delivery of a stillborn child and the court took into account the psychological damage the plaintiff had suffered.

In all these cases the plaintiff was the primary victim, ie the plaintiff was directly involved in the incident. If the plaintiff is a secondary victim, ie someone who witnesses the suffering of others, *Alcock and others v Chief Constable of South Yorkshire* [1992] 1 AC 310 is the seminal case. There, the plaintiffs had all suffered psychiatric trauma as a result of the Hillsborough disaster in 1989, none had sustained any physical injury and most of them were not even present at the ground. The court ruled that claims for nervous shock should be limited and to that end three criteria had to be satisfied.

The first criterion relates to the class of persons who could claim. It was held that what mattered was the degree of love and affection; such would be presumed in the case of close relatives and would be scrutinised in the case of more distant relatives. The court seemed to leave open the question whether a bystander could sue. Lord Keith said (at p 397):

> The case of a bystander ... is difficult. Psychiatric injury to him would not ordinarily ... be within the range of reasonable foreseeability, but could not perhaps entirely be excluded from it if the circumstances of a catastrophe occurring very close to him were particularly horrific.

However, in the recent case concerning the Piper Alpha disaster, *McFarlane v E Caledonia Ltd* [1994] 2 All ER 1, the court rejected a claim by a bystander. The plaintiff, who had previously suffered from depression, witnessed a massive explosion on a North Sea oil rig at least 100 metres away. At the time he was on a support vessel. The court held that, since there was no evidence that the plaintiff had close ties to any of the crew on the rig, he was simply a bystander and therefore his claim failed. This was so despite the fact that the plaintiff must have witnessed the horrific events knowing that there would be many deaths. However, he was held not to be involved with the disaster nor to be a rescuer and, as no one else on the support ship had suffered injury or was close enough to be in danger, the claim failed.

The second criterion is that there must be proximity of time and space. This has been held to cover the aftermath of the accident (see *McLoughlin v O'Brian* [1983] AC 410). In *Alcock,* the claim failed because it was nearly nine hours before the plaintiffs saw the victims and then only for formal identification. The same reasoning was applied in *Taylor v Somerset Health Authority* [1993] 4 Med LR 34 where the plaintiff alleged that she had suffered nervous shock after identifying her husband's body in the mortuary. Additionally, in *Alcock,* the court ruled that the medium by which the plaintiffs were informed of the ensuing events, ie television, did not come within the aftermath principle as the plaintiffs could only see a general picture of chaos and not the suffering of their own relatives. This principle, however, is not set in stone; it may be that parents who witness their children's injuries on television can succeed.

Just how far the aftermath principle stretches is not certain. In *McLoughlin,* the plaintiff was allowed to recover because she saw her family before they had been treated by the medical staff, something which is unlikely to happen in a medical negligence case. Certainly, in *Alcock,* the court refused to give 'aftermath' a precise definition. The conclusion appears to be that unless the plaintiff sees his relative in an injured state, preferably covered in blood, then the claim will probably fail.

The third criterion is that the nervous shock must arise from the negligence of the defendant which causes injury to the plaintiff or a third party. However, it is far from clear whether the court was ruling out claims in other types of cases, eg where the defendant suffers injury through his own fault which in turn causes the plaintiff to suffer psychiatric illness. What is clear is that the psychiatric illness must be induced by shock (see *Alcock and others v Chief Constable of South Yorkshire* [1992] 1 AC 310, at pp 215, 216). In *Jaensch v Coffey* (1984) 54 ALR 417, Brennan J gave two examples which would not qualify for compensation, namely an overworked spouse who had been caring for a husband who was injured by the defendant's negligence and as a result suffers from psychiatric illness, and a parent who suffers as a result of the behaviour of a brain-damaged child. There must be some shock which must be immediate or fall within the aftermath principle, and not simply a period of time spent caring for the plaintiff. With respect, subject to certain limits, we do not see any reason why the compensation should not be extended to cover the aforementioned situations. It is clearly foreseeable, so why the need for the shock element? The sufferer has still been placed in a position which he would not have been in but for the negligence of the tortfeasor.

The case of *Tredget and Tredget v Bexley Health Authority* [1994] 5 Med LR 178 may be taken as giving support to our proposition. There, the plaintiffs were allowed to recover damages for nervous shock caused by their child's death shortly after its birth. Although the birth itself was a horrifying event – at one point the child's shoulder had to be broken to allow the birth to take place – the shock arose from the parents spending two-and-a-half days knowing that something was gravely wrong until eventually the child's life support machine was switched off. Conversely, in *Sion v Hampstead Health Authority* [1994] 5 Med LR 170, a father was denied a claim for nervous shock which was allegedly caused by watching his son die as a result of medical negligence. The plaintiffs in *Tredget* and *Sion* clearly satisfied the aftermath test, but were their injuries reasonably foreseeable? Mrs Tredget was a diabetic and had already experienced one difficult delivery; therefore, it could be said that a difficult delivery and the events that followed were foreseeable. Additionally, it could be argued that the events that followed would cause shock in a person of reasonable fortitude. On the other hand it could be that this was just intense grief.

The question of foreseeability was considered more recently in *Page v Smith* [1995] 2 WLR 644 (for the facts see Chapter 6, Causation, at p 192). This was a claim by the plaintiff, a primary victim, who alleged that a road traffic accident had exacerbated a pre-existing condition of ME. The House of Lords found for the plaintiff by a majority of 3–2, Lord Lloyd held that where the plaintiff was a primary victim what must be foreseeable was personal injury of some type. This argument was endorsed by Lord Browne-Wilkinson who said that no distinction should be drawn between physical and psychiatric injury. What is interesting are the propositions put forward by Lord Lloyd for dealing with nervous shock claims. He said that it was important to distinguish between primary and secondary victims. As regards the latter, the law imposes certain control mechanisms to limit the number of claimants. However, the defendant will not be liable unless psychiatric injury is foreseeable in a person of ordinary fortitude, although in the case of a secondary victim it may be appropriate to use hindsight. Subject to these qualifications, a defendant will be liable to the plaintiff if it can be established that he can reasonably foresee that his conduct will expose the plaintiff to a risk of physical or psychiatric injury. Once the duty of care is established, the plaintiff must prove that the nervous shock resulted in a psychiatric illness; it does not matter that this illness is unusually severe; the defendant must take his victim as he finds him.

Whether these propositions will be adopted unequivocally in future cases remains to be seen; however, we can see no reason why they should not be applied successfully in a medical negligence claim

The argument against extending the '*Tredget*-like' claims would be that the courts could be confronted with a situation where the death of a neonate, or for that matter anyone, will lead to claims for nervous shock. We are of the opinion that it is justifiable that where there is a particularly serious lack of care by the hospital, and the plaintiff has to endure a traumatic period watching a loved one die knowing that the death could have been avoided; then, in such cases, the hospital should be held accountable for any lasting psychiatric damage caused to the plaintiff. There is an inbuilt safeguard in these claims – the plaintiff must show that he has suffered from a psychiatric illness and not mere grief. This is the way the law should progress. At present, however, a claim resulting from the negligence of the doctor or hospital will only have a good chance of success if:

(1) the claim is made by the victim of the alleged negligence (either as a result of receiving some horrific treatment while still conscious or, if he was unconscious, perhaps waking up to find that the wrong limb has been amputated); or

(2) a third party witnesses the horrific treatment; or

(3) the third party sees the victim in a distressed state as a result of the medical negligence.

REFERENCES

English case law

(1) Hotson v East Berkshire Health Authority [1987] AC 750; [1987] 2 All ER 909

See Chapter 6, Causation, at p 182, *et seq.*

(2) Jobling v Associated Dairies Ltd [1982] AC 794

The defendant's negligence resulted in the plaintiff sustaining a back injury. Three years later he found he was suffering from myelopathy. The defendant argued that its liability was extinguished by the onset of the myelopathy, an argument which ultimately found favour with the House of Lords.

(3) Hicks and others v Chief Constable of the South Yorkshire Police [1992] 2 All ER 65

See above, at p 203.

(4) Rourke v Barton (1982) The Times, 23 June

The plaintiff's husband was suffering from terminal cancer. She sustained an injury to her hip which prevented her from caring for her husband when he was at home. The distress caused to her was taken into account in the assessment of damages.

(5) Kralj v McGrath and St Theresa's Hospital [1986] 1 All ER 54

Considered at pp 242, 243.

(6) Ackers v Wigan Health Authority [1991] 2 Med LR 232

The plaintiff was not totally anaesthetised during a caesarian section. She was awarded £12,000 for pain and suffering and consequent psychological upset.

(7) Phelan v East Cumbria Health Authority [1991] 2 Med LR 419

The plaintiff was paralysed but fully conscious while his leg was opened, drilled and four screws inserted. He was awarded £5,000 for his experience on the operating table and £10,000 for the resulting psychological damage.

(8) Cooper v Nottingham Health Authority (1989) The Times, 17 March

The plaintiff was conscious during a caesarian section – she was awarded £15,000 for pain and suffering.

See also *Taylor v Worcester and District HA* [1991] 2 Med LR 215 at Chapter 5, Standard of Care, at p 162.

(9) Burton v Islington Health Authority; De Martell v Merton and Sutton Health Authority [1993] 4 Med LR 8; [1995] 6 Med LR 234

Both cases effectively restate the position under the Congenital Disabilities (Civil Liability) Act 1976 and are only relevant to those cases which predate the Act. See further, Chapter 3, Duty, at p 77.

(10) Wise v Kaye [1962] 1 QB 368

See above, at p 205. The plaintiff was aged 20 at the date of the accident. At the time of trial (three years later) she had not recovered consciousness and was unlikely to do so. The court awarded £15,000 general damages (other than future loss of earnings and loss of expectation of life).

(11) H West & Son Ltd v Shepherd [1964] AC 174

See above, at p 205.

(12) Lim Poh Choo v Camden and Islington Area Health Authority [1980] AC 174

The plaintiff sustained extensive and irremediable brain damage and was totally dependent on others. The House of Lords held that the domestic elements of the plaintiff's care should be deducted from the cost of care claim and that the expenses she would have incurred in earning her living should be deducted from the loss of earnings claim.

(13) Cookson v Knowles [1979] AC 566

This case involved a fatal accident in which the plaintiff's husband was killed.

(14) Page v Sheerness Metal plc (1996) The Times, 23 October; [1996] PIQR 26

At first instance, Dyson J held that the 4–5% discount rate was not a rule of law and adopted a 3% discount rate per annum. The plaintiff was 28 years old and would be expected to retire at 62. A multiplier of 19 was applied to future loss of earnings and 24 for future care. However, in the Court of Appeal the court held that it would continue to adopt a discount rate of 4.5%.

See also *Wells & Wells and Thomas v Brighton Health Authority* also reported at (1996) *The Times*, 23 October.

(15) Auty v National Coal Board [1985] 1 All ER 930; [1985] 1 WLR 784

See p 207.

(16) Smith v Manchester Corporation [1974] 17 KIR 1

See above, at p 207.

(17) Moeliker v A Reyrolle & Co Ltd [1976] ICR 253

In assessing damages for loss of earning capacity the court had to assess whether the risk was substantial (real) or whether it was fanciful or speculative. Where there is a real risk, the assessment of damages depends on the degree of the risk at the time when the loss of employment might occur and the factors affecting the plaintiff's prospects of obtaining another job. Each case would be decided on its individual facts.

(18) Foster v Tyne & Wear County Council [1986] 1 All ER 567

An adult plaintiff was awarded £35,000 for loss of earning capacity. Lloyd LJ said that, in determining the level of the award, it was necessary to weigh up all the chances in all the circumstances of a particular case.

(19) Pickett v British Rail Engineering [1980] AC 136

See above, at p 207.

(20) Harris v Empress Motors Ltd [1984] 1 WLR 212; [1983] 3 All ER 561

See above, at p 208.

(21) Phipps v Brooks Dry Cleaning Services The Times, 16 July 1996

See above, at p 208.

(22) Roberts v Johnstone [1988] 3 WLR 1247

See above, at p 209.

(23) Donnelly v Joyce [1974] QB 454

See above, at p 210.

(24) Housecroft v Burnett [1986] 1 All ER 332

See above, at p 210.

(25) Hunt v Severs [1994] 2 All ER 385

See above, at p 210.

Medical experts agreed that the plaintiff had a life expectancy of 25 years. The Court of Appeal therefore assessed damages for this fixed period. The House of Lords, however, ruled that this was inappropriate.

(26) Mehmet v Perry [1977] 2 All ER 529

The court may use the earnings of one parent who stays at home to look after the children as the multiplicand.

It was held that the plaintiff had acted reasonably in giving up work on the death of his wife and that it was reasonable that he should not take up employment until his youngest child reached the age of 15. (The plaintiff's two youngest children, H and S suffered from a rare blood disorder and required frequent blood transfusions.) In these circumstances, the damage for loss of the deceased's housekeeping services should be assessed by reference to the plaintiff's loss of wages, not by reference to the reasonable cost of employing a housekeeper, because the plaintiff's loss of wages represented the loss of providing the services of a full time housekeeper in substitution for his wife.

(27) Jones v Jones [1984] 3 WLR 862

The plaintiff suffered a severe personality change after his injuries which caused the breakdown of his marriage. The court awarded damages of £15,000 to compensate the plaintiff for the money he had paid to his wife and children to enable them to set up a new home. In fact, the plaintiff actually paid his wife £25,000 but the court only awarded him £15,000 to reflect the fact that the plaintiff would inevitably have paid his wife money in respect of the care that she had provided.

(28) Pritchard v Parrot (1985) The Times, 27 September

Initially, the court awarded £42,500 to a plaintiff whose marriage had broken down as a result of his injuries. The award was made to enable the plaintiff to purchase a new home, separate from his wife and family and for the cost of maintaining it. This ruling was reversed in the Court of Appeal, which held that the financial detriment suffered by the plaintiff was too remote, even though it was admitted that the divorce was a result of the plaintiff's personality change.

(29) Wright v British Railways Board [1983] 2 AC 773

In this case the court applied the guidelines for the award of interest as discussed, at p 212.

(30) Bagley v North Herts Health Authority [1986] 136 New LJ 1014

See Chapter 6, Causation, at p 186.

(31)Clark v McLennan [1983] 1 All ER 416

See Chapter 6, Causation, at p 179 and Chapter 5, Standard of Care, at p 139.

(32)Sutton v Population Services Family Planning Programme Ltd (1981) The Times, 7 November

See Chapter 6, Causation, at p 186 and above, at p 213.

(33) Allied Maples Group v Simmons and Simmons [1995] 1 WLR 1602

See Chapter 6, Causation, at pp 185, 187.

(34) Stovold v Barlows (1995) The Times, 30 October

See Chapter 6, Causation, at pp 185, 187.

(35) McGhee v National Coal Board [1973] 1 WLR 1; [1972] 3 All ER 1008

See Chapter 6, Causation, at p 174.

(36) McKay v Essex Area Health Authority [1982] QB 1166; [1982] 2 All ER 771

See Chapter 3, Duty, at p 79.

(37) Allen v Bloomsbury Health Authority [1993] 1 All ER 651

See p 214. The case involved the birth of a healthy child following a failed abortion.

(38) Fish v Wilcox [1994] 5 Med LR 230

The plaintiff gave birth to a handicapped child and brought a claim for loss and damage as a result of the birth and having to look after a seriously handicapped child. The plaintiff was later diagnosed as having MS and was unable to look after the child. The judge at first instance awarded the plaintiff £234,387 by way of damages for negligence, £34,167 was awarded for the nursing care the plaintiff had provided up until the date of trial. No award was made for loss of earnings, because the judge ruled that this would amount to double recovery. The plaintiff appealed against this. The appeal was dismissed, the court ruling that:

(1) The plaintiff could not do two jobs at once and she was not entitled to be paid for doing two jobs at once.

(2) That the judge had awarded on additional burden of looking after her child as opposed to the work the plaintiff had previously done.

In any event, the judge had awarded a substantial sum over and above the compensation for loss of earnings to reflect the additional burden of caring for a child.

In essence, it appears that these type of awards are subject to the ultimate discretion of the court as to whether to recompense the parent for loss of earnings or the value of services rendered.

Note that this case simply reiterates the decision in *Housecroft v Burnett* [1986] 1 All ER 332 but is the first medical negligence case on this point.

(39) Emeh v Kensington and Chelsea and Westminster Health Authority [1985] QB 1012; [1984] 3 All ER 844

See Chapter 6, Causation, at p 195.

(40) Reilly & Reilly v Merseyside HA [1995] 6 Med LR 246

The plaintiffs were trapped in the defendant's lift for over one hour. On appeal, it was held that there was no compensatable damage – claustrophobia and fear were normal human emotions.

(41) Salih v Enfield Health Authority [1991] 2 Med LR 235

A baby was born with congenital rubella syndrome because of the negligence of the defendant. The mother was awarded £5,000 for her pain and suffering although there was no evidence of any psychological effects or physical defects.

(42) Grieve v Salford Health Authority [1991] 2 Med LR 295

The plaintiff was delivered of a stillborn child. Liability was admitted by the Health Authority. The court took into account the effect on the plaintiff's personality of the stillbirth. The plaintiff had repeatedly been given inconsistent explanations as to the cause of her child's death.

(43) Alcock and others v Chief Constable of South Yorkshire [1992] 1 AC 310; [1991] 4 All ER 907

Actions were brought against the police for nervous shock arising out of the disaster at the Hillsborough football ground in April 1989 when 95 were killed and 400 injured by crushing. Too many people had been allowed to crowd into a confined area. The events were shown on live television and broadcast on the news. The actions were brought by those who were present at the ground, those who had witnessed the events on television and those who had identified the bodies at the mortuary. The claims were divided into two categories, those where the plaintiff was involved as a participant and those who had witnessed the accident. In the case of the latter, the court held that they must satisfy the three criteria discussed above, at p 215, *et seq.*

(44) McFarlane v E Caledonia Ltd [1994] 2 All ER 1

See above, at p 216.

(45) McLoughlin v O'Brian [1983] AC 410; [1982] 2 All ER 298

The plaintiff's family was involved in a road traffic accident – one child was killed and her husband and other two children were badly injured. The plaintiff was told about the accident some two hours later and taken to the hospital where she was told about the death of her child and saw the injuries to her family before they had been attended to. Clearly, most emphasis was placed on the fact that the plaintiff had seen her family in a distressed state before they had been cleaned up. We advocate that the views of Lord Bridge have some merit – is there really any difference between a mother who imagines the horrors of her family who have been subjected to a hotel fire and Mrs McLoughlin who has the misfortune of seeing them?

See also the potential liability of breaking bad news in *Furniss v Fitchett* [1958] NZLR 396 in Chapter 1, Medical Confidentiality, at p 4.

(46) Taylor v Somerset Health Authority [1993] 4 Med LR 34

The plaintiff's husband had a heart attack and was taken to hospital, where he later died. The plaintiff arrived 20 minutes later and identified her husband's body in the mortuary. She alleged that this caused her shock and she suffered from a psychiatric illness. The health authority admitted negligence in failing to treat the deceased's heart condition. However, the plaintiff's claim failed because she did not witness the accident within the defined aftermath principle. She had simply gone to the mortuary to dispel her disbelief that her husband was dead.

(47) Tredget and Tredget v Bexley Health Authority [1994] 5 Med LR 178

The plaintiffs claimed damages for psychiatric illness which contributed to the breakdown of their marriage. The illness had been caused by the death of their son two days after his birth. It was admitted by the defendant that they were liable for the child's death; however, they alleged that the breakdown of the plaintiff's marriage was the result of their grief rather than nervous shock. The plaintiffs were allowed to recover damages for nervous shock.

(48) Sion v Hampstead Health Authority [1994] 5 Med LR 170

The plaintiff's son was injured in a motor cycle accident. The plaintiff stayed at his son's bedside for some 14 days until his son died. He contended that the hospital were negligent in failing to diagnose bleeding from his son's kidney which led to his son lapsing into a coma. He alleged that as a result of the hospital's negligence in caring for his son he had suffered psychiatric illness and had had to give up work.

Held:: there was no shock. The plaintiff had merely been subjected to a continuing process, and his giving up work resulted from an abnormal grief reaction to his son's death. There was no 'sudden appreciation by sight or sound of a horrifying event which visibly agitates the mind' (*per* Lord Ackner in *Alcock and others v Chief Constable of South Yorkshire* [1992] 1 AC 310; [1991] 4 All ER 907, at p 401).

(49) Taylorson v Shieldness [1994] PIQR 329

The plaintiffs were the parents of a child who was involved in a road traffic accident. They were told of the accident and went to the hospital where although they did not see their son they glimpsed his face with blood on it on the way to intensive care. They did not see him for several hours and then saw him in intensive care over the next two days until his eventual death. Their claim for nervous shock failed because they failed to come within the immediate aftermath principle.

Query – is this case really distinguishable from *Tredget*?

(50) Page v Smith [1995] 2 WLR 644; [1995] 2 All ER 736

See Chapter 6, Causation, at p 192.

Foreign case law

AUSTRALIA

(1) Jaensch v Coffrey (1984) 54 ALR 517

The facts were similar to *McLoughlin v O'Brien* – a mother was informed of the death of her husband and children but did not witness the aftermath of the accident.

(2) CES Superclinics (Australia) Pty Ltd [1996] Med L Rev 102

See above, at p 214.

UNITED STATES

Lovelace Medical Center v Mendez (1991) 803 P (2d) 603

This case concerned a negligent tubal ligation.

It was held that damages could be recovered for the care of the child until he reached the age of majority. However, the court overruled the first instance decision that the interest of financial security and limiting the size of a family were not worthy of protection.

Note that in the United States there have been some successful claims in which the plaintiff has been allowed to recover for the fear of future disease without present physical injury. Generally most of these claims have failed as the plaintiff has failed to demonstrate a physical injury, but there have been some successes. In *Wisner v Illinois Central Gulf* (1988) RR 537 So (2d) 740, the court allowed recovery for fear of cancer following toxic fume exposure. However, the majority of cases reflect the decision in *Payton v Abbot Labs* (1982) 386 Mass 540, 437 NE (2d) 171. This was a class action brought by women who were exposed to diethylstilbestrol (DES) *in utero*. They claimed that they were more likely to suffer from abnormalities of the reproductive organs, but they presented no physical symptoms at the time of trial. It was held that to recover for negligently inflicted emotional distress, one of the factors that must be present is some element of physical harm.

Practice directions

Practice Direction (Damages: Personal Injuries) [1984] 1 WLR 1127

See Appendix C, at p 343.

Statutes/statutory instruments

(1) CONGENITAL DISABILITIES (CIVIL LIABILITY) ACT 1976

Sections 1, 1A – see Appendix A, at pp 264–65.

See also s 44 Human Fertilisation and Embryology Act 1990.

(2) ADMINISTRATION OF JUSTICE ACT 1982

Reduction of life expectancy

1(1) ...

    (b) if the injured person's expectation of life has been reduced by the injuries, the court, in assessing damages in respect of pain and suffering caused by the injuries, shall take account of any suffering caused or likely to be caused to him by awareness that his expectation of life has been so reduced.

Maintenance at public expense

5 In an action under the law of England and Wales or the law of Northern Ireland for damages for personal injuries (including any such action arising out of a contract) any saving to the injured person which is attributable to his maintenance wholly or partly at public expense in a hospital, nursing home or other institution shall be set off against any income lost by him as a result of his injuries.

(3) FATAL ACCIDENTS ACT 1976

See r 7(E) and Appendix A, at p 262.

(4) LAW REFORM (PERSONAL INJURIES) ACT 1948

Private medical costs

2(4) In an action for damages for personal injuries (including any such action arising out of a contract), there shall be disregarded, in determining the reasonableness of any expenses, the possibility of avoiding those expenses or part of them by taking advantage of facilities available under the National Health Service Act 1977 or the National Health Service (Scotland) Act 1978 or any corresponding facilities in Northern Ireland.

(5) SUPREME COURT ACT 1981

For interest on damages, see s 35A, Appendix A, at p 282.

(6) COUNTY COURTS ACT 1984

For interest on damages, see s 69, Appendix A, at p 286.

(7) CIVIL EVIDENCE ACT 1995

The admissibility of actuarial tables

10(1) The actuarial tables (together with explanatory notes) for use in personal injury and fatal accident cases issued from time to time by the Government Actuary's Department are admissible in evidence for the purpose of assessing, in an action for personal injury, the sum to be awarded as general damages for future pecuniary loss.

(2) They may be proved by the production of a copy published by Her Majesty's Stationery Office.

(3) For the purposes of this section:

(a) 'personal injury' includes any disease and any impairment of a person's physical or mental condition; and

(b) 'action for personal injury' includes an action brought by virtue of the Law Reform (Miscellaneous Provisions) Act 1934 or the Fatal Accidents Act 1976.

Note that the Act is reproduced in full at Appendix A, at p 315.

Practice points

Using the Ogden tables – multipliers

Pursuant to s 10 Civil Evidence Act 1995 (see above) the Ogden tables are now specifically admissible. See also the draft High Court and County Court Rules issued by the Supreme Court Rule Committee and County Court Rule Committee, RSC Ord 38, r 21; CCR Ord 20, r 15.

Interest

- In fatal accident cases, interest on the bereavement award is awarded at the full special investment rate from the date of death. Interest is also awarded on the dependency award on the pre-trial pecuniary loss of the dependants at the special investment account rate from time to time.
- *Note* that interest awarded on personal injury damages is not taxable as income pursuant to s 329 Income and Corporation Taxes Act 1988.
- A claim for interest must be pleaded (RSC Ord 18, r 8(4); CCR Ord 6, r 1A).
- For interim payments, the fact that interest will be awarded with the final award must be taken into account in making the final award.
- Finally, note that in *Wright v British Railways Board* [1983] 2 AC 773 (see p 212) the court indicated that in exceptional cases, where one party is guilty of gross delay,

the court could increase or decrease the amount of interest or alter the period for which it is allowed.

Nervous shock

- The plaintiff will have to adduce cogent psychiatric evidence that he has indeed been affected by nervous shock. As vulgar as this may seem, the plaintiff will have to adduce evidence that he loved the victim whose distress he witnessed. Be prepared for the fact that defence counsel could allege that there was in fact no love and affection and adduce evidence to the contrary.

- Finally, it appears that the success of the claim will often rest upon whether the plaintiff witnessed the actual injuries. Thus, in the case of a plaintiff who is merely told what has happened to her nearest and dearest, it is unlikely that the claim will succeed unless there is some unique factor. For medical negligence cases this may be the death knell for such claims.

RULE 7(B)

The plaintiff has a duty to mitigate his damages. The plaintiff must also give credit for any benefits he has received as a result of his injuries and these will be deducted from the final award.

Commentary

Mitigation

It is for the defendant to prove that the plaintiff has failed to mitigate his damages (see *McGregor on Damages* (15th edn) para 289):

> The onus of proof on the issue of mitigation is on the defendant. If he fails to show that the plaintiff ought reasonably to have taken certain mitigating steps, then the normal measure will apply.

Although the rule is expressed in terms of a 'duty to mitigate', the plaintiff will commit no wrong should he fail in this duty; however, his damages may be reduced. Consequently, if the plaintiff has lost his job or is unable to return to his employment because of his injuries, he should seek alternative employment if he is still capable of working; if he secures a lower paid job then it follows that he will only be able to recover his net loss ie the difference between what he was earning prior to his injuries and what he is now earning.

An interesting point is whether the plaintiff has an obligation to seek further medical treatment to alleviate or improve his condition. Whatever the treatment it must be reasonable, see Chapter 6, Causation, at p 195, this is why no plaintiff will be required to undergo an abortion, *Emeh v Kensington and Chelsea Area Health Authority* [1985] QB 1012. As for most questions concerning the plaintiff's conduct, the test is whether or not it was reasonable for him to refuse further treatment and, in assessing this, the court will look at the degree of risk and whether or not there is a predicted outcome. As the defendant has placed the plaintiff in the adverse position, it will be a rare for the court to find that the plaintiff has acted unreasonably. If there is conflicting medical advice, or if the risk is such that the doctors leave the final decision to the plaintiff as in

Selvanayagam v University of the West Indies [1983] 1 WLR 585, a refusal of treatment will invariably be considered reasonable.

If the court were to find that the plaintiff had acted unreasonably, then they have the problem of assessing damages especially where the prospect of success of the treatment was uncertain. In line with the loss of chance cases, see p 182, *et seq*, it may be that, where the operation has a less than 50% chance of succeeding, the court could refuse to take that into account in assessing damages. However, as the courts are accustomed to taking the slightest contingencies into account, it is submitted that they will simply have regard to the chances of the treatment succeeding as against the possibility of it failing. This was the approach used in the Canadian case of *Ippolito v Janiak* (1981) 6 DLR (4th) 1. However, a cautionary note should be introduced here – there have been cases where the courts have simply assessed damages on the principle that the operation would have been successful (see *McAuley v London Transport Executive* [1957] 2 Lloyd's Rep 500).

We wish to make two final points. Where the plaintiff cannot mitigate his damages because of impecuniosity, the defendant will be liable for the full loss. This could perhaps apply where the plaintiff requires some expensive treatment not ordinarily available on the NHS. Secondly, the reasonable plaintiff can recover the increased damages which result from his attempt to mitigate (see *Hoffberger v Ascot International Bloodstock Bureau Ltd* (1976) 120 SJ 130).

Benefits

The rule is that the plaintiff will not be allowed to recover twice for his injuries. Hence he must give credit for any benefits received. The rules are different depending on the size of the award, and if the payment is an 'exempt payment' (see below, at p 230).

Amounts over £2500

The scheme for the deduction of benefits is contained in Part IV Social Security Administration Act 1992 and the Social Security (Recoupment) Regulations 1990 (SI 1990/332). Pursuant to s 82(1) of the 1992 Act, the scheme applies to 'compensation payments' arising 'in consequence of an accident, injury or disease' whether or not these are tort damages. The accident or injury must have occurred on or after 1 January 1989 or, in the case of a disease, if the victim's first claim for a relevant benefit in consequence of the disease is made on or after 1 January 1989 (s 81(7)).

Certain small payments, eg less than £2500 are exempt under this Act, as are payments made under the Fatal Accidents Act 1976, payments made by the Criminal Injuries Compensation Board under the Criminal Injuries Compensation Scheme and payments made in respect of occupational sick pay (see further s 81(3)).

When the defendant (compensator) is ready to make a final award he will be able to deduct from the final award the amount of total benefit specified in the certificate. This certificate is obtained from the Compensation Recovery Unit (CRU) and details the amount of benefits the plaintiff has received from the day after the injury or accident or, in the case of disease, the first day the benefit is claimed. This period ends five years later or whenever the last compensation is paid whichever is the earlier (see further s 88(1)). The five year period may seem somewhat harsh for those plaintiffs who are in receipt of income support but equally it can operate fairly in relation to benefits such as mobility allowance where the benefit is not dependent on the plaintiff's pecuniary state. No allowance is made for the fact that the compensation payment may have already been reduced because of contributory negligence. The amount of benefits once deducted by the compensator is paid back to the CRU. Thus, the CRU will recoup money spent on the plaintiff's upkeep because of the accident. The compensator deducts this sum from the global award, not just from the loss of earnings element.

The relevant benefits are basically any benefit under the Social Security (Contributions and Benefits) Act 1992 (see also Social Security (Recoupment) Regulations 1990 SI 1990/322 and Part IV of the 1992 Act). They are:

- attendance allowance;
- constant attendance allowance;
- disability living allowance (from 6 April 1992);
- disability working allowance (from 6 April 1992);
- exceptionally severe disablement benefit;
- family credit;
- income support;*
- incapacity benefit (from 13 April 1995)
- industrial injuries disablement allowance;
- invalidity benefit (up to 5 April 1992) (from 13 April 1995 incapacity benefit replaced sickness and invalidity benefit);
- mobility allowance (up to 5 April 1992);
- Old Cases Act benefits;
- reduced earnings allowance;
- retirement allowance;
- severe disablement allowance;
- statutory sick pay (before 2 April 1994);
- sickness benefit (up to 12 April 1995);
- unemployment benefit.*

   * From October 1996 Jobseeker's allowance replaces Unemployment benefit and income support.

Note that the Statutory Sick Pay Act 1994 amended Part 1 Social Security (Contributions and Benefits) Act 1992, abolishing the right of employers to recover 20% of statutory sick pay paid to their employees from their remittance of national insurance contributions – see Statutory Sick Pay Act 1994 (Consequential) Regulations 1994 (SI 1994/730).

One important point which has only recently emerged is what happens where the victim was already receiving benefit at the date of the accident. In *Hassal and another v Secretary of State* [1995] 1 WLR 812, the claimant had been receiving income support prior to his accident. After his accident he continued to receive income support because he was sick and unable to work. The court ruled that the benefits received after the accident were recoupable despite the plaintiff's argument that, even without the accident, he would almost certainly have continued to receive income support and therefore it should not have been recoupable. The court also ruled that the portion of the benefit paid in respect of the members of the family was recoupable. Realising that this could cause some injustice, the court indicated that the plaintiff's solicitor should make a claim for lost benefits which, but for the accident, would not have been lost. It may well be that a solicitor who does not now make such a claim will be negligent.

Listed below, in no particular order, is a series of points concerning the recoupment of benefits which should be taken into account by both the plaintiff's solicitor and the compensator. Consider also the practice points, at p 251.

(1) Where a payment is made by the compensator which is not final, ie it is followed by a further payment, the deduction and recoupment required by the second payment is to be reduced by the amount deducted from the first payment. This rule only applies where at both stages the identity of the compensator is the same; if the compensator is different a deduction will be made at both instances (s 86(2)).

(2) Within 14 days of making the payment, the compensator must pay the recoupment payment to the State. However, if the Secretary of State does not furnish the compensator with a certificate of total benefit within four weeks of a request from the compensator, the compensator's liability is extinguished (s 96(1)(c)).

(3) With regard to a payment into court, the usual practice is for the compensator to obtain a certificate of total benefit and then to indicate on the notice of payment the amount deducted. However, the compensator may make a payment in before obtaining a certificate providing he applies for the certificate on the same day. The plaintiff must bear in mind that the benefits have not been deducted and the compensator must remember his liability to the state before making the payment in. A solicitor should always ensure that any settlement is clear as to the terms regarding deduction of benefits and that future benefits are not deducted; thus, it is advantageous that a settlement is reached earlier rather than later (s 93).

(4) While waiting for a certificate of total benefit the compensator may make a *Calderbank* offer (see *Calderbank v Calderbank* [1976] Fam 93, ie without prejudice as to costs). The offer is subject to whatever deduction is required and holds good for seven days after the certificate is received. In the county court, the offer must be lodged at the court in a sealed envelope. For further information, see RSC (Amendment No 2) 1990 SI 1990/1689; CCR Ord 11, r 10(2) amended by County Court (Amendment No 3) Rules 1990 SI 1990/1764.

Amounts of £2500 or less

Awards of £2,500 or less are still governed by the Law Reform (Personal Injuries) Act 1948 as amended. The main point here is that there is no reimbursement to the Secretary of State; therefore, the defendant may push for a settlement to avoid reimbursing the state.

Under s 2 of the Act, for a period of five years after the accident, 50% of certain benefits (sickness benefit, invalidity benefit, severe disablement allowance and (industrial) disablement allowance) are deductible, while those benefits that are not specified in s 2 of the Act are deductible in full, these include mobility and attendance allowance, unemployment benefit and family credit.

The Compensation Recovery Bill

The preceding paragraphs may soon be superceded by the new Compensation Recovery Bill which will allow plaintiffs to keep all of their damages for pain and suffering and the clawback provision will only apply to the loss of earnings element of the award. *Note*, however, that the small payments limit of £2,500 is to be removed – at present many claimants would try and settle at this sum to try and avoid the clawback provisions. It is proposed that reimbursement of state benefits should form a separate head of compensation. As yet, there are no plans to take account of the fact that the plaintiff may have been contributorily negligent.

Other benefits

Sometimes, as a result of his injuries, the plaintiff will benefit in monetary terms in other ways. Whether such sums are deductible is discussed below.

(1) Benevolence

Any gifts received either from public benevolence (eg a disaster fund) or private benevolence (eg a gift from a friend) are to be disregarded.

(2) Insurance moneys

These are also to be disregarded since the defendant cannot rely on the plaintiff's foresight and planning to reduce his liability. In *McCamley v Cammell Laird Shipbuilders Ltd* [1990] 1 WLR 963, the House of Lords ruled that, for this rule to apply, the plaintiff himself must have paid the premiums. In this case, the premiums had been paid by the defendant employer. Notwithstanding this, the court held that the insurance moneys were still to be disregarded as the payment was an act of benevolence by the employer.

(3) Redundancy payments

These are not deductible unless the plaintiff is made redundant because of his injuries.

(4) Pensions

Whether the pension is contributory or non-contributory it is not deductible (see *Smoker v London Fire and Civil Defence Authority* [1991] 2 All ER 449). Additionally, neither state pensions nor an *ex gratia* pension payable by the employer will be deductible. The plaintiff, however, must give credit if he is receiving a disablement benefit.

(5) Gratuitous payments by the defendant

It is still uncertain as to what extent payments made by the defendant which are not legally required are deductible. In *Hunt v Severs* [1994] 2 All ER 385, the court ruled that where the tortfeasor provided the defendant with a wheelchair he could not be charged with the cost of the wheelchair. However, where the defendant makes a payment into a disaster fund there is no deduction. There will be no deduction for sick pay where there is a clause in the plaintiff's contract of employment that the plaintiff will repay the money to the employer if his claim is successful.

(6) Maintenance at public expense

According to the Administration of Justice Act 1982, the plaintiff must give credit for any saving caused by his maintenance at public expense, eg because he is in a nursing institution. However, under the Law Reform (Personal Injuries) Act 1948, the plaintiff can claim the cost of private treatment notwithstanding the same is available on the NHS. The plaintiff must give credit for any savings to his living expenses; thus, in *Lim Poh Choo v Camden and Islington Area Health Authority* [1980] AC 174, where the plaintiff, who was totally dependent on others, brought a claim for loss of earnings and the cost of care, the House of Lords held that the domestic elements of the plaintiff's care should be deducted from the cost of care claim; also, the expenses the plaintiff would have incurred in earning a living, eg commuting, should be deducted from her loss of earnings claim.

(7) Compensation order made in the criminal courts

Any award of compensation made to or in respect of the victim by the Criminal Injuries Compensation Board under s 111 Criminal Justice Act 1988 is not deductible.

REFERENCES

English case law

(1) Emeh v Kensington and Chelsea and Westminster Area Health Authority [1985] QB 1012; [1984] 3 All ER 844

See Chapter 6, Causation, at p 195.

(2) Selvanayagam v University of the West Indies [1983] 1 WLR 585

The plaintiff refused to undergo an operation which, if successful, would have allowed him to recover 80% of his mortality and allowed him to resume his career as a professional engineer.

Held:: the question as to whether the plaintiff had failed to mitigate his damages was one of fact and the burden was on the plaintiff. (In this case, the court held that he had discharged this burden.)

See note 13–009 in *Kemp & Kemp* where the opinion is that this decision was made *per incuriam*.

(3) McAuley v London Transport Executive [1957] 2 Lloyds Rep 500

Jenkins LJ said that damages should be assessed on the assumption that had the plaintiff undergone the operation and it had been successful.

(4) Hoffberger v Ascot Intended Bloodstock Bureau Ltd (1976) 120 Sol Jo 130

See above, at p 227.

(5) Hassal & another v Secretary of State [1995] 1 WLR 812

See p 229.

(6) Calderbank v Calderbank [1976] Fam 93

See above, at p 229.

(7) McCamley v Cammell Laird Shipbuilders Ltd [1990] 1 WLR 963

An employer had taken out a personal accident policy for the benefit of his employees although the employees were unaware of this and in fact made no contributions to the premiums. The sum was payable as a lump sum.

Held:: the moneys payable under the policy should not be deducted from an award of damages made by the employer.

(8) Smoker v London Fire and Civil Defence Authority [1991] 2 All ER 449

The House of Lords held that pension benefits were deferred remuneration in respect of the plaintiff's past work and the defendant cannot appropriate the benefit of this.

(9) Hunt v Severs [1994] 2 All ER 385

See p 210.

(10) Lim Poh Choo v Camden and Islington Area Health Authority [1980] AC 174

See p 205.

Foreign case law

CANADA

Ippolito v Janiak (1985) 6 DLR (4th) 1

In this case, the mitigating operation which the plaintiff had refused to undergo had a 70% chance of success.

Held:: the 30% chance of it failing should be taken into account in assessing damages.

Statutes/statutory instruments

(1) SOCIAL SECURITY ADMINISTRATION ACT 1992

See Appendix A, at p 302. The main provisions are set out at CCR 1421–1431.

(2) SOCIAL SECURITY (RECOUPMENT) REGULATIONS 1990 SI 1990/332

See Appendix B, at p 323.

(3) SOCIAL SECURITY (CONTRIBUTIONS AND BENEFITS) ACT 1992

See above, at p 228.

(4) STATUTORY SICK PAY ACT 1994 (CONSEQUENTIAL) REGULATIONS 1994 SI 1994/730

See above, at p 228.

(5) RULES OF THE SUPREME COURT (AMENDMENT NO 2) REGULATIONS 1990 SI 1990/1689; CCR ORD 11, R 10(2); COUNTY COURT (AMENDMENT NO 3) RULES 1990 SI 1990/1764

See above, at p 229.

(6) FATAL ACCIDENTS ACT 1976

See Appendix A, at p 262.

(7) LAW REFORM (PERSONAL INJURIES) ACT 1948

Deduction of benefits for small claims

2(1) In an action for personal injuries (including any such action arising out of contract), where this section applies there shall in assessing those damages be taken into account, against them, one-half of the value of any rights which have accrued or probably will accrue to the injured person from the injuries in respect of:

(a) any of the relevant benefits, within the meaning of s 81 Social Security Administration Act 1992;

(b) any corresponding benefits payable in Northern Ireland,

for the five years beginning with the time when the cause of action accrued.

(1)(A) This section applies in any case where the amount of the damages that would have been awarded from any reduction under subsection (1) above is less than the sum for the time being prescribed under s 85(1) Social Security Administration Act 1992 (recoupment of benefit: exception for small payments).

(3) The reference in subsection (1) of this section to assessing the damages for personal injuries shall, in cases where the damages otherwise recoverable are subject to reduction under the law relating to contributory negligence or are limited by or under any Act or by contract, be taken as referring to the total damages which would have been recoverable apart from the reduction or limitation.

...

(6) For the purposes of this section disablement benefit in the form of a gratuity is to be treated as benefit for the period taken into account by the assessment of the extent of the disablement in respect of which it is payable.

Practice points

For assistance/queries on the recoupment of benefits, contact the Compensation Recovery Unit, DSS, Reyrolle Building, Hebburn, Tyne and Wear NE31 1XB.

RULE 7(C)

Damages are usually awarded as a lump sum. However, in certain instances, damages may be awarded on more than one occasion, in advance of the final resolution of the matter or in a form other than a lump sum.

Commentary

As already noted the plaintiff can only bring one action in respect of the alleged tort and any compensation is usually awarded in a lump sum. Such a method of payment can create problems where, eg the plaintiff's prognosis is uncertain or where the award is large. In such situations, the solicitor may wish to consider alternatives to the lump sum payment. These are considered below. However, before doing so there is another possibility which he may wish to consider, and that is a split trial where the issues of liability and *quantum* are tried separately. This may be appropriate in the case of a brain-damaged baby where it will be sensible to deal with liability at an early stage but resolve *quantum* when the child is older and his future needs will have become apparent.

Structured settlements

Structured settlements were introduced in England and Wales in 1987 following an agreement between the Association of British Insurers (ABI) and the Inland Revenue. Essentially, the settlement allows compensation to be paid in instalments for the life of the plaintiff who will also receive part of his damages as a lump sum payment.

What happens when a structured settlement is agreed? The defendant's insurer will agree to pay a lump sum to the plaintiff but additionally will agree that the majority of this lump sum will be paid by instalments tied to the Retail Price Index with a life office for an annuity on the plaintiff's life. The annuity is in fact paid to the defendant or the defendant's insurers, who then pay these sums to the plaintiff. The main advantage of such a scheme is that the plaintiff receives this sum tax free as it is regarded as a capital payment and consequently represents a considerable saving to him. Investment income from the lump sum is treated as income and therefore is subject to tax. It is possible that the defendant's insurers will attempt to negotiate a discount on the award, bearing in mind that the plaintiff will make a tax saving of some 45%.

The second advantage of a structured settlement is one of security, since there is an increasing worry that the damages may not cater for the plaintiff's life expectancy. Where the plaintiff has dependants, any structured settlement will usually provide for a minimum number of payments in case the plaintiff dies early, and will also provide a capital sum to cater for any contingencies. The plaintiff is also relieved of both the financial pressures of managing a large sum of money.

The defendant insurer is, however, under a disadvantage as he is required to pay the gross amount to the plaintiff, reclaiming the tax withheld at the end of the financial year. Therefore, although the plaintiff receives a tax free annuity, the defendant will suffer an administrative burden and the loss of cash flow in having to pay the gross amount before reclaiming the tax.

In considering whether to elect for a structured settlement, it would be an unwise solicitor who does not consider its potential disadvantages. Not necessarily a disadvantage but a point worth noting is that before making the structured settlement the parties usually estimate what the court would have awarded at trial; thus there is still a guessing element that goes with the lump sum award. Once set up, a structured settlement is there for the life of the plaintiff and cannot be changed. This can cause problems, eg where the plaintiff's condition deteriorates unexpectedly so that he now needs expensive treatment or where he can no longer be cared for at home and requires a place in a residential home. The contingency fund may cope with these problems, but the greater the amount placed in such a fund the less the tax benefit to the plaintiff; any income generated by the fund is subject to income tax. Finally, there will be no legacy left to the plaintiff's dependants on his death – this may be considered both an advantage or disadvantage depending on how you view the situation.

Many of these problems have been highlighted in a recent report by the Law Commission No 224 'Structured Settlements and Interim Payments'. That report was against the proposal that the court should have the power to impose a structured settlement, arguing that reform should be targeted at rationalising and building on the voluntary system (see paras 3.53–3.57). It also focused on what it perceived to be the two main problems with structured settlements:

(1) the problems encountered by the insurer, eg cashflow and administrative burdens; and

(2) the fears of the plaintiff concerning the security of the structured settlement.

The report's main recommendation was:

> A life office should be able to make payments free of tax direct to the Plaintiff as the annuitant under an annuity bought for her or him from the office by the defendant (or defendant insurer) who will apply for this purpose as part of the damages, which would be payable by the defendant to the plaintiff. (3.57)

This recommendation would be implemented by a stand-alone structured settlement scheme; in effect structured settlements would be put on a statutory basis. To implement such reform there would have to be an agreement between the plaintiff and the defendant (or defendant insurers) and both parties would have to agree that the damages (excluding the lump sum) would consist of periodic payments to the plaintiff for a fixed term or for life or both (with or without provision for indexation). There is no real change here. However, the report goes on to say that the defendant (or defendant insurer) must agree to purchase the annuities for the plaintiff. This is a change: at present the defendant will usually purchase an annuity, but he is not compelled to do so. Finally, the annuity payments received by the plaintiff will be free of tax in the same way that damages payable by instalments under a voluntary structured settlement are free of tax. In addition, under the Policyholders Protection Act 1975, it is recommended that, under a structured settlement arrangement a plaintiff should be protected to the full amount of the liability attributed to the policy.

In the medical negligence field, structured settlements have became more common following the changes introduced by the Crown Indemnity Scheme in 1990.

With regard to the Department of Health, the Law Commission noted that there had been an increase in structured settlements. The main problem with such schemes in this area was that the Crown did not usually insure but rather carried its own risks. An annuity was not usually purchased, instead the situation was to a large extent resolved by the provision of letters of comfort, in which NHS representatives gave assurances as to the security of the scheme. What is now proposed by the Law Commission is that the Secretary of State for Health should be empowered to give an appropriate Crown guarantee.

Provisional damages

The introduction of provisional damages remedied another deficiency in the lump sum award. Usually, the plaintiff received his compensation in one sum. The problem arises when, for example, five years after that payment, the plaintiff finds his condition deteriorating. He cannot go back to court and try to claim more compensation. An award of provisional damages allows the plaintiff to obtain some compensation and still return to court at a later date should his condition deteriorate. Pursuant to s 6 of the Administration of Justice Act 1982, both the High Court and the county court have the power to award provisional damages, see s 32A Supreme Court Act 1981 and s 51 County Courts Act 1984. For the relevant rules concerning this award, see RSC Ord 37, rr 7–10 and CCR Ord 18, r 3. See also Practice Direction (Provisional Damages: Procedure) [1985] 1 WLR 961 and Practice Note [1988] 1 WLR 654 (Appendix C, at pp 344, 346).

What situations will qualify for an award of provisional damages? The leading authority is the case of *Willson v Ministry of Defence* [1991] 1 All ER 638 which should be studied in detail by any solicitor contemplating an application under RSC Ord 37. In that case the court refused to make an award under Ord 37 because the plaintiff had not established that there was a serious deterioration in his condition as opposed to a chance of continuing deterioration of his condition. The court held that for an award of provisional damages to be successful:

(1) there had to be a chance of the injury or disease deteriorating and that possibility had to be measurable rather than fanciful; and

(2) the deterioration must be serious in that it was something beyond ordinary deterioration; that was a question of fact, depending on the circumstances of the case.

Thus, for example, a plaintiff who contracts HIV through contaminated blood could apply for provisional damages on the basis that at some time in the future he may develop AIDS; similarly, a plaintiff who has a disease which is now in remission may claim for the chance that the disease may reoccur. However, even if those two conditions were satisfied, the court still had a discretion as to whether to award provisional damages. In *Willson*, the court regarded the development of osteo-arthritis as a progressive condition. *Note* that the burden of proof is on the plaintiff to show there is a chance of deterioration.

At present, the plaintiff must give the defendant three months' notice of the application to apply for the award and then only one application may be made. Recently, the Law Commission No 224 Recommendation 11 (5.22–5.23) recommended that the plaintiff should be permitted to make more than one application where the disease or deterioration specified in the order occurs in more than one part of his body. This is a significant improvement because at present the plaintiff could be unjustly prejudiced if, eg cancer, later appears in a different part of the body from where it was discovered previously. Another recommendation was that s 1 Fatal Accidents Act 1976 should be amended so that where a person who was awarded provisional damages dies due to the negligence that gave rise to the award, the earlier award of provisional damages should not prevent an action under the Fatal Accidents Act; instead, in assessing the amount of loss claimed under the Act, the court should take into account any amount of provisional damages which were intended to compensate for pecuniary loss after the deceased's death. At present, whether the dependants can recover further damages under the 1976 Act is uncertain, see *Middleton v Elliot Turbomachinery Ltd* (1990) The Times, 29 October. In that case, it was held that a declaration that the award of provisional damages did not preclude a claim by the plaintiff's dependants under the Fatal Accidents Act 1976 for further damages in the event of the plaintiff's death was unlawful.

For further procedural points see p 262.

Interim payment

An interim payment is, as the name suggests, an interim award, an advance on the plaintiff's damages. In medical litigation the need for immediate compensation can be great, eg where the plaintiff requires nursing care or incurs other medical expenses; consequently interim awards are very important.

The relevant rules can be found at RSC Ord 29, r 10. The High Court Rules also apply in the county court where the amount claimed is greater than £1,000, see CCR Ord 13, r 12. Ord 29 stipulates the defendant must be:

(1) insured;

(2) a public authority; or

(3) a person whose means and resources are such that he is capable of making the payment.

Clearly, in medical litigation, this should not pose too many problems because in the majority of cases the defendant will be the Health Authority or Trust.

The court has a discretion as to whether to make the payment or not. The plaintiff must satisfy one of three grounds:

(1) that the defendant has admitted liability for the plaintiff's damages;

(2) that judgment has been entered against the defendant for damages to be assessed; or

(3) that, if the matter proceeded to trial, the plaintiff would be awarded substantial damages against that defendant.

Clearly, the last ground in effect asks the court to do little more than guess what will be the eventual outcome of the action and, therefore, the plaintiff must show that his case is as strong as possible.

Sometimes an interim payment will be coupled with an application for summary judgment under RSC Ord 14; CCR Ord 9; however, such an application should only be brought where liability is clear cut.

As the majority of points we wish to make with regard to interim payments are of a procedural nature they are all dealt with in the practice points, at p 239.

REFERENCES

English case law

(1) Willson v Ministry of Defence [1991] 1 All ER 638

See p 236.

(2) Middleton v Elliot Turbomachinery Ltd (1990) The Times, 29 October

See p 236.

(3) Hurditch v Sheffield Health Authority [1989] 2 All ER 869

See practice points below, at p 239.

(4) Stringman v McArdle [1994] 1 WLR 1653

See practice points below, at p 239.

(5) Smith v Glennon [1994] 5 Med LR 218

The plaintiff sought an interim payment of £160,000 out of a total damages award of £240,000. The defendant appealed against the decision at first instance awarding the interim payment contending that, among other things, the award was excessive. The defendant argued that the plaintiff had brought problems upon himself by moving to the United States and that the plaintiff had acted irresponsibly in the past having already dissipated two previous interim payments.

Held:: if the case was within Ord 29, r 10, it was of no concern to the court how the money was used or why the plaintiff needed it.

(6) Schott Kem Ltd v Bentley [1991] 1 QB 61

See practice points below, at p 240.

(7) Independent Broadcasting Authority v EMI Electronics (1981) 14 Build LR 1

See practice points below, at p 241.

Statutes / statutory instruments

(1) SUPREME COURT ACT 1981

Sections 32, 32A – interim payments and provisional damages. See Appendix A, at p 279.

(2) COUNTY COURTS ACT 1984

Sections 50, 51 – interim payments and provisional damages. See Appendix A, at p 283.

(3) RULES OF THE SUPREME COURT 1965

RSC Ord 29, rr 9–18 – interim payments. See Appendix D, at p 361.

RSC Ord 37, r 10 – provisional damages. See Appendix D, at p 366.

(4) COUNTY COURT RULES 1981

CCR Ord 13, r 12 – interim payments. See Appendix D, at p 379.

CCR Ord 18, r 3 – provisional damages. See above, at p 236.

(5) LEGAL AID (GENERAL) REGULATIONS 1989 in CRIMINAL AND CARE PROCEEDINGS SI 1989/344

Regulation 94(4), see below, at p 241.

(6) CIVIL LEGAL AID (ASSESSMENT OF RESOURCES) REGULATIONS 1989 SI 1989/338

Schedule 3 14B, see below, at p 241.

(7) INCOME SUPPORT (GENERAL) REGULATIONS 1987 SI 1987/1967

Regulation 45, Sched 9 para 22, see below, at p 241.

Practice points

Structured settlements

A structured settlement can be considered at any time up to when the parties enter into a binding contract to settle the case. There is no set minimum figure for the settlement but as a guide it is likely that the award will be in excess of £100,000. It is usual in any event to obtain the advice of a forensic accountant (after first obtaining authority from the Legal Aid Board/client). As for the formal approval, see Practice Direction [1992] 1 WLR 328. *Note* that approval will be required where the plaintiff is a minor or is incapable of looking after himself. See also *Hadfield v Knowles and another*, 16 May 1996 where the Court of Appeal looked at the appropriate procedure for structured settlements for plaintiffs under a disability.

In assessing whether or not the structured settlement is appropriate, the solicitor must first take into account the age of the plaintiff, the nature of the disabilities, life expectancy and the cost of future and care and equipment needed.

If the courts approval is required (eg in the case of a minor) counsel's opinion will have to be lodged at court. The opinion should assess the value of the claim and then consider the plaintiff's life expectancy based on medical opinion. Also, if applicable, the approval of the Court of Protection must be sought. Before giving such consent, the Master of the Court of Protection will require counsel's written advice in order to be able to confirm that the court would be prepared to approve the form of settlement.

A report from accountants or other financial experts as to the fiscal and investment advantages of a structured settlement should be sought and it must be considered as to whether the plaintiff has sufficient funds outside the structured settlement to meet any foreseeable capital need. The agreement should then be submitted in draft to the Inland Revenue for approval.

Provisional damages

We do not intend to go into the specific procedural requirements in any detail. Briefly, a claim for provisional damages should be pleaded and whether or not to make an award is at the discretion of the court. The parties should endeavour to agree that the award of provisional damages is appropriate; however, if they fail to reach an agreement, that in itself will not bar the court from making an award, the parties will simply be directed to file their respective medical reports. See on this point *Hurditch v Sheffield Health Authority* [1989] 2 All ER 869 where although there was no total agreement between the parties the court ruled there had been sufficient agreement in accordance with the rules. If the case goes to trial, then the judge's award of damages will recite the disability or, if the case is settled, a consent order will be required. If the case is settled before the commencement of proceedings it will not be necessary to start proceedings.

The court, if satisfied that the circumstances justify such an award, will specify the circumstances when an application may be made and the time limits for doing so. *Note* that, pursuant to RSC Ord 37, r 9; CCR Ord 22, r 6(a), the defendant may, after the plaintiff has made an application for provisional damages, make a written offer in satisfaction of the plaintiff's claim on the assumption that the plaintiff will not contract the specified disease or his condition will not deteriorate. The defendant must specify in his offer the said disease or deterioration. As a general rule, the procedure post-trial will be in accordance with the Practice Direction (Provisional Damage Procedure) [1985] 1 WLR 961.

Interim payments

The application itself is made by summons/notice of application supported by an affidavit. The requirements for the affidavit are set out at RSC Ord 29, r 10(1)(e), (f). The plaintiff's wish for the payment need not be taken into account, see *Stringman v McArdle* [1994] 1 WLR 1653. What is important is that the plaintiff has satisfied one of the criteria of Ord 29. The court is not even concerned about whether the plaintiff has dissipated previous payments (see *Smith v Glennon* [1994] 5 Med LR 218). The plaintiff must satisfy the court that he will succeed against the defendant. *Note*, however, that although the court indicated in *Smith* that it was not concerned with how the plaintiff used the money it did take note of what the plaintiff intended to do with the money (in this case purchase a home), Additionally, the court considered both the plaintiff's career and medical history, in particular, the court noted the number of jobs the plaintiff had applied for. Therefore, it is apparent that in any affidavit in support of the application this information should be included. To summarise, the following additional information should be included:

(1) All requirements as specified by RSC Ord 29, r 10 (1)(e), (i), ie the stage of the action, whether the defendant admits liability, has there been a payment into court, etc. *Note* that all pleadings should be exhibited and the plaintiff's age at the time of the accident should be included, similar to the rule for pleadings.

(2) Exhibit medical reports. In addition, the affidavit should summarise the effect and consequences of the accident, thereby saving the court from the task of ploughing through the medical report in meticulous detail. The affidavit should specify what treatment the plaintiff underwent as a result of the accident.

(3) Details of all special damages to date and all past and future loss of earnings.

(4) Details of the plaintiff's educational and career history, eg did the plaintiff spend several years qualifying, did he have a promising future, etc. If appropriate, the fact that the plaintiff has attempted to mitigate his damages should also be included.

(5) All letters to the DSS.

(6) With regard to the loss of amenity claim the plaintiff's lifestyle should be described in acute detail, what can he no longer do?

(7) In a Fatal Accidents Act case, the names and relationships of the deceased to the dependants.

(8) Pursuant to RSC Ord 29, r 11(2), a paragraph stating that the defendant has the means to make the payment should be included.

(9) Although the plaintiff need not show a need for the payment, if he can so much the better (see *Smith v Glennon* [1994] 5 Med LR 218).

Where there is more than one defendant, the court must be satisfied that a particular defendant or defendants are liable. However, the court will also make an order against more than one defendant if it is satisfied that each defendant is liable (see *Schott Kem Ltd v Bentley* [1991] 1 QB 61). Indeed, the court can apportion the award between the various parties (eg several partners in a general practice) providing the sums do not exceed the 'just amount'.

As stated above, the defendant must be able to meet the claim. Generally, any objection to the plaintiff's application will be made on the ground that the defendant is financially unable to meet the award, although the court could refuse to make the award on the grounds that the plaintiff has failed prove his case or that there is a serious doubt that the plaintiff would win substantial damages. In this regard, the court will take into account such matters as set-off, counterclaims or, perhaps more relevant to medical negligence claims, any allegation of contributory negligence.

As to the amount of the interim payment, the court will not order the defendant to pay more than a just amount not exceeding a reasonable proportion of the damages (and it is here that the court will take into account contributory negligence if any). Guidance is given as to the likely amount of the award in *The White Book* 29/11/2. Generally, the court will order that the amount of special damages already incurred and those anticipated up to the date of trial should be paid to the plaintiff, although if the plaintiff should want an amount in respect of his anticipated general damages that too may be awarded subject to the court's discretion. The overriding concern of the court is not to risk over compensating the plaintiff although, as previously indicated, it is not fatal if the plaintiff cannot show a need. Everything is subject to the court's discretion.

Listed below are some miscellaneous practice points regarding interim payments (generally see *The White Book* 29/11/1).

(1) The interim payment is usually payable to the plaintiff and there will be a time limit specified. Once received, the funds should be used as quickly as possible. It is conceivable that if the funds sit in court or the plaintiff's bank account, the defendant could argue that the interim payment should never have been made, eg the plaintiff does not really require the new accommodation or nursing care. The plaintiff must ensure that the interim payment is spent in accordance with his special damages schedule.

(2) If the plaintiff is under a disability, the court can order that the payment is paid into the Court of Protection. In *Stringman v McArdle* [1994] 1 WLR 1653, the court said that, eg where the only relief required was the application of the minor's property and there was no family dispute, the Court of Protection was to be preferred, especially if the minor was nearing majority. Generally, in the case of a plaintiff under a disability, the court will confine the amount of the interim payment to those sums required by the next friend for maintenance of the plaintiff until trial.

(3) The actual payment is usually made in a lump sum, although it may be paid in instalments (r 13(3)). If the plaintiff is legally aided, the interim payment will not attract the statutory charge although the final award will, see Legal Aid General Regulations 1989, reg 94(4). Also, the payment will be disregarded in the assessment of means in relation to the plaintiff's eligibility for legal aid. The Civil Legal Aid (Assessment of Resources) Regulations 1989 SI 1989/338 Sched 3 14B specifies that any capital payment made in relation to the incident giving rise to the dispute in respect of which legal aid is granted is to be ignored.

(4) Benefits must also be taken into consideration. Any award or settlement will be subject to the clawback provisions. If the client was receiving income support, he will cease to be entitled to this benefit if the capital awarded is £8,000 or greater (see Income Support (General) Regulations 1987 SI 1987/1967 reg 45). The way around this is to pay the sum into a discretionary trust which should be in place before the award. (*Note* the introduction of the jobseekers allowance, see p 228.)

(5) The court may award interest on the interim payment (see *Independent Broadcasting Authority v EMI Electronics Ltd* (1981) 14 Build LR 1). The court should specify how the award is made up.

(6) The secrecy rule regarding payment into court is waived if an interim payment application is made. In fact, it is usual for the payment to be used to make the award. If a payment in is made after the interim payment, it should state whether it has taken that into account (see *The White Book* 29/11/2 para 4).

(7) Finally, more than one application can be made.

Note that the Law Commission Report No 224 considers that interim payments and provisional damages awards could be structured, though as an interim payment is usually made for a specific purpose it does not seem appropriate for structuring.

RULE 7(D)

Damages are essentially compensatory in nature. In certain circumstances damages may not be compensatory.

Commentary

Damages may be contemptuous, nominal, exemplary or (aggravated) punitive. For the purposes of medical negligence, only the latter two are relevant.

Exemplary damages

These damages are awarded to teach the defendant a lesson (see *Rookes v Barnard* [1964] AC 1129). In practice, they are only awarded where:

(1) there has been oppressive, arbitrary or unconstitutional action by servants of the government; or

(2) the defendant's conduct has been calculated by him to make a profit for himself which may well exceed the compensation payable to the plaintiff; or

(3) they are specifically authorised by statute.

Furthermore, in *Gibbons and others v South West Water Services Ltd* [1993] QB 507, the courts decided that exemplary damages can only be awarded for those torts which were recognised as being appropriate for that particular claim before the decision in *Rookes v Barnard* [1964] AC 1129.

Exemplary damages have little or no part to play in medical negligence claims in England, but they do feature in other jurisdictions, in particular, the United States. The main thrust of the argument against their introduction is that it would cause confusion between civil and criminal law but, given that the number of cases where they may be applicable are few and far between, this argument seems untenable. For the method of calculating the award, see *Rookes v Barnard* [1964] AC 1129 and *Cassell & Co Ltd v Broome* [1972] AC 1027.

Aggravated (punitive) damages

Essentially aggravated damages are compensatory in nature, but when the court awards such damages it usually takes into account the way in which the plaintiff was injured, eg was the conduct of the defendant wilful and intentional and, consequently, was the plaintiff's injury and/or pride injured? In such circumstances, the court may award a higher level of damages. It seems that at present, the court is unlikely to award such damages in a medical negligence field. In *Kralj v McGrath and St Theresa's Hospital* [1986] 1 All ER 54 where the plaintiff suffered appalling treatment during childbirth, the court ruled that aggravated damages were inappropriate in a medical negligence case.

REFERENCES

English case law

(1) Rookes v Barnard [1964] AC 1129

See above, at p 242.

(2) Gibbons and others South West Water Services Ltd [1993] QB 507

This was an action for public nuisance. The defendant had allegedly caused injury to the plaintiffs by supplying contaminated water. As there was no similar claim for exemplary damages prior to 1964, the plaintiffs claim for exemplary damages was struck out.

(3) Broome v Cassell & Co Ltd [1972] AC 1027; [1971] 2 QB 354

The commission of a tort in a malicious, insulting or oppressive manner may aggravate the plaintiff's injury.

(4) Kralj v McGrath and St Theresa's Hospital [1986] 1 All ER 54

The plaintiff was pregnant with twins. Because of the defendant's negligence; one of the twins was born severely disabled and died eight weeks later. The plaintiff suffered a truly horrific time during the delivery and suffered shock at seeing the child's injuries and watching the child die over the eight week period following. The court ruled that aggravated damages were inappropriate in an action for negligence against a doctor and in addition no award was made in respect of the woman's grief, but the court took into account that the plaintiff's treatment might have increased her pain and suffering in relation to the death of her child.

See p 204.

See also *Devi v West Midlands Regional Health Authority* (1981) *Kemp & Kemp*, Vol 2, F5–018 and F5–107, where compensatory damages of £4,000 were awarded in a case of non-consensual sterilisation without any reference to aggravated damages. See further Chapter 2, Consent, at p 41.

Practice points

- A claim for exemplary damages must be specifically pleaded together with the facts relied on, RSC Ord 18, r 8(3), *The White Book* 18/8/7, although they need not be pleaded in the county court. *The White Book* specifies that the claim must be pleaded in the main body of the claim and must be made in addition to any other claim for damages. Also, the party must plead all facts in support of the claim. (This reverses the rule stated in *Broome v Cassell & Co Ltd* [1972] AC 1027; [1971] 2 QB 354.)

  It is probable that the same rules apply to a claim for aggravated damages; sufficient facts will have to be pleaded to establish a claim for aggravated damages and consequently the claim should be pleaded.

RULE 7(E)

Where a person has a cause of action against the defendant but dies before it has been resolved the defendant may still be liable to the estate of the deceased under the Law Reform (Miscellaneous Provisions) Act 1934, or to the dependants of the deceased under the Fatal Accidents Act 1976.

Commentary

Although these statutory claims have been grouped within one rule, for the sake of convenience they will be dealt with separately. However, the procedural aspects of both claims are dealt with together in the practice points section.

An action under the Law Reform (Miscellaneous Provisions) Act 1934

Section 1 of the 1934 Act does not create a cause of action, rather it allows the deceased's claim to survive after his death. In addition, s 1(4) of the Act allows an action to continue against a tortfeasor after the latter has died. For example where a GP negligently prescribes the wrong drug and dies before his patient has suffered damage from taking the drug over a long period, the patient will still have an action against the GP's estate.

Generally, the damages recoverable will be the same as if the plaintiff was still alive (eg loss of earnings and other pecuniary losses from the date of injury until death), except that neither exemplary damages nor any amounts in respect of loss of income after the deceased's death is recoverable, see s 1(2) of the Act. Claims prior to 1 January 1983 are outside the scope of this provision, see *Kemp and Kemp* 26–001 *et seq* for further guidance and *Gammell v Wilson and Swift & Co Ltd* [1982] AC 27 where the court allowed the estate to recover an amount in respect of the deceased's loss of earnings after his death. However, a bereavement claim is available under s 3 Administration of Justice Act 1982. In assessing a sum to reflect pain and suffering, damages cannot be recovered for pain which is suffered as a result of dying. See *Hicks v Chief Constable of West Yorkshire* [1992] 2 All ER 65, and s 1(2)(c) of the Act, where the death has been caused by the act or omission which gives rise to the cause of action, no account is to be taken of any loss or gain to the estate in the calculation of damages except that an additional claim may be made for funeral expenses if paid for by the estate.

Where it is the tortfeasor who dies, damages will be assessed in the normal way against his estate. In a medical negligence claim, this provision is effectively redundant, since the claim will usually be against the Health Authority, Trust, private hospital, or against the GP's practice, although in the latter case the claim can be brought against the deceased GP's estate as well as against his fellow partners.

An action under the Fatal Accidents Act 1976

Where the wrongful act of the defendant causes the death of the deceased, then a claim under this Act is possible. The claim is brought by the deceased's dependants and it is for the loss which has been suffered or is likely to be suffered. The claim may be brought by any dependant (for the definition of dependant see p 230) and is a new action in its own right. It will only subsist if the deceased whilst alive could have sued the tortfeasor for his injuries. Additionally, if the deceased had already accepted compensation for his injuries before his death or if his claim was statute barred (see Chapter 4, Limitation, at p 104) then the dependant(s) will have no claim.

The Act provides for three types of compensation: bereavement allowance, a claim for loss of dependency, and a claim for funeral expenses if paid by the dependants. The bereavement payment is fixed at £7,500 for deaths occurring after 1 April 1991, and £3,500 for deaths before that date. Interest will be payable on such a sum at the full rate.

The loss of dependency claim can be brought by a wide class of dependants and, generally, will cover any amounts which they could have reasonably expected from the deceased had he not died. Thus, the court must take into account the characteristics of the dependants, eg if the dependant has a short life expectancy. The benefit alleged to be lost must arise because of the relationship between the deceased and the dependant but, where the dependency occurs after the injury which causes the deceased's death, the spouse may still bring a claim under the Act (see *Phillips v Grampian Hospital Board* [1991] 3 Med LR 16 (a Scottish case)).

The usual approach in assessing the damages is to take the deceased's net income and from that deduct a figure which represents an amount which the deceased will have spent on himself. Any other benefits such as a company car or cheap mortgage should be added in calculating the net income. This figure is the multiplicand. The figure can only be an approximate one as it will often be very difficult to apportion expenditure between family members. Alternatively, the multiplicand may be calculated by building up a profile of the deceased's income and expenditure. In the case where a mother has died, there may be other factors to take into account in assessing the multiplicand and the proper award to the children dependants. Where the deceased did not provide any earnings but provided services such as caring for children, the usual figure will be either the cost of employing someone to look after the children (*Regan v Williamson* [1976] 1 WLR 305) or the earnings lost by the other parent in having to stay at home and look after the children (*Mehmet v Perry* [1977] 2 All ER 529) providing that the decision to stay home was reasonable. Where the children would be looked after by a relative, the wage should be net of tax and national insurance contributions. Where children had lost their mother, the court ruled in *Spittle v Bunney* [1988] 1 WLR 847 that the mother's services could not be valued at a constant figure for the whole of the child's dependency; it therefore raised the award by some 10%. *Note* that the multiplicand is assessed at the date of trial, ie the income the deceased would have been earning had he been alive. In practice, the court assesses the deceased's income at the date of his death and the degree of dependency of each claimant and then revises it in the light of his expected income at the date of trial.

Future loss of earnings is calculated in exactly the same way as for a living plaintiff (see p 208); however, the multiplier is a figure decided at the date of death and not the date of the trial as for a living plaintiff (see *Graham v Dodds* [1983] 1 WLR 808). Exactly what the multiplier will be depends on the characteristics of the dependants, eg age, health, expectation of working life, and was it foreseeable that the deceased's income would rise in the immediate future; if so, the multiplier is likely to be increased. In addition, the court must take into account any period which has elapsed between the death and the date of the trial. On this point, see *Corbett v Barking, Havering and Brentford Health Authority* [1991] 2 QB 408 where on appeal the multiplier was increased to reflect that the plaintiff was aged eleven-and-a-half at the time of trial (her mother died at her birth). In assessing the multiplier, no account is taken of inflation. Interest is awarded pre-trial at half the short-term investment rates current between the date of death and trial and there is no interest on future losses. Generally, the court assumes that the award will be invested to provide an annuity and will also take into account whether the award is likely to be subject to heavy taxation. As regards the dependant's future prospects, s 3 states that no account shall be taken of the widow's prospect of remarriage; however, the same does not apply for the widower's chances of remarriage, or for that matter a widow when assessing a child's dependency, however, it seems by the application of s 4 as substituted by s 3(1) Administration of Justice Act 1982, the same result is achieved by a widower, see below. With regard to a cohabitee, the court will take into account that there is no legal duty on the deceased to maintain the cohabitee and consequently reduce the damages accordingly. The court can take into consideration the likelihood that the parties might have divorced and in doing so the court will have regard to the fact that one-third of marriages end in divorce (see *Owen v Martin and Another* [1992] PIQR Q 151).

The court will disregard any benefits the dependants receive in calculating the compensation payable under the 1976 Act (s 4); this includes benefits which have accrued and those which will accrue. But exactly what constitutes a benefit has proved somewhat elusive. In *Stanley v Saddique* [1992] QB 1, the court ruled that the word 'benefit' should be given a wide meaning and in that case it was held to include care provided by a stepmother to a child which had lost his natural mother in an accident, notwithstanding that the care provided was better than that which could have been provided by the child's natural mother. The award, however, was still reduced to reflect the prospects of the services continuing.

The benefit lost must be as a result of the deceased's death and directly related to the relationship between the deceased and the dependant. In *Hayden v Hayden* [1992] 1 WLR 986, the defendant was the father of the infant plaintiff whose claim was in respect of the loss of her mother's care. The defendant had given up work to look after the child and it was held that this was not a benefit pursuant to s 4 but, rather, it was a factor to be taken into account in calculating the plaintiff's loss under s 3(1). This decision appears, at first, to be at odds with the cases of *Stanley* and *Hay v Hughes* [1975] QB 790 where the court, in considering the application of s 3(1), held that care provided by the deceased's grandmother could be disregarded as it was provided out of the generosity of the grandmother and not because of the deceased's death. *Stanley* was distinguished from *Hayden* on the ground that in the former an unstable relationship had been replaced by something rather better, whereas in the latter the father was simply carrying out his parental duties. However, it seems clear that the services were provided as a direct result of the mother's death and the court erroneously took into account the continuing benefit of her father's services. Whatever the artificial distinction, it now appears that the courts have resolved the dilemma by the approach adopted in *Donnelly v Joyce* [1974] QB 454 and *Hunt v Severs* [1994] 2 All ER 385. In *Donnelly*, the plaintiff was allowed to claim for his mother's loss of wages as a result of her giving up her employment to care for him, although the court held that such damages should be held in trust for the third party. In *Hunt,* it was held that there can be no claim for services rendered by the tortfeasor, despite the fact that he is insured. This seems a more sensible approach as it is illogical for a plaintiff to hold damages on trust for the defendant!

In assessing damages, the court will deduct any amount which they consider just to reflect contributory negligence by the deceased (s 5). Additionally, where the deceased's death was the fault of the deceased and one of the dependants, it seems likely that the dependant will have his compensation reduced to a degree proportionate to his responsibility. If the death was caused by the negligence of the dependant, this would debar him from claiming but it has no effect on the other dependants.

According to s 3(1), damages will be awarded to the dependants in proportion to the injury suffered, but the courts have said they will assess the loss as a whole and then apportion it between the dependants (see *Davies v Powell Duffryn Associated Collieries Ltd* [1942] AC 601). The case of *Harris v Empress Motors Ltd* [1984] 1 WLR 212 acts a as a useful guide (where there are no unusual features): if the husband is killed and the wife does not work, dependency will be approximately 66% of the husband's total income; if both spouses worked, dependency will be 66% of the joint income; if there are children, the figure rises to around 75%. However, this will only apply in a 'usual' case; so where the wife was earning a substantial sum before the deceased's death or perhaps has substantial private income, this rule may be inappropriate (see *Coward v Comex Houlder Diving Ltd* [1984] 1 WLR 212).

Recently, the Court of Appeal looked at the question of dependency in relation to state benefits and fraudulent earnings. In *Hunter v Butler* (1995) 19 December (unreported), the plaintiff's husband was killed in a road traffic accident. Before his death, he was in receipt of supplementary benefit and was also working part-time; however, he did not disclose these earnings to the DSS. The court held that since, after his death, the plaintiff had claimed a widow's allowance and a widowed mother's allowance, and continued to receive housing benefit as before, the death of her husband did not cause her any loss, she remained dependent on the State. Moreover, the court held that it would be contrary to public policy to allow dependency on the assumption that the deceased would have continued to claim benefits without disclosing his earnings. The plaintiff was privy to the deceased's conduct and had also committed an offence, hence she was precluded from recovering damages – see further *Kemp & Kemp* para 26–006.

Finally, a claim may be made for funeral expenses where those expenses have been paid by the dependants (s 3(3)). Regrettably, there is no definition of funeral expenses in either the 1976 Act or the 1934 Law Reform (Miscellaneous Provisions) Act; however, it will only be reasonable funeral expenses (see *Gammell v Wilson and Swift & Co Ltd* [1982] AC 27, *Quainoo v Brent and Harrow Area Health Authority* [1982] NLJ 1100 and *Smith v Marchioness/Bowbelle* (1993) *The Times,* 27 January).

REFERENCES

English case law

(1) Gammell v Wilson and Swift & Co Ltd [1982] AC 27

This case is set out in full at para 20–051 in *Kemp and Kemp*.

(2) Hicks and others v Chief Constable of the West Yorkshire Police [1992] 2 All ER 65

See p 203.

(3) Regan v Williamson [1976] 1 WLR 305

This case involved the death of a non-wage earning wife and mother. It was held that the court should value the husband's loss by taking the cost of employing a housekeeper plus the value of those services which were not replaceable.

(4) Mehmet v Perry [1977] 2 All ER 529

See above, at p 245.

(5) Spittle v Bunney [1988] 1 WLR 847

See above, at p 245. The award was increased from £25,000 to £47,500. The court ruled that it could not value the mother's services at a constant figure for the whole of the dependency.

(6) Graham v Dodds [1983] 1 WLR 808

See above, at p 245.

(7) Corbett v Barking, Havering and Brentford Health Authority [1991] 2 QB 408; [1990] 3 WLR 1037

A claim was brought for the benefit of a boy who was aged eleven-and-a-half at the date of the trial. The court applied a multiplier of 15 (normally a multiplier of 12 would have been used); the court, however, applied a multiplier of 3.5 for the post-trial loss.

(8) Owen v Martin (1992) The Times, 21 May; [1992] PIQR Q 151

See above, at p 246

(9) Stanley v Saddique [1992] QB 1

See above, at p 246

(10) Hayden v Hayden [1992] 1 WLR 986

See p 246.

(11) Hay v Hughes [1975] QB 790

See p 246.

(12) Donnelly v Joyce [1974] QB 454

See above, at pp 210, 246.

(13) Hunt v Severs [1994] 2 All ER 385

See pp 210, 247.

(14) Davies v Powell Duffryn Associated Collieries Ltd [1942] AC 601

See above, at p 247.

(15) Harris v Empress Motors Ltd [1984] 1 WLR 212; [1983] 3 All ER 561

See above, at p 247.

(16) Coward v Comex Houlder Diving Ltd [1984] 1 WLR 212

It was held that the judge at first instance had adopted the wrong approach in that it was not for the court to ask whether the evidence displaced the conventional or usual figure of two-thirds/one-third. The judge should have asked whether the evidence required or permitted him to take a larger figure into account. As he did not do so, it was up to the court to examine the findings of fact and the evidence to see whether any larger figure was justified. In this case, the amount of dependency should be calculated by reference to 60% of the net earnings instead of two-thirds.

(17) Hunt v Butler 19 December 1995 (unreported)

See above, at p 247.

(18) Quainoo v Brent and Harrow Area Health Authority [1982] NLJ 1100

This case involved the funeral of a member of the Ghanaian royal family. The cost of transporting the body back to Ghana and the cost of the relatives air fares and cars for the funeral procession were allowed, but not the costs of funeral cards, wreaths, photographer and the hire of a hall and funeral attire.

(19) Smith v Marchioness/Bowbelle (1993) The Times, 27 January

The plaintiff was allowed £400 for a reception of wine and canapes for 300 people after the funeral.

(20) Avery v LNER [1938] AC 606

See below, at p 250.

(21) Shepherd v Post Office (1995) The Times, 14 June

See practice points, at p 250.

Foreign case law

SCOTLAND

Phillips v Grampian Hospital Board [1991] 3 Med LR 16

Although this is a Scottish case, it is more than likely that the same principles would apply in English law. The deceased had begun an action against the defenders for failure to diagnose a testicular tumour. The defenders argued that as the pursuer had married the deceased knowing that he was suffering from a fatal illness she could not sue in respect of his death. Moreover, as her husband was already dying, the pursuer could not claim for loss of society or support because she never had any expectation of obtaining this in her marriage. The court rejected this argument, ruling that s 1(3) Fatal Accidents Act 1976 provided that damages were not simply awarded for an unexpected death but the pursuer had a right to be compensated for loss of support suffered or likely to be suffered as a result of the defender's omission. The date of the marriage was irrelevant because the assumption was that the deceased would not have died but for the negligence of the defenders.

Statutes / statutory instruments

(1) LAW REFORM (MISCELLANEOUS PROVISIONS) ACT 1934

See Appendix A, at p 261.

(2) FATAL ACCIDENTS ACT 1976

See Appendix A, at p 262.

(3) ADMINISTRATION OF JUSTICE ACT 1982 s 3(1)

Practice points

- The 1934 and the 1976 Acts are distinct: damages claimed under the former go to the estate, whereas any compensation recovered under the 1976 Act goes to the dependants. Usually, claims under both Acts will be brought together. If the death does not occur until sometime after the accident, it is likely that proceedings will have commenced prior to death. However, once death has occurred, the pursuance of the claim can be taken over by the personal representatives under the 1934 Act who should apply *ex parte* by affidavit, RSC Ord 15, r 7; CCR Ord 5; and the personal representatives' consent to be added as plaintiffs should also be produced. The pleadings under the Fatal Accidents Act should be amended.

  Note that a missing dependant cannot bring a second action under the 1976 Act (see *Avery v LNER* [1938] AC 606). Conversely, the defendant cannot rely on missing dependants to justify a lowering of the award to other dependants, since each dependant has a separate judgment debt.

- The definition of a dependant under the 1976 Act is set out at Appendix A and includes the following (s 1(3)):

  (a) the spouse or former spouse of the deceased;

  (b) a person who has been living with the deceased as 'husband or wife' in the same household two years prior to his or her death;

  (c) any parent, or other ascendant of the deceased including a person who was treated as a parent;

  (d) any child or other descendant of the deceased including a child treated as a child of the family by the deceased;

  (e) any person who is, or is the issue of, a sibling, uncle or aunt of the deceased;

  (f) an adopted/stepchild/illegitimate child of the deceased;

  (g) a common law spouse providing he or she has been living with the deceased two years prior to the accident. See the recent case of *Shepherd v Post Office* [1995] *The Times*, 14 June which held that a divorced woman who remarried but later returned to her first husband was capable of being a dependant under the Fatal Accidents Act 1976 as a former wife and did not have to show that she had been living with the deceased in the same household prior to his death. The courts now appear to be more concerned with the facts of the situation rather than being simply bound by the two year rule.

- A claim under the 1976 Act should be brought by the personal representatives of the deceased; however, if they fail to sue within six months of the deceased's death, then any dependant may bring the action in his own name or on behalf of himself and others (s 2). There is a time limit of three years which runs from the date of the deceased's death.

- Where death was instantaneous, damages under the Law Reform (Miscellaneous Provisions) Act will be limited to funeral expenses which in any event are recoverable under the Fatal Accidents Act; thus only a claim under the Act should be brought.

- Any proceedings will bear the name of the plaintiff, eg 'Jim Smith Widower and Administrator of the Estate of Edna Smith deceased'. The statement of claim should include all those matters as required for any personal injury pleading, eg date of birth of the deceased, date of the accident or injury, and the circumstances in which it occurred, details of injury (in this case, pre-death) and the consequences of the injury. Additionally, the pleading should state the date of the death of the deceased, details of the grant of probate or administration, details of the plaintiff's relationship with the deceased and details of all dependants.

- The schedule of special damages should cover all pre-death losses and losses suffered by the dependants.
- If there is to be an inquest, the client should be advised that legal aid will not be available and therefore any attendance will have to be paid for privately. *Note* that inquest evidence cannot be admitted as evidence at the trial unless both parties agree.
- Where there are claims under both Acts, the defendant may make one payment into court in respect of both claims and the court will have to apportion the payment between the two claims (see RSC Ord 22, r 1(6), *The White Book* 22/1/15).
- When the plaintiff wishes to accept the payment in satisfaction of a claim under either of the 1934 or 1976 Acts, he can only do so pursuant to an order of the court (see RSC Ord 22, r 4(d), and also *The White Book* 22/4/4).
- Pursuant to RSC Ord 80, r 10, where children are involved, there can be no settlement unless it is sanctioned by the court. The court has to apportion between the children and any surviving parent (see *The White Book* 80/15/4). Where there appears to be a conflict of interest between the dependants, the court can order that the question of apportionment be tried as a separate issue pursuant to RSC Ord 33, r 3. The court can also order that parties be added as plaintiffs or defendants or that infant plaintiffs be separately represented by the Official Solicitor.
- In assessing how the fund should be applied for a child dependant (see *The White Book* 80/12/7). At paras 80/12/6 and 80/15/3, the solicitor will find the general rules for the apportionment under the 1976 Act. The court will first estimate the cost of keeping the child until the age of majority from the date of the order, then apportion a payment out of the income and capital to cover this cost and to provide him with a sum to start life as an adult. This exercise will be repeated for each additional child; remaining money will go to the widow. If insufficient money is recovered, then the child's share will be reduced proportionately. *Note* that courts do not normally approve of apportioning all the funds to the widow since they are of the opinion that this is too risky: she might marry a wastrel.

GENERAL PRACTICE POINTS – RULES 7(A)–(E)

Many of the points listed below are dealt with in the paragraphs above in more detail. We do not propose to discuss in detail how a special damages schedule should be calculated; there are numerous texts which deal more than adequately with that subject. What follows is a ready reckoner on the subject; a checklist designed to act more as a reminder than anything else. As a final note it is suggested that the starting point should always be to send the plaintiff a questionnaire to encourage him to keep a record of his past and continuing loss.

DAMAGES SCHEDULE

Pain and suffering	[What was the nature of the injury? Was the plaintiff suffering from a previous injury or illness (see p 203 above).]
Amenity	[What effect has the injury had on the client's lifestyle (see p 204 above?) Consider what additional expenses have been generated by this claim.]

Psychiatric damage [Is there a recognisable illness? Do you need an expert report? Is it ongoing? (see p 215 above).]

Loss of chance [Unlikely to succeed; instead formulate as a *McGhee* claim if possible (see p 213).]

Wrongful birth: [Damages may be awarded for the birth of either a healthy or disabled child. It is important to find out what is the family's lifestyle (see p 213).]

The client's loss of earnings

- Has the client returned to work?
- Is the client a minor? You will have to speculate on what the client could have earned.

Generally, the following matters should be considered for loss of earnings to date:

(1) You need a six month comparison. Remember to check that the figures are truly comparable, eg overtime, promotion and fluctuating wage rates. Figures are usually obtained from the employer. Obtain an expert's report, if appropriate. Did the client have different employers? Do you need to contact the tax office (you will need client approval)?

If the client is returning to work, what will his salary be and what will be the date of his return? If he has already returned, what is his present salary? Has he returned to work less well paid?

(2) Obtain a copy of the client's contract of employment; check the position as regards statutory sick pay.

(3) Remember that income must be calculated net of tax; what is the client's personal allowance? Is he or she married? With non-MIRAS mortgages of up to £30,000 some of the interest is deductible for tax purposes. What was the client's personal allowance for each of the tax years? Do not forget national insurance contributions.

(4) Remember that the client must give credit for all benefits received. Will there be a Hassal type claim (see p 229) for those benefits received before the accident? Which benefits would he have continued to receive notwithstanding the accident?

Note the client must give credit for all earnings he receives as a result of the accident.

Special cases

If the client is self-employed you may need an accountant's or actuary's report (which will have to be disclosed). *Note* that the accountant or actuary will need all the client's personal details. Do not forget that actuarial tables can now be admitted pursuant to the Civil Evidence Act 1995.

Expenses because of the accident

It is very important that the client keeps an up-to-date record of all his expenses whether by diary or otherwise, eg bank or credit card statements. Such expenses might include:

(1) Transport (eg to and from hospital: how many visits, did other members of the family incur travelling expenses?)

(2) Special equipment such as handrails, ramps, etc.

(3) Private medical care (see s 2(4) Law Reform Personal Injuries Act 1948).

(4) Any special dietary requirements.

(5) Holidays.

(6) Heating/lighting/telephone.

(7) Damage to clothing; any special clothing required.

(8) Any accommodation losses (likely to be future losses).

(9) Cost of carer, eg member of the family (likely to be future losses).

(10)Wages lost by any other member of the family as a result of the accident.

Future losses

As above, but in particular consider:

(1) Accommodation – *Roberts v Johnstone* [1988] 3 WLR 1247 (see p 209).

(2) Cost of future care – not only for the client but also for the client's children, eg will someone be required to collect the children from school? Also consider who is to provide the care: if it is a member of the client's family the value of the service may be difficult to calculate – try using home help rates.

(3) Future medical treatment costs.

(4) Counselling – did the client suffer psychiatric damage?

(5) Therapy – this generic term covers all sorts of therapy, eg occupational, speech, physiotherapy, etc.

(6) Education – if the client is a minor or disabled will he now require any special educational needs, eg the purchase of a new computer, home tuition?

(7) Fees – will any fees be payable now or in the future, eg Court of Protection fees, fees payable for financial advice, etc?

(8) Child's earnings.

Loss of future earnings

There is not much to say here which has not already been said (p 205), except to reiterate that account should also be taken of the loss of earnings of anyone affected by the client's injuries.

Finally do not forget

(1) Interest – at applicable rates.

(2) Costs – agree if possible but remember they are always in the discretion of the court. Generally, no costs will be allowed in a claim less than £1,000 (*Azfal v Ford Motor Company Ltd* [1994] 4 All ER 720). This limit has been raised to £3,000 from 8 January 1996 for non-personal injury cases.

HOW THE CASE WILL PROCEED

As the discussion of the substantive law of negligence comes to an end it seems appropriate to conclude with some comments on the procedural aspects of a medical negligence claim. All solicitors will have access to *The White* and *Green Books* so what follows is by no means an exhaustive commentary; rather it is a guide to some of the more important points that should be borne in mind.

Discovery

Technically, this should have taken place before directions (ie one month after the close of pleadings) but in practice this often does not happen.

The defendant may ask whether the service of a list can be dispensed with given that the medical records have already been disclosed. It is possible to write to the defendant to confirm that he has no more documentation, but is this really worth the risk? It is far better to proceed with discovery by list despite the defendant reluctance.

The list should include all documents which were disclosed during pre-action discovery, together with all additional documents which have yet to be disclosed, eg there may be records of subsequent treatment. Beware of vague statements made by the defendant, especially when he is claiming privilege for documents. There may, for example, have been an internal hospital inquiry report; see Ministry of Health 55(66) circular which states: 'without a contemporaneous report it may not be possible to take action urgently needed to prevent the occurrence of the same mishap again.' These documents will only be privileged if the dominant purpose for which they were prepared was to obtain legal advice (see *Waugh v British Railways Board* [1980] AC 521). If the documents were made prior to the proceedings, they will not attract privilege.

Consider also the plaintiff's and defendant's evidence – does it indicate that further documentation needs to be disclosed?

Discovery should focus on updated medical records and those documents used to prove special damages, eg receipts, etc.

Finally, all solicitors must be alert to the legal consequences should they mistakenly disclose a privileged document. As a basic principle, once the document is disclosed the privilege is lost, although the decision as to whether the document can be used is ultimately at the discretion of the court (see *Derby v Weldon* [1990] 3 All ER 762). In *Pizzey v Ford Motor Co Ltd* (1993) *The Times*, 8 March, it was held that if the receiving party honestly and reasonably believed that the privilege had been waived the court would not intervene and prevent that party using the document at trial. The court further held that the onus was on the plaintiff to satisfy the court that a solicitor in the position of the defendant's solicitor would have realised that the document had been mistakenly disclosed. *Note* also Principle 16.07 Solicitors Practice Rules which obliges the solicitor to return a privileged document to the other side if it is obvious that it has been mistakenly disclosed. Finally, a party's solicitor may cover up parts of the document if the section is privileged or of no relevance to the action (see *GE Capital Corporate Finance Group Ltd v Bankers Trust Co* [1995] 1 WLR 172).

Directions

Automatic directions do not apply in the High Court (see RSC Ord 25, r 8(5)) unlike the county court (see CCR Ord 17, r 11). However, automatic directions are usually inappropriate in a medical negligence claim and an application for a pre-trial review should be made.

Under RSC Ord 25, r 1, the summons must usually be taken out within one month of the close of pleadings, or under RSC Ord 25, r 1(7), the plaintiff may take out a summons at any time (eg the defendant may require a lengthy extension to serve the defence). The usual directions that will be sought are:

(1) discovery (if this has not yet taken place);

(2) evidence, eg exchange of witness statements, expert reports, documentary evidence;

(3) service of special damages schedule; and

(4) the number of witnesses to be called, setting down, etc.

Recently, the standard form applying for a summons for directions has been extended from the former 12 paragraphs to 21 paragraphs with many of the additional directions in line with Practice Direction (Civil Litigation: Case Management) [1995] 1 WLR 262 (Appendix C, at p 347). Two of those directions, namely witness statements and expert evidence are considered in a little more detail below.

Witness statements

The witness statement will be an amalgamation of all the client's proofs of evidence adapted to meet the formal requirements of exchange, see RSC Ord 38, r 2A (*The White Book* para 38/2A/8) and Practice Direction (Evidence: Documents) [1983] 1 WLR 922 (*The White Book* 41/11/1). The initial statement taken from the plaintiff (proof of evidence) will contain all the evidence the plaintiff can remember, including hearsay and opinion evidence. The latter must be edited out of the witness statement which will be exchanged with the other side. However, at the time of writing, the Civil Evidence Act 1995 has just been enacted, although the rules of court have yet to be finalised (expected January 1997). Obviously, this will need to be borne in mind when drafting the witness statement since hearsay evidence will now be specifically admissible.

Pursuant to the Act, evidence will not be inadmissible on the ground that it is hearsay as defined under s 1(2)(b) as 'a statement made otherwise than by a person while giving oral evidence in the proceedings which is tendered as evidence of the matters stated'. There is no change in the rules governing the admissibility of opinion evidence.

Under s 2(1), (2) and (3), a party wishing to adduce hearsay evidence must normally give notice to the other side though the parties may choose to waive the notice procedure. Additionally, particulars of that evidence should be given. A failure to comply with the notice procedure will not render the evidence inadmissible but the court may take this into account in assessing the weight to be attached to the hearsay evidence and, further, may penalise a party in costs (s 2(4)).

Where a party adduces hearsay evidence but then decides not to call that person as a witness, the other side may call that person as a witness for cross-examination on that hearsay evidence as if the statement had been put in examination-in-chief. This is new, prior to the Act, no one could make use of the statement unless a party gave consent or the court gave leave.

With regard to the weight to be attached to the hearsay evidence, the court will consider whether it would have been reasonable and practical to call the witness instead; whether the statement was made contemporaneously; if the statement is multiple hearsay; if the maker has any motive to conceal or misrepresent facts; if the statement has been edited or is the product of collaboration with another; and, finally, if the statement is being adduced as hearsay evidence to try and circumvent a proper evaluation of its weight (see s 6(3)). *Note* that the rules regarding opinion evidence remain unchanged.

Finally, the formal requirements, eg the heading of the action should be at the top of the statement, all pages should be numbered and, although not strictly necessary, it should contain a statement that it is true to the best of the deponent's knowledge and belief.

It is important that all the witnesses who may be needed are contacted and witness statements prepared. The more witnesses who endorse the plaintiff's version of events the stronger the plaintiff's evidence becomes.

The witness statement must contain all the evidence which the witness intends to adduce; therefore it must be reviewed in the light of all the other evidence, eg pleadings, further and better particulars, medical reports and records; discrepancies between the two should be resolved. *Note* that the witness will be unable to adduce any evidence not contained in his statement without the leave of the court.

Tactically what should or should not go into the witness statement is a personal matter; but remember the court must not be misled. What should always be considered is that evidence detrimental to the plaintiff's case is likely to come out in cross-examination and therefore to lessen its effect it should be adduced as evidence-in-chief.

Whether or not it is counsel who draws up the statement will depend on the level of experience of the solicitor, but beware of any cost implications. In any event, it is usually advisable to have the statement checked by counsel and/or the expert.

Exchange of witness statements is made pursuant to RSC Ord 38, r 2A(4); CCR Ord 17, r 11(3). In the county court, if automatic directions apply, the statements should be exchanged within 10 weeks of close of pleadings.

As to the exchange process itself contact the other side and agree mutual exchange as early as possible and be alert to issue a summons for default of exchange. It is important that witness statements are exchanged in advance of exchange of medical reports so as to prevent the defendant from amending his statements to counter the plaintiff's medical evidence. Once exchange has taken place any inconsistencies between the plaintiff's evidence and the defendant's statements should be attended to; in addition, check that all the defendant's witnesses have given the same version of events. It may be that further statements will have to be taken if each side's evidence is completely different to the other. The statements should then be forwarded to the plaintiff's expert for consideration.

Expert reports

Clearly, the plaintiff will already have disclosed one medical report with his statement/particulars of claim. It may be that this is the only medical evidence that the plaintiff intends to rely on; however, in many cases a further report will be required to provide an update on the plaintiff's prognosis. For any report which the parties wish to rely on at trial, they must apply to the court for guidance for disclosure of that report (see RSC Ord 38, rr 36–44; CCR Ord 20, rr 27, 28). In the county court, since automatic directions will apply, no further application to the court is required unless the parties have made an application to vary the automatic directions (see above, at p 254). Exchange of reports should take place simultaneously as with exchange of witness statements. If the action is proceeding in the county court and the automatic directions apply, the report should be disclosed within 10 weeks of the close of pleadings.

Prior to exchange, each side should have gone through the other side's witness statements; in fact, all the evidence exchanged to date and the reports should have been reviewed in the light of that evidence. Remember that until the exchange of witness statements, each side is, in effect, in the dark about the other side's case and the final report should contain an opinion on these witness statements. If the other side's expert's opinion is revised in the light of seeing this further evidence it should be compared with all prior reports; if there is more than one expert each should be sent the other's revised comments. It is also important at this stage to check that the expert's opinion accords with the latest medical literature.

CCR Ord 17, r 11 – automatic striking out

Solicitors would do well to remember the Draconian penalty should they fall foul of this order. Briefly, the plaintiff's solicitor must, within six months of close of pleadings, request the court for a date for trial. But if no request is made, at the very latest within 15 months of close of pleadings or, if the court has varied this limit, nine months after the period fixed by the court, the action will be automatically struck out. No notice will be given to either party. Any application for an extension should be made before the expiry of the 15 months.

The two most often quoted cases on automatic striking out are *Rastin v British Steel plc* [1994] 1 WLR 732 and *Gardner v London Borough of Southwark* (1994) *The Legal Times*, 5 October, p 14 (also noted at [1996] 1 WLR 571) and both authorities should be studied in detail. In *Gardner*, the court reiterated that the obligation for progressing the case always lies with the plaintiff, and it is irrelevant that the defendant has employed delaying tactics. An order to strike out, however, does not amount to dismissal for want of prosecution.

Finally, although High Court cases escape the rigours of automatic striking out, the plaintiff's solicitor should remember that there are provisions which the defendant solicitor could employ to have the claim struck out: dismissal of the action for want of prosecution RSC Ord 19, r 1; default of statement of claim or summons for directions (Ords 25 and 34 respectively).

In all cases where the limitation period has not expired, the plaintiff is at liberty to bring fresh proceedings.

Preparation for trial

(1) We remind solicitors of the importance of Practice Direction (Civil Litigation: Case Management) [1995] 1 WLR 262 (Appendix C, at p 347) which must be adhered to. At present, this direction is only applicable in the High Court. Remember that in cases likely to last more than 10 days, a pre-trial review must be applied for and attended by all parties, and the solicitor is required to lodge a completed pre-trial checklist with the court no later

than two months before the date fixed for trial. Additionally, the parties are under an obligation to try to clarify and reduce the issues in dispute. This may mean that the opposing experts will have to meet on a more regular basis which adds to the court's power to convene a 'without prejudice' meeting of the experts pursuant to RSC Ord 38, r 38.

(2) The pre-trial conference should be used to resolve any ambiguities in both expert and factual evidence.

(3) Medical records will be adduced pursuant to s 1 Civil Evidence Act 1995.

(4) Consider the case of *National Justice Compania Naveria SA v Prudential Assurance Co Ltd (The Ikarian Reefer)* [1993] 2 Lloyds Rep 68 (see Cresswell J at p 81) for the presentation of expert evidence (see also Chapter 5, Standard of Care, p 167, *et seq*). It is vital that the expert understands that his evidence should be objective, unbiased and accurate. It is advisable that the expert is thoroughly familiar with the practice of cross-examination.

It is common in medical negligence cases for evidence of fact to be adduced before expert evidence. This is to avoid the plaintiff's expert being placed under an unfair advantage in having to give his evidence before hearing the defendant's witnesses. Both sides will therefore have to agree to the reorganisation of witnesses.

(5) Medical literature, visual aids, etc should also be organised. It is vital that any fresh evidence be disclosed to the other side as quickly as possible, and the judge's bundle is also updated.

(6) If the case is proceeding in the High Court then it will usually be listed as category B. In the county court, it will usually be heard before a circuit judge. Always consider the use of a split-trial coupled with an interim payment.

Persons under a disability

It is appropriate to include a brief section on the particular problems caused by minors, given that a significant number of medical negligence claims are brought on their behalf. See also RSC Ord 80, set out in Appendix D.

(1) Pursuant to RSC Ord 80, a person under a disability means a person who is an infant or a patient. A patient means a person, who, by reason of mental disorder within the reasoning of the Mental Health Act 1983 is incapable of managing and administering his property and affairs. See also s 1(1), (2) Family Law Reform Act 1969 and s 94 Mental Health Act 1983.

(2) A minor must sue by his next friend who assumes responsibility for the costs of the action. The solicitor should explain this liability to the next friend who should confirm that the minor is less than 18 years of age (by producing a copy of the birth certificate) and that there is no conflict of interest (RSC Ord 80, r 2).

The next friend will have to sign a consent form agreeing to act as a next friend. In the county court, this form must be witnessed by a solicitor. In the High Court, the solicitor signs a separate certificate which must be lodged at the court when the proceedings are issued.

(3) In the High Court, when the writ is issued, the next friend's consent must be lodged along with the certificate from the solicitor confirming that there is no conflict of interest.

(4) If the minor reaches full age during the course of the proceedings, he should serve a notice of adoption and file it at court. The court will then no longer be required to approve any settlement.

(5) For those patients certified under the Mental Health Act 1983, a copy of the order under Part VII of that Act and a certificate certifying that the plaintiff is under a disability should be filed.

(6) Where a compromise has been reached, the respective parties must obtain the court's approval. The reasons for seeking the court's approval are set out at RSC Ord 80, rr 10, 11; basically their purpose is to protect the plaintiff from any lack of skill or experience on the part of their legal advisers and to ensure that the money is properly invested.

(7) The procedure for approval, compromise or a settlement is set out at *The White Book* 80/10–11/3. The application is made by originating summons/originating application (before proceedings have commenced), or summons/notice of application after proceedings have commenced. The application for approval will be made under r 11 and for directions to deal with the fund under r 12 to the master/district judge if the settlement is reached after proceedings are begun but before trial or, if the settlement is agreed at/or during the trial, to the trial judge or master.

(8) In the Chancery Division, the summons and affidavit exhibiting counsel's opinion approving the settlement together with all relevant evidence is filed. In the Queen's Bench Division and the county court no affidavit is required.

(9) The procedure on compromise/settlement (see *The White Book* 80/10–11/4). Briefly, the following should be considered:

Liability – If this is admitted no further evidence need be presented; however, if it is still in dispute the content of the evidence should be presented by both sides along with counsel's opinion, if appropriate.

Quantum – this will be assessed according to the medical reports of both sides, all items making up special damages and in actions under the Fatal Accidents Act 1976, the age, occupation and earnings of the deceased, the ages of the widow and children, the amount, if any, of the deceased's estate and the extent to which the widower and the children were dependent on the deceased.

The court will consider if the settlement is reasonable and beneficial to the plaintiff and what the plaintiff would have obtained had the action gone to trial. If the court is not entirely satisfied with the settlement, it will adjourn the proceedings and give the parties a chance to re-negotiate or, if no further progress is made, it may give directions for the future conduct of the action.

Normally, an affidavit is not required except if the case is particularly difficult as to liability. The next friend may be present but in any event their approval to the settlement should be produced. The plaintiff is not usually present except where the injury involves cosmetic blemishes or there is a large sum involved. If there are several dependants under the Fatal Accidents Act, the application must be brought by all of them. If the action is not approved, the court will go on to give directions for proceedings to be issued or directions akin to the automatic directions. See also Practice Note (Structured Settlements (Courts Approval) [1992] 1 WLR 328.

Note that if the action is brought under the approval of the Court of Protection, then their approval must be produced. However, the final decision for approval is that of the court where the action was commenced. The damages may be administered by the Court of Protection (see RSC Ord 80, r 12(6)).

(10) The order will stipulate to whom the money is to be paid and what is to be done with it. Often the sum will be paid into court and invested there. From time to time, the plaintiff's guardian can simply apply to the court by letter requesting moneys for the plaintiff's care. Generally, the money should be applied for the purpose for which it was awarded. Often small amounts will be paid out immediately to cover current expenses; larger amounts may not be paid over to the parent/guardian and the court may insist that a solicitor be involved.

(11) With regard to costs, the parties should agree these if possible. If the parties do agree costs then, if the plaintiff is legally aided, any agreement by his solicitor to accept the costs paid by the defendant in satisfaction of his own costs requires the approval of the Area Director under reg 106 of the Civil Legal Aid (General) Regulations 1989. If there is no such agreement, then the order will be for the defendant to pay the costs to be taxed on a standard basis and, if the plaintiff is legally aided, an order for legal aid taxation.

In the case of a private client, costs will be taxed on an indemnity basis. The shortfall between these costs and the amount received from the defendant's solicitor will be met out of the plaintiff's compensation. In fact, the plaintiff's solicitor is unlikely to adopt this practice not only because of the expense of the taxation, but also because the *inter partes* costs will have to be taxed, which may not please the defendant's solicitor.

APPENDIX A

STATUTES

LAW REFORM (MISCELLANEOUS PROVISIONS) ACT 1934

Effect of death on certain causes of action

1(1) Subject to the provisions of this section, on the death of any person after the commencement of this Act all causes of action subsisting against or vested in him shall survive against, or, as the case may be, for the benefit of his estate: Provided that this subsection shall not apply to causes of action for defamation.

(1A) The right of a person to claim under s 1A Fatal Accidents Act 1976 (bereavement) shall not survive for the benefit of his estate on his death.

(2) Where a cause of action survives as aforesaid for the benefit of the estate of a deceased person, the damages recoverable for the benefit of the estate of that person:

    (a) shall not include:

        (i) any exemplary damages;

        (ii) any damages for loss of income in respect of any period after that person's death;

    (b) [Repealed.]

    (c) where the death of that person has been caused by the act or omission which gives rise to the cause of action, shall be calculated without reference to any loss or gain to his estate consequent on his death, except that a sum in respect of funeral expenses may be included.

(3) [Repealed.]

(4) Where damage has been suffered by reasons of any act or omission in respect of which a cause of action would have subsisted against any person if that person had not died before or at the same time as the damage was suffered, there shall be deemed, for the purposes of this Act, to have been subsisting against him before his death such cause of action in respect of that act or omission as would have subsisted if he had died after the damage was suffered.

(5) The rights conferred by this Act for the benefit of the estates of deceased persons shall be in addition to and not in derogation of any rights conferred on the dependants of deceased persons by the Fatal Accidents Act 1846–1908 or the Carriage by Air Act 1932, and so much of this Act as relates to causes of action against the estate of deceased persons shall apply in relation to causes of action under the said Act as it applies in relation to other causes of action not expressly excepted from the operation of subsection (1) of this section.

(6) In the event of the insolvency of an estate against which proceedings are maintainable by virtue of this section, any liability in respect of the cause of action in respect of which the proceedings are maintainable shall be deemed to be a debt provable in the administration of the estate, notwithstanding that it is a demand in the nature of unliquidated damages arising otherwise than by a contract, promise or breach of trust.

FATAL ACCIDENTS ACT 1976

Right of action for wrongful act causing death

1(1) If death is caused by any wrongful act, neglect or default which is such as would (if death had not ensued) have entitled the person injured to maintain an action and recover damages in respect thereof, the person who would have been liable if death had not ensued shall be liable to an action for damages, notwithstanding the death of the person injured.

(2) Subject to s 1A(2) below, every such action shall be for the benefit of the dependants of the person ('the deceased') whose death has been so caused.

(3) In this Act 'dependant' means:

    (a) the wife or husband or former wife or husband of the deceased;

    (b) any person who:

        (i) was living with the deceased in the same household immediately before the date of the death; and

        (ii) had been living with the deceased in the same household for at least two years before that date; and

        (iii) was living during the whole of that period as the husband or wife of the deceased;

    (c) any parent or other ascendant of the deceased;

    (d) any person who was treated by the deceased as his parent;

    (e) any child or other descendant of the deceased;

    (f) any person (not being a child of the deceased) who, in the case of any marriage to which the deceased was at any time a party, was treated by the deceased as a child of the family in relation to that marriage;

    (g) any person who is, or is the issue of, a brother, sister, uncle or aunt of the deceased.

(4) The reference to the former wife or husband of the deceased in subsection (3)(a) above includes a reference to a person whose marriage to the deceased has been annulled or declared void as well as a person whose marriage to the deceased has been dissolved.

(5) In deducing any relationship for the purposes of subsection (3) above:

    (a) any relationship by affinity shall be treated as a relationship of consanguinity, any relationship of the half blood as a relationship of the whole blood, and the stepchild of any person as his child, and

    (b) an illegitimate person shall be treated as the legitimate child of his mother and reputed father.

(6) Any reference in this Act to injury includes any disease and any impairment of a person's physical or mental condition.

Bereavement

1A(1) An action under this Act may consist of or include a claim for damages for bereavement.

(2) A claim for damages for bereavement shall only be for the benefit:

    (a) of the wife or husband of the deceased; and

    (b) where the deceased was a minor who was never married:

        (i) of his parents, if he was legitimate; and

        (ii) of his mother, if he was illegitimate.

(3) Subject to subsection (5) below, the sum to be awarded as damages under this section shall be £7,500.

(4) Where there is a claim for damages under this section for the benefit of both the parents of the deceased, the sum awarded shall be divided equally between them (subject to any deduction falling to be made in respect of costs not recovered from the defendant).

(5) The Lord Chancellor may by order made by statutory instrument, subject to annulment in pursuance of a resolution of either House of Parliament, amend this section by varying the sum or the time being specified in subsection (3) above.

Persons entitled to bring the action

2(1) The action shall be brought by and in the name of the executor or administrator of the deceased.

(2) If:

    (a) there is no executor or administrator of the deceased, or

    (b) no action is brought within six months after the death by and in the name of an executor or administrator of the deceased, the action may be brought by and in the name of all or any of the persons for whose benefit an executor or administrator could have brought it.

(3) Not more that one action shall lie for and in respect of the same subject matter of complaint.

(4) The plaintiff in the action shall be required to deliver to the defendant or his solicitor full particulars of the persons for whom and on whose behalf the action is brought and of the nature of the claim in respect of which damages are sought to be recovered.

Assessment of damages

3(1) In the action such damages, other than damages for bereavement, may be awarded as are proportioned to the injury resulting from the death to the dependants respectively.

(2) After deducting the costs not recovered from the defendant any amount recovered otherwise than as damages for bereavement shall be divided among the dependants in such shares as may be directed.

(3) In an action under this Act where there fall to be assessed damages payable to a widow in respect of the death of her husband there shall not be taken into account the re-marriage of the widow or her prospects of re-marriage.

(4) In an action under this Act where there fall to be assessed damages payable to a person who is a dependant by virtue of section 1(3)(b) above in respect of the death of the person with whom the dependant was living as husband or wife there shall be taken into account (together with any other matter that

appears to the court to be relevant to the action) the fact that the dependant had no enforceable right to financial support by the deceased as a result of their living together.

(5) If the dependants have incurred funeral expenses in respect of the deceased, damages may be awarded in respect of those expenses.

(6) Money paid into court in satisfaction of a cause of action under this Act may be in one sum without specifying any person's share.

Assessment of damages: disregard of benefits

4 In assessing damages in respect of a person's death in an action under this Act, benefits which have accrued or will or may accrue to any person from his estate or otherwise as a result of his death shall be disregarded.

Contributory negligence

5 Where any person dies as the result partly of his own fault and partly of the fault of any other person or persons, and accordingly if an action were brought for the benefit of the estate under the Law Reform (Miscellaneous Provisions) Act 1934 the damages recoverable could be reduced under s 1(1) Law Reform (Contributory Negligence) Act 1945, any damages recoverable in an action under this Act shall be reduced to a proportionate extent.

CONGENITAL DISABILITIES (CIVIL LIABILITY) ACT 1976

Civil liability to child born disabled

1(1) If a child is born disabled as a result of such an occurrence before its birth as is mentioned in subsection (2) below, and a person (other than the child's own mother) is under this section answerable to the child in respect of the occurrence, the child's disabilities are to be regarded as damage resulting from the wrongful act of that person and actionable accordingly at the suit of the child.

(2) An occurrence to which this section applies is one which:

(a) affected either parent of the child in his or her ability to have a normal healthy child; or

(b) affected the mother during pregnancy, or affected her or the child in the course of its birth, so that the child is born with disabilities which would not otherwise have been present.

(3) Subject to the following subsections, a person (here referred to as 'the defendant') is answerable to the child if he was liable in tort to the parent or would, if sued in due time, have been so; and it is no answer that there could not have been such liability because the parent suffered no actionable injury, if there was a breach of legal duty which, accompanied by injury, would have given rise to the liability.

(4) In the case of an occurrence preceding the time of conception, the defendant is not answerable to the child if at that time either or both of the parents knew the risk of their child being born disabled (that is to say, the particular risk created by the occurrence); but should it be the child's father who is the

defendant, this subsection does not apply if he knew of the risk and the mother did not.

(5) The defendant is not answerable to the child, for anything he did or omitted to do when responsible in a professional capacity for treating or advising the parent, if he took reasonable care having due regard to then received professional opinion applicable to the particular class of case; but this does not mean that he is answerable only because he departed from received opinion.

(6) Liability to the child under this section may be treated as having been excluded or limited by contract made with the parent affected, to the same extent and subject to the same restrictions as liability in the parent's own case; and a contract term which could have been set up by the defendant in an action by the parent, so as to exclude or limit his liability to him or her, operates in the defendant's favour to the same, but no greater, extent in an action under this section by the child.

(7) If in the child's action under this section it is shown that the parent affected shared the responsibility for the child being born disabled, the damages are to be reduced to such extent as the court thinks just and equitable having regard to the extent of the parent's responsibility.

Extension of s 1 to cover infertility treatments

1A(1) In any case where:

(a) a child carried by a woman as the result of the placing in her of an embryo or of sperm and eggs or her artificial insemination is born disabled;

(b) the disability results from an act or omission in the course of the selection, or the keeping or use outside the body, of the embryo carried by her or of the gametes used to bring about the creation of the embryo; and

(c) a person is under this section answerable to the child in respect of the act or omission, the child's disabilities are to be regarded as damage resulting from the wrongful act of that person and actionable accordingly at the suit of the child.

(2) Subject to subsection (3) below and the applied provisions of section 1 of this Act, a person (here referred to as 'the defendant') is answerable to the child if he was liable in tort to one or both of the parents (here referred to as 'the parent or parents concerned') or would, if sued in due time, have been so; and it is no answer that there could not have been such liability because the parent or parents concerned suffered no actionable injury, if there was a breach of legal duty which, accompanied by injury, would have given rise to the liability.

(3) The defendant is not under this section answerable to the child if at the time the embryo, or the sperm and eggs, are placed in the woman or the time of her insemination (as the case may be) either or both of the parents knew the risk of their child being born disabled (that is to say, the particular risk created by the act or omission).

(4) Subsections (5)–(7) of s 1 of this Act apply for the purposes of this section as they apply for the purposes of that but as if references to the parent or the parents affected were references to the parent or parents concerned.

Liability of woman driving when pregnant

2 A woman driving a motor vehicle when she knows (or ought reasonably to know) herself to be pregnant is to be regarded as being under the same duty to take care for the safety of her unborn child as the law imposes on her with respect to the safety of other people; and if in consequence of her breach of that duty her child is born with disabilities which would not otherwise have been present, those disabilities are to be regarded as damage resulting from her wrongful act and actionable accordingly at the suit of the child.

3(1) Section 1 of this Act does not affect the operation of the Nuclear Installations Act 1965 as to liability for, and compensation in respect of, injury or damage caused by occurrences involving nuclear matter or the emission of ionising radiations.

(2) For the avoidance of doubt anything which:

(a) affects a man in his ability to have a normal, healthy child; or

(b) affects a woman in that ability, or so affects her when she is pregnant that her child is born with disabilities which would not otherwise have been present, is an injury for the purposes of that Act.

(3) If a child is born disabled as the result of an injury to either of its parents caused in breach of a duty imposed by any of ss 7–11 of that Act (nuclear site licensees and others to secure that nuclear incidents do not cause injury to persons, etc) the child's disabilities are to be regarded under the subsequent provisions of that Act (compensation and other matters) as injuries caused in the same occasion, and by the same breach of duty, as was the injury to the parent.

(4) As respects compensation to the child, s 13(6) of that Act (contributory fault of person injured by radiation) is to be applied as if the reference there to fault were to the fault of the parent.

(5) Compensation is not payable in the child's case if the injury to the parent preceded the time of the child's conception and at that time either or both of the parents knew the risk of their child being born disabled (that is to say, the particular risk created by the injury).

Interpretation and other supplementary provisions

4(1) References in this Act to a child being born disabled or with disabilities are to its being born with any deformity, disease or abnormality, including predisposition (whether or not susceptible of immediate prognosis) to physical or mental defect in the future.

(2) In this Act:

(a) 'born' means born alive (the moment of a child's birth being when it first has a life separate from its mother), and 'birth' has a corresponding meaning; and

(b) 'motor vehicle' means a mechanically propelled vehicle intended or adapted for use on roads; and references to embryos shall be construed in accordance with s 1 Human Fertilisation and Embryology Act 1990.

(3) Liability to a child under s 1, 1A or 2 of this Act is to be regarded:

   (a) as respects all its incidents and any matters arising or to arise out of it; and

   (b) subject to any contrary context or intention, for the purposes of construing references in enactments and documents to personal or bodily injuries and cognate matters, as liability for personal injuries sustained by the child immediately after its birth.

(4) No damages shall be recoverable under any of those section in respect of any loss of expectation of life, nor shall any such loss be taken into account in the compensation payable in respect of a child under the Nuclear Installations Act 1965 as extended by s 3, unless (in either case) the child lives for at least 48 hours.

(4A) In any case where a child carried by a woman as the result of the placing in her of an embryo or of sperm and eggs or her artificial insemination is born disabled, any references in s 1 of this Act to a parent includes a reference to a person who would be a parent but for ss 27–29 Human Fertilisation and Embryology Act 1990.

(5) This Act applies in respect of births after (but not before) its passing, and in respect of any such birth it replaces any law in force before its passing, whereby a person could be liable to a child in respect of disabilities with which it might be born; but in s 1(3) of this Act the expression 'liable in tort' does not include any reference to liability by virtue of this Act, or to liability by virtue of any such law.

(6) References to the Nuclear Installations Act 1965 are to that Act as amended; and for the purposes of s 28 of that Act (power by Order in Council to extend the Act to territories outside the United Kingdom) s 3 of this Act is to be treated as if it were a provision of that Act.

Crown application

5 This Act binds the Crown.

Citation and extent

6(1) This Act may be cited as the Congenital Disabilities (Civil Liability) Act 1976.

(2) This Act extends to Northern Ireland but not to Scotland.

LIMITATION ACT 1980

PART I: ORDINARY TIME LIMITS FOR DIFFERENT CLASSES OF ACTION

Time limits under Part I subject to extension or exclusion under Part II

1(1) This part of this Act gives the ordinary time limits for bringing actions of the various classes mentioned in the following provisions of this part.

(2) The ordinary time limits given in this part of this Act are subject to extension or exclusion in accordance with the provisions of Part II of this Act.

Actions founded on tort

Time limit for actions founded on tort

2 An action founded on tort shall not be brought after the expiration of six years from the date on which the cause of action accrued.

Actions founded on simple contract

Time limit for actions founded on simple contract

5 An action founded on simple contract shall not be brought after the expiration of six years from the date on which the cause of action accrued.

Actions in respect of wrongs causing personal injuries or death

Special time limit for actions in respect of personal injuries

11(1) This section applies to any action for damages for negligence, nuisance or breach of duty (whether the duty exists by virtue of a contract or of provision made by or under a statute or independently of any contract or any such provision) where the damages claimed by the plaintiff for the negligence, nuisance or breach of duty consist of or include damages in respect of personal injuries to the plaintiff or any other person.

(2) None of the time limits given in the preceding provisions of this Act shall apply to an action to which this section applies.

(3) An action to which this section applies shall not be brought after the expiration of the period applicable in accordance with subsection (4) or (5) below.

(4) Except where subsection (5) below applies, the period applicable is three years from:

(a) the date on which the cause of action accrued; or

(b) the date of knowledge (if later) of the person injured.

(5) If the person injured dies before the expiration of the period mentioned in subsection (4) above, the period applicable as respects the cause of action surviving for the benefit of his estate by virtue of s 1 Law Reform (Miscellaneous Provisions) Act 1934 shall be three years from:

(a) the date of death; or

(b) the date of the personal representative's knowledge; whichever is the later.

(6) For the purposes of this section 'personal representative' includes any person who is or has been a personal representative of the deceased, including an executor who has not proved the will (whether or not he has renounced probate) but not anyone appointed only as a special personal representative in relation to settled land; and regard shall be had to any knowledge acquired by any such person while a personal representative or previously.

(7) If there is more than one personal representative, and their dates of knowledge are different, subsection (5)(b) above shall be read as referring to the earliest of those dates.

Actions in respect of defective products

11A(1) This section shall apply to an action for damages by virtue of any provision of Part I of the Consumer Protection Act 1987.

(2) None of the time limits given in the preceding provisions of this Act shall apply to an action to which this section applies.

(3) An action to which this section applies shall not be brought after the expiration of the period of ten years from the relevant time, within the meaning of s 4 of the said Act of 1987; and this subsection shall operate to extinguish a right of action and shall do so whether or not that right of action had accrued, or time under the following provisions of this Act had begun to run, at the end of the said period of ten years.

(4) Subject to subsection (5) below, an action to which this section applies in which the damages claimed by the plaintiff consist of or include damages in respect of personal injuries to the plaintiff or any other person for loss of or damage to any property, shall not be brought after the expiration of the period of three years from whichever is the later of:

(a) the date on which the cause of action accrued; and

(b) the date of knowledge of the injured persons or, in the case of loss of or damage to property, the date of knowledge of the plaintiff or (if earlier) of any person in whom his cause of action was previously vested.

(5) If in a case where the damages claimed by the plaintiff consist of or include damages in respect of personal injuries to the plaintiff or any other person the injured person died before the expiration of the period mentioned in subsection (4) above, that subsection shall have effect as respects the cause of action surviving for the benefit of his estate by virtue of s 1 Law Reform (Miscellaneous Provisions) Act 1934 as if for the reference to that period there were substituted a reference to the period of three years from whichever is the later of:

(a) the date of death; and

(b) the date of the personal representative's knowledge.

(6) For the purposes of this section 'personal representative' includes any person who is or has been a personal representative of the deceased, including an executor who has not proved the will (whether or not he has renounced probate) but not anyone appointed only as a special personal representative in relation to settled land, and regard shall be had to any knowledge acquired by any such person while a personal representative or previously.

(7) If there is more than one personal representative and their dates of knowledge are different, subsection (5)(b) above shall be read as referring to the earliest of those dates.

(8) Expressions used in this section or s 14 of this Act and in Part I of the Consumer Protection Act 1987 have the same meanings in this section or that section as in that part; and s 1(1) of that Act (Part I to be construed as enacted for the purpose of complying with the product liability Directive) shall apply for the purpose of construing this section and the following provisions of this Act so far as they relate to any action by virtue of any provision of that part as it applies for the purpose of construing that part.

Special time limits for actions under Fatal Accidents legislation

12(1) An action under the Fatal Accidents Act 1976 shall not be brought if the death occurred when the person injured could no longer maintain an action and recover damages in respect of the injury (whether because of a time limit in this Act or in any other Act, or for any other reason).

Where any such action by the injured person would have been barred by the time limit in s 11 or 11A of this Act, no account shall be taken of the possibility of that time limit being overridden under s 33 of this Act.

(2) None of the time limits given in the preceding provisions of this Act shall apply to an action under the Fatal Accidents Act 1976, but no such action shall be brought after the expiration of three years from:

(a) the date of death; or

(b) the date of knowledge of the person for whose benefit the action is brought; whichever is the later.

(3) An action under the Fatal Accidents Act 1976 shall be one to which ss 28, 33 and 35 of this Act apply, and the application to any such action of the time limit under subsection (2) above shall be subject to section 39; but otherwise Parts II and III of this Act shall not apply to any such action.

Operations of time limit under s 12 in relation to different dependants

13(1) Where there is more than one person for whose benefit an action under the Fatal Accidents Act 1976 is brought, s 12(2)(b) of this Act shall be applied separately to each of them.

(2) Subject to subsection (3) below, if by virtue of subsection (1) above the action would be outside the time limit given by s 12(2) as regards one or more, but not all, of the persons for whose benefit it is brought, the court shall direct that any persons as regards whom the action would be outside that limit shall be excluded from those for whom the action is brought.

(3) The court shall not give such a direction if it is shown that if the action were brought exclusively for the benefit of the person in question it would not be defeated by a defence of limitation (whether in consequence of s 28 of this Act or an agreement between the parties not to raise the defence, or otherwise).

Definition of date of knowledge for purposes of ss 11 and 12

14(1) Subject to subsection (1A) below in ss 11 and 12 of this Act references to a person's date of knowledge are references to the date on which he first had knowledge of the following facts:

(a) that the injury in question was significant; and

(b) that the injury was attributable in whole or in part to the act or omission which is alleged to constitute negligence, nuisance or breach of duty; and

(c) the identity of the defendant; and

(d) if it is alleged that the act or omission was that of a person other then the defendant, the identity of that person and the additional facts supporting the bringing of an action against the defendant; and knowledge that any acts or omissions did or did not, as a matter of law, involve negligence, nuisance or breach of duty is irrelevant.

(1A) In s 11A of this Act and in s 12 of this Act so far as that section applies to an action by virtue of s 6(1)(a) Consumer Protection Act 1987 (death caused by defective product) references to a person's date of knowledge are references to the date on which he first had knowledge of the following facts:

(a) such facts about the damage caused by the defect as would lead a reasonable person who had suffered such damage to consider it sufficiently serious to justify his instituting proceedings for damages against a defendant who did not dispute liability and was able to satisfy a judgment; and

(b) that the damage was wholly or partly attributable to the facts and circumstances alleged to constitute the defect; and

(c) the identify of the defendant; but, in determining the date on which a person first had such knowledge there shall be disregarded both the extent (if any) of that person's knowledge on any date of whether particular facts or circumstances would or would not, as a matter of law, constitute a defect and, in a case relating to loss of or damage to property, any knowledge which that person had on a date on which he had no right of action by virtue of Part I of that Act in respect of the loss or damage.

(2) For the purposes of this section a person's knowledge includes knowledge which he might reasonably have considered it sufficiently serious to justify his instituting proceedings for damages against a defendant who did not dispute liability and was able to satisfy a judgment.

(3) For the purposes of this section a person's knowledge includes knowledge which he might reasonably have been expected to acquire:

(a) from facts observable or ascertainable by him; or

(b) from facts ascertainable by him with the help of medical or other appropriate expert advice which it is reasonable for him to seek; but a person shall not be fixed under this subsection with knowledge of a fact ascertainable only with the help of expert advice so long as he has taken all reasonable steps to obtain (and, where appropriate, to act on) that advice.

Special time limit for negligence actions where facts relevant to cause of action are not known at date of accrual

14A(1) This section applies to any action for damages for negligence, other than one to which s 11 of this Act applies, where the starting date for reckoning the period of limitation under subsection (4)(b) below falls after the date on which the cause of action accrued.

(2) Section 2 of this Act shall not apply to an action to which this section applies.

(3) An action to which this section applies shall not be brought after the expiration of the period applicable in accordance with subsection (4) below.

(4) That period is either:

(a) six years from the date on which the cause of action accrued; or

(b) three years from the starting date as defined by subsection (5) below, if that period expires later than the period mentioned in paragraph (a) above.

(5) For the purposes of this section, the starting date for reckoning the period of limitation under subsection (4)(b) above is the earliest date on which the plaintiff or any person in whom the cause of action was vested before him first had both the knowledge required for bringing an action for damages in respect of the relevant damage and a right to bring such an action.

(6) In subsection (5) above 'the knowledge required for bringing an action for damages in respect of the relevant damage' means knowledge both:

(a) of the material facts about the damage in respect of which damages are claimed; and

(b) of the other facts relevant to the current action mentioned in subsection (8) below.

(7) For the purposes of subsection (6)(a) above, the material facts about the damage are such facts about the damage as would lead a reasonable person who had suffered such damage to consider it sufficiently serious to justify his instituting proceedings for damages against a defendant who did not dispute liability and was able to satisfy a judgment.

(8) The other facts referred to in subsection (6)(b) above are:

(a) that the damage was attributable in whole or in part to the act or omission which is alleged to constitute negligence; and

(b) the identity of the defendant; and

(c) if it is alleged that the act or omission was that of a person other than the defendant, the identity of that person and the additional facts supporting the bringing of an action against the defendant.

(9) Knowledge that any acts or omissions did or did not, as a matter of law, involve negligence is irrelevant for the purposes of subsection (5) above.

(10) For the purposes of this section a person's knowledge includes knowledge which he might reasonably have been expected to acquire:

(a) from facts observable or ascertainable by him; or

(b) from facts ascertainable by him with the help of appropriate expert advice which it is reasonable for him to seek;

(c) but a person shall not be taken by virtue of this subsection to have knowledge of a fact ascertainable only with the help of expert advice so long as he has taken all reasonable steps to obtain (and, where appropriate, to act on) that advice.

Overriding time limit for negligence actions not involving personal injuries

14B(1) An action for damages for negligence, other than one to which s 11 of this Act applies, shall not be brought after the expiration of 15 years from the date (or, if more than one, from the last of the dates) on which there occurred any act or omission:

(a) which is alleged to constitute negligence; and

(b) to which the damage in respect of which damages are claimed is alleged to be attributable (in whole or in part).

(2) This section bars the right of action in a case to which subsection (1) above applies notwithstanding that:

(a) the cause of action has not yet accrued; or

(b) where s 14A of this Act applies to the action, the date which is for the purposes of that section the starting date for reckoning the period mentioned in subsection (4)(b) of that section has not yet occurred; before the end of the period of limitation prescribed by this section.

PART II: EXTENSION OR EXCLUSION OF ORDINARY TIME LIMITS

Disability

Extension of limitation period in case of disability

28(1) Subject to the following provisions of this section, if on the date when any right of action accrued for which a period of limitation is prescribed by this Act, the person to whom it accrued was under a disability, the action may be brought at any time before the expiration of six years from the date when he ceased to be under a disability or died (whichever first occurred) notwithstanding that the period of limitation has expired.

(2) This section shall not affect any case where the right of action first accrued to some person (not under a disability) through whom the person under a disability claims.

(3) When a right of action which has accrued to a person under a disability accrues, on the death of that person while still under a disability, to another person under a disability, no further extension of time shall be allowed by reason of the disability of the second person.

(4A) If the action is one to which s 4A of this Act applies, subsection (1) above shall have effect as if for the words from 'at any time' to 'occurred') there were substituted the words 'by him at any time before the expiration of three years from the date when he ceased to be under a disability'.

(6) If the action is one to which ss 11 or 12(2) of this Act applies, subsection (1) above shall have effect as for the words 'six years' there were substituted the words 'three years'.

(7) If the action is one to which s 11A of this Act applies or one by virtue of s 6(1)(a) Consumer Protection Act 1987 (death caused by defective product), subsection (1) above:

(a) shall not apply to the time limit prescribed by subsection (3) of the said s 11A or to that time limit as applied by virtue of s 12(1) of this act; and

(b) in relation to any other time limit prescribed by this Act shall have effect as if for the words 'six years' there were substituted the words 'three years'.

Extension for cases where the limitation period is the period under s 14A(4)(b)

28A(1) Subject to subsection (2) below, if in the case of any action for which a period of limitation is prescribed by s 14A of this Act:

    (a) the period applicable in accordance with subsection (4) of that section is the period mentioned in paragraph (b) of that subsection;

    (b) on the date which is for the purposes of that section the starting date for reckoning that period the person by reference to whose knowledge that date fell to be determined under subsection (5) of that section was under a disability; and

    (c) section 28 of this Act does not apply to the action;

the action may be brought at any time before the expiration of three years from the date when he ceased to be under a disability or died (whichever first occurred) notwithstanding that the period mentioned above has expired.

(2) An action may not be brought by virtue of subsection (1) above after the end of the period of limitation prescribed by s 14B of this Act.

Postponement of limitation period in case of fraud, concealment or mistake

32(1) Subject to subsections (3) and (4A) below, where in the case of any action for which a period of limitation is prescribed by this Act, either:

    (a) the action is based upon the fraud of the defendant; or

    (b) any fact relevant to the plaintiff's right of action has been deliberately concealed from him by the defendant; or

    (c) the action is for relief from the consequences of a mistake;

the period of limitation shall not begin to run until the plaintiff has discovered the fraud, concealment or mistake (as the case may be) or could with reasonable diligence have discovered it.

References in this subsection to the defendant include references to the defendant's agent and to any person through whom the defendant claims and his agent.

(2) For the purposes of subsection (1) above, deliberate commission of a breach of duty in circumstances in which it is unlikely to be discovered for some time amounts to deliberate concealment of the facts involved in that breach of duty.

(3) Nothing in this section shall enable any action:

    (a) to recover, or recover the value of, any property; or

    (b) to enforce any charge against, or set aside any transaction affecting any property;

to be brought against the purchaser of the property or any person claiming through him in any case where the property has been purchased for valuable consideration by an innocent third party since the fraud or concealment or (as the case may be) the transaction in which the mistake was made took place.

(4) A purchaser is an innocent third party for the purposes of this section:

    (a) in the case of fraud or concealment or any fact relevant to the plaintiff's right of action, if he was not a party to the fraud or (as the case may be) to the concealment of that fact and did not at the time of the purchase know or have reason to believe that the fraud or concealment had taken place; and

(b) in the case of mistake, if he did not at the time of the purchase know or have reason to believe that the mistake had been made.

(4A) Subsection (1) above shall not apply in relation to the time limit prescribed by s 11A(3) of this Act or in relation to that time limit as applied by virtue of s 12(1) of this Act.

(5) Section 14A and 14B of this Act shall not apply to any action to which subsection (l)(b) above applies (and accordingly the period of limitation referred to in that subsection, in any case to which either of these sections would otherwise apply, is the period applicable under s 2 of this Act).

Discretionary exclusion of time limit for actions in respect of personal injuries or death

33(1) If it appears to the court that it would be equitable to allow an action to proceed having regard to the degree to which:

(a) the provisions of ss 11 [or 11A] or 12 of this Act prejudice the plaintiff or any person whom he represents; and

(b) any decision of the court under this subsection would prejudice the defendant or any person whom he represents;

the court may direct that those provisions shall not apply to the action, or shall not apply to any specified cause of action to which the action relates.

(1A) The court shall not under this section disapply:

(a) subsection 3 of s 11A; or

(b) where the damages claimed by the plaintiff are confined to damages for loss of or damage to any property, any other provision in its application to an action by virtue of Part I Consumer Protection Act 1987.

(2) The court shall not under this section disapply s 12(1) except where the reason why the person injured could no longer maintain an action was because of the time limit in s 11 or subsection (4) of s 11A.

If, for example, the person injured could at his death no longer maintain an action under the Fatal Accidents Act 1976 because of the time limit in Article 29 in Schedule 1 to the Carriage by Air Act 1961, the court has no power to direct that s 12(1) shall not apply.

(3) In acting under this section the court shall have regard to all the circumstances of the case and in particular to:

(a) the length of, and the reasons for, the delay on the part of the plaintiff;

(b) the extent to which, having regard to the delay, the evidence adduced or likely to be adduced by the plaintiff or the defendant is or is likely to be less cogent than if the action had been brought within the time allowed by s 11, s 11A or (as the case may be) by s 12;

(c) the conduct of the defendant after the cause of action arose, including the extent (if any) to which he responded to requests reasonably made by the plaintiff for information or inspection for the purpose of ascertaining facts which were or might be relevant to the plaintiff's cause of action against the defendant;

(d) the duration of any disability of the plaintiff arising after the date of the accrual of the cause of action;

(e) the extent to which the plaintiff acted promptly and reasonably once he knew whether or not the act or omission of the defendant, to which the injury was attributable, might be capable at that time of giving rise to an action for damages;

(f) the steps, if any, taken by the plaintiff to obtain medical, legal or other expert advise and the nature of any such advice he may have received.

(4) In a case where the person injured died when, because of s 11 or subsection 4 of s 11A, he could no longer maintain an action and recover damages in respect of the injury, the court shall have regard in particular to the length of, and the reasons for, the delay on the part of the deceased.

(5) In a case under subsection (4) above, or any other case where the time limit, or one of the time limits, depends on the date of knowledge of a person other than the plaintiff, subsection (3) above shall have effect with appropriate modifications, and shall have effect in particular as if references to the plaintiff included references to any person whose date of knowledge is or was relevant in determining a time limit.

(6) A direction by the court disapplying the provisions of s 12(1) shall operate to disapply the provisions to the same effect in s 1(1) Fatal Accidents Act 1976.

(7) In this section, 'the court' means the court in which the action has been brought.

(8) References in this section to s 11 or 11A include references to that section as extended by any of the preceding provisions of this part of this Act or by any provision of Part III of this Act.

PART III: MISCELLANEOUS AND GENERAL

New claims in pending actions: rules of court

35(1) For the purposes of this Act, any new claim made in the course of any action shall be deemed to be a separate action and to have been commenced:

(a) in the case of a new claim made in or by way of third part proceedings, on the date on which those proceedings were commenced; and

(b) in the case of any other new claim, on the same date as the original action.

(2) In this section, a 'new claim' means any claim by way of set-off or counterclaim and any claim involving either:

(a) the addition or substitution of a new cause of action; or

(b) the addition or substitution of a new party;

and 'third party proceedings' means any proceedings brought in the course of any action by any party to the action against a person not previously a party to the action, other than proceedings brought by joining any such person as defendant to any claim already made in the original action by the party bringing the proceedings.

(3) Except as provided by s 33 of this Act or by rules of court, neither the High Court nor any county court shall allow a new claim within subsection (1)(b) above, other than an original set-off or counterclaim, to be made in the course of any action after the expiry of any time limit under this Act which would affect a new action to enforce that claim.

For the purposes of this subsection, a claim is an original set-off or an original counterclaim if it is a claim made by way of set-off or (as the case may be) by way of counterclaim by a party who has not previously made any claim in the action.

(4) Rules of court may provide for allowing a new claim to which subsection (3) above applies to be made as there mentioned, but only if the conditions specified in subsection (5) below are satisfied, and subject to any further restrictions the rules may impose.

(5) The conditions referred to in subsection (4) above are the following:

(a) in the case of a claim involving a new cause of action, if the new cause of action arises out of the same facts or substantially the same facts as are already in issue on any claim previously made in the original action; and

(b) in the case of a claim involving a new party, if the addition or substitution of the new party is necessary for the determination of the original action.

(6) The addition or substitution of a new party shall not be regarded for the purposes of subsection (5)(b) above as necessary for the determination of the original action unless either:

(a) the new party is substituted for a party whose name was given in any claim made in the original action in mistake for the new party's name; or

(b) any claim already made in the original action cannot be maintained by or against an existing party unless the new party is joined or substituted as plaintiff or defendant in that action.

(7) Subject to subsection (4) above, rules of court may provide for allowing a party to any action to claim relief in a new capacity in respect of a new cause of action notwithstanding that he had no title to make that claim at the date of the commencement of the action.

This subsection shall not be taken as prejudicing the power of rules of court to provide for allowing a party to claim relief in a new capacity without adding or substituting a new cause of action.

(8) Subsections (3)–(7) above shall apply in relation to a new claim made in the course of third party proceedings as if those proceedings were the original action, and subject to such other modification as may be prescribed by rules of court in any case or class of case.

(9) [Repealed.]

Interpretation

38(1) In this Act, unless the context otherwise requires:

'action' includes any proceedings in a court of law, including an ecclesiastical court;

'land' includes corporeal hereditaments, tithes and rent-charges and any legal or equitable estate or interest therein, including an interest in the proceeds of the sale of land held upon trust for sale, but except as provided above in this definition does not include any incorporeal hereditament;

'personal estate' and 'personal property' do not include chattels real;

'personal injuries includes any disease and any impairment of a person's physical or mental condition, and 'injury' and cognate expression shall be construed accordingly;

'rent' includes a rentcharge and a rent service;

'rentcharge' means any annuity or periodical sum of money charged upon or payable out of land, except a rent service or interest on a mortgage on land;

'settled land', 'statutory owner' and 'tenant for life' have the same meanings respectively as in the Settled Land Act 1925;

'trust' and 'trustee' have the same meanings respectively as in the Trustee Act 1925; and

'trust for sale' has the same meaning as in the Law of Property Act 1925.

(2) For the purposes of this Act a person shall be treated as under a disability while he is an infant, or of unsound mind.

(3) For the purposes of subsection (2) above a person is of unsound mind if he is a person who, by reason of mental disorder within the meaning of the Mental Health Act 1983, is incapable of managing and administering his property and affairs.

(4) Without prejudice to the generality of subsection (3) above, a person shall be conclusively presumed for the purposes of subsection (2) above to be of unsound mind:

(a) while he is liable to be detained or subject to guardianship under the Mental Health Act 1983 (otherwise than by virtue of ss 35 or 89); and

(b) while he is receiving treatment as an in-patient in any hospital within the meaning of the Mental Health Act 1983 or mental nursing home within the meaning of the Nursing Homes Act 1975 without being liable to be detained under the said Act of 1983 (otherwise than by virtue of ss 35 or 89), being treatment which follows without any interval a period during which he was liable to be detained or subject to guardianship under the Mental Health Act 1959, or the said Act of 1983 (otherwise than by virtue of ss 35 or 89) or by virtue of any enactment repealed or excluded by the Mental Health Act 1959.

(5) Subject to subsection (6) below, a person shall be treated as claiming through another person if he became entitled by, through, under, or by the act of that other person to the right claimed, and any person whose estate or interest might have been barred by a person entitled to an entailed interest in possession shall be treated as claiming through the person so entitled.

(6) A person becoming entitled to any estate or interest by virtue of a special power of appointment shall not be treated as claiming through the appointor.

(7) References in this Act to a right of action to recover land shall include references to a right to enter into possession of the land or, in the case of rentcharges and tithes, to distrain for arrears of rent or tithe, and references to the bringing of such an action shall include references to the making of such an entry or distress.

(8) References in this Act to the possession of land shall, in the case of tithes and rentcharges, be construed as references to the receipt of the tithe or rent, and references to the date of dispossession or discontinuance of possession of land shall, in the case of rentcharges, be construed as references to the date of the last receipt of rent.

(9) References in Part II of this Act to a right of action shall include references to:

(a) a cause of action;

(b) a right to receive money secured by a mortgage or charge on any property;

(c) a right to recover proceeds of the sale of land; and

(d) a right to receive a share or interest in the personal estate of a deceased person.

(10) References in Part II to the date of the accrual or a right of action shall be construed:

(a) in the case of an action upon a judgment, as references to the date on which the judgment became enforceable; and

(b) in the case of an action to recover arrears of rent or interest, or damages in respect of arrears of rent or interest, as references to the date on which the rent or interest became due.

SUPREME COURT ACT 1981

Orders for interim payment

32(1) As regards proceedings pending in the High Court, provision may be made by rules of court, in such circumstances as may be prescribed, to make an order requiring a party to the proceedings to make an interim payment of such amount as may be specified in the order, with provision for the payment to be made to such other party to the proceedings as may be so specified or, if the order so provides, by paying it into court.

(2) Any rules of court which make provision in accordance with subsection (1) may include provision for enabling a party to any proceedings who, in pursuance of such an order, has made an interim payment to recover the whole or part of the amount of the payment in such circumstances, and from such other party to the proceedings, as may be determined in accordance with the rules.

(3) Any rules made by virtue of this section may include such incidental, supplementary and consequential provisions as the rulemaking authority may consider necessary or expedient.

(4) Nothing in this section shall be construed as affecting the exercise of any power relating to costs, including any power to make rules of court relating to costs.

(5) In this section, 'interim payment', in relation to a party to any proceedings, means a payment on account of any damages, debt or other sum, (excluding any costs) which that party may be held liable to pay to or for the benefit of another party to the proceedings if a final judgment or order of the court in the proceedings is given or made in favour of that other party.

Orders for provisional damages for personal injuries

32A(1) This section applies to an action for damages for personal injuries in which there is proved or admitted to be a chance that at some definite or indefinite time in the future the injured person will, as a result of the act or omission which gave rise to the cause of action, develop some serious disease or suffer some serious deterioration in his physical or mental condition.

(2) Subject to subsection (4) below, as regards any action for damages to which this section applies in which a judgment is given in the High Court, provision may be made by rules of court for enabling the court, in such circumstances as may be prescribed, to award the injured person:

(a) damages assessed on the assumption that the injured person will not develop the disease or suffers the deterioration in his condition; and

(b) further damages at a future date if he develops the disease or suffers the deterioration.

(3) Any rules made by virtue of this section may include such incidental, supplementary and consequential provisions as the rulemaking authority may consider necessary or expedient.

(4) Nothing in this section shall be construed:

(a) as affecting the exercise of any power relating to costs, including any power to make rules of court relating to costs; or

(b) as prejudicing any duty of the court under any enactment or rule of law to reduce or limit the total damages which would have been recoverable apart from any such duty.

Power of High Court to order disclosure of documents, inspection of property, etc in proceedings for personal injuries or death

34(1) This section applies to any proceedings in the High Court in which a claim is made in respect of personal injuries to a person, or in respect of a person's death.

(2) On the application, in accordance with rules of court, of a party to any proceedings to which this section applies, the High Court shall, in such circumstances as may be specified in the rules, have power to order a person who is not party to the proceedings and who appears to the court to be likely to have in his possession, custody or power any documents which are relevant to an issue arising out of the said claim:

(a) to disclose whether those documents are in his possession, custody or power; and

   (b) to produce such of those documents as are in his possession, custody or power to the applicant or, on such conditions as may be specified in the order:

      (i) to the applicant's legal advisers;

      (ii) to the applicant's legal advisers and any medical or other professional adviser of the applicant; or

      (iii) if the applicant has no legal adviser, to any medical or other professional adviser of the applicant.

(3) On the application, in accordance with the rules of court, a party to any proceedings to which this section applies, the High Court shall, in such circumstances as may be specified in the rules, have power to make an order providing for any one or more of the following matters, that is to say:

   (a) the inspection, photographing, preservation, custody and detention of property which is not the property of, or in the possession of, any party to the proceedings but which is the subject-matter of the proceedings or as to which any question arises in the proceedings;

   (b) the taking of samples of any such property as is mentioned in paragraph (a) and the carrying out of any experiment on or with any such property.

(4) The preceding provisions of this section are without prejudice to the exercise by the High Court of any power to make orders which is exercisable apart from those provisions.

Provisions supplementary to ss 33 and 34

35(1) The High Court shall not make an order under ss 33 or 34 if it consider that compliance with the order, if made, would be likely to be injurious to the public interest.

(2) Rules of court may make provision as to the circumstances in which an order under ss 33 or 34 can be made; and any rules making such provision may include such incidental, supplementary and consequential provisions as the rule-making authority may consider necessary or expedient

(3) Without prejudice to the generality of subsection (2), rules of court shall be made for the purpose of ensuring that the costs of and incidental to proceedings for an order under ss 33(2) or 34 incurred by the person against whom the order is sought shall be awarded to that person unless the court otherwise directs.

(4) Sections 33(2) and 34 and this section bind the Crown; and s 33(1) binds the Crown so far as it relates to property as to which it appears to the court that it may become the subject-matter of subsequent proceedings involving a claim in respect of personal injuries to a person or in respect of a person's death.

    In this subsection, references to the Crown do not include references to Her Majesty in her private capacity or to Her Majesty in right of Her Duchy of Lancaster or to the Duke of Cornwall.

(5) In ss 33 and 34 and this section:

'property' includes any land. chattel or other corporeal property of any description;

'personal injuries' includes any disease and any impairment of a persons physical or mental condition.

Power of High Court to award interest in debts and damages

35A(1) Subject to rules of court, in proceedings (whenever instituted) before the High Court for the recovery of a debt or damages there may be included in any sum for which judgment is given simple interest, at such rate as the court thinks fit or as rules of court may provide, on all or any part of the debt or damages in respect of which judgment is given, or payment is made before judgment, for all or any part of the period between the date when the cause of action arose and:

(a) in the case of any sum paid before judgment, the date of the payment; and

(b) in the case of the sum for which judgment is given, the date of the judgment.

(2) In relation to a judgment given for damages for personal injuries or death which exceed £200 subsection (1) shall have effect:

(a) with the substitution of 'shall be included' for 'may be included'; and

(b) with the addition of 'unless the court is satisfied that there are special reasons to the contrary' after 'given,' where first occurring.

(3) Subject to rules of court, where:

(a) there are proceedings (whenever instituted) before the High Court for the recovery of a debt; and

(b) the defendant pays the whole debt to the plaintiff (otherwise than in pursuance of a judgment in the proceedings),

the defendant shall be liable to pay the plaintiff simple interest at such rate as the court thinks fit or as rules of court may provide on all or any part of the debt for all or any part of the period between the date when the cause of action arose and the date of the payment.

(4) Interest in respect of a debt shall not be awarded under this section for a period during which, for whatever reason, interest on the debt already runs.

(5) Without prejudice to the generality of s 84, rules of court may provide for a rate of interest by reference to the rate specified in s 17 Judgment Act 1838 as that section has effect from time to time or by reference to a rate for which any other enactment provides.

(6) Interest under this section may be calculated at different rates in respect of different periods.

(7) In this section, 'plaintiff' means the person seeking the debt or damages and 'defendant' means the person from whom the plaintiff seeks the debt or damages and 'personal injuries' includes any disease and any impairment of a person's physical or mental condition.

(8) Nothing in this section affects the damages recoverable for the dishonour of a bill of exchange.

COUNTY COURTS ACT 1984

Interim payments in pending proceedings

Orders for interim payment

50(1) Provision may be made by county court rules for enabling the court, in such circumstances as may be prescribed, to make an order requiring a party to the proceedings to make an interim payment of such amount as may be specified in the order, with provision for the payment to be made to such other party to the proceedings as may be so specified or, if the order so provides, by paying it into court.

(2) Any county court rules which make provision in accordance with subsection (1) may include provision for enabling a party to any proceedings who, in pursuance of such an order, has made an interim payment to recover the whole or part of the amount of the payment in such circumstances, and from such other party to the proceedings, as may be determined in accordance with the rules.

(3) Any rules made by virtue of this section may include such incidental, supplementary and consequential provisions as the rule committee may consider necessary or expedient.

(4) Nothing in this section shall be construed as affecting the exercise of any power relating to costs, including any power to make county court rules relating to costs.

(5) In this section, 'interim payment', in relation to a party to any proceedings, means a payment on account of any damages, debt or other sum, (excluding any costs) which that party may be held liable to pay to or for the benefit of another party to the proceedings if a final judgment or order of the court in the proceedings is given or made in favour of that party; and any reference to a party to any proceedings includes a reference to any person who for the purposes of the proceedings acts as next friend or guardian of a party to the proceedings.

Provisional damages for personal injuries

Orders for provisional damages for personal injuries

51(1) This section applies to an action for damages for personal injuries in which there is proved or admitted to be a chance that at some definite or indefinite time in the future the injured person will, as a result of the act or omission which gave rise to the cause of action, develop some serious disease or suffer some serious deterioration in his physical or mental condition.

(2) Subject to subsection (4), as regards any action for damages to which this section applies in which a judgment is given in the county court, provision may be made by county court rules for enabling the court, in such circumstances as may be prescribed, to award the injured person:

    (a) damages assessed on the assumption that the injured person will not develop the disease or suffer the deterioration in his condition; and

    (b) further damages at a future date if he develops the disease or suffers the deterioration.

(3) Any rules made by virtue of this section may include such incidental, supplementary and consequential provisions as the rule committee may consider necessary or expedient.

(4) Nothing in this section shall be construed:

(a) as affecting the exercise of any power relating to costs, including any power to make county court rules relating to costs; or

(b) as prejudicing any duty of the court under any enactment or rule of law to reduce or limit the total damages which would have been recoverable apart from any such duty.

(5) In this section, 'personal injuries' includes any disease and any impairment of a person's physical or mental condition.

Discovery and related procedures

Powers of court exercisable before commencement of action

52(1) On the application of any person in accordance with county court rules, a county court shall, in such circumstances as may be prescribed, have power to make an order providing for any one or more of the following matters, that is to say:

(a) the inspection, photographing, preservation, custody and detention of property which appears to the court to be property which may become the subject-matter of subsequent proceedings in the court, or as to which any question may arise in any such proceedings; and

(b) the taking of samples of any such property as is mentioned in paragraph (a), and the carrying out of any experiment on or with any such property.

(2) On the application, in accordance with county court rules, of a person who appears to a county court to be likely to be a party to subsequent proceedings in that court in which a claim in respect of personal injuries to a person, or in respect of a person's death, is likely to be made , the county court shall, in such circumstances as may be prescribed, have power to order a person who appears to the court to be likely to be a party to the proceedings and to be likely to have or to have had in his possession, custody or power any documents which are relevant to an issue arising or likely to arise out of that claim:

(a) to disclose whether those documents are in his possession, custody or power, and

(b) to produce such of those documents as are in his possession, custody or power to the applicant or, on such conditions as may be specified in the order

(i) to the applicant's legal advisers; or

(ii) to the applicant's legal advisers and any medical or other professional adviser of the applicant; or

(iii) if the applicant has no legal adviser, to any medical or other professional adviser of the applicant.

(3) This section is subject to any provision made under s 38.

Power of court to order disclosure of documents, inspection of property, etc in proceedings for personal injuries or death

53(1) This section applies to any proceedings in a county court in which a claim is made in respect of personal injuries to a person, or in respect of a person's death.

(2) On the application, in accordance with county court rules, of a party to any proceedings to which this section applies, a county court shall, in such circumstances as may be prescribed, have power to order a person who is not a party to the proceedings and who appears to the court to be likely to have in his possession, custody or power any documents which are relevant to an issue arising out of the said claim:

(a) to disclose whether those documents are in his possession, custody or power; and

(b) to produce such of those documents as are in his possession, custody or power to the applicant or, on such conditions as may be specified in the order:

(i) to the applicant's legal advisers; or

(ii) to the applicant's legal advisers and any medical or other professional adviser of the applicant; or

(iii) if the applicant has no legal adviser, to any medical or other professional adviser of the applicant.

(3) On the application, in accordance with county court rules, of a party to any proceedings to which this section applies, a county court shall, in such circumstances as may be prescribed, have power to make an order providing for any one or more of the following matters, that is to say:

(a) the inspection, photographing, preservation, custody and detention of property which is not the property of, or in the possession of, any party to the proceedings but which is the subject-matter of the proceedings or as to which any question arises in the proceedings;

(b) the taking of samples of any such property as is mentioned in paragraph (a) and the carrying out of any experiment on or with any such property.

(4) The preceding provisions of this section are without prejudice to the exercise by a county court of any power to make orders which is exercisable apart from those provisions.

(5) This section is subject to any provision made under s 38.

Provisions supplementary to ss 52 and 53

54(1) A county court shall not make an order under ss 52 or 53 if it considers that compliance with the order, if made, would be likely to be injurious to the public interest.

(2) County court rules may make provision as to the circumstances in which an order under ss 52 or 53 can be made; and any rules making such provision may include such incidental, supplementary and consequential provisions as the rule committee may consider necessary or expedient.

(3) Without prejudice to the generality of subsection (2), county court rules shall be made for the purpose of ensuring that the costs of and incidental to proceedings for an order under ss 52(2) or 53 incurred by the person against whom the order is sought shall be awarded to that person unless the court otherwise directs.

(4) Sections 52(2) and 53 and this section bind the Crown; and s 52(1) binds the Crown so far as it relates to property as to which it appears to the court that it may become the subject-matter of subsequent proceedings involving a claim in respect of personal injuries to a person or in respect of a person's death.

In this subsection, references to the Crown do not include references to Her Majesty in Her private capacity or to Her Majesty in right of Her Duchy of Lancaster or the Duke of Cornwall.

(5) In ss 52 and 53 and this section:

'property' includes any land, chattel or other corporeal property of any description;

'personal injuries' includes any disease and any impairment of a person's physical or mental condition.

(6) This section is subject to any provision made under s 38.

Power to award interest in debts and damages

69(1) Subject to county court rules, in proceedings (whenever instituted) before a county court for the recovery of a debt or damages there may be included in any sum for which judgment is given simple interest, at such rate as the court thinks fit or as may be prescribed, on all or any part of the debt or damages in respect of which judgment is given, or payment is made before judgment, for all or any part of the period between the date when the cause of action arose and:

    (a) in the case of any sum paid before judgment, the date of the payment; and

    (b) in the case of the sum for which judgment is given, the date of the judgment.

(2) In relation to a judgment given for damages for personal injuries or death which exceed £200, subsection (1) shall have effect:

    (a) with the substitution of 'shall be included' for 'may be included'; and

    (b) with the addition of 'unless the court is satisfied that there are special reasons to the contrary' after 'given', where first occurring.

(3) Subject to county court rules, where:

    (a) there are proceedings (whenever instituted) before a county court for the recovery of a debt; and

    (b) the defendant pays the whole debt to the plaintiff (otherwise than in pursuance of a judgment in the proceedings), the defendant shall be liable to pay the plaintiff simple interest, at such rate as the court thinks fit or as may be prescribed, on all or any part of the debt for all or any part of the period between the date when the cause of action arose and the date of the payment.

(4) Interest in respect of a debt shall not be awarded under this section for a period during which, for whatever reason, interest on the debt already runs.

(5) Interest under this section may be calculated at different rates in respect of different periods.

(6) In this section, 'plaintiff' means the person seeking the debt or damages and 'defendant' means the person from whom the plaintiff seeks the debt or damages and 'personal injuries' includes any disease and any impairment of a person's physical or mental condition.

(7) Nothing in this section affects the damages recoverable for the dishonour of a bill of exchange.

(8) In determining whether the amount of any debt or damages exceeds that prescribed by or under any enactment, no account shall be taken of any interest payable by virtue of this section except where express provision to the contrary is made by or under that or any other enactment.

DATA PROTECTION ACT 1984

PART I: PRELIMINARY

Definition of 'data' and related expressions

1(1) The following provisions shall have effect for the interpretation of this Act.

(2) 'Data' means information recorded in a form in which it can be processed by equipment operating automatically in response to instructions given for that purpose.

(3) 'Personal data' means data consisting of information which relates to a living individual who can be identified from that information (or from that and other information in the possession of the data user), including any expression of opinion about the individual but not any indication of the intentions of the data user in respect of that individual.

(4) 'Data subject' means an individual who is the subject of personal data.

(5) 'Data user' means a person who holds data, and a person 'holds' data if:

(a) the data form part of a collection of data processed or intended to be processed by or on behalf of that person as mentioned in subsection (2) above; and

(b) that person (either alone or jointly or in common with other persons) controls the contents and use of the data comprised in the collection; and

(c) the data are in the form in which they have been or are intended to be processed as mentioned in paragraph (a) above or (though not for the time being in that form) in a form into which they have been converted after being so processed and with a view to being further so processed on a subsequent occasion.

(6) A person carries on a 'computer bureau' if he provides other persons with services in respect of data, and a person provides such services if:

(a) as agent for other persons he causes data held by them to be processed as mentioned in subsection (2) above; or

(b) he allows other persons the use of equipment in his possession for the processing as mentioned in that subsection of data held by them.

(7) 'Processing', in relation to data, means amending, augmenting, deleting or re-arranging the data or extracting the information constituting the data and, in the case of personal data, means performing any of these operations by reference to the data subject.

(8) Subsection (7) above shall not be construed as applying to any operation performed only for the purpose of preparing the text of documents.

(9) 'Disclosing', in relation to data, includes disclosing information extracted from the data; and where the identification of the individual who is the subject of personal data depends partly on the information constituting the data and partly on other information in the possession of the data user, the data shall not be regarded as disclosed or transferred unless the other information is also disclosed or transferred.

PART III: RIGHTS OF DATA SUBJECTS

Right of access to personal data

21(1) Subject to the provisions of this section, an individual shall be entitled:

(a) to be informed by any data user whether the data held by him include personal data of which that individual is the data subject; and

(b) to be supplied by any data user with a copy of the information constituting any such personal data held by him; and where any of the information referred to in paragraph (b) above is expressed in terms which are not intelligible without explanation the information shall be accompanied by an explanation of those terms.

(2) A data user shall not be obliged to supply any information under subsection (1) above except in response to a request in writing and on payment of such fee (not exceeding the prescribed maximum) as he may require; but a request for information under both paragraphs of that subsection shall be treated as a single request and a request for information under paragraph (a) shall, in the absence of any indication to the contrary, be treated as extending also to information under paragraph (b).

(3) In the case of a data user having separate entries in the register in respect of data held for different purposes, a separate request must be made and a separate fee paid under this section in respect of the data to which each entry relates.

(4) A data user shall not be obliged to comply with a request under this section:

(a) unless he is supplied with such information as he may reasonably require in order to satisfy himself as to the identity of the person making the request and to locate the information which he seeks; and

(b) if he cannot comply with the request without disclosing information relating to another individual who can be identified from that information, unless he is satisfied that the other individual has consented to the disclosure of the information to the person making the request.

(5) In paragraph (b) of subsection (4) above the reference to information relating to another individual includes a reference to information identifying that individual as the source of the information sought by the request; and that paragraph shall not be construed as excusing a data user from supplying so much of the information sought by the request as can be supplied without disclosing the identity of the other individual concerned, whether by the omission of names or other identifying particulars or otherwise.

(6) A data user shall comply with a request under this section within forty days of receiving the request or, if later, receiving the information referred to in paragraph (a) of subsection (4) above and, in a case where it is required, the consent referred to in paragraph (b) of that subsection.

(7) The information to be supplied pursuant to a request under this section shall be supplied by reference to the data in question at the time when the request is received except that it may take account of any amendment or deletion made between that time and the time when the information is supplied, being an amendment or deletion that would have been made regardless of the receipt of the request.

(8) If a court is satisfied on the application of any person who has made a request under the foregoing provisions of this section that the data user in question has failed to comply with the request in contravention of those provisions, the court may order him to comply with the request; but a court shall not make an order under this subsection if it considers that it would in all the circumstances be unreasonable to do so, whether because of the frequency with which the applicant has made requests to the data user under those provisions or for any other reason.

(9) The Secretary of State may by order provide for enabling a request under this section to be made on behalf of any individual who is incapable by reason of mental disorder of managing his own affairs.

Health and social work

29(1) The Secretary of State may by order exempt from the subject access provisions, or modify those provisions in relation to, personal data consisting of information as to the physical or mental health of the data subject.

(2) The Secretary of State may by order exempt from the subject access provisions, or modify those provisions in relation to, personal data of such other descriptions as may be specified in the order, being information:

(a) held by government departments or local authorities or by voluntary organisations or other bodies designated by or under the order; and

(b) appearing to him to be held for, or acquired in the course of, carrying out social work in relation to the data subject or other individuals; but the Secretary of State shall not under this subsection confer any exemption or make any modification except so far as he considers that the application to the data of those provisions (or of those provisions without modification) would be likely to prejudice the carrying out of social work.

(3) An order under this section may make different provision in relation to data consisting of information of different descriptions.

HOSPITAL COMPLAINTS PROCEDURE ACT 1985

Hospital complaints procedure

1(1) It shall be the duty of the Secretary of State to give to each health authority in England and Wales and to each Health Board in Scotland such directions under s 17 National Health Service Act 1977 or s 2(5) National Health Service (Scotland) Act 1978 (directions as to exercise of functions) as appear to him necessary for the purpose of securing that, as respects each hospital for the management of which that authority or Board is responsible:

(a) such arrangements are made for dealing with complaints made by or on behalf of persons who are or have been patients at that hospital; and

(b) such steps are taken for publicising the arrangements so made, as (in each case) are specified or described in the directions.

(2) No right of appeal, reference or review conferred under this section shall preclude an investigation under Part V of the said Act of 1977 or Part VI of the said Act of 1978 (investigation by Health Service Commissioners) in respect of any matter.

(3) In this section:

(a) in its application to England and Wales, expressions which are also used in the said Act of 1977 have the same meanings as in that Act;

(b) in its application to Scotland, expressions which are also used in the said Act 1978 have the same meanings as in that Act.

1A It shall also be the duty of the Secretary of State to give directions under paragraph 6(2)(e), Schedule 2 National Health Service and Community Care Act 1990 and paragraph 6(2)(e), Schedule 7A National Health Service (Scotland) Act 1978, to any NHS trust which is responsible for the management of a hospital, to comply with directions under s 1 above.

Short title, commencement and extent

2(1) This Act may be cited as the Hospital Complaints Procedure Act 1985.

(2) This Act shall come into force on such day as the Secretary of State may by order made by statutory instrument appoint.

(3) This Act does not extend to Northern Ireland.

ACCESS TO MEDICAL REPORTS ACT 1988

Right of access

1 It shall be the right of an individual to have access, in accordance with the provisions of this Act, to any medical report relating to the individual which is to be, or has been, supplied by a medical practitioner for employment purposes or insurance purposes.

Interpretation

2(1) In this Act:

'the applicant' means the person referred to in s 3(1) below;

'care' includes examination, investigation or diagnosis for the purposes of, or in connection with, any form of medical treatment;

'employment purposes', in the case of any individual, means the purposes in relation to the individual of any person by whom he is or has been, or is seeking to be, employed (whether under a contract of service or otherwise);

'health professional' has the same meaning as in the Data Protection (Subject Access Modification) (Health) Order 1987;

'insurance purposes', in the case of any individual, means the purposes in relation to the individual of any person carrying on an insurance business with whom the individual has entered into, or is seeking to enter into, a contract of insurance, and 'insurance business' and 'contract of insurance' have the same meaning as in the Insurance Companies Act 1982;

'medical practitioner' means a person registered under the Medical Act 1983;

'medical report', in the case of an individual, means a report relating to the physical or mental health of the individual prepared by a medical practitioner who is or has been responsible for the clinical care of the individual.

(2) Any reference in this Act to the supply of a medical report for employment or insurance purposes shall be construed:

(a) as a reference to the supply of such a report for employment or insurance purposes which are purposes of the person who is seeking to be supplied with it; or

(b) (in the case of a report that has already been supplied) as a reference to the supply of such a report for employment or insurance purposes which, at the time of its being supplied, were purposes of the person to whom it was supplied.

Consent to applications for medical reports for employment or insurance purposes

3(1) A person shall not apply to a medical practitioner for a medical report relating to any individual to be supplied to him for employment or insurance purposes unless:

(a) that person ('the applicant') has notified the individual that he proposes to make the application; and

(b) the individual has notified the applicant that he consents to the making of the application.

(2) Any notification given under subsection (1)(a) above must inform the individual of his right to withhold his consent to the making of the application, and of the following rights under this Act, namely:

(a) the rights arising under ss 4(1)–(3) and 6(2) below with respect to access to the report before or after it is supplied,

(b) the right to withhold consent under subsection (1) of s 5 below, and

(c) the right to request the amendment of the report under subsection (2) of that section, as well as of the effect of s 7 below.

Access to reports before they are supplied

4(1) An individual who gives his consent under s 3 above to the making of an application shall be entitled, when giving his consent, to state that he wishes to have access to the report to be supplied in response to the application before it is so supplied; and, if he does so, the applicant shall:

(a) notify the medical practitioner of that fact at the time when the application is made, and

(b) at the same time notify the individual of the making of the application; and each such notification shall contain a statement of the effect of subsection (2) below.

(2) Where a medical practitioner is notified by the applicant under subsection (1) above that the individual in question wishes to have access to the report before it is supplied, the practitioner shall not supply the report unless:

(a) he has given the individual access to it and any requirements of s 5 below have been complied with, or

(b) the period of 21 days beginning with the date of the making of the application has elapsed without his having received any communication from the individual concerning arrangements for the individual to have access to it.

(3) Where a medical practitioner:

(a) receives an application for a medical report to be supplied for employment or insurance purposes without being notified by the applicant as mentioned in subsection (1) above, but

(b) before supplying the report receives a notification from the individual that he wishes to have access to the report before it is supplied, the practitioner shall not supply the report unless:

(i) he has given the individual access to it and any requirements of s 5 below have been complied with, or

(ii) the period of 21 days beginning with the date of that notification has elapsed without his having received (either with that notification or otherwise) any communication from the individual concerning arrangements for the individual to have access to it.

(4) References in this section and s 5 below to giving an individual access to a medical report are references to:

(a) making the report or a copy of it available for his inspection; or

(b) supplying him with a copy of it; and where a copy is supplied at the request, or otherwise with the consent, of the individual the practitioner may charge a reasonable fee to cover the costs of supplying it.

Consent to supplying of report and correction of errors

5(1) Where an individual has been given access to a report under s 4 above the report shall not be supplied in response to the application in question unless the individual has notified the medical practitioner that he consents to its being so supplied.

(2) The individual shall be entitled, before giving his consent under subsection (1) above, to request the medical practitioner to amend any part of the report which the individual considers to be incorrect or misleading; and, if the individual does so, the practitioner:

(a) if he is to any extent prepared to accede to the individual's request, shall amend the report accordingly;

(b) if he is to any extent not prepared to accede to it but the individual requests him to attach to the report a statement of the individual's views in respect of any part of the report which he is declining to amend, shall attach such a statement to the report.

(3) Any request made by an individual under subsection (2) above shall be made in writing.

Retention of reports

6(1) A copy of any medical report which a medical practitioner has supplied for employment or insurance purposes shall be retained by him for at least six months from the data on which it was supplied.

(2) A medical practitioner shall, if so requested by an individual, give the individual access to any medical report relating to him which the practitioner has supplied for employment or insurance purposes in the previous six months.

(3) The reference in subsection (2) above to giving an individual access to a medical report is a reference to:

(a) making a copy of the report available for his inspection; or

(b) supplying him with a copy of it; and where a copy is supplied at the request, or otherwise with the consent, of the individual the practitioner may charge a reasonable fee to cover the costs of supplying it.

Exemptions

7(1) A medical practitioner shall not be obliged to give an individual access, in accordance with the provisions of ss 4(4) or 6(3) above, to any part of a medical report whose disclosure would in the opinion of the practitioner be likely to cause serious harm to the physical or mental health of the individual or others or would indicate the intentions of the practitioner in respect of the individual.

(2) A medical practitioner shall not be obliged to give an individual access, in accordance with those provisions, to any part of a medical report whose disclosure would be likely to reveal information about another person, or to reveal the identity of another person who has supplied information to the practitioner about the individual, unless:

(a) that person has consented; or

(b) that person is a health professional who has been involved in the care of the individual and the information relates to or has been provided by the professional in that capacity.

(3) Where it appears to a medical practitioner that subsection (1) or (2) above is applicable to any part (but not the whole) of a medical report:

(a) he shall notify the individual of that fact; and

(b) references in the preceding sections of this Act to the individual being given access to the report shall be construed as references to his being given access to the remainder of it; and other references to the report in ss 4(4), 5(2) and 6(3) above shall similarly be construed as references to the remainder of the report.

(4) Where it appears to a medical practitioner that subsection (1) or (2) above is applicable to the whole of a medical report:

(a) he shall notify the individual of that fact; but

(b) he shall not supply the report unless he is notified by the individual that the individual consents to its being supplied; and accordingly, if he is so notified by the individual, the restrictions imposed by ss 4(2) and (3) above on the supply of the report shall not have effect in relation to it.

Application to the court

8(1) If a court is satisfied on the application of an individual that any person, in connection with a medical report relating to that individual, has failed or is likely to fail to comply with any requirement of this Act, the court may order that person to comply with that requirement.

(2) The jurisdiction conferred by this section shall be exercisable by a county court or, in Scotland, by the sheriff.

Notifications under this Act

9 Any notification required or authorised to be given under this Act:

(a) shall be given in writing; and

(b) may be given by post.

Short title, commencement and extent

10(1) This Act may be cited as the Access to Medical Reports Act 1988.

(2) This Act shall come into force on 1st January 1989.

(3) Nothing in this Act applies to a medical report prepared before the coming into force of this Act.

(4) This Act does not extend to Northern Ireland.

ACCESS TO HEALTH RECORDS ACT 1990

Preliminary

'Health record' and related expressions

1(1) In this Act, 'health record' means a record which:

(a) consists of information relating to the physical or mental health of an individual who can be identified from that information, or from that and other information in the possession of the holder of the record; and

(b) has been made by or on behalf of a health professional in connection with the care of that individual; but does not include any record which consists of information of which the individual is, or but for any exemption would be, entitled to be supplied with a copy under s 21 Data Protection Act 1984 (right of access to personal data).

(2) In this Act, 'holder', in relation to a health record, means:

(a) in the case of a record made by, or by a health professional employed by, a general practitioner:

(i) the patient's general practitioner, that is to say, the general practitioner on whose list the patient is included; or

(ii) where the patient has no general practitioner, the Family Practitioner Committee or Health Board on whose medical list the patient's most recent general practitioner was included;

(b) in the case of a record made by a health professional for purposes connected with the provision of health services by a health service body, the health service body by which or on whose behalf the record is held;

(c) in any other case, the health professional by whom or on whose behalf the record is held.

(3) In this Act, 'patient', in relation to a health record, means the individual in connection with whose care the record has been made.

Health professionals

2(1) In this Act, 'health professional' means any of the following, namely:

(a) a registered medical practitioner;

(b) a registered dentist;

(c) a registered optician;

(d) a registered pharmaceutical chemist;

(e) a registered nurse, midwife or health visitor;

(f) a registered chiropodist, dietician, occupational therapist, orthoptist or physiotherapist;

(g) a clinical psychologist, child psychotherapist or speech therapist;

(h) an art or music therapist employed by a health service body; and

(i) a scientist employed by such a body as head of department.

(2) Subsection (1)(a) above shall be deemed to include any person who is provisionally registered under ss 15 or 21 Medical Act 1983 and is engaged in such employment as is mentioned in subsection (3) of that section.

(3) If, after the passing of this Act, an order is made under s 10 Professions Supplementary to Medicine Act 1960, the Secretary of State may by order make such consequential amendments of subsection (1)(f) above as may appear to him to be necessary or expedient.

(4) The provisions of this Act shall apply in relation to health professionals in the public service of the Crown as they apply in relation to other health professionals.

Main provisions

Right of access to health records

3(1) An application for access to a health record, or to any part of a health record, may be made to the holder of the record by any of the following, namely:

(a) the patient;

(b) a person authorised in writing to make the application on the patient's behalf;

(c) where the record is held in England and Wales and the patient is a child, a person having parental responsibility for the patient;

(d) where the record is held in Scotland and the patient is a pupil, a parent or guardian of the patient;

(e) where the patient is incapable of managing his own affairs, any person appointed by a court to manage those affairs; and

(f) where the patient has died, the patient's personal representative and any person who may have a claim arising out of the patient's death.

(2) Subject to s 4 below, where an application is made under subsection (1) above the holder shall, within the requisite period, give access to the record, or the part of a record, to which the application relates:

(a) in the case of a record, by allowing the applicant to inspect the record or, where s 5 below applies, an extract setting out so much of the record as is not excluded by that section;

(b) in the case of a part of a record, by allowing the applicant to inspect an extract setting out that part or, where that section applies, so much of that part as is not so excluded; or

(c) in either case, if the applicant so requires, by supplying him with a copy of the record or extract.

(3) Where any information contained in a record or extract which is so allowed to be inspected, or a copy of which is so supplied, is expressed in terms which are not intelligible without explanation, an explanation of those terms shall be provided with the record or extract, or supplied with the copy.

(4) No fee shall be required for giving access under subsection (2) above other than the following, namely:

(a) where access is given to a record, or part of a record, none of which was made after the beginning of the period of 40 days immediately preceding the date of the application, a fee not exceeding the maximum prescribed under s 21 Data Protection Act 1984; and

(b) where a copy of a record or extract is supplied to the applicant, a fee not exceeding the cost of making the copy and (where applicable) the cost of posting it to him.

(5) For the purposes of subsection (2) above the requisite period is:

(a) where the application relates to a record, or part of a record, none of which was made before the beginning of the period of 40 days immediately preceding the date of the application, the period of 21 days beginning with that date;

(b) in any other case, the period of 40 days beginning with that date.

(6) Where:

    (a) an application under subsection (1) above does not contain sufficient information to enable the holder of the record to identify the patient or, in the case of an application made otherwise than by the patient, to satisfy himself that the applicant is entitled to make the application; and

    (b) within the period of 14 days beginning with the date of the application, the holder of the record requests the applicant to furnish him with such further information as he may reasonably require for that purpose, subsection (5) above shall have effect as if for any reference to that date there were substituted a reference to the date on which that further information is so furnished.

Cases where right of access may be wholly excluded

4(1) Where an application is made under subsection (1)(a) or (b) of s 3 above and:

    (a) in the case of a record held in England and Wales, the patient is a child; or

    (b) in the case of a record held in Scotland the patient is a pupil, access shall not be given under subsection (2) of that section unless the holder of the record is satisfied that the patient is capable of understanding the nature of the application.

(2) Where an application is made under subsection (1)(c) or (d) of s 3 above, access shall not be given under subsection (2) of that section unless the holder of the record is satisfied either:

    (a) that the patient has consented to the making of the application; or

    (b) that the patient is incapable of understanding the nature of the application and the giving of access would be in his best interests.

(3) Where an application is made under subsection (1)(f) of s 3 above, access shall not be given under subsection (2) of that section if the record includes a note, made at the patient's request, that he did not wish access to be given on such an application.

Cases where right of access may be partially excluded

5(1) Access shall not be given under s 3(2) above to any part of a health record:

    (a) which, in the opinion of the holder of the record, would disclose:

        (i) information likely to cause serious harm to the physical or mental health of the patient or of any other individual; or

        (ii) information relating to or provided by an individual, other than the patient, who could be identified from that information; or

    (b) which was made before the commencement of this Act.

(2) Subsection (1)(a)(ii) above shall not apply:

    (a) where the individual concerned has consented to the application; or

    (b) where that individual is a health professional who has been involved in the care of the patient; and subsection (1)(b) above shall not apply where and to the extent that, in the opinion of the holder of the record, the giving of access is necessary in order to make intelligible any part of the record to which access is required to be given under s 3(2) above.

(3) Where an application is made under 1(c), (d), (e) or (f) of s 3 above, access shall not be given under subsection (2) of that section to any part of the record which, in all opinion of the holder of the record, would disclose:

(a) information provided by the patient in the expectation that it would not be disclosed to the applicant; or

(b) information obtained as a result of any examination or investigation to which the patient consented in the expectation that the information would not be so disclosed.

(4) Where an application is made under subsection (1)(f) of s 3 above, access shall not be given under subsection (2) of that section to any part of the record which, in the opinion of the holder of the record, would disclose information which is not relevant to any claim which may arise out of the patient's death.

(5) The Secretary of State may by regulations provide that, in such circumstances as may be prescribed by the regulations, access shall not be given under s 3(2) above to any part of a health record which satisfies such conditions as may be so prescribed.

Correction of inaccurate health records

6(1) Where a person considers that any information contained in a health record, or any part of a health record, to which he has been given access under s 3(2) above is inaccurate, he may apply to the holder of the record for the necessary correction to be made.

(2) On an application under subsection (1) above, the holder of the record shall:

(a) if he is satisfied that the information is inaccurate, make the necessary correction;

(b) if he is not so satisfied, make in the part of the record in which the information is contained a note of the matters in respect of which the information is considered by the applicant to be inaccurate; and

(c) in either case, without requiring any fee, supply the applicant with a copy of the correction or note.

(3) In this section, 'inaccurate' means incorrect, misleading or incomplete.

Duty of health service bodies , etc to take advice

7(1) A health service body or Family Practitioner Committee shall take advice from the appropriate health professional before they decide whether they are satisfied as to any matter for the purposes of this Act, or form an opinion as to any matter for those purposes.

(2) In this section, 'the appropriate health professional', in relation to a health service body (other than a Health Board) which is the holder of the record by virtue of s 1(2)(a) above) means:

(a) where, for purposes connected with the provision of health services by the body, one or more medical or dental practitioners are currently responsible for the clinical care of the patient, that practitioner or, as the case may be, such one of those practitioners as is the most suitable to advise the body on the matter in question;

(b) where paragraph (a) above does not apply but one or more medical or dental practitioners are available who, for purposes connected with the provision of such services by the body, have been responsible for the clinical care of the patient, that practitioner or, as the case may be, such one of those practitioners as was most recently so responsible; and

(c) where neither paragraph (a) nor paragraph (b) above applies, a health professional who has the necessary experience and qualifications to advise the body on the matter in question.

(3) In this section, 'the appropriate health professional', in relation to a Family Practitioner Committee or a Health Board which is the holder of the record by virtue of s 1(2)(a) above, means:

(a) where the patient's most recent general practitioner is available, that practitioner; and

(b) where that practitioner is not available, a registered medical practitioner who has the necessary experience and qualifications to advise the Committee or Board on the matter in question.

Supplemental

Applications to the court

8(1) Subject to subsection (2) below, where the court is satisfied, on an application made by the person concerned within such period as may be prescribed by rules of court, that the holder of a health record has failed to comply with any requirement of this Act, the court may order the holder to comply with that requirement.

(2) The court shall not entertain an application under subsection (1) above unless it is satisfied that the applicant has taken all such steps to secure compliance with the requirements as may be prescribed by regulations made by the Secretary of State.

(3) For the purposes of subsection (2) above, the Secretary of State may by regulations require the holders of health records to make such arrangements for dealing with complaints that they have failed to comply with any requirements of this Act as may be prescribed by the regulations.

(4) For the purpose of determining any question whether an applicant is entitled to be given access under s 3(2) above to any health record, or any part of a health record, the court:

(a) may require the record or part to be made available for its own inspection; but

(b) shall not, pending determination of that question in the applicant's favour, require the record or part to be disclosed to him or his representatives whether by discovery (or, in Scotland, recovery) or otherwise.

(5) The jurisdiction conferred by this section shall be exercisable by the High Court or a county court or, in Scotland, by the Court of Session or the sheriff.

Avoidance of certain contractual terms

9 Any term or condition of a contract shall be void in so far as it purports to require an individual to supply any other person with a copy of a health record, or of an extract from a health record, to which he has been given access under s 3(2) above.

Regulations and orders

10(1) Regulations under this Act may make different provisions for different cases or classes of cases including, in particular, different provision for different health records or classes of health records.

(2) Any power to make regulations or orders under this Act shall be exercisable by statutory instrument.

(3) Any statutory instrument containing regulations under this Act or an order under s 2(3) above shall be subject to annulment in pursuance of a resolution of either House of Parliament.

Interpretation

11 In this Act:

'application' means an application in writing and 'apply' shall be construed accordingly;

'care' includes examination, investigation, diagnosis and treatment;

'child' means an individual who has not attained the age of 16 years;

'general practitioner' means a medical practitioner who is providing general medical services in accordance with arrangements made under s 29 National Health Service Act 1977 or s 19 National Health Service (Scotland) Act 1978;

'Health Board' has the same meaning as in the National Health Service (Scotland) Act 1978;

'health service body' means:

- (a) a health authority within the meaning of the National Health Service Act 1977;
- (b) a Health Board;
- (c) a State Hospital Management Committee constituted under s 91 Mental Health (Scotland) Act 1984; or
- (d) a National Health Service trust first established under s 5 National Health Service and Community Care Act 1990 or s 12A National Health Service (Scotland) Act 1978;

'information', in relation to a health record, includes any expression of opinion about the patient;

'make', in relation to such a record, includes compile;

'parental responsibility' has the same meaning as in the Children Act 1989

Short title, commencement, and extent

12(1) This Act may be cited as the Access to Health Records Act 1990.

(2) This Act shall come into force on 1 November 1991.

(3) This Act does not extend to Northern Ireland.

THE COURTS AND LEGAL SERVICES ACT 1990

Conditional fee arrangements

58(1) In this section, 'a conditional fee agreement' means an agreement in writing between a person providing advocacy or litigation services and his client which:

    (a) does not relate to proceedings of a kind mentioned in subsection (10);

    (b) provides for that person's fees and expenses, or any part of them, to be payable only in specified circumstances;

    (c) complies with such requirements (if any) as may be prescribed by the Lord Chancellor; and

    (d) is not a contentious business agreement (as defined by s 59 Solicitors Act 1974).

(2) Where a conditional fee agreement provides for the amount of any fees to which it applies to be increased, in specified circumstances, above the amount which would be payable if it were not a conditional fee agreement, it shall specify the percentage by which that amount is to be increased.

(3) Subject to subsection (6), a conditional fee agreement which relates to specified proceedings shall not be unenforceable by reason only of its being a conditional fee agreement.

(4) In this section, 'specified proceedings' means proceedings of a description specified by order made by the Lord Chancellor for the purpose of subsection (3).

(5) Any such order shall prescribe the maximum permitted percentage for each description of specified proceedings.

(6) An agreement which falls within subsection (2) shall be unenforceable if, at the time when it is entered into, the percentage specified in the agreement exceeds the prescribed maximum permitted percentage for the description of proceedings to which it relates.

(7) Before making any order under this section, the Lord Chancellor shall consult the designated judges, the General Council of the Bar, the Law Society and such other authorised bodies (if any) as he considers appropriate.

(8) Where a party to any proceedings has entered into a conditional fee agreement and a costs order is made in those proceedings in his favour, the costs payable to him shall not include any element which takes account of any percentage increase payable under the agreement.

(9) Rules of court may make provision with respect to the taxing of any costs which include fees payable under a conditional fee agreement.

(10) The proceedings mentioned in subsection (1)(a) are any criminal proceedings and any proceedings under:

    (a) the Matrimonial Causes Act 1973;

    (b) the Domestic Violence and Matrimonial Proceedings Act 1976;

    (c) the Adoption Act 1976;

    (d) the Domestic Proceedings and Magistrates' Court Act 1978;

(e) sections 1 and 9 Matrimonial Homes Act 1983;

(f) Part III Matrimonial and Family Proceedings Act 1984;

(g) Parts I, II or IV Children Act 1989; or

(h) the inherent jurisdiction of the High Court in relation to children.

SOCIAL SECURITY AND ADMINISTRATION ACT 1992

PART IV: RECOVERY FROM COMPENSATION PAYMENTS

Interpretation of Part IV

81(1) In this part of this Act:

'Benefit' means any benefit under the Contributions and Benefits Act except child benefit and subject to regulations under subsection (2) below, the 'relevant benefits' are such of those benefits as may be prescribed for the purposes of this part of this Act;

'certificate of deduction' means a certificate given by the compensator specifying the amount which he has deducted and paid to the Secretary of State in pursuance of s 82(1) below;

'certificate of total benefit' means a certificate given by the Secretary of State in accordance with this part of this Act;

'compensation payment' means any payment falling to be made (whether voluntarily, or in pursuance of a court order or an agreement, or otherwise):

(a) to or in respect of the victim in consequence of the accident, injury or disease in question; and

(b) either:

(i) by or on behalf of a person who is, or is alleged to be, liable to any extent in respect of that accident, injury or disease; or

(ii) in pursuance of a compensation scheme for motor accidents, but does not include benefit of an exempt payment or so much of any payment as is referable to costs incurred by any person;

'compensation scheme for motor accidents' means any scheme or arrangement under which funds are available for the payment of compensation in respect of motor accidents caused, or alleged to have been caused, by uninsured or unidentified persons;

'compensator', 'victim' and 'intended recipient' shall be construed in accordance with s 82(1) below;

'payment' means payment in money or money's worth, and cognate expressions shall be construed accordingly;

'relevant deduction' means the deduction required to be made from the compensation payment in question by virtue of this part of this Act;

'relevant payment' means the payment required to be made to the Secretary of State by virtue of this part of this Act;

'relevant period' means:

    (a) in the case of a disease, the period of five years beginning with the date on which the victim first claims a relevant benefit in consequence of the disease; or

    (b) in any other case, the period of five years immediately following the day on which the accident or injury in question occurred; but where before the end of that period the compensator makes a compensation payment in final discharge of any claim made by or in respect of the victim and arising out of the accident, injury or disease, the relevant period shall end on the date on which that payment is made; and

'total benefit' means the gross amount referred to in s 82(1)(a) below.

(2) If statutory sick pay is prescribed as a relevant benefit, the amount of that benefit for the purposes of this part of this Act shall be a reduced amount determined in accordance with regulations by reference to the percentage from time to time specified in s 158(1)(a) Contributions and Benefits Act (percentage of statutory sick pay recoverable by employers by deduction from contribution).

(3) For the purposes of this part of this Act, the following are the 'exempt payments':

    (a) any small payment, as defined in s 85 below;

    (b) any payment made to or for the victim under s 35 Powers of Criminal Courts Act 1973 or s 58 Criminal Justice (Scotland) Act 1980;

    (c) any payment to the extent that it is made:

        (i) in consequence of an action under the Fatal Accidents Act 1976; or

        (ii) in circumstances where, had an action been brought, it would have been brought under that Act;

    (d) (applies to Scotland only);

    (e) without prejudice to s 6(4) Vaccine Damage Payments Act 1979 (which provides for the deduction of any such payment in the assessment of any award of damages), any payment made under that Act to or in respect of the victim;

    (f) any award of compensation made to or in respect of the victim by the Criminal Injuries Compensation Board under s 111 Criminal Justice Act 1988;

    (g) any payment made in the exercise of a discretion out of property held subject to a trust in a case where no more than 50% by value of the capital contributed to the trust was directly or indirectly provided by persons who are, or are alleged to be, liable in respect of:

        (i) the accident, injury or disease suffered by the victim in question; or

        (ii) the same or any connected accident, injury or disease suffered by another;

    (h) any payment made out of property held for the purposes of any prescribed trust (whether the payment also falls within paragraph (g) above or not);

(i) any payment made to the victim by an insurance company within the meaning of the Insurance Companies Act 1982 under the terms of any contract of insurance entered into between the victim and the company before:

(i) the date on which the victim first claims a relevant benefit in consequence of the disease in question; or

(ii) the occurrence of the accident or injury in question;

(j) any redundancy payment falling to be taken into account in the assessment of damages in respect of an accident, injury or disease.

(4) Regulations may provide that any prescribed payment shall be an exempt payment for the purposes of this part of this Act.

(5) Except as provided by any other enactment, in the assessment of damages in respect of an accident, injury or disease the amount of any relevant benefits paid or likely to be paid shall be disregarded.

(6) If, after making the relevant deduction from the compensation payment, there would be no balance remaining for payment to the intended recipient, any reference in this part to the making of the compensation payment shall be construed in accordance with regulations.

(7) This part of this Act shall apply in relation to any compensation payment made on or after 3 September 1990 (the date of the coming into force of s 22 Social Security Act 1989 which, with Schedule 4 to that Act, made provision corresponding to that made by this part) to the extent that it is made in respect of:

(a) an accident or injury occurring on or after 1 January 1989; or

(b) a disease, if the victim's first claim for a relevant benefit in consequence for the disease is made on or after that date.

Recovery of sums equivalent to benefit from compensation payments in respect of accidents, injuries and disease

82(1) A person ('the compensator') making a compensation payment, whether on behalf of himself or another, in consequence of an accident, injury or disease suffered by any other person ('the victim') shall not do so until the Secretary of State has furnished him with a certificate of total benefit and shall then:

(a) deduct from the payment an amount, determined in accordance with the certificate of total benefit, equal to the gross amount of any relevant benefits paid or likely to be paid to or for the victim during the relevant period in respect of that accident, injury or disease;

(b) pay to the Secretary of State an amount equal to that which is required to be so deducted; and

(c) furnish the person to whom the compensation payment is or, apart from this section, would have been made ('the intended recipient') with a certificate of deduction.

(2) Any right of the intended recipient to receive the compensation payment in question shall be regarded as satisfied to the extent of the amount certified in the certificate of deduction.

Time for making payment to Secretary of State

83 The compensator's liability to make the relevant payment arises immediately before the making of the compensation payment, and he shall make the relevant payment before the end of the period of 14 days following the day on which the liability arises.

The certificate of total benefit

84(1) It shall be for the compensator to apply to the Secretary of State for the certificate of total benefit and he may, subject to subsection (5) below, from time to time apply for fresh certificates.

(2) The certificate of total benefit shall specify:

(a) the amount which has been, or is likely to be, paid on or before a specified date by way of any relevant benefit which is capable of forming part of the total benefit;

(b) where applicable:

(i) the rate of any relevant benefit which is, has been, or is likely to be paid after the date so specified and which would be capable of forming part of the total benefit; and

(ii) the intervals at which any such benefit is paid and the period for which it is likely to be paid;

(c) the amounts (if any) which, by virtue of this part of this Act, are to be treated as increasing the total benefit; and

(d) the aggregate amount of any relevant payments made on or before a specified date (reduced by so much of that amount as has been paid by the Secretary of State to the intended recipient before that date in consequence of this part of this Act).

(3) On issuing a certificate of total benefit, the Secretary of State shall be taken to have certified the total benefit as at every date for which it is possible to calculate an amount that would, on the basis of the information so provided, be the total benefit as at that date, on the assumption that payments of benefit are made on the days on which they first become payable.

(4) The Secretary of State may estimate, in such manner as he thinks fit, any of the amounts, rates or periods specified in the certificate of total benefit.

(5) A certificate of total benefit shall remain in force until such date as may be specified in the certificate for that purpose and no application for a fresh certificate shall be made before that date.

(6) Where a certificate ceases to be in force, the Secretary of State may issue a fresh certificate, whether or not an application has been made to him for such a certificate.

(7) The compensator shall not make the compensation payment at any time when there is no certificate of total benefit in force in respect of the victim, unless his liability to make the relevant deduction and the relevant payment has ceased to be enforceable by virtue of s 96 below.

Exemption from deduction in cases involving small payments

85(1) Regulations may make provision exempting persons from liability to make the relevant deduction or the relevant payment in prescribed cases where the amount of the compensation payment in question, or the aggregate amount of two or more connected compensation payments, does not exceed the prescribed sum.

(2) Regulations may make provision for cases where an amount has been deducted and paid to the Secretary of State which, by virtue of regulations under subsection (1) above, ought not to have been so deducted and paid, and any such regulations may, in particular, provide for him to pay that amount to the intended recipient or the compensator or to pay a prescribed part of it to each of them.

(3) The reference in s 81(3)(a) above to a 'small payment' is a reference to a payment from which by virtue of this section no relevant deduction falls to be made.

(4) For the purposes of this section:

(a) two or more compensation payments are 'connected' if each is made to or in respect of the same victim and in respect of the same accident, injury or disease; and

(b) any reference to a compensation payment is a reference to a payment which would be such a payment apart from s 81(3)(a) above.

Multiple compensation payments

86(1) This section applies where:

(a) a compensation payment (an 'earlier payment') has been made to or in respect of the victim; and

(b) subsequently another such payment (a 'later payment') falls to be made to or in respect of the same victim in respect of the same accident, injury or disease (whether by the same or another compensator).

(2) In determining the amount of the relevant deduction and payment required to be made in connection with the later payment, the amount referred to in s 82(1)(a) above shall be reduced by the amount of any relevant payment made in connection with the earlier payment, or, if more than one, the aggregate of those relevant payments.

(3) In relation to the later payment, the compensator shall take the amount of the reduction required by subsection (2) above to be such as may be specified under s 84(2)(d) above in the certificate of total benefit issued to him in connection with that later payment.

(4) In any case where:

(a) the relevant payment made in connection with an earlier payment is not reflected in the certificate of total benefit in force in relation to a later payment; and

(b) in consequence, the aggregate of the relevant payments made in relation to the later payment and every earlier payment exceeds what it would have been had that relevant payment been so reflected, the Secretary of State shall pay the intended recipient an amount equal to the excess.

(5) In determining any rights and liabilities in respect of contribution or indemnity, relevant payments shall be treated as damages paid to or for the intended recipient in respect of the accident, injury or disease in question.

Collaboration between compensators

87(1) This section applies where compensation payments in respect of the same accident, injury or disease fall (or apart from this part would fall) to be made to or in respect of the same victim by two or more compensators.

(2) Where this section applies, any two or more of those compensators may give the Secretary of State notice that they are collaborators in respect of compensation payments in respect of that victim and that accident, injury or disease.

(3) Where such a notice is given and any of the collaborators makes relevant payment in connection with such a compensation payment, each of the other collaborators shall be treated as if the aggregate amount of relevant payments specified in his certificate of total benefit, as in force at the time of that relevant payment, or in a fresh certificate which does not purport to reflect the payment, were increased by the amount of that payment.

Structured settlements

88(1) This section applies where:

    (a) in final settlement of a person's claim, an agreement is entered into:

        (i) for the making of periodical payments (whether of an income or capital nature) to or in respect of the victim; or

        (ii) for the making of such payments and one or more lump sum payments; and

    (b) apart from this section, those payments would fall to be regarded for the purposes of this part of this Act as compensation payments.

(2) Where this section applies, this part of this Act (other than this section) shall have effect on the following assumptions, that is to say:

    (a) the relevant period in the case of the compensator in question shall be taken to end (if it has not previously done so) on the day of settlement;

    (b) the compensator in question shall be taken:

        (i) to have been liable to make on that day a single compensation payment of the amount referred to in s 82(1)(a) above reduced or increased in accordance with such of the provisions of this part as would have applied in the case of a payment on that day; and

        (ii) to have made from that single payment a relevant deduction of an amount equal to it; and

    (c) the payments under the agreement referred to in subsection (1) above shall be taken to be exempt payments.

(3) The intended recipient shall not by virtue of anything in this section become entitled to be paid any sum, whether by the compensator or the Secretary of State, and if on a review or appeal under ss 97 or 99 below it appears that the amount paid by a compensator in pursuance of this section was either greater or less than it ought to have been, then:

(a) any excess shall be repaid to the compensator instead of to the intended recipient; but

(b) any deficiency shall be paid to the Secretary of State by the intended recipient.

(4) Where any further compensation payment falls to be made to or in respect of the victim otherwise than under the agreement in question, subsection (2)(a) above shall be disregarded for the purpose of determining the end of the relevant period in relation to that further payment.

(5) In any case where:

(a) the person making the periodical payments ('the secondary party') does so in pursuance of arrangements entered into with another (as in a case where an insurance company purchases an annuity for the victim from another such company); and

(b) apart from those arrangements, that other ('the primary party') would have been regarded as the compensator, then for the purposes of this part, the primary party shall be regarded as the compensator and the secondary party shall not be so regarded.

(6) In determining for the purposes of this section whether any periodical payments would fall to be regarded as compensation payments, s 81(3)(a) above shall be disregarded.

(7) In this section, 'the day of settlement' means:

(a) if the agreement referred to in subsection (1) above is approved by a court, the day on which that approval is given; and

(b) in any other case, the day on which the agreement is entered into.

Insolvency

89(1) Where the intended recipient is subject to a bankruptcy order, nothing in the Insolvency Act 1986 shall affect the operation of this part of this Act.

(2) (Applies to Scotland only.)

Protection of legal aid charges

90(1) In any case where:

(a) the compensation payment is subject to any charge under the Legal Aid Act 1974 or the Legal Aid Act 1988, and

(b) after the making of the relevant deduction, the balance of the compensation payment is insufficient to satisfy that charge, the Secretary of State shall make such a payment as will secure that the deficiency is made good to the extent of the relevant payment.

(2) Where the Secretary of State makes a payment under this section, then for the purposes of s 84 above, the amount of payment shall be treated as increasing the total benefit.

(3) (Applies to Scotland only.)

Overpaid benefits

91 In any case where:

  (a) during the relevant period, there has, in respect of the accident, injury or disease, been paid to or for the victim any relevant benefit to which he was not entitled ('the overpaid benefit'); and

  (b) the amount of the relevant payment is such that, after taking account of the rest of the total benefit, there remains an amount which represents the whole or any part of the overpaid benefit, then, notwithstanding anything in s 71 above or any regulations under that section or s 53 of the 1986 Act, the receipt by the Secretary of State of the relevant payment shall be treated as the recovery of the whole or, as the case may be, that part of the overpaid benefit.

Death

92 In the case of any compensation payment the whole or part of which is made:

  (a) in consequence of an action under the Fatal Accidents Act 1976; or

  (b) in circumstances where, had an action been brought, it would have been brought under that Act; or

  (c) (applies to Scotland only),

regulations may make provision for estimating or calculating the portion of the payment which is to be regarded as so made for the purposes of s 81(3)(c) or (d) above.

Payments into court

93(1) Nothing in this part of this Act requires a court to make any relevant deduction or payment in connection with money in court.

(2) Where a party to an action makes a payment into court which, had it been paid directly to the other party, would have constituted a compensation payment, the making of that payment shall be regarded for the purposes of this part of this Act as the making of a compensation payment, but the compensator:

  (a) may either:

    (i) withhold from the payment into court an amount equal to the relevant deduction; or

    (ii) make such a payment into court before the certificate of total benefit has been issued to him; and

  (b) shall not become liable to make the relevant payment, or to furnish a certificate of deduction, until he has been notified that the whole or any part of the payment into court has been paid out of court to or for the other party.

(3) Where a person making a payment into court withholds an amount in accordance with subsection (2)(a)(i) above:

  (a) he shall, at the time when he makes that payment, furnish the court with a certificate of the amount so withheld; and

(b) the amount paid into court shall be regarded as increased by the amount so certified, but no person shall be entitled by virtue of this subsection to the payment out of court of any amount which has not in fact been paid into court.

(4) Where a payment into court is made as mentioned in subsection (2)(a)(ii) above, the compensator:

(a) shall apply for the certificate of total benefit no later than the day on which the payment into court is made; and

(b) shall become liable to make the relevant payment as mentioned in subsection (2)(b) above, notwithstanding that the relevant deduction has not been made.

(5) Where any such payment into court as is mentioned in subsection (2) above is accepted by the other party to the action within the initial period, then, as respects the compensator in question, the relevant period shall be taken to have ended on the day on which the payment into court (or, if there were two or more such payments, the last of them) was made; but where the payment into court is not so accepted, then:

(a) the relevant period as respects that compensator shall end on the day on which he is notified that the payment has been paid out of court to or for that other party; and

(b) in determining the amount of the relevant payment, that compensator shall be treated as if his payment into court had been made on that day.

(6) In subsection (5) above, 'the initial period' means the period of 21 days following the making of the payment into court (or, if there were two or more such payments, the last of them), but rules of court may make provision varying the length of that period.

(7) Where a payment into court is paid out wholly to or for the party who made the payment (otherwise than to or for the other party to the action) the making of the payment into court shall cease to be regarded as the making of a compensation payment.

(8) Rules of court may make provision regulating or prescribing the practice and procedure to be followed in relation to such payments into court as are mentioned in subsection (2) above.

(9) This section does not extend to Scotland.

Provision of information

94(1) Any person who is, or is alleged to be, liable in respect of an accident, injury or disease, or any person acting on his behalf, shall furnish the Secretary of State with the prescribed information relating to any person seeking compensation, or in respect of whom compensation is sought, in respect of that accident, injury or disease.

(2) Any person who claims a relevant benefit or who has been in receipt of such a benefit or, if he has died, the personal representatives of such a person, shall furnish the Secretary of State with the prescribed information relating to any accident, injury or disease suffered by that person.

(3) A person who makes any payment (whether a compensation payment or not) on behalf of himself or another:

(a) in consequence of any accident, injury or disease suffered, or any damage to property sustained, by any other person; or

(b) which is referable to any costs, or, in Scotland, expenses, incurred by any such other person by reason of such an accident, injury, disease or damage, shall, if the Secretary of State so requests him in writing, furnish the Secretary of State with such particulars relating to the size and composition of the payment as may be specified in the request.

(4) Any person:

(a) who is the employer of a person who suffers or has suffered an accident, injury or disease; or

(b) who has been the employer of such a person at any time during the relevant period, shall furnish the Secretary of State with the prescribed information relating to the payment of statutory sick pay in respect of that person.

(5) In subsection (4) above, 'employer' has the same meaning as it has in Part XI Contributions and Benefits Act.

(6) Any person furnishing information under this section shall do so in the prescribed manner, at the prescribed place and within the prescribed time.

Applications for certificates of total benefit

95(1) If at any time before he makes the compensation payment in question the compensator requests the Secretary of State to furnish him with a certificate of total benefit relating to the victim in question:

(a) the Secretary of State shall comply with that request before the end of the period of four weeks, or such other number of weeks as may be prescribed, following the day on which the request is, or is deemed in accordance with regulations to be, received; and

(b) any certificate so furnished shall, in particular, specify for the purposes of s 84(2)(a) above a date not earlier than the date of the request.

(2) Where the Secretary of State furnishes any person with a certificate of total benefit, he shall also provide the information contained in that certificate to the person who appears to him to be the victim in relation to the compensation payment in question.

(3) The victim may apply to the Secretary of State for particulars of the manner in which any amount, rate or period specified in a certificate of total benefit has been determined.

Liability of compensator unenforceable if certificate not issued within time limit

96(1) The liability of the compensator to make the relevant deduction and payment relating to the first compensation payment after the default date shall not be enforceable if:

(a) he has made a request under s 95(1) above which:

(i) accurately states the prescribed particulars relating to the victim and the accident, injury or disease in question; and

(ii) specifies the name and address of the person to whom the certificate is to be sent;

(b) he has in his possession a written acknowledgment, sent to him in accordance with regulations, of the receipt of the request; and

(c) the secretary of State does not, within the time limit referred to in s 95(1) above, send the certificate to the person specified in the request as the person to whom the certificate is to be sent, at the address so specified; and accordingly, where those liabilities cease to be enforceable, nothing in this part of this Act shall prevent the compensator from making that compensation payment.

(2) In any case where:

(a) the liability to make the relevant deduction and payment becomes unenforceable by virtue of this section; but

(b) the compensator nevertheless makes that deduction and payment, he shall be treated for all purposes as if the liability had remained enforceable.

(3) Where the compensator, in reliance on this section, does not make the relevant deduction and payment, then:

(a) he shall within 14 days of the default date give the Secretary of State notice of that fact together with such other particulars as may be prescribed; and

(b) in determining the amount of the relevant deduction and payment to be made in connection with any subsequent compensation payment made by the same or any other compensator, the amount which, apart from this section, would have fallen to be deducted and paid by him shall continue to form part of the total benefit and shall not be treated as if it had been paid.

(4) If, in the opinion of the Secretary of State, circumstances have arisen which adversely affect normal methods of communication:

(a) he may by order provide that no liability shall become unenforceable by virtue of this section during a specified period not exceeding three months; and

(b) he may continue any such order in force for further periods not exceeding three months at a time.

(5) In this section, 'the default date' means the date on which the time limit mentioned in subsection (1)(c) above expires.

Review of certificates of total benefit

97(1) The Secretary of State may review any certificate of total benefit if he is satisfied that it was issued in ignorance of, or was based on a mistake as to, some material fact or that a mistake (whether in computation or otherwise) has occurred in its preparation.

(2) On any such review the Secretary of State may either:

(a) confirm the certificate; or

(b) issue a fresh certificate continuing such variations as he considers appropriate, but he shall not so vary the certificate as to increase the total benefit.

(3) In any case where:

(a) one or more relevant payments have been made; and

(b) in consequence of a review under this section, it appears that the aggregate amount so paid exceeds the amount that ought to have been paid, the Secretary of State shall pay the intended recipient an amount equal to the excess.

Appeals

98(1) An appeal shall lie in accordance with this section against any certificate of total benefit at the instance of the compensator, the victim or the intended recipient, on the ground:

(a) that any amount, rate or period specified in the certificate is incorrect; or

(b) that benefit paid or payable otherwise than in consequence of the accident, injury or disease in question has been brought into account.

(2) No appeal shall be brought under this section until:

(a) the claim giving rise to the compensation payment has been finally disposed of; and

(b) the relevant payment, or where more than one such payment may fall to be made, the final relevant payment, has been made.

(3) Notwithstanding subsection (2) above, where:

(a) an award of damages ('provisional damages') has been made under or by virtue of:

(i) section 32A(2)(a) Supreme Court Act 1981;

(ii) (applies to Scotland only); or

(iii)section 51(2)(a) County Courts Act 1984; and

(b) the relevant payment or, where more than one such payment falls to be made, the final relevant payment in relation to the provisional damages so awarded has been made, an appeal may be brought under this section against any certificate of total benefit by reference to which the amount of that relevant payment, or any of those relevant payments, was made.

(4) Regulations may make provision:

(a) as to the manner in which, and the time within which, appears under this section are to be brought; and

(b) for the purpose of enabling any such appeal to be treated as an application for review under s 97 above, and regulations under paragraph (b) above may, in particular, provide that the circumstances in which such a review may be carried out shall not be restricted to those specified in s 97 above.

(5) If any of the medical questions arises for determination on an appeal under this section, the Secretary of State shall refer that question to a medical appeal tribunal, whose determination shall be binding, for the purposes of the appeal,

on any social security appeal tribunal to whom a question is referred under subsection (7) below.

(6) A medical appeal tribunal, in determining any of the medical questions, shall take into account any decision of any court relating to the same, or any similar, issue arising in connection with the accident, injury or disease in question.

(7) If any question concerning any amount, rate or period specified in the certificate of total benefit arises for determination on an appeal under this section, the Secretary of State shall refer that question to a social security appeal tribunal, but where any medical questions arising on the appeal have been referred to a medical appeal tribunal:

(a) he shall not refer any question to the social security appeal tribunal until he has received the determination of the medical appeal tribunal on the questions referred to them; and

(b) he shall notify the social security appeal tribunal of the determinations of the medical appeal tribunal.

(8) On a reference under subsection (7) above a social security appeal tribunal may either:

(a) confirm the amounts, rate and periods specified in the certificate of total benefit; or

(b) specify any increases, reductions or other variations which are to be made on the issue of the fresh certificate under subsection (9) below.

(9) When the Secretary of State has received the determinations of the tribunals on the questions referred to them under subsections (5) and (7) above, he shall in accordance with those determinations either:

(a) confirm the certificate against which the appeal was brought; or

(b) issue a fresh certificate.

(10) Regulations may make provision with respect to the procedure for the reference under this section of questions to medical appeal tribunals or social security appeal tribunals.

(11) An appeal shall lie to a Commissioner at the instance of the Secretary of State, the compensator, the victim or the intended recipient from a decision of a medical appeal tribunal or a social security appeal tribunal under this section on the ground that the decision was erroneous in point of law; and for the purposes of appeals under this subsection:

(a) section 23(7)–(10) above shall apply in relation to an appeal from the decision of a social security appeal tribunal; and

(b) section 48(3) above shall apply in relation to an appeal from the decision of a medical appeal tribunal.

(12) In this section, 'the medical questions' means:

(a) any question whether, as a result of a particular occurrence, the victim suffered an injury, sickness or disease;

(b) any question as to the period for which the victim suffered any injury, sickness or disease.

CIVIL EVIDENCE ACT 1995

Admissibility of hearsay evidence

1(1) In civil proceedings evidence shall not be excluded on the ground that it is hearsay.

(2) In this Act:

(a) 'hearsay' means a statement made otherwise than by a person while giving oral evidence in the proceedings which is tendered as evidence of the matters stated; and

(b) references to hearsay include hearsay of whatever degree.

(3) Nothing in this Act affects the admissibility of evidence admissible apart from this section.

(4) The provisions of ss 2–6 (safeguards and supplementary provisions relating to hearsay evidence) do not apply in relation to hearsay evidence admissible apart from this section, notwithstanding that it may also be admissible by virtue of this section.

Notice of proposal to adduce hearsay evidence

2(1) A party proposing to adduce hearsay evidence in civil proceedings shall, subject to the following provisions of this section, give to the other party or parties to the proceedings:

(a) such notice (if any) of that fact; and

(b) on request, such particulars of or relating to the evidence,

as is reasonable and practicable in the circumstances for the purpose of enabling him or them to deal with any matters arising from its being hearsay.

(2) Provision may be made by rules of court:

(a) specifying classes of proceedings or evidence in relation to which subsection (1) does not apply; and

(b) as to the manner in which (including the time within which) the duties imposed by that subsection are to be complied with in the cases where it does apply.

(3) Subsection (1) may also be excluded by agreement of the parties; and compliance with the duty to give notice may in any case be waived by the person to whom notice is required to be given.

(4) A failure to comply with subsection (1), or with rules under subsection (2)(b), does not affect the admissibility of the evidence but may be taken into account by the court:

(a) in considering the exercise of its powers with respect to the course of proceedings and costs; and

(b) as a matter adversely affecting the weight to be given to the evidence in accordance with s 4.

Power to call witness for cross-examination on hearsay statement

3 Rules of court may provide that where a party to civil proceedings adduces hearsay evidence of a statement made by a person and does not call that person

as a witness, any other party to the proceedings may, with the leave of the court, call that person as a witness and cross-examine him on the statement as if he had been called by the first-mentioned party and as if the hearsay statement were his evidence-in-chief.

Considerations relevant to weighing of hearsay evidence

4(1) In estimating the weight (if any) to be given to hearsay evidence in civil proceedings the court shall have regard to any circumstances from which any inference can reasonably be drawn as to the reliability or otherwise of the evidence.

(2) Regard may be had, in particular, to the following:

(a) whether it would have been reasonable and practicable for the party by whom the evidence was adduced to have produced the maker of the original statement as a witness;

(b) whether the original statement was made contemporaneously with the occurrence or existence of the matters stated;

(c) whether the evidence involves multiple hearsay;

(d) whether any person involved had any motive to conceal or misrepresent matters;

(e) whether the original statement was an edited account, or was made in collaboration with another or for a particular purpose;

(f) whether the circumstances in which the evidence is adduced as hearsay are such as to suggest an attempt to prevent proper evaluation of its weight.

Competence and credibility

5(1) Hearsay evidence shall not be admitted in civil proceedings if or to the extent that it is shown to consist of, or to be proved by means of, a statement made by a person who at the time he made the statement was not competent as a witness.

For this purpose, 'not competent as a witness' means suffering from such mental or physical infirmity, or lack of understanding, as would render a person incompetent as a witness in civil proceedings; but a child shall be treated as competent as a witness if he satisfied the requirements of s 96(2)(a) and (b) Children Act 1989 (conditions for reception of unsworn evidence of child).

(2) Where in civil proceedings hearsay evidence is adduced and the maker of the original statement, or of any statement relied upon to prove another statement, is not called as a witness:

(a) evidence which if he had been so called would be admissible for the purpose of attacking or supporting his credibility as a witness is admissible for that purpose in the proceedings; and

(b) evidence tending to prove that, whether before or after he made the statement, he made any other statement inconsistent with it is admissible for the purpose of showing that he had contradicted himself.

Provided that evidence may not be given of any matter of which if he had been called as a witness and had denied that matter in cross-examination, evidence could not have been adduced by the cross-examining party.

Previous statements of witnesses

6(1) Subject as follows, the provisions of this Act as to hearsay evidence in civil proceedings apply equally (but with any necessary modifications) in relation to a previous statement made by a person called as a witness in the proceedings.

(2) A party who has called or intends to call a person as a witness in civil proceedings may not in those proceedings adduce evidence of a previous statement made by that person, except:

(a) with the leave of the court; or

(b) for the purpose of rebutting a suggestion that his evidence has been fabricated.

This shall not be construed as preventing a witness statement(that is, a written statement or oral evidence which a party to the proceedings intends to lead) from being adopted by a witness in giving evidence or treated as his evidence.

(3) Where in the case of civil proceedings ss 3, 4 or 5 Criminal Procedure Act 1865 applies, which make provision as to:

(a) how far a witness may be discredited by the party producing him;

(b) the proof of contradictory statements made by a witness; and

(c) cross-examination as to previous statements in writing,

this Act does not authorise the adducing of evidence of a previous inconsistent or contradictory statement otherwise than in accordance with those sections.

This is without prejudice to any provision made by rules of court under s 3 above (power to call witness for cross-examination on hearsay statement).

(4) Nothing in this Act affects any of the rules of law as the circumstances in which, where a person called as a witness in civil proceedings is cross-examined on a document used by him to refresh his memory, that document may be made evidence in the proceedings.

(5) Nothing in this section shall be construed as preventing a statement of any description referred to above from being admissible by virtue of s 1 as evidence of the matters stated.

Evidence formerly admissible at common law

7(1) The common law rule effectively preserved by ss 9(1) and (2)(a) Civil Evidence Act 1968 (admissibility of admissions adverse to a party) is superseded by the provisions of this Act.

(2) The common law rules effectively preserved by ss 9(1) and (2)(b)–(d) Civil Evidence Act 1968, that is any rule of law whereby in civil proceedings:

(a) published works dealing with matters of a public nature (for example, histories, scientific works, dictionaries and maps) are admissible as evidence of facts of a public nature stated in them;

(b) public documents (for example, public registers, and returns made under public authority with respect to matters of public interest) are admissible as evidence of facts stated in them; or

(c) records (for example, the records of certain courts, treaties, Crown grants, pardons and commissions) are admissible as evidence of facts stated in them,

shall continue to have effect.

(3) The common law rules effectively preserved by ss 9(3) and (4) Civil Evidence Act 1968, that is, any rule of law whereby in civil proceedings:

(a) evidence of a person's reputation is admissible for the purpose of proving his good or bad character; or

(b) evidence of reputation or family tradition is admissible:

(i) for the purpose of proving or disproving pedigree or the existence of a marriage; or

(ii) for the purpose of proving or disproving the existence of any public or general right or of identifying any person or thing,

shall continue to have effect in so far as they authorise the court to treat such evidence as proving or disproving that matter.

Where any such rule applies, reputation or family tradition shall be treated for the purposes of this Act as a fact and not as a statement or multiplicity of statements about the matter in question.

(4) The words in which a rule of law mentioned in this section is described are intended only to identify the rule and shall not be construed as altering it in any way.

Proof of statements contained in documents

8(1) Where a statement contained in a document is admissible as evidence in civil proceedings, it may be proved:

(a) by the production of that document; or

(b) whether or not that document is still in existence, by the production of a copy of that document or of the material part of it,

authenticated in such manner as the court may approve.

(2) It is immaterial for this purpose how many removes there are between a copy and the original.

Proof of records of business or public authority

9(1) A document which is shown to form part of the records of a business or public authority may be received in evidence in civil proceedings without further proof.

(2) A document shall be taken to form part of the records of a business or public authority if there is produced to the court a certificate to that effect signed by an officer of the business or authority to which the records belong.

For this purpose:

(a) a document purporting to be a certificate signed by an officer of a business or public authority shall be deemed to have been duly given by such an officer and signed by him; and

(b) a certificate shall be treated as signed by a person if it purports to bear a facsimile of his signature.

(3) The absence of an entry in the records of a business of public authority may be proved in civil proceedings by affidavit of an officer of the business or authority to which the records belong.

(4) In this section:

'records' means records in whatever form;

'business' includes any activity regularly carried on over a period of time, whether for profit or not, by any body (whether corporate or not) or by an individual;

'officer' includes any person occupying a responsible position in relation to the relevant activities of the business or public authority or in relation to its records; and

'public authority' includes any public or statutory undertaking, any government department and any person holding office under Her Majesty.

(5) The court may, having regard to the circumstances of the case, direct that all or any of the above provisions of this section do not apply in relation to a particular document or record, or description of documents or records.

Admissibility and proof of Ogden Tables

10(1) The actuarial tables (together with explanatory notes) for use in personal injury and fatal accident cases issued from time to time by the Government Actuary's Department are admissible in evidence for the purpose of assessing, in an action for personal injury, the sum to be awarded as general damages for future pecuniary loss.

(2) They may be proved by the production of a copy published by Her Majesty's Stationery Office.

(3) For the purposes of this section:

(a) 'personal injury' includes any disease and any impairment of a person's physical or mental condition; and

(b) 'action for personal injury' includes an action brought by virtue of the Law Reform (Miscellaneous Provisions) Act 1934 or the Fatal Accidents Act 1976.

Meaning of 'civil proceedings'

11 In this Act, 'civil proceeding' means civil proceedings, before any tribunal, in relation to which the strict rules of evidence apply, whether as a matter of law or by agreement of the parties.

References to 'the court' and 'rules of court' shall be construed accordingly.

Provisions as to rules of court

12(1) Any power to make rules of court regulating the practice or procedure of the court in relation to civil proceedings includes power to make such provision as may be necessary or expedient for carrying into effect the provisions of this Act.

(2) Any rules of court made for the purposes of this Act as it applies in relation to proceedings in the High Court apply, except in so far as their operation is excluded by agreement, to arbitration proceedings to which this Act applies, subject to such modifications as may be appropriate.

Any question arising as to what modifications are appropriate shall be determined in default of agreement by the arbitrator or umpire as the case may be.

Interpretation

13 In this Act:

'civil proceedings' has the meaning given by s 11 and 'court' and 'rules of court' shall be construed in accordance with that section;

'document' means anything in which information of any description is recorded, and 'copy', in relation to a document, means anything onto which information recorded in the document has been copied, by whatever means and whether directly or indirectly;

'hearsay' shall be construed in accordance with s 1(2);

'oral evidence' includes evidence which, by reason of a defect of speech or hearing, a person called as a witness gives in writing or by signs;

'the original statement', in relation to hearsay evidence, means the underlying statement (if any) by:

(a) in the case of evidence of fact, a person having personal knowledge of that fact; or

(b) in the case of evidence of opinion, the person whose opinion it is; and

'statement' means any representation of fact or opinion, however made.

Savings

14(1) Nothing in this Act affects the exclusion of evidence on grounds other than that it is hearsay.

This applies whether the evidence falls to be excluded in pursuance of any enactment or rule of law, for failure to comply with rules of court or an order of the court, or otherwise.

(2) Nothing in this Act affects the proof of documents by means other than those specified in ss 8 or 9.

(3) Nothing in this Act affects the operation of the following enactments:

(a) section 2 Documentary Evidence Act 1868 (mode of proving certain official documents);

(b) section 2 Documentary Evidence Act 1882 (documents printed under the superintendence of Stationery Office);

(c) section 1 Evidence (Colonial Statutes) Act 1907 (proof of statutes of certain legislatures);

(d) section 1 Evidence (Foreign, Dominion and Colonial Documents) Act 1933 (proof and effect of registers and official certificates of certain countries);

(e) section 5 Oaths and Evidence (Overseas Authorities and Countries) Act 1963 (provision in respect of public registers of other countries).

Consequential amendments and repeals

15(1) The enactments specified in Schedule 1 are amended in accordance with that Schedule, the amendments being consequential on the provisions of this Act.

(2) The enactments specified in Schedule 2 are repealed to the extent specified.

Short title, commencement and extent

16(1) This Act may be cited as the Civil Evidence Act 1995.

(2) The provisions of this Act come into force on such day as the Lord Chancellor may appoint by order made by statutory instrument, and different days may be appointed for different provisions and for different purposes.

(3) An order under subsection (2) may contain such transitional provisions as appear to the Lord Chancellor to be appropriate; and subject to any such provision, the provisions of this Act shall not apply in relation to proceedings begun before commencement.

(4) This Act extends to England and Wales.

(5) Section 10 (admissibility and proof of Ogden tables) also extends to Northern Ireland.

As it extends to Northern Ireland, the following shall be substituted for subsection (3)(b):

(b) 'action for personal injury' includes an action brought by virtue of the Law Reform (Miscellaneous Provisions) (Northern Ireland) Act 1937 or the Fatal Accidents (Northern Ireland) Order 1977.

(6) The provisions of Schedules 1 and 2 (consequential amendments and repeals) have the same extent as the enactment's respectively amended or repealed.

MEDICAL (PROFESSIONAL PERFORMANCE) ACT 1995

Professional performance

1 After s 36 Medical Act 1983 (professional misconduct and criminal offences), there shall be inserted:

36A(1) Where the standard of professional performance of a fully registered person is found by the Committee on Professional Performance to have been seriously deficient, the Committee shall direct:

(a) that his registration in the register shall be suspended (that is to say, shall not have effect) during such period not exceeding 12 months as may be specified in the direction; or

(b) that his registration shall be conditional on his compliance, during such period not exceeding three years as may be specified in the direction, with the requirements so specified.

APPENDIX B

STATUTORY INSTRUMENTS

CIVIL LEGAL AID (GENERAL) REGULATIONS 1989 SI 1989/339

Exemptions from the statutory charge

94 The charge created by s 16(6) of the Act shall not apply to:

(a) any interim payment made in accordance with an order made under Order 29, rule 11 or 12 of the Rules of the Supreme Court 1965, or Order 13, rule 12 of the County Court Rules 1981, or in accordance with an agreement having the same effect as such an order;

CIVIL LEGAL AID (ASSESSMENT OF RESOURCES) REGULATIONS 1989 SI 1989/338
Schedule 3

14B In computing the amount of capital of the person concerned there shall be wholly disregarded any capital payment received from any source which is made in relation to the incident giving rise to the dispute in respect of which the legal aid application has been made.

SOCIAL SECURITY (RECOUPMENT) REGULATIONS 1990 SI 1990/322

PART I

General

Citation, commencement and interpretation

1(1) These Regulations may be cited as the Social Security (Recoupment) Regulations 1990 and shall come into force:

for the purposes of this regulation and regulations 5, 6, 7, 8 and 16 on 2 April 1990;

for the purposes of regulations 2, 9, 10, 13, and 15 on 9 July 1990; and for all other purposes on 3 September 1990.

(2) In these Regulations:

'the 1989 Act' means the Social Security Act 1989;

'Schedule 4' means Schedule 4 to the 1989 Act; and

'the Compensation Recovery Unit' means the Compensation Recovery Unit of the Department of Social Security at Reyrolle Building, Hebburn, Tyne & Wear.

(3) In these Regulations, unless the context otherwise requires, a reference:

(a) to a numbered regulation is to the regulation in these Regulations bearing that number; and

(b) in a regulation to a numbered paragraph is to the paragraph in that regulation bearing that number.

PART II

Benefits and payments

Relevant benefits

2(1) The following benefits are relevant benefits for the purposes of s 22 of the 1989 Act:

(a) attendance allowance,

(b) disablement benefit (including disablement pensions) payable in accordance with ss 57–63 of the Principal Act,

(c) family credit,

(d) income support, under Part II of the Social Security Act 1986, including personal expenses addition, special transitional additions and transitional addition as defined in the Income Support (Transitional) Regulations 1987,

(e) invalidity pension and allowance,

(f) mobility allowance,

(g) benefits payable under schemes made under the Old Cases Act,

(h) reduced earnings allowance,

(i) retirement allowance,

(j) severe disablement allowance,

(k) sickness benefit,

(l) statutory sick pay, subject to paragraph (3) below,

(m)unemployment benefit,

(ma) disability living allowance,

(mb) disability working allowance,

(n) any increase in any of the benefits mentioned above payable in accordance with the Social Security Acts 1975–1989 or the Old Cases Act or with any regulations, Order in Council, order or scheme made thereunder.

(2) In paragraph (1), references to, respectively, invalidity pension and allowance, severe disablement allowance, sickness benefit and unemployment benefit include also a reference to any income support paid with each of those benefits on the same instrument of payment, and for this purpose, income support includes personal expenses addition, special transitional additions and transitional addition as defined in the Income Support (Transitional) Regulations 1987.

(3) The amount of statutory sick pay for the purposes of s 22 of the 1989 Act (recovery of sums equivalent to benefit from compensation payments) is, in so far as it relates to any liability an employer may have to make a payment of statutory sick pay to an employee of his in respect of a day of incapacity for

work falling on or after 6 April 1991, 80% of the payment of statutory sick pay which the employer is liable to make.

Small payments

3(1) A person shall be exempted from liability to make the relevant deduction or the relevant payment where the amount of the compensation payment in question, or the aggregate amount of two or more connected compensation payments, does not exceed £2,500.

(2) Where an amount has been deducted and paid to the Secretary of State which, by virtue of paragraph (1), ought not to have been so deducted and paid, the Secretary of State:

(a) Where he is satisfied that the whole of the amount ought to have been paid to the intended recipient, shall pay the whole of that amount to that person; or

(b) Where he is not so satisfied, shall either pay the whole of the amount to the compensator or pay to the compensator that part of the amount which he would have been entitled to retain and to the intended recipient that part which he would have been entitled to receive had the amount not been so deducted and paid.

Exempt payments

4 The following payments shall be exempt payments for the purposes of s 22 of the 1989 Act:

(a) any payment made out of property held for the purpose of the charitable trust called the Macfarlane Trust and established partly out of funds provided by the Secretary of State to the Haemophilia Society for the relief of poverty or distress among those suffering from haemophilia;

(b) any compensation payment made by British Coal in accordance with the NCB Pneumoconiosis Compensation Scheme set out in the Schedule to an agreement made on the 13 September 1974 between the National Coal Board, the National Union of Mine Workers, the National Association of Colliery Overmen Deputies and Shot-firers and the British Association of Colliery Management;

(c) any payment made to the victim in respect of sensorineural hearing loss where the loss is less than 50 db in one or both ears; and

(d) any contractual amount paid to an employee or employer of his in respect of a day of incapacity for work;

(e) any payment made from the Macfarlane (Special Payments) Trust established on 29 January 1990 partly out of funds provided by the Secretary of State for the Benefit of certain persons suffering from haemophilia; and

(ee) any payment made from the Macfarlane (Special Payments) (No 2) Trust established on 3 May 1991 partly out of funds provided by the Secretary of State, for benefit of certain persons suffering from haemophilia and other beneficiaries;

(f) any payment made under the National Health Service (Injury Benefits) Regulations 1974 or the National Health Service (Scotland) (Injury Benefits) Regulations 1974;

(g) any payment made by or on behalf of the Secretary of State for the benefit of persons eligible for payment in accordance with the provisions of a scheme established by him on 24 April 1992 or, in Scotland on 10 April 1992.

PART III

Administration and adjudication

Information to be provided by compensator

5 A person who is, or is alleged to be, liable in respect of an accident, injury or disease, or any person acting on his behalf, shall furnish the Secretary of State with the following information in respect of that accident, injury or disease:

(a) the full name and the address of any person seeking compensation or in respect of whom compensation is sought;

(b) where known the date of birth or the national insurance number of that person, or both if both are known;

(c) where the liability arises, or is alleged to arise, in respect of:

    (i) an accident or injury, the date of the accident or injury; or

    (ii) a disease, the date the disease was diagnosed;

(d) the nature of the accident, injury or disease; and

(e) where known, whether at the time of the accident or injury or diagnosis of the disease, the person was employed under contract of service, and if he was, the name and address of his employer at that time and the person's payroll number.

Information to be provided by victim

6(1) A person who claims (whether on behalf of himself or another) a relevant benefit or has been in receipt of such a benefit, shall furnish the Secretary of State with such of the following information relating to any accident, injury or disease the victim has suffered as the Secretary of State requests:

(a) whether the accident, injury or disease resulted from any action taken by another person, or from any failure of another person to act, and if so, the full name and address of that other person;

(b) whether he has claimed or may claim a compensation payment, and if so, the full name and the address of the person against whom the claim was or may be made;

(c) the amount of any compensation payment and the date on which it was made;

(d) the relevant benefit claimed, the date from which benefit was first claimed and the amount of benefit received in the period beginning with that date and ending with the date the information is sent;

(e) in the case of a person who has received or is entitled to receive statutory sick pay during the relevant period, the name and address of any employer who is or was liable to make these payments to him during the relevant period and the dates the employment with that employer began and ended; and

(f) any changes in the medical diagnosis relating to the condition arising from the accident, injury or disease.

(2) In this regulation, 'person' includes a deceased person's personal representative.

Information to be provided by employer

7 Any person:

(a) who is the employer of a person who suffers or has suffered an accident, injury or disease; or

(b) who has been an employer of such a person at any time during the relevant period, shall furnish the Secretary of State with such of the following information relating to the payment of statutory sick pay as the Secretary of State requests:

(i) the amount of any statutory sick pay he is liable to pay or has paid to the victim since the first day of the relevant period;

(ii) the date the liability first arose and the rate at which statutory sick pay is or was payable;

(iii) the date that such liability terminated or is likely to terminate; and

(iv) the causes of the incapacity for work during any periods of entitlement to statutory sick pay.

Sending information

8 A person who furnishes the Secretary of State with information shall do so by sending it in writing to the Compensation Recovery Unit not later than 14 days after:

(a) where he is a person to whom regulation 5 applies, the date he receives a claim for compensation from the victim in respect of the accident, injury or disease;

(b) where he is a person to whom regulation 6 or 7 applies, the date the Secretary of State requests the information from him.

Particulars to be stated before liability of compensator becomes unenforceable

9 The following particulars are prescribed for the purposes of paragraph 15(1)(a)(i) of Schedule 4 (particulars to be stated before liability of compensator becomes unenforceable):

(a) the full name of the victim together with his address, and either his date of birth or national insurance number or both if both are known;

(b) unless already furnished to the Secretary of State in accordance with regulation 5:

(i) where the liability arises or is alleged to arise in respect of an accident or injury, the date of that accident or injury, or where it arises or is alleged to arise in respect of a disease, the date the disease was diagnosed;

(ii)   the nature of the accident, injury or disease; and

(iii)   where known, whether at the time of the accident or injury or the diagnosis of the disease the victim was employed under a contract of service, and if he was, the name and address of his employer at that time and the person's payroll number.

Acknowledgment of compensator's request

10 Where the compensator requests a certificate of total benefit in accordance with paragraph 15(1)(a) of Schedule 4, the Secretary of State shall send to the compensator, as soon as reasonably practicable, a written acknowledgment of the receipt of the request stating the day on which the request was received.

Appeals

11(1) Any appeal against a certificate of total benefit shall be in writing and shall be made by sending or delivering it to the Compensation Recovery Unit:

(a)   not later than three months after the date the compensator made the relevant payment; or

(b)   where the certificate was reviewed by the Secretary of State in accordance with regulation 13 not later than three months from the date the certificate is confirmed, or as the case may be, a fresh certificate issued.

(2) Any appeal under this regulation shall contain particulars of the grounds on which it is made.

(3) Where an earlier compensation payment has been made and subsequently one or more later payments are made to or in respect of the same victim in respect of the same accident, injury or disease (whether by the same or an other compensator), the date referred to in paragraph (1)(a) is the date of the last of those later payments.

(4) The time for making an appeal may be extended for special reasons by the chairman of the tribunal to which the appeal is referred, even though the time limit may have already expired.

(5) Any application for an extension of time under paragraph (4) shall be made in writing and shall be determined by the chairman.

(6) An application under paragraph (4) for an extension of time which has been refused shall not be renewed.

(7) Where it appears to the chairman of the tribunal to whom the appeal was referred that the appeal gives insufficient particulars to enable the question at issue to be determined, he may require the person making the appeal to furnish such further particulars as may reasonably be required.

Withdrawal of appeal

12 A person who has made an appeal under regulation 11 may withdraw that appeal:

(a)   before the hearing begins by giving notice in writing of his intention to withdraw the appeal to the Appeal Tribunal to whom the appeal was made and with the consent in writing of the Secretary of State;

(b) after the hearing has begun and before the determination is made, with the leave of the chairman of the Appeal Tribunal.

Review

13 The Secretary of State may treat any appeal as an application for review under paragraph 16 of Schedule 4, notwithstanding that the certificate of total benefit was not issued in ignorance of or based on a mistake as to some material fact or that a mistake (whether in computation or otherwise) has not occurred in its preparation.

PART IV

Miscellaneous matters

Benefits exceed compensation

14 Where, after the relevant deduction from the compensation payment, there is no balance remaining for payment to the intended recipient, any reference in Schedule 4 to the making of the compensation payment shall be construed as a reference to the acceptance by the intended recipient of an offer in respect of his claim against the compensator.

Foreign compensators

15 Where immediately before the making of a compensation payment, the compensator is not resident and does not have a place of business in Great Britain, than these regulations shall be modified in their application to the intended recipient in accordance with the following provisions:

(a) regulation 5 shall apply with the additional requirement that the intended recipient supply the Secretary of State with the name of the compensator and his address; and

(b) regulation 9 shall apply with the additional requirement that he supply the Secretary of State with details of:

(i) the amount of the compensation paid to him; and

(ii) whether that payment represents the final payment in respect of the accident, injury or disease.

Transitional provisions and saving

16(1) A compensator who may make a compensation payment after 2 September 1990 in respect of an accident, injury or disease which occurred on or after 1 January 1989 but before 2 April 1990, shall so inform the Secretary of State as soon as reasonably practicable.

(2) Where an accident or injury occurred or a disease was diagnosed before 1 January 1989 and a compensation payment in respect of that accident, injury or disease is or may be made after 2 September 1990, then:

(a) the provisions of s 2 Law Reform (Personal Injuries) Act 1948 shall apply to that payment as though the amendment made to it in paragraph 22 of Schedule 4 to the 1989 Act, had not been enacted; and

(b) the payment shall be calculated as if s 22(6) of that Act had not been enacted.

THE NATIONAL HEALTH SERVICE (GENERAL MEDICAL SERVICES) REGULATIONS SI 1992 1992/635

SCHEDULE 2: TERMS OF SERVICE FOR DOCTORS (Regulation 3(2))

General

3 Where a decision whether any, and if so what, action is to be taken under these terms of service requires the exercise of professional judgment, a doctor shall not, in reaching that decision, be expected to exercise a higher degree of skill, knowledge and care than:

(a) in the case of a doctor providing child health surveillance services under regulation 28, maternity medical services under regulation 31 or minor surgery services under regulation 33, that which any general practitioner included in the child health surveillance list, the obstetric list or, as the case may be, the minor surgery list may reasonably be expected to exercise; and

(b) in any other case, that which general practitioners as a class may reasonably be expected to exercise.

A doctor's patients

4(1) Subject to sub-paragraph (2) and to paragraphs 9,10 and 11, a doctor's patients are:

(a) persons who are recorded by the FHSA as being on his list;

(b) persons whom he has accepted or agreed to accept on his list, whether or not notification of that acceptance has been received by the FHSA, and who have not been notified to him by the FHSA as having ceased to be on his list;

(c) for the limited period specified in sub-paragraph (4), persons whom he has refused to accept;

(d) persons who have been assigned to him under regulation 21;

(e) for the limited period specified in sub-paragraph (5), persons in respect of whom he has been notified that an application has been made for assignment to him in a case to which regulation 21(3)(b) applies;

(f) persons whom he has accepted as temporary residents;

(g) in respect of services under paragraph 8, persons to whom he has agreed to provide those services;

(h) persons to whom he may be requested to give treatment which is immediately required owing to an accident or other emergency at any place in his practice are, provided that:

(i) he is not, at the time of the request, relieved of liability to give treatment under paragraph 5; and

(ii) he is not, at the time of the request, relieved, under paragraph 19(2), of his obligation to give treatment personally; and

    (iii) he is available to provide such treatment;

    (iv) and any persons by whom he is requested, and agrees, to give treatment which is immediately required owing to an accident or other emergency at any place in the locality of any FHSA in whose medical list he is included, provided there is no doctor who, at the time of the request, is under an obligation otherwise than under this head to give treatment to that person, or there is such a doctor but, after being requested to attend, he is unable to attend and give treatment immediately required;

(i) persons in relation to whom he is acting as deputy for another doctor under these terms of service;

(j) during the period of an appointment under regulation 25, persons whom he has been appointed to treat temporarily;

(k) in respect of child health surveillance services, contraceptive services, maternity medical services, or minor surgery services persons for whom he has undertaken to provide such services; and

(l) during the hours arranged with the FHSA, any person whose own doctor has been relieved of responsibility during those hours under paragraph 19 and for whom he has accepted responsibility under that paragraph.

(2) Except in a case to which head (h), (i) or (j) of sub-paragraph (l) applies, no person shall be a patient for the purposes of that sub-paragraph if the doctor has been notified by the FHSA that he is no longer responsible for the treatment of that person.

(3) Where a person applies to a doctor for treatment and claims to be on that doctor's list, but fails to produce his medical card on request and the doctor has reasonable doubts about that person's claim, the doctor shall give any necessary treatment and shall be entitled to demand and accept a fee accordingly under paragraph 38(f), subject to the provision for repayment contained in paragraph 39.

(4) Where a doctor refuses to accept for inclusion on his list a person who lives in his practice area and who is not on the list of another doctor practising in that area, or refuses to accept as a temporary resident a person to whom regulation 26 applies, he shall on request give that person any immediately necessary treatment for one period not exceeding 14 days from the date when that person was refused acceptance or until that person has been accepted by or assigned to another doctor, whichever period is the shorter.

(5) Where the FHSA has notified a doctor that it is applying for the Secretary of State's consent under regulation 21(3)(b), the doctor shall give the person proposed for assignment any immediately necessary treatment until the FHSA has notified him that:

(a) the Secretary of State has determined whether or not the person is to be assigned to that doctor; and

(b) either the person has been accepted by, or assigned to, another doctor or another doctor has been notified that an application has been made, in a case to which regulation 21(3)(b) applies, to assign that person to him.

5 A doctor who is elderly or infirm or who has been exempted by the FHSA under regulation 21(11) from the liability to have persons assigned to him, may be relieved by the FHSA of any liability to give treatment which is immediately required owing to an accident or other emergency between 7 pm on weekdays and 8 am on the following morning and between 1 pm on Saturday and 8 am on the following Monday to persons who are neither:

(a) on his list; nor

(b) temporary residents for whom he is responsible; nor

(c) accepted by him for the provision of maternity medical services.

Acceptance of patients

6(1) Subject to sub-paragraph (2), a doctor may agree to accept a person on his list if the person is eligible to be accepted by him.

(2) Where a doctor is responsible for treating the patients of another doctor whose name has been removed from the medical list, he may not consent to the transfer of any of those patients under regulation 22 to his own list or to that of his partner.

(3) Where a doctor has agreed to accept a person on his list, he shall, within 14 days of receiving this person's medical card or form of application, or as soon after the expiry of that period as it practicable:

(a) sign the medical card or, as the case may be, the form of application; and

(b) send it to the FHSA.

(4) Where, for the purposes of sub-paragraph (3), any person signs a medical card or a form of application on behalf of a doctor he shall, in addition to his own signature, specify the name of the doctor on whose behalf he is signing.

7 A doctor may:

(a) undertake to provide contraceptive services to a women who has applied to him in accordance with regulation 29;

(b) accept as a temporary resident a person who has applied to him in accordance with regulation 26(1);

(c) undertake to provide maternity medical services to a woman who has made an arrangement with him in accordance with regulation 31(2).

8 Notwithstanding that the person concerned is not on his list, a doctor may:

(a) take a cervical smear from a woman who would be eligible for acceptance by him as a temporary resident or for whom he has undertaken to provide maternity medical services or contraceptive services; and

(b) vaccinate or immunise a person who would be eligible for acceptance by him as a temporary resident.

Termination of responsibility for patients

9(1) A doctor may have any person removed from his list and shall notify the FHSA in writing that he wishes to have a person removed from his list and, subject to sub-paragraph (2), the removal shall take effect:

(a) on the date on which the person is accepted by or assigned to another doctor; or

(b) on the eighth day after the FHSA receives the notice,

whichever is the sooner.

(2) Where, at the date when the removal would take effect under sub-paragraph (1), the doctor is treating the person at intervals of less than seven days, the doctor shall inform the FHSA in writing of the fact and the removal shall take effect:

(a) on the eighth day after the FHSA receives notification from the doctor that the person no longer needs such treatment; or

(b) on the date on which the person is accepted by or assigned to another doctor,

whichever is the sooner.

10 Where a doctor informs the FHSA in writing that he wishes to terminate his responsibility for a temporary resident, his responsibility for that person shall crease in accordance with paragraph 9, as if the temporary resident were a person on his list.

11(1) A doctor with whom an arrangement has been made for the provision of any or all of the maternity medical services mentioned in regulation 31(1)(a) may agree with the woman concerned to terminate the arrangement, and in default of agreement the doctor may apply to the FHSA for permission to terminate the arrangement.

(2) On an application under paragraph (1), the FHSA, after considering any representations made by either party and after consulting the Local Medical Committee, may terminate the arrangement.

(3) Where a doctor ceases to provide any or all of the maternity medical services mentioned in regulation 31(1)(a), he shall inform any woman for whom he has arranged to provide such services that he is ceasing to provide them and that she may make a fresh arrangement to receive those services from another doctor.

Services to patients

12(1) Subject to paragraphs 3, 13, and 44, a doctor shall render to his patients all necessary and appropriate personal medical services of the type usually provided by general medical practitioners.

(2) The services which a doctor is required by sub-paragraph (1) to render shall include the following:

(a) giving advice, where appropriate, to a patient in connection with the patient's general health, and in particular about the significance of diet, exercise, the use of tobacco, the consumption of alcohol and the misuse of drugs or solvents;

(b) offering to patients consultations and, where appropriate, physical examinations for the purpose of identifying, or reducing the risk of, disease or injury;

(c) offering to patients, where appropriate, vaccination or immunisation against measles, mumps, rubella, pertussis, poliomyelitis, diphtheria and tetanus;

(d) arranging for the referral of patients, as appropriate, for the provision of any other services under the Act; and

(e) giving advice, as appropriate, to enable patients to avail themselves of services provided by a local social services authority.

(3) A doctor is not required by sub-paragraph (1) or (2):

(a) to provide to any person child health surveillance services, contraceptive services, minor surgery services nor, except in an emergency, maternity medical services, unless he has previously undertaken to the FHSA to provide such services to that person; or

(b) where he is a restricted services principal, to provide any category of general medical services which he has not undertaken to provide.

Provision of services to patients.

13 ...

Newly registered patients

14 ...

Patients not seen within three years

15(1) Subject to sub-paragraph (2), a doctor shall, in addition to and without prejudice to any other obligation under these terms of service, invite each patient on his list who appears to him:

(a) to have attained the age of 16 years but who has not attained the age of 75 years; and

(b) to have neither:

(i) within the preceding three years attended either a consultation with, or a clinic provided by, any doctor in the course of his provision of general medical services; nor

(ii) within the preceding 12 months been offered a consultation pursuant to this sub-paragraph by any doctor,

to participate in a consultation at his practice premises for the purpose of assessing whether he needs to render personal medical service to that patient.

(2) Sub-paragraph (1) shall not apply in the case of a doctor who is a restricted services principal.

(3) When inviting a patient to participate in a consultation pursuant to subparagraph (1) a doctor shall comply with the requirements of paragraph 14(3).

(4) Where a patient agrees to participate in a consultation mentioned in sub-paragraph (1), the doctor shall, in the course of that consultation:

(a) where appropriate, seek details from the patient as to his medical history and, so far as may be relevant to the patient's medical history, as to that of his consanguineous family, in respect of:

(i) illnesses, immunisations, allergies, hereditary disease, medication and tests carried out for breast or cervical cancer;

(ii) social factors (including employment, housing and family circumstances) which may affect his health;

    (iii) factors of his lifestyle (including diet, exercise, use of tobacco, consumption of alcohol, and misuse of drugs or solvents) which may affect his health; and

    (iv) the current state of his health;

(b) offer to undertake a physical examination of the patient, comprising:

    (i)   the measurement of his blood pressure; and

    (ii) the taking of a urine sample and its analysis to identify the presence of albumen and glucose; and

    (iii) the measurement necessary to detect any changes in his body mass;

(c) record, in the patient's medical records, his findings arising out of the details supplied by, and any examination of, the patient under this sub-paragraph;

(d) assess whether and, if so, in what manner and to what extent he should render personal medical services to the patient; and

(e) in so far as it would not, in the opinion of the doctor, be likely to cause serious damage to the physical or mental health of the patient to do so, offer to discuss with the patient the conclusions the doctor has drawn as a result of the consultation as to the state of the patient's health.

(5) In this paragraph, 'body mass' means the figure produced by dividing the number of kilograms in the patient's weight by the square of the number of metres in his height.

Patients aged 75 years and over

16 and 17 ...

Absences, deputies, assistants and partners

18(1) Subject to sub-paragraph (2), a doctor is responsible for ensuring the provision for his patients of the services referred to in paragraph 12 throughout each day during which his name is included in the FHSA's medical list.

(2) A doctor who was, prior to 1 April 1990, relieved by the FHSA of such responsibility in respect of his patients during times approved by the FHSA may continue to enjoy such relief for so long as his name is included in the medical list.

19(1) Subject to the following provisions of this paragraph, a doctor shall give treatment personally.

(2) Subject to sub-paragraphs (3), (5), and (6), a doctor (in this sub-paragraph referred to as 'the patient's doctor') shall be under no obligation to give treatment personally to a patient provided that reasonable steps are taken to ensure the continuity of the patient's treatment, and in those circumstances treatment may be given:

(a) by another doctor acting as a deputy, whether or not he is a partner or assistant of the patient's doctor; or

(b) in the case of treatment which it is clinically reasonable in the circumstances to delegate to someone other than a doctor, by a person whom the doctor has authorised and who he is satisfied is competent to carry out such treatment.

(3) Subject to sub-paragraph (4), in the case of maternity medical services a doctor on the obstetric list shall not arrange for the provision of such services by another doctor unless that doctor is a doctor on the obstetric list or satisfies one or more of the criteria set out in Part 1 of Schedule 5.

(4) Sub-paragraph (3) shall not apply where there has been a summons to an obstetric emergency.

(5) In the case of child health surveillance services, a doctor who has, pursuant to regulation 28, undertaken to provide such services shall not arrange for the provision of such services by:

(a) another doctor unless that doctor is included in a child health surveillance list; or

(b) any other person without the consent of the FHSA.

(6) In the case of minor surgery services, a doctor who has, pursuant to regulation 33, undertaken to provide such services shall not arrange for the provision of such services by:

(a) another doctor unless that doctor is included in a minor surgery list; or

(b) any other person.

(7) In this paragraph, 'a summons to an obstetric emergency' means a summons to the doctor by a midwife or on behalf of the patient to attend when medical attention is required urgently by a woman or her baby during pregnancy, labour or the post-natal period, as defined in regulation 31(7).

20(1) In relation to his obligations under these terms of service, a doctor is responsible for all acts and omissions of:

(a) any doctor acting as his deputy;

(b) any deputising service while acting on his behalf; and

(c) any person employed by, or acting on behalf, of him or such a deputy or deputising service expect where the act or omission is one for which a deputy is responsible under sub-paragraph (2).

(2) Where a doctor whose name is included in the medical list is acting as deputy to anther doctor whose name is also included in the list, the deputy is responsible for:

(a) his own acts and omissions in relation to the obligations under these terms of service of the doctor for whom he acts as deputy; and

(b) the acts and omissions of any person employed by him or acting on his behalf.

21(1) A doctor shall inform the FHSA of any arrangements for the engagement of a deputy on a regular basis unless the deputy:

(a) is an assistant of the doctor, or is a doctor included in the medical list of an FHSA; and

(b) is to carry out the arrangements at the doctor's practice premises.

(2) Where a doctor proposes to be absent form his practice for more that a week, he shall inform the FHSA of the name of any doctor responsible for his practice during his absence.

22(1) Before entering into arrangements with a deputising service for the provision of any deputy, a doctor shall obtain the consent of the FHSA.

(2) In giving its consent, the FHSA may impose such conditions as it considers necessary or expedient to ensure the adequacy of such arrangements.

(3) Before refusing its consent or imposing any such conditions, the FHSA shall consult the Local Medical Committee.

(4) The FHSA may at any time, and shall periodically, review in consultation with the Local Medical Committee any such consent given or conditions imposed in relation to any doctor under this paragraph, and may withdraw such consent or vary such conditions.

(5) A doctor may appeal to the Secretary of State against refusal of consent or the imposition of a condition under this paragraph or against withdrawal of consent or variation of conditions under this paragraph.

(6) An appeal under sub-paragraph (5) shall be made in writing within 30 days of the decision of the FHSA and shall set out the grounds of appeal.

(7) In determining an appeal under sub-paragraph (5) the Secretary of State may substitute for the FHSA's decision such decision and conditions as he thinks fit.

23 A doctor shall take reasonable steps to satisfy himself that a doctor whom he proposes to employ as a deputy or assistant is not disqualified under s 46 of the Act from inclusion in the medical list of the FHSA and he shall not knowingly employ a doctor who is so disqualified.

24(1) A doctor shall inform the FHSA of the name of any assistant he employs and of the termination of such employment, and shall not employ any one or more assistants for a total period of more than three months in any period of 12 months without the consent of the FHSA.

(2) The FHSA shall periodically review and may withdraw any consent given but, before refusing or withdrawing consent, the FHSA shall consult the Local Medical Committee.

(3) The doctor may appeal to the Medical Practices Committee against any refusal or withdrawal of consent.

(4) Any withdrawal of consent under this paragraph shall not have effect until the expiration of period of one month after the date of notification of the withdrawal, but if the doctor appeals to the Medical Practices Committee against the withdrawal and the Medical Practices Committee dismisses the appeal, the withdrawal shall not take effect until after such date as the Committee determines being a date falling not less than one month after the date of such dismissal.

25 A doctor acting as a deputy for another doctor may treat patients at places and at times other than those approved pursuant to paragraph 29 in relation to the doctor for whom he is acting, but when determining the places and times at which he is to provide such treatment, the deputy shall have regard to the convenience of the patients.

26 When issuing any document under these terms of service a deputy or assistant (other than a partner or assistant whose name is included in the medical list) shall, as well as signing the document himself, enter on it the name of the doctor for whom he is acting, if it does not already appear.

Arrangements at practice premises

27 A doctor shall:

    (a) provide proper and sufficient accommodation at his practice premises, having regard to the circumstances of his practice; and

    (b) on receipt of a written request from the FHSA, allow inspection of those premises at a reasonable time by a member or officer of the FHSA or Local Medical Committee or both, authorised by the FHSA for the purpose.

Employees

28(1) A doctor shall, before employing any person to assist him in the provision of general medical services, take reasonable care to satisfy himself that the person in question is both suitably qualified and competent to discharge the duties for which he is to be employed.

(2) When considering the competence and suitability of any person for the purpose of sub-paragraph (1), a doctor shall have regard, in particular, to:

    (a) that person's academic and vocational qualifications;

    (b) that person's training and his experience in employment; and

    (c) any guidance issued by the FHSA pursuant to regulation 39.

(3) A doctor shall afford to each employee reasonable opportunities to undertake appropriate training wit a view to maintaining that employee's competence.

Doctors' availability to patients

29 ...

Doctors' available for only four days a week

30 ...

Practice area

34 ...

Notification of change of place of residence

35 ...

Records

36 ...

Certification

37 ...

Fees

38 ...

Prescribing

43 ...

Practice leaflet

47 ...

Reports to medical officers, etc

48 ...

CONDITIONAL FEE AGREEMENTS ORDER 1995
SI 1995/1674

Citation and commencement

1 This order may be cited as the Conditional Fee Agreements Order 1995 and shall come into force on 5 July 1995.

Specified proceedings

2(1) The proceedings specified for the purpose of s 58(4) Courts and Legal Services Act 1990 (conditional fee agreements in respect of specified proceedings not to be unenforceable) are the following:

(a) proceedings in which there is a claim for damages in respect of personal injuries or in respect of a person's death, and 'personal injuries' includes any disease and any impairment of person's physical or mental condition;

(b) proceedings in England and Wales by a company which is being wound up in England and Wales or Scotland;

(c) proceedings by a company in respect of which an administration order made under Part II of the Insolvency Act 1986 is in force;

(d) proceedings in England and Wales by a person acting in the capacity of:

(i) liquidator of a company which is being wound up in England and Wales or Scotland; or

(ii) trustee of a bankrupt's estate;

(e) proceedings by a person acting in the capacity of an administrator appointed pursuant to the provisions of Part II of the Insolvency Act 1986;

(f) proceedings before the European Commission of Human Rights and the European Court of Human Rights established under article 19 of the Convention for the Protection of Human Rights and Fundamental Freedoms opened for signature at Rome on 4 November 1950, ratified by the United Kingdom on 8 March 1951, which came into force on 3 August 1953, provided that the client does not have legal aid in respect of the proceedings.

(2) Proceedings mentioned in paragraph (1) shall be specified proceedings notwithstanding that they are concluded without the commencement of court proceedings.

(3) In paragraphs (1)(b) and (1)(d), 'company' means a company within the meaning of s 735(1) Companies Act 1985 or a company which may be wound up under Part V of the Insolvency Act 1986.

(4) Where legal aid in respect of the proceedings to which a conditional fee agreement relates is granted after that agreement is entered into the proceedings shall cease to be specified from the date of the grant.

(5) In this article, 'legal aid' means representation under Part IV of the Legal Aid Act 1988.

Maximum permitted percentage increase on fees

3 For the purpose of s 58(5) of the Act, the maximum permitted percentage by which fees may be increased in respect of each description of proceedings specified in article 2 is 100%.

CONDITIONAL FEE AGREEMENTS REGULATIONS 1995 SI 1995/1675

Citation, commencement and interpretation

1(1) These Regulation may be cited as the Conditional Fee Agreements Regulations 1995 and shall come into force on 5 July 1995.

(2) In these Regulations:

'agreement', in relation to an agreement between a legal representative and an additional legal representative, includes a retainer;

'legal aid' means representation under Part IV of the Legal Aid Act 1988;

'legal representative' means a person providing advocacy or litigation services.

Agreements to compile with prescribed requirements

2 An agreement shall not be a conditional fee agreement unless it complies with the requirements of the following regulations.

Requirements of an agreement

3 An agreement shall state:

(a) the particular proceedings or parts of them to which it relates (including whether it relates to any counterclaim, appeal or proceedings to enforce a judgment or order);

(b) the circumstances in which the legal representative's fees and expenses or part of them are payable;

(c) what, if any, payment is due:

    (i)   upon partial failure of the specified circumstance to occur;

    (ii) irrespective of the specified circumstances occurring; and

    (iii) upon terminations of the agreement for any reason;

(d) the amount payable in accordance with sub-paragraphs (b) or (c) above or the method to be used to calculate the amount payable; and in particular whether or not the amount of any damages which may be recovered on behalf of the client.

Additional requirements

4(1) The agreement shall also state that, immediately before it was entered into, the legal representative drew the client' attention to the matters in paragraph (2).

(2) The matters are:

    (a) whether the client might be entitled to legal aid in respect of the proceedings to which the agreement relates, the conditions upon which legal aid is available and the application of those conditions to the client in respect of the proceedings;

    (b) the circumstances in which the client may be liable to pay the fees and expenses of the legal representative in accordance with the agreement;

    (c) the circumstances in which the client may be liable to pay the costs of any other party to the proceedings; and

    (d) the circumstances in which the client may seek taxation of the fees and expenses of the legal representative and the procedure for so doing.

Application of regulation 4

5 Regulation 4 shall not apply to an agreement between a legal representative and an additional legal representative.

Form of agreement

6 An agreement shall be in writing and, except in the case of an agreement between a legal representative and an additional legal representative, shall be signed by the client and the legal representative.

Amendment of agreement

7 Where it is proposed to extend the agreement to cover further proceedings or parts of them regulations 3–6 shall apply to the agreement as extended.

APPENDIX C

PRACTICE DIRECTIONS AND NOTES

PRACTICE DIRECTION (DAMAGES: PERSONAL INJURIES) [1984] 1 WLR 1127

1 Time is too often wasted at the trial of personal injury actions because the parties do not try to agree the items of special damage, or to find out to what extent they disagree and why, until the hearing is imminent or has actually started. To avoid this happening, the practice set out in paragraph 2 is to be followed in future.

2 In any personal injury action in which the damages claimed consist of or include a claim for: (a) loss of earnings; (b) loss of future earning capacity; (c) medical or other expenses relating to or including the cost of care, attention, accommodation or appliances; (d) loss of pension rights; particulars, where appropriate in the form of a schedule, shall be prepared by the party making such claim and not later than seven days after the case appears in the Warned List in London shall be served upon all other parties against whom such claim is made. Not later than seven days thereafter every party upon whom particulars have been served shall indicate in writing whether and to what extent each item claimed is agreed and, if not agreed, the reason why not and any counter proposals. When there is a fixed date for hearing, the plaintiff's particulars shall be served not less than 28 days before that date and the answer not later than 14 days thereafter.

The failure by a party to comply with these requirements may be taken into account in deciding any question of costs.

3 In cases of hearings outside London, the particulars referred to in paragraph 2 shall be served no later than the lodging of the certificate of readiness and the answer not later than 14 days thereafter.

1 August 1984

Lord Lane CJ

PRACTICE DIRECTION (PROVISIONAL DAMAGES: PROCEDURE) [1985] 1 WLR 961; [1985] 2 ALL ER 895

A Judgments for provisional damages after trial

The following practice will be followed:

Trial proceedings

1 The oral judgment of the Judge will specify the disease or type of deterioration: (a) which, for the purpose of the award of immediate damages, has been assumed will not occur; (b) which will entitle the plaintiff to further damages if it occurs at a future date.

2 The material parts of associate's certificate and the judgment entered pursuant to it will be in the following or similar form with such variations as may be necessary under RSC Ord 37, r 8:

> The judge awarded to the plaintiff by way of immediate damages [set out the award, differentiating between general and special damage, in the usual way] upon the assumption that the plaintiff would not at a future date as a result of the act or omission giving rise to the cause of action develop the following disease, namely [specify it] *or* suffer deterioration in his physical or mental condition of the following type [specify it]. And the Judge further ordered that if the plaintiff at a future date did so develop such disease or [did so suffer such deterioration] he should be entitled to apply for further damages.

3 The Judge will normally specify the period within which the application for further damages must be made and this will be set out in the associate's certificate and the judgment.

4 Documents – Case file

The Judge will also direct what documents are to be lodged and preserved as material for any further assessment. These documents are hereinafter called the case file. Subject to his directions the case file will normally include: (a) a copy of the associate's certificate; (b) a copy of the judgment drawn up on it; (c) the pleadings; (d) a transcript of the Judge's oral judgment; (e) all medical reports placed before the Court; (f) a transcript of such parts of the plaintiff's own evidence as the Judge may think necessary.

5 The contents of the case file shall be scheduled to the associate's certificate and to the judgment.

6 The associate shall have overall responsibility for the preparation and transmission of the case file. It shall be a secure file or folder and be clearly marked. The plaintiff's solicitor shall be responsible for procuring any transcripts or other documents directed to be placed on the case file.

7 In every case a judgment shall be drawn up and entered and a copy placed on the case file.

8 Transmission and preservation

The associate shall: (1) lodge the case file in the office in which the action is proceeding; (2) forward a copy of the judgment endorsed: 'Case file lodged in (name of office and date)', on to The Officer in Charge, Filing Department, Central Office, Royal Courts of Justice, Strand, London, WC2A 2LL.

9 Case files shall be filed and preserved as pleadings after trial.

B Orders without trial

Section 32A Supreme Court Act 1981 requires that immediate damages and provisional damages must be the subjects of awards by the court, if they are be enforced under that section. Accordingly, the following practice shall be followed in relation to settlements under that section:

10 Applications shall be made by summons for leave to enter judgment by consent in the terms of a draft annexed to the summons. If the plaintiff is under a disability, the approval of the court should be asked for in the summons and recited in the draft judgment.

11 The draft shall contain the particulars in paragraphs 1–3 hereof. It shall also contain a direction as to the documents to be placed on the case file. These will normally be: (a) a copy of the order made on the summons; (b) a copy of the judgment; (c) pleadings, if any; (d) an agreed statement of the facts; (e) agreed medical reports.

The contents of the case file shall be scheduled to the order and to the judgment. The terms of the order and judgment shall be subject to the court's approval.

12 The plaintiff's solicitor shall: (1) prepare the case file, which shall be secure and clearly marked; (2) draw up the order and judgment and place copies on the case file; (3) lodge the case file in the office in which the action is proceeding where it shall be preserved as though it were the pleadings of an action disposed of by trial; (4) forward a copy of the judgment as directed in paragraph 8(2) hereof.

Duties of the Central Office

13 The Filing and Record Department of the Central Office shall:

(1) File the copy judgments received in order of receipt, giving them file numbers;

(2) Maintain an index of the judgments under the initial letters of the plaintiffs' surnames and containing:

File number;

Action number;

Date of judgment;

Period within which application for further damages must be made;

Plaintiff's name;

Office where case file lodged.

14 This direction applies to all trial centres and offices of the High Court.

5 July 1985

Lord Lane CJ Skinner and Macpherson JJ

PRACTICE NOTE [1988] 1 WLR 654; [1988] 2 ALL ER 102

1 Where provisional damages are part of the relief claimed in an action, entry of judgment with or without leave is not permissible under Ord 13 or Ord 19 (see Ord 37, r 8(5)); and the following procedure should be adopted.

2 If the defendant does not give notice of intention to defend, the plaintiff should, if he has not already done so, serve a statement of claim. That may provoke appearance and defence out of time (see Ord 12, r 6(2)). The plaintiff should therefore apply promptly by summons for directions for trial (see *Austin v Wildig* [1969] 1 All ER 99). It might be prudent to include in the summons a prayer for an order that the defendant be precluded from contesting the issue of liability unless within a limited time he gives notice of intention to defend and serves a defence. Otherwise liability might be put in issue at a late stage by service of notice of intention to defend and of a defence out of time.

3 If a defendant, having given notice of intention to defend, fails to serve a defence, Ord 25, r 1(7) enables a summons for directions to be issued, and this should be done as soon as there has been default. On that summons the relief sought will be *mutatis mutandis* the same as in that referred to in the preceding paragraph.

4 At the trial, there will be in issue:

    (1) *quantum* of damage;

    (2) the question whether the case is an appropriate one for an award of provisional damages and if so, upon what terms.

14 April 1988

PRACTICE DIRECTION (CIVIL LITIGATION: CASE MANAGEMENT) [1995] 1 WLR 262; [1995] 1 ALL ER 385

1 The paramount importance of reducing the cost and delay of civil litigation makes it necessary for judges sitting at first instance to assert greater control over the preparation for and conduct of hearings than has hitherto been customary. Failure by practitioners to conduct cases economically will be visited by appropriate orders for costs, including wasted costs orders.

2 The court will accordingly exercise its discretion to limit: (a) discovery; (b) the length of oral submissions; (c) the time allowed for the examination and cross-examination of witnesses; (d) the issues on which it wishes to be addressed; (e) reading aloud from documents and authorities.

3 Unless otherwise ordered, every witness statement shall stand as the evidence-in-chief of the witness concerned.

4 RSC Ord 18, r 7 (facts, not evidence, to be pleaded) will be strictly enforced. In advance of trial, parties should use their best endeavours to agree which are the issues or the main issues, and it is their duty so far as possible to reduce or eliminate the expert issues.

5 RSC Ord 34, r 10(2)(a)–(c) (the court bundle) will also be strictly enforced. Documents for use in court should be in A4 format where possible, contained in suitably secured bundles, and lodged with the court at least two clear days before the hearing of an application or a trial. Each bundle should be paginated, indexed, wholly legible, and arranged chronologically and contained in a ring binder or a lever-arch file. Where documents are copied unnecessarily or bundled incompetently the cost will be disallowed.

6 In cases estimated to last for more than 10 days, a pre-trial review should be applied for or in default may be appointed by the court. It should when practicable be conducted by the trial judge between eight and four weeks before the date of trial and should be attended by the advocates who are to represent the parties at trial.

7 Unless the court otherwise orders, there must be lodged with the listing officer (or equivalent) on behalf of each party no later than two months before the date of trial a completed pre-trial check-list in the form annexed to this practice direction.

8 Not less than three clear days before the hearing of an action or application, each party should lodge with the court (with copies to other parties) a skeleton argument concisely summarising that party's submissions in relation to each of the issues, and citing the main authorities relied upon which may be attached. Skeleton arguments should be as brief as the nature of the issues allows, and should not without leave of the court exceed 20 pages of double-spaced A4 paper.

9 The opening speech should be succinct. At its conclusion, other parties may be invited briefly to amplify their skeleton arguments. In a heavy case, the court may in conjunction with final speeches require written submissions, including the findings of fact for which each party contends.

10 This direction applies to all lists in the Queen's Bench and Chancery Divisions, except where other directions specifically apply.

24 January 1995

Lord Taylor of Gosforth CJ and Sir Richard Scott V-C

PRACTICE NOTE (STRUCTURED SETTLEMENTS COURT'S APPROVAL) [1992] 1 WLR 328

1 This Practice Note applies only to proceedings in the Central Office and the Admiralty and Commercial Registry of the High Court. It concerns settlements of claims in respect of personal injury or death where approval of the court is required and which include a structured element. The practice set out below, adapted as indicated, is appropriate whether or not the Court of Protection is involved. It will apply, on an experimental basis, until further notice. If the plaintiff is under mental disability, then the additional steps set out in paragraphs 6(viii) and 8 of this Practice Note should be taken.

2 By this Practice Note it is intended to establish a practice to overcome the present administrative difficulty caused by the short period over which life offices keep open offers of annuities at a given price. It has proved difficult for plaintiff's solicitors to do all that is necessary to obtain the approval of the court within the period during which the annuity offer remains open.

3 As from 30 March 1992, all applications for approval in structured settlement cases will be listed for hearing on Friday mornings during term time.

4 After setting down, applications for the fixing dates for these purposes should be made to the Clerk of the Lists in Room W11.

5 Once a hearing date has been obtained, documents should be lodged in Room W11 not later than noon on the Thursday immediately before the Friday for which the hearings is fixed.

6 The following are the classes of document which should be lodged in accordance with paragraph 5 above: (i) copies of originating process or pleadings, if any; (ii) an opinion of counsel assessing the value of the claim on a conventional basis (unless approval has already been given) and, if practicable, the opinion of counsel on the structured settlement proposed; (iii) a report of forensic accountants setting out the advantages and disadvantages, if any, of structuring bearing in mind the plaintiff's life expectancy and the anticipated costs of future care; (iv) a draft of the proposed agreement as approved by the Inland Revenue (and by the Treasury where the defendant or other paying party is a Health Authority); (v) sufficient material to satisfy the court that enough capital is available free of the structure to meet anticipated future capital needs: particular reference to accommodation and transport needs will usually be helpful in this context; (vi) sufficient material to satisfy the court that the structure is secure and backed by responsible insurers; (vii) evidence of other assets available to the plaintiff beyond the award the subject of the application; (viii) in cases where the plaintiff is under mental disability the consent of the Court of Protection.

The classes of document required to be lodged should be separately bundled and clearly marked so that the presence of the appropriate classes of document (but not the adequacy of their content) may be checked by the clerks in Room W11.

7 If the proceedings are in the Admiralty and Commercial Registry, application should be made to the Admiralty Registrar in good time for the transfer of the

proceedings to the Central Office for the purpose of the application for approval only.

8 In cases where the plaintiff is under mental disability, the documents set out in paragraphs 6(i)–(vii) (inclusive) should be lodged in the Enquiries and Acceptances Branch of the Public Trust Office, Steward House, 24 Kingsway, London, WC2B 6JH, not later than noon on the Monday immediately before the Friday for which the hearing is fixed. Unless an application has already been made for the appointment of a receiver, there must also be lodged an application for the appointment of a receiver (form CP1) (in duplicate), a certificate of family and property (form CP5) and a medical certificate (form CP3). (Blank forms are available from the same address.) The Court of Protection's approval, if granted, will be available by 10.30 on the Thursday immediately before the Friday fixed for the hearing.

9 This Practice Note is issued with the approval of the Deputy Chief Justice, the Judge in charge of the non-jury list, the Admiralty Judge and the Master of the Court of Protection.

12 February 1992

APPENDIX D

RULES OF THE SUPREME COURT

ORDER 6, r 8

Duration and renewal of writ

8(1) For the purposes of service, a writ (other than a concurrent writ) is valid in the first instance:

    (a) if an Admiralty writ *in rem*, for 12 months;

    (b) where leave to serve the writ out of the jurisdiction is required under Order 11, for six months,

    (c) in any other case, for four months,

beginning with the date of its issue.

(1A) A concurrent writ is valid in the first instance for the period of validity of the original writ which is unexpired at the date of issue of the concurrent writ.

(2) Subject to paragraph (2A), where a writ has not been served on a defendant, the court may by order extend the validity of the writ from time to time for such period, not exceeding four months at any one time, beginning with the day next following that on which it would otherwise expire, as may be specified in the order, if an application for extension is made to the court before that day or such later day (if any) as the court may allow.

(2A) Where the court is satisfied on an application under paragraph (2) that, despite the making of all reasonable efforts, it may not be possible to serve the writ within four months, the court may, if it thinks fit, extend the validity of the writ for such periods, not exceeding 12 months, as the court may specify.

(3) Before a writ, the validity of which has been extended under this rule, is served, it must be marked with an official stamp showing the period for which the validity of the writ has been so extended.

(4) Where the validity of a writ is extended by order made under this rule, the order shall operate in relation to any other writ (whether original or concurrent) issued in the same action which has not been served so as to extend the validity of that other writ until the expiration of the period specified in the order.

ORDER 15, r 6

Misjoinder and nonjoinder of parties

6(1) No cause or matter shall be defeated by reason of the misjoinder or nonjoinder of any party; and the court may in any cause or matter determine the issues or questions in dispute so far as they affect the rights and interest of the persons who are parties to the cause or matter.

(2) Subject to the provisions of this rule, at any stage of the proceedings in any cause or matter the court may on such terms as it thinks just and either of its own motion or on application:

(a) order any person who has been improperly or unnecessarily made a party or who has for any reason ceased to be a proper or necessary party, to cease to be a party;

(b) order any of the following persons to be added as a party, namely:

(i) any person who ought to have been joined as a party or whose presence before the court is necessary to ensure that all matters in dispute in the cause or matter may be effectually and completely determined and adjudicated upon, or

(ii) any person between whom and any party to the cause or matter there may exist a question or issue arising out of or relating to or connected with any relief or remedy claimed in the cause or matter which in the opinion of the court it would be just and convenient to determine as between him and that party as well as between the parties to the cause or matter.

(3) An application by any person for an order under paragraph (2) adding him as a party must, except with the leave of the court, be supported by an affidavit showing his interest in the matters in dispute in the cause or matter or, as the case may be, the question or issue to be determined as between him and any party to the cause or matter.

(4) No person shall be added as a plaintiff without his consent signified in writing or in such other manner as may be authorised.

(5) No person shall be added or substituted as a party after the expiry of any relevant period of limitation unless either:

(a) the relevant period was current at the date when proceedings were commenced and it is necessary for the determination of the action that the new party should be added, or substituted; or

(b) the relevant period arises under the provisions of ss 11 or 12 Limitation Act 1980 and the court directs that those provisions should not apply to the action by or against the new party.

In this paragraph, 'any relevant period of limitation' means a time limit under the Limitation Act 1980 or a time limit which applies to the proceedings in question by virtue of the Foreign Limitation Periods Act 1984.

(6) Except in a case to which the law of another country relating to limitation applies, and the law of England and Wales does not so apply, the addition or substitution of a new party shall be treated as necessary for the purposes of paragraph (5)(a) if, and only if, the court is satisfied that:

(a) the new party is a necessary party to the action in that property is vested in him at law or in equity and the plaintiff's claim in respect of an equitable interest in that property is liable to be defeated unless the new party is joined; or

(b) the relevant cause of action is vested in the new party and the plaintiff jointly but not severally; or

(c) the new party is the Attorney General and the proceedings should have been brought by relator proceedings in his name; or

(d) the new party is a company in which the plaintiff is a shareholder and on whose behalf the plaintiff is suing to enforce a right vested in the company; or

(e) the new party is sued jointly with the defendant and is not also liable severally with him and failure to join the new party might render the claim unenforceable.

ORDER 15, r 7

Change of parties by reason of death, etc

7(1) Where a party to an action dies or becomes bankrupt but the cause of action survives, the action shall not abate by reason of the death or bankruptcy.

(2) Where at any stage of the proceedings in any cause or matter the interest or liability of any party is assigned or transmitted to or devolves upon some other person, the court may, if it thinks it necessary, in order to ensure that all matters in dispute in the cause or matter may be effectually and completely determined and adjudicated upon, order that other person to be made a party to the cause or matter and the proceedings to be carried on as if he had been substituted for the first mentioned party.

An application for an order under this paragraph may be made *ex parte.*

(3) An order may be made under this rule for a person to be made a party to a cause or matter notwithstanding that he is already a party to it on the other side of the record, or on the same side but in a different capacity; but:

(a) if he is already a party on the other side, the order shall be treated as containing a direction that he shall cease to be a party on that other side; and

(b) if he is already a party on the same side but in another capacity, the order may contain a direction that he shall cease to be a party in that other capacity.

(4) The person on whose application an order is made under this rule must procure the order to be noted in the cause book, and after the order has been so noted that person must, unless the court otherwise directs, serve the order on every other person who is a party to the cause or matter or who becomes or ceases to be a party by virtue of the order and serve with the order on any person who becomes a defendant a copy of the writ or originating summons by which the cause or matter was begun and of all other pleadings served in the proceedings and a form of acknowledgement of service in Form 14 or 15 in Appendix A, whichever is appropriate.

(5) Any application to the court by a person served with an order made *ex parte* under this rule for the discharge or variation of the order must be made within 14 days after the service of the order on that person.

ORDER 15, r 8

Provisions consequential on making of order under r 6 or 7

8(1) Where an order is made under r 6, the writ by which the action in question was begun must be amended accordingly and must be indorsed with:

- (a) a reference to the order in pursuance of which the amendment is made; and
- (b) the date on which the amendment is made; and the amendment must be made within such period as may be specified in the order or, if no period is so specified, within 14 days after the making of the order.

(2) Where by an order under r 6 a person is to be made a defendant, the rules as to service of a writ of summons shall apply accordingly to service of the amendment writ on him but, before serving the writ on him, the person on whose application the order was made must procure the order to be noted in the cause book.

(2A) Together with the writ of summons served under paragraph (2) shall be served a copy of all other pleadings served in the action.

(3) Where by an order under r 6 or 7 a person is to be made a defendant, the rules as to acknowledgement of service shall apply accordingly to acknowledgement of service by him, subject, in the case of a person to be made a defendant by an order under r 7, to the modification that the time limited for acknowledging service shall begin with the date on which the order is served on him under r 7(4) or, if the order is not required to be served on him, with the date on which the order is noted in the cause book.

(4) Where by an order under r 6 or 7 a person is to be added as a party or is to be made a party in substitution for some other party, that person shall not become a party until:

- (a) where the order is made under r 6, the writ has been amended in relation to him under this rule and (if he is a defendant) has been served on him; or
- (b) where the order is made under r 7, the order has been served on him under r 7(4) or, if the order is not required to be served on him, the order has been noted in the cause book;

and where by virtue of the foregoing provision a person becomes a party on substitution for some other party, all things done in the course of the proceedings before the making of the order shall have effect in relation to the new party as they had in relation to the old, except that acknowledgement of service by the old party shall not dispense with acknowledgement of service by the new.

(5) The foregoing provisions of this rule shall apply in relation to an action begun by originating summons as they apply in relation to an action begun by writ.

ORDER 15, r 9

Failure to proceed after death of party

9(1) If, after the death of a plaintiff or defendant in any action, the cause of action survives but no order under r 7 is made substituting as plaintiff any person in whom the cause of action vests or, as the case may be, the personal representatives of the deceased defendant, the defendant or, as the case may be, those representatives may apply to the court for an order that unless the action is proceeded with within such time as may be specified in the order the action shall be struck out as against the plaintiff or defendant as the case may be, who has died but, where it is the plaintiff who has died, the court shall not make an order under this rule unless satisfied that due notice of the application has been given to the personal representatives (if any) of the deceased plaintiff and to any other interested persons who, in the opinion of the court, should be notified.

(2) Where in any action a counterclaim is made by a defendant, this rule shall apply in relation to the counterclaim as if the counterclaim were a separate action and as if the defendant making the counterclaim were the plaintiff and the person against whom it is made a defendant.

NOTE

The following note is taken from *The White Book* 18/8/10

17 Limitation Act 1980 – In the ordinary run of actions for personal injuries, any question concerning the operation of the Limitation Act 1980 will very likely be dealt with and disposed of on affidavit evidence on the hearing of an appropriate summons at an early interlocutory stage of the action. This will apply as much to the question of 'the date of knowledge' if it is alleged to be later than the date of the accrual of the cause of action (see *Simpson v Norwest Holst Southern Ltd* [1980] 1 WLR 968; [1980] 2 All ER 471) as to the question of the power of the court to override the defence of limitation under s 33 (see *Chappel v Cooper* [1980] 1 WLR 958; [1980] 2 All ER 463). If, however, these questions are not disposed of in this summary manner, but are left to be dealt with either as a preliminary issue on the pleadings, etc or as issues arising in the action, careful regard will have to be had to the matter of pleading relating to these two questions.

As to the date of knowledge in an action for damages for personal injuries or under the Fatal Accidents Act 1976, the plaintiff who alleges that he was entitled to commence the action within three years from the date of knowledge which is later than the date on which the cause of action accrued, must in his statement of claim plead the facts and matters on which he relies to support his contention. He should not wait for the defendant to plead the defence of limitation and then serve a reply alleging the grounds entitling him to bring the action later than three years from the date of the accrual of the cause of action. In particular, the plaintiff should plead in the statement of claim the date as precisely as he can when he first knew of each of the facts and matters specified in s 14 and he should give particulars of the facts relating to such knowledge under Ord 18, r 12(4)(a). It should perhaps be emphasised that s 14 of that Act is cast in the conjunctive and not disconjunctive form, so that the plaintiff has to plead and prove the date on which he first had knowledge of each of the facts therein specified. It should, however, be noted that Bristow J stated in *Ogunsanya v Lambeth Area Health Authority* 3 July 1985 (unreported) that the proper pattern of pleading is that the plaintiff should make no mention of the limitation point in his statement of claim, but should leave this to be raised in the defence, to which the plaintiff should then serve his reply to raise the facts and contentions relied on as to date and knowledge and the power of the court to override the defence of limitation.

So far as the defendant is concerned in such actions, if he raises the defence of limitation and merely denies the facts alleged by the plaintiff as to the date of knowledge, he will merely put those facts in issue. If, however, the defendant intends to set up a positive case that the plaintiff first had knowledge of any of the specified facts before the date alleged by the plaintiff, it is incumbent upon him to plead such a defence expressly, and in particular he should plead the date as precisely as he can when he alleges the plaintiff first knew any of the facts specified and he should give particulars of the facts relating to such knowledge on the part of the plaintiff (Ord 18, r 12(4)(a)). Moreover, if the defendant intends to rely on provisions of s 14(3) of the Act, so as to show that the plaintiff's date of knowledge was or ought to be treated as having been before the date alleged by the plaintiff, the defendant must plead the facts and matters relied on to support his contention. Only in this way will the court be able to see and to be apprised of the precise issues between the parties on the question of the 'date of knowledge'.

As to the power of the court under s 33 of the Act to disapply the defence of limitation, unless the plaintiff has good reason for believing that the defence of limitation will not be raised, the better practice is for the plaintiff in his statement of claim to plead, in the alternative if necessary, all the facts and circumstances relied on, with all necessary particulars, to invoke the power of the court to allow the action to proceed and to direct that the provisions of ss 11, 12 of the Act should not apply to the action or to any specified cause of action to which the action relates, and indeed the plaintiff should include in his prayer a claim for such a direction. If such a direction is given by the court, it should be included in the judgment. Equally, if the defendant intends to contend that the court should not exercise its overriding powers under s 33 of the Act, he may deny the facts and circumstances alleged by the plaintiff and so put them in issue, but if he intends to rely upon additional facts or circumstances to support his contention, he should expressly plead such facts and circumstances; otherwise he may be precluded from adducing evidence relating thereto.

ORDER 18 r 12

Particulars of pleading

12(1) Subject to paragraph (2), every pleading must contain the necessary particulars of any claim, defence or other matter pleaded including, without prejudice to the generality of the foregoing:

(a) particulars of any misrepresentation, fraud, breach of trust, wilful default or undue influence on which the party's pleading relies;

(b) where a party pleading alleges any condition of the mind of any person, whether any disorder or disability of mind or any malice, fraudulent intention or other condition of mind except knowledge, particulars of the facts on which the party relies; and

(c) where a claim for damages is made against a party pleading, particulars of any facts on which the party relies in mitigation of, or otherwise in relation to, the amount of damages.

(1A) Subject to paragraph (1B), a plaintiff in an action for personal injuries shall serve with his statement of claim:

(a) a medical report, and

(b) a statement of the special damages claimed.

(1B) Where the documents to which paragraph (1A) applies are not served with the statement of claim, the court may:

(a) specify the period of time within which they are to be provided; or

(b) make such other order as it thinks fit (including any order dispensing with the requirements of paragraph (1A)) or staying the proceedings.

(1C) For the purposes of this rule:

'medical report' means a report substantiating all the personal injuries alleged in the statement of claim which the plaintiff proposes to adduce in evidence as part of his case at the trial;

'a statement of the special damages claimed' means a statement giving full particulars of the special damages claimed for expenses and losses already incurred and an estimate of any future expenses and losses (including loss of earnings and pension rights).

(2) Where it is necessary to give particulars of debt, expenses or damages and those particulars exceed three folios, they must be set out in a separate document referred to in the pleading and the pleading must state whether the document has already been served and, if so, when, or is to be served with the pleading.

(3) The court may order a party to serve on any other party particulars of any claim, defence or other matter stated in his pleading, or in any affidavit of his ordered to stand as a pleading, or a statement of the nature of the case on which he relies, and the order may be made on such terms as the court thinks just.

(4) Where a party alleges as a fact that a person had knowledge or notice of some fact, matter or thing, then, without prejudice to the generality of paragraph (3), the court may, on such terms as it thinks just, order that party to serve on any other party:

(a) where he alleges knowledge, particulars of the facts on which he relies; and

(b) where he alleges notice, particulars of the notice.

(5) An order under this rule shall not be made before service of the defence unless, in the opinion of the court, the order is necessary or desirable to enable the defendant to plead or for some other special reason.

(6) Where the applicant for an order under this rule did not apply by letter for the particulars he requires, the court may refuse to make the order unless of the opinion that there were sufficient reasons for an application by letter not having been made.

(7) Where particulars are given pursuant to a request, or order of the court, the request or order shall be incorporated with the particulars, each item of the particulars following immediately after the corresponding item of the request or order.

ORDER 20, r 5

Amendment of writ or pleading with leave

5(1) Subject to Order 15, rr 6, 7 and 8 and the following provisions of this rule, the court may at any stage of the proceedings allow the plaintiff to amend his writ, or any party to amend his pleading, on such terms as to costs or otherwise as may be just and in such manner (if any) as it may direct.

(2) Where an application to the court for leave to make the amendment mentioned in paragraph (3), (4) or (5) is made after any relevant period of limitation current at the date of issue of the writ has expired, the court may nevertheless grant such leave in the circumstances mentioned in that paragraph if it thinks it just to do so.

In this paragraph, 'any relevant period of limitation' includes a time limit which applies to the proceedings in question by virtue of the Foreign Limitation Periods Act 1984.

(3) An amendment to correct the name of a party may be allowed under paragraph (2) notwithstanding that it is alleged that the effect of the amendment will be to substitute a new party if the court is satisfied that the mistake sought to be corrected was a genuine mistake and was not misleading or such as to cause any reasonable doubt as to the identity of the party intending to sue or, as the case may be, intended to be sued.

(4) An amendment to alter the capacity in which a party sues may be allowed under paragraph (2) if the new capacity is one which that party had at the date of the commencement of the proceedings or has since acquired.

(5) An amendment may be allowed under paragraph (2) not withstanding that the effect of the amendment will be to add or substitute a new cause of action if the new cause of action arises out of the same facts or substantially the same facts as a cause of action in respect of which relief has already been claimed in the action by the party applying for leave to make the amendment.

ORDER 24, r 7A

Application under ss 33(2) or 34(2) of the Supreme Court Act 1981

7A(1) An application for an order under s 33(2) of the Act for the disclosure of documents before the commencement of proceedings shall be made by originating summons (in Form No 10 in Appendix A) and the person against whom the order is sought shall be made defendant to the summons.

(2) An application after the commencement of proceedings for an order under s 34(2) of the said Act for the disclosure of documents by a person who is not a party to the proceedings shall be made by summons, which must be served on that person personally and on every party to the proceedings other than the applicant.

(3) A summons under paragraph (1) or (2) shall be supported by an affidavit which must:

(a) in the case of a summons under paragraph (1), state the grounds on which it is alleged that the applicant and the person against whom the order is sought are likely to be parties to subsequent proceedings in the High Court in which a claim for personal injuries is likely to be made;

(b) in any case, specify or describe the documents in respect of which the order is sought and show, if practicable by reference to any pleading served or intended to be served in the proceedings, that the documents are relevant to an issue arising or likely to arise out of a claim for personal injuries made or likely to be made in the proceedings and that the person against whom the order is sought is likely to have or have had them in his possession, custody or power.

(4) A copy of the supporting affidavit shall be served with the summons on every person on whom the summons is required to be served.

(5) An order under the said ss 33(2) or 34(2) for the disclosure of documents may be made conditional on the applicant's giving security for the costs of the person against whom it is made or on such other terms, if any, as the court thinks just, and shall require the person against whom the order is made to make an affidavit stating whether any documents specified or described in the order, are, or at any time have been, in his possession, custody or power and if not then in his possession, custody or power, when he parted with them and what has become of them.

(6) No person shall be compelled by virtue of such an order to produce any documents which he could not be compelled to produce:

(a) in the case of a summons under paragraph (1) if the subsequent proceedings had already been begun; or

(b) in the case of a summons under paragraph (2) if he had been served with a writ of *subpoena duces tecum* to produce the documents at the trial.

(7) In this rule, 'a claim for personal injuries' means a claim in respect of personal injuries to a person or in respect of a person's death.

(8) For the purposes of rr 10 and 11, an application for an order under the said ss 33(2) or 34(2) shall be treated as a cause or matter between the applicant and the person against whom the order is sought.

ORDER 25, r 1

Summons for directions

1(1) With a view to providing, in every action to which this rule applies, an occasion for the consideration by the court of the preparations for the trial of the action, so that:

(a) all matters which must or can be dealt with on interlocutory applications and have not already been dealt with may so far as possible be dealt with; and

(b) such directions may be given as to the future course of the action as appear best adapted to secure the just, expeditious and economical disposal thereof,

the plaintiff must, within one month after the pleadings in the action are deemed to be closed, take out a summons (in these rules referred to as a summons for directions) returnable in not less than 14 days.

(2) This rule applies to all actions begun by writ except:

(a) actions in which the plaintiff or defendant has applied for judgment under Order 14, or in which the plaintiff has applied for judgment under Order 86, and directions have been given under the relevant order;

(b) actions in which the plaintiff or defendant has applied under Order 18, r 21, for trial without pleadings or further pleadings and directions have been given under that rule;

(c) actions in which an order has been made under Order 24, r 4, for the trial of an issue or question before discovery;

(d) actions in which directions have been given under Order 29, r 7;

(e) actions in which an order for the taking of an account has been made under Ord 43, r 1;

(f) actions in which an application for transfer to the commercial list is pending;

(g) actions which have been commenced, or ordered to be tried as, Official Referees' business;

(h) actions for the infringement of a patent;

(i) (revoked by RSC (Amendment No 3) Order 1980 SI 1980/1908)

(j) actions for personal injuries for which automatic directions are provided by r 8;

(k) actions in the Chancery Division in which the parties agree under r 9 that the only matters to be determined are the mode of trial and time for setting down.

(3) Where, in the case of any action in which discovery of documents is required to be made by any party under Order 24, r 2, the period of 14 days referred to in paragraph (1) of that rule is extended, whether by consent or by order of the court or both by consent and by order, paragraph (1) of this rule shall have effect in relation to that action as if for the reference therein to one month after the pleadings in the action are deemed to be closed there were substituted a reference to 14 days after the expiration of the period referred to in paragraph (1) of the said r 2 as so extended.

(4) If the plaintiff does not take out a summons for directions in accordance with the foregoing provisions of this rule, the defendant or any defendant may do so or apply for an order to dismiss the action.

(5) On an application by a defendant to dismiss the action under paragraph (4), the court may either dismiss the action on such terms as may be just or deal with the application as if it were a summons for directions.

(6) In the case of an action which is proceeding only as respects a counterclaim, references in this rule to the plaintiff and defendant shall be construed respectively as references to the party making the counterclaim and the defendant to the counterclaim.

(7) Notwithstanding anything in paragraph (1), any party to an action to which this rule applies may take out a summons for directions at any time after the defendant has given notice of intention to defend, or, if there are two or more defendants, at least one of them has given such notice.

Authors' note: RSC Ord 25, r 8 states that the automatic directions will normally apply in a personal injury action except RSC Ord 25 r 8(5)(b) stipulates that they shall not apply 'where the pleadings contain an allegation of a negligent act or omission in the course of medical treatment'.

ORDER 29, r 9

Interpretation of Part II

9 In this part of this Order:

'interim payments', in relation to a defendant, means a payment on account of any damages, debt or other sum (excluding costs) which he may be held liable to pay to or for the benefit of the plaintiff; and any reference to the plaintiff or defendant includes a reference to any person who, for the purpose of the proceedings, acts as next friend of the plaintiff or guardian of the defendant.

ORDER 29, r 10

Application for interim payment

10(1) The plaintiff may, at any time after the writ has been served on a defendant and the time limited for him to acknowledge service has expired, apply to the court for an order requiring that defendant to make an interim payment.

(2) An application under this rule shall be made by summons but may be included in a summons for summary judgment under Order 14 or Order 86.

(3) An application under this rule shall be supported by an affidavit which shall:

    (a) verify the amount of the damages, debt or other sum to which the application relates and the grounds of the application;

    (b) exhibit any documentary evidence relied on by the plaintiff in support of the application; and

    (c) if the plaintiff's claim is made under the Fatal Accidents Act 1976, contain the particulars mentioned in s 2(4) of that Act.

(4) The summons and a copy of the affidavit in support and any documents exhibited thereto shall be served on the defendant against whom the order is sought not less than 10 clear days before the return day.

(5) Notwithstanding the making or refusal of an order for an interim payment, a second or subsequent application may be made upon cause shown.

ORDER 29, r 11

Order for interim payment in respect of damages

11(1) If, on the hearing of an application under r 10 in an action for damages, the court is satisfied:

(a) that the defendant against whom the order is sought (in this paragraph referred to as 'the respondent') has admitted liability for the plaintiff's damages; or

(b) that the plaintiff has obtained judgment against the respondent for damages to be assessed; or

(c) that, if the action proceeded to trial, the plaintiff would obtain judgment for substantial damages against the respondent or, where there are two or more defendants, against any of them, the court may, if it thinks fit and subject to paragraph (2), order the respondent to make an interim payment of such amount as it thinks just, not exceeding a reasonable proportion of the damages which in the opinion of the court are likely to be recovered by the plaintiff after taking into account any relevant contributory negligence and any set-off, cross-claim or counterclaim on which the respondent may be entitled to rely.

(2) No order shall be made under paragraph (1), in an action for personal injuries if it appears to the court that the defendant is not a person falling within one of the following categories, namely:

(a) a person who is insured in respect of the plaintiff's claim;

(b) a public authority; or

(c) a person whose means and resources are such as to enable him to make the interim payment.

ORDER 29, r 12

Order for interim payment in respect of sums other than damages

If, on the hearing of an application under r 10, the court is satisfied:

(a) that the plaintiff has obtained an order for an account to be taken as between himself and the defendant and for any amount certified due on taking the account to be paid; or

(b) that the plaintiff's action includes a claim for possession of land and, if the action proceeded to trial, the defendant would be held liable to pay to the plaintiff a sum of money in respect of the defendant's use and occupation of the land during the pendency of the action, even if a final judgment or order were given or made in favour of the defendant; or

(c) that, if the action proceeded to trial, the plaintiff would obtain judgment against the defendant for a substantial sum of money apart from any damages or costs, the court may, if it thinks fit, and without prejudice to any contentions of the parties as to the nature or character of the sum to be paid by the defendant, order the defendant to make an interim payment of such amount as it thinks just, after taking into account any set-off, cross-claim or counterclaim on which the defendant may be entitled to rely.

ORDER 29, r 13

Manner of payment

(1) Subject to Order 80, r 12, the amount of any interim payment ordered to be made shall be paid to the plaintiff unless the order provides for it to be paid into court, and where the amount is paid into court, the court may, on the application of the plaintiff, order the whole or any part of it to be paid out to him at such time or times as the court thinks fit.

(2) An application under the preceding paragraph for money in court to be paid out may be made *ex parte*, but the court hearing the application may direct a summons to be issued.

(3) An interim payment may be ordered to be made in one sum or by such instalments as the court thinks fit.

(4) Where a payment is ordered in respect of the defendant's use and occupation of land the order may provide for periodical payments to be made during the pendency of the action.

ORDER 29, r 14

Directions on application under r 10

14 Where an application is made under r 10, the court may give directions as to the further conduct of the action, and, so far as may be applicable, Order 25, rr 2–7, shall, with the omission of so much of r 7(1) as requires the parties to serve a notice specifying the orders and directions which they require and with any other necessary modifications, apply as if the application were a summons for directions, and, in particular, the court may order an early trial of the action.

ORDER 29, r 15

Non-disclosure of interim payment

15 The fact that an order has been made under r 11 or 12 shall not be pleaded and, unless the defendant consents or the court so directs, no communication of that fact or of the fact that an interim payment has been made, whether voluntarily or pursuant to an order, shall be made to the court at the trial, or hearing, of any question or issue as to liability or damages until all questions of liability and amount have been determined.

ORDER 29, r 16

Payment into court in satisfaction

16 Where, after making an interim payment, whether voluntarily or pursuant to an order, a defendant pays a sum of money into court under Order 22, r 1, the

notice of payment must state that the defendant has taken into account the interim payment.

ORDER 29, r 17

Adjustment on final judgment or order or on discontinuance

17 Where a defendant has been ordered to make an interim payment or has in fact made an interim payment, whether voluntarily or pursuant to an order, the court may, in giving or making a final judgment or order, or granting the plaintiff leave to discontinue his action or to withdraw the claim in respect of which the interim payment has been made, or at any other stage of the proceedings on the application of any party, make such order with respect to the interim payment, and in particular:

(a) an order for the repayment by the plaintiff of all or part of the interim payment; or

(b) an order for the payment to be varied or discharged; or

(c) an order for the payment by any other defendant of any part of the interim payment which the defendant who made it is entitled to recover from him by way of contribution or indemnity or in respect of any remedy or relief relating to or connected with the plaintiff's claim.

ORDER 29, r 18

Counterclaims and other proceedings

18 The preceding rules in this part of this order shall apply, with the necessary modifications, to any counterclaim or proceeding commenced otherwise than by writ, where one party seeks an order for an interim payment to be made by another.

ORDER 32, r 9A

Application for a direction under the Limitation Act 1980

9A The jurisdiction to direct, under s 33 Limitation Act 1980, that ss 11 or 12 of that Act should not apply to an action or to any specified cause of action to which the action relates shall be exercisable by the court.

ORDER 33, r 3

Time, etc of trial of questions or issues

3 The court may order any question or issue arising in a cause or matter, whether of fact or law or partly of fact and partly of law, and whether raised by the pleadings or otherwise, to be tried before, at or after the trial of the cause or matter, and may give directions as to the manner in which the question or issue shall be stated.

ORDER 33, r 4

Determining the place and mode of trial

4(1) In every action begun by writ, an order made on the summons for directions shall determine the place and mode of the trial; and any such order may be varied by a subsequent order of the court made at or before the trial.

(2) In any such action different questions or issues may be ordered to be tried at different places or by different modes of trial and one or more questions or issues may be ordered to be tried before the others.

ORDER 37, r 7

Application and interpretation

7(1) This part of this order applies to actions to which s 32A of the Act (in this part of this order referred to as 's 32A') applies.

(2) In this part of this order, 'award of provisional damages' means an award of damages for personal injuries under which:

- (a) damages are assessed on the assumption that the injured person will not develop the disease or suffer the deterioration referred to in s 32A; and
- (b) the injured person is entitled to apply for further damages at a future date if he develops the disease or suffers the deterioration.

ORDER 37, r 8

Order for provisional damage

8(1) The court may on such terms as it thinks just and subject to the provisions of this rule make an award of provisional damages if:

- (a) the plaintiff has pleaded a claim for provisional damage; and
- (b) the court is satisfied that the action is one to which s 32A applies.

(2) An order for an award of provisional damages shall specify the disease or type of deterioration in respect of which an application may be made at a future date, and shall also, unless the court otherwise determines, specify the period within which such application may be made.

(3) The court may, on the application of the plaintiff made within the period, if any, specified in paragraph (2), by order extend that period if it thinks it just to do so, and the plaintiff may make more than one such application.

(4) An order for an award of provisional damages may be made in respect of more than one disease or type of deterioration and may in respect of each disease or deterioration specify a different period within which an application may be made at a future date.

(5) Orders 13 and 19 shall not apply in relation to an action in which the plaintiff claims provisional damages.

ORDER 37, r 9

Offer to submit to an award

9(1) Where an application is made for an award of provisional damages, any defendant may at any time (whether or not he makes a payment into court) make a written offer to the plaintiff:

    (a) to tender a sum of money (which may include an amount, to be specified, in respect of interest) in satisfaction of the plaintiff's claim for damages assessed on the assumption that the injured person will not develop the disease or suffer the deterioration referred to in s 32A and identifying the disease or deterioration in question; and

    (b) to agree to the making of an award of provisional damages.

(2) Any offer made under paragraph (1) shall not be brought to the attention of the court until after the court has determined the claim for an award of provisional damages.

(3) Where an offer is made under paragraph (1), the plaintiff may, within 21 days after receipt of the offer, give written notice to the defendant of his acceptance of the offer and shall on such acceptance make an application to the court for an order in accordance with the provisions of r 8(2).

ORDER 37, r 10

Application for award of further damages

10(1) This rule applies where the plaintiff, pursuant to an award of provisional damages, claims further damages.

(2) No application for further damages may be made after the expiration of the period, if any, specified under r 8(2), or of such period as extended under r 8(3).

(3) The plaintiff shall give not less than three months' written notice to the defendant of his intention to apply for further damages and, if the defendant is to the plaintiff's knowledge insured in respect of the plaintiff's claim, to the insurers.

(4) The plaintiff must take out a summons for directions as to the future conduct of the action within 21 days after the expiry of the period of notice referred to in paragraph (3).

(5) On the hearing of the summons for directions, the court shall give such directions as may be appropriate for the future conduct of the action, including, but not limited to, the disclosure of medical reports and the place, and date of the hearing of the application for further damages.

(6) Only one application for further damages may be made in respect of each disease or type of deterioration specified in the order for the award of provisional damages.

(7) The provisions of Order 29 with regard to the making of interim payments shall, with the necessary modifications, apply where an application is made under this rule.

(8) The court may include in an award of further damages simple interest at such rate as it thinks fit on all or any part thereof for all or any part of the period between the date of notification of the plaintiff's intention to apply for further damages and the date of the award.

ORDER 38, r 2A

Exchange of witness statements

2A(1) The powers of the court under this rule shall be exercised for the purpose of disposing fairly and expeditiously of the cause or matter before it, and saving costs, having regard to all the circumstances of the case, including (but not limited to):

(a) the extent to which the facts are in dispute or have been admitted;

(b) the extent to which the issues of fact are defined by the pleadings;

(c) the extent to which information has been or is likely to be provided by further and better particulars, answers to interrogatories or otherwise.

(2) At the summons for directions in an action commenced by writ, the court shall direct every party to serve on the other parties, within 14 weeks (or such or period as the court may specify) of the hearing of the summons and on such terms as the court may specify, written statements of the oral evidence which the party intends to adduce on any issues of fact to be decided at the trial.

The court may give a direction to any party under this paragraph at any other stage of such an action and at any stage of any other cause or matter.

Order 3, r 5(3) shall not apply to any period specified by the court under this paragraph.

(3) Directions under paragraph (2) or (17) may make different provision with regard to different issues of fact or different witnesses.

(4) Statements served under this rule shall:

(a) be dated and, except for good reason (which should be specified by letter accompanying the statement), be signed by the intended witness and shall include a statement by him that the contents are true to the best of his knowledge and belief;

(b) sufficiently identify any documents referred to therein; and

(c) where they are to be served by more than one party, be exchanged simultaneously.

(5) Where a party is unable to obtain a written statement from an intended witness in accordance with paragraph (4)(a), the court may direct the party wishing to adduce that witness's evidence to provide the other party with the name of the witness and (unless the court otherwise orders) a statement of the nature of the evidence intended to be adduced.

(6) Subject to paragraph (9), where the party serving a statement under this rule does not call the witness to whose evidence it relates, no other party may put the statement in evidence at the trial.

(7) Subject to paragraph (9), where the party serving the statement does call such a witness at the trial:

(a) except where the trial is with a jury, the court may, on such terms as it thinks fit, direct that the statement served, or part of it, shall stand as the evidence-in-chief of the witness or part of such evidence;

(b) the party may not without the consent of the other parties or the leave of the court adduce evidence from that witness the substance of which is not included in the statement served, except:

(i) where the court's directions under paragraph (2) or (17) specify that statements should be exchanged in relation to only some issues of fact, in relation to any other issues;

(ii) in relation to new matters which have arisen since the statement was served on the other party;

(c) whether or not the statement or any part of it referred to during the evidence-in-chief of the witness, any party may put the statement or any part of it in cross-examination of that witness.

(8) Nothing in this rule shall make admissible evidence which is other wise inadmissible.

(9) Where any statements served is one to which the Civil Evidence Acts 1968 and 1972 apply, paragraphs (6) and (7) shall take effect subject to the provisions of those Acts and Parts III and IV of this order.

The service of a witness statement under this rule shall not, unless expressly so stated by the party serving the same, be treated as a notice under the said Acts of 1968 and 1972; and where a statement or any part thereof would be admissible in evidence by virtue only of the said Act of 1968 or 1972, the appropriate notice under Part III or Part IV of this order shall be served with the statement notwithstanding any provision of those Parts as to the time for serving such a notice. Where such a notice is served a counter-notice shall be deemed to have been served under Order 38, r 26(1).

(10) Where a party fails to comply with a direction for the exchange of witness statements he shall not be entitled to adduce evidence to which the direction related without the leave of the court.

(11) Where a party serves a witness statement under this rule, no other person may make use of that statement for any purpose other than the purpose of the proceedings in which it was served:

(a) unless and to the extent that the party serving it gives his consent in writing or the court gives leave; or

(b) unless and to the extent that it has been put in evidence (whether pursuant to a direction under paragraph (7)(a) or otherwise).

(12) Subject to paragraph (13), the judge shall, if any person so requests during the course of the trial, direct the associate to certify as open to inspection any witness statement which was ordered to stand as evidence-in-chief under paragraph (7)(a).

A request under this paragraph may be made orally or in writing.

(13) The judge may refuse to give a direction under paragraph (12) in relation to a witness statement, or may exclude from such a direction any words or passages in a statement, if he considers that inspection should not be available:

(a) in the interests of justice or national security;

(b) because of the nature of any expert medical evidence in the statement; or

(c) for any other sufficient reason.

(14) Where the associate is directed under paragraph (12) to certify a witness statement as open to inspection he shall:

(a) prepare a certificate which shall be attached to a copy ('the certified copy') of that witness statement; and

(b) make the certified copy available for inspection.

(15) Subject to any conditions which the court may by special or general direction impose, any person may inspect and (subject to payment of the prescribed fee) take a copy of the certified copy of a witness statement from the time when the certificate is given until the end of seven days after the conclusion of the trial.

(16) In this rule:

(a) any reference in paragraphs (12) or (15) to a witness statement shall, in relation to a witness statement of which only part has been ordered to stand as evidence-in-chief under paragraph (7)(a), be construed as a reference to that part;

(b) any reference to inspecting or copying the certified copy of a witness statement shall be construed as including a reference to inspecting or copying a copy of that certified copy.

(17) The court shall have power to vary or override any of the provisions of this rule (except paragraphs (1), (8) and (12) to (16)) and to give such alternative directions as it thinks fit.

ORDER 38, r 35

Interpretation

35 In this part of this order, a reference to a summons for directions includes a reference to any summons or application to which, under any of these rules, Order 25, rr 2–7, apply and expressions used in this part of this order which are used in the Civil Evidence Act 1972 have the same meanings in the part of this order as in that Act.

ORDER 38, r 36

Restrictions on adducing expert evidence

36(1) Except with the leave of the court or where all parties agree, no expert evidence may be adduced at the trial or hearing of any cause or matter unless the party seeking to adduce the evidence:

(a) has applied to the court to determine whether a direction should be given under r 37 or 41 (whichever is appropriate) and has complied with any direction given on the application; or

(b) has complied with automatic directions taking effect under Order 25, r 8(1)(b).

(2) Nothing in paragraph (1) shall apply to evidence which is permitted to be given by affidavit or shall affect the enforcement under any other provision of these rules (except Order 45, r 5) of a direction given under this part of this order.

ORDER 38, r 7

Direction that expert report be disclosed

37(1) Subject to paragraph (2), where in any cause or matter an application is made under r 36(1) in respect of oral expert evidence, then, unless the court considers that there are special reasons for not doing so, it shall direct that the substance of the evidence be disclosed in the form of a written report or reports to such other parties and within such period as the court may specify.

(2) Nothing in paragraph (1) shall require a party to disclose a further medical report if he propose to rely at the trial only on the report provided pursuant to Order 18, r 12(1A) or (1B) but, where a party claiming damages for personal injuries discloses a further report, that report shall be accompanied by a statement of the special damages claimed and, in this paragraph, 'statement of the special damages claimed' has the same meaning as in Order 18, r 12(1C).

ORDER 38, r 38

Meeting of experts

38 In any cause or matter the court may, if it thinks fit, direct that there be a meeting 'without prejudice' of such experts within such periods before or after the disclosure of their reports as the court may specify, for the purpose of identifying those parts of their evidence which are in issue. Where such a meeting takes place the experts may prepare a joint statement indicating those parts of their evidence on which they are, and those on which there are not, in agreement.

ORDER 38, r 39

Disclosure of part of expert evidence

39 Where the court considers that any circumstances rendering it undesirable to give a direction under r 37 relate to part only of the evidence sought to be adduced, the court may, if it thinks fit, direct disclosure of the remainder.

ORDER 38, r 41

Expert evidence contained in statement

41 Where an application is made under r 36 in respect of expert evidence contained in a statement and the applicant alleges that the maker of the statement cannot or should not be called as a witness, the court may direct that the provisions of rr 20–23 and 25–33 shall apply with such modifications as the court thinks fit.

ORDER 38, r 42

Putting in evidence expert report disclosed by another party

42 A party to any cause or matter may put in evidence any expert report disclosed to him by any other party in accordance with this part of this order.

ORDER 38, r 43

Time for putting expert report in evidence

43 Where a party to any cause or matter calls as a witness, the maker of a report which has been disclosed in accordance with a direction given under r 37, the report may be put in evidence at the commencement of its maker's examination-in-chief or at such other time as the court may direct.

ORDER 38, r 44

Revocation and variation of directions

44 Any direction given under this part of this order may on sufficient cause being shown be revoked or varied by a subsequent direction given at or before the trial of the cause or matter.

ORDER 62, r 15A

Conditional fee agreements

15A(1) This rule applies to every taxation of a solicitor's bill to his own client where the solicitor and his client have entered into a conditional fee agreement as defined by s 58 of the Courts and Legal Services Act 1990.

(2) In this rule:

    (a) 'the base costs' means the costs other than a percentage increase;

    (b) 'percentage increase' means a percentage increase pursuant to a conditional fee agreement entered into between the solicitor and his client or, as the case may be, between counsel and the solicitor.

(3) On a taxation to which this rule applies, the client may apply for taxation of either the base costs or a percentage increase, or of both.

(4) Where the client applies for taxation of a percentage increase, he:

    (a) may give reasons why the percentage increase should be reduced; and

    (b) may state what he believes the percentage increase should be.

(5) On a taxation to which this rule applies:

    (a) where the client applies for taxation of the base costs, the base costs shall be taxed on an indemnity basis as if the solicitor and his client had not entered into a conditional fee agreement and r 15(2) shall apply to the taxation of the base costs;

    (b) where the client applies for taxation of a percentage increase, the percentage increase may be reduced where it is disproportionate having regard to all relevant factors, including:

        (i) the risk that the circumstances in which the fees or the expenses would be payable might not occur;

        (ii) the disadvantages relating to the absence of payments on account;

        (iii)whether the amount which might be payable under the conditional fee agreement is limited to a certain proportion of any damages recovered by the client;

        (iv)whether there is a conditional fee agreement between the solicitor and counsel.

(6) A percentage increase may be reduced notwithstanding that it does not exceed the maximum percentage permissible pursuant to s 58(2) Courts and Legal Services Act 1990.

(7) When considering the factors mentioned in paragraph (5)(b)(i) and (ii), the taxing officer shall have regard to the risk or disadvantage (as the case may be) as they reasonably appeared to the solicitor or counsel when the conditional fee agreement was entered into or at the time of any variation of the agreement.

(8) Taxations under this rule may be carried out only by a taxing master or district judge.

ORDER 80, r 1

Interpretation

1 In this order:

'the Act' means the Mental Health Act 1983;

'patient' means a person who, by reason of mental disorder within the meaning of the Act, is incapable of managing and administering his property and affairs;

'person under disability' means a person who is an infant or a patient.

ORDER 80, r 2

Person under disability must sue, etc, by next friend or guardian ad litem

2(1) A person under disability may not bring, or make a claim, in any proceedings except by his next friend and may not acknowledge service, defend, make a counterclaim or intervene in any proceedings, or appear in any proceedings under a judgment or order notice of which has been served on him, except by his guardian *ad litem*.

(2) Subject to the provisions of these rules, anything which in the ordinary conduct of any proceedings is required or authorised by a provision of these rules to be done by a party to the proceedings shall or may, if the party is a person under disability, be done by his next friend or guardian *ad litem*.

(3) A next friend or guardian *ad litem* of a person under disability must act by a solicitor.

ORDER 80, r 3

Appointment of next friend or guardian ad litem

3(1) (Revoked by RSC (Amendment No 4) 1971 SI 1971/1269.)

(2) Except as provided by paragraph (4) or (5) or by r 6, an order appointing a person next friend or guardian *ad litem* of a person under disability is not necessary.

(3) Where a person is authorised under Part VII of the Act to conduct legal proceedings in the name of a patient or on his behalf, that person shall be entitled to be next friend or guardian *ad litem*, as the case may be, of the patient in any proceedings to which his authority extends unless, in a case to which paragraph (4) or (6) or r 6 applies, some other person is appointed by the court under that paragraph or rule to be next friend or guardian *ad litem*, as the case may be, of the patient in those proceedings.

(4) Where a person has been or is next friend or guardian *ad litem* of a person under disability in any proceedings, no other person shall be entitled to act as such friend or guardian, as the case may be, of the person under disability in those proceedings unless the court makes an order appointing him such friend or guardian in substitution for the person previously acting in that capacity.

(5) Where, after any proceedings have been begun, a party to the proceedings becomes a patient, an application must be made to the court for the appointment of a person to be next friend or guardian *ad litem*, as the case may be, of that party.

(6) Except where the next friend or guardian *ad litem*, as the case may be, of a person under disability has been appointed by the court:

(a) the name of any person shall not be used in a cause or matter as next friend of a person under disability;

(b) service shall not be acknowledged in a cause or matter for a person under disability; and

(c) a person under disability shall not be entitled to appear by his guardian *ad litem* on the hearing of a petition, summons or motion which, or notice of which, has been served on him,

unless and until the documents listed in paragraph (8) have been filed in the appropriate office.

(7) The appropriate office for the purpose of paragraph (6) is the office of the Supreme court which has the conduct of the business of the division or court in

which the cause or matter is proceedings or, if it is proceedings in a district registry, that registry.

(8) The documents referred to in paragraph (6) are the following:

(a) a written consent to be next friend or guardian *ad litem*, as the case may be, of the person under disability in the cause or matter in question given by the person proposing to be such friend or guardian;

(b) where the person proposing to be such friend or guardian of the person under disability, being a patient, is authorised under Part VII of the Act to conduct the proceedings in the cause or matter in question in the name of the patient or on his behalf, an office copy, sealed with the official seal of the court of Protection, of the order or other authorisation made or given under the said Part VII by virtue of which he is so authorised; and

(c) except where the person proposing to be such friend or guardian of the person under disability, being a patient, is authorised as mentioned in sub-paragraph (b) a certificate made by the solicitor for the person under disability certifying:

(i) that he knows or believes, as the case may be, that the person to whom the certificate relates is an infant or a patient, giving (in the case of a patient) the grounds of his knowledge or belief; and

(ii) where the person under disability is a patient, that there is no person authorised as aforesaid; and

(iii) except where the person named in the certificate as next friend or guardian *ad litem*, as the case may be, is the official solicitor, that the person so named has no interest in the cause or matter in question adverse to that of the person under disability.

ORDER 80, r 10

Compromise, etc by person under disability

10(1) Where in any proceedings money is claimed by or on behalf of a person under disability, no settlement, compromise or payment and no acceptance of money paid into court, whenever entered into or made shall, so far as it relates to that person's claim, be valid without the approval of the court.

ORDER 80, r 11

Approval of settlement

11(1) Where, before proceedings in which a claim for money is made by or on behalf of a person under disability (whether alone or in conjunction with any other person) are begun, an agreement is reached for the settlement of the claim, and it is desired to obtain the court's approval to the settlement, then, notwithstanding anything in Order 5, r 2, the claim may be made in proceedings begun by originating summons and in the summons an application may also be made for:

(a) the approval of the court to the settlement and such orders or directions as may be necessary to give effect to it or as may be necessary or expedient under r 12; or

(b) alternatively, directions as to the further prosecution of the claim.

(2) Where in proceedings under this rule a claim is made under the Fatal Accidents Act 1976, the originating summons must include the particulars mentioned in s 2(4) of that Act.

(3) Without prejudice to Order 7, r 5, and Order 75, r 36(1), an originating summons under this rule may be issued out of any district registry notwithstanding that the proceedings are assigned to the Chancery Division.

(4) An originating summons under this rule shall be in Form No 10 in Appendix A.

(5) In this rule, 'settlement' includes a compromise.

ORDER 80, r 12

Control of money recovered by person under disability

12(1) Where in any proceedings:

(a) money is recovered by or on behalf of, or adjudged or ordered or agreed to be paid to, or for the benefit of, a person under disability; or

(b) money paid into court is accepted by or on behalf of a plaintiff who is a person under disability,

the money shall be dealt with in accordance with directions given by the court under this rule and not otherwise.

(2) Directions given under this rule may provide that the money shall, as to the whole or any part thereof, be paid into the High Court and invested or otherwise dealt with there.

(3) Without prejudice to the foregoing provisions of this rule, directions given under this rule may include any general or special directions that the court thinks fit to give and, in particular, directions as to how the money is to be applied or dealt with and as to any payment to be made, either directly or out of the amount paid into court to the plaintiff, or to the next friend in respect of moneys paid or expenses incurred for or on behalf or for the benefit of the person under disability or for his maintenance or otherwise for his benefit or to the plaintiff's solicitor in respect of costs.

(4) Where in pursuance of directions given under this rule money paid into the High Court to be invested or otherwise dealt with there, the money (including any interest thereon) shall not be paid out, nor shall any securities in which the money is invested, or the dividends thereon, be sold, transferred or paid out of court, except in accordance with an order of the court.

(5) The foregoing provisions of this rule shall apply in relation to a counterclaim by or on behalf of a person under disability, and a claim made by or on behalf of such a person in an action by any other person for relief under s 504 Merchant

Shipping Act 1894, as if for references to a plaintiff and a next friend there were substituted references to a defendant and to a guardian *ad litem* respectively.

ORDER 80, r 13

Appointment of guardian of child's estate

13(1) In any of the circumstances described in paragraph (2)(a)–(e) the court may appoint the Official Solicitor to be a guardian of the estate of a child provided that:

(a) the appointment is to subsist only until the child reaches the age of 18; and

(b) the consent of the persons with parental responsibility for the child (within the meaning of s 3 Children's Act 1989):

(i) has been signified to the court; or

(ii) in the opinion of the court, cannot be obtained or may be dispensed with.

(2) The circumstances referred to in paragraph (1) are:

(a) where money is paid into court on behalf of the child in accordance with directions given under r 12(2) (Control of money recovered by person under disability);

(b) where the Criminal Injuries Compensation Board notifies the court that it has made or intends to make an award to the child either under s 111 Criminal Justice Act 1988 or otherwise;

(c) where a court or tribunal outside England and Wales notifies the court that it has ordered or intends to order that money be paid to the child;

(d) where the child is absolutely entitled to proceeds of a pension fund;

(e) where such an appointment seems desirable to the court.

ORDER 80, r 15

Proceedings under Fatal Accidents Act: apportionment by court

15(1) Where a single sum of money is paid into court under Order 22, r 1, in satisfaction of causes of action arising under the Fatal Accident Act 1976, and the Law Reform (Miscellaneous Provisions) Act 1934, and that sum is accepted, the money shall be apportioned between the different causes of action by the court either when giving directions for dealing with it under r 12 (if that rule applies) or when authorising its payment out of court.

(2) Where, in an action in which a claim under the Fatal Accidents Act 1976 is made by or on behalf of more than one person, a sum in respect of damages is adjudged or ordered or agreed to be paid in satisfaction of the claim, or a sum of money paid into court under Order 22, r 1, is accepted in satisfaction of the cause of action under the said Act; then, unless the sum has been apportioned between the persons entitled thereto by the jury, it shall be apportioned between those persons by the court.

The reference in this paragraph to a sum of money paid into court shall be construed as including a reference to part of a sum so paid, being the part apportioned by the court under paragraph (1) to the cause of action under the said Act.

APPENDIX E

RULES OF THE COUNTY COURT

ORDER 13, r 5

Striking out pleadings

5(1) The court may at any stage of the proceedings in an action order the whole or any part of any pleading to be struck out or amended on the ground that:

    (a) it discloses no reasonable cause of action or defence, as the case may be; or

    (b) it is scandalous, frivolous or vexatious; or

    (c) it may prejudice, embarrass or delay the fair trial of the action; or

    (d) it is otherwise an abuse of the process of the court;

and may order the action to be stayed or dismissed or judgment to be entered accordingly, as the case may be.

(2) Any application for an order under paragraph (1) shall be made on notice to the party affected by it.

(3) This rule shall apply with the necessary modifications to a matter as it applies to an action.

ORDER 13, r 12

Interim payments

12(1) Subject to the following paragraphs of this rule, the provisions of RSC Order 29 Part II shall apply in relation to proceedings in a county court except where those proceedings stand referred for arbitration under Order 19, r 3.

(2) RSC Order 29, r 10 shall apply with the substitution in r 10(4), for the words 'not less than 10 clear days before the return day', of the words 'not less than seven days before the day fixed for the hearing of the application'.

(3) RSC Order 29, r 13(1) shall apply with the substitution, for the reference to RSC Order 80, r 12, of a reference to Order 10, r 11 of these rules.

(4) RSC Order 29, r 14 shall not apply but where an application is made for an order requiring the defendant to make an interim payment the court may treat the hearing of the application as a pre-trial review and Order 17 with the necessary modifications shall apply accordingly.

ORDER 17, r 11

Automatic directions

11(1) This rule applies to any default or fixed date action except:

    (a) an action for the administration of the estate of a deceased person;

    (b) an Admiralty action;

    (c) proceedings which are referred for arbitration under Order 19;

(d) an action arising out of a regulated consumer credit agreement within the meaning of the Consumer Credit Act 1974;

(e) an action for the delivery of goods;

(f) an action for the recovery of income tax;

(g) interpleader proceedings or an action in which an application is made for relief by way of interpleader;

(h) an action of a kind mentioned in s 66(3) of the Act (trial by jury);

(i) an action for the recovery of land;

(j) a partnership action;

(k) an action to which Order 48A applies (patent actions);

(l) a contentious probate action;

(m) [revoked, 1993];

(n) an action to which Order 5, r 5 applies (representative proceedings);

(o) an action to which Order 9, r 3(6) applies (admission of part of plaintiff's claim);

(p) an action on a third party notice or similar proceedings under Order 12;

(q) an action to which Order 47, r 3 applies (actions in tort between husband and wife);

(r) an action to which Order 48C applies (the Central London County Court Business List).

(1A) This rule applies to actions transferred from the High Court as it applies to actions commenced in a county court but (with prejudice to paragraph (2)) where directions have been given by the High Court, directions taking effect automatically under this rule shall have effect subject to any directions given by the High Court.

(2) In an action to which this rule applies:

(a) except where a pre-trial review is ordered pursuant to a direction given under paragraph (4)(a), the foregoing provisions of this order shall not apply and directions shall take effect automatically in accordance with the following paragraphs of this rule;

(b) where the court gives directions with regard to any matter arising in the course of proceedings, directions taking effect automatically under this rule shall have effect subject to any directions given by the court.

(3) When the pleadings are deemed to be closed, the following directions shall take effect:

(a) there shall be discovery of documents within 28 days, and inspection within seven days thereafter, in accordance with paragraph (5);

(b) except with the leave of the court or where all parties agree:

(i) no expert evidence may be adduced at the trial unless the substance of that evidence has been disclosed to the other parties in the form of a written report with 10 weeks;

(ii) subject to paragraph (7), the number of expert witnesses of any kind shall be limited to two; and

(iii) any party who intends to place reliance at the trial on any other oral evidence shall, within 10 weeks, serve on the other parties written statements of all such oral evidence which he intends to adduce;

(c) photographs and sketch plans and, in an action for personal injuries, the contents of any police accident report book shall be receivable in evidence at the trial and shall be agreed if possible;

(d) unless a day has already been fixed, the plaintiff shall within six months request the proper officer to fix a day for the hearing and r 12 shall apply where such request is made.

(3A) Paragraphs (4) to (16) of Order 20, r 12A shall apply with respect to statements and reports served under sub-paragraph (3)(b) as they apply with respect to statements served under that rule.

(4) Nothing in paragraph (3) shall:

(a) prevent the court from giving, of its own motion or on the application of any party, such further or different directions or orders as may in the circumstances be appropriate (including an order that a pre-trial review be held or fixing a date for the hearing or dismissing the proceedings or striking out any claim made therein); or

(b) prevent the making of an order for the transfer of the proceedings to the High Court or another county court;

and r 3 shall apply where an application is made under this paragraph as it applies to applications made on a pre-trial review.

(5) Subject to paragraph (6), the parties must make discovery by serving lists of documents and:

(a) subject to sub-paragraph (c), each party must make and serve on every other party a list of documents which are or have been in his possession, custody or power relating to any matter in question between them in the action;

(b) the court may, on application:

(i) order that discovery under this paragraph shall be limited to such documents or classes of documents only, or as to such only of the matters in question, as may be specified in the order; or

(ii) if satisfied that discovery by all or any of the parties is not necessary, order that there shall be no discovery of documents by any or all of the parties;

and the court shall make such an order if and so far as it is of opinion that discovery is not necessary either for disposing fairly of the action or for saving costs;

(c) where the liability is admitted or in an action for personal injuries arising out of a road accident, discovery shall be limited to disclosure of any documents relating to the amount of damages;

(d) the provisions of Order 14 of these rules relating to inspection of documents shall apply where discovery is made under this paragraph as it applies where discovery is made under that order.

(6) Discovery under paragraph (5) shall not apply in proceedings to which the Crown is a party.

(7) In an action for personal injuries:

(a) the number of expert witnesses shall be limited in any case to two medical experts and one expert of any other kind;

(b) nothing in paragraph (3) shall require a party to produce a further medical report if he proposes to rely at the trial only on the report provided pursuant to Order 6, r 1 (5) or (6) but, where a further report is disclosed, that report shall be accompanied by an amended statement of the special damages claimed, if appropriate.

(8) Where the plaintiff makes a request pursuant to paragraph (3)(d) for the proper officer to fix a day for the hearing, he shall file a note which shall if possible be agreed by the parties giving:

(a) an estimate of the length of the trial; and

(b) the number of witnesses to be called.

(9) If no request is made pursuant to paragraph (3)(d) within 15 months of the day on which pleadings are deemed to be closed (or within nine months after the expiry of any period fixed by the court for making such a request), the action shall be automatically struck out.

(10) Where the proper officer fixes a day for the hearing, he shall give not less than 21 days' notice thereof to every party.

(11) For the purposes of this rule:

(a) pleadings shall be deemed to be closed 14 days after the delivery of a defence in accordance with Order 9, r 2 or, where a counterclaim is served with the defence, 28 days after the delivery of the defence;

(b) 'a road accident' means an accident on land due to a collision or apprehended collision involving a vehicle;

(c) 'a statement of the special damages claimed' has the same meaning as in Order 6, r 1 (7).

(12) Unless the context otherwise requires, references in these rules to the return day in relation to a fixed date action to which this rule applies shall be construed as references to the date on which directions take effect under this rule.

ORDER 20, r 27

Restrictions on adducing expert evidence

27(1) Except:

(a) with the leave of the court;

(b) in accordance with the provisions of Order 17, r 11; or

(c) where all parties agree,

no expert evidence may be adduced at the trial or hearing of an action or matter, unless the party seeking to adduce the evidence has applied to the court to determine whether a direction should be given under r 37, 38 or 41 (whichever is appropriate) of RSC Order 38, as applied by r 28 of this order, and has complied with any direction given on the application.

(2) Nothing in paragraph (1) shall apply to expert evidence which is permitted to be given by affidavit or which is to be adduced in an action or matter in which no defence or answer has been filed or in proceedings referred to arbitration under s 64 of the Act.

(3) Nothing in paragraph (1) shall affect the enforcement under any other provision of these rules (except Order 29, r 1) of a direction given under this part of this order.

ETHICAL GUIDELINES

HIPPOCRATIC OATH

I will look upon him who shall have taught me this Art even as one of my parents. I will share my substance with him, and I will supply his necessities, if he be in need. I will regard his offspring even as my own brethren, and I will teach them this Art, if they would learn it, without fee or covenant. I will impart this Art by precept, by lecture and by every mode of teaching, not only to my own sons, but to the sons of him who taught me, and to disciples bound by covenant and oath, according to the Law of Medicine.

The regimen I adopt shall be for the benefit of my patients according to my ability and judgment, and not for their hurt or for any wrong. I will give no deadly drug to any, though it be asked of me, nor will I counsel such, and especially I will not aid a woman to procure abortion. Whatsoever house I enter, there will I go for the benefit of the sick, refraining from all wrongdoing or corruption, and especially from any act of seduction of male or female, of bond or free. Whatsoever things I see or hear concerning the life of men, in my attendance on the sick, or even apart therefrom, which ought not to be noised abroad, I will keep silence thereon, counting such things to be as sacred secrets.

DUTIES OF A DOCTOR (GUIDANCE FROM THE GENERAL MEDICAL COUNCIL)

Patients must be able to trust doctors with their lives and well-being. To justify that trust, we as a profession have a duty to maintain a good standard of practice and care and to show respect for human life. In particular, as a doctor you must:

- make the care of your patient your first concern;
- treat every patient politely and considerately;
- respect patients' dignity and privacy;
- listen to patients and respect their views;
- give patients information in a way they can understand;
- respect the rights of patients to be fully involved in decisions about their care;
- keep your professional knowledge and skills up-to-date;
- recognise the limits of your professional competence;
- be honest and trustworthy;
- respect and protect confidential information;
- make sure that your personal beliefs do not prejudice your patients' care;
- act quickly to protect patients from risk if you have good reason to believe that you or a colleague may not be fit to practice;
- work with colleagues in the ways that best serve patients' interests.

CONFIDENTIALITY – GUIDANCE FROM THE GENERAL MEDICAL COUNCIL

Principles of confidentiality

1 Patients have a right to expect that you will not disclose any personal information which you learn during the course of your professional duties, unless they give permission. Without assurances about confidentiality patients may be reluctant to give doctors the information they need in order to provide good care. For these reasons:

- When you are responsible for confidential information you must make sure that the information is effectively protected against improper disclosure when it is disposed of, stored, transmitted or received;
- When patients give consent to disclosure of information about them, you must make sure they understand what will be disclosed, the reasons for disclosure and the likely consequences;
- You must make sure that patients are informed whenever information about them is likely to be disclosed to others involved in their health care, and that they have the opportunity to withhold permission;
- You must respect requests by patients that information should not be disclosed to third parties, save in exceptional circumstances (for example, where the health or safety of others would otherwise be at serious risk);
- If you disclose confidential information you should release only as much information as is necessary for the purpose;
- You must make sure that health workers to whom you disclose information understand that it is given to them in confidence which they must respect;
- If you decide to disclose confidential information, you must be prepared to explain and justify your decision.

These principles apply in all circumstances, including those discussed in this booklet.

Disclosure of confidential information with the patient's consent

2 You may release confidential information in strict accordance with the patient's consent, or the consent of a person properly authorised to act on the patient's behalf.

Disclosure within teams

3 Modern medical practice usually involves teams of doctors, other health care workers, and sometimes people from outside the health care professions. The importance of working in teams is explained in the GMC's booklet 'Good Medical Practice'. To provide patients with the best possible care, it is often essential to pass confidential information between members of the team.

4 You should make sure – through the use of leaflets and posters if necessary – that patients understand why and when information may be shared between team members, and any circumstances in which team members providing non-medical care may be required to disclose information to third parties.

5 Where the disclosure of relevant information between health care professionals is clearly required for treatment to which a patient has agreed, the patient's explicit consent may not be required. For example, explicit consent would not be needed where a general practitioner discloses relevant information to a medical secretary to have a referral letter typed, or a physician makes relevant information available to a radiologist when requesting an X-ray.

6 There will also be circumstances where, because of a medical emergency, a patient's consent cannot be obtained, but relevant information must in the patient's interest be transferred between health care workers.

7 If a patient does not wish you to share particular information with other members of the team, you must respect those wishes. If you and a patient have established a relationship based on trust, the patient may choose to give you discretion to disclose information to other team members, as required.

8 All medical members of a team have a duty to make sure that other team members understand and observe confidentiality.

Disclosure to employers and insurance companies

9 When assessing a patient on behalf of a third party (for example, an employer or insurance company), you must make sure, at the outset, that the patient is aware of the purpose of the assessment, of the obligation that the doctor has towards the third parties concerned, and that this may necessitate the disclosure of personal information. You should undertake such assessments only with the patient's written consent.

Disclosure of information without the patient's consent

Disclosure in the patient's medical interests

10 Problems may arise if you consider that a patient is incapable of giving consent to treatment because of immaturity, illness, or mental incapacity, and you have tried unsuccessfully to persuade the patient to allow an appropriate person to be involved in the consultation. If you are convinced that it is essential in the patient's medical interests, you may disclose relevant information to an appropriate person or authority. You must tell the patient before disclosing any information. You should remember that the judgment of whether patients are capable of giving or withholding consent to treatment or disclosure must be based on an assessment of their ability to appreciate what the treatment or advice being sought may involve, and not solely on their age.

11 If you believe a patient to be a victim of neglect or physical or sexual abuse, and unable to give or withhold consent to disclosure, you should usually give information to an appropriate responsible person or statutory agency, in order to prevent further harm to the patient. In these and similar circumstances, you may release information without the patient's consent, but only if you consider

that the patient is unable to give consent, and that the disclosure is in the patient's best medical interests.

12 Rarely, you may judge that seeking consent to the disclosure of confidential information would be damaging to the patient, but that the disclosure would be in the patient's medical interests. For example, you may judge that it would be in a patient's interests that a close relative should know about the patient's terminal condition, but that the patient would be seriously harmed by the information. In such circumstances information may be disclosed without consent.

Disclosure after a patient's death

13 You still have an obligation to keep information confidential after a patient dies. The extent to which confidential information may be disclosed after a patient's death will depend on the circumstances. These include the nature of the information, whether that information is already public knowledge, and how long it is since the patient died. Particular difficulties may arise when there is a conflict of interest between parties affected by the patient's death. For example, if an insurance company seeks information about a decreased patient in order to decide whether to make a payment under a life assurance policy, you should not release information without the consent of the patient's executor or a close relative, who has been fully informed of the consequences of disclosure.

14 You should be aware that the Access to Health Records Act 1990 gives third parties right of access, in certain circumstances, to the medical records of a deceased patient.

Disclosure for medical teaching, medical research and medical audit

Research

15 Where, for the purposes of medical research there is a need to disclose information which it is not possible to anonymise effectively, every reasonable effort must be made to inform the patients concerned, or those who may properly give permission on their behalf, that they may, at any stage, withhold their consent to disclosure.

16 Where consent cannot be obtained, this fact should be drawn to the attention of a research ethics committee which should decide whether the public interest in the research outweighs patients' right to confidentiality. Disclosures to a researcher may otherwise be improper, even if the researcher is a registered medical practitioner.

Teaching and audit

17 Patients' consent to disclosure of information for teaching and audit must be obtained unless the data have been effectively anonymised.

Disclosure in the interests of others

18 Disclosures may be necessary in the public interest where a failure to disclose information may expose the patient, or others, to risk of death or serious harm. In such circumstances you should disclose information promptly to an appropriate person or authority.

19 Such circumstances may arise, for example, where:

- A patient continues to drive, against medical advice, when unfit to do so. In such circumstances you should disclose relevant information to the medical adviser of the Driver and Vehicle Licensing Agency without delay. Further guidance is given in Appendix 1.

- A colleague, who is also a patient, is placing patients at risk as a result of illness or another medical condition. Guidance on this issue, and on the rights of doctors who are ill, is contained in the GMC's leaflet 'HIV infection and AIDS: the ethical considerations' and in a separate note about the GMC's health procedures.

- Disclosure is necessary for the prevention or detection of a serious crime.

Disclosure in connection with judicial or other statutory proceedings

20 You may disclose information to satisfy a specific statutory requirement, such as notification of a communicable disease or of attendance upon a person dependent upon certain controlled drugs. You may also disclose information if ordered to do so by a judge or presiding officer of a court, or if you are summoned to assist a Coroner, Procurator Fiscal, or other similar officer in connection with an inquest or comparable judicial investigation. If you are required to produce patients' notes or records under a court order you should disclose only so much as is relevant to the proceedings. You should object to the judge or the presiding officer if attempts are made to compel you to disclose other matters which appear in the notes, for example matters relating to relatives or partners of the patient who are not parties to the proceedings.

21 In the absence of a court order, a request for disclosure by a third party, for example, a solicitor, police officer, or officer of a court, is not sufficient justification for disclosure without a patient's consent.

22 When a Committee of the GMC investigating a doctor's fitness to practice has determined that the interest of justice require disclosure of confidential information, you may disclose information at the request of the Committee's Chairman, provided that every reasonable effort has been made to seek the consent of the patients concerned. If consent is refused the patient's wishes must be respected.

Disclosure to inspectors of taxes

23 If you have a private practice, you may disclose confidential information in response to a request from an inspector of taxes, provided you have made every effort to separate financial information from clinical records.

Doctors who decide to disclose confidential information must be prepared to explain and justify their decisions.

APPENDIX 1

Disclosure of information about patients to the Driver and Vehicle Licensing Agency (DVLA)

1 The DVLA is legally responsible for deciding if a person is medically unfit to drive. They need to know when driving licence holders have a condition which may now, or in the future, affect their safety as a driver.

2 Therefore, where patients have such conditions you should:

- Make sure that the patients understand that the condition may impair their ability to drive. If a patient is incapable of understanding this advice, for example, because of dementia, you should inform the DVLA immediately.
- Explain to patients that they have a legal duty to inform the DVLA about the condition.

3 If the patients refuse to accept the diagnosis or the effect of the condition on their ability to drive, you can suggest that the patients seek a second opinion, and make appropriate arrangements for the patient to do so. You should advise patients not to drive until the second opinion has been obtained.

4 If patients continue to drive when they are not fit to do so, you should make every reasonable effort to persuade them to stop. This may include telling their next of kin.

5 If you do not manage to persuade patients to stop driving, or you are given or find evidence that a patient is continuing to drive contrary to advice, you should disclose relevant medical information immediately, in confidence, to the medical adviser at the DVLA.

6 Before giving information to the DVLA you should inform the patient of your decision to do so. Once the DVLA has been informed, you should also write to the patient, to confirm that a disclosure has been made.

HIV AND AIDS: THE ETHICAL CONSIDERATIONS

Guidance from the General Medical Council

The doctor/patient relationship

1 The doctor/patient relationship is founded on mutual trust, which can be fostered only when information is freely exchanged between doctor and patient on the basis of honesty, openness and understanding. Acceptance of that principle is, in the view of the GMC, fundamental to the resolution of the questions which have been identified in relation to AIDS.

2 The GMC has been impressed by the significant increase in the understanding of AIDS and AIDS-related conditions, both within the profession and by the

general public, which appears to have occurred. It seems that most doctors are now prepared to regard these conditions as similar in principle to other infections and life threatening conditions, and are willing to apply established principles in approaching their diagnosis and management, rather than treating them as medical conditions quite distinct from all others. The GMC believes that an approach of this kind will help doctors to resolve many of the difficulties which have arisen hitherto.

3 In all areas of medical practice doctors need to make judgments which they may later have to justify. This is true both of clinical matters and of the complex ethical problems which arise regularly in the course of providing patient care, because it is not possible to set out a code of practice which provides solutions to every such problem which may arise. The GMC would remind the profession of the statements of general principle which are set out for the guidance of doctors in its booklet 'Good medical practice'. In the light of that general guidance, the GMC has formed the following views on questions of particular significance in relation to HIV infection and the conditions related to it.

The doctor's duty towards patients

4 The GMC expects that doctors will extend to patients who are HIV positive or are suffering from AIDS the same high standard of medical care and support which they would offer to any other patient. It has, however, expressed its serious concern at reports that, in a small number of cases, doctors have refused to provide such patients with necessary care and treatment.

5 It is entirely proper for a doctor who has conscientious objection to undertaking a particular course of treatment, or who lacks the necessary knowledge, skill or facilities to provide appropriate investigation or treatment for a patient, to refer that patient to a professional colleague.

6 However, it is unethical for a registered medical practitioner to refuse treatment, or investigation for which there are appropriate facilities, on the ground that the patient suffers, or may suffer, from a condition which could expose the doctor to personal risk. It is equally unethical for a doctor to withhold treatment from any patient on the basis of a moral judgment that the patient's activities or lifestyle might have contributed to the condition for which treatment was being sought. Unethical behaviour of this kind may raise a question of serious professional misconduct.

7/8/9 Duties of doctors infected with the virus.

10 Rights of doctors infected with the virus.

Consent to investigation or treatment

11 It has long been accepted, and is well understood within the profession, that a doctor should treat a patient only on the basis of the patient's informed consent. Doctors are expected in all normal circumstances to be sure that their patients consent to the carrying out of investigative procedures involving the removal of samples or invasive techniques, whether those investigations are performed for the purposes of routing screening, for example, in pregnancy or prior to surgery, or for the more specific purpose of differential diagnosis. A

patient's consent may in certain circumstances be given implicitly, for example by agreement to provide a specimen of blood for multiple analysis. In other circumstances it needs to be given explicitly, for example, before undergoing a specified operative procedure or providing a specimen of blood to be tested specifically for a named condition. As the expectations of patients, and consequently the demands made upon doctors, increase and develop, it is essential that both doctor and patient feel free to exchange information before investigation or treatment is undertaken.

Testing for HIV infection: the need to obtain consent

12 The GMC believes that the above principle should apply generally, but that it is particularly important in the case of testing for HIV infection, not because the condition is different in kind from other infections but because of the possible serious social and financial consequences which may ensue for the patient from the mere fact of having been tested for the condition. These are problems which would be better resolved by a developing spirit of social tolerance than by medical action, but they do raise a particular ethical dilemma for the doctor in connection with the diagnosis of HIV infection or AIDS. They provide a strong argument for each patient to be given the opportunity, in advance, to consider the implications of submitting to such a test and deciding whether to accept or decline it.

13 In the case of a patient presenting with certain symptoms which the doctor is expected to diagnose, this process should form part of the consultation. Where blood samples are taken for screening purposes, as in ante-natal clinics, there will usually be no reason to suspect HIV infection but even so the test should be carried out only where the patient has given explicit consent. Similarly, those handling blood samples in laboratories, either for specific investigation or for the purpose of research, should test for the presence of HIV only where they know the patient has given explicit consent. Only in the most exceptional circumstances, where a test is imperative in order to secure the safety of persons other than the patient, and where it is not possible for the prior consent of the patient to be obtained, can testing without explicit consent be justified.

14 A particular difficulty arises in cases where it may be desirable to test a child for HIV infection and where, consequently, the consent of a parent, or a person in loco parentis, would normally be sought. However, the possibility that the child may have been infected by a parent may, in certain circumstances, distort the parent's judgment so that consent is withheld in order to protect the parent's own position. The doctor faced with this situation must first judge whether the child is competent to consent to the test on his or her own behalf. If the child is judged competent in this context, then consent can be sought from the child. If, however, the child is judged unable to give consent the doctor must decide whether the interest of the child should override the wishes of the parent. It is the view of the GMC that it would not be unethical for a doctor to perform such a test without parental consent, provided always that the doctor is able to justify that action as being in the best interests of the patient.

Confidentiality

15 Doctors are familiar with the need to make judgments about whether to disclose confidential information in particular circumstances, and the need to justify their action where such a disclosure is made. The GMC believes that, where HIV infection or AIDS has been diagnosed, any difficulties concerning confidentiality which arise will usually be overcome if doctors are prepared to discuss openly and honestly with patients the implications of their condition, the need to secure the safety of others, and the importance for continuing medical care of ensuring that those who will be involved in their care know the nature of their condition and the particular needs which they will have. The GMC takes the view that any doctor who discovers that a patient is HIV positive or suffering from AIDS has a duty to discuss these matters fully with the patient.

Informing other health care professionals

16 When a patient is seen by a specialist who diagnoses HIV infection or AIDS, and a general practitioner is or may become involved in that patient's care, then the specialist should explain to the patient that the general practitioner cannot be expected to provide adequate clinical management and care without full knowledge of the patient's condition. The GMC believes that the majority of such patients will readily be persuaded of the need for their general practitioners to be informed of the diagnosis.

17 If the patient refuses consent for the general practitioner to be told, then the doctor has two sets of obligations to consider: obligations to the patient to maintain confidence, and obligations to other carers whose own health may be put unnecessarily at risk. in such circumstances the patient should be counselled about the difficulties which his or her condition is likely to pose for the team responsible for providing continuing health care and about the likely consequences for the standard of care which can be provided in the future. If, having considered the matter carefully in the light of such counselling, the patient still refuses to allow the general practitioner to be informed then the patient's request for privacy should be respected. The only exception to that general principle arises where the doctor judges that the failure to disclose would put the health of any of the health care team at serious risk. The GMC believes that, in such a situation, it would not be improper to disclose such information as that person needs to know. The need for such a decision is, in present circumstances, likely to arise only rarely but, if it is made, the doctor must be able to justify his or her action.

18 Similar principles apply to the sharing of confidential information between specialists or with other health care professionals such as nurses, laboratory technicians and dentists. All persons receiving such information must, of course, consider themselves under the same general obligation of confidentiality as the doctor principally responsible for the patient's care.

Informing the patient's spouse or other sexual partner

19 Questions of conflicting obligations also arise when a doctor is faced with the decision whether the fact that a patient is HIV positive or suffering from AIDS

should be disclosed to a third party, other than another health care professional, without the consent of the patient. The GMC has reached the view that there are grounds for such a disclosure only where there is a serious and identifiable risk to specific individual who, if not so informed, would be exposed to infection. Therefore, when a person is found to be infected in this way, the doctor must discuss with the patient the question of informing a spouse or other sexual partner. The GMC believes that most such patients will agree to disclosure in these circumstances, but where such consent is withheld the doctor may consider it a duty to seek to ensure that any sexual partner is informed, in order to safeguard such persons from infection.

Conclusion

20 It is emphasised that the advice set out above is intended to guide doctors in approaching the complex questions which may arise in the context of this infection. It is not in any sense a code, and individual doctors must always be prepared, as a matter of good medical practice, to make their own judgments of the appropriate course of action to be followed in specific circumstances, and be able to justify the decisions they make. The GMC believes that the generality of doctors has acted compassionately, responsibly and in a well-informed manner in tackling the especially sensitive problems with which the spread of this group of conditions has confronted society. It is confident that they will continue to do so.

The authors extend their grateful thanks to the General Medical Council for permission to reproduce the above material.

GLOSSARY OF SOME COMMON ABBREVIATIONS AND HIEROGLYPHS

Common abbreviations

aa	of each (Greek)
AAL	Anterior Auxiliary Line
ac	before meals
ACTH	Adrenocorticotrophic Hormone
ad	up to
add	adduction
ADH	Antidiuretic Hormone
ADL	Activities of Daily Living
ad lib	to the desired amount
ADP	Adenosine Diphosphate
AE	Air Entry
AFB	Acid Fast Bacillus (TB)
AFP	Alpha-fetoprotein maternal serum and occasionally amniotic fluid levels tested in pregnancy to screen for neural tube defect in foetus
AID	Artificial Insemination–Donor
AIDS	Acquired Immune Deficiency Syndrome
AIH	Artificial Insemination–Husband
AJ	Ankle Jerk (reflex: see also BJ,KJ,SJ,TJ)
alt dieb	every other day
Al S	Alimentary System
anti-D	this gamma globulin must be given by injection to rhesus negative mother who delivers/aborts rhesus positive child/foetus, to prevent mother developing antibodies which would damage a subsequent rhesus positive baby
Apgar	Apgar score: means of recording baby's condition at birth by observing and 'scoring' (0,1 or 2) five parameters
applic	applications
aq	water
aq dest/ster	distilled water/sterilised
aq dest	distilled water
AR	Analytical standard of Reagent purity
ARC	Aids Related Complex (less damage can result in full blown AIDS)
ARDS	Adult Respiratory Distress Syndrome
ARM	Artificial Rupture of Membranes

ASD		Atrial Septal Defect
AST		Aspartate Aminotransferase
ATP		Adenosine Triphosphate
aurist		ear drops
A/V		Anteverted
bd		both
b.d.		twice a day
BJ		Biceps Jerk (reflex: see AJ)
B.S.		British Standard
blood sugar		normal 2.5–5.5 mmol/1
blood urea		normal 2.5–6.6 mmol/1
BMR		Basal Metabolism Rate
BNF (plus date)		British National Formulary (prescriber's bible supplied free to all NHS doctors).
BO		Bowels Open
BP (plus date)		British Pharmacopoeia
BP		Blood Pressure
BS	(i)	Breath Sounds
	(ii)	Bowel Sounds
	(iii)	Blood Sugar
	(iv)	British Standard
c		with (Latin: cum)
C2H5OH		alcohol
Ca	(i)	Carcinoma/cancer
	(ii)	Calcium
Caps		Capsules
CAT scan		Computed Axial Tomograph
cp		compare
CIN		Cervical Intraepithelial Neoplasia (cervical cancer)
CMV		Cytomegalovirus
CNS		Central Nervous System
CO		Complaining Of
CO2		carbon dioxide
COETT		Cuffed Oral Endotracheal Tube (see COT and ETT)
comp		compounded of
COT		Cuffed Oral Tube (endotracheal tube used for ventilating a patient who cannot breathe unaided)

CPD	Cephalo-pelvic Disproportion (baby too big to fit through pelvis)
crem	a cream
CSF	Cerebro-spinal Fluid
CTG	Cardiotocograph Trace (during labour–of baby's heart and mother's contractions)
CVA	Cardiovascular Accident (stroke)
CVS	Cardiovascular System
Cx	Cervix
CXR	Chest X-ray
D	Diagnosis (GOK–God Only Knows)
DES	Diethylstilbestrol
DIC	Disseminated Intravascular Coagulation (a serious complication of many conditions–relates to widespread thrombosis)
dil	dilute
DNA (i)	Did Not Attend
(ii)	Deoxyribonucleic Acid
D & V	Diarrhoea and Vomiting
DOA	Dead On Arrival
DOPA	Dopamine
DVT	Deep Vein Thrombosis
D/W	Discussed With
Dx	Diagnosis
ECG	Electrocardiography
ECT	Electroconvulsive Therapy
EDD	Expected Date of Delivery
emf	electromotive force
EM	Electron Micrography
EMG	Electromyo/gram/graph
emp	emplastrum (a plaster)
enem	enemata (enemas)
EOG	Electro-oculogram
ER	External Rotation
ERCP	Endoscopic Retrograde Cholangio-pancreatography/scope
ERPC	Evacuation of Retained Products of Conception
ERG	Electroretinogram

ESR	Erythrocyte Sedimentation Rate
Ex	Extension
FB	Finger's Breadth
FBC	Full Blood Count
FBS	Foetal Blood Sampling (ob)
FH	Family History
FHH	Foetal Heart Heard
FHHR	Foetal Heart Heard Regular
FHR	Foetal Heart Rate
Flex	Flexion
FLK	Funny Looking Kid
FMF	Foetal Movements Felt
FSE	Foetal Scalp Electrode
FSH	Family Social History or
	Follicle-stimulating Hormone
GA	General Anaesthetic
garg	gargles
glc	Gas Liquid Chromatography
GTT	Glucose Tolerance Test
GFR	Glomerular Filtration Rate
GIT	Gastrointestinal Tract
GM	Geiger Muller
GUT	Genitourinary Tract
Hb	Haemoglobin
HCG	Human Chorionic Gonadotrophin
HCO	History of Present Complaint (or HPC)
hn	hac nocte (Latin: tonight)
ha	hora somni (Latin: at bed time)
HS	Heart Sounds
HSA	Human Serum Albumin
HVS	High Vaginal Swab
Hx	History
ICF	Intracellular Fluid
ICS	Intercostal Space
IgA, IgB, IgG, IgM	Immunoglobins
IJV	Internal Jugular Vein

IM	Intramuscular
implant	implantation
in aq	in water
inj	injections
IP	Intraperitoneal
IR	Internal Rotation
irrig	irrigations
IVI	Intravenous Infusion
IVP	Intravenous Pyelogram
K	potassium
KJ	Knee Jerk
KPa	Kiloplascal, approx 7.5 mm Hg
L	Litre
LA	Local Anaesthetic
LATS	Long Acting Thyroid Stimulator
LFT	Liver Function Tests
LH	Lutenizing Hormone
LIH	Left Inguinal Hernia
linc	linctus
lin	liniments
liq	solutions
LMP	Last Menstrual Period
LN	Lymph Node
LOA	Left Occiput Anterior
LOC	Loss Of Consciousness
LOL	Left Occiput Lateral
LOP	Left Occiput Posterior
LSCS	Lower Segment Caesarean Section
LSK	Liver, Spleen, Kidneys
m	mix
mane	in the morning (Latin)
mcg	microgram
MCL	Mid Clavicular Line
ME	Myalgic Encephalomyelitis (chronic fatigue syndrome or post viral fatigue syndrome)
mg	milligram

mmttg	mm of mercury (unit of pressure)
ml	millilitres
MP	Melting Point
MS	Multiple Sclerosis
MSH	Melanophore Stimulating Hormone
MSU	Midstream Specimen of Urine
N & V	Nausea and Vomiting
NAD	Nothing Abnormal Detected
NBM	Nil By Mouth
Neb	a spray
ng	nanogram
NG	Neoplastic Growth
Ng	Nasogastric
NGT	Nasogastric Tube
NHL	non-Hodgkins Lymphoma
NMCS	No Malignant Cells Seen
NOF	Neck of Femur
N/S	Normal Size
O2	oxygen
occulent	eye ointment
OA	Occupito-anterior
od	daily
OD	Outside Diameter
OE	On Examination
om	every morning
oe	every evening
OP	Occupito-posterior
PR	Pulse Rate
Pa	Pascal
PAS	Periodic Acid–Schiff reaction
pc	after meals
PCG	Phonocardiogram
PCV	Packed Cell Volume
PERLA	Pupils are Equal and React to Light and Accommodation
PE	Pulmonary Embolism

pes	pessaries
PET	Pre-eclampsia Toxaemia
ph	acidity/alkalinity scale
PH	Past History
PID	Pelvic Inflammatory Disease or
	Prolapsed Intravertebral Disc
PMH	Past Medical History
PN(R)	Percussion Note (Resonant)
PNS	Peripheral Nervous System
PPI	paternal preconception irradiation
PO	Per–or by–mouth
PR	Per Rectum
PV	Per Vagina
PVS	Persistent Vegetative State
prn	as required/as occasion arises
RBC	Red Blood Cells
Rh	Rhesus
RH	Relative Humidity
RIA	Relative Immune Assay
RIH	Right Inguinal Hernia
ROA	Right Occupit Anterior
ROL	Right Occupit Lateral
ROM	Range of Movement
RPF	Renal Plasma Flow
RQ	Respiratory Quotient
RS	Respiratory System
RT	Reaction Time
RTI	Respiratory Tract Infection
S/B	Seen By
S/D	Systolic/Diastolic
SEM	Scanning Electron Microscope
SH	Social History
SJ	Jerk
SOA	Swelling Of Ankles
SOB	Shortness Of Breath
SOS	Si Opus Sit (if necessary) or See Other Sheet

SROM	Spontaneous Rupture of Membranes
SVC	Superior Vena Cava
SVD	Spontaneous Vaginal Delivery
TCI 3/52	To Come In three weeks time
TGH	To Go Home
THR	Total Hip Replacement
TID	Three Times a Day
TJ	Triceps Jerk
TFTS	Thyroid Function Tests
TSH	Thyroid Stimulating Hormone
U & E	Urea and Electrolytes
ung	ointments
UG	Urogenital System
URTI	Upper Respiratory Tract Infection
VE	Vaginal Examination
VF	Ventrical Fibrillation
VT	Ventrical Tachycardia
V/V	Vulva and Vagina
WBC	White Blood Count/Corpuscle

Common hieroglyphs

#	fracture
Δ	diagnosis
R_x	treatment
o	nil/nothing
$\uparrow$	up
$\downarrow$	down
1/7	one day
2/52	two days
3/12	three months

The authors extend their grateful thanks to AVMA for permission to reproduce this list of common abbreviations and hieroglyphs.

APPENDIX H

MISCELLANEOUS

Injury	Expert
Brain damage/head injury	Neurologist/neurosurgeon preferably at a hospital with brain scan equipment.
Mother and baby	Obstetrician and gynaecologist, paediatrician.
Wrong drug treatment	Pharmacologist (and toxicologist if necessary) and appropriate expert.
Negligent surgery	A general surgeon expert in the field.
Chest complaints	Chest physician – most teaching hospitals have large chest clinics with modern equipment and post graduate expertise.
Ear, nose and throat	Otolaryngologist.
Eyes	Ophthalmologist.
Personality disorders	Psychiatrist/clinical psychologist.
Waterworks and related piping	Urologist.
Bones	Orthopaedic consultant expert in knees, hips, etc.
Children	Paediatrician, eg specialist in neurology, urology and note educational psychologist.
'Wrongful birth cases'	May involve haematologist, geneticist.
In anaesthetic cases	Anaesthetist as well as the speciality within which the anaesthetic problem arose.
In nursing cases	A senior nursing officer.
In GP cases	An experienced GP and/or university teachers of general practice.

APPLICATION ON BEHALF OF PATIENT FOR HOSPITAL MEDICAL RECORDS FOR USE WHEN COURT PROCEEDINGS ARE CONTEMPLATED

This should be completed as fully as possible

Insert Hospital Name and Address	**TO: Medical Records Officer** **Hospital**

1 (a)	Full name of patient (including previous surnames)	
(b)	Address now	
(c)	Address at start of treatment	
(d)	Date of Birth	
(e)	Hospital ref no if available	
(f)	NI number, if available	
2	This application is made because I am considering:	
(a)	a claim against your hospital as detailed in para 7 overleaf	YES/NO
(b)	pursuing an action against someone else	YES/NO

3	Department(s) where treatment was received	
4	Name(s) of Consultant(s) at your hospital in charge of the treatment	
5	Whether treatment at your hospital was private or NHS, wholly or in part	
6	A description of the treatment received, with approximate dates	
7	If the answer to Q2(a) is 'Yes', details of the likely nature, and grounds for, such a claim, and approximate dates of the events involved	
8	If the answer to Q2(b) is 'Yes' insert: (i) the names of the proposed defendants	
	(ii) whether action yet begun	YES/NO
	(iii) if appropriate, details of Court and action number	
9	We confirm we will pay (i) reasonable copying charges (ii) a reasonable administration fee	YES/NO YES/NO

10	We request prior details of: (i) photocopying and administration charges for medical records (ii) number of, and cost of copying, X-ray and scan films	YES/NO YES/NO
11	Any other relevant information particular requirements, or any particular documents not required (eg copies of computerised records)	
	Signature of Solicitor	
	Name	
	Address	
	Ref	
	Telephone Number	
	Fax number	

		Please print name beneath each signature. Signature by child over 12 but under 18 years also requires signature by parent
	Signature of patient:	
	Signature of parent or next friend, if appropriate:	
	Signature of personal representative where patient has died:	

LORD WOOLF'S ACCESS TO JUSTICE
RECOMMENDATIONS ON MEDICAL NEGLIGENCE

A Summary

(1) The training of any health professionals should include an introduction to the legal context of medical work, including an indication of what is involved in a claim for negligence.

(2) The General Medical Council and other regulatory bodies should consider whether a rule of professional conduct is needed to clarify the responsibility of healthcare professionals to their patients when they discover an act or omission in which they may have been negligent in their care and treatment.

(3) The NHS should consider tackling the problem of tracing former hospital staff, by improving hospital record systems or making more use of existing information.

(4) A pre-litigation protocol for medical negligence cases should be developed. As part of the protocol, claimants should be required to notify defendants of a firm intention to sue in a letter before action. The letter should include the fullest available information about the basis of the intended claim, and should wherever possible give at least three months' notice that statement of case is to be served. If liability is disputed, defendants should be required to provide a reasoned answer.

(5) The use of alternative dispute resolution mechanisms should be encouraged in medical negligence, especially for smaller claims. Solicitors acting for patients should not automatically advise litigation but should inform their clients of all the available options, including the Health Service Ombudsman, and consider the possibility of alternative dispute resolution at all stages.

(6) The specialist lists in the Queen's Bench Division of the High Court and county court level should include a separate medical negligence list.

(7) Outside London, medical negligence cases at both High Court and county court level should be handled at specially designated court centres.

(8) There should be regional lists, or a single national list, to facilitate the flexible allocation of cases for trial and reduce delay.

(9) The Judicial Studies Board should investigate, with appropriate medical experts, the scope and content of training in medical issues for procedural and trial judges, and organise the necessary training.

(10) Standard tables should be used wherever possible to reduce the cost of quantifying complex medical negligence (and other personal injury) claims.

(11) There should be a practice guide to indicate how the new rules on case management and procedure will apply in detail to medical negligence litigation. The guide should be developed by the new 'umbrella' organisation for medical negligence or under the aegis of the Civil Justice Council.

(12) The Court service should facilitate a pilot study of the various options for dealing with medical negligence claims below £10,000, to establish which is the most effective procedure for enabling these cases to be litigated on a modest budget.

Reproduced with kind permission of the Lord Chancellor's Department.

LETTER SEEKING PRE-WRIT VOLUNTARY DISCLOSURE

MK/MR/006

9 November 1996

The General Manager
Westcastle Area Health Authority
Westcastle
WE5 1SY

Dear Sir

Re Miss Sarah Smith of 22 Reldon Street, Westcastle.

D.O.B. 14/9/74

Hospital No [IF KNOWN]

[ENSURE THAT THE CLIENT IS EASILY IDENTIFIABLE]

Pre-Action Disclosure of Medical Records - ss 33 and 35 Supreme Court Act 1981

We act for Sarah Smith under Legal Aid Certificate Number ...... in connection with a proposed claim against the Health Authority for damages for personal injuries suffered as a result of negligent medical treatment following the birth of her baby son on 14 May 1996.

On 13 May 1996, our client was admitted to Westcastle General Hospital in readiness for the birth of her child. The baby was delivered by caesarian section at approximately 2.40am on 14 May 1996. Our client believes that she was under the overall supervision of a Mr Green. [INSERT, IF KNOWN, WHO HAD CARE OF THE CLIENT]

Our client was discharged on 18 May 1996.

On 28 June 1996, our client suffered ... [AND THEN DETAIL THE CLIENT'S INJURIES DEALING WITH EACH EVENT IN A CHRONOLOGICAL ORDER. THE LETTER SHOULD CONTINUE WITH THE ALLEGATIONS OF NEGLIGENCE FOR EXAMPLE ...]

We anticipate that the claims to be made on behalf of our client, after we have had access to the hospital records and obtained expert advice, will include allegations as to unreasonable failure to diagnose and/or treat our client's condition resulting in the injuries which, with due care and skill, would have been avoided.

We have set out sufficient particulars to make it clear that our client may well have a claim for negligence arising out of the treatment which she received, and also to make it clear that this is a case where medical records should be disclosed to this firm without it being necessary to make an application to the court under s 33(2) Supreme Court Act 1981.

We enclose a schedule setting out those documents which, where appropriate, should be included. [NOW THERE IS THE OPTION OF SIMPLY REFERRING TO THE LAW SOCIETY'S STANDARD PROTOCOL]

We are not prepared to agree to disclosure being limited to a nominated medical adviser and disclosure should be made to us so that we may advise our client properly as to whether personal injury proceedings brought by her would have reasonable prospects of success.

We therefore seek from you, pursuant to s 33(2)(b), copies of all such documents. If any such documents were once but are not now in your possession, custody or power, please itemise them, state when you parted with them, and what has become of them.

We shall therefore be grateful if you will:

(a) Let us have confirmation within 21 days that you will provide such a list and that the records shall be disclosed to us within six weeks of the date of this letter;

(b) Let us have within those six weeks either a list of documents or confirmation by reference to the enclosed schedule that the documents are all those which are or ever have been in your possession, custody or power;

(c) Let us have either the original documents upon our undertaking to copy them and return them to you within 10 working days or complete copies upon our undertaking to pay the reasonable photocopying charges involved;

(d) Notify us if you believe that any of the relevant documents are in the possession, custody or power of someone else, identifying that other person;

(e) Ensure that the relevant documents will be preserved in their entirety pending production, inspection and trial, notifying us immediately if it is not your intention to do so.

We enclose Miss Smith's signed authority.

If it becomes necessary to make an application for pre-action discovery, we will place this letter before the court when dealing with the substance of the application and the question of costs.

Yours faithfully

Khan & Robson
Encs

The authors are grateful to the firm of Loomba & Burke, Solicitors, Newcastle Upon Tyne for permission to reproduce this pro-forma letter.

ADVANCE DIRECTIVE

TO MY FAMILY AND MY PHYSICIAN

This Declaration is made by me (full name and address) at a time when I am of sound mind and after careful consideration.

If I am unable to take part in decisions about my medical care owing to my physical or mental incapacity and if I develop one or more of the medical conditions listed in Item 3 below and two independent physicians conclude that there is no prospect of my recovery, I declare that my wishes are as follows:

1. I request that my life shall not be sustained by artificial means such as life support systems, intravenous fluids or drugs, or by tube feeding.

2. I request that distressing symptoms caused by illness or by lack of food or fluid should be controlled by appropriate sedative treatment though such treatment may shorten my life.

*3. The said medical conditions are:
   (1) Severe and lasting brain damage sustained as a result of injury, including stroke, or disease.

   (2) Advanced disseminated malignant disease.

   (3) Advanced degenerative disease or of the nervous and/or muscular systems with severe limitations of independent mobility, and no satisfactory response to treatment.

   (4) Senile or pre-senile dementia, eg Alzheimer or multi-infarct type.

   (5) Other condition of comparable gravity.

* Cross out and initial any condition you do not wish to include.

I further declare that I hereby absolve my medical attendants from any civil liability arising from action taken in response to and in terms of this Declaration.

I reserve the right to revoke this Declaration at any time.

Signature:.....................

Date:...........................

Witnessed by:

Signature:.......................... Signature:..........................

Name:......................... Name:.........................
(please print) (please print)

Address:.......................... Address:.......................

....

....

The authors extend their appreciation to the Voluntary Euthanasia Society for giving their permission to reproduce their sample advance directive.

CONSENT FORM

For medical or dental investigation, treatment or operation

Health Authority .... **Patient's Surname**..............................

Hospital .... **Other Names**.....................................

Unit Number.................................... **Date of Birth**..

Sex: *(please tick)* Male ☐ Female ☐

DOCTORS OR DENTISTS *(This part to be completed by doctor or dentist. See notes on the reverse)*

TYPE OF OPERATION INVESTIGATION OR TREATMENT

I confirm that I have explained the operation investigation or treatment, and such appropriate options as are available and the type of anaesthetic, If any (general/regional/sedation) proposed, to the patient in terms which in my judgement are suited to the understanding of the patient and/or to one of the parents or guardians of the patient.

Signature..................................... Date .../.../...

Name of doctor or dentist ....

PATIENT/PARENT/GUARDIAN

1. Please read this form and the notes overleaf very carefully.

2. If there is anything that you don't understand about the explanation, or if you want more information, you should ask the doctor or dentist.

3. Please check that all the information on the form is correct. If it is, and you understand the explanation, then sign the form.

I am the patient/parent/guardian *(delete as necessary)*.

I agree	■ to what is proposed which has been explained to me by the doctor/dentist named on this form.
	■ to the use of the type of anaesthetic that I have been told about.
I understand	■ that the procedure may not be done by the doctor/dentist who has been treating me so far.
	■ that any procedure in addition to the investigation or treatment described on this form will only be carried out if it is necessary and in my best interests and can be justified for medical reasons.
I have told	■ the doctor or dentist about any additional procedures I would <u>not</u> wish to be carried out straightaway without my having the opportunity to consider them first.

Signature ....

Name..

Address ....

(if not the patient) ....

....

INDEX